2068

C000047310

VIOLENCE AND
IN THE WESTERN S

Andrew Linklater's *The Problem of Harm in World Politics* (Cambridge University Press, 2011) created a new agenda for the sociology of states-systems. *Violence and Civilization in the Western States-Systems* builds on the author's attempts to combine the process-sociological investigation of civilizing processes and the English School analysis of international society in a higher synthesis. Adopting Martin Wight's comparative approach to states-systems and drawing on the sociological work of Norbert Elias, Linklater asks how modern Europeans came to believe themselves more 'civilized' than their medieval forebears. He investigates novel combinations of violence and civilization through a broad historical scope from classical antiquity, Latin Christendom and Renaissance Italy to the post-Second World War era. This book will interest all students with an interdisciplinary commitment to investigating long-term patterns of change in world politics.

ANDREW LINKLATER is Woodrow Wilson Professor of International Politics at Aberystwyth University, a Fellow of the British Academy and a member of the Academy of Social Science and of the Learned Society of Wales. He has published extensively on theories of international relations and on the importance of process sociology for the study of international society. His previous books include *Men and Citizens in the Theory of International Relations, Beyond Realism and Marxism, The Transformation of Political Community, The English School of International Relations* (co-authored with Hidemi Suganami) and *The Problem of Harm in World Politics.*

VIOLENCE AND CIVILIZATION IN THE WESTERN STATES-SYSTEMS

ANDREW LINKLATER

Aberystwyth University

CAMBRIDGE
UNIVERSITY PRESS

CAMBRIDGE
UNIVERSITY PRESS

University Printing House, Cambridge CB2 8BS, United Kingdom

Cambridge University Press is part of the University of Cambridge.

It furthers the University's mission by disseminating knowledge in the pursuit of
education, learning and research at the highest international levels of excellence.

www.cambridge.org
Information on this title: www.cambridge.org/9781316608333

First published 2016

Printed in the United Kingdom by Clays, St Ives plc

A catalogue record for this publication is available from the British Library

ISBN 978-1-107-15473-5 Hardback
ISBN 978-1-316-60833-3 Paperback

And now for lords who understand, I'll tell
A Fable; once a hawk, high in the clouds
Clutched in his claws a specked nightingale.
She, pierced by those hooked claws, cried, 'Pity me'.
But he made scornful answer: 'Silly thing,
Why do you cry? Your master holds you fast,
You'll go where I decide, although you have
A minstrel's lovely voice, and if I choose,
I'll have you for a meal or let you go.
Only a fool will match himself against a
Stronger party, for he'll only lose
And be disgraced as well as beaten'

Hesiod, *Works and Days*, II 202–211

Two principles in human nature reign:
Self-love, to urge, and Reason, to restrain

Pope, *An Essay on Man*, Epistle II-II

CONTENTS

vii

PREFACE AND ACKNOWLEDGEMENTS

The following investigation extends the argument for a comparative sociology of states-systems that was developed in the final chapter of *The Problem of Harm in World Politics: Theoretical Investigations* (Cambridge 2011). A central aim is to analyse the extent to which agreed standards of self-restraint that were linked with shared conceptions of civility or civilization have shaped the development of Western states-systems. A related objective is to determine whether the dominant patterns of self-restraint in the contemporary international system are radically different from those that existed in the preceding arrangements. It is to show what modern standards of restraint owe to their predecessors and to begin to explain the key differences.

The inquiry is designed to advance Martin Wight's comparative approach to states-systems by drawing on the considerable resources of Eliasian or process sociology. The latter provided a provisional explanation of how modern Europeans came to regard themselves as more 'civilized' than their medieval forebears and more 'advanced' than surrounding 'barbarians'. The general pattern of social development was said to be evident in an overall decline in the level of interpersonal violence over approximately five centuries, and in an attendant growing aversion to pain and suffering. It identified changes in what is permissible and what is forbidden within state-organized societies. The argument was that continuity rather than change has been the norm in the relations between political communities. In several publications, Elias referred to mounting pressures on societies to resolve their differences peacefully and to collaborate to deal with the problems of interconnectedness that faced them all. He described the ways in which the idea of civilization had shaped modern Western attitudes to violence including genocide. What was missing, however, and is still in need of elaboration, is an account of how far changing conceptions of permissible and impermissible violence are evident not only within modern nation-states but in the relations between them.

Elias wrote extensively about civilizing processes but paid little attention to international societies of states including the modern one. He did not see them as particular forms of social and political integration with distinctive civilizing processes and standards of restraint. It is nevertheless essential to understand his analysis of the process of civilization in order to explain the Western-initiated global 'civilizing process' that has shaped the modern states-system over the last few decades and centuries. For his part, Wight suggested that international societies have only emerged in regions where the constituent parts thought they belonged to a cultural zone that was clearly distinguished from the world of the 'barbarians'. That sense of civilization, the argument was, made it easier for states to reach common understandings about, *inter alia,* diplomatic procedures and rules of war that should be upheld in the relations between 'advanced' peoples, but could be placed to one side in conflicts with 'inferiors'. Wight noted how the idea of civilization had influenced common understandings of the permissible and the forbidden in world politics. But his works do not contain a systematic analysis of the impact of ideas of civilization on international societies. Shared cultures or civilizations were described as background conditions that facilitated the development of societies of states rather than as processes – of which those forms of world political organization were an important part – that unfolded over many centuries. There was no discussion then of how the modern society of states was not simply embedded in, but an important feature of, the longer civilizing process that Elias attempted to explain.

Wight's vision of a comparative study of states-systems and Elias's analysis of the European civilizing process are magisterial contributions to the social sciences. But they are limited achievements because they did not explore the connections between civilizing processes and societies of states. Elias's investigation of how the dominant beliefs about what is permissible and what is forbidden changed in the modern period suggests specific avenues of research. To use a term that was introduced in *The Problem of Harm in World Politics,* the sociological challenge is to understand the dominant harm conventions in different states-systems. That inquiry drew attention to certain universals of social life, including the reality that all societies have harm conventions that distinguish between harmful and harmless acts, and between justifiable and unjustifiable harm. The same is true of international societies. They possess harm conventions that can be divided into those that are designed to preserve order between separate states (international harm conventions) and those that have been created to protect individuals and non-state groups (cosmopolitan harm conventions) in their own right. A central question in the chapters below is how far shared conceptions of civilized conduct shaped, and were influenced by, the dominant harm conventions in world politics. Such an investigation must examine the complex interconnections between domestic and international patterns of change. Ideas about civilization, their relationship with harm conventions that embody general understandings about civilized behaviour, and their impact on the prevalent ideas about the permissible and the forbidden within and between state-organized societies belong to one overall pattern of social and political development. But inquiries into those interrelationships barely exist, and this is also true of explorations of the basic social-scientific concepts that can be used to compare civilizing processes in international societies.

One of the functions of the comparative sociology of states-systems therefore is to ascertain how far societies have agreed that certain harm conventions should be upheld everywhere because of shared understandings of civility or civilization, or because of equivalent social ideas that expressed their conviction in having progressed beyond a 'barbarous' past and neighbouring 'savages'. The argument is that process sociology has a crucial part to play in that analysis, despite the limitations noted earlier. The details will be discussed in the introduction. Suffice it to note that Elias did not develop a conceptual system that was confined to investigations of the relations between members of the same society – which was the customary object of analysis in sociological inquiry. His writings were critical of sociological orthodoxy that presumed that changes within societies could be understood without investigating their interdependencies with the domain of inter-societal relations. He developed certain concepts in order to cast light on the ways in which people are bound together in diverse social 'figurations', including families and primary associations, local communities, nation-states and international organizations. The chapters in this work employ that mode of analysis in order to understand the relationship between violence and civilization in different international societies.

The inquiry draws heavily on Elias's writings but is critical of their claims about the differences between ancient and modern attitudes to violence and suffering. It provides a detailed discussion of core features of Elias's study of the civilizing process with the aim of establishing as precisely as possible what it contributes to the sociology of states-systems but also to show how its approach to long-term patterns of development can be taken further by engaging with the analysis of states-systems. The intended readership includes process and historical sociologists, students of international relations, historians with an interest in the analysis of long-term social and political patterns of development, and scholars who are engaged in building connections between those fields of investigation. Process sociologists will find much that is familiar in the sections that draw on Elias's writings, but hopefully they will discover much that is new in the attempt to extend his examination of the civilizing process. Students of international relations will have encountered many of the themes that are considered in the sections on the modern states-system, but they should also find much that is novel in the attempt to take forward the comparative analysis of societies of states through an engagement with process sociology. Specialist historians will not discover much that is novel in the chapters that rely heavily on scholarly works in their fields. But few will be familiar with the intellectual synthesis that is developed in a preliminary fashion in this work. It is important to stress that the following discussion shares a central ambition of process sociology which is promoting higher levels of synthesis in social-scientific inquiry at a time when increasing specialization and the fragmentation of knowledge are prevalent. The exploration of linkages between process sociology, international relations and specialist historical narratives is undertaken in that spirit.

There is one further point to make in concluding this preface. The contention has been that Wight and Elias had different intellectual preoccupations, the former focussing on international societies, the latter analysing processes of civilization with only passing references to the relationship between violence and civilization in world politics. But in one fundamental respect, Wight and Elias were broadly agreed about the nature of international relations. That convergence of opinion is evident in certain contrasts they drew between international relations in the Graeco-Roman world and in the modern period. Each provided examples of attitudes to violence at the end of the Second World War and in the post-war era that suggested that the modern society of states is fundamentally different from the states-systems of antiquity. They maintained that modern assumptions about the need for restraints on violence revealed important changes of normative orientation. Wight was explicit that such differences were linked with more 'civilized' standpoints on violent harm; Elias did not express the point in exactly the same manner but, as will be shown later, a similar standpoint runs through his writings.

Such comments are perplexing – and raise interesting questions for the sociology of states-systems – when considered in conjunction with other features of their general reflections on international relations. In some of their writings, they suggest that the similarities between different phases in the history of international relations are greater than the differences. Both emphasized long-term trends in different eras towards the concentration of military strength in the hands of a diminishing number of great powers that drifted into the final conflict that destroyed earlier states-systems and culminated in empire. From that perspective, all past advances in restraining the behaviour of the great powers turned out to be fragile and short-lived. The same may be true of the modern states-system, notwithstanding the ways in which ideas about civilization have fostered the belief that societies should cooperate to ensure that behaviour that was once permitted – including conduct that has come to be known as war crimes or human rights violations – is forbidden. The references in Wight's and Elias's writings to supposedly modern sensibilities about violence reveal that there is a great deal of unfinished business to undertake to ascertain what is distinctive about the contemporary society of states and what may be unique about the relationship between violence and civilization in the most recent phase of its development.

Elias and Wight may not have been entirely consistent on whether there have been limited progressions in particular domains of world politics. They did not answer questions that were posed in the final chapter of *The Problem of Harm in World Politics*, which outlined an empirical research programme for the sociology of states-systems. They included the extent to which great powers assumed that they could behave more or less as they pleased under conditions of insecurity, thought that everything is permissible or that nothing should ever be ruled out under conditions of military necessity, or believed that cosmopolitan moral commitments demanded collective efforts to spare enemy combatants and civilian groups needless suffering. Related questions considered how far racist, xenophobic and similar representations of outsiders legitimated acts of violence that were largely forbidden within the societies involved, and whether solidarity with other peoples restrained foreign policy behaviour. Those questions can be rephrased to highlight the issue of how far notions of civility or civilization constrained violent harm or were tied to conceptions of social superiority that justified unlimited violence against 'barbarians'.

It has been noted that Wight and Elias were not optimistic that the modern states-system will avoid the destructive fate of its predecessors. But some of Elias's remarks about powerful tendencies in the modern world invite discussion of whether societies today confront some parallels to the challenges that faced peoples in early modern Europe and resulted in an unplanned civilizing process. It may be that such parallels distinguish the modern states-system from its predecessors and inspire cautious optimism that cosmopolitan standards of self-restraint are now part of a tenuous global 'civilizing process' that may make it possible for the modern states-system to escape the violent end of its predecessors. In the course of human history the standards of self-restraint that have applied in relations between societies have invariably been less demanding than the principles that governed relations between members of the same society. Perhaps that has changed in fundamental respects. One of the functions of the comparative sociology of states-systems is to shed light on what has altered and to endeavour to understand the basic reasons.

Numerous debts have been incurred in the process of writing this book. Several colleagues at Aberystwyth read draft chapters or an earlier version of the volume as a whole. I thank Ken Booth, Ian Clark, Andre Saramago and Kamila Stullerova for their expert advice and comments. Further afield, Josuke Ikeda, Makoto Sato and Giorgio Shani provided the opportunity to deliver work-in-progress papers at symposia held at Ritsumaiken University in Kyoto and the International Christian University in Tokyo in 2012 and 2014. Thanks to Giorgio, an earlier version of Chapter 11 was published in the *Journal of Social Science* in April 2015. I am also deeply grateful to Chris Reus-Smit for organizing a two-day workshop on the problem of harm in world politics at the European University Institute in Florence in April 2012. I thank members of the vibrant doctoral community for engaging sympathetically and critically with drafts of Chapters 5, 6 and 7, and Dirk Moses for his guidance on Chapter 9. Also invaluable was the opportunity to present the penultimate version of the last chapter at the Middle Eastern Technical University in Ankara. I thank Nuri Yurdesev for the invitation to present the keynote lecture at the Conference on *Multiple Paradigms/Multiple Worlds* that was held there in June 2014.

I have profited from seminar discussions in many centres – in my own Department in Aberystwyth, the University of Copenhagen (thanks to Norman Gabriel and Lars Bo Kaspersen), the University of Glasgow (thanks to Maurizio Carbone), Leicester University (thanks to Jason Hughes), Lisbon University (thanks to Isabel David and Andre Saramago), Sheffield University (thanks to Jonathan Joseph) and Xiamen University (thanks to Biwu Zhang).

At a critical point in the project, Barry Buzan and John Hobson provided indispensable feedback on the penultimate draft of the manuscript. John in particular has been a source of wise counsel, inspiration and encouragement. Stephen Mennell read the entire manuscript and offered profound insights on the conversation with Elias that runs through the following pages. Two anonymous referees skilfully advised on how to improve the penultimate draft. I thank John Haslam at Cambridge University Press for his faith in the project as well as for his guidance and patience.

I am grateful to my own university for the gift of time in the shape of research leave that made it possible for me to work on the manuscript. Finally, I thank Jane for her constant love and support, and tolerance and under-standing – in the hope they will survive just one more volume.

~

Introduction

The central question in the following discussion is whether modern ethical attitudes to the use of force are significantly different from the prevalent assumptions about violence and suffering in the earlier Western states-systems. A few comments about specific writings on that subject will explain how that problem arises; they point the way towards a solution. Wight speculated that the ancient Greeks and Romans appear to have had little or no conception of 'international ethics' that restrained violent harm. He highlighted the differences between the states-systems of classical antiquity and the modern international order where moral sensitivities to the use of force appear to be more developed. In support of the conjecture, Wight (1966: 126) referred to the Allies' rejection of Stalin's suggestion that the German General Staff should be liquidated at the end of the Second World War. The implication was that peoples of classical antiquity were less troubled by the summary execution of enemy leaders. There is a striking parallel with Elias's observation about the differences between 'ancient' and 'modern' responses to what has come to be known as genocide. Information about the Holocaust produced shock and revulsion amongst 'civilized' peoples, not least because of the realization that one of them – another advanced, technological society – had organized mass slaughter on an industrial scale. But, Elias argued, massacres were commonplace in classical antiquity, and usually passed without comment or condemnation.

Those comments are puzzling for these reasons. As will be discussed below, Wight maintained that international relations constitute 'the realm of recurrence and repetition', while Elias stated in one place that little seems to change in world politics apart from the methods of killing and the number of people involved. Modern 'civilized' peoples, the latter added, are still living much as our ancestors did 'in the period of their so-called "barbarism"' (Elias 2013: 190). The level of domestic pacification had increased in European societies over recent centuries, but the tolerance of force in relations with enemies had not been significantly reduced. The presumption was that a global equivalent to the European civilizing process that had forbidden many practices that had once been permitted is unlikely to occur in the absence of a higher monopoly of coercive power that can provide levels of security that are comparable to the peaceful conditions that are largely taken for granted in 'civilized' societies.

Similar tensions are evident in more recent writings on international relations. Many authors have maintained that liberal societies have eradicated force from their relations with each other. The global spread of liberal democratic values, it is contended, can be expected to lead to the gradual pacification of international society as a whole, assuming that non-liberal societies can undergo a successful transition to liberalism. However, such restraints on using force in relations with other liberals have not been observed assiduously in conflicts with illiberal regimes that are presumed to lack political legitimacy (Doyle 1983). Liberal governments have been criticised by groups that are alarmed by basic contradictions between liberal values and the continuing tolerance of force, particularly where it leads to what the relevant publics regard as unnecessary suffering. For some analysts, liberal experiments have demonstrated how the international system can be pacified; for realist critics, such images have not substantially altered the basic dynamics of world politics.

Arguably, most scholars occupy a mid-position between those standpoints. Few would claim that international relations have barely changed across the centuries apart from successive revolutions in the instruments of warfare; few would contend that the relationship between morality and politics is the same today as it was in earlier phases in the history of the modern states-system, or in the earlier systems of states in the West. On the other hand, few scholars have maintained that international society has changed so profoundly that one can point to a complete and perhaps irreversible break with the past. In the main, such orientations are largely impressionistic and do not rest on systematic comparisons between states-systems; indeed, there has been little empirical research that sheds light on, *inter alia,* what is, and what is not, distinctive about 'international ethics' in the modern period. This work aims to fill that curious gap in the literature by trying to answer three questions: first, whether the most recent phase of the modern states-system is different from classical antiquity (and from the earlier states-systems in the West); second, how far conceptions of civilization, and related ideas about self-restraint in preceding eras, explain basic differences between those states-systems; and, third, what the analysis of the states-systems in the West suggests are the social and political preconditions of ethical restraints on violence that mark the rise of a more 'advanced' civilization.

Those introductory remarks therefore raise important questions about whether the similarities between the Western states-systems are greater than the differences, and about how any fundamental differences are best explained. The revival of interest in the 'English School' since the early 1990s has not been accompanied by efforts to build on Wight's vision of a sociology of states-systems which is the obvious starting point for the quest to understand shifts in what is and is not permissible in international politics across long time intervals. The work that comes closest in general orientation was less engaged with perspectives on ethics and world politics than with shifts in the distribution of military power over the last five millennia (Watson 1992). The argument is that an examination of the relationship between violence and civilization can clarify whether and how far social attitudes to force have changed in the history of the Western states-systems.

The importance of that relationship is suggested by Elias and Wight's references to attitudes to force during and after the Second World War. As will be explained later, Elias referred to growing external compulsions on modern states to exercise greater self-restraint and foresight than their predecessors did. The upshot of the analysis is that there are interesting parallels between the 'civilizing process' in early modern Europe, when people were forced together in longer webs of interconnectedness, and the related challenges of contemporary globalization. Elias did not contend that pressures to restrain violence will lead inexorably to the pacification of relations between the great powers. The future remained open. But his comments about the dominant responses to the Nazi genocides clearly implied that the civilizing process had transformed attitudes to the use of force in the modern states-system. Indeed, it would be peculiar if modern 'civilized' standpoints on violence and suffering had made no impression on foreign policy behaviour whatsoever.

As for Wight's example from the Second World War, the implication appeared to be that the Western allies could not endorse a course of action that so obviously clashed with cherished civilized self-images. Such links between violence and civilization are implied by his conjecture that all societies of states appear to have emerged in regions where the governing elites believed that they were part of a cultural zone that was superior to neighbouring 'backward' societies (Wight 1977: 33–5). Shared beliefs about society and politics ensured levels of mutual comprehension that might not have existed otherwise; they made it easier to reach lasting diplomatic agreements. In relations with 'barbarians', those societies did not feel compelled to observe the ethical restraints on violence that they generally upheld in their own international relations (Wight 1977: ibid.). The 'double standard of morality' was especially evident in the age of European conquest. The gulf between the principles that were valued in relations between members of the same state-organized society and the 'ethic' that governed relations with other 'civilized' groups was even greater in the relations between self-defining civilized, colonizing peoples and subject populations. The latter were conquered by force, liquidated, or enslaved, exploited and harmed in other ways that were largely prohibited in 'civilized' enclaves.

Wight and Elias identified crucial links between violence and civilization but each focused on one dimension of a broader pattern of social and political change, and their respective positions need to be brought together in a more synoptic approach to long-term processes of development. For example, Wight argued that a pre-existing sense of belonging to a shared culture or civilization smoothed the way to creating an international society, but he did not analyse civilization in processual terms: he did not discuss how societies came to have specific values in common or explain how shared 'civilized' beliefs influenced – and were shaped by – the ways in which states were bound together in an international society. No account of how the society of states gave shape to, and was part of, a larger process of civilization was provided.

Elias's remarks about modern attitudes to genocide indicated how the civilizing process has influenced attitudes to violent harm in relations between societies. His comments are part of a broader argument that all societies that have made the transition from autocratic to democratic rule have had to wrestle with the question of how universalistic and egalitarian moral principles should guide the conduct of foreign policy. Such societies have confronted tensions that did not arise for preceding social groups (Elias 2013: 175–6). Those comments resonate with Wight's discussion of how the moral foundations of domestic legitimacy changed over the last few centuries as states went through the transition from dynastic to democratic and nationalist principles of government (Wight 1977: ch. 6). Those observations are the counterpart to the claim that principles of legitimacy that specify which political units have the right to belong to the society of states, and dictate how they should behave, are an obvious point of intersection between domestic and international politics (Wight 1977: ibid.).

The process-sociological analysis of how actions that were once permitted came to be forbidden shows how that discussion can be extended, and how the comparative study of states-systems can be taken forward. But its investigation of violence and civilization can be developed by incorporating key insights from English School analyses of international society. It is necessary to add that Elias did not make the mistake of thinking that the development of European conceptions of civilization was a wholly endogenous process that took place within separate or autonomous societies. He stated that the ruling elites in early modern Europe belonged to a 'supra-national court society' (Elias 2010: 3–4), but he did not regard that figuration as a crucial precursor of the modern society of states. One problem was that Elias did not regard modern conceptions of diplomacy as part of a larger European civilizing process that spread from the French absolutist court to other European societies and then to other parts of the world. He analysed the impact of earlier notions of courtesy and civility on the rise and development of European notions of civilization, but neglected how specific conceptions of self-restraint in the earlier Western states-systems left a cultural inheritance that included modern conceptions of 'civilized' statecraft. In short, process sociology is incomplete without considering what the comparative sociology of state-systems can contribute to understanding modern images of civilization.

The upshot is that an inquiry into modern conceptions of violence and civilization must analyse the ways in which societies have been tied together in long-term processes in which, for example, classical Greek and Roman ideals of self-restraint influenced Renaissance and early European ideas of civility and later conceptions of civilization. What has not been documented in detail are the ways in which later states-systems were shaped by reflections on the political experience of earlier examples – not just by efforts to emulate their military achievements but also by endeavours to learn from their conceptions of restraint. What the English School adds to comprehending the relationship between violence and civilization is the recognition that international society is a crucial realm in which different societies discover the extent to which they can agree on what Elias called 'social standards of self-restraint'. The very fact that genocide is now forbidden by international law is an illustration of powerful normative shifts within the contemporary society of states. It is an important example of a Western-inspired global 'civilizing process' that was obscured by the corollary of Elias's contention that the rise of state monopolies of power over force and taxation was crucial for the whole European process of civilization, namely that a global equivalent is improbable in the absence of a higher monopoly of power that can compel states to comply with specific standards of restraint. What several members of the English School have called the 'civilizing' effect of international society and its core institutions such as diplomacy and international law was missing from the analysis.

As already noted, Elias stated that sociologists could not regard societies as separate entities that had been shaped by entirely endogenous patterns of development. European societies, for example, did not first reach their independent positions on their 'civilized' condition, and only then ask how they were set apart from, and should behave towards, less 'civilized' peoples and towards each other. Although Elias devoted little attention to this point, their interactions with subject peoples were critical in forming 'civilized' identities and in constructing the society of states. The nineteenth-century European 'standard of civilization' is evidence of how 'civilized' sensibilities were embedded in international society. It shows how Elias's explanation of the civilizing process and the English School analysis of international society can be combined in a 'higher level synthesis' that strengthens the former's account of how specific patterns of social and political change between the fifteenth and twentieth centuries transformed not just the European continent but the entire world.

In this discussion, the comparative analysis of states-systems considers the issue of how far their constitutive civilizing processes were expressed in the dominant international or cosmopolitan harm conventions – in the prevalent beliefs about permissible and forbidden forms of violence. The English School approach contains a battery of concepts that can be employed to comprehend those dimensions of world politics. The analysis of the Hobbesian, Grotian and Kantian tradition of international thought described competing approaches to the level of restraint in foreign policy and their different levels of optimism or pessimism about future possibilities (Wight 1991). Distinctions between the pluralist and solidarist images of international society have been used to draw attention to diverse philosophical, legal and diplomatic assumptions about the extent to which sympathy for, and solidarity with, vulnerable peoples can drive the states-system beyond the quest for order and stability between the major powers towards collective action to alleviate human suffering (Bull 1966). Those concepts were developed to characterize and classify types of international society. They are useful for describing different approaches to the relationship between violence and civilization, but they do not explain the crucial differences. Process sociology, on the other, possesses a range of concepts with precisely that explanatory ambition. It is important to stress that the central categories were not designed to explain the core features of world politics but were deemed to be invaluable for understanding social figurations of any kind, whether local, national or global (Elias 2009). Three concepts will guide the following discussion. They are 'we feeling' or 'the scope of emotional identification', the 'we–I balance', and 'social constraints towards self-restraint'. Those ideas which were central to the comparative study of civilizing processes can contribute to an analysis of harm conventions in different international states-systems that extends the preceding investigation of the problem of harm in world politics. They can support the endeavour to ascertain whether the relationship between violence and civilization in the contemporary world is testimony to distinctive accomplishments in restraining the power to cause violent harm.

The concept of 'we-feeling' – an alternative term is 'we-identity' – refers to solidarity between people that is most apparent in collective attachments to 'survival units' such as kin-based associations, city states, universal empires or nation-states (Kaspersen and Gabriel 2008). It highlights the role of emotions in binding people together in such entities. Examples are the extent to which shame or guilt can be aroused by violating – or contemplating the transgression of – social norms, by the degree to which pity or compassion develops by witnessing others' suffering and pain, and the extent to which collective fear, hatred, anger or indignation can be provoked by perceived threats to security or by assaults on 'group pride'. The idea of 'scope' captures the reality that the ties that bind are invariably connected with morally significant dichotomies between 'social superiors' and 'social inferiors' within the relevant groups as well as stark contrasts between the society as a whole and other peoples. In a parallel discussion, Deutsch (1970) argued that, in international security communities, the level of we-feeling and the associated desire to resolve differences peacefully reflect a weakening of such pernicious distinctions in the relations between the peoples involved. The same is true of international societies and their core understandings about who enjoys the right of membership (and who can be excluded); the same is true of related beliefs about who should be protected by the dominant harm conventions (and who is denied the associated rights).

The second concept enlarges on the idea of 'we-feeling' by recognizing that a 'we-identity' is compatible with very different understandings of the relationship between the individual and society. Elias coined the expression, the 'we–I balance', to analyse the relationship between 'we' and 'I' in different figurations and, more specifically, to establish how far human groups have recognized and respected individual demands for free expression or privacy, or for maximizing personal wealth and promoting material self-interest. The contention was that most societies in human history have been very different from the highly-individuated societies that developed in Europe from the Renaissance. The sense of 'we' was predicated on radically different assumptions about the power balance between the collectivity and its individual members. The idea that the latter have 'natural rights' that cannot be overridden for the sake of the larger community was foreign to societies where rights and responsibilities were attached to specific social roles. The conviction that the individual could have rights that existed independently of society was entirely alien.

The notion of the we–I balance is relevant to the analysis of international societies and specifically to understanding the relationship between 'we' (where 'we' refers to international society or to some conception of humanity, and 'I' (where 'I' refers to the separate state). There are sharp differences between the pluralist conception of international society in which the we–I balance involved certain restrictions on national sovereignty for the sake of maintaining international order, and the solidarist alternative in which restraints on sovereign power are derived from ethical commitments to universal human rights. In general, the sense of 'we-feeling' in societies of states has usually been low relative to the claims that have been asserted in defence of the 'I' (the independent political community). For that reason, a central issue is how far the dominant understandings of the we–I balance in the most recent phase of international society represent a significant break with earlier arrangements.

The third concept, social standards of self-restraint, is best considered by recalling that in every society, infants have to learn how to control the 'animalic' impulses that govern their behaviour. In the course of routine patterns of socialization, children learn to internalize the standards of self-restraint in their society; in the course of 'conscience formation', they learn how to attune their emotional dispositions and behaviour to others in the same group. Elias mainly concentrated on explaining the European idea of civilization but he observed that all societies have civilizing processes whether or not they not they possessed the idea of civilization (that only came to the forefront of political theory and practice in Western Europe in the last quarter of the eighteenth century). All societies have civilizing processes, Elias maintained, in the technical, non-evaluative use of the concept because their members are required to observe particular standards of self-control and to tame violent and aggressive behaviour – though clearly not in the same way or to the same degree – if they are to live together in the same society. The idea of a socialization process might appear to be perfectly adequate for explaining those features of human existence; the seemingly more neutral idea of collective learning processes may be a preferable term (Linklater 2011: 244ff.). But neither concept quite captures the reality that dichotomies between the 'responsible' or 'deviant' or 'dangerous' members of the societies are core features of the ways in which people are bound together in the same society and central elements of the socialization processes they go through in early life. Those oppositions are invariably interwoven with distinctions between 'advanced' and 'backward' societies that construct individual and collective identities. The idea of a civilizing process is preferred because it captures those elementary, universal normative realities that are integral to 'conscience formation' in all ways of life.[1]

That broader concept was also used in connection with changes that affected the species as a whole as cultural development gradually took over from biological evolution as the main determinant of human history. That orientation to the past highlighted social transformations that occurred over many hundreds of thousands of years as early humans or proto-humans were freed from the instinctual drives that governed the behaviour of the 'animalic' species from which they emerged. It drew attention to the process of 'symbol emancipation' from the domination of nature that was evident in the early phases of human evolution when peoples made the first advances in restraining 'animal' aggression (Elias 2011). That process continues. Societies no longer face the problem of taming the aggressive impulses that were part of the 'animal' nature of early humans, although the potential for violence remains a fundamental part of their biological inheritance. They confront instead the greater challenge of restraining violent dispositions that are the product of increased social complexity in human history.

---

[1] In the following pages, the civilizing process will therefore be used to refer to two different phenomena – to the development of European images of cultural superiority, and to conceptions of self-restraint that exist in all human societies. How the term is used will be evident from the specific context. In neither case is the term used to express approval of the arrangements under discussion. Where necessary, the term has been placed in quotation marks to make that point clear.

The problem of controlling violence is not the same for modern humans as it was for their distant ancestors, but their respective challenges are part of one interconnected chain of events. Early humans were steadily freed from the genetic constraints on aggression and compelled to develop substitutes in the form of internal and external restraints on violent and aggressive impulses. They protected themselves from some forms of violent harm in the process, but many became exposed to new dangers as a result of success in creating strong intra-societal restraints on violence. The greater collective power that those agreements made possible could be turned against opponents in the same society and used against external enemies. Societies have not succeeded in solving the problem of violent harm that emerged as early humans became emancipated from the genetic constraints on violence that determine the behaviour of other species. Perhaps they never will. However, the idea of a global civilizing process in the technical sense of the term can be used to describe the extent to which there have been such achievements in relations between the societies into which the species is divided. The concept does not refer to some normative vision of 'civilized' existence but to shifts in the standards of self-restraint that people have imposed on themselves and on each other in the course of responding to the new potentials for organizing harm that occurred as cultural development replaced biological evolution as the principal influence on the history of the species. Important questions arise about the part that different forms of world political organization such as empires have played in shaping global civilizing processes. They include the place of international societies in the development of social standards of self-restraint that have addressed the recurrent problem of harm in world politics.

As with the level of 'we-feeling' and the 'we–I balance', the standards of self-restraint vary enormously from society to society, and shift over time in the history of every human group. In the explanation of the European civilizing process, Elias drew various contrasts between the medieval and modern periods that will be considered in the later discussion of the differences between the international relations of Latin Christendom and the ensuing European states-system. The argument was that medieval knights were free to carry and to use weapons more or less as they pleased; restraints on violent and aggressive behaviour were not as strong as those that regulate the behaviour of the members of modern highly pacified, 'civilized' societies. Over several centuries, it was argued, the influence of external constraints and the fear of state coercion on human action declined relative to the power of inner restraints and the dictates of 'conscience'. Coercion did not disappear from the most stable, pacified societies, but was stored 'in the barracks' from which it re-emerged to deal with significant threats to public order (Elias 2012: 411). It could not be assumed that the internalized sources of individual restraint would survive in any future crisis where people fear for their security or survival – where, for example, they believe that public institutions cannot or will not protect them. Similar anxieties have often appeared in the relations between societies where self-reliance is the norm and where the dominant standards of self-restraint that are associated with international society or with the idea of humanity have been less demanding than in the domestic domain. Social attitudes to what is permissible and what is forbidden in the relations between members of the same society have not been thought to apply directly to foreign policy as a matter of principle. Weaker restrictions on force have characterized that sphere.

Elias observed that it is possible to imagine a future condition where people trust each other to observe very high levels of self-restraint, and where they are confident that they can coexist non-violently without the need for external coercion. Such a state of affairs, he argued, would be a 'very advanced form of civilization' indeed; that form of life seems unattainable at present, and may never be realized, but it is important to try to achieve it (Elias 2007: 141). The contention was linked with a rare open display of a normative commitment in Elias's sociological writings that stated that humanity is at present undergoing 'a great collective learning process', and that 'the task that lies before us is to work towards the pacification and organized unification of humankind' in the face of the reality that, for the most part, people's 'self-regulation is ... geared to the identification with small sub-units of humankind' (Elias 2008: 89ff.). That formulation is an example of a recurrent theme in Elias's writings, which is that ruling elites have long acted on the principle that they must have the freedom which citizens do not ordinarily have in their relations with each other to depart from the dominant intra-societal restraints on force. Acts of violence that are often prohibited or strictly regulated within social groups have been deemed necessary to conquer or defeat external foes. Violations of the usual taboos against force have been actively encouraged and have brought social rewards to the warriors involved.

Those points provide a reminder that throughout human history, 'survival units' have rarely been bound together by a powerful sense of we-feeling (Elias 2010a: 194ff.). Where some degree of solidarity has existed – as in the case of the Hellenic and modern states-systems where there was a strong sense of belonging to the same civilization or international society – the we–I balance strongly favoured the individual survival units. Such conceptions of their place in the world have usually failed to restrain states that faced major external threats to security or survival. In those circumstances, societies insisted that it is entirely legitimate, if not absolutely necessary, to use forms of violence that had been eliminated from relations within the relevant 'survival unit' where a high level of control of violent tendencies had developed. Internalized ethical restraints on using force against enemies – as opposed to restraints that are based entirely on the fear of external sanctions – were weaker.

As noted at the beginning of this introduction, questions arise about whether, or how far, the rigorous control of 'violent impulses' was largely missing from the international systems of classical antiquity. A central issue is whether the most recent phase of the modern states-system has made important advances in embedding ethical restraints on those impulses and whether they are testimony to the influence of 'civilized' notions on how states should behave towards each other and towards their respective populations. A related question is whether some of the pressures that gave rise to a distinctive civilizing process and unique harm conventions in early modern European societies are being replicated at the global level in response to increasing human interconnectedness.

Such comparisons are made easier by trying to establish whether there have been changes in we-feeling, in the we–I balance and in the dominant social standards of self-restraint in the different Western states-systems. The discussion of 'integration–disintegration tensions' throughout human history and in the current phase of the modern states-system also contributes to that investigation (Elias 2010a: 147ff.). Profound ambiguities in the contemporary condition stand out more clearly as a result. Rising levels of interconnectedness have created pressures to exercise greater self-regulation and self-restraint (and especially in response to the threat of nuclear war and the challenges of global economic interdependence and climate change). They have introduced incentives to acquire more realistic understandings of other people that have often been blocked under conditions of conflict where adversaries embraced 'highly emotive' world views that were suffused with pernicious representations of outsiders (Elias 2007: 159ff.). On the other hand, ancient rivalries and animosities have not exactly disappeared. Routine socialization processes continue to promote strong emotional attachments to the nation-state which is, for most people, the indispensable 'survival unit'. Collective fears about the loss of national power or autonomy, or resentment about external challenges to group pride and cherished self-images, have often led to 'counterthrusts' and 'decivilizing processes' that may well acquire the upper hand as a result of integration–disintegration tensions in world politics (Mennell 1990; van Benthem van den Bergh 2001).

The apparent tension within Wight's and Elias's positions that was discussed earlier can be resolved by noting how modern 'civilized' peoples became both more and less dangerous to each other as part of the same process of development. In the course of European state formation, societies became less tolerant of 'cruelty' and unnecessary suffering within their borders but they were also increasingly exposed to the danger of physical destruction through interstate warfare. With the pacification of society, modern states acquired levels of destructive power that distinguish the most recent phase in the history of the Western states-systems. The great powers converted themselves from 'survival units' into 'annihilation units' (Elias 2010a: 186–7). The revolutionary transformation of the power to harm more and more people over greater distances created pressures and incentives to tame traditional struggles for power and security. But the subsequent taming of the great powers was intertwined with fundamental changes within many core states. State monopolies of power had led to demands on subjects that included the taxation of wealth and income and conscription into national armies. Those pressures from above led to popular resistance that was inspired by ethical commitments to human equality and individual rights that were gradually embedded in international society during the nineteenth and twentieth centuries. The most recent period in the history of the society of states has been characterized by the prominence of cosmopolitan harm conventions – as in the example of the condemnations of genocide that were discussed earlier – that have the function of minimizing unnecessary suffering whether it is caused by the state's domestic rule or by foreign policy conduct. That development which reflected the moral sensibilities that were integral to the European civilizing process occurred alongside the emergence of 'annihilation units' that took classical great power rivalries to new levels. The interplay between those internal and external forces and the changing balance of power between those dynamics gave rise to a unique phase in the history of the Western states-systems.

   Ethical visions of an international society that reduces unjustifiable suffering have been connected with the idea of civilization since the concept first emerged in France in the late eighteenth century. Confidence in their 'civilized' condition led many Europeans to believe they could treat 'uncivilized' peoples as they wished but, for others, colonial cruelties had to be condemned because they clashed with the pretence of belonging to a 'higher civilization'. As previously noted, related images of civilized practices have influenced various features of world politics such as the humanitarian laws of war and the universal human rights culture. Those innovations reflected the troubled recognition that human ingenuity with respect to the ability to cause violent harm had outpaced inventiveness with regard to effective agreements on global standards of self-restraint. Humanitarian advances have not been the direct result of levels of civilization that 'simpler' peoples were somehow incapable of reaching; they have been connected with the political problems that engulfed 'civilized', state-organized societies with unprecedented military power. What might be called 'moral progress' has to be understood in connection with unique challenges that demand a melancholic refrain on core features of long-term social and political developments (Linklater 2011: 250ff.). The modern states-system may seem no different from its predecessors in crucial respects – or the main differences may be thought to consist of extraordinary advances in the capacity to inflict violent harm. But, for that very reason, societies have been pushed towards restraining the use of force in ways that increased the political influence of the prevalent images of 'civilized' behaviour.

Western conceptions of the relationship between violence and civilization have dominated world politics in the modern period. That is the reason for concentrating on Europe and its moral and political legacy in this work; the final volume in this trilogy will broaden the discussion. As discussed in the previous study of harm, the modern states-system has been one of the main driving forces behind rising levels of global interconnectedness over the last few centuries. Western ideas about international relations have defined the 'global covenant' that regulates the relations between independent political communities in the current era (Jackson 2000). Those Western principles have become embedded in the first universal society of states that will remain, for the foreseeable future, the highest 'steering mechanism' that the species can employ in the struggle to control global forces. What is important is how far the dominant principles and practices of any international society enable the constituent political parts to coexist with reduced levels and prospects of violence, and how far they lay the foundations for additional moral and political advances. Western ideas of territorial sovereignty, non-intervention, diplomacy and international law were accepted by the overwhelming majority of the colonized territories that became full members of international society in the post-Second World War era. The former imperial powers and the colonies have been linked by egalitarian principles that replaced the earlier 'hegemonial' conceptions of international society where one political system demanded that all others submit to its higher authority or 'standard of civiliza-tion' (Bull and Watson 1984). Agreements about the relevant international harm conventions have been accompanied by several cosmopolitan harm conventions that are part of the deeply contested legacy of the European civilizing process. What from that civilizing process will survive in the emerging 'post-Western' society of states, and what will be thrown to one side, is impossible to predict. Classical notions of sovereignty and non-intervention command general support; other Western values including liberal doctrines of human rights clearly do not enjoy the same status. The human rights culture may be so deeply embedded in international society and so certain of support from non-governmental organizations in world society that the drift back to a more basic pluralist society of states can be discounted in the immediate future (Hurrell 2007). Even so, the most influential Western perspectives on violence and civilization – on what is permissible and unac-ceptable in the relations between peoples – will not survive indefinitely. New centres of political power can be expected to press for revisions to the dominant harm conventions in the light of their political interests, collective identities and ethical preferences. New standards of social restraint are likely to appear along with novel conceptions of the we–I balance and transformations in we-feeling that characterize a new phase in the history of the modern international states-system.

The harmonious renegotiation of the organizing principles of world politics will require careful attention to an important theme that was raised in passing in Elias's *On the Process of Civilization,* namely that the constitutive units in the international system do not have the same understandings about the principles of self-restraint that should govern their relations with each other (or the relations between the state and its citizens or subjects). As will be discussed below, the societies in question have undergone different civilizing processes with distinctive harm conventions. Those patterns of change have not developed autonomously but have been interwoven in manifold ways that are only partly understood, but which can become more intelligible as a result of further advances in world or global history (Burke 2003; Hobson 2004; Nelson 1973). All that need be added is that systematic analysis of non-Western civilizing processes is in its infancy (Mennell 1996). That inquiry is essential not just for comprehending past struggles against Western political dominance but for understanding the contemporary challenge of reconstructing international society so that it is more responsive to the needs and aspirations of radically different, but increasingly interconnected, peoples.

Significant advances on that front are to be welcomed for several reasons. They are critical for breakthroughs in understanding how societies can become attuned to each other's needs and interests in the context of unprecedented levels of human interdependence that seem likely to rise in the decades and centuries that lie ahead; they are essential for advances in learning how to increase the capacity to think from the distinctive standpoints of different peoples, and to identify with all humans, irrespective of national origins; and they are vital for establishing the potentials for global agreements on social standards of self-restraint that can enable peoples to live together in relations of mutual respect and trust. One of the purposes of social-scientific investigation is to throw light on the conditions under which such global civilizing processes can develop. For that reason, the following inquiry is designed to contribute to Elias's conception of modes of social inquiry that provide humans with a larger fund of 'reality-congruent knowledge' that can assist them in gaining more control over largely unregulated global processes (Elias 2007: introduction). Elias insisted on a social-scientific 'detour of detachment' and protested against partisan social inquiry that overlooked inconvenient features of human societies in the haste to explain supposedly underlying harmonies between ethical ideals and basic social realities or historical tendencies. But as noted earlier, an unmistakeable normative dimension to Elias's inquiry is apparent in the conviction that one of the functions of social inquiry is to increase the fund of knowledge that can be harnessed to build a more 'advanced' global civilization.

Elias was opposed to forging close connections between normative and sociological inquiry. His vision of higher-level synthesis in the social sciences was limited accordingly. But without articulating the point exactly in the following terms, he recognized the connection between the contemporary condition in which analysis lags behind synthesis and the political problem where creativity with respect to the invention and deployment of violent technologies has often outstripped collective learning in restraining the power to harm. Advances towards higher levels of human interconnectedness have often outpaced measures to control the relevant processes so that harm to people and the natural environment is reduced if not eliminated. To some degree, there have been progressions in appreciating that some basic similarities between peoples – namely their common, but far from equal, vulnerability to mental and physical harm – can underpin the more accessible forms of human solidarity that can be expressed in agreements on cosmopolitan standards of self-restraint that deal with, amongst other things, the problem of global environmental harm. There is perhaps a greater sense than in the past that the moral importance that has been attached to cultural differences in the history of struggles for power and prestige has obscured such potentialities. However, material interconnections between peoples have not been accompanied by radical changes of outlook that express a collective desire for new forms of political community that protect people everywhere from avoidable violent and non-violent harm. It is important nonetheless to ask how far modern understandings of common vulnerabilities and unjustified suffering that are central to many global harm conventions distinguish the modern society of states from past international systems.

The argument of the preceding volume on harm was that the movement towards a more synoptic standpoint depends on a double integration – between the Eliasian analysis of civilizing processes and the English School inquiry into international society, and between those combined realms of inquiry and Frankfurt School critical theory. The sociological examination of the problem of harm in world politics should be understood in that context. The aim is to discover more about the 'civilizing' role of harm conventions in the states-systems of the West, to analyse the principal similarities and differences, to explain the conditions that favour processes of civilization in relations between societies, and to reflect on what the Western international political experience reveals about the prospects for a more 'advanced civilization' in which a 'cosmopolitan harm principle' is centre-stage in collective efforts to respond to the inescapable challenges of global interconnectedness.

There are a few additional points to make about the following discussion prior to providing an overview of the individual chapters. Writing a work such as this has involved engaging with a large literature to reach provisional conclusions. The exponential growth of the literature on the Holocaust provides a window onto a larger and growing problem in the social sciences. It has been reported that the standard bibliographical guide on Nazism grew from 25,000 to 37,000 items in 4–5 years; the literature on the Holocaust may have grown even faster (Evans 2003: preface; Stone 2010: introduction). It is clearly impossible to do more than consult a fraction of the relevant work in those areas. They may form a unique case, but rapid rates of expansion in other fields of investigation point to the 'double-bind processes' that scholars face in many disciplines. The sheer volume of literature creates pressures to research highly specialized areas, and to add to the published work that others will feel the same compulsion to master in the relentless narrowing of horizons and the greater fragmentation of knowledge. Increasing specialisms can result in a collective failure to make the connections between fields of investigation that are necessary to make more substantial advances in the specific areas in question. Crucial here is the need to consider the significance of long patterns of development – often extending not just over several decades but over centuries or millennia – for understanding particular historical eras and contemporary events. There is also the related issue of how advances in comprehending specific episodes and eras, now and in the past, can contribute to the larger stock of knowledge about very long-term processes of social and political change.

Process sociology is standard-setting in advancing a vision of the social sciences that considers the interconnections between diverse forms of human interaction in long-term perspective. A central conviction is that the most sophisticated realms of sociological inquiry are necessarily historical, and the most profound forms of historical explanation are sociological by virtue of utilizing precise social-scientific categories to show how particular epochs and events fit within long-run patterns of change. From that standpoint, every historical period is significant for comprehending what the species has become and is capable of. As a result, the contemporary era should not be privileged just because 'we' have a clear stake in the outcomes of various political struggles. Its meaning becomes clearer by comprehending not just 'what it means for us' but what it reveals about the point that humanity has reached in the long history of social and political development.

Obvious pitfalls await those who enter this field of inquiry. Critics of historical sociology and world history have stressed the danger of selecting evidence that provides convenient support for pre-existing and precarious assumptions about overall trends and tendencies. They have emphasized that such studies are derivative enterprises that depend on specialist inquiries that approach primary sources with methodological commitments that reduce the polluting effect of highly 'personalized', idiosyncratic interpretations. But the problems are not confined to those who stray from primary sources that many historians correctly regard as vital for explaining 'relatively short' and 'man- ageable' historical periods since those scholars also engage in intellectual abstraction, albeit at a lower level (Elias 2007a: 152ff.). The artificial division of the past into 'realistic' segments divorces specific areas from long historical processes that hold the key to grasping their essential characteristics. The upshot of intellectual partitioning is that synthesis in the social sciences continues to lag behind disparate and often unconnected modes of analysis. Few advances have taken place in constructing conceptual frameworks that support the integration of research findings in different areas of inquiry with the aim of promoting a more systematic accumulation of knowledge across the generations (Elias 2007a: ibid.). The following discussion is therefore undertaken in what process sociologists have described as the spirit of 'research-theorizing', where 'theory' and 'history' develop in tandem (Dunning and Hughes 2013: 49). As discussed in the volume that precedes this work, a central objective is to contribute to process sociology as well as to the English School analysis of international society, and to incorporate their main strengths in a higher synthesis that includes – contrary to the dominant positions in both areas of inquiry – the emancipatory ideals of Frankfurt School social theory.

The latter commitment runs contrary to the claims for detachment that are central to process sociology, although, as previously noted, its normative ambitions are evident in the contention that higher-level synthesis in the social sciences can add to the fund of knowledge that the species can employ to acquire greater control over poorly regulated global processes. From that standpoint, the relative paucity of sociological analyses of long-term patterns of change and the related problems that stem from the continuing fragmentation of knowledge do not only impoverish the social sciences; they contribute to the social forces that block the human potential to exercise more control over the relations that bind people together in lengthening webs of interconnectedness. One of the purposes of contemporary social science is to build conceptual frameworks that contribute to the larger challenge of orientating people to the attendant global uncertainties and challenges. One of the primary objectives is to promote 'education and knowledge-transfer' that is not confined to the short-term preoccupations of particular societies but has 'humanity as its horizon' (Elias 2008a). Those normative considerations are central to the following approach to the sociology of states-systems.

As for the organization of this book, the first chapter discusses the international politics of Ancient Greece. The analysis offers an assessment of Wight's contention that 'simpler civilizations' including the classical Greek world lacked any real counterpart to modern 'international ethics'. It is also framed by Elias's related statement that acts of genocide were prevalent in Ancient Greece and rarely attracted the moral condemnation that similar atrocities arouse today. Such claims clash with the main findings of the more recent literature on the Greeks at war that emphasize the constraining effects of identification with Hellenic international society. They are in tension with Thucydides' explanation of how the 'decivilizing' rivalry between Athens and Sparta threw an earlier long-term Hellenic civilizing process into reverse. Those points stress the need for a more complex analysis of the tensions between civilizing and decivilizing processes – and between integrative and disintegrative tendencies – in the Hellenic states-system. Central process sociological concepts that were discussed earlier are invaluable for an analysis of the shifting relationships between violence and civilization in classical antiquity that breaks with the one-dimensional image of the high tolerance of inter-societal violence that was noted above.

The second chapter is in two main parts. The first analyses the relationship between violence and civilization in the period between the rise of Macedonian hegemony over the Greek cities and the disintegration of Alexander's empire into the component parts of the Hellenistic states-system. The second focuses on the period between the emergence of Rome's dominance in Italy and the consolidation of its empire. The discussion heeds warnings against too rigid a separation between states-systems and empires (Watson 1992: 13ff.). It draws attention to levels of violence that appear to confirm arguments about the absence of equivalents to modern conceptions of international ethics in the ancient states-systems. But it is important to consider influential ideas about restraining political power and acting with moderation and mercy that formed a bridge between the classical Greek world and medieval and early modern court societies. Those concepts influenced the development of 'civilized' attitudes to violence within modern European states, and they were important factors in two interrelated developments that Elias did not investigate – the early disputes about the rights and duties of imperial governance and the considerations of the standards of restraint that should be observed in the European society of states that was emerging in that period. Highlighting the tolerance of force in the ancient states-systems obscures the respects in which earlier conceptions of violence and civilization influenced later debates and developments that helped to define the modern society of states.

Chapter three considers the relationship between civilizing and decivilizing processes in Latin Christendom, specifically noting the Church's efforts to tame the medieval warriors through the doctrinal fusion of violence and piety, and by attaching traditional notions of chivalry to a public ideology of 'decivilizing', crusading warfare. Medieval violence and cruelty have often been contrasted with the more peaceful and secure conditions of recent times (Elias 2012: 186ff.). Many, though not all, historians of the period now contest or reject that interpretation. What is indisputable, as recent scholarship in International Relations has emphasized, is that the stark dichotomy between the 'medieval' and 'modern' world detracts attention from long patterns of change that emerged as early as the eleventh and twelfth centuries. As Elias argued, they included the rise of new power monopolies that would conduct violent 'elimination contests' over larger areas in the coming centuries. But various images of chivalry that influenced the development of the just war doctrine demonstrate that the violence of the medieval age was not exactly free from the influence of 'international ethics'. It is important to consider whether the traditional focus on medieval violence did not only exaggerate the level of tolerance of physical force but also detracted attention from the influence of medieval constitutionalism on the formation of European international society and on parallel images of the 'civil empire'.

Chapter four discusses the interconnections between civil strife and intercity conflict in the Italian city-state system, in a critical phase in the process of state formation and in the overall 'civilization' of conduct in Europe. Efforts to pacify relations within the cities – and the appearance of various ideals of the civil life – are discussed. The chapter considers the high tolerance of violence in the Italian Renaissance, but it highlights features of the city-state system that were not included in Elias's explanation of the European civilizing process but have long been central to English School analysis – specifically the use of diplomacy in attempts to pacify a city-states system that was connected with, and would become subsumed within, the larger web of European great power rivalries. The humanistic exploration of the relationship between *Fortuna* and necessity is investigated because it signified changing orientations towards the social and political world that would be taken further by Enlightenment thinkers in a new phase of the European civilizing process. At the heart of the inquiry was the problem of how far societies could tame struggles for power and prestige within the cities and in their external relations by acquiring a deeper understanding of the laws and patterns of human affairs. A key issue is whether the idea of the Renaissance as the 'first Enlightenment' reveals the distant origins of the quest to promote a civilizing process that has been a major distinguishing feature of the modern society of states in recent decades.

Beginning with Elias's comments on the rapacious nature of warfare in early modern Europe, chapter five discusses a turning point in the history of the West – and in the social and political development of humanity as a whole – namely, the process of state formation and the accompanying 'civilizing' of conduct that first occurred in 'court society'. The point has been made that Elias's reflections on the violent nature of relations between states largely ignored the restraining influence of international society in the modern period and in the preceding eras. That theme will be extended by considering the Northern humanist images of 'civilized' foreign policy. Elias attached particular importance to Erasmus's explorations of civility which he regarded as a key influence on, and reflection of, the emergent European civilizing process. But he did not consider the significance of his reflections on international relations for ethical debates about violence and civilization that arose in the Italian Renaissance and continue to this day. Nor did he explore one of the main features of the European civilizing process which is considered in this chapter, namely the construction of conceptions of diplomatic restraint that have been highlighted in English School analyses of modern international society. Those images revealed how links between court society and civilization that were central to Elias's analysis of the configuration of the modern state also shaped the 'civilized' European society of states.

Disputes about the rights and wrongs of imperial rule which were a second offshoot of the civilizing process are the subject of discussion in chapter six. European peoples forged their 'civilized identities through stark contrasts with 'social inferiors' in the non-European regions. As far as related attitudes to violence were concerned, they firmly believed that in relations with 'savages', 'civilized' peoples were not obliged to abide by the restraints on force that they generally observed amongst themselves. Images of civilization placed restraints on some forms of violence and authorized others. But that was not their only effect on relations between imperial and colonized peoples. Throughout the history of the colonial era, notions of civility and civilization were a powerful weapon in the hands of critics of imperial violence that led to organized campaigns against the cruelties of the Atlantic slave trade and chattel slavery. They were later extended to include public opposition to empire itself that represents a new phase in the relationship between violence and civilization in the Western states-systems.

Chapter seven turns to the role of 'radical Enlightenment' thinkers in the transformation of 'civilized' self-images not least because they advanced the claim that those who inflicted colonial cruelties forfeited the right to be regarded as civilized. European peoples had long believed that they were morally entitled to 'civilize' other peoples, but central strands of the 'radical Enlightenment' shifted the focus to the transformations that Europeans had to undergo in order to 'civilize' themselves. The chapter considers how the interplay between analyses of lengthening chains of human interconnectedness, compassionate cosmopolitanism and universal histories gave rise to novel positions on violence and civilization. New images were formed of a future global civilizing process in which relations between interdependent societies were steadily pacified – in which war-prone absolutist societies were replaced by what has come to be known as the 'liberal peace'.

Enlightenment conceptions of the future have been criticized for their naive faith in the inevitability of progress. That is a simplistic interpretation of the main patterns of thought. Nevertheless, as discussed in chapter eight, the rise of the nation-in-arms and 'total warfare' in the aftermath of the French Revolution undermined the confidence in the progressive nature of modern societies that is often associated with the European Enlightenment. The discussion considers the appearance of the 'nationalization of suffering' that unfolded in tandem with the 'nation in arms'. It explains how attitudes to violence and civilization were refashioned as aerial bombardment brought warfare from the remote battlefield into the heartland of industrial societies. The social transformation of warfare was a product of the radical extension of state power that is one of the direct outcomes of the European civilizing process. One of its consequences was an increase in the pressures on states to tame international struggles for power and to introduce global harm conventions in a concerted attempt to minimize 'unnecessary suffering' and 'superfluous injury' to military personnel and civilian communities. Global 'civilizing offensives' that were unknown in earlier states-system became more central as a result of the interplay between those international developments and the domestic transformation of the societies involved.

Chapter nine discusses the phenomenon of 'industrial killing' that distinguished the Nazi genocides from earlier examples of mass slaughter. That dimension of modern societies led to major debates about the European civilizing process. They include disputes about whether genocidal violence demonstrated a latent potential for 'civilized barbarism' that plainly contradicted Elias's analysis or revealed the importance of its inquiry into the 'breakdown' of civilized restraints on force for which European peoples were unprepared. From the latter standpoint, the leading societies had deceived themselves into thinking that 'civilization' was a natural condition that was bound to survive rather than a process that had to be protected and could be reversed. They were duped into supposing that mass slaughter was confined to 'savage' groups. The first images of the death camps produced widespread revulsion that highlighted, according to Elias, the gulf between ancient and modern attitudes to genocide. Certainly, feelings of shock and repugnance were part of the civilizing process in which people became more sensitive to public violence and to what was designated as cruelty. They found expression in demands for social and political institutions that would guard against the peculiar dangers that 'civilized' peoples face as a result of the extraordinary growth and possible breakdown of state monopolies of the instruments of violence. In large part because of the Nazi genocides, core elements of the European civilizing process have been embedded in cosmopolitan harm conventions in the international society of states. The 'civilizing' aversion to unnecessary pain and suffering is most clearly expressed in the universal human rights culture and in associated innovations in international criminal law that separate the contemporary society of states from its predecessors.

Chapter ten extends that last point by discussing efforts to build a cosmopolitan version of the liberal harm principle into international law and diplomatic practice. It analyses efforts to reconfigure the principle of national sovereignty – a central concept in the European civilizing process that helped legitimate the state's monopolies of power – and to invest it with new moral and political responsibilities given the multiple challenges that are inherent in the current phase of global integration. The taming of sovereigns through planned 'civilizing' strategies to eradicate militarism, and through other global measures to restrain violent harm, has been a principal feature of the recent phase of the 'civilizing process'. Those initiatives are as central as the 'taming of the warriors' or the 'civilizing' of imperial sovereignty were in an earlier age. They are part of the same pattern of development and they are a reminder of how state-building, imperialism and international society formed three sides of one overall European civilizing process. The chapter highlights some parallels between the early modern period and the contemporary era where lengthening and deepening webs of interconnectedness have created major incentives to make the exercise of state power answerable to global standards of restraint that represent a new phase in the history of the idea of sovereignty. Efforts to construct innovative conceptions of global responsibility are evidence of growing pressures to establish novel relations between sovereignty, civilization and international society – to devise new standards of restraint in conjunction with a transformed 'civilized' we-identity and parallel changes in the we–I balance.

Chapter eleven draws together Elias's reflections on international relations with the aim of advancing the process-sociological account of civilizing processes in the contemporary international society, one that focuses specifically on attitudes to permissible and forbidden conduct. It notes that, with exceptions, process sociologists have concentrated on explaining the absence of a global equivalent to the European civilizing process. What has been missing is an engagement with reflections on the nature of international society and an exploration of how deliberations about the permissible and the prohibited have shaped conceptions of civilization and 'conscience formation' within that figuration. The final chapter identifies four distinguishing features of the modern society of states in the attempt to show how a synthesis of process sociology and English School analysis helps to explain key 'civilizing' dynamics. Looking forward to the final volume in this trilogy of books on the problem of harm, it considers the reappearance of grand narratives that trace the development of the species as a whole in an attempt to enable people to orientate themselves to the challenges of global connectedness. Such narratives address the disjuncture between increasing material interdependencies between human groups and continuing powerful emotional attachments to traditional 'survival units'. They are indispensable for the development of a more cosmopolitan we-identity and 'civilized' practices in which the social standards of self-restraint are higher than they are today, and in which the state, international society and humanity form a we–I balance in which cosmopolitan harm conventions acquire much greater importance. That is one of the principal stakes in the analysis of violence and civilization in the Western states-systems.

1

The Hellenic City-States System

The Ancient Greeks ... who are so often held up to us as models of civilized behaviour, considered it quite a matter of course to commit acts of mass destruction, not quite identical to those of the National Socialists but, nevertheless, similar to them in certain respects. The Athenian popular assembly decided to wipe out the entire population of Melos, because the city did not want to join the Athenian colonial empire. There were dozens of other examples in antiquity of what we now call genocide. The difference between this and the attempted genocide in the 1930s and 1940s is at first glance not easy to grasp. Nevertheless, it is quite clear. In the period of Greek antiquity, this warlike behaviour was considered normal. It conformed to the standard.

(Elias 2013: 445–6)

The contrasts that Elias drew between ancient and modern warfare must be treated with considerable caution. His observations about the greater tolerance of genocide in classical Greece and Rome captured certain features of the wars between Athens and Sparta, but serious doubts must be raised about whether they provided an accurate summation of the main patterns of development across the whole history of the Hellenic city-states system. The comments about genocide seem to imply that international relations in ancient Greece were remarkably static: an interpretation that is supported in some but not all quarters (see the contrasting views of van Wees 2004; Connor 1988; and Low 2007). If those who reject the interpretation that 'total war' was endemic are correct, then, paradoxically, Elias's comments were at odds with his processual standpoint – with a long-term perspective on social interaction that analysed recurring geopolitical competition and war in conjunction with shifting relations between civilizing and decivilizing processes or integrative and disintegrative tendencies.

Elias's remarks on ancient and modern attitudes to genocide certainly stressed that social attitudes to violence had changed over time. Commenting on the *pankration* – literally, 'total force' or 'no holds barred', or a form of ground wrestling in which participants were not infrequently killed – Elias (2008b: 117–18) speculated that the 'standards of violence in fighting may have fluctuated' over the thousand year period in which the Olympic Games were held. But his comments were designed to emphasize that modern ethical sensitivities to violent harm are very different from the standards that prevailed in classical antiquity where great value was attached to success in agonistic competition in the intertwined spheres of sport and warfare (Pritchard 2013: 176ff.).[1] Those observations were not meant to imply that modern peoples are intrinsically 'better' than ancient Greeks; they did not deny the existence of peculiarly modern forms of 'barbarism' or rule out the possibility of 'regression' to the mass slaughter of whole populations. Moreover, Elias's remarks about the distinctively 'modern' repugnance towards genocide – and his statement that such feelings indicated that 'human societies have undergone a civilizing process, however limited in scope and however unstable its results' (Elias 2008b: 125) – did not suggest that the Greek world was entirely devoid of 'civilizing spurts' that had tamed struggles for power. It is important to extend the point. Any emphasis on the differences between the ancient Greek and the modern states-systems should not obscure the latter's debt to 'civilizing' themes in the international relations of earlier eras including classical antiquity. They included not only the contrasts between 'civilized' and 'savage' peoples or 'natural slaves' that influenced attitudes to European conquest but also the emphasis on the virtues of self-restraint in political affairs that Roman-Christian civilization inherited and transmitted to the modern world.

To understand the Hellenic city-state system, it is necessary to analyse the distinctive civilizing process that bound the poleis together. It has been argued that the city-states system was superimposed on extensive personal networks which survived, *inter alia*, in the idea of *xenia* or guest friendship that had a 'civilizing' influence on the relations between societies (Herman 1987: 6). The analysis illustrates Wight's observation that all societies of states emerged within cultural zones where a pre-existing we-identity supported agreements on principles of coexistence (Wight 1977: ch. 1). It is essential however to understand the long-term patterns of social change that led to identification with the 'civilized' world of Hellas; it is important to stress that 'civilized' self-images were linked with intercity harm conventions that rested on clear distinctions between permissible and impermissible violence. Finally, it is necessary to analyse what they disclosed about the forms of vulnerability and suffering that aroused moral concern in ancient Greece. Although disputes continue about its historical accuracy, Thucydides' account of the wars

---

[1] A central theme in process sociology is that attitudes to violence in sport are not sealed off from other social processes but encapsulate wider understandings about acceptable levels of violence in relations within the group and in conduct towards outsiders – unsurprisingly, given that sport has long been a training ground for war. Elias and Dunning (2008: 77) refer to the 'controlled decontrolling of restraints on emotions' to describe the measured relaxation of the customary taboos against aggression in contact sports such as boxing and wrestling (see also Poliakoff 1987 and Spivey 2004).

between Athens and Sparta remains the principal extant source for interpreting those features of relations between the ancient poleis (Hornblower 1987). The *Archaeology* which opens his account of the wars provided an overview of the formation of a unique and highly prized Hellenic civilizing process. The core of that work explained how conflict between the Athenians and the Spartans unleashed 'decivilizing' processes that eroded conventional restraints on warfare that had been integral to collective identification with Hellas. Efforts to portray Thucydides as one of the founders of political realism ignore his central objective which was to understand the conditions under which 'civilized' societies flourish as well as the pressures that can lead to the rapid dissolution of 'civilized' constraints on human conduct (Rahe 2002). Thucydides' narrative discussed the decline of we-feeling and the changing we–I balance between Hellas and the polis which was the fundamental 'survival unit'; it combined that endeavour with an investigation into 'integration–disintegration tensions' not only during the conflicts between Athens and Sparta but across the preceding centuries. As far as the Peloponnesian Wars were concerned, those tensions included the fluctuating role of moral and religious constraints on force, the 'decivilizing' effects of appeals to strategic necessity and the rise of stark insider–outsider dualisms and destructive masculinities that, dispensing with the customary laws of warfare, plunged Hellas into catastrophic violence.

On that interpretation, Thucydides (1.23) lamented the unparalleled destructiveness of the wars between Athens and Sparta that reversed the process of Hellenic civilization (Kokaz 2001; Lateiner 1977). Not that the Greeks described the wars in those terms. They did not possess the modern idea of civilization but they used several concepts that had clear affinities with it (Lebow 2003: 117n4). Thucydides' history stated that the periods of greatest ferocity were not the historical norm but were radical departures from traditional customs and practices. Contemporary scholarship maintains that those violent episodes disrupted an older 'civilizing process' that was recovered in the final stages of Greek history before Macedon subjugated the city states. But advances in learning how to coexist more peacefully appeared too late in the day to save the polis from the consequences of Macedonian and Roman expansion.

To consider those matters in more detail, the following discussion describes the customs and beliefs that bound the city states together in the Hellenic international society. It then analyses the dominant attitudes to violence and suffering in the domestic and international spheres (subject to the standard caveats about the accuracy of surviving sources and about the degree to which speculations about such orientations can be imputed to all Greeks across the generations). The idea of collective social learning is introduced in the next section, which lays the groundwork for some provisional conclusions about the Hellenic civilizing process that have two main purposes – to assess Elias's statements about the differences between ancient and modern states-systems, and to advance preliminary reflections on what this overview of the Hellenic city-states system contributes to understanding the preconditions of global civilizing processes.

An International Society?

In the fifth century BC, the Greeks regarded the polis as the pinnacle of a long pattern of development from the simple, scattered settlements in which their ancestors lived in the era before the Hellenes clearly distinguished themselves from the barbarians (Thucydides 1.3). Pride in a Hellenic civilizing process is evident in the customs that Thucydides (1.6) described as indicators of how civilized Greeks – and Athenians in particular – distanced themselves from the less 'advanced' societies of Hellas and adjacent 'barbaric' peoples. Thucydides (4.126) referred to the Greeks' contempt for 'barbarian' warfare where both flight and attack were 'equally honourable' and where the attempt to intimidate adversaries from afar was preferred to the noble trials of hand-to-hand combat. In the period before the emergence of Hellas, piracy was a common profession; Hellenes and barbarians plundered unprotected cities out of greed or to support their poorest members (Thucydides 1.5; also de Souza 1999: ch. 2). Far from being condemned as disgraceful, piracy was deemed to be honourable; it survived, Thucydides (1.5) argued, as the route to social esteem 'even to-day' in several parts of the Greek mainland. Various settlements had used their material wealth to build walled cities, but armed robbery endured in many areas (Thucydides: 1.4–7). The ancient custom of carrying weapons in the age when homes were 'unprotected' and 'intercourse with each other was unsafe' lived on in some parts of Hellas (Thucydides 1.6). Athens had been the first to abandon the practice of carrying arms at all times that remained the rule 'among foreigners' (Fisher 1998; van Wees 2004: 37ff.). Even so, each household had its supply of weapons, in part because policing in classical Athens and in other societies was largely a vigilante operation (Cohen 1995).

Thucydides' history stressed that the most advanced societies had made significant progress in pacifying the world at least within the city walls; travel especially by sea contained its own hazards that included the risk of kidnap (see Rihll 1993). He added that in other respects, as in the case of their mode of dress, the ancient Hellenes were 'tribes' that lived in the manner of the 'barbarians' of that time (Thucydides 1.2). The latter survived without 'any of the basic elements of civilization, viz. commerce, agriculture, surplus capital, walled cities or fixed settlements, or political organization of any complexity' that distinguished Hellas (Price 2001: 335). Other parts of the *Archaeology* that opened Thucydides' history of the Athenian–Spartan wars indicate that he was not only interested in what each city had won for itself but also in what they had contributed, individually and collectively, to the most remarkable achievement of all – the civilization of Hellas (Price 2001: ch. 7; Lebow 2003: ch. 4). The discussion constituted a grand narrative that explained how progress came to be undone by its own instruments, the city states (Price 2001: 376). Herodotus had described the Hellenes' success in harnessing advances in collective social power in response to the Persian military threat. Thucydides (1.8) explained in intricate detail how the idea of Hellas was driven forward by powerful cities that were able to project their political and military power across greater distances with contradictory results (Parry 1989). The upshot is that Thucydides was one of the first analysts of society and politics to reflect on 'the great tragedy of social life (which is) that every extension of solidarity, from family to village' and beyond to the world of cities, states and empires, created the potential for 'organized hatred on a larger scale' (Stinchcombe 1975: 601ff.). He was amongst the first to consider the ambiguities of rising levels of interconnectedness, namely how the pacification of larger-scale societies developed in tandem with their entanglement in more violent 'elimination contests' that were conducted over larger areas (de Romilly 1977).

The Hellenic civilizing process included advances in pacification within cities though not in their external relations to the same extent (Orwin 1994: 30–2). Early Greeks had exercised a 'right of reprisal' in dealings with outsiders. As with many early societies, the Greeks used financial settlements to deter acts of reprisal (Garlan 1976: 39). But 'man seizure' (*androlepsia*) was standard as citizens captured one or more foreigners in retaliation for killing one of their own and where there was no prospect of compensation (Bederman 2001: 123ff.). Reprisals had been a core feature of the 'self-help' system in the period described by Homer, although public authorities would later restrain 'private' wars that could plunge an entire community into violent conflict (Pritchett 1991: 358ff.). The dominant strata became relatively restrained in comparison with their pre-classical ancestors (Elias 2008b: 127–8). A significant development was the increased reliance on judicial means of settling disputes. The institution of *isopoliteiai* which gave the citizens of other cities the right of access to courts in the pursuit of justice was one such initiative that was designed to bring an end to uncontrollable cycles of revenge.

Changing attitudes to piracy and looting were no less central to the Hellenic civilizing process. In the Homeric age, raiding was generally held to be 'legitimate': there were no religious prohibitions against piracy, although custom dictated that sacred sites and occupants should not be harmed (Jackson 1993: 68–9). As previously noted, Thucydides (1.5) contended that raiding could still win a man considerable prestige in those regions where 'the habit of carrying arms is a survival of their old freebooting life'. In the classical period, wars between the cities were usually described as morally just responses to wrongs that others had inflicted. By that point, the 'unprovoked raids' that had been 'a matter of glory' in Homeric times had lost much of their former legitimacy (Austin 1993: 201). Piracy flourished where weak political structures were unable to prevent it, but, according to Thucydides, it had been driven to the margins of Hellas with advances in territorial pacification, only to resurface during the Peloponnesian War (Garlan 1976: 33; Ormerod 1978: ch. 4).

The 'common laws of Hellas' that had their origins in Homeric times were fundamental to the belief in a long-term civilizing process. Thucydides (1.3) maintained that Hellas 'engaged in no enterprise in common' before the Trojan War. Until then, the Hellenes did not even have a common name that distinguished them from 'barbarians'. Significantly, changing self-images that emphasized self-restraint were inextricably connected with negative conceptions of other peoples, and specifically the Persians' alleged comparative lack of self-control. The Greek distinction between *hybris* and *sophrosyne* captured the essential point. The former term referred to an assault on another's honour that risked provoking anger or shame, and it stressed the obsession with exacting revenge. As the opposite of *sophrosyne* (self-restraint), *hybris* was held to be a threat to civilized ways of life that was dramatized by the distinctions between Hellenes and the 'barbaric' Persian invader, 'the epitome of *hybris*' (Fisher 1992: 111ff., 500ff.). The identity of a distinctive Hellenic civilizing process was evident in political efforts to transform the relationship between 'individualistic values' that revolved around the male 'preoccupation with ... honour' that could easily trigger violence in response to actual or perceived insults and the 'other regarding' or 'humane' values that were defended in the attempt to control traditional rights of 'self-assertion' (Cairns 1993: 240–1). The individualistic side of honour was hard to reconcile with a collective interest in civil order because there were inbuilt dangers of acting with excess, in going beyond what adversaries could regard as reasonable or right (Cohen 1995: 66–68). On at least one account, the male citizens of democratic Athens went through a civilizing process that elevated individual self-restraint above the pursuit of honour that resulted in excessive force (Herman 2006: 201ff.). That 'sea change' in social attitudes to violence placed constraints on destructive masculinity for the sake of 'communal' principles. It represented a relocation of the 'threshold principle' – a decisive shift in the point at which 'honour [was] deemed to have been impugned' (Herman 2006: 165). The contention that 'self-control is the chief element in self-respect' (Thucydides 1.84) was an illustration of a changing we–I balance, but one that did not greatly influence the conduct of foreign policy which continued to be governed by permissive rules regarding violence (Herman 2006: 360ff.).

Central issues surrounding the male right of 'self-assertion' were at the heart of the Hellenic civilizing process. They had been highlighted in the

Iliad where Homer (Books 22–4) described Achilles' vengeful act of dese-crating the body of the Trojan, Hector. Apollo was said to have accused Achilles of failing to heed 'the voice of mercy'. He ordered him to accept ransom in exchange for Hector's body and warned that the failure to do so would incur Zeus' wrath. Such passages have been regarded as evidence that the mutilation of an enemy corpse was anathema to the Greeks and a marker of their perceived superiority to barbarians. In the classical period, permit-ting the enemy to bury its war dead was a core element of we-feelings that were enshrined in the warriors' honour code. The conditions that Hector had attached to his challenge to the Achaeans exemplified the longstanding social significance of that chivalric or 'civilizing' norm: 'And here are the conditions I lay down, with Zeus for witness. If your man kills me . . . he can strip me of my arms . . . but he must let them bring my body home, so that the Trojans and their wives may burn it in the proper manner. If Apollo lets me win and I kill your man, I shall strip his armour off . . . but I shall send back his corpse . . . so that the long-haired Achaeans may give him burial rites and make a mound above him by the broad Hellespont. Then one day some future traveller . . . will say: "This is the monument of some warrior of an earlier day who was killed in single combat by illustrious, Hector." Thus my fame will be kept alive for ever' (Homer *Iliad*, Book 7).

Those observations about war raise the question of whether the Greeks found 'a pleasure in attacking' (*Angriffslust*) that has been regarded as typical of warrior codes including the medieval version that was tamed in the course of the European civilizing process (Elias 2012: 189ff.). It has been argued that, in Homer's writings, the concept of *charmei gethosunoi* described the thrill of combat rather than the joys of killing (Coker 2007: 27). Achilles was con-demned for his lack of restraint, and for failing to control *thumos*, the seat of anger (Lintott 1992). Far from standing in judgment of Achilles, Homer may have hoped to encourage sympathy and understanding on the grounds that even the best of men can do 'bad things' (*kakaerga*) 'in their grief and fury' (Elias 2008b: 126).

The term, *schetlios*, was used to describe actions that were thoughtless and ruthless, indicating that embryonic conceptions of later ideas of cruelty in war existed in the heroic age described by Homer (Lintott 1992). As already noted, the broader point is that the warriors' quest for honour could provide the motive for displaying noble self-restraint but it could trigger violent revenge against attacks on a person's social standing that had predictable 'decivilizing' results. The connection between those orientations and foreign policy is evident in the claim that the 'Athenians saw their city as a Homeric warrior *writ large*, dedicated to violent revenge and possessed of a touchy sense of honour', but they recognized that cities, just like individuals, should strive to resolve disputes in a 'civilized' way, without recourse to war (Hunt 2010: 2–3).

In the classical period, the victorious army erected a trophy to commemorate its military success before collecting its dead. Enemy corpses were stripped of weapons and precious objects prior to allowing the survivors to recover the bodies and to perform the funerary rites befitting fallen warriors. The Hellenic civilizing process dictated that bodies were returned unmutilated (Pritchett 1985: 249). Violations of that practice are mentioned in the *Iliad* but it has been argued that 'by the classical period, the Greeks forbade such outrages even when they were dealing with barbarians' (Garlan 1976: 61). In the main, combatants buried their dead the day after the battle, but conflict could be suspended when one side requested a temporary truce before the outcome of the struggle had been decided (Garlan 1976: ibid.). Such agreements to permit the rapid retrieval of bodies and the identification of those who had died in battle undoubtedly reflected the speed with which bodies decomposed in the summer heat (Vaughn 1991). Truces that were agreed at the time of religious festivals upheld similar civilizing restraints. Breaches certainly occurred, but religious prohibitions on violence often prevailed over strategic calculations of the 'necessities of defence' (Pritchett 1971: 125–6).

As with the earlier Sumerian city-states system, treaties derived their binding force from the convention of pledging oaths before the gods who acted as 'third party' guarantors; it was presumed that they were harmed by infringements and disposed to side with the injured party (Garlan 1976: 55; Dover 1974: 248ff.). Reflecting their critical role in the preservation of social restraints, shame and stigma were attached to those who violated sacred duties. Collective disgrace that was caused by leaders who disregarded restraints that were integral to the Hellenic we–I balance could blight a city for generations. The desire to avoid shame (*aidos*) was central to the Greek honour code (Cairns 1993). Its role was to establish the point at which immoderate, civic 'self-assertion' trampled on another's honour and invited self-reproach (Cairns 1993: introduction, 432). Departures from customary rules often occurred when internal or external restraints on cities were powerless to check the pursuit of military advantage. The absence of a higher court of appeal above the cities meant that there was ample scope for acrimony when interests and presumed entitlements clashed. A striking example was the Boeotian refusal to return the Athenian dead after the battle of Delium on the grounds that Athens had earlier seized and fortified a Boeotian temple in contravention of the Hellenic laws of war. As part of their defence, the Athenians proclaimed that they had occupied the temple for reasons of military necessity, and asserted that the gods 'would look indulgently on any action done under the stress of war and danger' (Thucydides 4.97–101; Pritchett 1985: 191). The rapid corruption of such 'civilizing' restraints on violence was a central theme in Thucydides' history of the Peloponnesian Wars (Thucydides 7.75). The incident was the solitary example that Thucydides provided of a refusal to return an adversary's fallen warriors, and one of only two reported instances in the entire classical Greek era (Orwin 1994: 90).

Crucial dimensions of the Hellenic process of civilization were identified in Herodotus' passage on the Athenians' efforts to reassure the Spartans that they would decline Persia's invitation to enter into a separate peace. The Athenians proclaimed that the Hellenes enjoyed 'a kinship . . . in blood and speech', and enjoyed a 'likeness of our way of life' that was most apparent in 'the shrines of gods and the sacrifices that we have in common'. Athens referred to such we-feeling when describing its responsibility to avenge the Persian decisions to burn temples and desecrate the images of the gods (Herodotus 4.8.144). Emotional identification with Hellas (*homonoia* or 'same-mindedness') was also embodied in religious festivals, such as the Pan-Hellenic games at Olympia and in the amphictyonies which included the Oracle of Apollo at Delphi (Spivey 2004: 184ff.). In the passage cited above, Herodotus stated that the latter union was cemented by an oath not to destroy a member polis, or 'starve it out', or 'cut off its running water in war or in peace'. The shared understanding was that those that violated the oath, plundered the shrine or had designs upon it deserved punishment. Amphictyonies were unions of cities that usually came together for religious purposes but also arranged truces to ensure that festivals and games, and oracles and shrines, were free from military assault. Wight observed that the Delphic amphictyony acted as arbitrator in intercity disputes. The purpose of arbitration appears to have been to restore friendly relations rather than to attempt to reach a 'critically satisfactory settlement' of the relevant disputes (Wight 1977: 52). But amphictyonies were evidence of the conviction that disputes between cities could be resolved through a civilized appeal to the customary principles that were embedded in those institutions (Hunt 2010: ch. 9).

Commenting on Herodotus' remarks about the Delphic amphictyony, Wight (1977: 50) stated that the pledge regarding the non-violation of water supplies was 'practically ineffective, since its imputed violation by one party released the others from its obligations'. Others have added that such harm conventions did not exist throughout Hellas. However, shared commitments including the belief that killing a person who had been granted religious sanctuary was an assault on the temple and an offence against the gods demonstrated that the Greeks did not regard 'the destruction of cities [in war] as inevitable' or honourable (Luard 1976: 288; Kern 1999: 136). At least – and the point has far-reaching significance for the analysis of violence and civilization in states-systems – they did not adopt such policies where reciprocity provided some guarantee of general compliance with the relevant civilizing restraints (Low 2007: ch. 2).

City states formed a society that consisted of kinship ties and special agreements that expressed friendship or *philia*. Endemic competition was moderated by such manifestations of we-feeling, by religious prohibitions and by considerations of personal and collective honour (van Wees 2001). The Hellenic world did not have the permanent institutions that modern societies use to determine the restraints that should be placed on national self-assertion. There was no equivalent of contemporary international organizations, codified international law, resident ambassadors that enjoy diplomatic immunities and privileges, a contrived balance of power, or the belief that the great powers are collectively responsible for preserving order between ostensibly sovereign equals. Reflecting those realities, the dominant strands of Greek moral and political thought argued that the good life could only be found within the polis which was the summit of a long pattern of development that was celebrated for taming the Homeric warrior ideal (Elshtain 1987: 49ff.). In the era of Plato and Aristotle, political theory focused almost exclusively on life within the polis in large part because relations between cities appeared to be 'unpredictable' and 'unmanageable' (Dawson 1996: 104–5).

Even so, the city states formed an international society, albeit one that lacked the complex legal and diplomatic institutions that have distinguished the contemporary society of states (Kokaz 2001). The Greeks relied on heralds and messengers who enjoyed special rights, and they invented the practice of conferring 'guest-friendship' on the citizen of another city state (Wight 1977: 53ff.; Mitchell 1997: 28ff.). By acquiring that special status, the person concerned, the *proxenos*, became responsible for assisting citizens who visited his city. The institution promoted a degree of we-feeling and fostered civilized relations between the members of different city states. Supporting mechanisms included modes of arbitration, and *philia* or diplomatic friendship where specific cities made express commitments not to injure or indeed to assist each other (Bauslaugh 1991: 63; Reus-Smit 1999: ch. 3; Wight 1977: 52; see Karavites 1992: ch. 2 on the Homeric origins of *philia*). There was no Hellenic conception of answerability to 'world public opinion', no cosmopolitan conception of humanity that demanded restraint on the part of city states and no counterpart to the modern idea that what is now called genocide should 'shock the conscience of humankind' (Wight 1977: 67ff.). But there were times when conquered cities pleaded for mercy and argued that their destruction would cause widespread indignation (Thucydides 3:57). The nearest thing to world public opinion was evident in outrage at such transgressions of 'the common law of Hellas' as burning temples or entering religious sanctuaries to seize the property of the gods (Wight 1977: 47–8; Garlan 1976: 58). Thucydides regarded the violation of truces surrounding religious festivals, the spoliation of temples, and the murder of neutral merchants who traded with enemies as shameful assaults on Hellenic civilization (Price 2001: 217ff.; Bederman 2001: 227ff.). He described such abominations as examples of *stasis* or civil war as much as *polemos* or interstate conflict; Hellas as a whole was the 'casualty' of the regression to 'barbarism' (Price 2001: 77). Herodotus had shown how a Hellenic we-identity was forged from collective repugnance at Persian violations of sacred sites. Thucydides' expressions of despair at the Greeks' sacrilegious behaviour showed how the symbolic boundaries between the 'civilized' and the 'barbarian' became blurred or indistinct in the struggle between Athens and Sparta (Price 2001: 233ff.). As a result, the we–I balance shifted dramatically from Hellas towards the short-term interests of the cities concerned and their ruthless governing elites. The standards of self-restraint that distinguished Hellenic civilization broke down in the process.

The 'civilized/barbarian' distinction provides a reminder of how the scope of emotional identification between the members of an international society is intertwined with the sense of 'cultural differentiation' from the outlying world, and of how 'civilized' self-images can legitimate violence against social 'inferiors' (Wight 1977: 33ff.; Wight 1991: ch. 4). Prior to the Persian wars, the idea of *barbaros* had been used in a non-pejorative way to describe those who spoke unintelligible languages. Homer's portrayal of the Trojans or Herodotus' observations about radically different peoples were largely free of pernicious distinctions between 'civilized' Hellenes and 'barbarian' outsiders. Herodotus (6.97; 7.134ff.) stressed that the Persians under Xerxes treated envoys with 'magnanimity'. Recent scholarship confirms that it was widely believed that harming ambassadors, whether they were Greek or 'barbarian', was an outrage even though there was no conception of an automatic right to diplomatic inviolability (Bederman 2001: 110, 251). But Herodotus' favourable comments about the Persians, which are sometimes regarded as a precursor of modern cultural relativism, were at odds with the dominant cultural stereotypes of the following era (Baldry 1965: 22–3).

Announcing the rise of 'ethnocentrism', the 'discourse of barbarism' was a conscious attempt to bring the boundaries of Hellas into close alignment with the 'boundaries of decency' or civilization (Hall 1989: ix, 166). Expressions of revulsion against 'barbaric' practices of disfiguring the body were central to Hellenic civilized self-images, and no doubt they helped to promote the sense of we-feeling that was expressed in the ideals and practice of mutual restraint in war. In the classical age, Greeks regarded the removal of the ears, eyes, noses and tongues as quintessentially barbaric acts, while punishment by impalement was associated with tyranny (Hall 1989: 26). Although disgusted by the Persian mutilation of bodies, the Hellenes engaged in forms of punishment that have long been regarded as barbaric in the recent period. They disfigured slaves (Hartog 1988: 142ff.). Punishment included throwing criminals off cliffs (Hall 1989: 158; see Dover 1974: 289–90 on offences that attracted the death penalty). Infanticide – particularly female infanticide – seems to have been widespread throughout the Greco-Roman world (Harris 1982). Nevertheless, the Greeks' disgust at 'barbarian' cruelty is evident in Eratosthenes' condemnation of the Carthaginians who (allegedly) were in the habit of drowning strangers, a comment that led Wight (1977: 103–4) to compare Greek images of

Carthage to nineteenth-century European perceptions of China that rested on a similar 'standard of civilization'. There were many parallels between Greek images of an 'effeminate, despotic and cruel' Persia and later European imperial conceptions of 'barbarians' (Hall 1989: ch. 1). Discourses of barbarism drew a stark contrast between Persian hierarchy, excess and 'unrestrained emotionalism', and the 'egalitarian, austere, and self-disciplined Greek character' (Hall 1989: 80). The Platonic concept of *sophrosyne*, variously translated as control of the passions, moderation, gentleness or mercy was opposed to *akolasia*, or surrender to the emotions that was typical of the 'uncivilized'. That social ideal was contrasted with *oloophron*, a concept that has been translated as possessing 'destructive thoughts' (Ferguson 1958: 32ff.; Hall 1989: 44, 125). *Sophrosyne* was a critical dimension of the emotional self-controls that were regarded as having 'tamed the warriors' and attuned them to life in the civilized, post-Homeric polis (North 1966: ch. 1). The concept is stressed here because it influenced medieval notions of civility and courtesy and the later European civilizing process via the Roman idea of *temperantia* that celebrated moderation, restraint and considerateness that, in Cicero's words, gave 'a certain polish to life' (Jaeger 1985: 116; also North 1966: ch. 9 on early Christian understandings of the concept).

References to the Persians 'unrestrained emotionalism' illuminate Hellenic notions of the relationship between masculinity and warfare. Artistic representations of the conflicts with Persia compared military success to sexual conquest; the masculinity of the Greeks was depicted as subjugating effeminate Persians (Hall 1993). Xenophon observed that the Greeks concluded that 'fighting against them (the Persians) would be much the same thing as having to fight with women' (*Hellenica* 3.4.19). Contemporary scholars have referred to Spartan public displays of naked Persian captives to demonstrate the differences between the athleticism of the Greek warrior and the unmuscular bodies of adversaries who had not been subjected to the discipline of the gymnasium (Spivey 2004: 123). Those standpoints were intertwined with the dominant conceptions of male athleticism and beauty (Spivey 2004: ch. 2). The ancient Greek concept, *kalokagathia*, emphasized the physical and moral traits that distinguished the ideal, young male warrior-citizen; it was at the same time an 'instrument for the exclusion of non-citizens, foreign ethnic and social-fringe groups' (Weiler 2002; Garland 1995).

Contrasts between the 'civilized' and the 'uncivilized' male body were projected back in time with the result that the Trojan War came to be portrayed as a struggle between 'civilization' and 'barbarism'. Aeschylus' play *The Persians* may have been the first extant tragedy to portray the Persians as barbarians (Hall 1989). A degree of sympathy for the Persian invaders who were humbled by war is evident in that work (Tritle 2000: ch. 6). But the restraints on violent harm that were valued in hoplite warfare were not widely observed in military conflicts with the Persians. In the period between 490–478 BC, when the Greeks feared for their survival, heralds were executed; warriors did not follow the convention of returning the war dead; they often pursued fleeing enemy forces in an attempt to maximize slaughter (Ober 1994: 18).

In an important passage in *The Republic*, Plato (469–471) referred to a natural state of war with the 'barbarian', and used the term, 'civil strife', to describe conflicts between 'natural friends', the Greeks. He distinguished between *polemos* (war with non-Greeks) and *stasis* (war between Greeks). In Plato's *Menexenus* (242), Socrates announces that Athens spared the lives of Spartan leaders because they believed that 'although they had it in their power to destroy them ... they deemed that against fellow Greeks it was right to wage war only up to the point of victory, and not to wreck the whole Greek community for the sake of a city's private grudge, but [it was right] to wage war to the death against the barbarians'. His contention that it was improper for Greeks to enslave each other, but entirely reasonable to make slaves of barbarians, reaffirmed the 'double standard of morality' that was intrinsic to the 'civilized' Hellenic we-identity. The conventional assumption amongst the more 'enlightened' social strata prior to the Peloponnesian War was that fellow Greeks had to be ransomed rather than enslaved. Aristotle's doctrine of natural slavery and his advice to Alexander the Great on the question of how to treat 'barbarians' are well known, not least because of their influence on the sixteenth-century debates about the rights of the 'newly discovered Indians'. Such observations cast light on the scope of emotional identification, the we–I balance and the dominant social standards of self-restraint in that period.

In an appeal to Philip of Macedon to lead the Hellenes in a war against the 'barbarians', Isocrates harnessed the 'civilized/barbarian' dualism to an imperial project that has some similarities with the nineteenth-century European 'civilizing mission'. Underlying his position was the conviction that Hellenic achievements came down to culture rather than race, and the confidence that the Greeks could elevate non-Greeks to their level through a deliberate process of civilization (Baldry 1965: 66ff.). As with most universalizing ideologies, the 'discourse of barbarism' was a favoured instrument of sectional interests. The Athenians employed it in the fifth century to forge a democratic identity in opposition to 'despotic' Sparta. Convinced that their interests were at one with the common laws of Hellas, they used pan-Hellenic ideals cynically in an attempt to justify their hegemony (Perlman 1976).

So strong was emotional identification with the polis – it has been argued that there was no place for conscientious objection to warfare or indeed 'to anything else (Dover 1974: 158) – that pan-Hellenism had little more than marginal influence on the evolution of the city-states system. The latter has been described as a 'triple power network' in which devotion to the polis existed alongside pride in the achievements of Hellas and a 'hesitant' notion of belonging to an all-encompassing community of humankind (Mann 1986: ch. 7). On that interpretation, the Greeks were 'too outward-looking' to develop 'a consistent sense of their own superiority', no doubt because they were aware of their cultural indebtedness to other societies (Mann 1986: ibid.). No sense of we-feeling centred on humanity restrained the polis or supported universalistic visions of the future political development of Hellas. The idea of intervention to protect distant strangers who faced a 'supreme humanitarian emergency', and the notion of international criminal law to ensure that what was once permissible was forbidden, would have been as alien to them as they were to modern peoples until quite recently. Most Greeks would have been bemused by the Kantian notion of a collective project to advance towards perpetual peace over many centuries. But more universal sensibilities were not completely devoid of political influence. No city state succeeded in subordinating those wider images of society to its particularistic world view. Moreover, more inclusive notions of community were too weak to curb the love of political autonomy or to shake the conviction that the polis was the highpoint of social evolution. The upshot was that 'Greek ideology was complex and highly contradictory' (Mann 1986: 211).

Recurrent difficulties arose in reconciling portrayals of the Persians as barbarians with their abundant achievements (Mann 1986: 214). It is unclear whether those images of the barbarian shared later European notions of race and racism (see Snowden 1983; Isaac 2004; Eliav-Feldon, Isaac and Ziegler 2009). Less controversial is the evidence that many Greeks had ambivalent attitudes about the Hellenic civilizing process that included the belief that history was possibly best regarded as a fall from a more 'primitive' condition in which humans had been closer to the gods (Hall 1989: 149; Dodds 1973: ch.1). Sharp dichotomies between the civilized and the barbarian were rejected by several thinkers. Alcidamas was one of the first and one of the few philosophers to reject slavery on the grounds that 'God has left all men free; nature has made no man a slave' (cited in Baldry 1965: 60). The sophist, Antiphon, appears to have rejected distinctions between Greeks and barbarians on the grounds that all people breathe the same air. That emphasis on shared biological conditions was also fundamental to the cosmopolitanism of the Hippocratic School that may have been an important influence on Thucydides' historical narrative (Baldry 1965: 43ff.; Jouanna 1999: ch. 6). Such viewpoints that appear to have won new admirers in the fourth century articulated traditional convictions in Greek moral and political thought that non-Hellenes had made important contributions to human advancement. The superior features of the Hellenic civilizing process were not the product of innate natural qualities that other peoples lacked and were unable to develop (Baldry 1965: 66).

It is impossible to know whether and how far those universalistic motifs might have transformed the Greek city-states system had it not become subject to Macedonian and Roman power. Classical scholars have provided several examples of civilizing measures to introduce restraints on traditional rights of civic self-assertion – not unlike those that developed within the polis – that were designed to offer protection from unnecessary harm. Late in the development of the city-state system, *eirene* came to signify not just the absence of violent conflict but a collective desire to build an enduring peace that was explored through at least eight efforts at multilateral pacification (Wight 1977: 71; Ryder 1965: 5–6). Several experiments in quasi-federal unions occurred in the same period, none so extensive as to relax the grip of the polis on the Greek political imagination. They did not encourage systematic reflections on a Hellenic civilizing offensive that placed radically new international or cosmopolitan harm conventions at the heart of the political order. In the main, what there were in the way of calls for Greek political unity tended to provoke 'genuine abhorrence' (Watson 1992: 49).

Traditional assumptions about the polis combined broadly egalitarian convictions (but far removed from the modern doctrine of the legal equality of states) with the supposition that the system had a 'natural leader', known as *prostates tes Hellados*, or *hegemon* (Wight 1977: 65). For Greeks, there was no contradiction between the virtue of political autonomy and the desire to rule over others. It was taken for granted that a polis that had the potential to acquire hegemony would pursue that objective (Dawson 1996: 66ff.). Cities were motivated by *pleonexia* – the 'desire for more' that was the impetus behind efforts to extend their influence, not least through colonization, as a means of winning honour as well as power and wealth (van Wees 2001; Robinson 2006: ch. 2). Competition for power and honour would prove to be a fatal flaw. Such struggles were limited in the classical era of hoplite warfare (see the discussion of war casualties in Krentz 1985), but became more difficult to restrain as threat levels increased. Thucydides (I.88) described the core problem when he maintained that Sparta's fear of the growth of Athenian power was the principal cause of the Peloponnesian Wars. The main Greek cities were not prepared for conflicts that could spiral out of control; they did not foresee that the 'desire for more' that entrenched competition and conflict between self-regarding societies would have devastating results. That is one reason for the absence of a contrived balance of power that depended on the generalized willingness to restrain political ambitions that would emerge in the Renaissance and modern states-systems. There was little, if any, awareness that increasing one's power would inevitably incite fear in others, and little recognition of the civilizing virtue of acting in concert to maintain an international political order that was critical for the security of the constituent parts. The latter may only develop when states have approximately equal levels of military power or when they face a common external threat that can only be overcome by acting in concert. Elements of such an orientation emerged from the struggle against the Persian invasion, but before long the joint leadership of

Athens and Sparta was replaced by a relentless 'struggle for primacy'. It was widely believed that hegemony was the price that the weakest cities had to pay for their security (Watson 1992: 49).

The King's Peace of 387/386 BC represented a sharp movement towards recognition of the equality of all states – not because moral support for that ideal had suddenly increased but because of the pragmatics of reaching a lasting settlement with Persia. The Peace declared that all states, and not only the signatories to the treaties that explicitly supported that principle, should be 'free and autonomous' without 'time-limit' (Ryder 1965: xvi, 1). The initiative came from Persia which claimed the right to control Greek cities in Asia (their revolt against its suzerainty had led to the first Persian Wars) in exchange for a pledge to stay out of mainland Greece as long as the city states relinquished the aspiration to 'dominate the Aegean' (Ryder 1965: 29). The Persian King was committed to a 'self-cancelling balance of independent states outside his control' that brought solid gains for many smaller city states (Ryder 1965: 102). In that period, Sparta and Athens supported self-rule to weaken the other's alliances and to enhance their own prestige (Ryder 1965: ch. 1). By recognizing the political autonomy of allied cities, the Athenians turned their back on policies that had converted the Delian League into a tributary empire (Ryder 1965: 55). For more than two decades following its establishment in 378 BC, the Second Athenian Confederacy attempted to adapt 'the old form of hegemonial alliance, which small cities still needed for their security', to new principles of international legitimacy that defended self-rule (Ryder 1965: 55ff.; de Romilly 1958). Similar changes occurred in Sparta (Ryder 1965: 67). Those developments signified the recognition that strategic interconnectedness had reached a point where the poleis had to compromise traditional assumptions about political autonomy, to become more attuned to each other's interests and to cooperate more closely to safeguard the order that affected them all – in short, to introduce patterns of self-restraint that reflected a changing we-identity and we–I balance (Osiander 2007: 84). However, the limited number of calls for political unity in response to the rise of Macedon failed. The continuing influence of Greek ideals of self-government blocked the creation of 'an effective voluntary union . . . to avert an imposed unification by force' (Wight 1977: 76). Small sacrifices of autonomy had been made to placate Persia but at that point, the Greek city-states system was nearing its end. Philip II of Macedonia defeated the city states at Chaeronea in 338 BC and incorporated them in the League of Corinth that was proclaimed to be the solution to the problem of incessant, intercity warfare.

Emotional Responses to Suffering

The Greek city states belonged to an international society with a high tolerance of violence. Between the Persian Wars (490 and 480/479 BC) and the battle of

Chaeronea in 338 BC, Athens was at war for about two years in every three – and at no point did it enjoy more than ten consecutive years of peace (Garlan 1976: 15). But generalized warfare does not seem to have been endemic prior to the fifth century (Connor 1988). Even so, as with slavery, war was regarded not as an 'aberration' but as a simple 'fact of life'; military combat was 'celebrated as the manliest of occupations' (Shipley 1993: 18). At least the wars were usually short (Hanson 1998). Did the severity as well as the frequency of Greek warfare distinguish the Hellenic order from the modern states-system? As the citation at the beginning of this chapter indicates, Elias believed that the Greeks had little compunction in initiating 'acts of mass destruction' that were typified by Athens' ruthless behaviour towards Melos. Facing imminent defeat in the conflict with Sparta, the Athenians did not expect to avoid the fate they had imposed on many cities, and 'saw nothing but slavery in front of them' (Xenophon, Hellenica: 2.2.14). The 'unexpected moderation' of the Spartans may have reflected their conviction that mercy would serve their long-term interests as the hegemon in Greece (Panagopolous 1978: 22). Nevertheless, there were perhaps dozens of examples of mass destruction in the Hellenic system (Elias 2008b: 125). The wholescale massacre of enemies may have 'aroused pity' at times, but outbursts of 'widespread condemnation' were rare (Elias 2008b: ibid.). The level of 'moral' repugnance against what is now called 'genocide' and 'the level of internalized inhibitions against physical violence' were lower than they are today – and perhaps 'they were entirely lacking' (Elias 2008b:126). Such 'warlike behaviour was considered normal'; it conformed to the standards of the time (Elias 2013: 446; also Wight 1966: 126 for a broadly similar interpretation).

Did Elias exaggerate the cruelty of ancient Greek warfare? More recent inventories of what might now be regarded as genocide suggest that he was not exactly wide of the mark. At least two dozen cities were annihilated in the classical period (van Wees 2001: 34; Eckstein 1995: ch. 5). On some accounts, in the fourth century 'repression, treachery and brutality were . . . more prevalent than in the fifth' (Pritchett 1971: 70ff.). Moreover, Wight's comments about the absence of 'international ethics' in the Graeco-Roman period appear to be confirmed by the decline of the restraints on warfare that accompanied the rise of Macedon (see Hammond 1989: 111ff. for illustrations; also Pritchett 1971: 70ff. and Pritchett 1991: 203ff. for an overview of the typical fate of war captives). There was no shortage then of acts of mass destruction. The important question as far as the Hellenic system is concerned is whether they were a frequent occurrence throughout its history or were concentrated in particular periods, and especially during the Peloponnesian Wars.

Elias's comment that 'warlike behaviour' including genocide 'was considered normal' in Greek antiquity raises complex issues about collective emotions, and specifically about whether the Greeks felt compassion or pity for the victims of violent harm. A useful starting point is Wight's previously cited contention that the modern states-system is weak in giving expression to sympathy for foreign peoples: a comment that applies with at least equal force to the Hellenic international order. It has been stated that 'it might have been flattering for an Athenian jury to be told that it characteristically demonstrated compassion towards disabled veterans and widows of the war dead', but 'the same body sitting in the Assembly would have found it insulting to be told that their decisions were habitually determined by pity towards the weak when foreign policy was being debated' (Garland 1995: 35ff.). Sympathy for fellow Greeks and collective pride in a Hellenic civilizing process were not sufficiently strong to promote a joint response to the Persian threat. Many city states resorted to 'medizing' – to aligning with Persia for self-interested reasons rather than out of solidarity with all Hellenes (Wight 1977: 75–83). *Xenia* or guest friendship, as found in the archaic period described by Homer, did link particular members of different poleis. It moderated the hardships of war, but the thirst for vengeance with the attendant dangers of unrestrained cycles of violence was a recurrent factor in the relations between city states (Bauslaugh 1991: 60; Lendon 2000). The institution of *proxenos* seems to have provided a focal point for the growth of emotional identification between the citizens of the cities involved. Solidarity between democratic or oligarchic factions in different cities was also important, as Thucydides observed. But the part that emotional identification with Hellas played in restraining city states was not accompanied by parallels to the 'campaigns of compassion' (including the efforts to abolish the slave trade and chattel slavery) that developed as part of nineteenth-century European 'civilizing offensives' (Linklater 2011: 189ff.).

The dominant modes of punishment provide a window onto the role of pity and compassion in the dominant harm conventions in any society. Judicial torture in Greece and Rome revealed 'great cruelty' and 'a profound failure of compassion in regard to the suffering of fellow human beings' (Konstan 2001: 23). In Athens, punitive measures ranged from killing by stoning, slow death through being bound to a stake and, as noted earlier, throwing offenders from cliffs (Peters 1995: 5; also Herman 2006: ch. 8 on the evidence of a distinctive 'Athenian civilizing process' that condemned those practices). In classical antiquity, corporal punishment was generally restricted to slaves – hence Demosthenes' remark that the greatest difference between the free man and the slave was the latter's answerability 'with his body for all offences' (cited in Finley 1980: 93ff.). An important step towards a public 'ideology of cruelty' can be found in Solon's critique of the injustice of the strong. But any more general condemnation of cruel behaviour may have been motivated as much by distaste for the lack of self-control on the part of tyrannical rulers as by emotional identification with, and compassion, for the suffering victims (Lintott 1992; Lintott 1982: 14ff.). Aristotle's discussion of pity suggests that those feelings were restricted to kin-members and close associates, and that the extermination or enslavement of other peoples rarely aroused moral criticism (Konstan 2001: 13, 49–50, 65; Pritchett 1991: 312). Time and time again, communities that were facing conquest took their own lives to escape their probable fate (Pritchett 1991: 219ff.). There was no 'independent concept of the prisoner of war' in the classical period; victory erased the distinction between the free person and the slave; the subdued were placed at the mercy of their conquerors, although 'ransom and release' were commonplace (Sage 1996: 104). Humanitarian concerns were not entirely absent from such relations (Pritchett 1971: 81–2), but it appears that serious ethical problems rarely arose in conjunction with violent harm between city states (Lintott 1992: 16). Even so, in Thucydides' writings, the idea of *omos* was used, conceivably for the first time, to condemn needlessly violent action. The term was employed to describe Athens' cruelty towards Mytilene. Supporting the city's destruction, Cleon argued that 'sweet reasonableness' (*epieikeia*) had no place in dealings with enemies (Lintott 1992). Thucydides may have wanted to demonstrate how ideals of self-restraint, reasonableness and even pity (*eleos*) for the pitiable (*oiktos*) that had become more prominent in Athenian moral and political thought had been casually pushed to one aside during the conflict with Sparta (Lintott 1992).

An examination of the prevalent attitudes to suffering should not conclude that all Greeks would have been entirely perplexed by contemporary forms of compassion or by the associated phenomenon of guilt for causing unnecessary harm. Expressions of pity may have been regarded as unmanly, but civilization and compassion were often linked. The evidence is that many Greeks 'took pride in their capacity for pity and (in) their humanity toward the vanquished or afflicted' (Konstan 2001: 23; Sternberg 2005). There is an important link with the contribution of Greek tragedy to preserving the civil way of life that was thought to occupy 'a "mediate" position between the "savage" life of the beasts ... and the eternal happiness of the blessed gods' (Segal 1981: 2). The tragic plays stressed the precarious nature of 'civilization' which was 'the fruit of man's struggle to assert his humanness in the face of the impersonal forces of nature' and in response to his 'own potential violence' and 'the remote powers of the gods' (Segal 1981: ibid.). Dramatists such as Euripides sought to 'unleash pity and compassion as civilizing forces'; they were architects of *paidea,* or 'an education in the civilizing connections with others that pity represents' (Alford 1993: 262ff.). The 'civilizing' role of women was a central theme in plays such as *Lysistrata* in which Aristophanes contrasted the unrestrained brutality of men with the moderating behaviour of women. In several dramas, support for good will based on recognition of the unifying role of common suffering was not insignificant especially in reflections on relations within the polis, but remorse at the destruction of a city was not unusual

(Dover 1974: 272; Kern 1999: 150). Euripides' dramatic representation of the suffering of the women of Troy may have aroused the sympathy of an audience that felt ashamed when recalling Athens' destruction of Melos. Other works such as Aeschylus' *Seven against Thebes* described the cruelties of Hellenic warfare and the dark side of civilization. In that tragedy, Aeschylus described the fate of a captured city, 'made slave and [subject to the] booty of the spear'. The tragedy referred to the plight of women who had to endure 'a captive's woeful bed', and stressed that 'the dead . . . have a happier fate than they' (Aeschylus, *Seven Against Thebes*: 333–67; Schaps 1982). Aeschylus' *The Persians* affirmed the need to treat the enemy with respect and to sympathize with people who were suffering – as the Athenians were – from the devastation of warfare (also Kaimio 1992).

It has been argued that one of Euripides' ambitions as the 'pre-eminent *political* theorist of pity' (Alford 1993: 275, italics in original) was to invite young male spectators to become 'a woman in thought', and to recognize the plight of those who had been raped in war. Euripides' 'war plays' highlighted the pain and cruelty that had been inflicted on the Trojan women. The dramas criticized the 'inevitable tensions between military, civic and human values' that had been largely silenced by the doctrine that 'might is right' (Hardwick 1992: 236–7). The 'extension of empathy required of an ancient Greek spectator [was] remarkable', it has been stated, 'given the extremely hierarchical, male-dominated character of Athenian society' (Nussbaum 2001: 429–30). Analysts can only speculate about how far such sentiments expressed genuine compassion for outsiders and regarded 'excessive' violence as incompatible with civilized ways of life. An additional question is how far the desire to highlight cruelty and to dramatize suffering was motivated by a collective fear that aggressive impulses could spill over into the city and disrupt civil order. Herodotus (6. 21) had observed that the Athenians felt 'deep grief' at the Persian capture of Miletus which led to the death of male citizens and the enslavement of the women and children. But he may have regarded such displays of close emotional identification as so extraordinary as to deserve special comment.

Remorse for causing suffering, and pity for the victims, cannot easily be disentangled from the fear that at some future point the perpetrators might face a similar fate (Sternberg 2005). Seemingly, the 'awareness of human ignorance and weakness, the unpredictability of the future, and the great and sudden reversals to which . . . fortunes are subject was a strong current which ran all through Greek civilization and found expression at all levels, sophisticated and popular alike' (Dover 1974: 269). Respect for the levelling role of fate was tied up with the religious conviction that the gods, despite their concern for some humans, were disposed to treat them as playthings, and to humiliate and in other ways harm them at will. Jealousy was one motive, as was the desire to punish humans for exhibiting *hybris*, for getting above themselves, and for failing to display the restraint that befitted mere mortals. Many believed that the gods looked kindly on those who were 'gentle in victory' and conquered 'softly' (Dover 1974: 75ff., 133ff., 254). The Greeks were not unique in thinking that the imperatives of warfare required acts of violence that were regrettable and that there should be sympathy for the victims, but they did not conclude that such behaviour deserved moral condemnation. Of greater concern, as is clear from Thucydides' discussion of the Mytilenean dialogue, was the recognition that needless cruelty could spread hatred that damaged the long-term interests of the responsible city (see below, pp. 43–4). A similarly pragmatic faith in the benefits of justice underpinned the defence of *eunoia* as a virtue in foreign policy in the third and fourth centuries BC. *Eunoia* may have been the bridge to the positive support for mercy (*clementia*) or humanity (*humanitas*) that appeared in the Hellenistic period and in Rome as a result of Stoic influences that would also shape medieval notions of civility and modern ideas of civilization (Hahm 2000).

War, Booty and Slavery

It is useful to comment further on the harm conventions that governed the more civilized era of hoplite warfare prior to considering in the next section the role of the Peloponnesian War in eroding traditional restraints on war as well as in deepening the moral and political engagement with pain and suffering in the so-called Greek Enlightenment. Widespread acceptance of the use of force did not mean that traditional hoplite warfare was a free-for-all (Garlan 1976: 23, Pritchett 1974: ch. 7). According to many sources, the standard practice was the prearranged pitched battle 'of the fair and open kind' that was idealized by later thinkers such as Demosthenes and leaders such as Alexander the Great, who dismissed the advice to ambush Darius' forces on the grounds that it was as dishonourable as the 'craft . . . of petty robbers and thieves' and robbed the victor of his deserved glory (Connor 1988; Pritchett 1974: 148, 174–5). In the main, Greek citizen warriors were opposed to forms of warfare such as archery that demanded harm at a distance, or cavalry assaults that made it difficult for defeated forces to flee (Osiander 2007: 59). Resistance to those forms of military engagement was critical to the identity of the male warrior and to the goal of social esteem that could only be gained by demonstrations of personal courage (see van Wees 2004, however). There is a parallel with the medieval knight's low regard for bowmen and with the contempt (that seems to have been widespread as late as the early seventeenth century) for 'cowardly' reliance on firearms (van Crefeld 1989: 71ff.).

Hoplite wars had the quality of a 'mass duel' in which rivals recognized the folly of refusing to surrender when clearly facing defeat. As a general rule, victors were content to prevail on the battlefield, and did not pursue the enemy to achieve total annihilation; they had in any case a limited ability to give chase, and no established practice of enslaving vanquished forces (Hanson 1999; Sage 1996: 95ff. and also Pritchard 2013: 168, who presents a different picture of defeated hoplite forces that were hunted down and killed). Demonstrations of submission took the form of a request for the return of the dead which, if accepted, usually limited the scale of the violence (Sage 1996: 98). Battles were usually won or lost in a single day. If an adversary declined to leave the city to engage in pitched battle, the opponent might ravage and plunder the adjacent countryside before returning home. Farmers who comprised the hoplite armies could not leave their lands unattended for long in order to wage protracted conflicts (Bauslaugh 1991: ch. 5; Hanson 1998). In short, in that period the Greeks were rather less warlike – or less given to waging total warfare – than they are often assumed to have been. Perspectives on war, including Sparta's, were not suffused with militarist beliefs that valued warfare as an unqualified collective good (Goodman and Holladay 1986). It has been said that the Greeks had an ambivalent attitude to war, at one and the same time deploring and praising it, as is evident in Homer's observation that wars are 'hateful', 'tearful' and 'baleful' but bring 'glory to man' and permit 'the joy of the fight' (Pritchett 1974: 187). As a general rule, hoplite warfare had some of the qualities of the restrained, orchestrated duel rather the bloody fight to the death. The upshot was that wars of annihilation appear to have been rare (Shipley 1993; Osiander 2007: 58ff.; also Ober 1994 on the post-Homeric rules of war).

The dissenting standpoint is that warfare in the period between Homer and Aristotle may well have approximated the conditions as described by Elias (van Wees 2004: introduction, 116–17). If so, it is impossible to distinguish clearly between periods of immense brutality and eras that were marked by greater moderation and restraint (van Wees 2004: ch. 11). The dominant harm conventions granted the victor absolute rights over defeated forces as long as religious obligations had been observed during the conflict, and as long as no prior agreement between the relevant cites tied the victor's hands. Unless a polis decided to fight to the last, in which case extermination was possible, the weaker party usually capitulated and pleaded for mercy. Victor's prerogatives were often exercised, but slaughtering the captured was far from 'routine', and may have been unusual in the period immediately before the Peloponnesian War (Price 2001: 211). References in the fifth and four centuries BC to laying waste to the land did not usually describe a 'scorched earth' policy, but referred to seizing the enemy's annual harvest, to general plunder, and to burning farm buildings so that adversaries were then burdened with supporting displaced farmers and livestock (Hanson 1998; Pritchett 1971: 38ff.; but see van Wees 2004: 121). Efforts to defeat a besieged city through starvation were rarely made, and would have been hard to organize in any event because of the seasonal nature of warfare.

Major changes in the conduct of warfare have been traced back to the Second Persian invasion of 480–479 BC when the Greeks turned to a key instrument of Persian strategy (siege warfare) to oust the Persians from their cities (Kern 1999: 93ff.). Prior to the last decade of the fifth century, assaults on fortified cities were unusual and rarely successful, but blockades often caused immense suffering (Adcock 1957: 58; Kern 1999: 139ff.). The outcome of siege warfare seems to have been largely dependent on the 'whims of individual commanders' and on calculations of the costs and benefits of destroying a city as opposed to displaying mercy (Kern 1999: 150). If there was a general rule – and it applies to siege warfare across the ages – it was that a city that surrendered quickly was more likely to be treated leniently than one that held out to the end and increased the costs of victory for enemy forces (Kern 1999: 147–8). Leniency before the Athenian–Spartan wars often took the form of ransom and release; massacre and enslavement were not standard practice (Sage 1996: 104).

Seemingly, by the sixth century, the massacre of defeated populations was not as commonplace as it appears to have been in Homer's day (Kern 1999: 139). Massacre may have followed defeat in about a quarter of all recorded cases compared with half of all cases in the Peloponnesian Wars (Garlan 1976: 71; Panagopoulos 1978: 219). Recalling Elias's claim about mass killing, the overwhelmingly evidence is that almost all of the massacres of captured forces took place during the three decades of that particular conflict (Price 2001: 211–12). The obvious material benefits of enslavement often moderated the use of force. That appears to have been the case at least until the outbreak of the Peloponnesian war when the 'harsher standards of siege warfare' prevailed, at the same time shifting 'the moral implications of total war' closer to the forefront of Greek consciousness (Kern 1999: 140). *Realpolitik* could decide whether or not a city was destroyed. The Spartan decision at the end of the Peloponnesian War not to destroy Athens, whose survival helped to balance the power of Thebes, was one such calculation, though some Spartans favoured mercy because of its earlier service to Hellas in resisting Persia (Watson 1992: 51–2; Forrest 1968: ch. 12).

It has been argued that popular morality largely revolved around the 'assumption that one should help one's friends and harm one's enemies' (Blundell 1989: 26; Dover 1974: 180ff.). The statement that the aim of warfare was 'to inflict maximum damage on the enemy while producing maximum advantage for one's own side' (Blundell 1989: 52) resonates with the claim that 'the threshold of sensitivity with regard to the infliction of physical injuries' was higher than it is in liberal democracies today, while the level of emotional identification between people was significantly lower (Elias 2008b: 118; Dover 1974: ch. 6). Greeks certainly did not conceal the pleasure that was derived from exacting revenge – nor did they conceal enmity – but it would be wrong to conclude that magnanimity was never valued (Dover 1974: 180ff.). Athenians might seem to have been 'lacking in compassion' and to have been disinclined to become involved in alleviating the 'misfortunes of others', but in large part that was because human setbacks were assumed to be 'divinely caused' (Dover 1974: 201). Even so, they were accustomed to acts of violence that have been outlawed or '*removed behind the scenes of social life*' in modern 'civilized' societies (Elias 2012: 122, italics in original; also Fisher 1998). For that very reason, the individual's journey from peace to war was less demanding psychologically than it is for the inhabitants of modern highly pacified, 'civilized' societies. Greater tolerance of violence did not mean that the Greeks lurched from one act of mass destruction to another in frenzied pursuit of the joys in killing.

What is not in dispute is that city states were geared towards the violent appropriation of wealth; the proceeds of war were often directed towards building temples (Pritchett 1971: 98ff.). In Aristotle's words, war was a natural mode of acquisition, the route to personal fortune and the means of securing individual autonomy (Aristotle, *Politics*, 1256B; Pritchett 1971: ch. 3). In the absence of mutual dependence, there was 'no economic reason' to refrain from profiting from others 'by stealing from them rather than trading with them' (Osiander 2007: 39). Enthusiasm for 'the toil of the spear (as) a valid mode of production' was especially evident in acts of colonization that led to serfdom or slavery and to displacing native peoples (Rihll 1993; Pritchett 1991: 445ff.). Slaves were the most valuable form of plunder. Most were obtained through military success (perhaps 70 per cent of the total number); the social consensus was that it was entirely legitimate to take possession of the captured in that way (Pritchett 1971: 80ff.). As in the case of Athens' treatment of the people of Melos in 416 BC, it was not unusual to impose *andrapodismos* which involved killing the adult males and enslaving the women and children. As part of their degradation, slaves were reduced to mere bodies or *somata* (Dover 1974: 283ff.; Hopkins 1978: 144). The branding of captives took place, but not without challenge. Towards the end of the classical era, branding slaves who had been condemned to a life of forced labour, often in the mines, came to be viewed as unnecessarily harsh, though changing moral sensibilities did not significantly alter behaviour towards 'barbarians'. Slave conditions in the mines and torturing slaves prior to giving evidence in court were examples of what is now widely regarded as cruelty although in many cities legal safeguards gave slaves some protection in keeping with civilized standards (Hammond 1967: 329). What there was in the way of humanity towards slaves did not ensure freedom from sexual availability, which was a clear manifestation and stark reminder of the slave's ultimate answerability with the body (Cole 1984).

Greek wars would have been unusual in the history of military conflict if women had not been regarded as the 'spoils of war', or if colonists had not relished opportunities for sexual exploitation (Pritchett 1991: 238ff.; Rihll

1993: 101). It may have been that the 'sexual violation of women was largely a characteristic of siege warfare' which also led to the demise of the old funeral customs, but the attendant 'impurity' troubled many Greeks (Kern 1999: 159). However, Athenian law regarded female suffering that resulted from sexual violence as less significant than the damage caused to the honour of the relevant male kin. Moreover, in ancient Greek there was no concept for rape as 'sexual intercourse committed by force' (Cole 1984: 98). The dominant attitudes were an expression of the plain reality that cities did not care a great deal about the wellbeing of other peoples. The Greek conscience was not especially troubled by profiting from human misery in warfare.

But women and children who had been captured in war were not entirely invisible from the moral point of view. Reflecting the broad consensus that their massacre was deplorable (Kern 1999: 157ff.), Euripides' plays, and *The Trojan Women* in particular, raised the ethical issue of pity for vulnerable, conquered peoples – possibly, as noted earlier, because of vivid memories of the previous year's destruction of Melos (see, however, Hall 2010: 268ff.). The audience for such dramas may have had complex motives. The Greeks may have enjoyed theatrical representations of suffering, and evidently poets from Homer onwards were well aware that 'tears and grief about past events . . . could be positively pleasurable' (Stanford 1983: 107). Nevertheless, the dramas, along with Thucydides' tragic narrative, openly discussed the human consequences of violent conflict. They highlighted the tension between power struggles and ethical ideals. They described the 'decivilizing' processes that erased the distinctions between Greeks and 'barbarians' that had been integral to the Hellenic civilizing process (Bozeman 1960: ch. 2; Tritle 2000: ch. 6). It may have been that the most important aspect of the tragedians enquiry into the suffering of warfare was their attempt to arouse 'pity and fear' (Hall 2010: 6), and not least because, as noted earlier, they forced the audience to confront the very real possibility that they could succumb to a similar fate.

The Peloponnesian Wars

The key to the psychological or 'psychogenetic' dimensions of the Hellenic civilizing process may well lie in the observation that the dominant personality types 'thought in terms of the particular Greek cities and their rivalries, the contrast between Ionian and Dorian, the superiority of men over women, the division into free men and slaves, the traditional cleavage between high and low . . . and the newer, but . . . generally accepted, antithesis between Greek and barbarian' (Baldry 1965: 33). Sharp distinctions between 'established' and 'outsider' groups were central features of a unique Hellenic civilizing process (see Elias and Scotson 2008 for a discussion of those concepts). They coexisted with universalistic elements in Greek culture that might well have become more influential had the city-state system survived. But struggles for power, security and honour between the very 'survival units' that had created Hellenic civilization threw their shared civilizing process into reverse.

Thucydides discussed how the polis had acquired the power to project military power over greater distances and how the resulting entanglements promoted fear and distrust between Athens and Sparta whose competition for power swept all of the Greek cities, including neutrals, into an all-encompassing military conflict. Elias's comments about genocide that were cited at the beginning of this chapter raised the question of whether the Hellenic system was more violent than the modern states-system. The case is not proven for reasons that were outlined earlier. There is strong evidence for the judgment that genocide 'was far from the only or normal outcome of hostile inter-group relations in the ancient world' and for the accompanying claim that there is 'enough information to show that mass executions were far rarer than mass enslavement' (van Wees 2010: 249). But there is no doubt that the massacres of captives during the Peloponnesian conflict reflected an increased tolerance of violence within Hellenic civilization; they revealed a general coarsening of attitudes towards human suffering (Panagopoulos 1978). Complex questions remain. It is hard to establish whether the wars between Athens and Sparta constituted a short 'decivilizing' interregnum between an earlier process of civilization and a later phase in which city states explored creative ways of resolving major differences non-violently. As noted earlier, key authorities disagree about such matters. On some accounts, the destruction of cities in the manner that Elias described was a recurrent feature of Greek warfare from around the eighth century (see van Wees 2004:124ff. for further discussion). Some authorities maintain that the atrocities that were committed in the Athenian–Spartan wars represented a clear break with the civilized harm conventions that governed hoplite warfare. Some have maintained that the brutalities increased immediately prior to, and during, the Peloponnesian wars, but declined in the period prior to the death of Philip II of Macedon in 336 BC. Others have argued that the lurch towards greater ruthlessness was more or less permanent (see Hanson 1995: ch. 8; Pritchett 1971: 70ff.).

The contention that the conflict between Athens and Sparta was a major turning-point in the development of the Greek city-state system has pointed to a profound shift from hoplite warfare centred on pitched battles, where no massacres have been recorded, to the era of siege warfare in which at least nine cases occurred (Kern 1999: 152–3). A major weak-ening of respect for the old harm conventions led to the unusual practice of the permanent occupation of defeated territories that was coupled with unprecedented destruction, rape and enslavement (Hanson 1991: 4–5; Kagan 2003). It is possible that Thucydides concentrated on the fate of the 'strategically insignificant island' of Melos because that was the first occasion when Athens asserted its right to disregard the traditional civilized restraints on force (Bauslaugh 1991: 25). Moreover, his emphasis on the 'unusual brutality and cruelty, seemingly arbitrary murder and violence, and violations of religious, social and ethical norms' in areas of minor strategic importance (such as Melos, Plataea, Mytilene and Mycallesus) highlighted the unprecedented suffering that was unleashed by a war that rapidly and unexpectedly spiralled out of control, morally and geographically (Price 2001: 210ff.).

As stated above, Elias may not have been wide of the mark when he emphasized the violent nature of Greek international politics. But the question remains of whether his comments about genocide captured the realities of Hellenic intercity politics over many centuries or reflected the lurch towards mass killing in an atypical period that was the result of a major 'decivilizing process'. Either way, Thucydides' decision to position the conflict in the longer struggle between 'civilizing' and 'decivilizing' processes in the Hellenic world has special significance for the present discussion. It was the first processual account of the changing relationship between violence and civilization over several decades and centuries – and the first to cast light on the unplanned development and precarious nature of civilizing restraints on violent behaviour in the struggles for power, honour and security between largely autonomous but interdependent political communities. It remains a model for understanding international relations in other historical periods.

To demonstrate how quickly traditional harm conventions were weakened, Thucydides famously described how the Athenians' argued in the Melian debate that destroying the city was entirely consistent with the general principle that each city had the right to act to the limits of its physical power. Reference has already been made to their contention that the gods (let alone fellow men) accepted that, in desperate circumstances, nothing could be 'sacred in war'. Other passages in Thucydides' narrative showed how heightened fear, insecurity and anger led to inflated claims about the absence of political choice – alternatively, how the restraining hand of civilized distinctions between what was 'forced' on leaders by military necessity and what was merely convenient or advantageous broke down (Linklater 2011: 122ff.). Significantly, none of the major figures portrayed by Thucydides initiated a public debate about the ideal relationship between morality and war (Price 2001: 223).

The Mytilenean dialogue had particular significance because it was entirely framed by calculations of political advantage and necessity. All larger issues about the relationship between power and morality were swept aside. Angered by the revolt of its ally, Mytilene in 427 BC, and fearful that similar desertions would weaken the empire, the Athenians were at first disposed to accept Cleon's remonstration to make an example of Mytilene by eliminating the

male population (Thucydides 3.37–40). They rescinded their impulsive decision the following day out of repentance for the 'cruel and monstrous' intention to punish the entire populace for the behaviour of those who had
spearheaded the revolt (Thucydides 3.36, 3.49). In opposition to Cleon's
assertion that devastating harm was essential to maintain Athenian dominance, Diodotus contended that its long-term interests were best served by
'punishing moderately', a policy that would encourage surrender and avoid the
burden of the prolonged siege (Thucydides 3.42–48). Athens would not be
secure if those who had risen against it were convinced that they had nothing
to lose by holding out until the last, and if they could be virtually certain that
defeat would result in their execution. (In the end, according to Thucydides
(3.50), the Assembly spared the city but killed over one thousand Mytileneans).
The debate over the strategy of annihilation revolved wholly around pragmatic
calculations about the course of action that would best serve Athens' long-term
interests; there was no moral dispute about permissible and impermissible
harm and human suffering.

In its later dispute with Scione, which defected from an alliance in 421 BC
to side with Sparta, the Athenians slaughtered the male inhabitants and
condemned the rest of the population to slavery (Thucydides 4.120–123,
5.32). In so doing, they accepted Cleon's argument that 'deterrence through
terror' was essential if future defections were to be prevented (Kagan 2003:
179). Six years later, Athens decided that destroying the neutral city of Melos
was vital to preserve its empire – the fear being that neutrals would ally with
Sparta. The Melian Council argued that it was in Athens' long-term interest
'not to destroy a principle that is to the general good of all men – namely, that
in the case of all who fall into danger there should be such a thing as fair play
and just dealing'. They implored the Athenians to recognize that destruction
would be 'visited by the most terrible vengeance' that would forever stand as
'an example to the world'. The response was that the stability of the alliance on
which their very survival depended gave the Athenians no choice but to
compel Melos to join the empire or be destroyed. Accepting its neutrality
would be widely interpreted as a sign of political weakness that would tempt
other allies to secede. Following the city's unconditional surrender, almost all
men of military age were killed, the women and children were sold into slavery,
and the island was reduced to a colony (Thucydides 5.84–116). Athens did not
exactly monopolize slaughter. On at least two occasions, the Spartans behaved
in much the same way (Thucydides 4.116 and 5.83).

In some respects, Athens did not move radically from the position it
adopted in the debate at Sparta in 432 BC – the year before the war broke
out – when it argued that questions of right and wrong had never dissuaded
cities from seizing the opportunity to extend their power through superior
strength. But it professed to admire the self-restraint that was displayed by
those who, 'considering their power', had been 'more observant of justice' than

circumstances demanded (Thucydides 1.76). As noted earlier, the hardening of social attitudes to violence was linked with the descent into ever expansive conceptions of political necessity – with a blurring of distinctions between real and 'pseudo-necessities', or between actions that secured a temporary advantage and behaviour that all might regard as essential to avoid defeat and destruction (Orwin 1994: ch. 9; Pouncey 1980). Athens proclaimed that it was necessary to reduce the three chief determinants of its foreign policy to two. Considerations of honour had to be placed to one side, leaving fear and self-interest in the driving seat (Pouncey 1980: 21). Conceptions of permanent emergency led Athens to abandon earlier protestations about the ennobling role of mercy and restraint, to contract the realm where moral choice and political deliberation held sway, and to become ever more tolerant of policies that caused immense suffering (Kern 1994: 140).

The coarsening of sensibilities during the Athenian–Spartan wars was furthered by civil conflicts between oligarchic and democratic groups in different cities. Thucydides argued that civil war (*stasis*) so overturned the moral order that what was once 'a thoughtless act of aggression' became an emblem of personal courage for members of the same political faction. Advising patience, caution and self-restraint came to be regarded as the path of the coward; appeals for moderation were described as veils that were designed to conceal an 'unmanly character'; an aptitude for appreciating the different sides of a conflict raised questions about loyalty or judgment that disqualified the person from public office; 'frantic impulsiveness' became the hallmark of the real man (Thucydides 3.82). One of the distinguishing features of the narrative was the account of how the disintegration of Hellenic international society was linked with the rise of new conceptions of authentic masculinity that revolved around cruel and destructive 'states of mind' (Price 2001: 347).

The transformation of relations between the city states developed hand in hand with 'a general deterioration of character throughout the Greek world'; the unprecedented cruelty and suffering of civil strife and interstate war reflected a steady decline of normative commitments that was evident in the corruption of language and collective emotions; crucially important was the ascent of the worst human types, the unscrupulous leaders – those of a 'meaner intellect' – who placed their own reputation and self-interest ahead of the wellbeing of the polis and the ancient laws of Hellas (Thucydides 3.83; Price 2001: 236ff.). In short, 'decivilizing' processes transformed the dominant harm conventions. Standards of self-restraint were relaxed; the sense of we-feeling and the scope of emotional identification contracted, and the power of 'we' (Hellas) relative to 'I' (the polis or the ruling strata) declined. With the reversal of the civilizing process, actions that had been forbidden became permissible. A central theme – arguably the central theme of the entire analysis – was that fear and insecurity can quickly strip away the civilized veneer of social existence, release baser passions from 'the social standards of self-restraint' that hold sway in more secure periods, and normalize behaviour that would not have occurred – and would not have been contemplated – in secure and peaceful periods.[2]

Thucydides broke off his account of the Sicilian expedition to describe the most appalling act of violence of the entire conflict – the sequence of events that demonstrated the sheer scale of the descent into gratuitous killing. The episode in question was the assault on Mycalessus that had been initiated by Thracians on their return home under the command of the Athenian general, Dieitrephes. The disaster that awaited the people was, 'for the size of the city', as 'deplorable' as any other incident in the war (Thucydides 7.27–30). With the active complicity of Dieitrephes, who had been ordered to employ them to cause as much harm as possible, the Thracians 'fell to plundering the houses and the temples and butchering the people, sparing neither old nor young, but killing all whom they met just as they came, even children and women . . . pack animals also and whatever other living things they saw' (Thucydides 7.29). 'Like the worst *barbarians*' who were at their bloodiest when there was 'nothing to fear', the Thracians 'fell upon a boys' school, the largest in the town, which the children had just entered, and cut down all of them' (ibid.; italics added). In that remarkable passage, Thucydides added that the people suffered a calamity that was as pitiable as anything that occurred during the entire war. The reference to the death of innocent children encapsulated his broader stance on the moral decline of Hellas, and of Athens in particular. The result was the exposure of vulnerable communities with no direct involvement in the war to the horrors of indiscriminate killing at the hands of those who had lost all respect for the traditional aristocratic principles of honourable and civilized self-restraint (Price 2001: 215; Quinn 1995).

Thucydides may not have been particularly surprised by the behaviour of the Thracians; what may have been most shocking was Athens' involvement in the massacre at Mycalessus. In an important passage, he observed that all Greeks had once behaved like the Thracians, but the rise of 'Greekness' had suppressed such 'barbarous' impulses (Orwin 1994: 135). During the Peloponnesian conflict, the Hellenes rediscovered their ancestral savagery and the pleasures of killing. Thucydides (3.84) gave the example of the civil war in Corcyra in 427–426 BC to show how duress can lead humans to repeal 'the common principles' on which 'every man's own hope of salvation'

---

[2] This is an appropriate moment to add that Thucydides' analysis of the interplay between 'sociogenetic' and 'psychogenetic' forces – between changes in domestic and international power relations and in emotional attitudes to violent harm and human suffering – was one of the earliest examples of the kind of higher-level synthesis that Elias (2007a: 176) defended in reaction to increasing specialization in the social science (see also the analysis of Elias's conception of 'historical social psychology' in Linklater 2011: ch. 5).

ultimately depends 'should he ... be overtaken by misfortune'. The plague in Athens had shown how the distinctions between citizen and slave, man and woman, Greek and barbarian that were earlier described as critical to the Hellenic features of the 'civilizing process' were rapidly stripped of all meaning when people were exposed to the torments of the body. It demonstrated how quickly the fragile constraints of civilized communities can yield to the impulses and indulgences of the moment when humans are governed by 'necessity' and do not expect to survive long enough to be punished for giving free rein to 'savage' dispositions. Thucydides stressed how self-restraint (*sophrosyne*) and foresight (*pronoia*) were replaced by short-term, callous considerations (see the discussion in Chapter 2, pp. 86, 92–4 and 103 for the importance of those concepts for later analyses of violence and civilization in the Western states-systems). The effects of the large-scale erosion of self-restraint on the long Hellenic civilizing process have been noted. Significantly, the Peloponnesian wars ended as a result of the siege of Athens in which many inhabitants starved to death, seeing 'no future for themselves except to suffer what they had made others suffer, people of small states whom they had injured not in retaliation for anything they had done but out of the arrogance of power and for no reason except that they were in the Spartan alliance' (Xenophon, *Hellenica*: 2.2.10–11).

As Thucydides (3.82–83) contended, under conditions of 'peace and prosperity both states and individuals have gentler feelings, because men are not then forced to face conditions of dire necessity; but war, which robs men of the easy supply of their daily wants, is a rough schoolmaster and creates in most people a temper that matches their condition'. Such brutal realties, he proceeded to argue, were the most 'significant lesson' of the war. It was one of the principal reasons for Thucydides' claim that his account of the war that engulfed Hellas was a 'possession' forever – a reminder to future generations who believed they were bound together in civilized societies that they would not be immune from similar regressions to barbarism (Pouncey 1980: 22).

Thucydides (1.23) maintained that the Peloponnesian War was the greatest disturbance (*kinesis*) in the history of the Hellenes; at no other time had 'so much human blood been shed, whether in the course of ... war itself or as the result of civil dissensions' (Price 2001: 208ff.). The narrative analysed the evolution of Hellas – the apex of human achievement – and traced how it became the cherished stake in the struggle against Persian rule, only to become trapped in violent conflicts that eventually rendered it indistinguishable from the 'barbarian' world. It has been noted that Greek tragedy had a civilizing role by confronting the immorality of organized violence, by opposing the crude reduction of moral principle to physical power, and by remonstrating against the substitution of prudential calculations about the most effective route to military success for ethical reflections on the qualities of the good life

(Bozeman 1960: ch. 2). Public discourses about the excesses of war drew on what have been described as the 'earliest roots of humanism', namely the belief in the universal vulnerability to pain that was central to the Hippocratic School and, specifically, to the collective pledge to 'abstain from all intentional wrong-doing and harm' to other persons, irrespective of social status (Jouanna 1999: ch. 6). Those ethical sentiments may have influenced Thucydides' comments on the general laws of humanity that exist to protect all people in distress – the standards that the Athenian generals at Melos contemptuously dismissed as an argument for justice that the weak and desperate use to compensate for the lack of military power (Jouanna 1999). Thucydides' humanism was not linked to a specific political project of restoring Greek unity or elevating Hellas to a new plane (Price 2001: 377). But it was similar in some respects to *eunoia* whose moderating role would be defended by various fourth-century thinkers. The practical influence of that civilizing concept in that period may have influenced patterns of cooperation such as the Second Athenian Confederation and the League of Corinth (de Romilly 1958). There is evidence that wars became more moderate at that time, that harm conventions govern-ing tribute were relaxed (at least in relations between Greeks) and that the severities of slavery were reduced. The evidence is that no Greek city state was massacred, nor were its inhabitants enslaved, by any other city in the period between 335 and 223 BC (Sage 1996: 116). The highpoint of violence and pillage may therefore have been reached in the preceding decades. The belief in the virtues of peace may have become widespread in the first part of the fourth century. Highly pacified cities were able in that period to turn to bolder experiments in international pacification.

The city states that comprised the Chalcidian League that was estab-lished early in the Peloponnesian War later formed a *sympolity* that rested on common citizenship. Proposals to create a federal system were drawn up (Hammond 1967: 468–9). Some cities introduced *isopolity*, which was the practice of granting the citizens of other cities rights of access to domestic courts to secure justice (Walbank 1981: 151). The regions that made most progress in experimenting with federal and quasi-federal associations were those where the polis had never been particularly strong in the first place (Walbank 1981: 152–3). Civil strife and interstate war had weakened the city states, but old attachments to the autonomous, self-regarding polis retained their ability to thwart efforts to advance Pan-Hellenic political cooperation (Perlman 1976). The old we–I balance did not change radically. Left to themselves, the Greeks might have succeeded in creating an international political order that expressed humanistic commitments to harm conven-tions that were designed to minimize needless suffering. Potentials for such a civilizing thrust certainly existed in Hellenic culture alongside dangerously competitive elements. But they were always weak. The rise of Macedon and Rome meant that 'time ran out' for those who believed that lasting political advances in that direction were possible (Walbank 1981: 157–8).

The Hellenic Civilizing Process

How different was the Hellenic system from the modern states-system with respect to the tolerance of violent harm, and what light do any differences shed on the conditions that favour the development of global civilizing processes? Elias's comments about attitudes to genocide in classical antiquity and in the period since the end of the Second World War are a useful place to begin. They described central features of the wars between Athens and Sparta, but whether they provide an accurate account of Hellenic intercity relations over the centuries is harder to ascertain. The evidence does not suggest that the Greeks lurched from one act of mass destruction to another or disregarded all moral and religious constraints on violent harm because of the pleasure in killing.

It is erroneous to suppose that the main dynamics of intercity relations can be reduced to a few basic principles that exist in every states-system, or to argue that the Greeks followed one simple trajectory of development that culminated in the ultimate violence of the wars between Athens and Sparta. The Western states-systems have shared several characteristics such as 'elimination contests' that resulted in fewer great powers that then engaged in a struggle to control the whole system. But such long-term patterns have to be understood in connection with the upward and downward curves of civilizing processes and changing attitudes to human suffering and violent harm. As with its later counterparts, the Hellenic pattern of civilization was highly contradictory. One set of social standards applied to the relations between citizens of the same polis; a less demanding code with fewer restraints on violence applied in relations between cities. The tolerance of violence in everyday life and in international relations was much greater than it is in highly pacified and secure liberal democracies today. Even so, hoplite forces were bound together by aristocratic principles of restraint that exemplified the Greek's distinctive response to 'the problem of harm in world politics'.

But the Greeks faced a different problem from the one that defines the modern era. There are five interrelated points to make about that subject. Firstly, they did not face the same external compulsions to restrain their behaviour that only developed in the age of industrialized warfare. The 'social constraints towards self-restraint' were lower; Greek armies were much freer to act violently than are modern industrial societies in their relations with each other. That is not to imply that they were unmoved by suffering or entirely indifferent to indiscriminate slaughter. But, secondly, the sense of we-feeling was too weak; the we–I balance was so clearly tilted towards the interests and honour of the polis and, as Thucydides revealed in intricate detail, the social standards of self-restraint were inadequate as the more powerful cities became entangled in uncontrolled struggles for dominance that were conducted over larger areas. The Hellenic civilizing process was characterized by low levels of sympathy for 'outsiders' – for women and slaves in the polis, for the inhabitants of other cities, and for 'barbarians' – and by the high tolerance of exploitation of other people that underpinned the routine harshness and hardships of social and political life. The institution of slavery reveals that the exploitation of the weak was not a central ethical problem in the Greek world – nor was the acquisition of war booty, or the colonization or the displacement of defeated peoples. None of those features of the Hellenic world aroused collective unease or provoked widespread opposition.

Thirdly, because of the hold of the polis on the Greek political imagination, Hellenic international society lacked the level of institutional complexity that has made it possible for modern states to develop collective solutions to the problem of violent harm. Emotional identification between Greeks was too low to support pan-Hellenic institutions that could help pacify struggles between cities. The latter resented all challenges to autonomy. The more powerful were wedded to the belief that the quest for hegemony was the most rational strategy. Fourthly, so powerful were the moral and political emotions and convictions mentioned above that the Greeks barely paused to consider alternative forms of intercity coexistence. No extant philosophical treatise deals with the ethics of warfare. The city states were so deeply involved in their immediate preoccupations that the moral and cultural resources that could have facilitated the quest for collaborative approaches to the problem of violent harm were largely missing. Loyalties to the polis and involvement in immediate power struggles meant that Greeks lacked the relevant detachment that is essential if societies are to make significant advances in bringing unregulated processes under greater control – the kind of detachment that is evident in Thucydides' endeavour to cast light not just on the fate of his own city, Athens, but on developments that had affected Hellas as a whole and that might reappear to trouble future generations. As was true of Western political thought until recently, reflections on international political theory were sparse or non-existent, but it is erroneous to argue that there was no 'international ethic' in the Hellenic system. Conceptions of *philia* and of *eunoia* that became highly valued in fourth-century philosophical circles were testimony to the importance of moral ideals that were bequeathed via Roman and Christianized ideas of *clementia* (mercy) and *philanthropia* (the love of humankind) to later generations (de Romilly 1974; Ferguson 1958: chs. 6 and 10). They were also important dimensions of the Hellenic 'civilizing' legacy.

A fifth and final point is that low levels of mutual dependence between different social strata in the same polis freed the dominant groups from many of the demands and restraints that have been integral to modern 'civilizing' practices. Political pressures to accommodate the interests of less powerful groups were weak, as were major incentives to sympathize with the vulnerable. Universal and egalitarian principles that became important in modern societies as a result of reductions in power disparities had little impact on domestic institutions and practices, and even less influence on the conduct of foreign policy than they have today, in large part because of the constraints on state behaviour that developed as a result of the devastating consequences of the industrialization of war. Therein lies one of the main differences between the ancient system and the most recent phase of the modern international order, and therein lies one of the main explanations of the different characters of their respective inter-societal civilizing processes.

2

New Territorial Concentrations of Power in Antiquity

Part I The Rise and Fall of the Hellenistic States-System

the social dynamic which drives states over and over again to progress from the desire for freedom from domination by other states and for equality with them, to an urge to be stronger than all the others, to gain predominance over them ... drives them into a struggle for hegemony which sooner or later, and again and again, must be fought out with military violence.

(Elias 2010c: 98)

Elias's observation about the 'social dynamic' that has driven successive quests for political supremacy and empire was central to his overview of key features of international politics in the ancient world. He described the struggle for hegemony in which Athens, Corinth, Sparta and Thebes competed for domination. The ensuing military stalemate was followed by the unification of reluctant city states under Macedonian rule (Elias 2010c: 119–20). A similar dynamic was evident in Alexander's relentless conquest to subdue ever more distant peoples that was undertaken in the belief that, at some future time, on the edges of the empire, armies would acquire total control over an 'absolutely secure frontier' (Elias 2010c: 93–4). A parallel orientation explained Rome's domination of neighbouring groups that, by their very existence as independent societies, were portrayed as endangering the imperial peace (Elias 2010c: 91–5). Elias's argument was that struggles for security and 'hegemonic intoxication' entangled states in geopolitical rivalries that could only be resolved – or so they believed – by violence. The three international systems described above collapsed for that reason. The stalemate between the major Greek city states, following a series of debilitating wars and the conflict with Persia, left the Hellenes entirely at the mercy of a new territorial concentration of power – Macedon. Alexander's empire collapsed because rapid expansion created a sprawling empire of diverse peoples that could not be unified symbolically, ruled effectively from a central administrative point, or guaranteed security from external threats (Elias 2010c: 93–4). Rome's initial expansion responded to what it regarded as challenges to its 'physical security and integrity' but, gripped by 'hegemonic intoxication' and convinced of its 'superiority and invincibility', it proceeded to launch a wave of military campaigns to subdue outlying groups. As with Alexander's expansion into Asia, the long-term result was an imperial order that could neither be governed from the centre nor secured from a myriad of threats on the imperial frontiers (Elias 2010c: 91ff.). Because of those endemic weaknesses, all three states-systems turned out to be 'evolutionary dead-ends' (Runciman 1990).

It is useful to recall the argument that states-systems appear to be destined to be destroyed by violence because of internal elimination contests and/or imperial conquest by a contiguous power (Wight 1977: ch. 1). An example was Philip II's victory at Chaeronea in 338 BC which led to Macedonian dominance of the Greek city states. Philip's hegemony was a turning point in the evolution of larger territorial concentrations of military and political power. The rise of Macedon was a major 'scaling up' of social and political organization that was accompanied by the development of new conceptions of civilization. The capacity to govern a larger-scale society from a central point created new opportunities for mobilizing collective social power that made the domination of Greece and the later Alexandrine imperial project possible. The whole pattern of social and political development raised new issues about the relationship between the greater destructive capabilities that were available to larger monopolies of power and the dominant understandings of the restraints that should be observed in relations with peoples who were deemed to be less civilized. Macedonian expansion into Asia posed the question of whether traditional conceptions of social and political life were suitable for administering a large, multicultural empire. Under Alexander's rule, the challenge of controlling vast imperial territories in which the Macedonians were plainly the minority led to the search for symbolic frameworks that could unite Macedonians, Greeks and Persians. The exercise was short-lived. Following his death in 323 BC, the empire was divided between the principal military commanders and quickly fragmented into warring Hellenistic kingdoms that were modelled on the earlier Macedonian state. The Hellenistic states-system survived from 300 BC to the initial period of Roman expansion in which the Macedonian state was relegated to an imperial province. A distinctive civilizing process took place in the Greek world, now reduced to a regional subsystem in the larger sphere of geopolitical interaction. Its core features included concerted efforts to tame violence, to create judicial mechanisms for resolving public and private disputes in the context of growing social and economic interconnections, and to reflect on how rational, universal principles could bring order and harmony to human society as a whole. Western ideas of civilization from the medieval period to the present day bear the imprint of the assorted breakthroughs in the legal and moral discourses of the age. As noted in Chapter 1, they were transmitted to later generations by Roman thought and practice, and specifically by

Stoic-Christian influences that shaped late medieval and early modern expressions of admiration for Rome's political and cultural achievements.

To explain that crucial legacy, this chapter provides an overview of the two eras that preceded the Hellenistic states-system: Alexander's empire and the earlier phase of Macedonian state formation which is usually overlooked in studies of ancient states-systems. Of central importance are the dominant attitudes to violence and civilization in those preceding epochs, and in the Hellenistic international system. As is the case in most times and places where there have been low levels of mutual dependence between the rulers and the ruled, Alexander's empire and the successor states displayed little compunction in combining 'hegemonic intoxication' with the ruthless exploitation of conquered peoples. Significant intellectual countertrends emerged amongst the Greek city states. As they struggled to adapt to their incorporation in longer chains of interconnectedness, various Greek political thinkers and associations constructed world views that broke with the old dichotomies between insiders and outsiders. Cosmopolitan moral orientations included the belief that shared vulnerabilities to pain and suffering provided the most direct method of widening the scope of emotional identification between diverse peoples. Those standpoints emerged in an era when the polis had lost much of its significance as a survival unit, and when the main challenge was to find new principles of coexistence between social groups that had been forced together by imperial expansion. Cosmopolitanism emerged in a world of more impersonal social relations where increased exposure to external forces meant that the polis provided little meaning and comfort for people who struggled to orientate themselves to rapidly changing circumstances. Success in creating wider symbolic frameworks of reference made the further scaling-up of social and political organization possible; the capacity to project military and political power over greater distances increased accordingly. The whole process that began with Macedonian state formation and expansion reached its apogee with the rise of Rome (Mann 1986: ch. 9).

The final parts of this chapter consider the incorporation of the Hellenic–Hellenistic system in Rome's sphere of influence. The decision to focus on core features of Roman social and political development requires brief explanation. The Roman world is usually regarded as an imperial order and not as a states-system; it may therefore seem to fall outside the scope of the comparative analysis of violence and civilization in the Western systems of states. But as Watson (1992: ch. 1) stated, most international systems have conformed neither to an idealized model of a highly centralized imperial order nor to the image of a political domain comprising approximate military equals. Most forms of world political organization tended towards the middle of a 'spectrum' that extends from 'absolute independence' to 'absolute empire' (Watson 1992: 13). From that perspective, the supposition that empires are free from the constraints that states confront as members of an international system or society is false; the 'freedom of action' that imperial governments enjoy is not unlimited but is checked 'by the constraints which involvement with other communities imposes' (Watson 1992: 16). That was one of the hallmarks of the 'suzerain state-system' that Rome dominated after it con-quered Macedon in 168 BC (Wight 1977: 23).

The rise of the Roman Empire should be considered in that context. Rome emerged as a small city within a larger multi-actor international system and gradually acquired military and political dominance through the ruthless application of force. But various ideas about restrained govern-ment developed in response to the challenge of conducting relations with conquered peoples that often preserved some political autonomy – as in the case of the Greek city states. Such beliefs also arose because Rome had relations with various societies on the frontier that were hard to control or to govern directly (Watson 1992: 100). Those political realities indicate that Rome was never a closed imperial system but was embedded in longer networks of social and political interaction that constrained its freedom of action. Various conceptions of restraint that enjoyed support as a way of pacifying the peoples who had been forced together within the empire did not always have much influence on external relations. But they were transmitted to the medieval period where they influenced natural law con-ceptions of constitutional authority as well as the language that was used to define the principles of a civilized society of states and to defend its core practices of diplomacy and international law (Bull 1990: 73–4). It is not possible to understand the relationship between violence and civilization in the modern states-system without recognizing that legacy.

Roman imperial experience also shaped early modern European images of empire that developed alongside the idea of international society (see Canny 1973). Many regarded Rome as a model of imperial self-restraint. They were aware that, during its rise to power, Rome combined great violence with shrewd pragmatism that aimed to woo the consent of conquered peoples. Romans often congratulated themselves on public demonstrations of mercy and moderation that distinguished their 'civilized' habitus from 'barbarian' practices. In large part because of the influence of Stoicism, conceptions of limited power won the support of the aristocracy during the Roman Republic. *Clementia* and *civilitas* were core elements of a distinctive civilizing process that combined support for the republican peace with the conviction that force was necessary to tame 'barbarian' warriors. Those social ideas were integral to the *Pax Romana,* and to the assurance that Rome served humanity by bringing peace and stability to the whole inhabited world. Those moral and political concepts were transmitted through the medieval courts to early modern Europe where they influenced state formation and the civilizing process, as well as the discourse of 'civil empire' and the language of international society that was mentioned earlier. To understand later phases of European development, it is necessary to analyse the relationship between violence and civilization in late antiquity, and to focus specifically on how new languages regarding restraints on force evolved in the period between the rise of Macedon and Rome's ascent to power in Italy and its subsequent dominance of the Mediterranean region. That was the era in which new territorial concentrations of power eclipsed the polis and replaced the ancient states-systems as a result of the social dynamics that have been noted. The latter also gave rise to new conceptions of civility and restraint that continue to be evident in the core practices of modern international society.

Macedonian State Formation

Over twenty-three years of rule, Philip transformed Macedonia from a backward society on the fringes of 'civilized' Hellenic society to the efficiently organized state that controlled the majority of the Greek city states through the League of Corinth (McQueen 1995). Established in 337 BC, the League was intended to advance Philip's interests by pacifying Greece and by legitimating action to liberate the Greek city states in Asia Minor. According to Arrian (7.9), pride in a distinctive Macedonian civilizing process was evident in the speech that Alexander the Great gave to his unruly armed forces at Susa. 'Philip', he proclaimed, 'found you a tribe of impoverished vagabonds, most of you dressed in skins, feeding a few sheep on the hills and fighting, feebly enough, to keep them from your neighbours – Thracians and Triballians and Illyrians. He . . . brought you down from the hills into the plains; he taught you to fight on equal terms with the enemy on your borders . . . he made you city-dwellers; he brought you law; he *civilized* you. He rescued you from subjection and slavery, and made you masters of the wild tribes who harried and plundered you' (italics added). The nomadic warrior tribes that existed in northern Greece in the sixth century attached great importance to a life dedicated to 'war and rapine' (Hammond and Griffith 1979: 23). The traditional warrior custom that 'a man wore a halter round his waste until he had killed an enemy was typical of that stage of civilization' (Hammond and Griffith 1979: ibid.). The Macedonian association of monarchy with a higher state of civilization went against the grain of the dominant patterns of Greek political thought that defended the ideal of the self-government of adult male citizens. Leaving aside Sparta, kingship was regarded as an example of the despotism that befitted craven, subservient barbarians (Walbank 1981:74–5). Relatively isolated from Greece, Macedonia had seemed barbaric to Greeks because it was governed by 'tribal monarchies' that often disintegrated into warring factions that pursued rival claims to govern (Heskel 1997). The shortcoming of the exclusive citizenship of the polis was a restricted ability to increase military forces and to integrate the diverse social groups that Philip and Alexander had at their disposal (Sekunda 2007: 325).

The historian, Curtius, observed that the Macedonian kings were distinguished by the 'observance of traditional customs, healthy self-restraint and self-discipline, and a citizen-like bearing' (Hammond 1989: 177). The Companions who drank, hunted and fought alongside the king were used to speaking frankly at the court, perhaps because the Assembly of the Macedonians had responsibility for electing a new king and often took it upon itself to depose an existing one. The king may have consulted the inner circle and behaved as *primus inter pares*, in recognition of the need to maintain their loyalty but, in the main, he controlled them in a warrior court society (Hammond 1989: 53ff., 140ff.; also Hamilton 1973: 24 and Herman 1997).

The 'tribal roots' of the Macedonian state were expressed in the convention that kings fought alongside their men (Serrati 2007: 461). Philip and Alexander were both wounded at the front. The latter's attempts to inspire the troops with displays of personal courage struck Arrian (6.13) as the reckless pursuit of the 'pleasure of battle' that could have led to his death and the total disarray of the armed forces. During the early military campaigns, Alexander was described as embodying the ideal of 'wild Homeric duelling around the king, to the exclusion of any coherent overview of the battle as a whole' (Sabin 2007: 407). The narrative altered with respect to later conflicts where he was portrayed as combining the roles of the 'battle manager' and the 'heroic leader' who only moved to the centre of the struggle at the critical stage (Sabin 2007: 407). Alexander's approach has been contrasted with Roman generals who were 'models of patience and restraint' with regard to siege warfare (de Souza 2007: 448). The point suggests that there was an overall trend away from the leader's personal involvement in fighting towards a more detached analysis of the battle as a whole. As will be discussed later, that movement is best regarded as one dimension of a broader transformation of world views – a civilizing process – that accompanied the rise of new territorial monopolies of power.

But Macedonian warrior society was still at the stage where such self-restraint would have been costly for the leaders. The failure to fight side by side with the army and to display personal courage in the front line of battle would have breached the harm conventions that underpinned the warriors' we-identity (Hamilton 1999). Macedonia's political unity, which was the key to levels of imperial expansion that the Greek city states with their vulnerability to civil strife could not match, owed a great deal to consensual rule that secured personal loyalty – as did the military triumphs of Philip and Alexander which were regarded as crucial evidence that they had 'won the favour of the gods' (Hammond 1989: 176–7). Certain parallels between the Hellenistic and early medieval European court societies have been identified (see Herman 1997), but what is perhaps most striking is the low level of self-restraint and the limited extent of the civilizing process when compared with the taming of the warriors in the early modern European courts (see Elias 2006: 98–9, 121–2; also Chapter 5 herein). The king surrounded himself with a Council, the so-called Friends, who performed various military, administrative and other tasks while remaining firmly under his direct control. For the most part, Philip's court was drawn from the Macedonian nobility, but persons from different regions of the Hellenistic world were recruited, though not to a level that risked alienating the traditional warrior aristocracy (Walbank 1981: 83). With the 'scaling up' of social and political organization, the challenge was how to lower the barriers to advancement that faced subordinate groups, and how to promote the symbolic unification of the conquerors and the conquered – again, without producing the disaffection of members of the traditional elite who were unwilling to relax their monopoly control of the instruments of power. As Alexander would later discover following the conquest of Persia, the challenge was how to create and maintain a delicate balance of power between the 'established' and the 'outsiders'.

Having been held hostage in Thebes for three years, Philip had first-hand experience of the hegemonic principle in Greek politics that would govern his perspective on foreign policy (Heskel 1997). Philip's behaviour towards the Balkan captives who were brought within the kingdom has been said to display racial and religious tolerance, respect for local autonomy, and the conviction that subordinate groups had to be capable of rising to high office in the service of the king (Hammond 1989: 194–5). The Macedonian civilizing process meant that wars were 'more humane' than their neighbours'; it was rare for victory to lead to the widespread massacre and enslavement of adversaries (Hammond and Griffith 1979: 164). Ending 'the life of a city was repugnant by the standards of the time' although that did not prevent Philip from destroying Olynthus in 348 BC. The strategy shocked the Greeks though many seized the opportunity to accumulate more slaves (Hammond and Griffith 1979: 324–5).

For the most part, Philip displayed generosity towards the allies in the League of Corinth that was explicitly committed to liberating Greek cities in Asia Minor. Philip was elected leader of the military expedition but assassinated before the invasion plans could be completed. Uncertainty exists about his long-term ambitions with respect to Persia. The assumption that there was a civilizing role to play – a 'sacred mission' – was emphasized by Isocrates (1928) in the *Oration to Philip* that implored him to lead a Greek expedition against 'barbarous' Persians. His appeal reflected changing attitudes towards monarchy and larger territorial monopolies of power that were exceptional given the Greeks' traditional attachment to the small-scale polis. The failure to overcome their political differences, and the collective inability to punish Persia for the ways in which it had 'injured Hellas', led Isocrates (1928a: 237) in the *Panegyricus* to argue that only Macedon could assume the role of saviour of the Hellenes that had once belonged to Athens. Moreover, in the process Macedon could liberate Greece from the scourge of mercenaries and miscreants who, as a result of war and civil strife, roamed the country in search of the means of survival, freely 'committing outrages' on those they encountered (Isocrates 1928: 319). In an interesting parallel with the belief that the First Crusade would free Christendom from untamed warriors, Isocrates (1928: 319) argued that a unifying war of revenge against Persia, and the establishment of new cities in conquered lands, would absorb the energies of a growing multitude which, if unconstrained, threatened 'to be a terror no less to the Hellenes than to the barbarians'.

Isocrates clearly believed then that it was no longer possible for the city states – individually or collectively – to use force to seek revenge against the Persians. His standpoint drew on distinctions between civilized and barbaric peoples that had emerged during the Persian Wars. The conviction that 'compulsion' was 'useful' in relations with barbarians, while the art of 'persuasion' was 'helpful' in relations between Greeks, restated an earlier belief that Persian inferiority was embodied in blind obedience to despotic government that was anathema to most Hellenes (Isocrates 1928: 255). That assumption also harboured the belief that the modernized state led by Philip would show 'self-control' and 'kindness' in relations with the Greeks as opposed to the 'force' that Athens had used against 'weaker' cities at the height of its ascendancy (Isocrates 1928a: 167–8). Philip won support amongst the Greeks for acts of restraint that included ransoming Athenian prisoners on at least three occasions instead of killing or enslaving them in accordance with the established Hellenic rules of war (McQueen 1995: 332). Isocrates' hope that the Macedonians would become Athens' heir as the civilizing *hegemon* in Greece – simultaneously promoting 'concord' within the Hellenic world and launching a 'campaign against the barbarian' – looked to the new territorial concentration of power to promote pan-Hellenic ideals (Isocrates 1928: 255, 331). Noteworthy was his supposition that Macedonian hegemony would promote rule by a 'king' rather than a 'tyrant' – or at least that the plea to Philip to adopt 'a policy of kindness to the Hellenes', and to seek honour in displaying 'gentleness and humanity' rather than 'harshness', would secure their political loyalty (Isocrates 1928: 317, 338–9).

Restraints on kingly rule in Philip's time were noted earlier in connection with the question of whether there were parallels between patterns of self-restraint in the courts of Philip and Alexander and in early modern Europe. The point was made in the light of the contention that there has often been a close link between court society and civilization (Elias 2006b). The literature on Alexander's court provides further clues to the nature and scope of civilized and restrained behaviour amongst the ruling elite. Arrian (4.8ff.) protested that court flatterers encouraged Alexander to orientalize the court by asserting a divine foundation for rule, and to act on the maxim that whatever the king decided was intrinsically just. Seemingly objecting to efforts to orientalize the court, Cleitus (who appears to have belonged to a faction that was intent on preserving the traditional rights of Macedeonian nobles) enraged Alexander, who killed him with his own hand, an action that clashed with quasi-egalitarian attitudes to relations within the ruling elite. The act of killing Cleitus may have been prompted by Alexander's desire to cast aside the old restraints of Macedonian court politics. In a profile of Alexander, Plutarch (1919: L–LII) maintained that his decision to mock the recently defeated Macedonians in full view of 'barbarians' provoked the rage of Cleitus and other members of the establishment. Wherever the truth may lie, Alexander's conduct breached the conventions that upheld something like a right of free speech in Macedonian court society, though his murderous act was hardly a radical departure from traditional court politics. Growing political tensions within the governing elite illustrated the problem that Alexander faced in creating a mode of rule that effectively integrated two radically different court societies (Hamilton 1973: ch. 10, 163–4). Major disputes broke out over Alexander's efforts to orientalize the Macedonian court by proposing the introduction of the Persian ritual of physical prostration (*proskynesis*) before the king (see also pp. 71–2 below). There was a danger of the eruption of the violent conflict that had been one of the main features of Macedonian court society. Philip was assassinated by a member of his inner circle, and later court conspiracies included attempts to kill Alexander. Celebrating his father's achievements, Alexander emphasized the civilizing role of the Macedonian state. However, a warrior ethos dominated Macedonian court society that revolved around a distinctive union of a high level of tolerance of violence and a culture of self-restraint. Comparisons will be made later with the 'taming of the warriors' in the later European court societies – with the rise of new conceptions of civilized behaviour that shaped state structures, the development of 'civil' empire, and the evolution of the European society of states.

Significantly, the clear political–military superiority of the Macedonian state, and confidence that the monarchical system of government would sooner or later prevail everywhere, promoted innovative philosophical reflections on society and politics. Subject to Macedonian domination after Chaeronea, the Greek cities had an obvious stake in moderating or civilizing the king's behaviour – in promoting ideals of restraint and conceptions of *praotes* or even-temperedness (Harris 2001: 234–5). Those themes would influence later phases in a long-term European civilizing process, most obviously through Roman and medieval treatises on princely or imperial rule that sought to check royal anger and to encourage moderation.

It is important to note how accounts of Alexander's unruly court and his violent and impulsive behaviour shaped the Roman civilizing process and later political theories of imperial government. Reflecting the influence of his Stoic teacher, Epictetus, Arrian (4.8ff.) argued that conquests that win admiration do not bring happiness unless the leader also acquires 'victory over himself': a theme repeated in Seneca's observation that Alexander was perfectly capable of dominating whole nations but was unable to conquer his own violent dispositions (Dawson 1996: 135). Arrian also commented on the low level of self-control over impulsive behaviour amongst members of the Macedonian ruling cohort, and maintained that Alexander was 'a slave of anger and drunkenness' and especially prone to 'barbaric excess'. Considerable license in the treatment of defeated cities echoed the freedoms that the king enjoyed within Macedonian court society. That combination drew the attention of Greek political thinkers following Chaeronea. Alexander won Arrian's approval for displaying remorse for his violent actions as against justifying them in the manner of court flatterers such as Anaxarchus who professed that whatever a king does is *ipso facto* right. Curtius (Bk 6: 6) regarded Alexander's drunkenness as evidence of the moral collapse that followed his gravitation towards Persian customs, but praised his 'great restraint' towards Darius' captured family – and specifically towards women of noble birth (Curtius 3.12.12; 17, 18, 21; also Arrian 4.19ff.). The latter reported Darius' astonishment on learning that Alexander had not raped his captured wife – an instance of civilized self-control that Arrian singled out for comment and, in so doing, provided a dark reminder of the usual fate of women who were seized by Alexander's forces. According to Curtius, he outshone all other kings in his 'self-control and clemency' but, as his power increased, 'self-restraint and abstinence' steadily declined. Greek writers were often ambivalent about Alexander, applauding his heroic exploits and personal courage while condemning his violent nature and susceptibility to the rage that led to the decision to destroy Thebes in 335 BC and to the enslavement of the surviving population (Harris 2001: 236–7; Brunt 1977). His character was condemned by Cicero and by Seneca who advanced Stoic ideals of restrained rule. The conviction that Alexander was 'a slave of anger and drunkenness' may have been a Stoic fabrication – a convenient method of underlining the threat that male warriors posed to 'civilized' society, of defending emergent ideals of merciful government, and assuring the thinkers involved that there had been progress beyond the 'barbarism' of earlier times. But evidence of the actions that led to that caricature is not exactly hard to find (Hamilton 1973: 164ff.). Issues regarding Alexander's character were important in later debates on the relationship between civilized government and imperial court society, but their significance extends well beyond the controversies of the ancient world. Reflections on Alexander's lack of self-control and excess were transmitted by the Stoics and by various medieval authorities to Enlightenment thinkers such as Adam Smith who regarded Alexander as a symbol of the 'devastating effects' of 'excessive self-estimation' – as a leader who had been admired for 'daring' projects that were 'devoid of justice' (Hanley 2009: 165ff.). The civilizing of human aspirations depended on the ability to separate 'the violence and injustice' and 'intrepid valour' of 'great conquerors' from genuine 'magnanimity' (Hanley 2009: 169–70). That is one of many examples of how Alexander's lack of restraint was used in attempts to give direction to future stages of the European civilizing process.

Alexander's Empire

There were many reasons for the decision to attempt to conquer Persia: the desire to seek vengeance, the joys of fame, glory and adventure that could only be satisfied by projecting physical power to the edge of the known world, and the simple quest for personal enrichment. On crossing the Hellespont in 334 BC, Alexander visited Troy to dramatize the pan-Hellenic nature of the enterprise, and to underline his claims to be the leader of Hellas rather than Macedon. Also important was the ideal of liberating not only Greeks, but other peoples, from Persian despotic rule, a 'civilizing' mission that was linked in the early phase of the conquest with commands that prevented victorious troops from looting, with demonstrations of respect for enemy leaders, for example, by ensuring that they were granted an honourable burial, and by lifting social barriers so that the upper echelons of defeated armies could join the imperial forces (Hammond 1989: 206; Hammond 1993). Conquest was also secured by eliminating rivals including the Persian satraps who were crucified. Arrian (2.7) stated that Alexander invoked familiar distinctions between the civilized and the barbarian when rallying his troops before the first major engagement with Darius' forces. The Persians, it was stated, were no different from slaves. They lived 'soft and luxurious lives', and were not hardened like the Macedonians who were 'free men' fighting for Greece. Arrian made it clear that he did not approve of Alexander's 'excessive severity', which only revealed that he was emulating 'Eastern extravagance and splendour, and the fashion of barbaric kings of treating their subjects as inferiors' (Arrian 4.7–8). Early in his reign, Alexander demonstrated that rebellious cities such as Thebes could assume that there would be no mercy towards women and children as well as military foes; in the first phase of the campaign in Asia Minor, the Macedonians massacred the Persian forces in Miletus; they crucified about six thousand enemy soldiers after defeating Tyre in 332 BC. Those acts encouraged other cities to submit, just as displays of mercy often induced opponents to surrender quickly and to avoid what would otherwise be a predictably cruel fate (de Souza 2007: 460; Kern 1999: 203–4). Siege warfare followed the usual patterns of the ancient world. Surrender was often rewarded by clemency; annihilation awaited those who chose to hold out (Kern 1999: chs. 8–9).

Many historical narratives have documented the scale of the atrocities that were committed against defenceless populations in Persia and India (see Arrian Book 4 for further details). Looting was endemic, as was the practice of living off the land that must often have resulted in mass starvation (Bosworth 1996: 184–5). Atrocities against various cities revealed that pleasure was found in destruction and frenzied killing – 'at times verging on massacre for its own sake' – that was often justified as the legitimate response to failures to send envoys to submit to Alexander's rule (Bosworth 1996: v, 23, 94ff., ch. 5; Arrian 6.6ff.). Many Macedonians were ashamed by the indiscriminate killing that often accompanied imperial conquests (Bosworth 1996: ibid.). Nevertheless, the belief that force was necessary to 'civilize' nomadic peoples was influential, as was the related belief that the traditional laws of war did not apply in struggles with 'inferiors' (Bosworth 1996: 92ff., 146). The mass killings of that period were intertwined with images of cultural superiority that foreshadowed the European colonial genocides and the fifteenth- and sixteenth-century Doctrine of Discovery that the colonial powers used to justify sovereign rights in the newly found territories (Miller 2010). The relationship between violence and civilization was encapsulated in the belief that 'primitive' groups had few, if any, rights against their Macedonian 'civilizers'. In one of the more intriguing encounters with non-Greek peoples, Alexander the Great asked a group of Indian Sages why they had stamped their feet on the ground as he approached. The response was that they were acting in the belief that no-one should possess more than the surface of the earth that he was standing on. Harmful ambition had driven Alexander to seize more and more land, but after his death, the sages observed, the natural order of things would be restored. Then he would 'own just as much of this earth as will suffice to bury you' (Arrian Book 7:2; also Diodorus 1954: volume 10, Book 19:97 on the protest of the Nabataean nomads). That was by no means the first or indeed the last critique of 'higher' civilization by people who wished to preserve a 'simpler' way of life. It was one of the outcomes of the rise of larger territorial monopolies of power and widening inequalities between 'advanced' peoples who asserted unlimited rights of colonial expansion and 'backward' peoples who were exposed to the 'barbarism' of 'civilization'.

The mass killings that took place during the waves of expansion raise serious problems for the 'Tarn thesis' which maintained – when focusing on the relations between Greeks, Macedonians and Persians – that Alexander's empire represented the progress of cosmopolitan principles of association (Tarn 1933, 1948). The idea that a commitment to moral and political cosmopolitanism explains Alexander's treatment of subjugated peoples has long been rejected, and not least because of a tendency to take ancient eulogistic portraits of 'Alexander the civilizer' at face value (Bosworth 1996: ch. 1; also

Badian 1958). Recent writings have switched attention to the limited control that ancient empires had over remote territories. Because the capacity for directly administering distant regions was restricted, ruling strata had little choice but to rely heavily on local intermediaries. In Alexander's case, a combination of calculated threats and incentives was used to incorporate conquered regional elites into the imperial governing apparatus. Allegiance, or 'compulsory cooperation', was secured by the promise of the continuation and/ or augmentation of wealth and privilege, by the clear threat of removal, or by physical elimination as punishment for revolt or resistance (Mann 1986: ch. 6). Alexander appointed Persians as 'civil governors' of the former regions of the empire (the satrapies); however, military and financial power remained firmly in the hands of the Macedonian armed forces (Davis and Kraay 1973: 27).

The supposed cosmopolitanism of Alexander's approach to governing Persia owed less then to the influence of proto-Stoic ethical attachments than to the practical difficulties of administering an empire that had out-grown Macedonia – it resulted from the recognition that the social principles that had bound together different groups during the process of state formation and in earlier phases of territorial expansion were inadequate for governing a multicultural empire that far exceeded the boundaries of its predecessors. That does not alter the reality that Alexander initiated a civilizing process in an attempt to bridge the cultural divides between Greek, Macedonian and Persian elites and to integrate them in relations of mutual trust and respect. The 'Tarn thesis' has the merit of identifying a deliberate project of creating new frameworks of thought and action in response to a major 'scaling up' of social and political organization. That political initiative is best characterized as an experiment in constructing a novel discourse of we-feeling and emotional identification as well as parallel changes in the we–I balance and in the social standards of self-restraint. Alexander's instruments of rule included the search for universal symbols that would legitimate empire by appealing to the rulers and the ruled alike. They were inspired by the quest to integrate 'subordinate' ideas or practices in a cross-cultural code that would have meaning and significance at least for the ruling strata of subjugated groups (Eisenstadt 1963). There were important parallels between Alexander's 'quest for internationally effective principles of cohesion' and the traditional Persian practice of restrained rule given the common problem of administering an empire that had forced extraordinarily diverse peoples together (Bozeman 1960: 92–3; Mann 1986: 237ff.). Personal authority and a 'universalistic' code developed hand in hand, in acknowledgment of the reality that the concepts that had been used to justify political power in Macedonia or Greece were ill-suited to the new imperial realities. Belief in the brotherhood of all peoples may not have been the driving force behind what was once regarded as Alexander's trailblazing appeal at the banquet in Opis in 324 BC for concord (*homonoia*) between Macedonians and Persians (Tarn 1933). Pragmatic concerns led to a degree of detachment from Macedonian and Greek organizing political principles. The alternative was not a form of cosmopolitanism that granted all peoples equal moral standing. The appeal to *homonoia* recognized the need for an inclusive symbolic framework that could fuse the cultural horizons of the dominant strata in the conquering and subjugated societies. What Alexander desired was that 'Persians and Macedonians might rule together in harmony as an imperial power' (Arrian 7.12). For that reason, his call for *homonoia* at Susa deserves to be included in any study of the emergence of universalistic modes of reasoning that found more abstract formulation in Roman law and which the Stoic-Christian ethical tradition transmitted to later generations.

Alexander encouraged the marriage of members of the Macedonian and Persian elites at Susa in 324 BC. Observing Persian rituals, he married Barsine, Darius' eldest daughter. On some accounts, ninety-two members of the Companions took Persian wives; dowries were granted to around ten thousand men who married native partners (Walbank 1981: 36–8). At times, Alexander and other members of the ruling cohort wore Persian dress – but avoiding what Macedonians regarded as offensive garments (Hamilton 1973: 163). Especially troubling in their view was the attempt to establish a version of the Persian court ritual of *proskynesis* (Bosworth 1996: 109ff.; Curtius Bk VI: vi; Bk VIII: v). The dominant tendency amongst the Greeks was to regard prostration before the king as a contemptible barbarian practice. It conferred a divine status on a fellow human that had no place in relations between free Greeks, but was reserved exclusively for relations with the gods. Macedonians were in the main hostile to a social practice that was associated with ruler worship and 'intolerable servility' (Bosworth 1996: 109). Alexander's wish to introduce Persian court practice may have had less to do with asserting divine status than with placing Macedonians and Persians on a more equal footing in an attempt to consolidate his personal power (Spawforth 2007). He may have feared that the Persians would conclude that he had renounced his authority if he did not insist on prostration. The relevant rituals, which were designed to solve the problems involved in administering a multi-ethnic empire – and in making the transition from 'king of Macedon to king of Asia' – created major political divisions within the Macedonian ruling strata (Bosworth 1988: 273). The latter's response to the plan to introduce prostration may have had less to do with ideological objections to an alien practice than with collective fears about the loss of social status that were intensified as a result of Alexander's decision to employ elite Persians in the machinery of imperial governance. All such measures were part of the controversial strategy of incorporating elements of Persian court society in a new cultural order that prompted Alexander's critics to contrast traditional kingship in

Macedonian court society with increasingly autocratic personal rule. Their objection was that government in that earlier era had observed the custom of proceeding with the consent of the Companions whereas Alexander, with the approval of some court officials, was intent on a fundamental alteration of the traditional balance of power (Hammond and Griffith 1979: 385–6, 396). In any event, the proposal to introduce *proskynesis* was abandoned because of the opposition of court officials such as Callisthenes who argued – appealing to tradition – that Alexander's attendants were not advisers to a 'Cambyses or Xerxes but [to] Philip's son ... a man whose forebears came from Argos to Macedonia, where they long ruled not by force but by law'.[1]

Particularly threatening in the eyes of the Macedonians were measures to create a 'cosmopolitan international force' that owed direct loyalty to Alexander, policies that anticipated the 'personal monarchies of the Hellenistic age' (Walbank 1981: 37; Badian 1958). Macedonian resentment at threats to traditional powers and privileges increased following the parade at Susa in 324 BC of approximately thirty thousand Iranian youths (the *Epigoni*) who had undergone Macedonian military training. Discontent was reinforced by the decision to incorporate Orientals in the Companion Cavalry and to create elite Persian forces that threatened the traditional Macedonian monopoly of power and influence (Bosworth 1988: 271ff.; Hammond 1989: 229). Such innovations did not amount to an endeavour to create a new ruling class that combined Macedonians and Persians as social equals. The latter's incorporation within, and greater stake, in the armed forces – but usually only within the lower ranks – was designed to win their acceptance of imperial structures. By establishing separate Persian forces, Alexander acquired a degree of independence from the Macedonian army but aroused suspicions that Persian ranks might be deployed against an imperial military establishment that was fearful of the loss of power and prestige. However, marriage to Persian women was a symbolic expression of new forms of political domination that sought to preserve, on both sides, social continuity and acquiescence (Bosworth 1988: 157–8; Arrian 7.30). Such measures were responses to the problem of legitimacy that invariably attends the 'scaling up' of social and political organization; they expressed an awareness of the need for principles of coexistence that were no longer tethered to the old 'ethnic' base. But as previously mentioned, Alexander's attempt to connect new forms of we-feeling with his personal rule alienated sections of the traditional Macedonian elite. Tensions came to a head at Opis in 324 where large sections of the army protested against the changing power balance between Macedonian and Persian social strata. Alexander had declared his intention

---

[1] See Bosworth (1996: 111–12) who adds that, revealingly, Callisthenes was tortured and crucified for opposing Alexander's plans to introduce *proskynesis*.

to govern as an 'absolute monarch, ruling in a markedly oriental style' (Bosworth 1988: 158). His response to what he regarded as an intolerable challenge to his authority clashed with the greater openness of traditional Macedonian court society.

Opposition rapidly melted away. Alexander offered Persians command positions that Macedonians had once monopolized (and confronted them with the danger that Persian forces might indeed be deployed against them); thirteen Macedonian leaders were executed (Bosworth 1988: 160). The feast of reconciliation at Opis followed where, according to Arrian, Alexander prayed before the nine thousand who gathered there that Persians and Macedonians might join together in harmony in an imperial power bloc. The endeavour to create points of unity between the imperial forces and the conquered elites was anchored in the belief that integration should take place through a civilizing process in which Persians transformed themselves into Greeks. Although Persians outnumbered them in the lower ranks, Macedonians continued to hold the most powerful and prestigious command positions. The evidence is that, following the disintegration of the empire, attention turned to ousting Persians from higher posts so that Macedonians re-established their monopoly control of the fruits of victory. That was the main political outcome of the power struggle in which the Macedonian nobility attempted to protect its traditional privileges during the expansion of the Alexandrine empire.

Even so, the whole process that Alexander initiated can be described as a tilt towards greater detachment from traditional politico-cultural horizons that accompanied the rise of larger territorial concentrations of power. A similar development shaped different spheres of life including the emergence of the conviction that the king should combine the traditional role of heroic warrior with the more detached standpoint of the 'battle manager' who decided how to use destructive power most effectively. Cosmopolitan ideologies appeared as part of the same long-term pattern of social and political development. Those movements emerged as part of the growing interweaving of radically different peoples. They were examples of the need for new forms of orientation to the world as 'small-scale' groups with 'short interdependence chains' were replaced by 'more populous social units with very long and closely knit interdependence chains' (Elias 2009a: 121). Concepts that were 'more impersonal and more detached' became invaluable as people became entangled in, and had to become attuned to, unanticipated higher levels of interconnectedness (Elias 2007a: 118ff.). Some of those changes occurred in the ethical sphere. Other developments provided new conceptions of the past. They were the universal histories that offered an explanation of the long-term trend towards unprecedented levels of social and political integration (see pp. 90–1 below).

Those cultural shifts towards more universalistic perspectives were there-fore inextricably connected with the emergence of larger and more destructive monopolies of physical power such as the Macedonian state and Alexander's empire. Their 'civilized' condition had legitimated the violent conquest of 'inferior' peoples. As in the case of Alexander's conception of empire, more detached perspectives that were part of the attempt to move beyond the traditional Macedonian conceptions of rule were orientated towards the organization of imperial power. But conceptions of just kingship and moderate rule would become important as is evident in the Stoic portraits of Alexander's lack of self-control that were mentioned earlier. The images of civilization that were set against his violent temperament influenced Roman conceptions of republican government and imperial order. They would have less impact on the dominant conceptions of how to conduct relations with other peoples. Nevertheless, certain tendencies were apparent in the recognition of tensions between the negative and positive dimensions of lengthening social interconnections – between acknowledgment of the possibilities for violence and exploitation over larger areas and consideration of the benefits of mercy and moderation, if only to secure the support of subjugated groups and to assure the imperial ruling elite that it was the custodian of 'civilized' values that could be disseminated across human society as a whole. The question was posed in the introduction to this work of whether contemporary attitudes to genocide distinguish the most recent phase of world politics from the ancient states-systems. The issue is whether the relationship between violence and civilization has changed significantly with the result that 'civilized' self-images have acquired an unprecedented role in constraining rather than legitimating violence. It is how far there has been a change in the power balance between the political quest to minimize restraints on the development and employment of more devastating forms of violent harm and the ethical conviction that 'civilized' principles can provide the foundations for an international order in which different peoples are free from indefensible violence. The tensions that appeared within the Alexandrine empire and in later interpretations of his character were manifestations of those deeper political problems. To develop the theme, the discussion now turns to international relations in the Hellenistic and Roman international systems.

The Hellenistic States-System

Following Alexander's death, the empire was divided between the Macedonian generals. Harmony did not govern the relations between the Successors (*Diadochoi*). For around a century, the Wars of Succession that broke out in 322 BC embroiled the Hellenistic states in almost permanent violent competition (Baker 2005: 386). In the absence of any agreed successor to Alexander, the leading generals, who belonged to the old warrior cultures with their dedication to the 'toil of the spear', competed for control of the conquered territories. Partitioning the former empire into separate dynastic states was not the result of a diplomatic agreement but the product of the plain reality that no single power could subjugate the rest. The Hellenistic kings were wedded to the 'fourth-century hegemonic ideal' that had been promoted by Athens, Thebes and Sparta, and was now projected over a much larger territorial area (Baker 2005: 376). The coalition that defeated Antigonus at the Battle of Ipsus in 301 BC (the only successor with some prospect of acquiring mastery of the old imperial territories) ensured that the empire was split between competing dynasties in Egypt, Babylonia and northern Syria, and in Macedonia and Greece. The areas that were controlled by the dynasties in the final years of the fourth century survived for around two centuries until they were incorporated within the Roman Empire.

Hellenistic rulers governed their territories according to the right of conquest. As with Alexander's claim on Persia, it was 'spear-won land' (*doriktetos chora*) that generated continuous warfare and the widespread fear of conquest and reduction to slavery. All of the governing elites continued Alexander's practice of plundering conquered cities; they preserved the ancient tradition of 'Homeric raiding on a grand scale' (Green 1990: 367). One of the aims of Alexander's imperialism had been to appropriate the wealth of the Persian kings, a strategy that had financed additional conquests. Similar calculations dominated international relations within the Hellenistic states-system. There was no counterpart to the modern separation of the 'economic' and 'political' spheres. War was the pathway to wealth based on harsh economic exploitation; the wealth that was acquired through conquest was crucial for increasing military and political power in the context of fierce interstate competition (Austin 1986).

The fact that no dynasty could impose its will on the others has led to the observation that a *de facto* balance of power existed in that period (Eckstein 2007). Rulers were not blind to the strategic advantages of forming alliances to thwart 'overambitious' rulers (Green 1990: 119–21). However, imperial expansion remained integral to the kingly ideal, and essential for preserving the loyalty of armies that clearly expected to share in the spoils of war (Serrati 2007: 479ff.; Austin 1986 and Green 1990: ch. 8). It has been argued that a 'natural' balance of power was formalized as part of an attempt to ensure a modicum of respect for international standards of self-restraint. Hellenistic diplomacy depended on 'international friendship networks' – on personal representatives of the king who were bound together, however loosely, in a 'supranational' court society. Those ties underpinned the belief in 'limited warfare' that may have been influenced by fourth-century Greek views that cities should not cause each other's destruction (Billows 2007: 304; Austin 1986). Amidst the violence was the belief that wars that preserved enemy property, if not enemy lives, were more profitable than wars of unlimited conflict and revenge (Walbank 1981: 48, 240; Roth 2007: 375). Distinctions between Greek and 'barbarian' attitudes to warfare, and the belief that the massacre of women and children was typical of the 'uncivilized', may have contributed to restraints on violence in this period (Roth 2007: 396). There was a civilizing process of sorts. Shared beliefs in the need for restraint may have expressed an element of we-feeling, but the we–I balance did not involve close cooperation to establish a balance of power and to act in concert to protect equilibrium from imperial challengers. Hellenistic states were far more belligerent than the idea of a 'contrived' as opposed to a merely 'fortuitous' balance of power suggests (Eckstein 2008: 16; Bull 1977: 104ff.). The upshot was a sequence of temporary stand-offs between societies that were highly attuned to violence (Eckstein 2008: ch. 4; Walbank 1981: 48; also Green 1990: 216–17, 307ff. on the atrocities in the Hellenistic wars of the fourth and third centuries).

The large, unified Macedonian kingdoms created the conditions in which commercial relations and the money economy could expand across the Hellenistic world, and in which new religious and political ideas were free to circulate. The movement of people had a profound effect on popular religious beliefs, on philosophical attitudes towards nature and society, and on ethical views about how peoples that had been thrown together by Macedonian military expansion could coexist peacefully. Those developments signified the increasingly 'cosmopolitan' ethos of the ancient Near East (Chaniotis 2005: 149; Green 1990: 589).

The most radical consequences would be evident in the increasingly pacified Greek world. As far as Greek wars were concerned, the massacre of the populations of defeated cities was now much less common than it had been during the military conflict between Athens and Sparta (Chaniotis 2005: 125). The relatively humane treatment of captured Greeks was a manifestation of more civilized harm conventions. According to Polybius, no war between Greeks ended in the destruction of a city in roughly the century after Alexander's death – a marked contrast, if he was correct, with the conflicts between Athens and Sparta during the Peloponnesian Wars (Roth 2007: 396). In addition, the existence of long supply chains that supported the Hellenistic armies removed some of the hardships that civilian populations had suffered because of the earlier practice of living off the land (Roth 2007: 382).

The Greek city states preserved something of their former autonomy in exchange for acknowledging the superiority of their Hellenistic 'benefactors' who tried to build a reputation for restraint by propagating the idea of kingship as government over a 'willing people' who had been won over by' beneficence and humanity' (Bringmann 1993: 7; Stevenson 1992). The region would prove to be a crucial engine-room as far as the taming of violent dispositions was concerned. Greek city states developed various mechanisms for pacifying their interconnected world. *Symbolai* were intercity agreements that afforded the citizens of each state a right of legal redress in the others' courts of law (Billows 2007: 307). A significant backlog of cases in some cities led to the formation of itinerant judicial commissions (*dicasts*) that understood the laws in different cities and promoted the convergence of legal codes. The introduction of sophisticated forms of interstate arbitration reflected the same general tendency, as did the proliferation of *proxenies* and the introduction of *aslyos,* namely the freedom from *syle* (seizure or reprisals) that religious sanctuaries had enjoyed, albeit precariously, and which the cities where they were located now sought for themselves (Ager 1996; Billows 2007: 310–11; de Souza 1999: 69; Walbank 1981: 145ff.). The civilizing institution of *isopolity* gave citizens political rights in each other's cities; in the case of *sympolity,* two or more communities merged into a single association (Billows 2007: 309; Walbank 1981:150ff.). Rome was the conveyor belt that passed on such achievements to Western Europe where they would influence the later civilizing process (Walbank 1981: 251). Rome also transmitted various philosophical doctrines that shaped Christian conceptions of the customs that were common to all peoples (*ius gentium*) and notions of the laws of reason (*ius naturale*) that would inspire later theories of the state, empire and international society.

Moral and intellectual responses to the Hellenistic age reflected a sense of being inexorably entangled in social processes that individuals could not control, or hope to influence, following the demise of the city state. One outcome was the conviction that chance (*tyche*) governed human affairs; a related development was the belief in the need for rituals to placate or please, *Fortuna,* the goddess who could exercise a benign, but perhaps more commonly a malevolent, influence on human affairs (Green 1990: 400). The sense of alienation from a joyless public world, and the feeling that there was no emotional compensation for the main economic and political patterns of change, presented people with the choice between withdrawing from public life and adapting and attuning themselves to changing political arrangements. In different ways, Cynicism and Epicureanism opted for detachment whereas Stoicism supported compromise with the political *status quo.* The former displayed an attitude of indifference to worldly affairs or they espoused a version of cosmopolitanism that expressed disinterest in fulfilling traditional civic and military obligations although disengagement from the polis was often linked with a lurch towards egalitarianism and support for the idea of the 'potential kinship' of humanity as a whole (Green 1990: 312; Moles 2000: 427).

Some fundamental ethical themes straddled such different endeavours to orientate people to the compulsions of growing interconnections. In various parts of the 'civilized' Greek world, individuals found solace in the 'negative virtues' proclaimed by different schools of Hellenistic philosophy – in virtues such as the absence of pain (*aponia*); the avoidance of psychological unease or the loss of equanimity (*ataraxia*), and in non-suffering or in freedom from the emotions (*apathia*) (Green 1990: 55–6; Walbank 1981: 179; Long 1993: 142). With Epicureanism (which had parallels with Stoicism) those sensibilities underpinned a social morality that maintained that the virtuous life was to be found in compliance with a 'no harm' principle (Green 1990: 624ff.). The lowering of ethical aspirations entailed disillusionment with the public world. The upshot was a vision of basic, negative obligations emptied of emotional warmth and social solidarity that can be contrasted with the classical Greek doctrine that those who eschewed the public life of the polis were 'do-nothings' (*apragmones*) or 'idiots' (*idiotai*) (Green 1990: 56). The historian is left with 'the grim suspicion that the best *anyone* felt able to hope for, spiritually or politically, was some limited relief from suffering' (Green 1990: 624; italics in original).

Apathy had no appeal to those who were nostalgic for the communal life of the polis (Green 1990: 388). But the prevalence of the preoccupation with the quest for personal happiness in isolation from the life of the active citizen revealed that human loyalties had not extended outwards to keep pace with the emergence of larger territorial power monopolies and lengthening webs of interconnectedness. Stoicism offered an alternative to the philosophical standpoints that were discussed above by emphasizing, first, the inadequacy of the Greek cities in the context of the significant 'scaling up' of social and political organization and, second, the failure of the Hellenistic kingdoms to provide a substitute for earlier forms of collective identification. Stoic thought was an attempt to 'replace old, lost city state loyalties with allegiances of a wider, indeed a more cosmic, nature' and, in some formulations, with some support for traditional ideals of the 'good man' who was actively engaged in deliberations about the 'public life' (Green 1990: 603). Many Stoics defended a vision of the 'morally responsible ruler' who displayed 'moderation and self-control', and assiduously enforced principles of justice. As noted earlier, they condemned Alexander for his unbridled arrogance and cruelty, a criticism that would find support in medieval writings on the Christian ruler ethic (Cary 1956; Hahm 2000). The whole movement would have a major impact on, and find new expression in, Rome. Of particular significance was support for *humanitas*, a concept that described what it was to be a 'civilized' Roman and which, in several Stoic renditions, affirmed the ethical duty to take account of the interests of every member of the species (Green 1990: 640; Wolff 1998: 54ff.). Influenced by Stoicism, Cicero contrasted *humanitas* with rusticity. The former concept referred to the fusion of knowledge and oratory in the shape of 'civilized' learning that equipped humans for community with others and for serving society through public office. Its proponents supported mercy as a constraint on the desire for angry retribution. They defended 'gentleness' of spirit as a restraint on brutality in war. Cicero's comment that 'not only nature, which may be defined as international law, but also the particular laws by which individual peoples are governed similarly ordain that no one is justified in harming another for his own advantage' is worth noting because of the powerful influence of its 'civilized' ethic of restraint on later theories of sovereign authority, humane imperial rule and responsible membership of international society (Cicero, *De Officiis*, 144). That orientation represented a major turning point in the history of the Western states-systems.

Part II The Rise of Rome

A The Roman Republic

The architects of international law in early modern Europe looked back to Roman legal and political thought in the search for a moral framework for organizing relations between the emergent sovereign polities and for justifying their dominion over the colonized world. Many believed that the manner in which the Empire has conducted its relations with the different peoples under its rule held the key to understanding how Europeans should organize their external affairs (Kingsbury and Strauman 2010: introduction). In particular, Roman conceptions of the just war and empire were important influences on the early modern civilizing process. With those themes in mind, this section deals with the transitional period in which Rome was more than the dominant city state in Italy but less than an empire. That was the era in which the gradual mastery of the societies in its vicinity led to various entanglements in an extensive network of geopolitical relations that embraced Sicily, the Hellenistic states, and Carthage which regarded one another as civilized societies (Bederman 2001: 41ff.). Illustrating the double standard of morality that was intrinsic to the dominant harm conventions, Rome adopted one code of conduct in relations with 'tribal enemies', and another in dealings with 'advanced' groups such as the Hellenistic kingdoms and Carthage – although the Carthaginians were often portrayed as 'cruel' and deceitful' in order to persuade wavering allies to regard Rome as a trustworthy and indispensable protector (Stepper 2001: 73ff.). In the first case, military commanders could decide to wage wars 'on the spot without consulting the authorities in Rome'; in the latter, wars were usually 'preceded by diplomatic exchanges and authorized by war votes passed in the Senate and in the assembly of the Roman people, and commonly ended with a formal peace treaty' (Rich 2001: 63–4).

Rome became the leading power in the Mediterranean system by destroying Carthage and then by prosecuting military campaigns against the two Hellenistic powers that had gained most from the collapse of Ptolemaic Egypt: Macedon under Philip V and the Seleucids under Antiochus III. Unrestrained violence was a recurrent feature of Rome's ascent to power – and here Elias's comment on the high levels of tolerance of violence in the ancient world is confirmed. But from the earliest times, Roman expansion was accompanied by alliances within Italy and with the Greek cities that paint a more complex picture. Rule was based on bilateral treaties (*foedera*) with Italian allies – the *amici et socii populi Romani*, or 'friends and associates of the Roman people' (Stepper 2001: 73). Alliances reduced their political autonomy but offered protection without demanding tribute or imposing especially onerous requirements to provide troops (Osiander 2007: 96). Rome's skill in 'alliance-management' that co-opted neighbouring peoples in the project of expansion provided the model for organizing future imperial relations (Eckstein 2008: 304).

With respect to the world to the east, there were few contacts between Rome and the Hellenistic states prior to the late third century. Their fate became closely intertwined between 264–146 BC when Rome was locked in a fight to the death with Carthage. Of crucial importance was the alliance between Philip V and Carthage in 215 BC in which the former committed Macedon to support Hannibal in any future conflict with Rome (Polybius 7.9; also Eckstein 2008: 83ff.). Philip's policy, which was grounded in the judgment that Carthage would ultimately prevail, led Ptolemaic Egypt to take the Roman side (see Polybius 5.104 on how the fusion of the Western and Eastern states-systems led to unprecedented levels of social and political integration). The Romans feared that Philip's opportunistic foreign policy would be followed by a direct military challenge. The punitive war against Philip's decision to ally with Hannibal revealed how Rome and the Hellenistic kingdoms became tied together in wider strategic entanglements with all their attendant insecurities. The conflict with Macedon led to large-scale atrocities on both sides to which the small Greek cities were particularly vulnerable (Eckstein 2008: 281ff.). The Second Macedonian War against Philip – the conflict started in 200 BC – marked the beginning of the end of the Hellenistic states-system. The succeeding conflict that began in 172 BC resulted in Rome's political dominance – in a 'suzerain state-system' in which one dominant state claims authority over, and exacts tribute from, subordinates.

Following Rome's victory over Carthage, the Greek cities in southern Italy looked to it to banish Illyrian piracy from the Adriatic and to stabilize the Hellenistic world that had been thrown into chaos by the collapse of Ptolemaic Egypt (Eckstein 2008). Roman triumph over the Illyrians in the late third century inaugurated a new phase of interaction with the mainland cities that was organized around *amicitia*. That concept expressed cordiality and good will rather than a commitment to entering into treaties between social equals, but the Greeks may well have mistaken it for *philia* or friendship between peers (Lesaffer 2002: 77ff.). As a result of its growing influence at the start of the second century, Rome found itself subject to frequent appeals from Greek cities to become the arbiter in their various squabbles. Those requests were dealt with positively in the manner of a 'superior' who dispensed favours to 'social inferiors', but they rarely involved impartial judicial procedures that could harm the interests of specific *amici* (Ager 1996; Billows 2007). Rome assumed that the Greeks would exhibit deference in proportion to its benevolence. It did not attempt to control the Hellenic world or to neutralize the region. The more modest objective was to acquire a sphere of influence without the burden of governing a province or administering a protectorate. The clear preference was for relying on compliant, allied Greek politicians rather than on military occupation. The cities were *amicitia* rather than client states, and they were expected to use their freedom responsibly in relations with their Roman benefactor. The strategy paved the way to hegemony in Greece by avoiding actions that were likely to provoke hostile protests against 'barbarian conquerors' (Eckstein 2008: 285ff., 297ff.; Erskine 1995: 375; Rich 2001: 64).

The interweaving of Rome and the Hellenic/Hellenistic worlds was attended by an element of contempt for each other's customs and practices. Greeks often referred to the 'western barbarians', while their Roman counterparts portrayed Greeks as untrustworthy and disputatious and, in a later period, as having a corrupting influence on the Roman way of life (Gruen 1984: ch. 7; Green 1990: 318–9). Even the most Hellenized Romans found it advantageous to mute their enthusiasm and, in any case, admiration for Greek cultural achievements did not necessarily diminish confidence in Rome's overall superiority or lead to sympathetic foreign policy. Philhellenism had the consequence that the Roman aristocratic elite believed that the Greeks were different from other enemies, but not so different as to be spared considerable violence in the event of fundamental conflicts of interest. That was the dominant mentality of the ruling strata that fully appreciated the 'psychological effect of brutality' (Roth 2007: 397).

For their part, the Greeks were often dismayed by perceived Roman inconsistencies – by the wish to avoid being embroiled in local conflicts, by a recurrent tendency to treat Greeks as mere underlings, and by sudden outbursts of shocking ruthlessness and war atrocities that had become rare in the Greek world during the fourth century, surpassing even the worst atrocities of the Hellenistic world (Gruen 1984: ch. 10; Harris 1979: 51–2). Roman atrocities in Sicily in the fourth and third centuries which were amongst the worst in ancient history increased fear and anxiety amongst the inhabitants of the city states. The reputation for exceptional violence was consolidated by the devastation of Carthage in 146 BC, the same year in which Rome laid waste to Corinth (Roth 2007: 397; Gruen 1984: 297–8). Acts of violence in later periods including the devastation of the Greek city, Epirus, circa 168 BC were a harsh reminder of the costs of violating agreements with Rome. Seventy towns were destroyed, 150,000 captives were enslaved and a vast booty was seized by Roman forces (Gruen 1984: 516). Indeed, the vast increase in the number of slaves was one of the defining features of the mid third-century international system (Green 1990: chs. 22, 30). Commenting on Rome's appetite for violence, Polybius (10.15), described the war against New Carthage in 209 BC when the army was commanded 'to exterminate every form of life they encountered', and to 'inspire terror' so that 'when cities are taken by the Romans you may often see not only the corpses of human beings but dogs cut in half and the dismembered limbs of other animals', a level of carnage that was 'especially frightful' in the case of Carthage 'because of the large size of the population'. Razing cities to the ground was standard practice (Harris 1979: 52). Even surrender did not guarantee immunity from slaughter. In a period of restrained warfare in many parts of the Hellenic world, Rome acquired an appetite and reputation for ruthlessness that often resulted in the complete annihilation of enemies (Harris 1979, Mattern 1999: ch. 5; Oakley 1995: 15–16).

To cultivate that reputation for unrelieved violence, Roman armies preferred to conclude specific battles with the cavalry charge that was designed to inflict as much harm as possible on retreating, defeated armies, that being the phase in which most of the casualties occurred. The sacking of cities and the devastation of farms were often as brutal as possible, and troops were permitted to cast off the customary taboos on violence in retaliation for failures to submit. Severed heads were fired into besieged cities, and captives were crucified close to the walls in the attempt to persuade enemies to concede defeat. Sexual violence and plunder were seen as the hard-won entitlements of victors who often resorted to the ancient practice of killing the adult male population, and occasionally slaughtered all inhabitants (see Ziolkowski 1995 on the Roman idea of *direptio*, the sacking of cities which, in line with its etymological origins, referred to the lifting of restraints from above on the armies' behaviour). Such atrocities led Livy (25.31.9; 28.19.6–8) to reflect on how 'shameful examples of anger and . . . greed' had weakened the constraints on violence, and on how 'cruel anger went even so far as to slay infants'. Demands for unconditional surrender (*deditio*) expressed the victorious commander's as well as Rome's appetite for prestige, but submission could spare a city the violence that armies were prepared to inflict on enemies (Mattern 1999: 217–8).

It has been argued that the Romans were amongst the most ferocious of the 'politically advanced' peoples of the ancient Mediterranean and that a convincing explanation of their cultural sadism is long overdue (Harris 1979: 51ff.). The sheer 'density of images of violence' in Roman society and the marked 'festive pleasure in looking at the images of massacres perpetrated by Roman soldiers on war enemies' clashed with the prevailing Greek attitudes to force (Zimmermann 2006: 345ff.). Those public representations of violence revealed that rape in war was commonplace; destructive masculinity and sexual conquest went hand in hand (Dillon 2006). Material rewards were important incentives for going to war (Rich 1995: 58ff.; Harris 1979: chs. 2–3).

The promise of financial gain ensured substantial support for military conflict amongst the army and in the wider society. For many, life in the legions provided a welcome escape from endemic poverty and hardship (Adams 2007: 209, 222). As in the case of Alexander's empire, imperial expansion and plunder created an economic surplus that could support larger armies; new recruits could then be deployed to extend power over greater areas as part of the further 'scaling up' of social and political organization. The intensification of violent conflict in the Mediterranean region from the fourth century onward was reflected in the high rates of military recruitment for war under the Republic. Between ten and fifteen per cent of the adult male population served in the army in any one year; the enlisted were obliged to remain in arms for between a four- and seven-year period (Cornell 1995: 156; Serrati 2007: 482ff.). That policy made it easier for Rome to directly impose its will on subject peoples, so releasing it from the precarious system of indirect rule through intermediaries that had been the practice in earlier periods, and in the ancient empires (Serrati 2007: 482ff.).

The concept of *pax* was missing from Roman political ideals – or at least in the third and second centuries BC, peace had no meaning apart from the military subjugation of enemies (Harris 1979: 35). During its rise to power, Rome demonstrated that it was not averse to recognizing the autonomy of cities in Italy or Greece as long as they did not harm its interests. But its general disposition was antithetical to the idea of the 'coequal interaction of independent societies', or to any conception of international society with its distinctive combination of we-feeling and standards of restraint (Stepper 2001: 79). Annihilation was the usual fate of any society that 'refused to be assimilated into the Roman system' (Stepper 2001: 79). Reflecting the conviction that political order depended on submission, Roman forces demanded total capitulation which placed adversaries at their mercy (see Rosenstein (2007: 227ff.) who maintains that, for the best part of five centuries, Roman policy resembled Athenian violence at Melos). Coercion and intimidation were used to dispel any impressions of Roman hesitancy, weakness or vulnerability.

As noted earlier, some have highlighted the Romans' exceptional ferocity and cultural sadism, while others have argued that the larger Mediterranean states-system to which Rome belonged and which it would dominate was an 'exceptionally cruel interstate anarchy' (Eckstein 2006: 3, 2006a). The latter have stated that Rome was surrounded by the 'Mediterranean chaos' that was the result of incessant struggles between the larger Hellenistic kingdoms and by attacks from outside – from the Goths and from Carthage – that almost led to its destruction. Certainly, two centuries of attack down to 340 BC that included the sack of Rome in 390 BC shaped the dominant social attitudes to military expansion and the high tolerance of brutality. There was a persistent fear of attack from numerically greater 'barbarian' forces that could only be dealt with, it was supposed, by maintaining highly disciplined forces that could overwhelm disorganized enemies with their supposed tendency to disintegrate in the chaos of frenzied killing or *paranomia* (Eckstein 1995: ch. 5). 'Barbarian' atrocities led to sharp contrasts between 'civilized' peoples and the 'animal' cruelty of 'savages'. The destructive events of 390 BC therefore gave rise to an unwavering determination to combine destructive power with an indisputable reputation for ruthlessness that would ensure that a city that was acutely aware of the precariousness of social systems would never again face serious threats to its survival. Debates continue about whether Rome's aggressive foreign policy was largely fuelled by a domestic culture of violence ('offensive imperialism') or was mainly a fearful response to the insecurities and challenges of international anarchy ('defensive imperialism'), but there is no reason to suppose that either internal or external forces were the ultimately decisive causal factor (see Rich 2001). International systemic forces pushed Rome to behave as violently and ruthlessly as most other states in the Mediterranean region (Eckstein 2006). However, Rome elevated military aggression to new heights. Elias's observation about the prevalence of 'hegemonic wars' and 'hegemonic intoxication' in the ancient world come to mind (Elias 2010c: 91), as does Wight's comment about 'simpler civilizations' such as Rome that appear to have had no counterpart to modern 'international ethics'.

But there was more to it. For all its brutality, which was usually at its height when dealing with rebellious forces and enemies that showed no mercy towards its own people, Rome was well aware of the military and political benefits that could accrue from exercising self-restraint in struggles with adversaries (Gilliver 1996). An astute combination of exceptional force and measured clemency was central to the relationship between violence and civilization. Promises of leniency were issued to urge adversaries to submit; regard for honour demanded that such commitments were kept. The period beginning in 168 BC saw the inauguration of an imperial era in which other societies were reduced to client states, but citizenship was often conferred on dependent peoples. The practice brought benefits but also substantial costs to the peoples involved since granting citizenship rights came with the duties of military service (Bederman 2001: 45). No less important were Rome's efforts to demonstrate that war was a just response to threats, insults and actual attacks, or obligatory to honour commitments to allies. The conviction that only just wars should be fought should not be dismissed as self-serving and disingenuous – although restraining the personal ambitions of military commanders and ensuring that their thirst for personal glory did not lead them to challenge Republican institutions were contributory factors (Robinson 2006: 40). The Roman preoccupation with legality and legitimacy had a long history and originated in the *ius fetiales* (the *fetiales* were special priests with responsibility for matters of war and peace) that governed Rome's relations with other peoples (Rich 2001: 67–8; Lintott 1968: 29, ch. 3). Ancient custom included the *rerum repetitio*, the formal declaration of war as demanded by the gods. That 'civilizing' practice had to be accompanied with an explanation of the reasons for deciding that war was justified, and with a formal proclamation of the terms on which Rome would settle the relevant dispute (Eckstein 2008: 69; Billows 2007: 314ff.). Especially because of the Gallic sack of Rome in 390 BC, the moral test of the justice of war was relaxed to remove any trace of vacillation or weakness in relations with enemies and to avert awkward tensions between conceptions of justice in war and security interests or considerations of expediency (Rosenstein 2007: 229ff.). Moreover, restraints on force were often set aside when the prospect of glory lay to hand. As a result of those competing tendencies, Romans at war were 'startlingly modern' in some respects and 'undoubtedly ancient' in others (Robinson 2006: 35).

Republican Rome in the third and second centuries recognized the high standing and social importance of military virtues, and, indeed, for much of its history, there was no meaningful distinction between politicians and generals. Demonstrated success in war was essential for attaining public office (Harris 1979: 10ff.; Serrati 2007: 482ff.). The traditional aristocracy received little more than military training. Not until the time of Cicero and Caesar did young aristocrats travel to Greece for a broader education and for engaging in what were regarded as valuable non-military pursuits (Harris 1979: 14–15). By the end of the first century BC, Greek had become an 'obligatory second language' for the Roman nobility; it was a symbol of 'aristocratic refinement' (Lomas 1995). In the late Republic, military success, although still more highly regarded than other achievements, no longer provided the crucial route to political positions. At the start of Cicero's career, political leadership roles could be acquired by proven competence in oratory and jurisprudence. In the late republic, expertise in Greek rhetorical and oratorical skills was the key to excelling in the Senate. The social importance of displays of courage on the battlefield suffered relative decline as part of a distinctive republican 'civilizing process' (Rosenstein 2007a).

A major transformation of the dominant harm conventions that was connected with new orientations towards violence and civilization was evident in the revised understandings of the personal quality known as *virtus*, the attribute of male courage or manliness in battle that was believed to include honesty and trustworthiness that had also been central to the influential Greek concept, *andreia*. The notion of *virtus* was linked with *vis* and *vires* (which referred to physical power, vitality, or violent and forceful action) and with *viriditas* or youthfulness (Barton 2001: 40ff.). That distinctive combination of personal attributes reflected the social importance of the 'rite de passage' of single combat, which was the standard method of displaying the masculine ideal of *virtus* (Lendon 2007: 509ff.). Young men or *velites* were placed in the front of the battle where they could test themselves in hand-to-hand combat (Oakley 1985). On some accounts, *virtus* was understood to mean 'aggressive manliness' rather than 'military courage'. The cult of *Virtus* which was instituted towards the end of the third century BC as part of a broad effort to weaken 'aristocratic restrictions on power and glory' has been regarded as a window onto the dominant masculine self-images that celebrated 'extraordinary martial prowess' (Welch 2006; McDonnell 2006: ch. 7, especially 236).

The link between *virtus* and force was challenged by Cicero and Sallust who refashioned the concept in the belief that the Republic could not survive on male aggression and military prowess alone (McDonnell 2006: ch. 10). Traditional notions of 'aggressive manliness' and 'aggressive courage' were criticized in the quest to tame a warrior ethos that was deemed to threaten civil order. The aristocracy was urged to embrace ethical virtue as part of a new pattern of conscience formation. Significantly, that republican 'civilizing offensive' succeeded in restraining the warrior code for three centuries even though no 'centralized peacekeeping force' had the power to restrain the traditional ruling strata (McDonnell 2006: 71, 195ff.). Its members imposed valued social constraints on themselves and on each other because of moral commitments to 'civilized' restraints on violence.

The Republic's survival owed a great deal to the *disciplina Romana*, to respect for decorum that was held in place by a civilizing 'government of shame' and a moderating 'shared public sense' that was not unlike an Orwellian regime of 'mutual surveillance and inhibition' (Barton 2001: 23). The ideal of *verecundia* (associated with shame or modesty) which insisted on the social importance of individual self-restraint demanded limits to rights of 'self-extension'; the metaphor of not intruding into a space that was not one's own became central to an aristocratic we-identity that was linked with ideals of civil conduct in the late republic and in the early years of the empire (Kaster 2005: chs. 1–2). As opposed to endorsing the violent response to some insult, aristocratic honour and virtue became associated with self-restraint or *sophrosyne* – with renouncing revenge through 'duels, vendettas, or blood-feuds' that had come to be identified with the 'barbarism' of the unruly 'lower' orders (Lendon 1997: 41–2). But greater expectations of restraint did not affect aristocratic behaviour in its totality. Less demanding social standards applied in relations with 'social inferiors' whose assaults on aristocratic *dignitas* invariably led to retaliatory violence (Lendon 1997: 247ff.; Lintott 1982: ch. 3). There was a clear link with attitudes to peoples who were believed to have insulted (*iniuria*) Roman honour (Robinson 2006: 42). 'Civilized' aristocratic harm conventions therefore restrained some forms of violence but authorized and demanded others.

In the Republican era, the right to hold a triumphal procession (where, over as many as three or four days, plundered wealth was paraded before the populace) was the highest accolade that Rome could confer on a victorious commander. The public execution of defeated leaders was a central part of the ritual (Flower 2004). Because the award of such a victory procession partly depended on the number of enemy casualties, Roman forces were encouraged at times to indulge in 'blood lust' (Gilliver 1999: 119, 156). Revealingly, no republican treatise ever contested the legitimacy of warfare and imperial expansion (Woolf 1995: 183). There was an acute sense of the tensions between the quest for personal glory through military exploits and republican political stability. The Republic was so named because it brought an end to the rule of kings and rested on the public principle that no person should be allowed to become so powerful as to be able to dominate state institutions (Flower 2004: 338). The changing power balance between civil and military attributes provided a major contrast with the preceding era where personal courage and prowess in war were highly valued. Many of the concerns about the legitimacy of war must be understood in that context. Military leaders who instigated a war for personal glory without first winning the approval of the Senate and the Assembly of the Roman people risked punishment, especially if the conflict was deemed to have 'brought dishonour upon Rome' (Robinson 2006: 39–40). Specific political tensions were built into the republic by the rule that military consuls should be appointed for one year. That decision restricted the opportunities to initiate wars for the sake of personal glory. The convention often restrained military leaders, but the rivalries that accompanied the quest for individual advancement through conquest ultimately led to the collapse of the Republic (Robinson 2006: 42).

It is important to stress that Republican imperial expansion produced astonishing material resources (Flower 2004: 328). Military leaders who acquired such wealth secured the personal loyalty of their troops and were eventually drawn into power struggles that plunged the republic into civil war. In the last decades of the republic, those who fought for Pompey and Caesar, or for Brutus and Cassius, were motivated by a desire for land and booty rather than by a commitment to republican principles including *libertas* (Campbell 2002: ch. 5). 'Decivilizing' processes were unleashed as support for public institutions was weakened along with the customary taboos on violence. Rome had long faced the challenge of reconciling its role as a small city state with the problem of administering a sprawling empire. Over time, the dynamics of imperial rule and conquest led to the replacement of the republican ideal of the civilian militia with professional armed forces that became increasingly isolated from the rest of society and would engulf Rome in civil war (Cornell 1991). The Principate that was established by Augustus in 31 BC ended the civil conflict and earned the gratitude of a war-weary population that became convinced that empire, peace and security were inextricably linked (Campbell 2002: ch. 6).

Roman warfare therefore displayed extraordinary violence. For the most part, open contempt awaited enemies who begged for clemency. But ruthlessness was combined with displays of mercy and self-restraint and there were occasions on which cruelty aroused the Senate's indignation (several examples are provided in Rich 1995). Romans continued to believe that war had to have a just cause in the period after the *ius fetiales* had fallen into disuse. The ancient laws of war were granted new ethical foundations by philosophers such as Panaetius who was the first Stoic in Rome to argue for greater self-restraint in warfare, but seemingly with little immediate effect. Poseidonius may have had more success in persuading senators that only defensive wars could be just (Harris 1979: 173–4). Crucial was the role of Cicero and his contemporaries who used the idea of *humanitas* to promote the idea of just war and who contended that when morality and power come into conflict, the former should prevail (Robinson 2006: 38). In *De Officiis*, Cicero (1.11) argued that 'in the case of a state in its external relations, the rights of war must be strictly observed. For since there are two ways of settling a dispute: first, by discussion; second, by physical force; and since the former is characteristic of man, the latter of the brute, we must resort to force only in case we may not avail ourselves of discussion. The only excuse ... for going to war is that we may live in peace unharmed; and when the victory is won, we should spare those who have not been bloodthirsty and barbarous in their warfare' (also Cicero, *De Officiis*, 3.29; and Dawson 1996: 124–5 on Cicero's influence on medieval political thought).

Those developments illustrate the point that was made earlier about the complex relationship between more universalistic conceptions of society and politics and the rise of larger and more destructive monopolies of power such as Macedon. Movement beyond the traditional Macedonian conceptions of rule occurred in order to administer the Alexandrine empire. Conceptions of just kingship and moderate rule would become important in the Hellenistic period, often in conjunction with the condemnation of Alexander's impulsiveness and lack of self-control. Such images influenced Roman conceptions of republican government and imperial order. They reflected a growing awareness of the tensions within the lengthening human interdependencies, specifically between the increased potential for inflicting violence over larger areas and the need for self-restraint and moderation to secure the acquiescence of the conquered to imperial rule while reassuring the ruling strata that they were the custodians of 'civilizing' values that could be shared with grateful peoples. The whole Stoic and Ciceronian 'civilizing offensive' should be seen in that context.

The analysis can be extended by considering Elias's discussion of how lengthening webs of human interconnectedness encouraged greater

detachment from immediate or short-term events and higher levels of reflectiveness about the forces that bind people together. Greater interdependencies
increased the value of the capacity to see oneself and to observe others
from a distance as well as the power of foresight and the ability to learn from
understanding long-term social and political processes (Elias (2012: 418ff.);
Elias (2007: 162ff.). One illustration was the development of complex forms
of time measurement that enabled people to attune themselves to others
over greater distances, to calculate how their actions might affect and be
affected by others, to synchronize their behaviour over long time intervals
and to orientate themselves in a more disciplined, self-regulating way to
remote institutions such as state structures. The approach to the dynamics of
extending webs of human interconnectedness helps to explain how seemingly
separate phenomena belong to one overall civilizing process. Three other
illustrations are considered here, beginning with changing aspects of the
conduct of warfare.

New conceptions of battle management broke with the warrior ideal that
had limited the effectiveness of Hellenistic armies (Beston 2000). Roman
military authorities contrasted Alexander's role as 'heroic leader' with the
Roman 'integrated ideal' in which the commander 'exposed himself in personal combat' but also appeared to be 'everywhere' at once, in possession of
a 'complete grasp of the progress of the battle' that enabled him to direct 'the
action as though he were watching it from a distance', and with considerable
detachment. It was deemed more rational for generals to consider the course of
the battle from afar 'with a methodical temperament' that avoided the risks of
hand-to-hand combat; patience and restraint were imperative to prevent 'rash
and costly decisions' that needlessly increased the number of Roman casualties
(Gilliver 1999: 120; de Souza 2007: 448–9).

No less important were advances in organizing more efficient armies.
The ability to employ highly disciplined and tightly organized professional
military forces to overwhelm larger, but poorly organized, 'barbarian' enemies
was a clear manifestation of the Romans' conception of their unique civilizing
process. Rome's confidence in its evident superiority over 'barbarians' was
apparent in the claim by the fourth-century military writer, Vegetius (Book I.i)
that the Roman people conquered the whole world because of superior
'drill-at-arms, camp-discipline, and military expertise'. Clear advantages over
disorganized 'tribal warriors' were apparent in new approaches to military
engagement. As battle managers, Philip and Alexander first considered the
most effective role for different military units and only then devised a more
holistic perspective of the method of deployment. With more uniform and
highly disciplined legions at their disposal, Roman generals relied for their
success on established battle drills that reduced the need to devise new battle
plans for each military encounter (Sekunda 2007: 348–9). Similar developments were the appearance in the second century of 'a high level of abstract

strategic thinking' that has parallels with the modern idea of the indirect approach in which military objectives could be realized through operations that were remote from the immediate scene of battle (Roth 2007: 370). No less important with respect to increased detachment was intelligence-gathering. Roman generals were more 'proactive' than their Hellenistic predecessors in gathering 'geographical information' that could be turned to their military advantage (see Roth 2007: 391 and Goldsworthy 2007: 99 for a different emphasis). All of those advances in longer-term and more detached stand-points were critical to Rome's military success.

Key dimensions of the relationship between imperial monopolies of power, longer social webs and changing cognitive outlooks carried forward Alexander's recognition that Macedonian cultural exclusiveness was a barrier to organizing a large, multicultural empire – hence the aspiration to integrate Macedonian and Persian social elites in joint rule. The critical development was uncoupling citizenship rights from membership of an exclusionary polis and ensuring that certain basic legal rights were shared by all, Romans and non-Romans, the conquerors and the conquered alike (until in AD 212 all free-born inhabitants of the empire were granted citizen status in the attempt to legitimate imperial rule). The advantages were distributed unequally. The Romans 'rejected juridical equality, the equality of all citizens before the law' just 'as they rejected political equality' (Garnsey 1974: 165). A process that began with the unification of Italy – a response to the challenge of adapting traditional institutions and practices to the larger scale of social and political organization – was an indication of how Rome 'solved' the problems that had undermined the ancient city and the Hellenistic kingdoms (Lomas 2004). The polis had been held together by a strong we-identity between citizens, but it was too small to compete in a world dominated by larger territorial Hellenistic concentrations of power; the latter were large and powerful, but vulnerable to collapse because of low social cohesion. Alexander sought to square the circle in the ways that have been described. By providing access to basic legal rights, Rome succeeded in uniting more and more people in the greatest increase in collective power that had occurred up to that point in the Western world (Mann 1986: 254, 293). Its success in combining territorial expansion with high levels of social and political integration was a major advance beyond the earlier ancient empires (Mann 1986: ch. 9).

Other manifestations of greater detachment in the form of a quest for more universal orientations and concepts that befitted the widening of social horizons included ethical doctrines such as Stoic cosmopolitanism and the appropriately named 'universal history'. As in the case of Polybius' narrative, the standpoint stood back from specific events in particular places in order to comprehend the overall trend towards the greater interweaving of peoples that culminated in Rome's imperial domination. There is no space here to consider those phenomena that were additional, interlinked expressions of one long-term pattern of development that included the unprecedented centralization of physical power, advances in the interweaving of human societies, confidence in reaching unparalleled levels of civilized existence and the presumed right to promote distinctive civilizing missions. A specific configuration of violence and civilization surfaced for the first time. It rested on images of violence as an expression of a higher 'civilization' but also on conceptions of civilized interaction that were designed to restrain the immense destructive capabilities that Rome commanded. The tensions between those dimensions of the relationship between violence and civilization would resurface again and again in the future development of the Western states-systems.

B *Pax Romana*

Symbols of peace and the public celebration of *concordia* in the later phases of Augustus' rule (with the *Pax Augusta)* marked the transition from the earlier period of outward extension to the internal pacification of the empire and the establishment of secure outposts along the frontiers. As a result of that shift of orientation, the 'interludes of comparative peace became longer and more frequent, and . . . major imperialist ventures became increasingly rare' until the invasions from the north and defeats in the east from the third century altered the course of social development (Cornell 1995: 158). Six centuries elapsed between Hannibal's threat to Rome in 212–211 BC and the next major external threat to the city. Notwithstanding various civil and international wars, it has been argued, the five hundred year period between Pompey's defeat of the pirates in 67 BC and the Vandal seizure of Carthage in AD 439 was the longest period of peace that Mediterranean societies have ever enjoyed (Ward-Perkins 2005: 133).

The 'civilizing process' embodied in the idea of *Pax Romana* expressed the conviction that the empire's frontiers constituted a 'moral barrier': on one side, *humanitas* (arts, discipline and humanity) prevailed; on the other side, *barbaritas* or *feritas* (wildness, savagery and irrationality) reigned (Sidebottom 2007: 5). In fact, social boundaries were not so clear-cut (Woolf 1995: 178). The recurrent practice was to assimilate 'barbarians' into the imperial forces, wherever possible, or to form strategic alliances to stabilize frontier zones. Support for *humanitas* – for virtues that had been defended in Greece – was linked with the self-assurance that the empire had a civilizing mission that surpassed anything the Greeks had achieved (Veyne 1993). The consolidation of the imperial frontiers led thinkers such as Pausanias to contend that the entire civilized world had been brought under the control of the empire; only the unworthy remained outside (Dawson 1996: 140). Illustrating a collective belief in having pioneered a process of civilization, Cicero maintained that 'scourging, the executioner's hook, the dread of the cross' became obsolete with the expulsion of kings with their 'cruel ways' from the lives of a 'free people', and with the shift from 'savage punishments' to the 'humane laws' that safeguarded liberty (cited in Bauman 1996: 1). But the 'civilizing' tilt was limited. Subjecting low-ranking citizens (*humiliores*) to an excruciatingly painful death was not thought to be a terrible assault on their dignity; indeed, the objective was to inflict suffering and humiliation (Bauman 1996). Punitive measures including mutilation became more severe as a result of increasing social distance between 'the established' and 'the outsiders'; the former were convinced that they would never experience the pain and anguish that their 'social inferiors' had to endure (MacMullen 1990). In that way, the 'ultimate restraint was thus lost: the restraint of inner pain and horror felt vicariously' (MacMullen 1990: 215).

The idea of *humanitas* was presumed to hold the key to the division between peaceful and civilized coexistence within the empire and the violence of the barbaric exterior. The concept was embedded in the imperial ideology that contended that barbarians had the potential for organizing themselves in accordance with Rome's 'civilized' standards. A central assumption was that Rome had surpassed Greece in its ability to spread civilized standards of behaviour to the barbaric regions, even though only a small elite in the subjugated societies was believed to be capable of reaching that cultural level (Hingley 2005: 62ff.).

The notion of *humanitas* seems to have been imported into Rome in the second century BC as a result of contacts with the Stoic, Panaetius, and through the influence of Polybius (Bauman 1996: 14). It described the aristocratic attributes that revealed Rome's 'historical progress' and justified imperial expansion to elevate 'imperfect' humans (Wolff 1998: 55ff.). Some have observed an affinity with Greek concepts: with *philanthropia* which is similar to modern notions of common humanity, and with *paedeai* which described the outlook of educated, cultured persons. Social refinement was associated with urban existence – with *urbanitas* that was contrasted with *rustica* that signified the cruder ways of rural peoples, and distinguished Romans from 'barbarous' humanity (Woolf 1998: 106; also Ramage 1960, 1961, 1963 on how Cicero's writings transmitted such concepts to Christian thinkers in the first century AD). A common belief was that the empire had moved 'barbarians' from the wildness of the open hills into settlements where they could be pacified. As a result, the sphere of *humanitas* increased while the realm of *feritas* contracted. The imperial army was positioned on the 'moral frontier' where the two worlds often collided. The 'civilizing' power of *humanitas*, which Cicero linked with the earlier Greek notion of *sophrosyne* or self-restraint, was one of the core aristocratic ethical virtues. The concept was employed to challenge the practice of using force to gain power and esteem amongst members of the ruling elite (Lendon 1997: 41ff.; North 1966: ch. 8).

Dominant social images of the pirate or the bandit were important in constructing an imperial ideology that celebrated Rome's achievements in protecting its inhabitants from the threats that were lurking in the 'uncivilized' world – in the case of pirates, from the menace of those who stood outside the law and whose predatory behaviour was 'inimical to civilization' (Braund 1995: 196–7). The level of hostility towards pirates is evident in the punishments that were handed out. Crucifixion was standard (Braund 1995: 198). Caesar was praised for his clemency when he ordered that captives should have their throats cut first. Rome under Augustus and his successors succeeded in controlling, but not in eliminating, piracy from various parts of the Mediterranean, an achievement that was declared to be a contribution to civilization and that was regularly cited in justification of imperial expansion (Braund 1995: 203ff.; de Souza 1999: 195ff.). A striking example was Tertullian's claim that was made shortly after the death of Marcus Aurelius: 'The world is every day better known, better cultivated and more civilized than before', and it was also more pacified (cited in Wells 1992: 220). Celebrations of empire declared that 'there are no wars any longer, nor battles, no brigandage on a large scale, nor piracy, but at any hour we may travel by land, or sail from the rising sun to its setting' (Epictetus 3.13.9).

As a result of imperial pacification and the expulsion of force to the periphery, war no longer intruded into the everyday lives of many citizens; it became the preserve of military specialists that were ever more divorced – both geographically and emotionally – from the rest of Roman society (Cornell 1995: 164). The successful incorporation of the former enemies in the provinces into the imperial army led to the 'multinational' forces that protected the empire (Rankov 2007: 42). The result was 'the increasing unpopularity of military service among ordinary citizens' and a probable 'general decline in Roman belligerence' (Harris 1979: 50). It seems that 'the warlike tradition of the Roman people faded out of existence' to the point where 'the warrior spirit survived only in a distorted and artificial form, as people took vicarious pleasure in reconstructions of battles in the writings of historians and poets, and in the bloody spectacles of the arena' (Cornell 1995: 165; Kyle 1998). The upshot was an educated aristocratic elite that had little or no experience of war and little sympathy for those who had in an increasingly 'civilian society' (Cornell 1995: 166–7). A ruling stratum that once owed its political power and social status to physical courage and excellence in war now found greater meaning and satisfaction in Roman ideals such as *humanitas* (Woolf 1995: 190).

Changing attitudes to anger and the call for new levels of anger control appeared early in the imperial era. Such imperatives had little place in the traditional warrior codes of antiquity where violent expressions of rage and the pleasures of vengeance were often applauded. The historical background is worth recalling. Classical Greek discussions of the Homeric warrior ideal had underlined the tension between the old personality traits such as the appetite for vengeance and the greater demand for self-restraint (*sophrosyne*) and self-control as levels of social and economic interdependence increased within the polis (Harris 2001: 26, chs. 5–8; van Wees 1992: 161ff.). The rise of the Hellenistic dynasties led to the exemplary treatise of the era – the commentary on the merciful king (the forerunner of medieval and Renaissance 'mirrors of the prince') that sought to limit the harm that was caused by royal anger. Such appeals had limited effect in the era of the Hellenistic kingdoms. It has been noted that reappraisals of Alexander's method of rule reflected a marked change of direction in early imperial Rome. An example was Seneca's comment that Alexander was 'a robber and looter of nations, ruin to foes and friends alike … whose highest good was to terrify the whole of mankind' (Seneca, *On Favours*: 1.13; *On Anger*: Book 3.17). In addition to moderation (*abstinentia*) and restraint, clemency acquired positive value in the late Republic, when the term first rose to prominence, and then under the rule of Augustus (Konstan 2005). As heir to Caesar's claim to have ended civil conflict through acts of mercy and generosity, Augustus asserted that his rule was free from the outbursts of anger towards adversaries that had condemned republican Rome to internal strife. *Clementia* was one of four virtues that were imputed to Augustus on his honorific shield (Griffin 2000: 540). The supposition that Roman Emperors exercised greater self-restraint than Hellenistic rulers had – or 'barbarian' leaders did – became central to imperial propaganda. Notable was the thesis that the critical difference between the tyrannical ruler and the merciful king consisted in the higher level of self-control that kings observed even in the absence of external compulsions.

Reflections on court etiquette addressed the acute tensions that were inherent in imperial government. Emperors were above the law, but their social standing depended in part on avoiding the arrogance towards 'inferiors' that was associated with oriental kingship. *Civilitas* was the concept that linked moderate rule with *comitas*, or friendly behaviour towards subordinates. Its meaning included the idea that the liberty of the ordinary citizen was protected by law rather than subject to imperial whim, and it affirmed at least the principle that the emperor (the 'civil prince' or *princeps civilis* discussed by Pliny) should walk among equals, avoiding harm or giving offence to aristocrats. *Civilitas*, which emerged as a respected social ideal in the second century AD, was combined with *humanitas* to underline the difference between Roman imperial rule and brutal tyranny. It pointed to a degree of parity between the emperor and the upper social strata on which imperial power and authority ultimately depended (Wallace-Hadrill 1982).

The point was made earlier that the Stoic and Ciceronian 'civilizing offensive' reflected a growing consciousness of the tensions between the potential for inflicting violence over greater areas and the need for observing levels of self-restraint that helped to legitimate imperial government while convincing the dominant social strata that they were the guardians of 'civilizing' values that should be exported to other peoples. Also important was the conflict between images of civilization that were used to justify the use of force and conceptions of civilized interaction that underpinned commitments to controlling violence. The construction of social ideals that expressed the tilt towards the second conception of the social world was bound up with distinctions between civilized and barbarian peoples. The former displayed *humanitas*; the latter, it was argued, lack the capacity to control 'animal' passions. Imperial government would provide instruction in acquiring levels of rational self-control that backward cultures would otherwise fail to develop (Harris 2001: ch. 9). But to fulfil that role, imperial rule had to comply with the political principles that distinguished 'civilized' society.

That orientation was explicit in Cicero's correspondence with his younger brother, Quintus, on the matter of his forthcoming governance in Asia. He advised on governing with due restraint should he acquire 'authority over Africans or Spaniards or Gauls, wild and barbarous nations' that would require concern for 'their comforts, their needs and their safety' (Woolf 1999: 60ff.). Action fuelled by anger clashed with *humanitas* which was vital for 'the dignity of imperial office' (Harris 2001: 204–5). A distinction was drawn between *patrocinium* and *imperium* to underline the difference between protection and mere rule (Cicero, *De Officiis* 2.26). Imperial legitimacy was to be measured by respect for the law and by sympathetic responses to provincial claims against imperial injustices. As for exporting *humanitas*, Pliny (3.5.39) argued that Italy had been chosen by the gods to 'unite scattered empires, to make manners gentle, to draw together in converse by community of language the jarring and uncouth tongues of so many nations, to give mankind civilization, and in a word to become throughout the world the single fatherland of all peoples'. Denying others 'the license to do harm (*iniuriarum licentia*)' was legitimate in the case of 'wicked people' who 'would be worse off if they had not been conquered' (Cicero, cited in Kingsbury and Strauman 2010: 8). The 'civilizing' sensibilities that were regarded as a model for the rest of humanity owed much to the intricacies of social relations within the imperial court, and particularly to a delicate power balance between the emperor and court officials that would break down in later eras. The former influenced the governance of the provinces – where there was little beyond self-restraint on the part of the ruling strata to protect subjects from acts of cruelty (Woolf 1998: 68) – as well as the treatment of slaves. But overwhelmingly, the focus was not on treating social inferiors in accordance with 'higher' ethical ideals but on the practical utility of minimizing harshness so that they did not protest against or disturb social and political order (Brunt 1978). The recurrent theme was that such behaviour could provoke angry responses that would complicate the lives of individual slave-owners (who often lived in fear of assassination by their slaves) and precipitate slave revolts that might endanger stability. However, pragmatism did not entirely rule the day in commentaries on how to 'civilize' the ruling strata in their relations with social 'inferiors'. Stoics such as Seneca (*On Mercy*:1:18) maintained that humanitarianism had intrinsic moral worth, a position that was exemplified by the statement that slave-owners were legally entitled to treat slaves as they chose, and 'yet there are things which the law common to all living creatures forbids you to do to a human being'. Along with Stoics more generally, Seneca had no 'in principle' objection to slavery, but did speak out against routine cruelties.

In the main, the Stoics did not protest against the violence of the game contests that pitched gladiators against each other, or in which slaves were killed – nor did they object to forms of punishment that satisfied the public lust for witnessing extreme pain, the collective appetite for vengeance, and the pleasures of dramatic demonstrations of the invulnerability of the empire that required the destruction of enemies. Such realities have often been contrasted with 'conditions' in modern 'civilized' societies where 'identification with other people [and] sharing in their suffering and death' are fundamentally different from the Roman world where no 'feeling of identity' seemed to bind spectators to those 'in the bloody arena [who]were fighting for their lives' (Elias 2010c: 4). If some high-ranking citizens deplored the violence and goriness of the gladiatorial games, it was invariably to highlight the gulf between their civility and the vulgarity of the masses. Seneca, for example, appeared to be less troubled by the effects of violence on the victims than by its corrupting effect on the spectators (Kyle 1998: 3–4). He professed to feel 'crueller and less humane' when witnessing the crowd-pleasing 'murder pure and simple' of combatants who had 'nothing to protect them' (Seneca 2004: Letter 7). Stark contrasts between Roman attitudes to public cruelty and modern, 'civilized' sensitivities to violence have often been noted (see Kyle 1998: 160). While the Nazis largely sought to conceal evidence of atrocities against the Jews, the Romans turned cruelty to people and animals into a lurid 'spectator sport'. Victims were usually stripped, although decorum dictated that women should be executed behind the scenes, usually by strangling, the executioner having exercised an established right to deflower virgins (Bauman 1996: 18). Nevertheless, 'civilized' Romans seemed to prefer that violence was mediated, with victims killing each other or being torn apart by wild animals. As for social attitudes to non-human species, the public display and slaughter of exotic creatures advertised Rome's mastery of the natural world. Those who had challenged the political order were often punished by being thrown to the beasts; as enemies of 'civilization', they forfeited the right to be protected from predatory animals (Wiedemann 1992: ch. 2).

The dominant social attitudes to the games may have revealed then that many Stoics were more concerned with preserving the 'civilized' self-image of the powerful strata than with the welfare of those who were under Roman control, but evolving elite attitudes to shame and decorum influenced the ways in which 'enlightened' strata behaved towards slaves and women. Transformed male attitudes to women represented a significant 'civilizing' advance (Elias 2009b). The character of the Roman civilizing process in this period has been illustrated with reference to the changing balance of power between the sexes, and specifically with regard to the contrast with early Rome where warriors were allowed to take women by force (Elias 2009b: 244–5). Recent support for that interpretation points to the evidence that the traditional custom in which a husband could kill an adulterous wife had probably faded away by the first century BC (Harris 2001: 219ff.; see Bauman 1996: 32ff. and Hopkins 1983: 88ff. on changing attitudes and behaviour towards 'women of property').

From the second half of the second century, more impartial legal codes and egalitarian ideologies were two core central features of 'a higher level of civilization' in the sense of a significant tilt in the direction of greater self-restraint on the part of the ruling strata (Elias 2009b: 244, 250ff., 258ff.). The 'high-point of the reforming impulse' was reached when later emperors such as Antoninus Pius introduced laws to protect slaves from cruelty. Although somewhat limited in effect, they urged greater self-restraint on the part of slave-owners (Harris 2001: 331–2; Hopkins 1978:118ff.; Brunt 1998: 141–2). What there were in the way of official prohibitions on violence declined as the empire fell into the hands of autocrats who were prone to arbitrary and cruel behaviour. When personal interest and survival were at stake, rather less was heard from courtiers about the virtues of restraining imperial anger.

The 'civilized' ethos did not disappear entirely with the destruction of imperial state institutions at the hands of the Germanic tribes. *Romanitas* survived in the 'laws of the barbarians' (*leges barbarorum*) and was mobilized in a later 'civilizing spurt' when the rediscovery of Roman law influenced the early phase of European state formation (Elias 2009b: 261ff.). Roman political ideals were passed down to the medieval courts in texts that combined pagan and Christian influences and circulated freely across society. Important examples were the ideals of the merciful and compassionate king in the eighth century, and 'the mirrors of princes' of the Carolingian age (Althoff 1998).

An additional part of that legacy included the philosophical claim that the just society was, in the words of Epicurus, organized around the moral imperative of 'not harming one another and not being harmed' (Schofield 2000: 440). The Stoics – many sought influence in the imperial court and, in Seneca's case had influence as tutor to Nero at the start of his principate – defended an ethic in which the duty to refrain from harm was the foundation of civil order (Schofield 2000; Griffin 2000). In Seneca's comment that the 'power to hurt is foul and detestable', and in his statement that cruelty is especially 'loathsome' because 'it goes beyond the bounds first of custom and then of humanity', one can see anticipations of the later natural law conviction that reason equips all humans with the capacity to grasp universal moral principles that enable people to coexist harmoniously under the governance of the same harm conventions (Seneca, *On Anger*: 2. 31.6; *On Mercy*: 1.25).

Seneca's support for *clementia* was grounded in those convictions. Clemency required 'mental self-control in one who has the power to exact revenge' and a similar 'disposition towards mildness in exacting punishment' (cited in Konstan 2005: 339). It demanded that the powerful overlook certain harms caused by others – or respond with due restraint – in order to preserve civility. The enemy of clemency was anger that paved the way for cruelty (Griffin 2000: 538–9). The emphasis was on moral obligations that should be observed across human society as a whole. Many Stoics regarded war as an aberration from the normal condition of peace, an orientation that was largely out of step with the dominant beliefs of the time (Sidebottom 2007: 27). For Cicero, the scope and significance of cosmopolitan morality was limited by the reality that people found their most meaningful social ties in relations with the family, or in the bonds of friendship, or in emotional identification with a particular city (*De Officiis*, 1.17). He contended that there was nothing reprehensible about pursuing imperial glory, or indeed about the elimination of enemies as long as the plundering and razing of cities were subject to control (Cicero, *De Officiis*, 1.11; 1.24). The duty to conduct war honourably and to treat defeated forces leniently was derived from the general duty not to seize an advantage for oneself or one's associates that imposed disproportionate and therefore unjust costs on others (Cicero, *De Officiis*, 1.14). Cicero (*De Officiis*, 1.45) argued that 'there are some acts either so repulsive or so wicked, that a wise man would not commit them, even to save his country'. The failure to distinguish between morality and the seemingly expedient often led to wrongs in relations between states, as in the case of Rome's destruction of Corinth (Cicero, *De Officiis*, 3.11). No action could be truly advantageous if it contradicted the fundamental virtues of 'propriety, moderation, temperance, self-restraint [and] self-control' (Cicero, *De Officiis*, 3.33). In a similar manner, Seneca referred to 'the crime of glory' when condemning the practice of punishing murderers by hanging while lavishing praise on leaders such as Alexander who had slaughtered whole populations (Dawson 1996: 135). Such reflections about justice in war that were refined by medieval political thinkers and handed down to the modern world contended that humans had to balance obligations to two cities: to their place of birth or city of residence, and to the community of humankind – the cosmopolis that was united by speech and reason (Seneca, *On the Private Life*: 4.1; Cicero, *De Officiis*, 1.16). Accordingly, conceptions of civilization as a constraint on violence required that Rome abstain from the cruel treatment of foreign subjects who were also members of the inclusive society of humankind (Seneca, *On Anger*: 2: 34.4).

The Stoic affirmation of the moral obligation to avoid unnecessary harm was incorporated into Roman law and conveyed to later periods by methods that have already been discussed. Roman law 'became the chief carrier of the idea of universality' throughout the Mediterranean region (Bozeman 1960: 211). The crucial innovation of the idea of contract released people from their 'dependency on local groupings', thereby facilitating 'the formation of greater unions' (Bozeman 1960: 197). Because it elaborated the privileges that were the monopoly of Roman citizens, the civil law (*ius civile*) did not apply to disputes with outsiders. The *praetor peregrines* had specific responsibility for settling disputes between citizens and foreigners. Occupants of the role laid the foundations for the *ius gentium,* the laws that were held to be common to all peoples. Initially described as an appendage to the civil law, those principles would be transformed by the Stoics into the original higher law of nature or *ius naturale* with which the civil law had to conform (Bozeman 1960: 207ff.; Stein 1999: 12–13). Those legal refinements helped to forge a cohesive ruling class culture. The Romanization of local elites was often so complete that it was often impossible after approximately a century of imperial government 'to detect local cultural survivals among elites of the western provinces' (Mann 1986: 269).

The empire continued to 'export' violence to the periphery where the 'barbarians' bore the brunt of the traditional appetite for violence that was justified in terms of the rights of the 'higher civilization'. The contradiction did not go unnoticed. Tacitus (*Agricola*, 79ff.) portrayed Calgacus rallying his fellow Britons in a war against the Romans with their 'lust for power' and 'indiscriminate plunder' to which 'they give the lying name of "government"; they create a desolation and call it peace' (see de Souza 2008). Roman society had long believed that barbarians had few if any rights, and not least because they were regarded as willing to use any method, however cruel, to achieve their military objectives. Few of the extant accounts expressed serious moral qualms about the suffering that imperial expansion inflicted on conquered peoples. To return to the question of whether the 'simpler civilizations' of Greece and Rome possessed an international ethic – the answer must take account of the reality that, for the most part, Roman armies did not wage wars of extermination against 'barbarian' groups in the period under discussion. Many became trusted allies in defending the imperial frontiers (Goldsworthy 2007: 96, 119).

Roman society had long regarded warfare not as a regrettable departure from convention but as the normal state of affairs. Peace was deemed to be the prize that came with imperial domination – to pacify (*pacare*), was a euphemism for 'to defeat'. Amicable coexistence with other peoples as equals had little place in the dominant harm conventions (Goldsworthy 2007: 112–3). Collective pride in the complex governing structures and military prowess that had led to the achievements of empire were at the heart of Roman civilized self-images. Rome frequently used dramatic displays of its highly organized armed forces and its lavish wealth to intimidate 'barbarian' enemies. Such self-confidence and sense of superiority over other peoples also influenced the empire's revealingly complex relations with Parthia from the beginning of the first century until its disintegration and subsequent annexation by the Sassanid Persians in AD 224.

The Romans were not attuned to dealing with societies that had the military capability and the determination to withstand its imperial ambitions. In the course of its transformation into an imperial power, Rome successfully created dependent client states on its frontiers, incorporated defeated peoples within the victorious armies or conferred citizenship as an incentive to participate in the consolidation and expansion of the empire. That is one reason why Rome's relations with the Parthian empire provide an interesting 'test case' of how far suzerain state-systems can form a larger, 'secondary' states-system (Wight 1977: 24). Parthia was often depicted as 'barbarian' or 'semi-barbarian' with the result that Augustus' diplomatic overtures to Parthia, and his implicit recognition of its equal standing (or something close to it), had to be communicated to fellow Romans as a response to Parthian deference to an obvious superior (Brosius 2006: ch. 3). Roman views about Parthia, which was heir to the Persian Empire, were influenced by classical Greek conceptions of the fifth-century wars with Persia, and by Alexandrine and Macedonian 'orientalist' constructions of the 'barbarian Other' (Hardie 2007). In his travels to the eastern provinces, Augustus avoided high-level summitry with the Parthian king lest it gave the impression that Rome recognized the latter's equality. Relations with Parthia demonstrated that the ruling elite found it easier to absorb others into the empire or sphere of influence than to create new forms of we-feeling with others as social equals. But the realities of the exchange displayed some of the civility and self-restraint that are associated with the attitudes and behaviour of peoples who have found some common ground as members of an international society. They were illustrated by the reciprocal respect that underpinned diplomatic rituals and formal agreements about zones of influence that were later violated by the emperor, Trajan (Campbell 1995). Advances towards more egalitarian relations with Parthia were tentative. They did not prevent Trajan from regarding the death of the Parthian leader, Parthamasirius, who was killed in a struggle with a Roman escort, as fitting given the explicit breach of agreements (see Fronto II: 215 who drew on established imperial images of the virtues of restraint and moderation when stating that 'it is far better to pass by an injury and have public opinion on your side than to avenge one and have it against you'). The whole episode highlighted the dangers involved in relations between aristocratic rulers who could decide at any moment to 'exercise their inexplicable whim without restraint' (Campbell 1995: 237–8). But imperial arbitrariness must be seen in long-term perspective. The Roman tendency to cling to traditional self-images that were fundamental to the whole imperial 'civilizing process' and the sense of superiority over barbarians exemplified a recurrent problem in the relations between human groups. It is the difficulty in acquiring more detached or decentred world views that are necessary for the peaceful coexistence of societies with relatively equal power resources that have been drawn unexpect-edly into longer webs of interaction that none can control. The issue once again is how far the dominant conceptions of civilization provide a restraint on, or the pretext for, violence against adversaries.

Rome and Parthia did succeed in coexisting peacefully between 31 BC and the early part of the second century AD – in marked contrast to the period between AD 113–217 when they engaged in four military conflicts. It is clear that Rome was unconditionally wedded to the belief that security depended on hegemony. Attunement to more equal power configurations that were hard to dominate did not come easily to it. However, Rome may have engaged in rather more diplomatic activity than its reputation for violence suggests, as is evident from strategic alliances in the first and fourth centuries with German kings in the Danube region who provided support in protecting the imperial frontier (Campbell 2001; Pitts 1989). There were parallels with the notion of the *amici* (the 'friends and associates of the Roman people') that Rome had devised during its rise to power within Italy.

Also instructive were relations with the Sassanid Persians in the fifth century when Roman foreign policy relied heavily on diplomacy to avoid becoming dangerously entangled in wars on several fronts (Humphries 2007). Significant advances in civility were the manuals on diplomacy that stressed the merits of avoiding arrogant behaviour. Safe passage without the need to carry arms was valued. Maltreatment of embassies was regarded as violating universal laws in the manner of 'barbarians' (Humphries 2007: 257ff.). Small advances occurred in the face of external restraints in moving beyond the classical doctrine that security was unattainable without hegemony – in recognizing the need for standards of restraint and principles of reciprocity that are more typical of the harm conventions in an international society where no great power can dominate the others. Perhaps those changes of orientation would not have occurred but for the earlier taming of the Roman aristocracy that had occurred by transforming the meaning of concepts such as *virtus*.

Not that the later stages of the empire were dominated by a more general lurch towards civility (Fear 2007). The empire evolved into what has been called 'a para-military state' where the army enjoyed a degree of autonomy that had not existed since the last years of the Republic. Military forces were portrayed as wolves that preyed on the vulnerable in society. Disputes continue about the reasons for the shift towards a parasitical relationship with society that would have astonished Romans in the first century AD, one that involved the brutal requisitioning of property and increased violence against powerless civilians. Some have traced those shifts to the 'barbarianization' of the military forces, and specifically to the substantial increase during the fourth century in the number of recruits from beyond the traditional boundaries of the empire, some rising to command positions, and most lacking emotional ties with the wider communities that would have underpinned significant self-restraint in dealings with them.

Wherever the explanation lies, the army became increasingly divorced from the rest of society in an era when military service was no longer a core civic obligation. The level of discipline that had been central to Roman conceptions of the 'civilized' realm declined, leading some to lament the demise of *temperamentia*. Those problems intensified as the imperial monopoly of power disintegrated. The centre became ever more dependent on 'barbarian' armed forces that had little if any emotional attachment to Rome (Stickler 2007). The imperial monopoly of violence collapsed in the third and fourth centuries as local military commanders won the personal loyalty of armies that were under their direct control. In the Western provinces, the rise to power of local warlords brought new insecurities to civilian communities (Liebeschuetz 2007). The collapse of the Western empire resulted in a breakdown of 'complexity' that included the destruction of long-distance economic and social ties; one result was the decline of major urban centres that had been integral to Roman ideals of the civilized life (Ward-Perkins 2005). Enormous violence often attended the collapse of the Western empire but it would be inaccurate to suggest that there was an abrupt transition from Roman order and civility to 'barbarian' chaos in all the former provincial territories (Liebeschuetz 1995, 2007). For some peoples, life in the areas that came under the dominion of unfamiliar 'barbarian' armies was preferable to conditions in the regions that remained subject to the 'savage' injustice of Roman authorities. Support for *Romanitas* was often preserved by Germanic courts in territories where the collapse of imperial authority was followed by experiments in adapting traditional Roman legal and political practice to new circumstances (Ward-Perkins 2005: ch. 4). The 'civilizing' role of the 'Stoic-Christian tradition' did not disappear entirely.

Several 'barbarian' leaders converted to Christianity and adapted many Roman practices in systems of government that presided over heavily militarized societies. 'Roman bureaucracy and legal procedure' were dismantled in many areas but several features 'persisted in peaceful fashion as a repertoire of ways of exercising authority from which Europe's early medieval power brokers could pick and choose' (Smith 2005: 30). Many 'barbarian' rulers transmitted respect for *Romanitas* to the Middle Ages by emphasizing their Roman heritage; they defended their claims to legitimacy as providers of public order and the rule of law (Chrysos 1997; Murray 2006; Pohl 1997). Western Europe in AD 500 is therefore best regarded as 'post-imperial' rather than 'post-Roman' (Smith 2005: 2; also Drake 2006; Barnwell 1997: conclusion; Hen 2007).

The Christianization of the imperial court up to the early fifth century increased the influence of monks, bishops and ascetics (Cameron 1993: ch. 5). In that period, the Greek concept of *sophrosyne* appears to have had more influence on attitudes to sexual morality rather than on images of public order (North 1966: chs. 8–9). Nevertheless, such social ideals were important in early medieval writings on 'civilizing ... the nobility' and also in treatises that provided instruction for knights in the manner of the 'mirror of princes' (Scaglione 1991: 52ff., 83). Echoes of earlier notions of restrained kingship were evident in the doctrines that expected the emperors 'to strike the difficult balance between dignity and affability, between justice and severity' (Cameron 1993: 102–3). Under Constantine and his immediate successors, pagan and Christian authors (the latter drawing extensively on Hellenic sources) constructed ideals of imperial authority that were directly modelled on the beneficence of the ruler of the universe (Downey 1955). From the sixth century onward, the ideal of *philanthropia* featured prominently in assorted philosophical reflections on the differences between kings and tyrants; the former, however autocratic, were expected to observe the rule of law in accordance with God's will. Commitments to *philanthropia* were central to the Church's effort to preserve what it could of the *pax Romana*, amended to emphasize spiritual limits on civil authority as embodied in the compromise between early Christian pacifism and the exigencies of defending the Christianized Empire that led to formulations of the idea of the just war. The latter was an important development in the long struggle between the permissive and restraining faces of civilization (Swift 2007; Scaglione 1991: 56ff.).

By those routes, core features of the Roman civilizing process such as *humanitas* were handed down to a later age. But so were the ambiguities of collective images of having scaled the heights of civilization. On the one side was the conviction that in their relations with 'civilized' peoples, the 'barbarian' had no rights; and on the other, the belief that their 'civilized' commitments demanded that 'advanced' societies act with self-restraint and share their cultural accomplishments with other groups, in keeping with the principle of *humanitas*. Therein resides the dual legacy of Roman images of civilization that would shape, *inter alia*, later European attitudes to the overseas empires.

Civilizing Processes in the Hellenistic and Roman Worlds

The larger territorial concentrations of power that eclipsed the Greek city states in the Hellenistic and Roman worlds were capable of what is now widely regarded as exceptional cruelty and excessive violence. But 'civilizing' efforts to control the use of force also developed. Various notions of moderate rule and the merciful treatment of enemies were important features of ancient processes of civilization. Some phases in the development of larger monopolies of power were undoubtedly more committed than others to 'taming the warriors'. The ruthless use of force was regarded as critical for survival and its legitimacy was endorsed by the supposed absolute rights of a higher civilization. But it was necessary for the societies involved to control the unprecedented collective powers at their disposal. The difficulty of governing the diverse peoples that had been forced together in the Alexandrine and Roman empires created incentives to govern with restraint. It was in the self-interest of the ruling strata to secure the support, or at least the acquiescence, of subject peoples in 'scaled up' forms of social and political organization. Alexander's role in attempting to anchor personal monarchy in more 'universal' principles of association that were designed to bridge major differences between Greeks, Macedonians and Persians was a turning point in the ancient world. Rome's ingenuous response to the challenge of incorporating different peoples within the empire included the breakthroughs in extending Roman citizenship and in promoting the more 'universal' legal and moral orientations that were captured by notions of *civilitas* that would have a lasting influence.

The previous chapter concluded by asking how different was the Hellenic system from the modern states-system with respect to the tolerance of violent harm, and what light do any differences shed on the conditions that favour the development of civilizing processes in world politics. As with the Greeks, the societies in the period that has been surveyed did not face equivalents to the immense external pressures to restrain their behaviour that emerged with the industrialization of warfare. Hellenistic and Roman armies were much freer to act violently than are modern industrial societies in their relations with each other. There was little systematic analysis of how independent political communities could learn to coexist peacefully. There was no imperative to reflect on how different societies could live harmoniously as equals. The hegemonic principle that had been central to the Hellenic system was perpetuated by Macedon under Philip and Alexander, by the Hellenistic kingdoms, and by Rome. Hegemonic wars were regarded as just and inevitable. For Romans with their confidence in their civilized superiority, subduing other peoples was the natural state of affairs just as it was for the majority of European peoples in their relations with non-Europeans until around the middle of the twentieth century. The entitlement to use whatever violence was needed to overwhelm adversaries was also taken for granted but it was not always enforced, not because of a sense of answerability to international society or accountability to humanity – which were entirely alien modes of reasoning – but for pragmatic reasons. There was no broader 'we' with claims that had to be reconciled with the interests of Macedon, Alexander's empire, the Hellenistic kingdoms or Rome in the relevant harm conventions.

The Hellenic and Hellenistic states-systems, and the Alexandrine and Roman empires, turned out to be 'evolutionary dead ends'. But international systems do not wither away without trace – without leaving behind a 'civilizing' legacy that can be used to construct new forms of world political organization, whether empires or societies of states, at a later date. In Rome's case, various perspectives on the virtues of the moderate exercise of political power contributed to the formation of European images of international society in the context of a more even power distribution between interdependent groups. They also influenced later doctrines of 'civil empire'. Those standpoints represented no more than a partial shift in the relative power of the 'progressive' and the 'regressive' dimensions of civilizing processes, but they were evidence nonetheless that for all their violence, earlier peoples were not entirely indifferent to 'international ethics'.

3

The International Relations of Latin Christendom

> Leaving aside a small elite, rapine, pillage and murder were standard practice in the warrior society of (the) time ... Outbursts of cruelty did not exclude one from social life. They were not outlawed. The pleasure in killing and torturing others was great, and it was a socially permitted pleasure. To a certain extent, the social structure even pushed its members in this direction, making it seem necessary and practically advantageous to behave in this way
>
> (Elias: 2012: 189)

The medieval political order did not consist of relatively autonomous political units that were bound together by shared understandings about standards of restraint that can be found in the international states-systems of antiquity, or the Italian Renaissance city-states system, or the modern global figuration of sovereign political communities. As a result of identification with the *societas christiana*, 'unity rather than separateness' – 'hierarchy rather than equality' – characterized relations between the constituent units (Wight 1977: 25–7). So powerful were we-feelings organized around the idea of 'the normative unity of the Christian world' that the physical 'separation ... into kingdoms and duchies was considered illegitimate by most and epiphenomenal even by the temporal rulers who benefited from it' (Fischer 1992:435–6). If there was a medieval states-system, it consisted of the 'triangular relationship between Eastern Christendom, Western Christendom and the Islamic world', but one that was complicated by the reality that none of those political entities formed a 'singular power-bloc' (Wight 1977: 25). Latin Christendom is perhaps best regarded as a 'uniquely complicated dualistic or double-headed suzerain state-system' in which the empire and papacy asserted rival claims for authority over the subordinate parts (Wight 1977: 29). Many of those actors would go onto assert and acquire rights of sovereignty that altered the we–I balance between Latin Christendom and particular 'survival units'. During the wars of religion, the restraining effect of earlier shared universal convictions declined sharply (Phillips 2011: chs. 4–5). Prior to that era, the papacy came closest to displaying the basic hallmarks of a state (Wight 1977: 28; also Davies 2003; Reynolds 1997, 2003 and Larkins 2010).

Those comments suggest that there are no exact parallels between medieval principles of political differentiation and the familiar dichotomies between the 'inside' and the 'outside', or the 'domestic' and 'international', that constitute modern political life (Teschke 1998: 353). Latin Christendom was distinguished by a complex web of overlapping political jurisdictions and multiple loyalties rather than by territorial concentrations of sovereign power and popular identification with specific nations or states. The term 'neo-medieval' has been coined to describe a supposedly emergent system of authorities and loyalties that resemble the political topography of Latin Christendom, but such interpretations are criticized for ignoring the 'positive role' of the state in the modern period (Bull 1977: 254–5; Bull 1979). The core contention is that many welcomed the rise of the sovereign state as an escape from the violent turmoil of the late medieval world. Whether such sharp contrasts between medieval and modern levels of violence are valid is one of the issues to explore in this chapter.

There is a short step from that observation about neo-medievalism to the analysis of a European civilizing process in which violence and lawlessness were replaced by the following conditions – internal pacification, lengthening chains of interconnectedness, and increased incentives to control violence and exercise all-round self-restraint (Elias 2012: 186ff.). Disputes have arisen about whether the Eliasian interpretation of state-formation and distinctive patterns of civilization exaggerated the level of medieval violence and cruelty and made the modern world seem more distinctive and peaceful than is in fact the case (Baraz 2003; Rosenwein 1998). A related criticism is that the approach underestimated the impact of religious beliefs on the European civilizing process, and specifically the role that the medieval courts played in the long-term exercise in 'taming the warriors' (Bax 1987; Goudsblom 2004; Turner 2004). But it is important to recall that Elias (2007a: 119) emphasized that there is no 'zero point' as far as any civilizing process is concerned – no clear juncture at which the history of 'barbarism' comes to an end and a new pathway of 'civility' begins (Elias 2012: 319; Elias 2013a: 253). The observation highlighted that in the course of 'the long-term gradual and continuous transformation of human groups' the people who have become bound together in new ways can lose sight of their indebtedness to earlier generations (Elias 2006b: 249). They may raise themselves above their 'savage' ancestors as they celebrate their supposedly 'uniquely civilized' accomplishments and disregard their own 'barbarism' (Elias 2012: 464ff.). The question is whether modern representations of the medieval period are guilty of such self-serving distortions.

Elias's approach advised against introducing stark contrasts between a static 'medieval' period and the supposedly more dynamic and fast-changing modern world. Far from being a 'petrified forest', the medieval era was marked by 'an alteration of expanding phases and sectors', some 'moving in precisely the direction . . . which the modern age has continued' (Elias 2012: 263). Such comments shed little light on the international relations of Latin Christendom. As already noted, the centrality of ideas of unity and hierarchy is one reason for hesitancy regarding that epoch as a states-system. That orientation resonates with the contention that the Middle Ages were distinctive because the constituent social units were bound together by a 'communal discourse' that revolved around feelings of belonging to a universal Christian empire that prized the rule of law (Fischer 1992: 434). That characterization is in harmony with the interpretation that maintains that the principal society in the Middle Ages was 'the supra-national society' of Christendom, and adds that the constituent 'Christian kingdoms' were 'dependent members' linked together in a larger community of faith (Keen 1965: 240). The absence of a 'visible head' may suggest that the unity of the medieval order was 'chimerical', and that the we–I balance favoured the parts over the whole. But those who stress unity and coherence can point to the evidence that a single law of arms was 'accepted as binding on soldiers throughout [the] length and breadth' of Latin Christendom (Keen 1965: ibid.). Those laws were 'more than a vague set of principles of loyalty and honour'; they were regarded as part of the civilizing inheritance of Roman law, and they were 'accepted and enforced in properly constituted courts' where the legal 'intricacies' were debated by 'trained lawyers' (Keen 1965: 240–1).

Others concur that a 'communal discourse' was integral to emotional identification with a universal Christian order that was held together by a code of law, but they stress profound similarities between the medieval order and various states-systems (Fischer 1992: 434). From a perspective that emphasizes the importance of 'I' over 'we', Latin Christendom consisted of 'functionally differentiated' units that were locked in struggles for power and security with all the 'decivilizing' potentials that exist whenever such entities face external threats (Teschke 1998: 351). Those reflections on different features of the medieval world invite discussion of whether the relationship between violence and civilization changed significantly over the centuries and, if so, how the variations are best explained.

It has been claimed that the papal conferral in AD 800 of the title of 'new Roman emperor' on Charlemagne expressed the Church's vision of a universal Christian society and advanced its conception of political and religious unity (Fischer 1992: 436ff.). However, Charlemagne's reign as king of the Franks (AD 768–814), which brought unity to most of Christian Europe, was short-lived; the idealized 'communal discourse' of the Carolingian empire did not become the dominant influence on the longer-term course of events. Between the ninth and eleventh centuries, the main trend was the steady disintegration of the Frankish empire – its dismemberment following the Treaty of Verdun in 843 into ever smaller 'survival units'. The balance of power shifted in favour of 'decivilizing processes', fuelled by unremitting conflicts between 'local strongmen' locked in violent competition for 'exclusive control of people and land' (Fischer 1992: 461). From that standpoint, the distribution of military power largely determined the outcomes of major conflicts of interest.

Especially during the twelfth and thirteenth centuries, competition for power and wealth was governed by the 'monopoly mechanism' that was central to Elias's explanation of European state formation and the 'civilizing process' – of long-term patterns of social and political development that extended over approximately a thousand years (see Chapter 5). That observation is in harmony with recent scholarship that argues for considering the medieval and modern worlds as part of one extended historical process that came into being around 1300, the point at which the rough outlines of a sovereign states-system were coming into existence (Latham 2012: 3, 58). Such works advance the critique of the supposition that the 1648 Peace of Westphalia was the decisive moment at which the modern sovereign states-system replaced the medieval political order. They stress the need to 'mainstream' the study of medieval international relations rather than to regard it as a prelude to modernity with little more than 'historical interest' for contemporary students of world politics. An important claim is that many elements of Hobbes and Bodin's political theory of sovereignty had been formulated – though less systematically – many centuries earlier (Latham 2012: 72ff., 134; Larkins 2010: 90ff.). There was, in short, no sharp dividing line between the medieval and the modern states-systems – or if there was a break in the history of the last thousand years, it occurred around 1300 when a world of interconnected medieval states first began to take shape.

The increased power of the kings relative to the nobles in the twelfth century was evident in the 'pacts among equals' that often conveyed notions of friendship or *amicitiae* in which the royal courts reached agreements not to seize one another's castles or to provide refuge for others' enemies (Pascua 2008; Geary 1994). Displays of *amicitia* never entirely disappeared from 'treaty practice' in the medieval period; they became rare during the High and Late Middle Ages, only to become central once again during the Italian Renaissance (Lesaffer 2002). The Roman-influenced discourse of princes as 'brothers and cousins' that underpinned restraints on the power to harm was evidence of 'the supranational court society' that was the precursor of the international society of states that lay ahead (see Chapter 5, p. 195). Within that political framework, the Church combined its role as spiritual leader with assorted civil responsibilities. Its political powers may have been limited, but it was committed to a project of pacifying the relations between kings that traditional preoccupations with the violence of the Middle Ages have often ignored. Even so, realist analysis has emphasized the disjuncture 'between feudal discourse, which portrayed Christendom as a harmonious unity without internal violence' and the typical behaviour of feudal polities that freely 'disregarded the communal discourse' because they were immersed 'in power politics in the manner of modern states' (Fischer 1992: 434–5, 443). The explanation of that competition stresses the creation of localized 'public fortresses' between the eighth and the tenth centuries when no central political authority could defend the frontier from threats posed by the Vikings, Saracens and Magyars (Fischer 1992: 437). Norse invasions in the ninth and ten centuries led the nobility to assert its claims over Church property (Hall and Kratochwil 1993: 482–3). The financial means of buying off the Vikings had to be acquired quickly, and drawing reserves from wealthy monasteries (that had often been endowed by the nobles in the first place) was a standard solution. Those developments suggest that the political disintegration of Latin Christendom was the consequence of the inner workings of an international anarchic system but one that included medieval polities and invading societies, and in which none of the parts formed a 'singular power-bloc' (Fischer 1993: 494).

The contention that no sector of medieval society was untouched by 'the violent reality of everyday life' (Fischer 1992: 464) resonates with the orthodox interpretation of many writers including Bloch (1962) and Elias (2012) that insisted that violence and insecurity were much greater in the Middle Ages than in present day 'civilized' societies. It supports the argument that the level of violence was significantly higher in the period before stable monopolies of power could pacify their respective territorial domains.[1] The approach seems to be at odds with descriptions of the 'communal' features of medieval politics. But those positions are complementary rather than contradictory. In many states-systems, competing political units have believed that they are part of a higher civilization such as Hellas, Christendom or Europe. They understood the 'problem of harm' in comparable ways, at one and the same time acquiring the 'power to hurt' and wrestling with the issue of how to restrain violence, and how to use their power to bring 'civilization' to other societies. In the case of the medieval era, the weakening of royal power following the 'barbarian invasions' led the Church to become active, especially from the end of the ninth century, in trying to restore public order by going 'over the head of formally constituted secular authority to deal directly . . . with the knighthood' (Keen 1984: 47). Positive evaluations of violence in the context of the Church's endeavours to tame the knights appeared around that time (Keen 1984: ch. 3). Evidence that competing forces shaped the development of medieval society is clear from the emergence – from around the middle of the twelfth century – of critiques of 'arbitrary lordship' that were linked with new doctrines of merciful rule. They appeared – and there is an interesting parallel with Elias's analysis of

---

[1] By way of example, the historical evidence suggests that between the thirteenth and sixteenth centuries the homicide rate in England declined by around fifty per cent (Becker 1988: 5). In the case of British ducal families in the fourteenth and fifteenth centuries, around forty-six per cent of male children that reached the age of fifteen suffered a violent death. Three hundred years later, and as a consequence of 'the domestication of the European nobility', the death rate fell to around four per cent.

the European civilizing process – alongside increasing interdependencies between members of the upper strata in the 'courtly cultures of power' (Bisson 2009: 79ff.). A 'newly organized sociability of power' that relied on experts in Roman law emerged in response to the incentives to pacify or 'civilize' intra-court relations (Bisson 2009: 438ff.). Some parallels with the Roman political experience will be evident, as will major contrasts with Macedonian court society.

Whether perspectives that emphasize the greater violence of the Middle Ages can be accepted without major qualifications is an important issue, as is the question of whether the violence of the era is explicable entirely as a result of a self-help system that was forced on societies by the perilous circumstances of international anarchy. On many accounts, the clergy furthered its objectives through inflated claims about the ingrained violence of a lawless nobility, but high levels of violence as a result of the proliferation of armed nobles following the collapse of the Carolingian Empire were real enough (Bisson 2009). However, it is essential to consider whether 'structural' explanations that stress the recurrent dynamics of anarchic orders can explain some of the major contrasts between states-systems that revolve around differences in the 'threshold of repugnance' towards violence. The question is how far such perspectives reveal the extent to which people found pleasure in killing and destruction or were shocked by cruelty or excessive force; it is how far such approaches provide insights into the changing power balances between the patterns of thought and action that bound people to their respective egoistical 'survival units' and the visions of human solidarity that transcended political differences and divisions.

Some debates in the study of international relations about the medieval international anarchy are worth noting in that context. A central aim of the structural realist interpretation has been to refute the constructivist thesis that a major transformation of the basic principles of political life occurred as the Middle Ages gave way to the modern era (see Ruggie 1983). It has been to argue that the violence of the former period confirms the neo-realist claim that international politics have been remarkably similar across the millennia because the same struggles for power and security are endemic in the condition of anarchy. It has been to reinforce the pessimistic conviction that 'civilizing' cosmopolitan political projects that aim to reduce unnecessary suffering are 'unlikely to succeed' (Fischer 1992: 465–6). But as noted earlier, the approach does not explain dimensions of human interaction that are central to a comparative sociology of harm conventions that analyses the dominant constructions of violence and civilization. They include social attitudes to the body, vulnerability and suffering that are clearly not identical in all eras, conceptions of permissible and impermissible forms of violence that change over time, and understandings of the possibilities for transnational solidarity that demonstrate that anarchy does not dictate identical patterns of behaviour across all historical periods (Linklater 2011: chs. 1 and 5; Wendt 1992). Progress in comprehending those dimensions of the relations between societies requires a detailed investigation of the relationship between violence and civilization in different states-systems that considers the interdependencies between domestic social forces and international dynamics; it requires an analysis of recurrent tensions within 'civilized' attitudes to permissible and forbidden violence that does not abandon, as neo-realism does, the quest to understand the conditions that facilitate the development of significant global 'civilizing processes'.

The remainder of this chapter begins by discussing competing interpretations of the violence of the Middle Ages. A short overview of prevalent emotional responses to violence, cruelty and suffering follows. The inquiry then turns to the social functions of chivalry and assesses the degree to which religious conceptions of we-feeling dampened aggressive impulses and the lust for killing amongst the knights. Of central importance was the Church's endeavour to 'tame the warriors' through the 'civilizing' fusion of piety and violence that fuelled crusading warfare – hence the statement that 'an echo of Latin Christendom and the knightly feudal Crusade' ran through later conceptions of European civilization, however secularized (Elias 2012: 61). The expansion of medieval international society is considered in that light. The chapter concludes with an overview of tensions between 'civilizing' and 'decivilizing' processes across the medieval period that can be linked with later discussions of the 'Janus-faced' character of 'processes of civilization'.

Order, Violence and Suffering

Following Bloch, Duby, Dumezil and other pioneering medieval historians, contemporary scholars have emphasized the feudal discourse from around the eleventh century that portrayed society as an organic whole that consisted of three functionally interdependent strata: 'the *oratores*, or clergy, who were to provide the community with divine grace; the *bellatores*, or knights, who were to protect it against external and internal foes; and the *laboratores*, or peasants, who were to procure its economic sustenance' (Fischer 1992: 443–4). With its codification by Adalbéron, Bishop of Laon in the early eleventh century, and by Gerard, Bishop of Cambrai, in the same period, that ternary division gave systematic expression to medieval images of social order. The tripartite distinctions were principally a statement about an ideal social organization rather than an accurate reflection of the existing state of affairs, but they would influence later articulations of the chivalric code (Keen 1984: 4). The ideology of the three orders was designed to assert the superiority of the clergy over the knights, but it was also geared towards redefining the former's role at a time when many lesser clerics carried arms, resorted to looting during military campaigns, and participated in banditry (Frassetto 1998; King 1998). There was virtually unanimous agreement that those who fought occupied a higher position in the social order than those who laboured merely to survive (Bloch 1962: 291–2). The evidence is that the knights did not hesitate to regard their position as more important than the missions that united the specialists in prayer but, at the time, few depictions of the *bellatores* celebrated the ennobling ideals of chivalry. That 'civilizing' conception of violence would appear later.

The political power and social importance of the knights have been underlined by studies of the role of blood vengeance and feuding in communities where no higher authority could resolve conflicts and enforce justice (Fischer 1992: 454–7). Indeed, 'much early medieval warfare was merely an extension and enlargement of feuds, themselves endemic in the aristocratic societies of Latin Europe'; moreover, accompanying all forms of warfare including conflicts with 'heathen attackers' and struggles for power between lords was 'the simple quest for wealth' (Leyser 1994: 33; Geary 1994). The prevailing warrior ethos granted lords the right to settle disputes 'by force of arms'. A long-established culture of resistance to restraints on a supposedly natural entitlement to violence as well as to protect honour through force and to seek vengeance has been identified as the main reason for institutionalized feuding (Teschke 1998: 347; Rouche 1987: 498ff.). The general consensus is that 'public peace always stood on the shaky ground of the noble right to armed resistance'; outside England, especially, monarchs rarely succeeded in eliminating aristocratic feuding, although one of their recurrent objectives was to tame what was widely regarded as a lawless nobility (Teschke 1998: 347; Vale 1988: 318ff.; White 1986; Dean 2001: conclusion).

Trial by battle was often the preferred strategy of knights locked in bitter conflict (Fischer 1992: 456; Kagay 1998; Vale 2000). The Church opposed the practice as it involved shedding Christian blood and violated the obligations of charity. It may have declined from the thirteenth century as a result of the greater availability of effective judicial procedures (Bartlett 1986: ch. 6). Courts attempted to suppress the desire for retribution by proposing adequate compensation for injured parties, but legal procedures, which varied enormously in their effectiveness and legitimacy, were often biased in favour of members of the dominant social strata who used them strategically (Davies and Fouracre 1986: conclusion). In the profoundly unequal medieval society, the power resources and status of the different parties in dispute invariably had more influence on judicial outcomes than the intrinsic merits of the specific case (Fischer 1992: 456–7). The lack of stable, centralized monopolies of power that could enforce legal decisions meant that the social elite frequently bypassed the judicial process entirely, preferring instead to rely on force to secure justice. Reflecting their strength in relation to weak judicial institutions, the lords resorted to trial by ordeal in their dealings with the peasantry. The practice survived from the ninth to the thirteenth centuries, at which point it was replaced by judicial torture – by a rerouting of violence in the early phases of modern state formation (Bartlett 1986). To the extent that clear distinctions were drawn between feuding and warfare (and the differences seemed to reflect the intensity of conflict rather than any intrinsic qualities), they did not alter the reality that the idea of human equality or a sense of universal we-feeling had no place in the harm conventions that regulated dispute-settlement in feudal society (Teschke 1998: 347; Elias 2012: 202).

Popular hopes for the alleviation of suffering surfaced from time to time in the form of assorted millenarian movements – peasant revolts against class exploitation that reduced them to starvation were not unusual – but medieval society was basically inhospitable to reformist political projects that resemble modern 'campaigns of compassion' that are orientated towards protecting 'ordinary life' (Le Goff 1988: 194). The relatively low level of emotional identification with others irrespective of social origins must be noted here. Lepers, the crippled and the diseased were regarded as undergoing rightful punishment for sinful conduct; the condition of hunger was portrayed in similar terms. Women were associated with the temptation of Adam and with original sin. Distrust was directed at strangers who had no identifiable place within the dense network of oaths that defined each person's social responsibilities and entitlements. The prevailing 'established–outsider' dualisms were entirely antithetical to meliorist political projects (Le Goff 1988: 235–6, 285–6, 321–2).

According to some interpretations, fighting was not an 'occasional duty' undertaken for the sake of 'lord, or king or family'; it 'represented much more – their whole purpose in life' (Bloch 1962: 292). Joy in fighting, Elias (2012: 186ff.) contended, was absolutely central to the collective identity of the male warrior class. Its members did not require the lengthy preparation for warfare and the appropriate psychological fashioning that citizens of modern 'civilized' societies who are far less attuned to violence in everyday life must undergo (Elias 2007: 145; Keegan 1991: ch. 2). Whether such portraits of the bellicosity of the nobles simplified and distorted medieval social realities is a matter to discuss later. It is clear that the tensions and attempted compromises between, on the one hand, the dominant attitudes to violence amongst members of the warrior aristocracy and, on the other hand, the world view of the Church shaped medieval civilizing processes in general, and influenced the relations between 'survival units' in particular. The Church held that the knights did not have a license to act violently without regard for the Christian virtues of mercy and charity. The expectation was that they would honour Christ's command to 'love thy neighbour as they selfe' (Fischer 1992: 443ff.). As part of the Church's endeavour to entrench chivalric duties, knights were authorized 'to use force solely to protect the unarmed parts of society . . . such as clerics, peasants, widows and orphans' (Fischer: ibid.). That conception of the knights' role embodied the hope and conviction that the Germanic warrior ethos could be harnessed to sacred purposes, that the we–I balance would not favour the knights' freedom of action over wider social considerations and responsibilities, and that the power to injure could be tamed accordingly by the relevant harm conventions and by new patterns of conscience formation.

That ethical aspiration had its origins in the late Roman Empire in the fifth century when elements of the ruling strata believed that Christian conversion would civilize 'barbarian' outsiders (Jones 1971: 381ff.; Le Goff 1988: ch. 1). The critical term, *civilitas,* described the commitment to the rule of law that had been derived from the 'civilizing' ideal of *Romanitas,* and that had all but been lost in several regions as a result of the 'barbarian' invasions and the crumbling of imperial political institutions. Those 'decivilizing' forces released aggressive tendencies that had been restrained to some degree in the preceding epoch. The consequence was a level of cruelty that may have exceeded even Rome's notorious treatment of the Christian martyrs (Le Goff 1988: 32–3). The point has been made that the Church attempted to assume some of the responsibilities of civil government in the face of social upheaval and political fragmentation, or tried to support and give direction to re-emergent civil authorities (Goetz 1992). Papal initiatives were undertaken to resolve disputes between Christian princes, and not necessarily for self-interested reasons (see Heath 1995: 129–30 who argues that their level of success is hard to gauge because the preoccupation with medieval violence has overshadowed the scholarly analysis of pacifying offensives). As early as the sixth century, and as heir to Roman ideas of civilization, religious authorities constructed doctrines of moderate Christian rule, social discipline and personal obedience in a conscious attempt to promote a 'civilizing offensive' (Le Goff 1988: 34). Between the eighth and sixteenth centuries, nostalgia for the 'civilizing' aspects of the Roman Empire appears to have increased albeit in tandem with the conviction that a more 'civilized' form of life may have been lost forever (Le Goff 1988: 36).

Religious authorities relied on the fear of excommunication and the prospect of eternal damnation in an attempt to control the knights' violent dispositions. Concurrently, images of sinfulness and the desire for penance won support amongst the warrior class. Medieval society was the outcome of a 'meeting and the fusion of two worlds' that were already 'evolving towards each other' (Le Goff 1988: 23). New social ideals emphasized the virtue of harnessing violence to religious objectives such as waging 'penitential' wars against the 'enemies of Christ' and engaging in crusading warfare to free Jerusalem and Eastern Christians from 'infidel' domination (Tyerman 2005: 19ff.). Religious taboos on violence within a 'civilized' world that was presumed to be surrounded by barbarians were expressed in the *Peace of God* that was formulated at the Councils of Le Puy and Charroux in AD975 and 989, and in the *Truce of God* that was proclaimed at the Councils of Elne (or Toulouges) in 1027 and Arles circa 1041. Those two 'civilizing' initiatives are best regarded as a reaction to the increased feuding and violence that followed the disintegration of the Carolingian empire and not as a monument to concrete achievements in taming the warriors by instilling respect for more exacting self-control and by promoting substantial changes in the we–I balance (Bredero 1994: ch. 4). The relevant harm conventions were introduced at a particular historical juncture when the end of the invasions created opportunities for the partial pacification of society by injecting sacred ideals into the traditional warrior codes (Le Goff 1988: 57). Their development reflected 'the Church's gradual admission from about AD 1000 of the Germanic warrior ethos into the orbit of Christianity' (Blake 1970: 12). Given the power of the warrior aristocracy, 'the ecclesiastical order had to bend traditional Christian rules of life and exegesis to assign [it] a protective function long recognized in rulers as preservers of peace' (Blake 1970: ibid.). The religious defence of the First Crusade used the rhetoric of the *Peace of God* to cement a relationship with the warriors that promised various spiritual and material rewards in exchange for vanquishing 'Christ's enemies'. The endeavour to reconfigure the warrior ethos focused on prohibiting fighting on days of religious significance, promoting respect for church property and instilling the commitment to refrain from harming the clergy and its parishioners. In reality, the knights were more often engaged in subjugation and pillage than in complying with religious demands to protect other groups. The result of trials of ordeal – in which peasants were required to prove their rights by undergoing painful experiences – was the large-scale upper-class appropriation of land. The upshot was that much of Western Europe was almost entirely devoid of free peasants by the end of the twelfth century (Fischer 1992: ibid.).

Whether Latin Christendom was always quite as violent as those observations suggest is a moot point that raises familiar questions about the reliability of sources and the accuracy of such classic studies as Bloch (1962). One engagement with the historical sources to develop a neo-realist analysis of medieval international anarchy has been criticized for generalizing the findings of analyses of violence in a specific and far from typical area – the Maconnais in the southeastern region of France (Fischer 1993). The objection is that it is illegitimate to assume that the level of conflict and insecurity that existed in that area was representative of medieval society as a whole, or evident in territories where the monopolization of power was sufficiently advanced to rein in violent impulses (see however Fischer 1993: 495–6). Others have gone further by drawing on specialist works on the region that suggest that a complex mesh of cross-cutting allegiances, ultimately anchored in faith and the fear of divine retribution, helped to restrain violence and to promote the peaceful reparation of harms that were caused by robbery and theft (Osiander 2007: 226ff.). Several studies of eleventh- and twelfth-century France were far too indebted, it has been argued, to church narratives that exaggerated the threats to religious interests or emphasized the contrasts between religious ideals and the brutality, corruption and sinfulness of every-day life (Reynolds 1984: 118; Bachrach 1999). Medieval representations of violence may often have had less to with providing an accurate description of social life than with demonizing members of the lower strata that were held responsible for, *inter alia*, the peasants' revolts. For example, in 1233, Pope Gregory IX compared the peasants in the Bremen region to wild beasts, ignoring their claims to be resisting unjust assaults on customary practice (see P. Freedman 1998, who maintains that the whole purpose of such narra-tives was to establish the lords' right to defend established interests by force). Unlike the later wars of religion in Western Europe, medieval violence was, according to some accounts, invariably 'localized socially and geographically' (Baraz 2003: 143). The violence of the early medieval world is not in doubt, but whether it was more or less violent than preceding and succeeding eras is, on some accounts, 'less easy to state and, perhaps, less profitable to consider' (Halsall 1998: 4).

In any event, the Church was far from powerless in its relations with the knights, even where levels of violence seem to confirm later stereotypes of the lawlessness of the Middle Ages. Partly in response to attacks on its wealth, the clergy invented the doctrine of the Three Orders; its aim was 'to pacify lordly aggressiveness internally and to deflect it into external conquest' (Teschke 1998: 333). Such measures had only limited success. Although there were exceptions, medieval warfare was rarely 'total', uprooting whole populations in the process and reducing many to slavery that had often been the fate of the inhabitants of conquered cities in classical antiquity. At times, conceptions of chivalry and the just war commanded sufficient respect to grant non-combatants some protection in periods of conflict. Medieval peoples were not permanently in the grip of unrelenting warfare despite the widespread absence of the rule of law and the prevalence of the insecurities that were fuelled by the warriors' celebration of the martial virtues. Military conflict may have been no more violent and destructive than the interstate wars of the sixteenth and seventeenth centuries (Contamine 1984: 306).

As noted earlier, high levels of violence in Latin Christendom have been cited to support the structural realist account of the power struggles that are inherent in anarchic systems. Feudal 'international politics', the thesis is, were 'largely governed' by the same forces that have governed every states-system (Fischer 1992: 461). The absence of 'central protection' compelled feudal actors 'to strive for exclusive control over manpower and ... territory in order to maximize the chances for survival' (Fischer 1992: ibid.). The interpretation has been criticized for failing to recognize the deeper reality of the exploitative nature of feudal property relations. From the vantage-point of historical materialism, 'extra-economic compulsion' is the 'central analytical concept' for understanding medieval conflict (Teschke 1998: 338). The conviction that it was entirely legitimate to appropriate wealth by force explains violent competition for land along 'three axes': in the relations between the peasantry and the lords, in interactions between the lords and in the struggles between the 'collectivity of lords' (in the form of the 'feudal state') and external 'survival units' (Teschke 1998: 326). That approach rejects the neo-realist thesis that medieval international politics can be explained as the effect of a 'transhistorical systemic logic' that can be understood in 'abstraction from the social relations of lordship' (Teschke 1998: 342). The point is to identify differences between the medieval and modern international systems and to highlight the latter's distinctive features and potentialities. One major difference is that the organizing principles of the modern states-system have broken with the belief that economic appropriation by force is permissible (although such behaviour remained acceptable in relations between Europe and the outside world long after it had been forbidden within Europe). As historical materialists argue, that metamorphosis was largely the product of the bourgeois ideological claim that capitalist social relations are entered into by free and equal contractors (Teschke 1998: 353–4; Linklater 2011: 139ff.). The argument can be extended by noting that the struggle for land and wealth was integral to the competition for male and family honour. Competition for power and honour was rarely 'a Hobbesian struggle of all against all', but reflected deep-seated beliefs about justice, about what the participants regarded as theirs, as 'of right' (Honig 2001: 118–19; Hall and Kratochwil 1993: 488–9).

Those contrasting approaches rest on different interpretations of human motivation that raise familiar questions about the relative causal importance of economic and political factors, and about the comparative influence of material interests and ideational forces. Drawing on Hobbes, neo-realism portrays agents as egoistical interest-maximizers. Leaning towards the focus of the *Annales School* in comprehending the dominant mentalité of any era, social constructivists argue that the self – its identity and interests – is embedded in, and constituted by, normative social frameworks (Hall and Kratchowil 1993). Fittingly, structural realists explain the physical appropriation of the monasteries' land and wealth during the invasions in 'power-political' terms. Such behaviour was scarcely surprising when no higher authority could restrain the competition for security (Fischer 1993). To explain the knight's enthusiasm for crusading warfare, it is argued, there is no need to look further than the desire for material gain (Fischer 1992, 1993). Without denying the importance of such motives, others maintain that crusading frequently appealed to the devout who were motivated by religious condemnations of social disorder and evidently anxious to follow the Church's remonstrations that crusading warfare could atone for past sins and provide the route to salvation (Hall and Kratchwil 1993: 488). Innocent III argued that the knights of God could secure remission for sins by diverting violence away from pride or greed towards conquering the 'enemies' of Christendom (see Kaeuper 1999: 75ff. on the sin of killing fellow Christians when force could be deployed to overwhelm the 'enemies of Christ'). Important then was the power and authority that stemmed from the Church's 'monopoly of the most basic means of orientation', namely its controls of 'revealed religion, in large parts of Europe' (Elias 2009a: 135–6). The 'monopoly over the means of salvation' and the attendant right of 'excommunication' had more than 'spiritual connotations'; excommunication entailed 'exclusion from the legal community, usually with devastating social and material consequences' that can be usefully compared with 'the loss of citizenship today' (Teschke 1998: 348). Many crusaders who participated in religious warfare in the hope of absolution were prepared to bear significant material costs and to turn away from opportunities for personal enrichment that lay closer to hand (Tyerman 2005: 56; also Riley-Smith 2002 and Bumke 2000: 293ff. for a discussion of crusader motives). The observation that many regarded crusading warfare as 'an expression of Christian vocation second only to monasticism itself' has been interpreted as 'startling testimony' to how 'the power of ideas' shape conceptions of self-interest (Tyerman 2005: 57 and 70).

Efforts to demonstrate the importance of religious values and ideals, or to show that the central power struggles resemble those that inexorably develop in any self-help system, or to emphasize the influence of property relations, usually ignore the role of collective emotions in medieval 'civilizing' and 'decivilizing' processes. Sociological investigation must include the scope of identification between people and the psychological, as well as the social dimensions of the we–I balance and the related standards of self-restraint. Disputes between the advocates of different approaches to international relations often proceed without considering emotional attitudes to pain and suffering that are a central element of the dominant harm conventions in every society and fundamental to individual conscience formation. They are silent about the prevalent emotional responses to mental and physical suffering, and about what is permitted and forbidden with respect to the power to kill, injure, humiliate, exploit and in other ways harm people. They are reticent about whether or not the emotional world – the social habitus – of the ruling strata was indifferent to collective measures to reduce unnecessary suffering, recognized even the pragmatic utility of commitments to improve the circumstances of the vulnerable, or embraced such projects in an enthusiastic attempt to realize a vision of the good society (Linklater 2011: ch. 5). They neglect the ways in which, inter alia, feelings of shame or guilt, or pity or compassion, influence individual and collective behaviour. Examining those aspects of social and political interaction is crucial for a sociology of states-systems that is orientated towards understanding the complex relationship between violence and civilization in different eras.

Those last comments shape the following approach to portraits of medieval attitudes to violence and suffering that have been advanced by several major historical studies. On the one hand, there was the Church's role in endeavouring to secure or maintain domestic peace, to alleviate pain and personal anguish and to facilitate personal salvation. Christian doctrines of a community of the suffering united by the agonies of Christ found expression in the alms-houses, hospitals and related institutions that provided protection for the homeless, the sick, the orphaned, the abandoned and the insane (Sennett 2002: 158). Through those social inventions, some forms of Christianity revealed that they 'allied [themselves] ethically with poverty, with the weak, and with the oppressed – with all those who are vulnerable bodies' (Sennett 2002: 132). The emphasis on 'the equality of the humble' and on 'the power of poverty' was derived from religious constructions of Christ's body; perceived as 'low-born' and 'weak', his 'martyrdom was meant in part to restore honour' to those who were imprisoned by similar misfortunes in this world (Sennett 2002: ibid.). The association of Christ's suffering with the conditions of the oppressed led to ideologies of the 'universal vulnerability of the body, to which all men and women were liable, independent of class and civic status' (P. Brown 1990: 316). Affirming the connection between vulnerability and social solidarity – which is one link between the ancient Hippocratic School and contemporary moral and political philosophy – St Francis stated that 'in our bodies we contain the ethical yardstick for judging rules, rights, and privileges in society: the more these cause pain, the more our bodies know they are unjust' (Sennett 2002: 161). More recent secular variants that regard suffering as the most accessible point of solidarity between strangers are direct descendants of those theological standpoints (Linklater 2011: 105ff.). In the recent period, they have altered the balance of power between the two core understandings of the relationship between violence and civilization that was discussed earlier (see Introduction, p. 11ff., and Chapter 11, p. 426ff.).

But as stated earlier, no collective political project emerged that was designed to eradicate senseless suffering for its own sake. Crucially important was an embedded 'pessimism' about the prospects for reducing suffering in a world in which widespread misery seemed to be the natural order of things and where fortune dominated and 'resignation' prevailed (see Le Goff 1988: 165ff. who links the limited role of meliorist policies with the prevalent conceptions of time that included the widespread tendency to look back to an imagined Golden Age and to suppose that the world was coming to an end). Unlike the inhabitants of stable, affluent societies that have largely eradicated serious disease, medieval populations were necessarily attuned to suffering caused by famine, pestilence and war. It is hardly surprising that the threshold of repugnance for human suffering was higher than it is today. But other factors were also relevant. Unlike modern societies that have turned health and physical wellbeing into the highest social ideals, medieval peoples were gripped by dolorist world views that displayed great ambiguity towards, if not plain contempt for, the body – the tarnished vessel whose principal value was that it provided a container for the immortal soul. The temporary sufferings of the body were little compared with each person's potential destiny – eternal salvation or damnation. Powerful strands of thought portrayed suffering as a personal test of faith, or exalted pain as a means of participating in the suffering of Christ, or maintained that the experience of physical anguish was essential for enjoying unity with others in a community of the suffering that struggled together in the hope of ultimate redemption (Merback 1999: ch. 4).

Systems of punishment provide a window onto civilizing processes and specifically onto collective beliefs about pain and suffering, and to interrelated distinctions between permissible force and intolerable violence; they illuminate the larger tapestry of harm conventions and the dynamics of conscience formation (Linklater 2011: chs. 1 and 4). Severe punitive methods that were prevalent for around a millennium included hanging for theft, breaking on the wheel for murder, rape and aggravated theft, burning at the stake in the case of witchcraft, heresy or sodomy, drowning for such offences against religious morality as adultery, as well as decapitation for robbery, manslaughter, incest and infanticide (Merback 1999: 140). 'Horrific torture-executions' that could last for hours were reserved for arch-criminals who had been found guilty of regicide or of attempted assassination (Merback 1999: ibid.).

Difficult issues have arisen around efforts to determine how far pleasure was derived from witnessing what is now regarded as cruel punishment. There seems little doubt that enormous satisfaction was derived from observing the application of *lex talionis* (the principle of an 'eye for an eye'), but the usual caveats apply. Generalizations across whole periods and across all regions are dangerous. It has been argued that torture in Paris from 1250 onwards was not as 'casual' as it had been before, and that 'torturers sought ecclesiastical assurances that they were causing pain to the devils inside, not to the person in whose body they lodged' (Sennett 2002: 162). Prolonged torture was often designed to afford the offender ample opportunity to confess publicly and to avoid suffering in Hell; it had 'a religious and in a certain way charitable purpose' (Sennett 2002: 298). There appears to have been more to witnessing public acts of vengeance than is suggested by the assumption that pleasure was found in theatrical spectacles of pain and suffering. Displays of the injured body demonstrated the justice of punishment. Making 'an act of violence public' declared 'its legitimacy', and 'might alleviate its consequences', whereas concealing the body could arouse suspicions that there was something to hide, and created the danger of retaliation that could spiral out of control (Halsall 1998: 15–16). The collective importance of the public spectacle of suffering is worth noting in the light of the later civilizing process. As Elias (2012: 77) maintained, one of the hallmarks of the Middle Ages was the public nature of so much conduct that, in the course of the civilizing process, came to be regarded as private, and as offensive or embarrassing if exposed to others (see Chartier 1989). An example is nudity. The same is true of punishment. In medieval communities, concealing judicial torture, execution and so forth would have clashed with social standards and expectations whereas, in line with 'civilized' mores, capital punishment is concealed from public view in the few remaining liberal societies where the practice still survives.[2]

For the reasons that have already been outlined, many advise caution with respect to Foucault's claims about the sharp rupture between the violent punishment of the body before the Enlightenment and the punitive methods of modern societies where the scope of emotional identification between people is wider than it was only a few centuries earlier (Dean 2001: ch. 6). The suffering of the martyrs and Christ's endurance on the cross gave the gruesome end to the criminal's earthly existence a collective symbolic significance that went beyond mere delight in public demonstrations of agonizing punishment. Enormous importance was attached to the good death (*bene moriendi*) in which, through final acts of repentance, offenders found peace with God and restored ruptured connections with their communities. Physical torment possessed redemptive and restorative qualities that ensured not only satisfaction in the spectacle of world-shattering pain but comfort in the renewal of social solidarity through the criminal's open admission of guilt in the presence of others and before God. By the same token, the suffering of those who failed to repent dramatically symbolized the plight that awaited the damned in hell (Merback 1999: 19–20, 221ff.).

Observations about the psychological state of the witnesses to such public rituals are necessarily speculative. Obvious difficulties arise in trying to establish whether the agents of violent punishment and the spectators thought they were cruel or unnecessarily harsh by the standards of the time (Merback 1999: 102, 143–4). With the Renaissance, the act and the suffering it caused rather than the underlying intention were foregrounded in moral and political thought as part of changing social orientations towards 'the

---

[2] Interesting tensions arise in relations between liberal and illiberal societies. The Western media displayed images of Saddam Hussein being led to the scaffold, but they did not show the hanging itself. With regard to the public display of the dead bodies of Hussein's two sons – in violation of what many regarded as 'civilized' standards of behaviour, US officials stated that it was essential for the Iraqi government to demonstrate that two leading representatives of the Ba'athist regime had indeed been killed ('Saddam's Sons Bodies Displayed', *The Guardian*, 15 July 2003). In short, the public nature of certain actions can produce shock or disgust in 'civilized' societies whereas in other communities the real offence is concealment.

body and the physical aspects of existence' (Baraz 2003: 25, 179). The threshold of repugnance with respect to violence was lowered as part of the civilizing process, as Elias argued. From the standpoint of many people in medieval communities, public displays of a greater aversion to pain would have been regarded as an abandonment of duties of care and as an assault on theological doctrine. Consequently, witnesses may have regarded some punitive acts as cruel and disgusting, as involving excessive violence against the body, but as essential because of the greater collective responsibility for the fate of the offender's immortal soul. Moreover, the focus was less on the deed than on the intention behind it. The moral purpose of saving souls by inflicting physical pain was central. Devout onlookers may have found emotional satisfaction in the successful use of the technologies of moral purification and may even have felt compassion for victims whose misconduct was regarded as evidence of their seizure by satanic forces (Merback 1999: 19–20; also Evans 1997: 104ff. on parallels with early modern Europe). With respect to witchcraft from the thirteenth century onwards, it has been stated that the witch was presumed to be linked with the Devil and controlled by demonic forces. The purpose of torture 'was to break that grip' so that the 'witch who confessed and perished in the flames had at least a chance of purging his or her guilt and achieving salvation' (Cohn 1993: 233). An insight into such strands of medieval thought can be found in Augustine's judgment that it was more loving to punish those who were 'injured by their sins' than to permit such a state of affairs to go unchecked, but it was wrong to derive pleasure from the victim's suffering or to act from the 'hatred which seeks to harm' rather than 'the love that seeks to heal' (Mastnak 2002: 63; Riley Smith 2002a: 42ff.). 'On the Augustinian model', pagan cruelties that inflicted pain on the body could be described as less cruel than abstentions from violence that jeopardized personal salvation (Baraz 2003: 17–19). An additional clue to medieval thinking is contained in Jerome's claim that, on occasion, the surgeon must be cruel to be compassionate – to cauterize rotten flesh to preserve the body, just as the Church had to cut out ailing members for the good of the whole (Baraz 2003: 17–18). Associating disease with sin, a quasi-medical discourse that justified violence against lepers could be extended to all those who were found guilty of corrupting society (Nirenberg 1996: ch. 2).

Elias referred to the widespread delight in 'ferocity, murder, torture, destruction and sadism' in the Middle Ages, and contrasted the abrupt emotional swings between 'kindness' and 'cruelty' in that period with the more evenly restrained lives of modern people whose emotions tend towards the midpoint of the spectrum, and who are more disposed to identify with each other as social equals (see Chapter 5). His account of the lust for violence and fluctuation between emotional extremes reflected what were at the time certain standard representations of the violent Middle Ages (see

Huizinga 1955: ch. 1, Bloch 1962: 410ff.). Although such interpretations of the medieval habitus have been criticized in recent years (Dean 2001: ch. 6), few quarrel with the claim that the inhabitants of medieval societies were accustomed to much greater violence than the members of 'civilized' societies are today, and attuned to the carefully contrived reputation for brutality that various groups created to intimidate or terrify enemies (Bartlett 1993: ch. 4). Elias maintained that the absence of stable monopolies of power was the main reason for permanent insecurities and for the joys of combat and the attunement to violence that was integral to the male warrior code. Attitudes to sexual violence are revealing. Rape (particularly group rape) and female abduction seem to have been commonplace in medieval settlements. The 'practice of seizing and making off with heiresses and other desirable women plagued early medieval society', despite various efforts by kings and bishops to prevent it (Brundage 1987: 148). High-ranking men could subject low-ranking women to sexual violence with relative impunity whereas 'the rape of noble women by men of lower classes' produced 'horror and outrage' (Murray 1996; also Bumke 2000: 327ff. and Dean 2001: 82ff.).

Ferocity in wars with outsiders – heretics and other outcasts as well as foreigners – was widespread in the period before state formation brought about the significant pacification of society. Even so, the question often arises of whether portraits of the violence of the age and claims about abrupt swings between cruelty and kindness and explosive outbursts of anger wrongly ascribed an infantilism to medieval populations that was supposedly left behind by the patterns of social refinement and maturation that lay ahead (Febvre in Burke 1973: 16–17). But wild emotional swings were not explained in terms of childishness or immaturity; for Elias, they were the consequence of specific social conditions such as recurrent violence, famine and plague that 'gave life a quality of permanent insecurity' (Elias 2012: 194ff.; Bloch 1962: 73).

According to some recent approaches, public outbursts of aristocratic anger often had the contrived strategic goal of communicating moral outrage at 'unjustifiable harm'; they were calculated responses to injury rather a childlike surrender to basic emotions (Peyroux 1998). The contention is that anger was deployed to convey the belief that a major rupture of social relations had occurred and to express the desire to reach an agreement about the terms of future non-violent coexistence (Barton 1998; White 1998). Displays of anger and violence were designed to draw attention to intense feelings about specific disputes, to rally support for the relevant cause and to declare an interest in third-party arbitration where no higher authority could enforce the judicial settlement of differences (Halsall 1998: 21). Calculated displays of anger publicized the intention to use force, but they may have helped to facilitate the 'civilized' resolution of disputes, although the danger of violent escalation was undoubtedly much greater than in modern 'civilized' societies where angry dispositions and threatening behaviour are largely discouraged and suppressed.

The assumption that anger displays were largely strategic runs the risk of regarding medieval people as basically similar in their emotional makeup to the members of modern civilized societies despite different social conditions. It is as if the angry posture was adopted for specific purposes, and that anger may not have been experienced by those involved. That they behaved in such ways is highly improbable. Interpreting the 'inner' states of mind of people in other periods is necessarily a highly speculative matter, but it is likely that disputants responded angrily and aggressively to assaults on their honour even though they may have been willing to explore opportunities to resolve major differences non-violently (Honig 2001: 121). Even so, any strategic dimensions to the deployment of anger are consistent with Elias's contention that medieval restraints on anger were weaker than in later 'civilized' societies. Anger was not condemned as a negative emotion that was associated with low levels of self-control and with the attendant dangers of avoidable and unwarranted violence – which is how it is generally understood in 'civilized' societies today (Linklater 2014).

The evidence suggests that anger displays rather like the pleasures of fighting – though not necessarily accompanied by joy in killing – were central to the knight's personal identity and social esteem (Thomas 2009: ch. 2). Revealingly, knights in England and Northern France *circa* 1050–1225 appear to have 'enjoyed fighting' but they were expected to combine courage with modesty, and to avoid pride (which was described as a Saracen vice) as well as recklessness (Bennett 1999). Averting risk was approved; rashness was not highly regarded. The honour code valued courage, prowess in battle and the acquisition of glory and posthumous fame in war or in the tourna-ment. The need for rigorous self-control in order to suppress personal fear (which was almost certainly shared with warrior groups in other eras) may have been more central to the habitus of the knight than the lust for killing (Bliese 1989; A. Taylor 1999; Verbruggen 1977: 39ff.). Avoiding shame as a result of displays of cowardice on the battlefield was crucial; the resulting social disgrace could blight the families of those involved for generations (Strickland 1996: ch. 4; Contamine 1984: 253ff.). Moreover, an appetite for cruelty, though rarely condemned, was not greatly valued amongst large sections of the warrior elite.

The Church repeatedly condemned cruel behaviour in its struggle to 'tame the warriors', but academic disputes continue about how far the Church was motivated by theological commitments to non-violence, by an ethical concern for the wellbeing of the vulnerable, and by the pragmatic objective of control-ling warriors who posed a threat to its specific interests and overall authority. Elias's analysis of the process of civilization did not devote much attention to its 'civilizing' role although it was noted, in passing, that the Church promoted 'the downwards diffusion of behavioural models' by flooding society with tracts on *civilité* (Elias 2012: 105). Elias stressed that sixteenth- and seventeenth-century notions of civility had come down from medieval notions of courtesy and courtliness. The relevant treatises formed a bridge to sixteenth- and seventeenth-century reflections on the virtues of civility that paved the way for later conceptions of civilization (Jaeger 1985).

How did the social preconditions of civility and civilization develop? One answer highlights parallels with classical Greek efforts to tame the Homeric warrior, to moderate the violent consequences of the honour code and to encourage the internalization of social expectations of greater, all-round self-restraint. Distinctions between good and bad anger illustrated how the clergy attempted to project Christian virtues across society by offering instruction in governance to the kings. Good anger stood against injustice, while bad anger was a destructive force because it was uncoupled from the obligations of civility and self-restraint (Barton 1998; Hyams 1998; Jaeger 1985; Knox 1991). The 'civilizing' role of the medieval courts must be considered in that light, as should religious efforts to promote a 'Christian ruler ethic' in the 'mirrors to princes' treatises that can be traced back to the seventh century and to the Carolingian era (Bumke 2000: 277-8; Althoff 1998: 61). Those writings were 'a reminder of the enduring legacy of the Roman belief that self-restrained moral conduct was the necessary precondition' for the rightful 'exercise of authority over others' (Smith 2005: 239ff.).

The 'Christian ruler ethic' that defended mercy and compassion advocated restraint or *disciplina*, a concept that was influenced by Roman ideas of urbanity that had been passed down by the writings of Seneca and Cicero (Stacey 2007: ch. 2). The discourse was linked with a larger movement in eleventh- and twelfth-century court society to distinguish between good rulers who displayed *clementia* and bad rulers or tyrants whose behaviour was governed by cruelty or *ferocitas* (Baraz 2003: ch. 4; also Althoff, Buhrer-Thierry, Hyams, and Little in Rosenwein 1998; Jaeger 1985: 129ff., 204ff.). According to the influential ideologies of kingship that circulated widely in the twelfth century, Christian rulers were exhorted not to 'oppress anyone unjustly by force', but to act as the 'defender of strangers, orphans, and widows', and to 'protect the churches and feed the poor'; moreover, from the thirteenth century, the influence of Seneca's writings reflected a growing 'cultural preoccupation with cruelty' that Renaissance thinkers would set against *humanitas* (Baraz 2003: 26, ch. 4). With images of Rome to hand, Christian thinkers drew on earlier ideas of merciful rule and moderate behaviour to forge the discourse of courtliness (*curialitas*) and related chivalric ideals. They constructed a distinctive vocabulary of politics that included ethical ideals such as the twelfth-century concept, *mansuetudo* – 'the civic virtue par excellence' – that owed more to Cicero's conception of aristocratic 'self-display' than to Christian notions of humility with their stress on human 'wretchedness' (Jaeger 1985: 36ff.). The concept was part of a broad cultural offensive to tame warrior impulses, to suppress anger and wrath and to encourage the renunciation of vengeance – they were elements of a collective quest to promote 'civilized interaction' (Jaeger 1985: ibid.).

Twelfth-century images of knighthood revolved around the virtues of *courtoisie*, or the manners and standards of restraint that befitted members of the court (Keen 1984: ch. 2). Early discourses on chivalry explicitly linked courtesy and combat, as represented by late twelfth-century ideals of 'courteous combat' or 'civil warfare' that helped to convert the 'knight as warrior' into 'the knight as courtly gentleman'.[3] Pertaining specifically to the knights was the notion of *mezura* that was designed to construct the boundaries between permissible and forbidden violence that warriors were expected to observe (Scaglione 1991: 50, 92). Also significant was Cicero's concept of *kalokagathia*, now transformed in accordance with Christian ideals to proclaim the inner virtues that were vital for the pacification or 'civilization' of the dominant personality traits of the knights (Jaeger 1985: 114ff; see also Chapter 1, p. 34). Linking the ruler ethic and the transformation of the warriors was the just war doctrine that upheld a 'civilizing' distinction between sheer necessity and the moral imperatives of self-restraint (Johnson 1981; Johnson 1987; Russell 1975). As will be discussed later, those ethical standpoints gave rise to a 'Janus-faced' civilizing process. The good ruler was thought to combine the commitment to upholding justice within the realm with the determination to use force against the enemies of Christendom and to enlist the knights in a 'holy war' or religious crusade.

Several authors have maintained that the medieval 'civilizing process' had its origins in the ethos of courtliness that developed between the ninth and thirteenth centuries (Elias 2006b: 201, 249; Elias 2012: 68–9; Vale 2001; Bartlett 2000: 580ff.). The secular elites in the twelfth- and thirteenth-century court societies whose orientation towards the world 'does not quite accord with the standard picture of the Middle Ages today' would influence not just that period but the whole civilizing process that was to come (Elias 2012: 191; Gillingham 2002: 287). Central to courtly practice was the ideal of

---

[3] Restraints on violence in relations between the knights became a crucial part of the honour code. However, 'even an increasingly courteous chivalry was fully compatible with and partially responsible for the practice of armed self-help, vengeance and private war which knights carried on with enthusiasm for centuries; it formed no barrier to the highly destructive campaigning by the armies of powerful proto-states as England and France filled more than a hundred years of later medieval history with their costly and destructive warfare' (Kaeuper 2000: 25).

controlling 'the reckless assertiveness of the European feudal nobility', limiting its 'freedom in manners and morals', restraining 'individual wilful-ness' and elevating the warrior class 'from an archaic and primitive stage of social and political life to a higher stage, imbuing it with ideals of modesty, humanity, elegance, restraint, moderation, affability, and respectfulness' (Jaeger 1985: 3; also Karras 2003 on the civilizing of 'knightly masculinity'). *Urbanus* ('Civilized Man') produced by Daniel of Beccles in the twelfth century – conceivably the first such courtesy book in England – has been described as asserting 'a new self-consciousness about etiquette and decorum', and about 'bodily restraint and self-control', in the relations between superiors and inferiors (Bartlett 2000: 582ff.). Those courtesy books may have been as much 'a monument to anxiety' as a guide to 'self-assurance'. They suggested that 'the civilized man' was 'a careful, controlled and worried individual' given that his was 'a touchy world, in which offence could be taken easily' (Bartlett 2000: 580ff.).

Anxiety and unease may have been intensified by twelfth- and thirteenth-century 'books of conduct' that argued for the 'feminizing of knighthood' and aimed to replace 'hypermasculine aggressiveness' with cultured behaviour especially in the presence of women at the royal courts (Bumke 2000: 196; Nicholls 1985). Sections of the warrior elite along with the conservative clergy resisted the 'feminizing' initiatives of the courts on the grounds that they would destroy the traditional 'fighting spirit' (Bumke 2000: chs. 5–6; Jaeger 1985: chs. 1 and 9). In the twelfth century, Ordericus Vitalis criticized the French court for promoting 'wanton youth . . . sunk in effeminacy', and for undermining the 'ways of men of honour from earlier days' (Jaeger 1985: 179ff.). Significantly, counterthrusts against such 'civilizing offensives' that equated the ideals of self-restraint with cowardice and unmanliness emerged as the Church launched the *Peace of God* (Jaeger 1985: 193–4). There is an important conclusion to draw for the analysis of medieval violence. Discussions of the ferocity of the medieval era that fail to mention the 'civilizing' influence of notions of *courtoisie* in elite circles perpetuate misleading divisions between the medieval, Renaissance and modern periods (Jaeger 1985: 15). Longer-term continuities that connect those phases are then concealed.

That is not to contend that references to the violence of the Middle Ages are wholly unreliable. The courtly ideal may have appealed to the warrior not only to restrain 'natural urges within the confines of the court' but also to live by new principles on the battlefield; in the latter domain, 'the splitting of skulls and the breaking of arms was a pleasure that was left to him only under strictly demarcated circumstances' – ideally, 'when the urge to indulge in it survived a sifting through ideals like humanity, compassion, gentleness, the renuncia-tion of revenge, and the service of justice, fair ladies and God' (Jaeger 1985: 211). But those aspirations did not completely transform the world of the knights, particularly those who escaped the influence of the courts (Bumke 2000: 311ff.). Classical notions of manliness as courage (*'viriliter'*) remained a powerful influence on the eighth- and ninth-century warrior ethos. Efforts to encourage 'persistence in faith and humble supplication' did not displace older social ideals that valued 'boldness in battle' (Stone 2011: 79–80). From the depths of that 'troubled epoch', Bloch (1962: 412) observed, there emerged a longing for kings to enforce the peace. In twelfth-century France, the *Peace of God* began to mutate into the *King's Peace,* the doctrine that royal power was indispensable in order to provide lasting relief from endemic violence and insecurity (Cowdrey 1970). The King's Peace has to be understood as part of a broader cultural shift in which 'courtliness and courtly humanity' and associated Christian ideals became 'the most powerful civilizing forces in the West' since Roman times (Jaeger 1985: 261). They gave shape to an early phase in the pacification of the European warriors.

Chivalrous Warfare

All societies must address the problem of how to distinguish between licit and illicit force in their harm conventions, but the medieval world had more reason than most – not because the level of violent harm was necessarily higher than in other epochs but because of the lasting influence of pacifist commitments in the early Church (Johnson 1987: ch. 1). From the earliest phases of its history, the apostles and missionaries who were described as the soldiers of Christ (*milites Christes*) or the soldiers of God (*milites Dei*) played a key role in determining Christian theory and practice (Bumke 2000: 290ff.). Participation in struggles to win converts to Christianity ruled out involvement in secular affairs – the knighthood of Christ (*militia Christi*) was separated from, and elevated above, the knights (*militia saecularis*) until approximately the end of the eleventh century when the conviction that secular violence could serve the faith gained support. The idea of the 'meritorious knighthood of God' (the new knighthood or *nova militia*) that replaced traditional images of 'secular robber-knights' was proclaimed by Bernard of Clairvaux in 1146 (Bumke 2000: 294ff.). Making the worldly requirement to kill in war entirely compatible with otherworldly considerations regarding salvation was a central problem for a 'faith-inspired' civilizing process. Early church proclamations that warriors should undergo penance for taking life, and cleanse themselves of impure motives such as fighting for personal gain or from anger or hatred, were often observed in practice – at least before the crusades significantly downgraded the duty not to kill with wrongful intent (Lowe 1997: 44; Tooke 1965). Penitential measures have been cited as evidence of attempts to restrain violence by denying the legitimacy of secular warfare (Verkamp 1993: ch. 2). But because of the positive evaluation of violence against heretics and other enemies, those practices were more or less obsolete by the end of the eleventh century (Verkamp 1993: ch. 3). Directed at the practices of secular chivalry, religious chivalry (a central influence on the civilizing process of the tenth and eleventh centuries) was held to be the key to reconciling the violence of the knight's mode of existence with public order. The *bellatores* were condemned for attacking the defenceless; they were urged to infuse their role with religious significance by protecting the *pauperes* (the poor, orphaned and widowed), and by displaying mercy on the understanding that enemies had rights (Kaeuper 1999: ch. 1). At the Council of Troyes in 1128, Bernard of Clairvaux condemned the chivalry of the 'secular militia' for institutionalizing the sin of homicide and for risking death without the possibility of final repentance. The new chivalric code enshrined in the harm conventions governing the Knights of the Templar that were established at Troyes integrated the obligations of the monastic and military ways of life. In response to the question of whether the Templars were monks or knights, Bernard announced that 'in truth they are worthy of both' (Contamine 1984: 74–5).

The religious transformation of secular chivalry therefore asserted that knights should become the 'strong right arm of the church' (Keen 1984: 4). Such was the influence of traditional knightly ideals that, initially, few responded to invitations to adopt that vocation. The Knights Templar and the Teutonic, Hospital and Spanish military orders were exceptions (Keen 1984: 49, 77). The condemnation of the tournament by Innocent II at the Council of Clermont in 1130, and the decision to deny participants the right to a Christian burial – because they had diverted military endeavours from religious ends – injected a sacred dimension into secular life that valued the standard virtues of courage, honour and military prowess. Opposition to the tournament may have done more to 'promote standards of civilized behaviour between belligerent forces' than other 'papal prohibitions, issued in the name of restraining undisciplined violence', ever did (Keen 1984: 94ff.). In any case, Pope John XXII revoked the ban in 1316. Although that particular project failed, the Church promoted the doctrine that, suitably civilized, the life of the warrior offered a pathway to salvation without retreating from the world in the manner of the monastic orders.

Knights frequently observed restrictions on force, but usually only in their relations with each other as a result of the 'we feeling' that bound them to their military caste but also because the Church could threaten to use its power of excommunication (Frassetto 1998). An example of mutual restraint was the practice of ransoming rather than killing prisoners of war. Ransom replaced the earlier practice of killing captured knights in England in the second quarter of the twelfth century (Hyams 1998: 107). Lacking all monetary value, 'commoners' were often put to death although they were spared when required to labour in conquered lands given that 'nobody wanted to rule over a desert'

(France 1999: 10ff.). The practice of ransom – which was often so severe as to bankrupt the families of those involved or to create penury through lasting debt – revealed the influence of material motives. Cruel ransoms that reduced women and children to poverty were condemned – at least early in the fifteenth century (Allmand 1998: 84). The chronicler, Honoré Bovet argued that not only should captives be spared, but both imprisonment and ransom should be 'courteous' and not lead to penury for the captive and his family. Nevertheless, the effect was that knights often departed for war knowing that it was very possible that their lives would be spared. Ransom may have reflected the influence of Christian values but it was also anchored in reciprocity – in the plain fact that warriors might meet again and that acts of cruelty might well rebound upon the perpetrators (Contamine 1984: 255–6). In general, they could presume that most adversaries would honour the social standards of self-restraint that protected captured knights from ill-treatment. Violations of the law of ransom were often regarded as amongst the 'most heinous of atrocities in war'; 'habitual cruelty on a large scale' towards knights seems to have been the exception rather than the rule in major conflicts although private feuds did not always respect the same constraints on violence (Strickland 1996: 199ff.). Needless to say, the relevant harm conventions were often breached, but estimates of war casualties suggest that they had a significant 'civilizing' effect. On one calculation, as few as seven knights per thousand were killed in a single year of conflict in the Flanders' regions *circa* 1127 (Contamine 1984: 256). Some regard for fellowship in war rather than joy in killing is suggested by such statistics. Chivalric standards of restraint were internationalized. Reflecting the scope of emotional identification, an aggrieved French knight could appeal, at least in principle, to English military authorities or to a court of chivalry with responsibility for enforcing the rules of ransom (Keen 1965: chs. 3–4; Strickland 1996: 46ff.).

Especially from the thirteenth century, deliberations about chivalry inquired into the ethics of attacking the defenceless; they addressed the practice of group assaults on a solitary opponent which many condemned as the disgraceful transgression of the 'civilized' convention of single combat (Kaeuper 1999: 170). As previously noted, those sensibilities did not always prevent mass slaughter, especially in pitched battles, infrequent though they were in the age of the knights (Bumke 2000: 165ff.). The Swiss and German mercenary forces seldom gave quarter, nor did Henry V at Agincourt, or political authorities in struggles with rebellious movements (Vale 1981: ch. 5). Believing that the arrival of additional enemy forces was imminent, Henry broke with customary practice in Anglo-French wars by ordering the execution of most of the French prisoners, contrary to the wishes of English knights who looked forward to the rewards of ransom. For that task, Henry turned to the bowmen who did not subscribe to the knights' code of conduct. Even so, there was very 'little contemporary criticism of his action'

(Keen 1984: 221).[4] More generally, the greater involvement of groups that were not drawn from the knights led to the steady decline of the traditional restraints on violence (Lowe 1997: 56; see Rogers 1993 on how the rise of the archers created the fear that the 'knightly' civilized code was in terminal decline). Estimates of the effect on war casualties are imprecise. As noted above, they were often low in medieval conflicts, but in the Hundred Years War, and especially during the fourteenth and fifteenth centuries, the number killed in battle may have risen to approximately twenty to fifty per cent of the forces involved. One of the consequences was that pitched battles became comparatively rare (Contamine 1984: 257–8).

The laws of chivalry certainly did not spare the 'lower orders' the miseries of warfare. During the Hundred Years' War, the sense of we-identity between knights from different societies was probably stronger than feelings of solidarity between 'social superiors' and 'inferiors' in the particular regions to which they belonged (Barnie 1974: 70ff.; Meron 1998:7). War chronicles contain many illustrations of the slaughter of innocents and the devastation that was inflicted on human settlements as the knights attempted to maximize the profits of warfare through seizing booty (Keen 1965: ch. 11). The expenditure of equipping themselves with weaponry and armoury, and the physical dangers of conflict, led many to regard the spoils of war as their just reward. Armies often levied protection money (*appatis*) from local communities in exchange for offering some guarantee of freedom from pillage (Allmand 1998: 85). The frequent absence of military discipline, combined with the lack of regular payment, often led soldiers to organize as 'freelance bands' that lived off the land, but even the best-equipped armies lacked the resources to remain deep in enemy territory for long.

The increased use of mercenary forces in the later Middle Ages had the effect that, at war's end, disbanded troops were free to pillage the areas they travelled through. The adverse effects of peace were especially evident when demobilization led, as in France, to levels of violence in the countryside that were only partly ended with the rise of standing armies *circa* 1445 in the reign of Charles VII. In that period, a central 'monopoly over the raising and maintenance of troops in the kingdom' remained difficult to enforce (Vale 1988: 323). Mercenary companies were especially hard to control. The need

---

[4] Bohemian knights protested that the Austrians violated the laws of nobility at the battle of Laa in 1246 by using arrows that pierced their armour (Bumke 2000: 173). Their words fell on deaf ears. In 1139 The Second Lateran Council prohibited the use of various weapons against co-believers, including the crossbow, in an attempt to deal with the increasing problem of mercenaries who showed little regard for the rules of war (Bumke 2000: 174; also Johnson 1987: 89). The Church decided in 1179 to excommunicate mercenaries who were 'fighters in their own right' and not subject to the public authorities that were entitled to use force (Percy 2007: 80).

to live off the land – in order to avoid starvation at times – goes some way towards explaining their low levels of compassion for powerless victims (Zajac 1997).

But as the discussion has shown, mercenaries did not monopolize looting. Critics of that practice were often motivated not by revulsion at the lack of humanity, or by emotional identification with the victims, but by outrage at the collapse of military discipline (Kaeuper 1999: 185) Whole areas could be subjected to 'the indiscriminate pillaging' by a soldiery that may have observed chivalric restraints in their relations with each other while behaving more or less as they wished towards the *pauperes* (Keen 1984: 228ff.). Such violence was not deemed to transgress the rules of chivalry. Religious authorities tried to persuade the knights of their social responsibilities for protecting the weak, but they usually ignored such pressures in the face of what they regarded as the imperatives of warfare (Strickland 1996: ch. 10). The devastation wrought by passing armies has been compared to a plague. Armies in the fifteenth century often stripped the land like swarms of locusts, and public authorities were often unable to stop them. There was no sharp dividing line 'between normal military service and brigandage, between an army company and a robber band' (Geremek 1990: 358). That reality had been pronounced during the Hundred Years' War when whole societies were subjected to large-scale violence. As in the case of the cavalry raids (*chevauchées*) that were initiated by Edward, the Black Prince, brutality against local communities in France was intended to destroy morale before delivering the *coup de grace* on the battle-field (Allmand 1998: 2; Rogers 2002). The growing trend in the thirteenth century towards levying war contributions from non-combatant communities made conflict a societal phenomenon in which the barriers between military and non-military life broke down (Allmand 1999: 260ff.). Individual lives might be spared, but property was invariably seized as of right. Those examples of excessive force did not completely destroy the humanitarian impulse. The slaughter of the inhabitants of Limoges in 1370 by the army of the Black Prince was condemned for its cruelty by chroniclers such as Froissart who inquired how the victors could be so pitiless towards the three thousand or more men, women and children who 'were dragged out to have their throats cut' (cited in Barnie 1974: 7ff. who states that the sack of that particular city, while 'certainly vicious' was 'not outstandingly so' by the standards of the time). The moral concern for the wellbeing of non-combatants that became more pronounced during the late fourteenth century expressed 'fellow-feeling if not ... compassion', but earlier human calamities had not always passed unnoticed (Allmand 1998: 132; Allmand 1999: 271). Chroniclers condemned what they saw as impermissible violence, or as an insistence on victor's rights that ignored the requirement for mercy, but there was less criticism of armies who stormed cities. As was the practice in the ancient world, sympathies declined when the inhabitants decided against surrender, bringing the risk of destruction on themselves. Victorious armies hoped to overwhelm such cities in order to seize substantial booty. Siege warfare created the very real possibility of death and dispossession, physical displacement and slavery during the Crusades.

Violence against women warrants particular attention because rape (rarely mentioned in the first three centuries of Christian moral thinking) became a serious ethical issue for medieval canonists and jurists. At the end of the eleventh century, canon law classified rape as a crime against the female victim although the civil law usually defined it as a crime against kindred males (Brundage 1987: 73, 107, 209–10, 311ff.). Women were typically prizes in war – property to be seized or assets to be defended for the sake of honour. The forced appropriation of women was commonplace in the early Middle Ages but comparatively rare in later times (Klapisch-Zuber 1990). Medieval writings often celebrated the chivalric defence of women from rape and supported the punishment of rapists in addition to highlighting the particular dangers that women faced when knights seized them from each other. The idealized three orders of society took no account of the circumstances of women. The harm conventions that dealt with their treatment by men were split between the code that applied to aristocratic women and the more permissive standards regarding low-status women who were largely 'outside the debate' (Kaeuper 1999: 225ff.). Tensions over sexual violence were a manifestation of the more general problem of maintaining self-restraint in male warrior cultures (Kaeuper 1999: 225ff.). The difficulties are captured in the observations in Chretien's Lancelot that the dominant customs dictated that 'any knight meeting a damsel who is alone should slit his own throat rather than fail to treat her honourably, if he cares about his reputation'. The knight who seized a woman 'by force' would be 'shamed forever in all the courts of all lands'. But if a woman was taken by another, and 'some knight desires her [and] is willing to . . . fight for her in battle, and conquers her, he can without shame or blame do with her as he will' (cited in Kaeuper 1999: 227). Efforts to refine chivalric codes to restrain violence against women reaffirmed gender inequalities by constructing the idealized male protector of the 'damsel in distress'. Even so, with 'the spread of courtly culture' during the twelfth century, romantic images of 'courtly love' and the desire to 'serve his lady and win honour for her' exercised a 'civilizing' influence on the knights (Robinson 2006: 62, 77–9).

Many later medieval texts raised concerns about the particular dangers to which women were especially exposed, and reflected a more general interest in the plight of the vulnerable in military conflicts. Around 1416, the Norman, Alain Chartier, described war from the perspectives of four women, and highlighted the devastating effects that Agincourt had on them and on their families (Allmand 1999: 268–9). The ordinances of war that had been promulgated by Henry V in 1419, as well as earlier codifications of chivalry, prohibited rape and affirmed the warrior's duty to protect women (Meron 1998: 5). Such treatises on chivalry warrant attention alongside the manners books that Elias examined in his explanation of the civilizing process (Cardini 1990: 109; see also Chapter 5 herein). Social restrictions on rape were usually subject to the qualification that women had not previously been captured in siege warfare. Under those circumstances, the triumphant seemed to subscribe to the principle that 'anything goes' with the 'right of storm' but, frequently, they were prepared to negotiate surrender with the special proviso that 'Christian captives [should] not be enslaved' (see Meron 1998: 56, 72, who adds that different standards applied in relations with Eastern Christians during the crusades; see also Strickland 1996: ch. 8).[5]

Religious opposition to secular violence was embodied in the *Peace of God* and in the *Truce of God*.[6] They were the main forms of ecclesiastical legislation of the time that symbolized the Church's efforts to deal with the disorder that followed the collapse of public authority (especially south of the Loire). The *Peace of God* was intended to protect non-combatants, and specifically priests, merchants and labourers from violent harm. Particular emphasis was placed on respecting church buildings and property that knights were often inclined to appropriate, on safeguarding the clergy, and on protecting agricultural production in the context of recurrent famine (Frassetto 1998). The *Peace of God* did not contain a vision of equal entitlements to personal security. There was no universal declaration of the rights of peasants to be protected from violence as fellow human beings: they only deserved consideration because of their value as labourers (Goetz 1992). Nor did the peace outlaw feuding in self-defence (Goetz 1992). For its part, the *Truce of God* initially banned warfare between Saturday evenings and Monday mornings. The prohibitions were later extended to include all periods of religious significance, and their geographical scope was enlarged from the diocese of Elne and the county of Roussillon to all parts of Latin Christendom. The *Truce of God* restricted violence between Christians but authorized the use of force against heretics and infidels (for example during the crusades). Although it organized peace militias, the Church lacked the coercive resources to enforce the *Truce of God*, but its role in defining enemies of the faith demonstrated its

---

[5] Henry V is said to have applied the following reading of Deuteronomy: when advancing on a city, 'make an offer of peace'; if it surrenders, 'all the people in it shall be put to forced labour'; if stormed, it is legitimate 'to put all its males to the sword', to take the cattle, women and dependents, and to rape and plunder freely (Bradbury 1992: 302, 317).

[6] On their antecedents, see Johnson (1987: 79ff.) who refers to the Council of Le Puy in 975, where Bishop Guy of Anjou imposed an oath on the knights to respect the possessions of the peasants as well as the Church, and the Council of Charroux in 989 that diminished the responsibility to peasants and upgraded the duty to protect ecclesiastical persons and property.

power to channel violence in particular directions, and that may have been its greatest influence (Johnson 1987: 87–8).

In its defence of a 'new, higher universality' at the ecclesiastical council in Narbonne in 1054 the Church decreed that 'no Christian should kill another Christian, for whoever kills a Christian undoubtedly sheds the blood of Christ' (Mastnak 2002: 36ff.). With the *Peace* and *Truce of God*, religious authorities made a concerted effort for the first time to limit armed hostilities, bypassing secular leaders in the process and dealing directly with the knights. Their support was essential for pacification, and praise was lavished on those who placed their arms in the service of the church. The sacralization of violence created a condition in which the relevant authorities could steer the use of force towards the religious and political objectives that animated successive crusades (Keen 1984: 27, 47). Exporting violence was one of the ways in which the Church promoted pacification, apparently with some success (Keen 1984: 48–9). Medieval chroniclers were 'well aware that at the start of a crusade the people at home in the old countries always breathed more freely, because now they could once more enjoy a little peace' (Bloch 1962: 296).

What became apparent then, as in earlier eras, was that enlisting the knights in religiously sanctioned violence invariably combined Christian virtues with the sinister practices of the marauders and booty-hunters. There was no systematic attempt to keep the two roles apart, and indeed there was a general tendency to muddy the waters regarding the practical obstacle of reconciling the ethics of chivalry with the predictable consequences of the power disparities between knights and the settlements that were plagued by passing or disbanded armies. Similarly, there was little serious consideration of the probable relations between victorious Christian forces and defeated Saracens during the crusades. Many knights took what they wanted from religion to dignify their military role, and they ignored anything that challenged their 'honour and entitlement' (Kaeuper 1999: 47). Notwithstanding their civilizing dimensions, notions of chivalry prolonged conflict by idealizing the male warrior and encouraging violence to acquire material gains. They helped to turn warfare into a business that ensured that the horrors of war were 'endemic' (Keen 1976: 45).

The Church assumed that God in his wisdom would draw the moral distinctions that secular authorities were unwilling to make and largely powerless to enforce. As for the knights, they believed that God would forgive temporary lapses from the chivalric code that occurred during periods of personal hardship and danger that constituted a form of penance (Keen 1984: 232–3; Kaeuper 1999: 50). Donations to the Church – including proceeds from booty – and deathbed contrition were calculated to appease the clergy and to solicit prayers for salvation (Kaeuper 1999: 86–7). Critics of religiously legitimated violence lamented the decline of chivalry, and expressed anxieties about the marriage of force and the faith. Huizinga (1955: 102) expressed a widely held conviction that chivalry was often little more than a charade, but it appears that, at times, it moderated violence and preserved the commitment to mercy if only to exhibit the knights' love of honour (Keen 1965). Whether it placed a 'serious check on the looting, widespread destruction, and loss of non-combatant lives that seem to have been the constant companions of warfare' is a different matter (Kaeuper 1999: 185). The evidence is that ransom 'helped to prevent unnecessary bloodshed in the field' but, as noted earlier, circumstances were very different for those who did not belong to the military elite: 'the civilians, and above all the humble, suffered untold hardships in war. The awful tales in descriptions of . . . men hung, roasted, or dragged behind horses in order to extract a few pennies of ransom from them, testify to conduct which can only be described as barbaric and inhuman' (Keen 1965: 243). However, chivalry and the just war doctrine with which it would be allied were important features of medieval civility and significant influences on the later process of civilization. Forged in the context of multiple authorities rather than centralized power, they upheld ethical ideals about restraining violence and avoiding unnecessary suffering that contributed to advances in domestic pacification (Elias 2012). But that was not their only effect. Further revealing the ambiguities of civilizing processes, they unleashed 'decivilizing processes' that reached their apogee with the crusades and that would have the longer-term effect of increasing support for doctrines of national chivalry that were used to channel human loyalties towards emergent state structures. The whole process would give new shape to the tensions within 'civilized' approaches to violence that were described earlier.

Crusading Warfare

Following Constantine's conversion to Christianity in AD 312, the idea of the just war was formulated as a compromise between the pacifism of the first Christian thinkers and the necessity of defending the Roman Empire. Pacifism continued to enjoy monastic support but two political pressures – dealing with the 'Christianized Germanic military elite' and resisting 'new external threats' from Vikings, Magyars and Muslims following the demise of Charlemagne's empire in the ninth century – led to the doctrinal accommodation with violence (Tyerman 2005: 70ff.). However much it tried to Christianize the warrior groups that had become the dominant political-military actors, the Church had no choice in its own eyes but to come to terms with the prevailing martial virtues. As previously stated, efforts at converting the Germanic peoples involved Christianizing the warrior ethos but not without a corresponding militarization of the Church that took place because of the laity's physical capacity to resist the 'barbarian' invasions (Erdmann 1977: introduction; Housley 2002: ch. 1; Tyerman 2005: 71). Even so, pacifism and the belief that violent 'combat remained sinful' remained influential within the Church.

From Carolingian times, religious authorities distinguished between publicly authorized legitimate warfare (*bellum*) and illicit private feuds (*guerra*). Those involved in the former modes of conflict received 'lighter penances' in that particular understanding of the relationship between civilization and violence (Tyerman 2005: 73).

The peaceful dissemination of Christian beliefs had been preferred to conversion by the use of the sword but, as in the case of crusading warfare against Muslims and early thirteenth-century struggles against the Albigensian 'heretics' in the Languedoc, force became the chosen method of promoting a religious 'civilizing process' east of the Elbe. Religious violence would become linked in the course of subsequent crusades with the weakening of distinctions between the infidel and the heretic, and with a shift towards the corrective use of force by the 'civilized' against heathens who were characterized as 'apostates and rebels, despisers of Christianity and traitors' (Johnson 1975: 574). The crucial outsider would become the heretic who was the presumed repository of evil and the cause of *maleficium* (harm by occult means). If the trial of heretics was conducted in order to reconcile the guilty party with God, the extermination of the infidel was undertaken to eradicate the evil that resulted from open pacts between wrongdoers and the devil or from the covert infiltration of demonic influences (Cohn 1993). Discourses that promoted the 'Christianization of war' described the destruction of evildoers as 'malicide' (Cardini 1990: 88; Russell 1975: 36ff.). Their representations of the 'infidel' influenced early twelfth-century Christian ideas about the morality of force that found distinctive expression in St Bernard's depiction of the Knights Templar. By killing the 'enemies of Christ', the thesis was, the Templars did not commit evil but ended the oppression of true believers who were in danger of being led towards iniquity (Contamine 1984: 75).

The use of physical violence to convert or subdue non-Christians represented a major change in the *jus ad bellum* provisions of the just war. The relevant articles had restricted the use of force to self-defence, to recovering seized property and to ending injustices (Johnson 1981, 1987). The final part of that rationale for force had not permitted public authorities to wage war against infidels if they were innocent of causing the harms that have just been listed. But in formulating the idea of a 'holy war', those who instigated the crusades inflated the meaning of harm. That was most explicit in the stance taken by Cardinal Odo of Chateauroux who, in the 1240s, advanced a 'harm principle' in defence of crusading warfare. He asked what was to be made of a believer who turned his back on crusading on the grounds that 'the Muslims have not hurt me at all'. If such a person 'thought well about, it he would understand that the Muslims do great injury to every Christian' (cited in Riley-Smith 1992: 24). The early defence of the crusading vocation employed that enlarged conception of harm to describe the permanent injury that arose from 'infidel' occupation of lands that had once belonged to Christians. Justifications appealed to familial obligations and to love for fellow men. They exploited duties to assist the lords and they traded on emotional traits that resonated with the obligatory rituals of the aristocratic feud. Parallels between crusading warfare and the 'blood feud' to protect honour were evident in the principle of taking up arms for Christ and in settling accounts with those who had 'harmed members of Christ's family' (Riley-Smith 2002a: 49). Willingness to fight was portrayed as a demonstration of love for fellow Christians who had been compelled to submit to infidel domination, and as dutiful conduct that aimed at recovering the Lord's inheritance. The upshot was the deliberate fusion of piety and violence (Tyerman 2005: 105–6). Papal declarations referred to the 'crime of infidelity' in failing to assist the Lord in need. According to Innocent III, a temporal king had the right to condemn unfaithful subjects who had failed to assist him if he was deposed and captured. In a similar manner, Christ could reasonably chastise those who repaid his love with 'the vice of ingratitude' and with the refusal to participate in restoring his legitimate authority (Riley-Smith 2002a: 36–7). The decision not to join the struggle to liberate the Holy Land was described then as unworthy resignation to preventable injury to the family of Christ, as a reprehensible version of 'omissive harm' (Linklater 2011: 102–3).

Efforts to release Muslims from sinful error were similarly described as displaying love and compassion for 'fellow men', although it must immediately be stressed that, in the writings of Peter Lombard and others, the duty to love one's enemies was a supplement to the primary obligation to assist Christians in the East (Riley-Smith 2002a). From the standpoint of the Church leaders, the violence of crusading warfare could be 'civilized' by ensuring that justice was observed, and that military conduct was not suffused with cruelty and hatred but assiduously observed the standards of self-restraint that were required by the principles of *ius in bello*. Crusading warfare was to be conducted for the benefit of the foe as well as to promote the just cause of the instigators; love for the enemy would ensure that war would be free from the unnecessary cruelties that occurred in wars that were fuelled by hatred. Anger and enmity had to be expunged from warfare, as St Augustine had argued (Contamine 1984: 264–5). Whenever they intruded, confession and atonement were imperative.

How far were crusaders from the late eleventh century onwards motivated, or held in check, by those fine conceptions of 'civilized' self-restraint? To what extent did crusaders habitually disregard Church prohibitions against killing from impure or sinful motives, and how far were they wedded to the doctrine that 'the barbarian had no rights' that would be so central to 'realist' thought in the age of European colonial expansion (Wight 1991: ch. 4)? To what extent was a deepening of insider–outsider dualisms that would become more pronounced in the future course of the 'civilizing process' the main legacy of the crusades? The questions draw attention to the dynamic relationship between two faces of the religious civilizing process. In the first case, civilization acted as a restraint on violence at least between Christians, as required by the Peace and Truce of God; in the second, it authorized the use of force against unbelievers in which the righteous were bound to claim special – if not absolute – liberties to depart from the customary restraint in wars between Christians. How the crusading forces negotiated the tensions between the two perspectives to violence and civilization is the interesting question.

Just war thinkers believed that a crusade had to comply with the central tenets of *ius in bello*, but the violence of successive crusades reflected the widespread belief amongst the crusading ranks that almost any act was permissible if it helped defeat the 'infidel'. The process of rethinking earlier theological standpoints on the use of violence against heretics and infidels had led to the emphasis on the penitential rewards for involvement in the Eastern crusades (similar views about the spiritual gains of waging crusading wars against heretical Christians would develop later). The orthodox conviction that the warrior should undergo penance for taking life from impure motives such as hatred or personal gain was steadily downgraded (Lowe 1997: 44). Those who decried the decision to promise salvation to those who fought against other Christians lamented what Sigebert of Gembloux called the 'window of wickedness' that had been 'opened to mankind' (Housley 2002a). Suffice it to add that later revulsion against the fanaticism of the crusades has long influenced the view that the Middle Ages in their entirety were consumed by levels of violence and cruelty that modern 'civilized' societies have largely eradicated (Baraz 2003: conclusion).

Initiating the first crusade in a sermon at Clermont on 27 November 1095, Urban II appealed to the devout to aid Eastern Christians who faced a growing Turkish threat (a request for military assistance had been made by envoys of the Byzantine emperor, Alexius I, earlier that year). Gregorians such as Leo IX (1049–54) and Gregory VII (1073–85) had prepared the way for such a plea by arguing that violence was praiseworthy in a good cause, a stark contrast with the latter's councillors who argued 'against the use of force even in defence of the faith or in the struggle with heretics' (Kaeuper 1999: 64). Crusading warfare was linked with older conceptions of chivalry in the hope and expectation that the knights would be absorbed into, and reconciled with, the world of Christianity. They were implored in their new role, and with new responsibilities to free Christ's tomb in Jerusalem from Muslim control, to expand Western Christian influence and to seize the opportunity to reunite the Church.[7] According to the cleric, Baudri of Bourgueil, who was present at

---

[7] Historians have debated whether Urban was mainly concerned with assisting the Eastern Church as opposed to liberating Jerusalem. No text with the exact words of the sermon at Clermont exists (see Cowdrey 2002; Blake 1970 and also Erdmann 1977).

Clermont, Urban called on 'you oppressors of orphans, you exploiters of widows, you murderers, you temple thieves, you pillagers of property not yours' to relinquish the love of violence or to use it against the infidel, if they cared for their souls (Osiander 2007: 226). Similar reformist ideals to those that were expressed in the Peace and Truce of God informed the dominant discourse of crusading warfare (Keen 1984: 48). By sanctifying violence as a means of atoning for past sins, the Peace introduced themes that would become central to the public ideology of the first crusade (1096–1102), namely that participating as pilgrims in a 'devotional war' could secure absolution (Lowe 1997: 28).

As noted above, the Peace outlawed force between Christians while authorizing its use against infidels. Urban II linked the violence of the crusade with the vision of pacifying Christendom that had been proclaimed at Narbonne (Cowdrey 1970). The overall level of violence may well have increased in the eleventh century as the Church attempted to restrain force within its jurisdiction while permitting the warrior to indulge traditional warlike pursuits in other regions (Stacey 1994). That was the unsurprising consequence of a religious 'civilizing offensive' to alter the conventional we–I balance by calling on the warriors to identify with an 'established' Christian brotherhood that was set against Muslim 'outsiders'. Moreover, according to some interpretations, Urban's vision of a crusade represented a break with the past by introducing dehumanizing images of Islam that were centred on the alleged cruelties of 'the Saracen' (Asbridge 2004: 33). Whether he did or not, devotional warfare combined pilgrimage and penance; it offered the knightly aristocracy the prospect of relief from the guilt and fear of sinning that were intrinsic features of the life of violence; and it restated the principle that 'Christianized' force offered the warrior a pathway to salvation. But, unsurprisingly, what some regarded as a virtuous combination of sacred violence and brotherly love as expressed in the ideal of dying for fellow Christians was, for the critics, a disastrous compromise with the laity that weakened the necessary moral constraints on hatred and greed (Riley-Smith 2002). Their complaint was that efforts to harmonize the Christian ethos with the knights' warrior culture led to the former's 'martial contamination' (Heath 1995). Undoubtedly, the acquisition of land and booty was an important part of crusader motivation. Given the dominant harm conventions regarding the spoils of war, it is safe to presume that crusaders expected to gain their share of the booty that was taken from captured cities in the Holy Land. Presumably Urban II recognized as much, despite preaching at Clermont that those who profited in that way would jeopardize their spiritual reward although, on some accounts, he held out the promise of such wealth to rally support for the crusade (see Bumke 2000: 294; also Zajac 1997 and Duncalf 1969: 244–5). Still, there is ample evidence that many knights were motivated by religious idealism rather than pecuniary ambitions and the desire for plunder, and incurred substantial financial costs by participating in crusading warfare (Riley-Smith 2002a).

A distinctive 'civilizing process' underpinned the ideology of crusading warfare, but how far traditional 'civilized' self-images that urged restraints on force influenced practice is another matter. Questions arise about the degree to which warriors observed – or were expected to obey – the eleventh-century law of arms (*jus armorum*) that enunciated the basic principles concerning obligations to non-combatants (Lowe 1997: 2). Urban II may have assumed that the knights who implemented the Church's policy towards the Holy Land would comply with the relevant provisions of the laws of war. But the reformist fervour of the period encouraged people from various social strata to answer the papal call for arms with extraordinary zeal. Significant numbers were indifferent to those laws and were, in any case, beyond the control of the Church and indeed of any secular power that might have wished to restrain violence (Kaeuper 1999: 147). It is probable that many church leaders were surprised, if not exactly shocked, by the violence against the Jews that began with the pogroms of 1096 in the Rhineland and Northern France (Katz 1994: 323ff.). When reports of the violence reached the east, several Jewish groups anticipated the outcome of crusader victory, and immediately sought refuge in the larger fortified settlements. Their defensive measures did not prevent the conquest from becoming 'as much a calamity for the Jewish communities as it was for the Muslims'; Jews died defending Jerusalem in 1099 and Haifa in 1100, and many were exterminated along with the rest of the population of the cities of Antioch, Jubail and Beirut (Prawer 1985: 95).

The violent sack of Jerusalem in 1099 seems to leave no doubt that the standard customs of war did not apply to Muslims although several scholars have argued that warfare within Christendom and crusading warfare did at times proceed along similar lines, that certain standards of self-restraint crossed the 'boundaries of race and religion', but that the 'terms of surrender' were usually 'much harsher' in conflicts between Christians and Muslims than in struggles between Christians (France 2008: 168; Bradbury 1992: 190–1; 297; Kedar 2002: 243). The traditional harm conventions prevailed in that a city's failure to surrender risked massacre or enslavement, which was the fate of the Muslim and Jewish inhabitants of Jerusalem and Haifa, and of the 'outsiders' in at least four other cities between the end of the eleventh and the middle of the following century. In Haifa, the Muslim and Jewish populations seem to have been offered the choice between conversion to Christianity (in which case they could retain their property and other rights) and maintaining their religious convictions (in which case they were forced to accept the terms of Frankish rule or face exile). Rejecting capitulation, the city was stormed, the population was massacred and, in a parallel with the classical 'toil of the spear', homes were taken in accordance with the existing 'law of conquest' that recognized the rights of the first person to leave their mark upon them (Kedar 2002: 243;

Prawer 1985a: 130). Sieges that ended with a negotiated surrender often allowed Muslims to move to areas under Muslim control although Genoese allies of the Franks turned the exodus at Acre in 1104 and at Tripoli in 1109 into massacres (Kedar 2002: 243). Harm conventions in areas under crusader rule prohibited the enslavement of Latin Christians, but enslaving Muslims, Jews and Eastern Christians who had been captured in war was widespread. Freedom from servile status could be secured through conversion, although many slave-owners rejected that course of action because of a material interest in perpetuating slavery. One proposal that was contained in a letter from Pope Gregory IX to the patriarch, Gerald of Jerusalem, was that baptism should be made conditional on the slave's pledge to remain 'in the state of their former serfdom' (Prawer 1985: 113). During the first crusade, liberating the Holy Land and assisting the Eastern Church mattered rather more than converting 'infidels'.

Putting prisoners of war to death was standard practice for both Christian and Muslim forces, although the traditional principles regarding ransom often limited the severity of violence. As in the case of wars within Christendom, the social status of the captive was crucial. Enemies who displayed courage were valued; women were often raped in war although the high-ranking were spared if the captors believed they could be usefully traded for ransom (Friedman 1995, 2001). After the customary massacres, the Franks sought a *modus vivendi* with local communities (Kedar 2002). Because of the need for labour-power, several crusader leaders tried to persuade the Muslim population to remain in conquered cities, and many (mostly peasants rather than the earlier ruling strata) chose to stay in some urban settlements where they were obliged to hand over one half of their produce to the administering authorities. However, many refugees were actively involved in an 'anti-Frankish jihad' (Kedar 2002: 243–4, 263).

The public principles governing sexual conduct also provide insights into relations between the principal communities. Resulting from decisions of the Council of Nablus in 1120, Frankish legislation prohibited sexual intercourse between Muslims and Christians, and prescribed equal punishment for transgressors, irrespective of faith (Kedar 2002: 254ff.; Nirenberg 1996: ch. 5). In twelfth-century Jerusalem, castration was the penalty for a Latin male who was found guilty of miscegenation with a Saracen woman; her proscribed punishment was removal of the nose (Brundage 1987: 207). From some perspectives, crusaders almost certainly felt a stronger emotional bond with eastern Christians than with the devotees of other religious communities, and consistently 'showed them more favour' (Prawer 1985: 70–1).

Pragmatic considerations often dictated religious tolerance. Muslims and Jews had the same right as Christians to visit Jerusalem but were prohibited – at least in theory – from residing there (Phillips 1995: 115).

Muslims might be granted the freedom to practise their religion but they were treated as inferior to Franks and Oriental Christians. Although not permitted to live in Jerusalem, Jews were allowed to reside in other towns with the same legal status as other native residents, which is not to suggest that religious tolerance was pervasive (Prawer 1985: 95). Reflecting the scope of emotional identification, every Frank, it has been argued, believed that 'even the poorest and the lowest [of them] ranked well above the wealthiest of the native population' (Prawer 1985a: 121). The 'decisive factor' was 'European origin' (Prawer 1985a: 121).

Moslems witnessed the destruction of their religious sanctuaries or their transformation into Latin churches; in some cases, mosques became lodgings for crusading populations (Prawer 1985: 71). Synagogues in Jerusalem were burned down without regard for the lives of Jews who had gathered there, seeking refuge in prayer (Prawer 1985: ibid.).[8] Although pernicious representations of Muslims were central to crusading propaganda, and notwithstanding the fact that the first crusade was conducted in the manner of a 'vendetta' against the occupants of Jerusalem who had dishonoured Christ (Riley-Smith 1986: 48), it is far from certain that many participants in the first crusade took part because of a special hatred of Muslims. As the crusading imperative gave rise to a 'common identity' and 'shared cultural tradition', it also 'heightened the exclusive world view in which Latin Christian cultural superiority was taken for granted' and 'dramatically increased the xenophobic streak within Western culture, hitherto relatively dormant' (S. Lloyd 1995: 64). The 'frenzy' associated with a 'holy war', coupled with the reality that many crusaders had not previously encountered Muslim 'otherness', left a dark 'legacy of revulsion and hatred' that survives, *mutatis mutandis*, in the contemporary era (Kedar 2002: 244, 263).

The first crusade intensified the belief that membership of Latin Christendom transcended all regional differences. The other side of the widening of the scope of emotional identification between Latin Christians was the belief in joint superiority over other peoples that would have a profound impression on later European conceptions of civilization and its relationship

---

[8] In his *Historia Francorum*, Raymond D'Aguiliers described the ecstasy of the massacre at Jerusalem and the slaughter on the Temple Mount. He wrote that 'it was a just and splendid judgement of God that this place should be filled with the blood of the unbelievers, since it had suffered so long from their blasphemies' (Section XII: The Frankish Victory). Crusader leaders reported the gory details to Pope Paschall II, seemingly unburdened by remorse or shame. William of Tyre said it was impossible 'to look upon the vast numbers of the slain without horror . . . Still more dreadful was it to gaze upon the victors themselves, dripping with blood from head to foot'; but comfort could be found in the 'spiritual joy' that was derived from witnessing 'the pious devotion . . . with which the pilgrims drew near to the holy places' (William of Tyre 1943: vol. 1. 372–3).

with violence. To promote enthusiasm for taking part in the repossession of Christian lands, the discourse surrounding the Peace of God may have used disparaging representations of Muslims that equated paganism with low levels of control over violent impulses (Lotter 1989: 274–5). Distinctive civilizing and decivilizing processes developed in tandem. Negative representations of Eastern Christians that were part of that larger social transformation also developed during the first crusade. They stressed their perceived untrustworthiness as well as the obstructiveness of the Byzantine Church and its alleged effeteness or unmanliness. Demeaning images replaced initial astonishment at the grandeur of Constantinople. Some Church leaders, but not the papacy, portrayed the eastern Greeks as heretics without rights (Barber 1992: 491ff.). The sack of Constantinople in 1204 was justified as the legitimate punishment of schismatics (Housley 2002: ch. 2; Phillips 2004 and Tyerman 2005: 37ff.). The 'Saracen stereotype' appeared contemporaneously, fuelled by the belief that the Muslim occupation of the Holy Land and the atrocities against Christians issued from false belief. Such images were moderated by 'a degree of mutual tolerance' that was anchored in shared commitments to chivalry and in the belief that at least the Saracen possessed an admirable fighting spirit that the 'effete' Byzantine clearly lacked (Barber 1992: 498ff.).

Although the principal antagonisms in medieval society were religious, social conflicts were often interlaced with tensions between culturally 'advanced' and 'backward' groups that led to atrocities against Finnic, Baltic, Russian and Lithuanian peoples. The success of the first crusade which was presumed to have been assisted by God brought those convictions to the forefront of the medieval order. Similar insider–outsider dualisms blew back into Latin Christendom in the form of wars against heretics and Muslims in Spain (see Tyerman 2005: 43ff. on how the indulgences that the Church granted the crusaders during the first crusade were extended from the 1130s onwards to all who waged wars against papal enemies). What began as a war against heresy could quickly mutate into 'land seizure' involving considerable brutality. Similar crusades 'against heretics remained in the Church's arsenal for the rest of the Middle Ages and beyond'; they were a major reason for the rise of 'a closed, intolerant society' and a 'persecuting mentality' that marked the Church's desire for doctrinal uniformity and shaped the secular powers' quest for legitimacy (Tyerman 2005: 44ff., 83, 134). The German Christian conquests of pagan Slavs and other Baltic peoples displayed an embryonic nationalism that rested on pernicious distinctions between 'civilized' Christian and 'barbarous' non-Christian groups, and encouraged what has come to be known as genocide – the physical extermination of Slavic peoples and the virtual destruction of their cultures (Bloch 1962: 433; Gillingham 1992; Johnson 1975). Of particular importance – and not least because they foreshadowed the 'two faces' of the later civilizing process in the age of European overseas expansion – were the contrasting perspectives on Christian international society proposed by Paulus Vladimiri and Hostiensis in the thirteenth century (Bull 1984: 120; also see Chapter 6). Vladimiri claimed that infidels such as the pagan Lithuanians enjoyed the right to property and political independence. According to Hostiensis, the use of force to dispossess infidel communities of their lands was legitimate. In that dispute lie the antecedents of sixteenth-century debates about the rights and responsibilities of Christian society to non-Christian peoples. The seeds of a later division are apparent in the conflict between the thesis that 'civilized' societies are obligated by their prevalent self-images to observe self-restraint in relations with 'outsiders' and the conviction that 'inferior' groups must yield to the representatives of a 'superior' civilization. The divergence between those standpoints was one of the defining characteristics of Latin Christendom – one respect in which it sharpened the contrasts between ethical orientations to 'difference' that originated in the discourses of 'civilization' and 'barbarism' in the Hellenic, Hellenistic and Roman worlds.

The inability to control the free companies – which was the outcome of the Church's decision to enlarge the offensive to include wars against heretics – encouraged the belief that powerful civil authorities were essential to control the chaotic forces that had been unleashed by religiously sanctioned violence (Lowe 1997: 34). New doctrines of national chivalry developed in the process. In England, following the collapse of chivalry during the Hundred Years' War, humanistic learning advanced ideals of responsible citizenship with the aim of bringing the 'chivalric code . . . under the discipline of monarchs' (Lowe 1997: 50ff., ch. 5). The principle that the truly noble should serve the nation and promote public order was a central theme in Bouvet's late fourteenth-century work, *The Tree of Battles*, that seems to have reflected a growing consensus on the importance of the principle of non-combatant immunity with regard to women, children, the aged and infirm as well as peasants and the clergy (Johnson 1987: 79ff.). The treatise argued for levels of restraint in warfare that went beyond the knights' understandings of their traditional privileges and entitlements. It revealed 'the growing impact of the chivalric code as a limitation on knightly violence', and it demonstrated how just war doctrines had come to provide the basis for 'a broad cultural agreement on the justification and restraint of violence and war' (Johnson 1987: 79ff.). Medieval chivalry has been described as one of the 'civilizing' tributaries that led to the modern laws of war (Meron 1998: 6; also Huizinga 1955: 100ff.). It was one of the mechanisms by which conceptions of restraints on the use of force that had developed in the ancient states-systems were refined and transmitted to modern societies that proceeded to develop new interpretations of the relationship between violence and civilization.

Its influence in court society grew in the fifteenth century as England and France turned their attention to constructing 'national chivalries' and ideals of 'princely discipline' (Wright 1976). Crucial was the belief that had been defended in the previous century that core ideas in the military manuals of republican and imperial Rome and in the tenth- and eleventh-century peace movements could be combined in new doctrines of chivalry that foregrounded the aristocratic obligation to ensure public order. The synthesis of classical and Christian moral and political beliefs was used to defend the idea of the 'public good' whose ultimate guardian was the prince (Wright 1976: 27ff.). The process of European state formation was influenced by endeavours to distinguish 'national 'chivalry from the traditional warrior code and to infuse it with a new civil ethic so that 'an increasingly pacified aristocracy' would find honour and nobility in serving the commonwealth (Lowe 1997: 191). A related trend from around the fourteenth century was the connection between crusading and 'national' wars that would shape the dominant mentalities in later religious conflicts; it also influenced European expansion into Africa and the Eastern Atlantic in the fifteenth century; and it was a central theme in the struggles against the Ottomans up to the seventeenth century.

Medieval Civilizing Processes

The first two chapters of this volume considered the claim that the 'simpler civilizations' of Greek and Rome devoted little if any attention to questions of 'international ethics'. The discussion stressed that recurrent power struggles and 'elimination contests' were conducted with what modern 'civilized' peoples generally regard as excessive violence. Conceptions of self-restraint in relations with others were not without political influence although they had little impact on the long-term development of the ancient states-systems. Turning to Latin Christendom, many standard accounts of 'the medieval period' have pointed to levels and forms of violence and cruelty that clash with contemporary 'civilized' commitments and with the higher level of order and security that citizens of stable liberal-democratic societies enjoy in the present era. There were undoubtedly substantial differences with respect to the tolerance of violence. Throughout the medieval era, physical violence was widely regarded as an inescapable part of life; large numbers of people were accustomed to it. But it is also true that, for long intervals, medieval societies were actively engaged in a religiously inspired quest to tame the warriors – in a distinctive 'civilizing offensive'. It was argued earlier that no extant Greek treatise on moral and political philosophy deals with the ethics of war. In the Roman world, there was little systematic analysis of how independent political communities could coexist peacefully. No such claims can be made about Latin Christendom where the problem of violent harm was inescapable as were core ethical questions about the rights and wrongs of using force.

Recent scholarship in International Relations has questioned any sharp division between the medieval and modern worlds. The emphasis falls on specific processes such as state-formation that developed over the best part of a millennium. Other approaches go further by questioning the very existence of a single medieval period. An illuminating example of that standpoint maintains that the overall medieval trajectory 'may be likened to the curve of a graph, arching from points low on the vertical axis (the sixth and seventh centuries), rising steadily upwards and reaching an apex (the twelfth and thirteen centuries) before changing course and tending downwards, though never returning to its lowest levels (before) the direction of our curve anticipates another upward turn sometime around the end of the fifteenth century'; what is more, the overall general trend suggests that, in several respects, the relationship between the medieval and modern eras is 'one of continuity' (Delogu 2002: 65). That thesis is supported by evidence of the rise and fall of levels of violence across the medieval period. The Carolingian wars appear to have been less cruel than the conflicts of the preceding Merovingian era. The collapse of Charlemagne's empire resulted in a major upsurge of violence. The Church initiated a significant pacification process with the *Peace* and *Truce of God*, and it harnessed knightly valour to crusading warfare that led to the atrocities against non-Christians and 'heretics'. The fanaticism of the 'religious wars' led many to look on with relief as state power monopolies imposed public order. The medieval international system turned out to be an 'evolutionary dead end' like the other international systems that have been discussed thus far. They did not disappear without leaving a 'civilizing' legacy – nor did Latin Christendom. However, greater controls on intra-societal violence in later periods often led to major distortions of the medieval era.

When comparing those international political orders, one is not comparing like with like. The power of the Church and Christian doctrine ensured a prominent political role for universalistic values and human sympathies. They were in tension with the practical realities that exist wherever people depend on their own power resources for their security and to resolve major disputes, and where there is a high risk that participants will take great pleasure in violent revenge and in causing human suffering. But largely because of Church efforts to 'tame the warriors' by fusing violence and piety, many knights did not act on violent impulses without any regard for the dictates of the 'Christian conscience'; the use of force could not be separated from the question of salvation or from considerations of justice.

The religious universalism of the period was plainly double-edged since it played a part in limiting violence within Christendom by constructing a 'we-identity', a related we–I balance and associated standards of restraint that were designed to increase controls over the knights. No such common identity restrained the knights in their dealings with the lower strata. Medieval society was profoundly unequal and exploitative, as were the preceding international orders. Moreover, no such collective identity unified believers and non-believers. Between the tenth and fourteenth centuries, medieval communities were heavy with distinctions between the heightened sense of Christian solidarity that crusading warfare had forged, and various conceptions of the barbarian, pagan, infidel, heretic or apostate that were used to justify violence on a more destructive scale (Bartlett 1993: ch. 9). Later generations would draw the conclusion that the key to domestic and international order was the elimination of wars against 'enemies of the faith', a strategy that involved turning religious belief into a matter of personal conscience and separating the public and private spheres. A new vision of 'civilized' existence first becomes evident in the Italian city-state system.

4

The Renaissance City-State System

> In the process of transformation and innovation that we designate by the term, 'Renaissance', what was regarded as 'fitting' and 'unfitting' in human intercourse no doubt changed to a certain degree. But the rupture was not marked by a sudden demand for new modes of behaviour opposed to the old.
>
> (Elias 2012: 86)

Italian Renaissance thinkers invented the idea of Middle Ages to describe the period of 'barbarism' that intervened between classical antiquity and their era. Leading humanists regarded their epoch as one of rebirth and renewal through the discovery of ancient texts and the reacquaintance with lost traditions. The idea of the Renaissance was a mid-nineteenth-century innovation, introduced by the French historian, Michelet, to characterize an intellectual and cultural movement rather to describe a unique historical era with a definite beginning and end (Brotton 2006: 8ff.; Burke 1987). Whether the term can be usefully employed to describe a clearly delineated epoch has long been debated. In the following discussion, the Renaissance refers to the period of Italian history that lasted from around 1350 to 1550 (see Caferro 2011: 22ff.). A central issue is whether the Renaissance differed substantially from the so-called Middle Ages, or was so closely interconnected with, or indebted to, the medieval world that it is misleading to regard it as the birth of the modern era (Larkins 2010: ch. 6). Huizinga (1955) described it as a crucial phase in the waning of the Middle Ages. Nineteenth-century thinkers such as Michelet and Burckhardt portrayed the Renaissance not as a discrete epoch but as a mentality or 'spirit' that was centred on the rise of individuality and signified the appearance of novel understandings of what it meant to be 'civilized' (Brotton 2006: 9ff.).

Burckhardt's thesis that Renaissance views of 'the state as a work of art' and the alleged celebration of individuality were evidence of distinctively modern attitudes to the world have long been rejected. Major cultural 'breakthroughs' are now presented as having paved the road to 'modernity'. Few subscribe to Burckhardt's contention that the leading figures of the Italian Renaissance were 'the first modern people of Europe', although his emphasis, it should be noted, was on bold 'speculations on freedom and necessity' that were advanced in 'violent and lawless political circumstances' where 'evil' often seemed to prevail with the result that 'their belief in God began to waver, and their view of the government of the world became fatalistic' (Burckhardt 1944 [1860]: 303). Renaissance thinkers adopted means of orientating themselves to the world by looking back to antiquity for inspiration. Collective efforts to recover ancient knowledge, and to derive key cultural bearings from the period before the collapse of Rome and the ascendancy of the Church, were distinctive because of the recognition of the extent to which Europe had fallen behind other regions, and specifically the Islamic world with its more continuous patterns of 'civilized' development (Goody 2010: ch. 8).

If the idea of modernity refers to a cultural standpoint that displays confidence in a progressive conception of change then the leading thinkers of the Italian Renaissance cannot be said to have satisfied that condition; they did not openly embrace such an image of their place in history. Employing ancient Rome as a yardstick for measuring social and artistic progress is not exactly what 'modernity' has come to connote (Burke 1998: introduction). As so often happens during periods of apparently large-scale social and political transformation, 'the new was added to the old rather than substituted for it' (Burke 1999: 17). A collective perception of belonging to a progressive era was a powerful theme amongst certain Italian humanists who spearheaded what Petrarch called the quest to discover the 'way back to the clear splendour of the ancient past' (Burke 1998: 24). Bringing classical works 'back to light' was central to the belief in participating in an age of Enlightenment (Skinner 1978: 111). 'Self-congratulatory exaggeration' meant that Renaissance thinkers often ignored 'the intense interest in antiquity' during the ninth-century Carolingian Renaissance (Greenblatt 2011: 116ff.; Southern 1970). In the *Della Vita Civile*, which was most likely written in the mid-1430s, the Florentine humanist, Matteo Palemieri, maintained that 'the solid foundation of all civilization' – letters and liberal studies – had been 'lost to mankind for eight hundred years and more. It is but in our day that men dare boast that they see the dawn of better things' (cited in Hay 1977: 12). Renaissance conceptions of the past invariably combined the sense of cultural breakthrough and revival with a cyclical approach to history in which forward movement was followed by inexorable social decline, and then by a new epoch of renewal and predictable decay in an endless and almost natural flow of events. In short, 'the idea of history as an ascending process was not part of the equipment of a Renaissance mind'; far too much was invested in the observable 'tendency for all composite bodies to disintegrate' (Butterfield 1940: 46ff.). Machiavelli expressed a conventional strand of argument when he argued that the state, stability and prosperity were no more than a temporary triumph over the normal order of things, and when he added – anticipating later Enlightenment thinkers – that the exercise of political imagination might at least defer probable decline. Similar themes were central to many branches of Renaissance moral and political thought, and particularly to influential reflections on the intricate relations between individual freedom, social constraints and the possibility of controlling wayward historical forces. Important developments occurred in representing the social world and its constraints as the product of individual and collective agency, and in openly confronting the question of what societies could hope to bring under their control and what might defy such transformative efforts. They were core features of the civilizing process of the era that foreshadowed Enlightenment convictions that the essence of political action was the struggle to end the tyranny of largely unregulated social processes.[1]

That complex orientation to the world represented a clear break with leading strands of Christian theology including the thesis that Pope Innocent III had advanced in *On the Misery of Human Life*. The treatise reflected the tradition of thought that maintained that physical decay and excrescence were the appropriate fate of the contemptible human body (Nauert 2006: 66). Influenced primarily by Petrarch's celebration of humanity's immense creativity, the dominant humanist position rejected religious disgust for the body and interlinked disdain for worldly achievements (Nauert 2006: 65–6). Pico della Mirandola's 1486 *Oration on the Dignity of Man* is generally regarded as the pivotal treatise that proclaimed the idea of the 'sovereign man' standing over non-human creation (Martines 1979: 216). He prized the individual's capacity to be 'the maker and moulder of thyself', and celebrated his unique power 'to have what he wishes, to be whatever he wills'. Confidence in *vir virtutis* – the 'creative social force' with which humans could elevate themselves to a higher level of existence – clashed with the Augustinian doctrine that Innocent had restated. The belief in the potential for self-improvement rejected its contention that righteousness in man was the result of 'the grace of God' rather than the outcome of individual thought and struggle (Skinner 1978: 91). However, the humanists' faith in human dignity did not reject the doctrine of original sin or deny the need for grace (Kristeller 1972). Mirandola and others who rejected the Augustinian perspective regarded their own endeavours as strengthening rather than undermining Christianity. They reflected the focus on the nobility and beauty of humans that had been expressed in earlier strands of medieval art and thought, and which revealed that the Middle Ages and the Renaissance were 'complementary' rather than 'contradictory' (Burke 1999: 202). The powers and liberties

---

[1] The belief that the Renaissance broke with the medieval world and announced the rise of modernity was once advanced by historians of ideas such as Cassirer who portrayed the Renaissance as the first Enlightenment (see Burke 1998: 232 who offers the alternative interpretation that the Enlightenment is perhaps best regarded as a second Renaissance).

that Mirandola described included the potential to reduce oneself to the level of the brutes and to raise oneself in the direction of the divine. Such comments reflected a sharpening sense of the positive value of individual and collective commitments to a process of civilization.

Because there was no sharp rupture with the 'medieval period, the Renaissance is best regarded as a distinctive movement within a broader course of development that extended from 1000 to 1800' (Burke 1987: conclusion; Burke 1997 and Goody 2010: 38ff.). That approach emphasizes the 'partial secularization' of thought that occurred in medicine and the natural sciences as humanists questioned the validity and 'appropriateness' of the dominant religious forms of orientation towards the world. It stresses the greater reliance on reason as opposed to faith. But it also recognized important continuities with the immediate past as Renaissance humanists attempted to build bridges between antiquity and Christianity and engaged in an exercise in 'rationalizing religion' that promoted the 'demystification of knowledge' that Weber and others would later regard as a distinguishing feature of Western modernity (Goody 2010: 9, 85). From that perspective, the Renaissance is best understood as a phase within European history in which the rapid acceleration of earlier social and political tendencies took place in Italy, and to a far greater extent than in other parts of Europe. It was a crucial part of the broader patterns of state formation and the larger process of civilization that will be discussed in the next chapter (Burke 1998: 200n40).

The importance of the Renaissance for that process provides the key to the organization of the following discussion. Section one discusses the rise of the city and the idea of a civilizing advance (modelled on the Roman Republic) that informed approaches to government. The defence of *virtus* (the moral example of manly virtue) rather than *vis* (brute force) was heir to the Ciceronian ideal and to the Christian ethic of princely rule that were considered earlier (Skinner 1988: 414ff.). How far that ethos influenced the conduct of foreign relations is a matter for consideration in the second section. Interwoven intercity and intra-city conflicts that were intensified by the reliance on mercenary armies encouraged some rulers to consider how earlier achievements in bringing political order and stability to their respective cities could be emulated at the international level. 'Elimination contests' reduced the number of major powers to just five principal cities that became dangerously entangled in the wider European rivalries in large part because rival cities cultivated external allies in their attempts to realize conflicting political objectives. Those are matters to discuss in part three. The last two sections discuss the role of humanism in forging core elements of the Italian civilizing process which included systematic efforts to understand the relationship between chance and necessity, and between statecraft and the power to control events. The conclusion argues that framing the central problem of politics in that way was a defining feature of a Renaissance civilizing process that influenced later moral and political responses to the problem of harm in the relations between states that became ever more pronounced as a result of the European Enlightenment.

City and Civilization

Italian city states had their origins in the medieval commune: in the 'sworn association of free men collectively holding some kind of public authority' that emerged in the late tenth and early eleventh centuries (Martines 1979: ch. 1). Many ruling elites turned to Roman law and ancient political texts in response to the complex legal problems that developed with the greater specialization and differentiation of functions in more urbanized environments. They were adamant that the chivalric code that prevailed amongst the knights had little relevance for the new patterns of interdependence that appeared in the period between 1000 and 1250. The civic ideal of peaceful coexistence was set against the traditional aristocratic code that licensed the right to use force to gain revenge, especially in response to slights to personal honour. Crucial was the belief amongst members of the post-chivalric elite in the existence of close parallels between the Roman republic and the urban communes. The related conviction was that the works of Cicero and Seneca shed considerable light on how their inhabitants could become attuned to one another in a more self-consciously civilizing manner (Stacey 2007: ch. 2; Witt 2000: 14–15, 55ff.). The thirteenth-century treatises that were written by the judge, Albertano da Brescia, who drew heavily on Seneca's works, were amongst the first post-classical treatises to defend a civic way of life in which revenge and the vendetta were replaced by the 'civilized' rule of law (Witt 2000: 58ff.). Identification with 'the superior culture of *Romanitas* intensified' in that period (Witt 2000: 65).

The largest urban settlements had populations of around ten to twenty thousand persons. Between classical antiquity and the late twelfth and thirteenth centuries, no Occidental city had more than thirty thousand inhabitants (Spufford 2003: 93). At the beginning of the thirteenth century, there were two to three hundred small urban complexes in north and central Italy. Estimates are that twenty-three cities in those regions had populations at the higher end of the spectrum mentioned above (Burke 1999: 1). As a result of population growth, cities such as Florence had around one hundred thousand inhabitants by the end of that century; several large cities had populations of about half that number. It seems that those were the largest urban communities in Europe at the time. Venice may well have been the world's largest merchant city at the beginning of the fifteenth century. The scale of urbanization was unmatched in other parts of Christendom. Between Lisbon and Moscow, it is improbable that there were more than twenty cities of comparable size (Burke 1999: 226ff.).

The reasons for the emergence of cities are complex and varied. The 'vacuum theory' of the state contends that such political entities are most likely to emerge in regions where central authorities are weak; they flourish for a time in the interstices between areas under great power control (Brown 1982: ch. 1; Burke 1986). There was no overarching political structure in Italy in the post-Carolingian era, a welcome condition for supporters of communal self-government. In the second half of the tenth century, and in the aftermath of the Carolingian empire, the bishops' power and authority was the nearest thing to an organized political system. Technically, cities were 'mere vassals of the empire' which, in the late twelfth and early thirteenth centuries, aggressively advanced its claims over northern Italy (Skinner 1988: 390). From the middle of the eleventh century, political tensions between the papacy and the empire created new opportunities for urban self-assertion. Cities came to be ruled by 'wealthy merchants and modest tradesmen and artisans' until, from the thirteenth century onwards, despotic rule became increasingly standard (Nauert 2006: 5).

In the political vacuum, forceful demands for communal self-government were advanced in opposition to the two dominant forms of government: aspiring empires and feudal monarchies. Legal and political theorists constructed the philosophical foundations of republican self-government in direct opposition to enunciations of the legitimacy of empire advanced by thinkers such as Dante (Skinner 1988: 390ff.). Advocates of the republican ideal celebrated the ideal of civic politics as espoused by Aristotle's *Politics*, recently rediscovered in Europe and employed by Bartolus of Sassoferato amongst others to defend a new and more civilized form of life. The other side of the defence of communal independence was the conviction that Italy was rightly divided into independent cities that were inescapably entangled in struggles for power, honour and security. As an alternative to the thesis that empire was the precondition of peace, many humanists envisaged an international league of princes united by Christian we-feeling and by a common desire to uphold the peace – the *pax* that was associated with the Roman Empire (Yates 1975: part one). Not that the Renaissance humanists looked back to the 'imperial city' that the medieval authorities admired since it had created the environment in which Christianity had flourished. The Florentine republican and one time Chancellor, Leonardo Bruni, stated that the empire had crushed the Italian cities which had to wait for its collapse before they could regain their earlier political powers (Grafton 1991: 12ff.). Others observed that the Italian peoples had remained free under the Roman republic, and not least by acquiring citizenship rights. The ancient social model that was most admired but not slavishly emulated was republican Rome in the first century BC which had combined political independence with republican government (Blythe 2000; Hörnqvist 2000). Humanists rejected the case for empire in a period when there was no reason to suppose – if the long-term development of the Hellenic and Hellenistic states-systems was any guide – that separate political communities could coexist peacefully for long or escape the ultimate fate of imperial domination. The presumption that levels of violence would be tolerable, at least for the most powerful cities, was the implicit wager in implementing the republican political ideal.

The vacuum theory maintains that cities can retain their autonomy for decades and even for centuries under specific power configurations that are unusual and prone to collapse. Their survival is precarious. Many will disappear because of 'elimination contests', or as a result of the military expansion of neighbouring powers or, as in the Italian case, because of their combined effect. The question is how far effective civilizing restraints on violent harm can develop in those conditions, both within the cities and in their external relations.

To discuss those issues in more detail, it is necessary to consider some of the principal challenges to the autonomy of cities in the early tenth century. Declining imperial structures that were unable to enforce their traditional territorial claims conferred specific privileges and liberties on many communes but stopped short of granting permanent rights to political independence (Barber 1992: ch. 10). In 1152, Frederick Barbarossa attempted to re-establish a presumed legal entitlement to exercise imperial rule in Lombardy, and he sought to justify the endeavour by contending that the main objective was to liberate the region from the scourge of private warfare. His ambitions which were mainly directed at weakening rather than eliminating local political authorities were thwarted after several decades of resistance by the communal movement that enjoyed most support in Lombardy and Tuscany (Martines 1979: ch.2). Its initial successes included the formation of the First Lombard League in 1167, followed by the Peace of Constance of 1183 in which the communes gained the power to appoint consuls and the right of fortification in exchange for token recognition of imperial authority (Martines 1979: ibid.). Political independence was linked with the emergence of court cultures that defended new civic ideals and, in so doing, anticipated 'the civilizing effects of court life in the larger territorial lordships of northern Europe' (Witt 2000: 40–1; Raccagni 2010).

Frederick II revived the imperial claims in 1235, and proceeded to impose his will on several cities after the defeat of the Lombard League in 1237. His aspirations were thwarted by an alliance led by Milan. In 1310–13, Henry VII resumed the attempt to re-establish imperial governance and claimed to be the rightful arbiter of recurrent intercity disputes. So strong was the desire for communal self-assertion that disputes between cities were preferred to whatever peace an imperial order could impose from above. That was the last significant political attempt to gain imperial control of the Italian peninsula. The Pact at Bologna in 1311 which was largely the outcome of the Florentine initiative to resist Henry VII was pivotal in securing the rights of city states as self-governing, autonomous 'survival units'.

From the earliest period, local patriotism fuelled by intercommunal rivalry was strong, but many communes were riddled with factionalism and violence. The level of internal pacification, which was low when compared to the later state of affairs in Western Europe, reflected the limited development of central monopolies of physical power that could maintain public order (Martines 1979: chs. 2–3). Even so, several communes in the early thirteenth century required citizens to pledge not to carry weapons and to avoid public brawls given the high probability of injury or death (Martines 1979: 34). The extraordinary 'patchwork quilt' of ecclesiastical authorities, noble principalities and several other groupings and factions makes it misleading to describe Italy as a system of unitary states (Martin 2007: 14). References to the Italian Renaissance state have often exaggerated the level of political innovation: bureaucratic structures were still embryonic in nature (Burke 1999: 218ff.). Specialist judges who expressed a bourgeois preference for the governance of impersonal rules in the cities of Mantua and Ferrara clashed with the prevailing aristocratic disposition to conflate public and private interests. The formers' proposed judicial reforms constituted an early civilizing endeavour to free public office from the stranglehold of sectional interests and traditional privileges (Chambers and Dean 1997: conclusion). Images of the 'incorruptible' public servant made little headway in what was an early stage in the transition to the modern legal-rational state. They demonstrated the very limited and precarious nature of Renaissance state bureaucracies.

The problem of order was the resident crisis in most cities. Florence was not unusual in facing 'chronic violence' inside the town and in adjoining rural areas (Becker 1976). Abolishing the carrying of arms was a major priority for cities with low levels of policing, ineffective prisons, and limited controls over 'local bullies' (Bowsky 1967; Dean 1994). Restraints on vendettas grew in tandem with increases in state power. The establishment of a constabulary in Florence in the latter part of the fourteenth century reflected a broader trend towards the monopolization of force in European societies (Zorzi 1994). At that time, crimes against the person and property (but not 'political violence') decreased (Becker 1976). Nevertheless, in most cities, levels of violent crime were high when compared to the prevailing conditions in later 'civilized' societies. As always, differences of class and gender require more detailed comparisons. In the main, women had fewer rights and far less civil protection than men (Hay and Law 1989: 39). They were more likely to die as a result of abandonment or infanticide (Hale 1981: 141).

As always, modes of punishment for serious crimes offer insights into the dominant emotional attitudes to violent harm and suffering. They are a window onto the prevalent harm conventions and onto the nature of the relevant civilizing process. State institutions decided that public spectacles of gruesome violence were essential for the maintenance of order, and urban populations were attuned to witnessing acts of punishment that inflicted immense suffering. Most societies relied heavily on organized fear to control 'unmanageable' social elements (Chambers and Dean 1997: ch. 1; Elias 2012: 403ff.). Standard methods of punishment included public beheading, hanging as well as burning on occasion, the amputation of hands, feet or tongues or the gouging of eyes for less serious offences, as well as public humiliation by parading the guilty through the streets. Judicial torture was standard in many cities (Chambers and Dean 1997: introduction; Hay and Law 1989: 78; Edgerton 1985).

There is substantial evidence that certain movements in Florentine art 'helped raise peoples' consciousness concerning the inhuman brutality of legalized torture and public execution', although the development should not be confused with modern humanitarian sensitivities to the 'barbaric' death penalty (Edgerton 1985: 14, 172ff.). They may not have altered the general view that capital punishment was the just reward for the worst offences. By the end of the fourteenth century, especially harsh punishments including burial alive, blinding, castration and amputation had become rare in some cities in large part because of the tendency to substitute a utilitarian system of fines (Dean 1994; Zorzi 1994). Cities attempted to introduce various means of providing for physical security given that central powers were limited, political factions could be quick to use force, and vendettas were rife. Investing power in the *signore* represented a shift towards the monopolization of force that would become the dominant trend across the European continent. Renaissance cities faced immense obstacles in raising the taxes that were indispensable for the consolidation of territorial concentrations of power. However, many succeeded in significantly pacifying their respective territories, notwithstanding weak and fragile state structures.

Whether the absence of stable highly centralized state authorities was connected with the tendency for people to swing between emotional extremes, as Elias maintained in his reflections on medieval society, is debated (see Chapter 3, pp. 123–4). With respect to Venice – though the discussion has broader application – society at large was laden with possibilities for 'explosive violence' (Ruggiero 1980: 113). The traditional nobility was the most violent of all social strata given its devotion to 'honour or status' and dedication to maintaining 'power and prestige' (Ruggiero 1980: 120). In many cities, the victim of offence or injury faced the stark choice between 'fight' or 'flight', which inevitably brought shame to the person involved (Muir 1998: introduction). City inhabitants were invariably quick to take offence, and often displayed little control over aggressive inclinations. Some authors have insisted that there is an 'unfortunately Huizinga-esque' flavour to such observations which make large generalizations about social behaviour that reflect official judicial reports that exaggerated the level of 'spontaneous, impulsive violence'

(Dean and Lowe 1994: 5–6). But studies that emphasize the volatility of the emotional lives of the populace in Venice and elsewhere are not exactly divorced from the collective self-understandings of the period (Burrow 2007: 281). Public investments in extending policing to deal with crimes of passion seem to have coincided with the conviction that significant numbers of people were so quick to act from passion that they were unlikely to be deterred by other measures that were designed to internalize 'rational' perspectives on relations between people (Ruggiero 1980: 154–5). Such claims support the view that the greater all-round control of the emotions lay ahead, in the period when the 'civilizing' of conduct occurred in conjunction with state formation.

The Renaissance city state did not enjoy the legal, political and fiscal power monopolies that many later European states would have at their disposal. They could not enforce the peaceful settlement of interpersonal disputes. They lacked the capacity to use a complex bureaucratic apparatus to survey and regulate social interaction from a central political-administrative point (Mattingly 1973: 55). But whereas early modern states had a limited ability to control everyday behaviour, the Italian cities had the advantage of consisting of relatively small-scale and densely populated communities; major advances in centralizing political and administrative power that could take such initiatives first occurred there (Mattingly 1973: ibid.). Despite limited powers, many central authorities enacted communal legislation in an attempt to regulate 'all imaginable aspects of life' (Denley 1988: 250ff.).

How far it is legitimate to describe the Renaissance city as a state is an important question for the comparative sociology of states-systems (Chabod 1964). Important doubts have already been raised. Patron–client relationships, endemic factionalism and frequent vendettas inhibited the formation of the monopolies of power that would later dominate Europe. Italy was not short of court societies where human loyalties were directed towards the prince rather than to impersonal state institutions. The princely household was not separate from 'public' bodies which were unable to function effectively without conferring various privileges including significant legal immunities on the most powerful family groups and social factions. Nor could political authorities operate without extensive patronage and corruption in the form of the sale of public offices. Significant concessions were vital if elite groups were to be persuaded that they had a major interest in preserving civil order and in protecting the 'public good' (Chambers and Dean 1997: 16, 232; Hay and Law 1989: 111).

State formation may have developed earlier and further in Renaissance Italy than in most other parts of Europe, but 'impersonal administration was impossible' where factionalism and corruption were so endemic (Burke 1999: 221ff.; Chojnacki 1972 and Covini 2000). Loyalties to the quarter or ward were paramount in what were essentially face-to-face societies (Burke 1999: 223).

Powerful families safeguarded their economic and political interests by maximizing their control over state institutions that did not possess the dual monopolies of force and taxation that are amongst the most distinctive features of the modern state (see Chapter 5). Little more than restricted centralized control of the instruments of violence was possible for the majority of cities. The ability to tax was constrained because powerful families were opposed to extensions of public authority that would erode power, prestige and influence. Efforts to increase taxation were often counterproductive because they fuelled revolt in regional areas (Chambers and Dean 1997: 165–6). Forced loans (*prestanze*) that were imposed on dominant family groups was a strategy that Florence amongst others employed in times of war. The *catasto*, the attempted inventory of wealth that was undertaken by the Florentine state between 1427 and 1430, is worth noting in this context. The simple fact that it took almost three years to compile an incomplete record is testimony to the limited capabilities of central institutions, but it was an intriguing prelude to one of the critical features of Western European state formation in the following centuries (Hay and Law 1989: ch. 6).

In many fourteenth-century Italian cities, 'squares and streets – all public places – became stages on which [male] honour could be won or lost', and where personal insult could prompt individuals to seek instant revenge (Rossiaud 1990: 152–3). Insecurities were compounded by the apparent joys of participating in vendettas (Dean 2001: 23). Some historians have argued that a civilizing process gathered pace in the fourteenth century that was exemplified by changes in the standard male response to assaults on honour. As discussed above with respect to earlier eras, revised images of 'honourable masculinity', especially within court circles, severed the link between masculinity and the thirst for vengeance; the more or less automatic resort to vendetta in the spirit of revenge amongst aristocratic males slowly gave way to ritualized duelling in the Northern Italian cities (Spierenburg 1998). But several decades would pass before the civilizing of aristocratic male behaviour through recourse to prearranged duels to settle major interpersonal disputes would become commonplace. 'New standards of civility' that emerged in the fourteenth century found expression in support for judicial efforts in the 'modernizing states' to 'limit and focus the violence required to protect [male] honour and masculinity from insult' (Strocchia 1998: 59). The 'courtly ethic of humanism' promoted the diffusion of new forms of we-feeling and associated ideals of individual and collective self-restraint; its 'civilizing' ethos was largely responsible for changing the prevailing attitudes towards force and for reinforcing a trend towards condemning revenge as uncontrolled 'madness'. A tilt towards dealing with insults to male honour in courts of law encouraged many humanists to imagine a new civil order that shook off the constraints of insular loyalties to families as well as poisonous attachments to dangerous factions.

Movements in those directions were not without dangers for those involved since they could safely assume that many peers would condemn a decision to opt for the peaceful resolution of disputes as weak and 'unmanly' (Muir 1994: 80). Injured parties became entangled in a 'double-bind process'. To retaliate violently created the predictable danger of cycles of revenge that could be hard to end, coupled with the additional risk of investigation and punishment by public authorities. To do nothing at all because of the fear of public sanctions could jeopardize a man's reputation and social standing (Muir 1994). As already noted, duelling, which 'dramatically reduced levels of interpersonal violence and even more importantly eliminated many of the remnant effects of vendetta practices', offered an escape route from a perilous double bind (Muir 1994: 80). The 'gentleman' could then respond to insults to honour by complying with the 'civilized' values of the courts without risking the accusation of succumbing to the 'unmanly' traits that many nobles mocked as exemplifying 'the beginnings of a feminisation of public life' (Muir 1994: ibid.). As in classical antiquity and across Latin Christendom, the political question was how to tame the destructiveness of male warriors through new and appealing modes of conscience formation; it was whether harm conventions could be introduced that dampened the customary practice of using force to protect honour.

Urban dominance of the countryside (*contado*) grew out of political strategies to weaken the feudal lords; controls were anchored in the high levels of taxation of rural groups (*contadino*) that were denied citizenship rights (Hay and Law 1989: ch. 4). Local resistance checked the centre's ability to project its political power into rural areas but unrest was often fostered by rival cities in the attempt to settle disputes over territory and to organize trade on favourable terms. Familiar dichotomies between urban civility and rustic wildness that betrayed ancient Roman influences thrived in that environment (Martines 1979: 166). An increasingly prevalent view in the fifteenth century was that the world outside the city walls was inhospitable to civilized existence (*vivere civilmente*). The princely task of controlling the 'uncivil' domain was often compared to taming wild animals and the forces of nature. Linked with 'virility' and fearlessness, that endeavour was undertaken in an effort to protect' the better sort' who were committed to *ben vivere*, or to life without the persistent fear of violence and robbery (Chambers and Dean 1997: 40ff.; Viroli 1990). The pronounced trend towards urban control and exploitation of rural populations reflected the commune's interest in ensuring a reliable supply of troops, taxes and food, and in repulsing attempts by adversaries to encroach on vital strategic and economic zones (Waley 1969: ch. 4). The whole process was driven along by the 'monopoly mechanism' (Elias 2012: 301ff.). Often, increased urban power over adjacent territories was achieved not through violent subjugation but through 'voluntary' submission in the face of intimidation, but the effect was the same, namely successive 'elimination contests' between cities (Waley 1969: ch. 4).

High levels of violence in many communes were caused by powerful feudal lords who resented measures to compel them to submit to a central political authority. Personal security within the city tended to rest on a self-help system in which armed family networks (*consorterie* or tower-societies), neighbourhood groups, guilds and similar associations competed to control urban space in order to protect affiliates (Martines 1979: ch. 6). Loyalties were directed towards the critical 'survival units' which, for the noble families, were centred on the towers and fortresses that offered protection. Rivalries between political factions could rapidly degenerate into lawlessness. For that reason, many humanists admired the Roman Republic for making civic commitments central to an aristocratic we–I balance that successfully defused competitive pressures that could so easily lead to violence. As already noted, as is standard in self-help systems, efforts to restrain the warriors involved the social reconstruction of the dominant images of masculinity – as had occurred in Republican Rome – in conjunction with the promotion of emotional identification with a public realm with significant independence from the morass of factional pressures.

One attempted solution to the problem of pacifying urban space and controlling the violence of the nobility was the practice of electing a leader (the *podesta*). Typically an appointee from another city with no personal involvement in local conflicts, the *podesta* was authorized to use specific legal powers to promote the public good. By the end of the twelfth century, most cities had invested judicial powers in the *podesta,* principally in order to deal with the disruptive effects of the migration of nobles to the towns. [Venice relied on the Doge – an insider who was appointed for life and whose powers usually exceeded those of the *podesta* in large part because of the greater social cohesion of the population (Lane 1973: 97ff.)]. The 'civilizing' role of the *podesta* had only limited success however. Rudimentary public authorities were rarely free from colonization by assertive noble families which were usually able to resist efforts by the *popolo* which consisted of two ascending classes – the 'little people' (*popolo minuto*) comprising artisans and shopkeepers, and the 'fat people' (*popolo grasso*) consisting of merchants and landowners – to secure their share of political influence, whether peacefully or by force. Those rising social groups tried to promote civility by reducing the power and status of the nobles – by insisting on sharing the rights and privileges that they monopolized (Denley 1988: 244ff.; Lane 1973: 103–4; Martines 1979: ch. 5). Members of the two strata were unified in opposing the powers and lawlessness of the nobility, but they were weakened by their own struggles to monopolize political power.

During the thirteenth and fourteenth centuries, several rulers initiated 'a project of territorial "centralisation", involving the reclassification of the city as a peaceful place, the demolition of private military installations, and the banishment of violent malefactors' (Vigneswaran 2007: 428). Many cities restricted or outlawed private methods of seeking revenge or justice; capital and corporal punishment were introduced for the most violent of crimes; legal mechanisms for investigating disputes were created although, unsurprisingly, the dominant strata were often unwilling to let the judicial process run its course when they suspected the outcomes would harm their interests; many were quick to use violence against officers of the law when traditional prerogatives and privileges were threatened (Chojnacki 1972). But responses varied. Members of the 'merchant-banker elite' in four-teenth-century Venice who were wedded to elements of the old feudal honour code became reliant on a more stable and 'more controlled environment'; the result was that 'socially acceptable levels of violence became much more narrowly defined throughout the cities of northern Italy at this time' (Ruggiero 1980: 4). Compared with earlier times, violence came to have less to do with the desire for 'vengeance' than with 'rational punishment' – with the utilitarian calculus that was mentioned earlier that applied the rationality of the commercial sphere to the challenge of preser-ving public order (Ruggiero 1980: 44–5). The Venetian 'merchant-banker nobility' was strongly disposed towards greater 'moderation and restraint' at a time when a 'new emphasis on cruelty and terror' was evident in many other cities (Ruggiero 1980: ibid.). The merchant-banker elite often shared the values of 'the courtly world' but was adamant that the nobles' tradition-ally 'violent way of living' and singular preoccupation with honour had to be 'modified by their economic mode of life' (Ruggiero 1980: 65–6). Fines and imprisonment became more prevalent as a result of the influence of utilitarian approaches to punishment and because of political strategies with more 'rational' or 'civilized' objectives. As in several other cities, the permanent danger was that efforts to impose such sanctions would incite 'the proud' to take up arms (Ruggiero 1980: 68ff.).

Striking parallels with the courtesy books that Elias used to explain the evolving relationship between state formation and the process of civilization can be found in the advice books of the period (see Chapter 5). They reflected the practical concerns with formulating new standards of civility or courtesy in a period in which people had to wrestle with the problem of how to live together in emerging urban environments where the power of family and faction often clashed with and overpowered civic attachments (Burke 1987: conclusion). They were symbols of an emergent civilizing process in which conceptions of civil virtue and self-restraint that had been derived from ancient Roman texts were transmitted to the court societies that would even-tually dominate Western Europe. The 'primers of conduct' that were compiled by members of the popolo (*popolani*) had the express aim of promoting 'urbanity' amongst the so-called new men – the *gente nuevo* or rising merchant families that the traditional nobility regarded as social inferiors (Martines 1979: 63). Early 'advice books' highlighted the importance of anchoring rule in respect for public office, and in gratitude for mercy and moderation, rather than in the fear of violence and cruelty that more or less guaranteed that governance was resented and short-lived (Skinner 1978: 33–4). The overall trend was to promote what were widely regarded as core Christian values, but Cicero's writings influenced the general quest to define and disseminate 'civilized' virtues (Skinner 1978: ch. 2). From the early fourteenth century, the 'advice books' were not only aimed at the *podesta*; they offered instruction in the civil responsibilities of all holders of public office (Skinner 1978: 88ff.). As with the forms of 'rational' punishment described earlier, the codes of conduct have been interpreted as monuments to an increasing confidence in the human capacity to mould fate through reason that was noted earlier in the writings of Petrarch and Mirandola (Skinner 1978: 94ff.). They exemplified a degree of optimism that a civilizing spurt could free the cities from the violence that was inherent in the nobility's way of life (Becker 1967).

For the reasons that were noted earlier, the 'civilizing' role of the *podesta* rarely succeeded in ending internal strife or in suspending it for long (Chambers and Dean 1997; Waley 1969: ch. 3). Persistent violence was the product of struggles over the distribution of political power between noble families, merchant groups and other social units. In the early thirteenth century, the result was the general collapse of support for republican institutions and its replacement with the 'strong man' – the *signore* to whom the social elites turned in the thirteenth century in the quest to end public disorder (Skinner 1978: ch. 2). Some of the new breed of leaders displayed 'exceptional cruelty' and were 'a foretaste of what was to come' (Denley 1988: 248). Despotic rule would become standard in the late fifteenth- and early sixteenth-century city states (Skinner 1978: ch. 5).

Even so, many cities did undergo a long-term civilizing process in the intervening period with the result that internal disputes were settled not by force but by votes in the early fifteenth-century council halls (Becker 1988: 191). Of special importance for the investigation of the relationship between violence and civilization in the city-state system – and for understanding the longer-term European civilizing process – were the new advice books that the humanists produced for the *signori* and which they would provide for the growing number of courtiers in the final part of the fifteenth century. The result was that the Italian courts came to have a pivotal role in disseminating specific principles of 'court rationality' across Europe as a whole (Skinner 1988: 423ff.; Hay 1977: ch. 7; Muchembled 2002). Their awareness of parallels between the social and political problems that had first emerged in the eleventh century and the tensions and struggles of the late Roman Republic was one reason for turning to Cicero's defence of aristocratic civility or *urbanitas* for inspiration and guidance (Burke 1987: conclusion).

Humanists made a related case for the moral virtues of princely rule in political discourses that advanced a concrete vision of the civil life (*la vita civile*). At the heart of the princely code was *virtus*, the Ciceronian ideal of moderation, wisdom and excellence in the service of the commonwealth that had been rediscovered by Petrarch (Skinner 1978: 88ff.; Scaglione 1991; Burke 1999: 201–2). The relevant 'mirrors-for-princes' texts combined the exercise in legitimating the public functions of the *signore* with the effort to promote broader cultural transformations (Becker 1968: 36ff.; Stacey 2007: 37, ch. 2). The latter included measures to control speech through respect for the protocols of 'civil conversation' (*la civile conversazione*) in a society where trading public insults could rapidly descend into factional violence (Ruggiero 1980: ch. 8; Burke 1993; Becker 1988: 767). Those social innovations were component elements of the political project of constructing *la vita civile* through an exercise in collective self-education or 'communal *paideia*' that was deemed to distinguish the 'civilized' from the 'barbarians from the north' – the '*gente barbara*' (Becker 1967: 142ff.). A clear sense of collective superiority over those who were not directly descended from the Roman world was at the heart of the civilized self-images that ran through the entire period (Hay 1977: 23; Larkins 2010: 137ff.). As was the case in ancient Greece, confidence in sharp distinctions from 'barbarians' underpinned certain shared practices including the protocols of diplomacy, but it was never strong enough to weaken attachments to the city state and to introduce a new we–I balance that found expression in close political cooperation and in exacting standards of self-restraint.

Moreover, struggles to 'civilize' life within the cities contributed to the violent nature of their external relations. A common practice was forcing internal adversaries into exile given that alternative strategies including the execution of enemies usually led to violent turmoil (Ruggiero 1980: 7). The exiled (*fuorusciti*) who could number as many as a thousand persons from any one city at any given time often found willing allies in neighbouring towns. Displaced factions could launch effective military challenges from the outlying regions. Pacifying strategies therefore 'stymied *intra*-city violence' but often 'tended to exacerbate *inter*-city violence by creating a class of armed, vengeful wanderers' that formed 'antagonistic coalitions' to seize control of the *patria* from which they had been banished (Vigneswaran 2007: 435ff.). In the Peace of Lodi of 9 April 1454, cities agreed not to support exiled factions, but the consequence was a substantial rise in the number of bandits – the *banniti* or *banditi* – many of whom found employment in the mercenary forces which will be discussed later (Davis 2007). Those dynamics reveal that no clear distinction between domestic and international affairs existed in the Renaissance city-state system.

Relations Between the City States

A version of the 'split' within modern civilization in which the ethic that governs relations between citizens of the same state is deemed to have little or no relevance in the competitive sphere of international politics existed in the Renaissance city-state system (see Chapter 5, p. 207). As in other periods, brutalizing conflicts sharpened the divisions between the principles that are often observed within communities and the principles that govern their external relations. To provide one illustration, in many Italian cities, the rape of unmarried women – and certainly from the lower strata – was 'unimportant' in courts of law (Ruggiero 1980: 168). It is scarcely credible that those who took part in warfare felt a stronger imperative to observe more 'civilized' standards regarding the treatment of women when they crossed the city walls to take part in warfare. It is reasonable to suppose that the social standards of restraint that at least the members of the ruling strata followed in their relations with each other had rather less influence on the conduct of their relations with external adversaries. Nevertheless, it is necessary to ask whether the 'tilt towards civility' within many urban communities had any impact at all on intercity relations.

In the mid-fifteenth century, a gradual and uneven shift from the non-permanent mission to resident ambassadors reflected the growing importance of taming international politics (Lubasz 1964). Also important was collective recognition of the value of collaboration to preserve the balance of power. Some parallels to the measures to promote internal pacification were evident in a regional civilizing process. A parallel development was the appearance of a fourth estate of officials who were distinguished from the clergy, nobility and the masses by a we-identity or *esprit de corps* that found expression in efforts to separate the public interests of the state from the personal ambitions of the ruler. From the dominant standpoints of the time, the idea of *stato* was not associated with images of political community and with associated notions of a public sphere. *Stato* referred to the personal dominion of the prince or royal household (Larkins 2010: ch. 7; Loughlin 2003). The idea of the state, by contrast, has come to denote the public monopolies of violence and taxation that are exercised over a population that is enclosed within precisely delineated territorial borders. It refers to the impersonal, legal-bureaucratic structures of authority that are the hallmark of the modern state.

Even so, as noted earlier, 'local patriotism' or *campanilismo* which was intensified by struggles with neighbouring societies and by the competition for control of the adjacent rural areas was a major element in the configuration of the early communes (Burke 1999: 222; Waley 1969: ch. 4). The idea of Italy had little importance, and did not have the symbolic value that 'Europe' would come to possess for the states that would be bound together in the 'civilized' international society of the eighteenth and nineteenth centuries. Revealingly, thirteenth- and fourteenth-century historical narratives focused on describing, usually in flattering terms, the development of the city to which the author belonged. The fact that chroniclers did not trace the history of Italy as a whole is testimony to the standard we–I balance. The major exception to the general trend, Guicciardini's *History of Italy*, was written in the aftermath of the French invasion in 1494 by which the time the common fate of most cities was abundantly clear. More will be said about such matters at a later stage of the discussion.

The movement of exiles promoted a sense of cultural unity, as did the mobility of humanists searching for gainful employment in the courts; the circulation of hired mercenaries consolidated the trend. It was noted in the previous section that the 1454 Peace of Lodi addressed the problem of political instability that resulted from exiled groups that could find support amongst rival governments. Based on relations between Venice and Milan, the Peace metamorphosed into a wider league including Florence, and in 1455 into a mutual non-aggression pact that extended to Naples and the papacy (Fubini 1995). A system of collective security that was established in case of attack from beyond the Alps or in the event of a Turkish invasion represented a significant movement towards the dream of 'European pacification' (Wight 1977: 133). When invasion came in the form of French aggression in 1494, it owed a great deal to the actions of Milanese and other exiles in France (Hay and Law 1989: ch. 2). Higher levels of concerted political action emerged in reaction to the challenges of increasing strategic interconnectedness between the cities and in response to their fateful incorporation within the European states-system. However, experiments in international pacification had only a partial effect on levels of internecine violence (Hay and Law 1989: 162). Few cities were as troubled by the danger of external intervention by one of the major European powers as they were by the threats posed by neighbouring cities and traditional enemies.

Several ruling elites were perfectly aware of the larger international political environment and of the dangers of wider entanglements which some cities tried to turn to their advantage. Following the pattern of trying to draw in external powers when it suited their interests, Ludivoco Sforza, the Duke of Milan, was instrumental in encouraging French involvement in local power struggles. Scholars have therefore rejected the thesis that was once advanced by Mattingly (1973) and others that the city-state system developed in a virtual 'political vacuum' that came to a sudden end with the French invasions (Goffman 2007; Mallett 1974: ch. 9).[2] Venetian expansion had alarmed the

---

[2] Mattingly (1973: 56–7) was closer to the mark when stating that the cities had little understanding of the scale of the social systems that were developing outside the peninsula, were far too confident in their capacity to involve outsiders for specific purposes and to despatch them after the preferred time interval, and were wholly unprepared for the devastation that was to come.

great powers north of the Alps (Larkins 2010: 136). The majority of cities were not as insulated from, or as blind to, wider political trends as some analysts once suggested. In addition, the growing power of the Ottoman Turks who captured Constantinople in 1453 encouraged the formation of we-feeling between cities as well as deliberations about collective security measures. That was one reason for the greater reliance on visiting embassies, and to a limited degree on permanent missions that would become a distinguishing feature of European state formation and a core institution of European international society (Hay and Law 1989). The Italian League (30 August 1454–25 February 1455) which was established shortly after the Peace of Lodi reflected the recognition in Venice, Milan and Florence in particular that Italy would remain vulnerable to external intervention as long as the cities failed to resolve major political differences (Ilardi 1986). The alliance was instrumental in developing a we-identity, as conveyed by the idea of *Italianita*. Recognition of an interdependent fate encouraged the upward curve of diplomatic communication and 'a more articulated sense of the balance of power' that recognized that international equilibrium need not be the unintended consequence of power struggles but could be the product of rational design, of skills in bringing unregulated processes within an unstable 'international' system under partial collective control (Bull 1977: 104–5; Hay and Law 1989: ch. 2, 158ff.).

No account of the constraints that the cities faced, and no discussion of the main obstacles to a system-wide civilizing process, is complete without discussing the destructive impact of mercenary forces (the free companies, or Companies of Adventure as they were called in Italy). In the early commune, citizens were expected to serve in the militia although many cities entered into temporary arrangements with mercenaries to augment their political and military power. The role of the mercenary captains – the *condottieri* who were hired by contract (*condotta*) became more prominent towards the end of the thirteenth century when they tied their armies to any city that was prepared to pay for them. The reasons for the increased significance of such armed forces relative to the civilian militias have been debated (Mallett 1974). Their greater power and influence on the struggles between the cities may have had much to do with growing civilian distaste for engaging in war and with the desire to shun 'all contact with the professional soldier' that was increasingly evident throughout 'the most civilized parts of Europe', and not least because of growing pacific tendencies amongst the merchant classes (Gilbert 1943: 7; Hay and Law 1989: 84ff.). Mercenary forces had special appeal to ruling factions that feared that civilian militias might turn against them, but immense dangers came with hiring mercenaries as well as in trying to protect the city without them.

Machiavelli condemned the mercenary forces for conducting wars with the primary aim of minimizing their own suffering. Calculations about future employment meant that they could not be trusted to promote the interests of the city that employed them. The role of mercenaries raised rather different, ethical, questions for many Christians. The morality of accepting payment for military service without regard for considerations of justice was an important issue at the start of the fifteenth century (Percy 2007: 71ff.).[3] As for the wars in which they were involved – for the most part, battles were not fought to the death, and casualties were usually far lower amongst the heavily armed knights than among the 'lower' ranks (Mallett 1974: 197ff.). With respect to the behaviour of the *condottieri*, Guicciardini observed that mercenary wars were limited before the arrival of the Spanish; 'licentiousness was restrained within tolerable bounds' (cited in Mallett 1974: 85–6,191–2). The atrocities that were committed by the Breton companies, which included the mass slaughter at Cesena in a three-day orgy of killing in 1375, appear to have been especially shocking by the standards of the time (Caferro 1998: 11). Ruling elites that feared the political ambitions of *condottieri* often arranged for their murder or execution. However, the long-term trend was to employ mercenary forces on a more permanent basis. That development, which was complicated by the reality that many mercenary forces were untrustworthy and under limited government control, meant that standing armies appeared in Italy as early as in other parts of Europe (and often much earlier).

The centralization of political and military power was designed to reduce the threats posed by large companies of mercenaries that were compounded at the end of the Hundred Years' War by the influx of discharged, foreign warriors into the peninsula (Caferro 1998: 87–8). With respect to their social origins, many mercenaries who went to Italy were recruited from 'the *petite noblesse*, impoverished by hard times'; given their desperate plight, distinctions between the 'chivalrous knight' and the 'predatory mercenary' were blurred; knights could fight for a commune for a period but then turn against it in order to raise additional booty (Caferro 1998: 5–6). Free companies lived by extortion. The sheer size of such military forces (the largest in 1354 consisted of about ten thousand men that survived by plundering the fertile, central Italian regions) becomes clearer by noting that no more than six thousand troops fought in the English army at Agincourt.

Several ruling elites responded to the political dangers by raising local taxes that were used to negotiate salaries that bound mercenaries to the city for an agreed period. Short-term contracts were perilous for the cities involved. There was no guarantee that the companies would stay loyal when the relevant arrangement expired. Hired mercenaries were

---

[3] The commander of the Great Company, Werner of Urslingen, had the words, 'Enemy of God, Pity, and Mercy' inscribed in gold on his armour (Caferro 1998: xiv).

notoriously unreliable – Niccolo Piccinino deserted the Florentines in the war against Milan in 1424, and almost brought down the republic (Skinner 1978: 75). Competition between *condottieri* could further complicate matters, and their rivalries for the control of territory prolonged several power struggles well into the fifteenth century (Denley 1988: 272ff.). Many cities created leagues to defend themselves against mercenaries, but most alliances had limited success because of irreconcilable internal differences (Caferro 1998: 99–100).

The evolving relationship between cities and mercenary companies was intertwined with the 'monopoly mechanism' that drove the long-term trend towards fewer, but larger, territorial concentrations of power (Denley 1988: 271ff.). That is the subject of the next section. By the 1380s, most of the companies had all but disappeared. As observed earlier, several company leaders became integrated into more powerful state structures. Five great powers existed in that phase and many condottieri became tied to them by longer-term contracts. The legendary English condottieri, John Hawkwood, entered into such an agreement with Florence from around 1378; Jacopo dal Verme fought for the Milanese ruler, Giangaleazzo Visconti, for most of his career (Caferro 1998: 13). The main solution to the 'decivilizing' effect of the mercenaries was the shift towards regular standing armies in the more stable and prosperous cities of the early fifteenth century. In that way, higher-level 'survival units' were formed. That 'civilizing' political innovation ensured a quasi-monopoly of civil control over mercenary forces that brought an end to free market extortion and the perils of short-term contracted employment. Those who lagged behind the main trend in cities such as Venice – Florence and Genoa were two examples – remained exposed to a high risk of violence. The transformation of the relationship between city and mercenary is most apparent in public works of art, as in the memorials that celebrated the condottieri who became permanently attached to a grateful city. Colleoni was commemorated by Verrocchio's equestrian statue in Venice (his will provided the necessary resources). Gattamelata was honoured by an equestrian statue by Donatello. Hawkwood and Tolentino were accorded similar honours in Florence.

Power Monopolization, Territorial Expansion and Elimination Contests

Throughout their history, the Italian cities struggled to control violent harm – whether initiated by the warring nobles and rival factions within the towns, or by the mercenaries who flocked to the peninsula or, to the extent that they constituted a separate domain, by intercity rivalries. The long-term result was the rise of territorial concentrations of power that had a greater capability to restrain violence within the city walls and to project military power beyond them. Italy experienced a sequence of 'elimination contests' that dramatically reduced the number of major cities. But there were also various measures to tame violence in the relations between communities; they amounted to a 'civilizing' project that restrained war for several decades, until the French and Spanish invasions of the late fifteenth and early sixteenth centuries totally transformed the peninsula. Key questions arise about whether there was an overall trend towards limiting violence and reducing suffering in the period in which the cities belonged to a relatively autonomous regional system, whether collective measures to stabilize relations between the cities represented a major advance beyond the states-systems of classical antiquity, and whether the humanist engagement with the Roman legacy led to a unique civilizing legacy of systematic reflections on the relationship between violence and civilization that shaped later European conceptions of statecraft and 'international ethics'.

Increased confidence in reason – in *ragione* which referred to the 'rational, calculating (and) prudent' perspectives on social interaction – was linked with lengthening financial and commercial webs. Powerful tendencies within Renaissance societies encouraged the rationalization of orientations to society and politics that included greater sophistication in 'controlling themselves and manipulating others' as well as in calculating the possible ramifications of developments in other cities (Burke 1999: 203ff.). The twin imperatives of monitoring potentially dangerous trends in other cities and exploring the prospects for diplomatic collaboration to preserve the balance of military power were part of that larger process (Frigo 2000). They were an illustration of how lengthening webs of mutual dependence create pressures and incentives for people to become attuned to each other in new ways with corresponding changes in the psychological dispositions of those involved (Elias 2012: 379ff.).

Greater foresight and more refined patterns of self-restraint emerged as a result of those patterns of development within Italian urban communities and in their relations with each other. They suffused the diplomatic arrangements that were employed to survey social and political developments across an increasingly interconnected states-system (Burke 1999: 204ff.). Stronger commitments to individual and group restraint, awareness of the importance of the ability to anticipate events (*anteverde*), and recognition of the necessity of exercising care (*pensatamente*) and prudence (*prudente*) appeared in that context. They were features of orientations to the social world that would become ever more prominent in later phases of the European civilizing process. Diplomatic works reflected the more general trend, as is evident in the defence of 'even-temperedness' or *equanimitas* in Bernard Du Rosier's 1436 *Short Treatise About Ambassadors* that enumerated the skills and the specific attribute for self-restraint that were critical for the successful performance of ambassadorial functions (for a summary, see Mattingly 1973: 26ff.).

Broad civilizing movements in that direction were constrained by the continuing difficulties in maintaining order within many cities. 'Internal' and 'external' dynamics were so closely interwoven because of the challenges posed by exiled factions that there was no qualitatively distinctive 'problem of harm in world politics' – no separate problem of order in the relations between the Renaissance city states. Cities had taken control of surrounding areas and exploited the inhabitants in the unending competition for security and survival. But the moment they faced external attack, disaffected groups were tempted to seize the opportunity to challenge central authorities or to strive for political independence (Gilbert 1965: 45). Ruling strata could be faced simultaneously with 'external' assaults on the territories they had acquired by force and with 'internal' attempts to appropriate some of their powers or to expel them from office. What there was in the way of a regional civilizing process was restricted then by low levels of intra- and intercity political stability. There were inevitable consequences for diplomacy that were illustrated by the fear in Florence and elsewhere that 'visits from foreign princes' could disturb 'urban tranquillity', or result in assassinations, coups or the seizure of political power (Trexler 1980: 297ff.; Mastenbroek 1999: 50ff.). The prospects for the diplomatic resolution of intercity disputes were limited at a time when the entry of foreign representatives into the city often raised deep suspicions about their ultimate motives and objectives (Trexler 1980: ch. 9).

Nevertheless, high levels of political and strategic interdependence created major incentives to collaborate in the attempt to stabilize relations between the most powerful cities. Their success in controlling and pacifying the areas under their control had the effect of 'filling up' the political space, especially in northern Italy around 1400; the 'margins and cushions' between the affected cities shrank with the result that they came to regard themselves as locked together in relations that were unstable and difficult to control (Mattingly 1973: 55–7, 82ff.). That condition had major ramifications for the diplomatic apparatus that was in place across Italy in 1450 and which spread to the rest of Europe about five decades later. It was a creative response to the challenges of higher levels of strategic interconnectedness; its principal achievement was intercity cooperation to maintain the balance of power (Hay 1977: 117; Mattingly 1973: 10).

Many cities had concluded by the 1430s and 1440s that the problem they confronted was not how to resist the hegemonic aspirations of any single leader who was hell-bent on military and political expansion. What they faced instead was the more general problem of how to enable cities to increase their power given their respective fears and insecurities, but to a moderate degree so that others did not respond by using force, fearing imminent attack

(Mattingly 1973: ch. 7; Fubini 1995). The solution was the recognition that the interests of the city were best promoted through the joint management of the balance of power – through a new we–I balance that involved the civilizing dispositions of collective foresight and mutual restraint. Guiccardini (1969 [1561]: 3ff., 8–9) credited Lorenzo de' Medici with the political insight of recognizing that 'the Italian situation should be maintained in a state of balance' through the collective exercise of moderation and restraint, and by adopting the appropriate policy of 'not leaning more toward one side than the other' and of 'being diligently on the watch' lest 'one of the major powers should extend their area of dominion' (Little 2007: 74ff.; Mattingly 1973: ch. 8; Witt 2000 :455). What was crucial was the breakthrough to understanding that any lasting solution to the problems faced by the cities had to be organized on a 'peninsular scale' (Mattingly 1973: chs. 7–8). The strategy also faced out-wards and sought to dissuade the French king from intervening in Italian affairs (Fubini 1995).

Several sixteenth-century writers looked back to the era of Lorenzo Medici when the balance of power was understood to be the most rational method of seeking to deal with common dangers – to the period before the city states were divided once again by power struggles and by the rise of the 'demonic' types in the tumultuous early sixteenth century (Gilbert 1965: 113ff., 282ff.; Burrow 2007:291ff.). Guicciardini, for example, maintained that Italy had been more peaceful at the end of Lorenzo's rule than a century earlier. Wars had been more limited as was the number of casualties, and the impact on civilians had been less severe. In the main, Italian warfare, while 'far from bloodless', was 'rarely unnecessarily brutal'; cruelty to prisoners was so unusual that it was often condemned as 'bad war' by the standards of the time (Mallett 1974: 200). It continued to be glorified rather than portrayed as 'deplorable' (Hale 1960: 105ff.). Revealingly, in the late fourteenth and early fifteenth centuries, 'the once terrifying god of war became tamed and dandyfied'; Mars was identified with the 'chivalrous ideal of knighthood and he was seen less as the warrior than the lover of Venus', not least in paintings such as Botticelli's that 'played with the familiar antithesis of cruelty and tenderness, the fashionable image of beauty taming cruelty, mildness subduing ferocity' (Hale 1960: ibid.). As in classical antiquity, limited civilizing initiatives arrived too late to alter the general course of events. Moreover, the prevalent Italian practice of deploying small mixed armies engaged in 'attritional warfare' was overwhelmed by the French who relied on large cavalry forces and massed pike infantry to inflict 'the crushing blow' in 'the set-piece battle' (Mallett 1974: conclusion). By skilfully fusing the two techniques, the Spanish emerged as the ultimate victors. That shift in military techniques was accompanied by greater brutality that was exemplified by repeated refusals to take prisoners. 'Unheard-of cruelty and callousness' at the hands of the French and Spanish invading armies was all the more shocking (Hale 1960: 105ff.).

Several scholars have identified two long-term trends in fourteenth-century Italy: the general collapse of republican government other than in cities such as Venice, Florence and Siena; and a steady reduction in the number of city states (Denley 1988: 272–3). In 1200, around two to three hundred political units could reasonably be regarded as city states in Italy. From around 1300, their numbers declined as a result of successive 'elimination contests'. In the course of geopolitical struggles in the early fourteenth and early fifteenth centuries, Florence took possession of Arrezo and then Pisa. Milan gained control of Brescia and Cremona. Venice annexed Verona and Padua. Each of those weaker cities had previously conquered smaller settlements before being subjugated in turn (Mattingly 1973: 54; Hay and Law 1989: 112ff.). By the early fifteenth century, only five great powers (Venice, Florence, Naples, Milan and the papacy) remained (Denley 1988: 273).

The destruction of smaller states and the concentration of military power in a few great powers have been regarded as dominant tendencies in all states-systems (Wight 1977: ch. 1). In the case of the Italian cities, the reduction in the number of great powers simplified the task of maintaining equilibrium. The civilizing role of the balance of power which was a major advance in managing great power relations through 'continuous consultation' owed much to that material reality (Hay 1977: 117). The existence of a shared civilizational discourse made it easier to reach agreements about, for example, the diplomatic rituals that should be followed in exploring the prospects for the non-violent resolution of disputes (Grubb 1991). The upshot was a condition in which the relations between the cities became 'more manageable', resulting in several years of peace (Denley 1988: 272–3). Having reached the outer limits of meaningful expansion, the five dominant powers turned to consolidating their gains through a 'non-aggression pact'. In 1453, Milan and Venice finally agreed to a peace that was extended the following year by the Peace of Lodi which had the consequence of making Italy 'the most peaceful area in the west' until the 1494 invasions ushered in an entirely 'new era' (Hale 1998: 15). In the years prior to the Peace, more restrained and forward-looking leaders such as Alfonso of Aragon and Cosimo de' Medici appeared on the political scene. The *condottieri* were under tighter political control. The Peace endured for forty years, not least because of financial exhaustion, but it did not eliminate warfare completely. Six violent conflicts took place between the 1454 agreement and the French invasion in 1494. Four were the result of internal instability or civil unrest that led other cities to intervene militarily. Although wars still occurred, they were less frequent (three out of every four years between the Peace of Lodi and the invasions were relatively peaceful). They were less destructive than in the past. No city was sacked in that period (Mattingly 1973: ch. 9; Grubb 1991).

The balance of power system collapsed in the last years of the fifteenth century as a result of the French invasion (an earlier rift between Florence and the other cities had helped to unravel it). Many humanists regarded French intervention as marking the return of the 'barbarians', but the cities were incapable of uniting against them, not least because the ruling elites did not command the legitimacy of the lower strata and were compelled to devote considerable resources to maintaining internal order for the reasons that were outlined later. When the invasions came, each city concentrated on its immediate security interests and survival, as in the case of Venice's decision to side with France. The cities were as divided as the Greek city states were when they were faced with Persian expansion. The French invasion (followed by the Spanish assault, which was welcomed by many cities in the attempt to balance France) was the outcome of the same processes that had shaped the long-term development of the Italian city-state system – the rounding out of organized political space, increasing strategic interconnectedness, and the compulsion to project power further afield in the quest for power, glory, security and wealth. 'Elimination contests' that had reduced the number of states in Italy were 'taken to [their] logical conclusion' (Denley 1988: 279). The consequence was that the peninsula was plunged into several decades of some of the most violent conflicts that Europe had ever seen. 1494 marked the beginning of the Wars of Italy. The Sack of Rome in 1527 that led to the death of at least 10,000 of its inhabitants at the hands of the imperial army and its mercenary forces is usually thought to mark the end of the Italian city-state system (Hook 2004).

The shock of the invasions produced a widening of horizons as the cities fully appreciated the extent of their interdependence with the territorial states north of the Alps. Initial responses displayed some confidence in forming a temporary alliance to resist the military challenge (Gilbert 1965: 182ff., 255ff.). Not until the early sixteenth century did the leading intellectuals recognize that the 1494 invasion had changed the Italian city-state system forever. It is hardly surprising that, following the invasions, the idea that force was not just one factor, but the decisive element, in human affairs moved to the forefront of Renaissance political thought (Gilbert 1965: 128ff.). War had ravaged the peninsula in the early part of the sixteenth century. Public order collapsed in many cities from the middle of the century. Several areas were consumed by systematic violence that had not been witnessed since the pre-communal area (Davis 2007: 398–9). After 'three generations of warfare', violence became 'a form of eloquent expression' and 'even casual thuggery seemed like a noble calling' (Davis 2007: 398–9). Violence may have reached its peak in the papal states around 1550–1600 when 'society at times appeared on the edge of a complete breakdown' (Davis 2007: 398–9). One major effect was the 'crisis of assumptions' that is evident in the transition from the earlier humanist confidence in using reason to exercise greater control over the social world to the resigned perspective which maintained that largely unpredictable and unmanageable forces dictated the course of events. The break with the past was most dramatically expressed by Machiavelli's writings, and not least in changing attitudes towards *Fortuna*.

Renaissance Humanism

The Renaissance humanist movement which had its origins in the medieval period had special significance for the theory and practice of the civilizing process in Italy, and for later analyses of the relationship between the human will, social constraints and the possibility of controlling patterns of change. Many humanists were employed by ruling elites that used their skills for the narrow purposes of government, but court service created opportunities for disseminating notions of the 'ideal state' and 'ideal civic conduct' that drew explicitly on Cicero's standard-setting image of the responsible citizen-orator (Denley 1988: 291; also Hay 1977: 108ff., 157ff. on the rise of the Italian courts and courtiers, and Vale 1988: 297ff. on their influence on the later Renaissance monarchies). Most humanists advocated fusing Christian values with the civic virtues of classical antiquity, and they contended that rulers faced a straightforward choice between Roman conceptions of the civilized society and the medieval 'wildness' or Gothic 'rudeness' that was the root cause of the violence of the age (Hankins 1996). Humanists were closely tied to emerging state structures and to efforts to promote internal pacification and to secure the rule of law, but many posed fundamental ethical questions about the conduct of foreign policy in the face of inescapable interdependencies.

The humanist civilizing process that was evident in systematic reflections on civility and civil conduct was not shaped by commitments to *humanitas* in the sense of compassion for others that runs through modern humanitarian campaigns. With respect to slavery, the overwhelming majority followed the ancients in thinking that *humanitas* in the sense of sympathy for others did not extend beyond merciful or lenient treatment (Vogt 1974: ch. 10). Italian humanists celebrated the notion of *humanitas* as human feeling but it was mainly linked with preserving the power and dignity of the ruling aristocratic strata. Many reflected on the human condition – *conditio humana* – but the usual focus was on philology rather than philosophy, or on 'the criticism of texts rather than the criticism of society' (Burke 1998: 31). Identification with an 'international "republic of learning"' through the exchange of letters (*respublica litteraria*) was widespread (Burke 1998: 88), but that should not be mistaken for the Kantian community of *philosophes* entrusted with bringing human rights violations anywhere to the attention of the world. Humanism referred to training in the *studia humanitatas* (specifically ethics, poetry, history, grammar and rhetoric) that included understanding how to use learning for practical purposes such as serving public authorities with their growing need for officials with expertise in translation, letter-writing and public-speaking – and in the case of diplomacy, with particular competence in oratory and Latin (Brotton 2006: 40; Hay and Law 1989: 110; Reus-Smit 1999: ch. 4). Humanists were largely dependent on the patronage of rulers, wrote on the education of princes, and generally assumed that their primary responsibility was to encourage political acquiescence and obedience (Brotton 2006: 45, 53ff.). They developed ideals of the 'cultivated' or 'civilized' self, educated in the classics, and equipped for success in politics, trade or religion (Brotton 2006: 39). Their world view was unashamedly elitist. 'No humanist educator', it has been stated, would have felt at home 'in the age of the common man' (Hay 1977: 210; Hankins 1996).

The case for civility rested on the conviction that social and political institutions were 'not god-given but man-made and . . . could be changed', although radical proposals were treated with considerable suspicion (Burke 1999: 193ff.; Gilbert 1965: 94ff.). Court humanists promoted the ethos of civility. Their 'civilizing' ambitions were spread across many courts rather than concentrated in one standard-setting centre, as in the case of the Versailles court in the early eighteenth century (Elias 2006b; Kempers 1992: 8–9). In addition to reflecting on princely rule, a 'plethora of treaties' in the late fourteenth century celebrated courtesy and moderation as part of the broader consideration of 'virtuous behaviour' (Kempers 1992: 209ff.). Those writings were motivated by the desire to construct a specific conception of human subjectivity: the individual with the voice and tone, the gestures, composure and comportment that embodied the ideal of responsible citizenship. The concept of *humano* referred specifically to courtesy and to the studious observance of the finer details and distinctions of social rank that exemplified courtliness (Martines 1979: 200ff., 236). Such refined attributes would prove to be crucial for conducting diplomacy – for the polished manners and cultivated bearing that befitted the ambassador whose primary role was to protect and enhance the honour of the prince (Biow 2002: ch. 4). In Florence, practical experience in the noble courts was valued because the acquisition of important 'skills and manners' made it easier for those involved to 'consort more easily with lords' in other cities (Trexler 1980: 291–2). The diplomatic community may have done more than absorb the social standards that were integral to the civilizing process within the courts; it may have shaped in its own right an international courtly etiquette that would eventually spread across the major European capitals. Be that as it may, the etiquette of receiving and meeting foreign representatives was invariably intended to advertise the wealth and splendour of the city; one challenge was to display a 'strong and virile posture' that had to be very carefully balanced by careful controls on 'arrogance' that could cause insult and incite 'anger' with all too predictable results (Trexler 1980: ch. 9).

The greatest legacy of that development – the most important bridge between Italian Renaissance humanism and later European conceptions of court diplomacy – was Castiglione's treatise, *Book of the Courtier,* which was first published in 1528 although written around ten to fifteen years earlier (Burke 1995; Hay 1977: ch. 7). The several dozen translations that appeared during the seventeenth and eighteenth centuries indicate that 'interest in Italian models of good behaviour' was even greater than the fascination with Italian art or architecture (Burke 2002: 97). Castiglione's work was a major influence on the education of the European courtier: he had himself been a member of several courts as well as embassies to England, France and Spain (Henshall 2010: 65ff.). His treatise has been described as one of the last major attempts to present a vision of restrained government and the gentleman courtier in an era of increasing violence – a 'civilized' utopian image of how, through the creativity of the 'ideal prince', societies could emancipate themselves from the turmoil and capriciousness that characterized 'savages' (Muchembled 2002: 163–4; Martines 1974). It provided a window onto the larger 'process whereby knights became metamorphosed into courtiers, and ultimately into gentlemen' (Anglo 1977; Skinner 1978: ch. 5). The fourth book, in particular, outlined the courtier's civilizing purpose in persuading the prince to govern virtuously, subordinating passions such as anger and vengefulness to temperance and moderation, and exhibiting similar restraint in the conduct of foreign policy (Castiglione 1959 [1528]: 310ff.). Castiglione defended a specific perspective on the relationship between civilization and violence in a period of social and political chaos that helped to transmit ancient Roman conceptions of *humanitas* to the modern world *via* the writings of later European humanists such as Erasmus and Thomas More which will be discussed in the next chapter.

Fortune and Necessity

The fifteenth-century advice books that celebrated the princely virtues of mercy, temperance and related virtues in the manner of the writings of Cicero and Seneca contended that morality and expediency were entirely compatible (Skinner 1978: ch. 2). Princely rule was required to maintain public order and justice which required the avoidance of *iniuria* – 'the doing of harm contrary to right' whether through the brutal treatment of subjects or the failure to honour one's word. Humanists asserted the possibility of 'moral greatness' through 'the exercise of reason' (Stephens 1990: ch. 3; 112). They stated that rulers who kept faith and displayed mercy would reap the reward of being loved rather than feared (Skinner 1988: 415–16). They also stressed that the prince had the responsibility to preserve the 'civilized' life within 'the necessities of Fortune' (Skinner 1988: ibid.). That formulation was a reference to the goddess, *Fortuna,* recovered by humanists to explain unexpected events without relying on the conventional theological doctrine of divine intervention in human affairs. The principal challenge to their conception of the relationship between violence and civilization – and to their approach to *Fortuna* – was Machiavelli whose writings are considered here from a sociological point of view. As with other works of social and political theory that will be discussed below, they are regarded as significant 'social facts' that reflect broader societal developments and provide special insights into changing orientations to the world. From that standpoint, Machiavelli was in the vanguard of the 'first great wave of reflection' that 'raised the age-old social customs of warrior groups to a higher level of synthesis' by skilfully 'recasting' them 'as a set of prescriptions' (Elias 2013: 131). His chief purpose was not 'to discover how the uncontrollable mechanisms of interstate rivalries and suspicions might be brought under better human control; the facts of power politics themselves appeared to him as unalterable'; the aim was to use the 'inquiry into the unintended mechanisms of the power game' in order to become proficient in 'the more skilful and deliberate playing of the game' (Elias 2013: 151ff.).

Considered from that vantage-point, Machiavelli's writings set out to criticize, as part of a major re-evaluation of 'civilized' standards, the 'effeminating effect' of humanist ideals of 'civility'; they remonstrated that 'the refinements of life' had a corrupting influence on the city; and they contended that the commercial virtues that many humanists admired posed a serious threat to the city's prospects of success in military conflicts (Gilbert 1943: 15). One of the objectives was to demonstrate that 'civilization, politics, history are human enterprises built in opposition to natural impulse and entropy; yet they must acknowledge, use, and transform rather than reject or deny the forces they oppose' – such as the ineradicable drives for security, glory and honour (Pitkin 1984: 233, 320ff.). Machiavelli challenged the supposition that cities could hope to survive without confronting the ethical compromises that were assumed to be dictated by violent competition for security or survival (Hale 1993: 368–9). The goal was to subvert rival humanist standpoints such as those that regarded the Roman republic as the model for any society that hoped to combine liberty and territorial expansion with justice in the relations with subjugated peoples (Hörnqvist 2012). Machiavelli similarly drew contemporary political lessons from ancient authorities – specifically from the writings of Livy – to argue that it was morally irresponsible for the prince to flinch from doing what was necessary in the face of 'necessity' to overwhelm adversaries. Machiavelli did not celebrate violence for its own sake or maintain that Christian virtues should be 'gratuitously ignored' (Skinner 1978: 136). But his writings displayed obvious contempt for those who 'ignored in a self-consciously *civilized* manner' the evidence that the existence of the city state often required unbridled violence (Skinner 1978: 128ff., italics added). In the *Discourses* (Book 1: ch. 26), Machiavelli (1950) argued that the demolition of cities and the transportation of people as part of state-building 'are cruel and destructive of all civilized life, and neither Christian nor even human, and should be avoided by everyone'. The 'life of a private citizen', he added, is preferable to that of a king who is responsible for the ruin of so many fellow human beings. However, at times, the preservation of the city ruled out all other alternatives. Complying with Christian ethical virtues without regard for the political consequences could be disastrous. Moral qualms about violence and cruelty could paralyse actions that were necessary to safeguard the only viable 'survival unit'. Machiavelli wished to restore respect for the ancient value of *virtu* which integrated civic ideals such as action to promote the common good with manliness in war; those were the essential political values that had been scorned by the representatives of Christianity who had made men 'contemplative', 'feeble and 'effeminate' (Machiavelli 1950, *Discourses* Book II: ch. 2). The pagans had been more 'ferocious in their actions', more familiar with 'the slaughter of many animals' and more attuned to the 'bloody nature' of warfare; by contrast, Christianity glorified 'humility, lowliness and a contempt for worldly objects' that made it easier for people 'to suffer than to achieve great deeds'; it left them 'easy prey to evil-minded men' because, in the hope of 'gaining Paradise', they were 'more disposed to endure injuries than to avenge them' (Machiavelli 1950, *Discourses* Book II: ch. 2).

In chapter twenty-five of *The Prince*, Machiavelli (1950) stated that male virtue could tame *Fortuna* which was compared to a woman who was governed by capriciousness rather than reason, and characteristically impulsive unless beaten into submission. The meaning and significance of *Fortuna* changed in that period. The Roman goddess, *Fortuna*, had been linked with good fortune after *fors* for luck; the connection with wilfulness and unpredictability was a later invention that did not jettison the belief that supplicants could influence the goddess to some degree (Pitkin 1984: ch. 6). In the Roman world, *Fortuna* was a potential ally who could be won over with displays of *virs* – 'true manliness' exemplified by masculine courage (Skinner 1981: 25ff.). The Italian Renaissance gave rise to the idea of *Fortuna* as a 'storm' that humans could partially master if, as Machiavelli argued, they demonstrated strength. It would totally overpower them if they exhibited cowardliness and displayed weakness.

Medieval chroniclers usually explained events in terms of the actions of prominent individuals or as the result of divine intervention – few constructed 'middle range explanations' that would only come to the forefront of social and political analysis in the eighteenth century (Burke 1969: ch. 4). But some anticipations of precisely that more sociological orientation can be observed in the transformed meaning of *Fortuna* which declared that the social world was governed by 'impersonal forces' that had to be comprehended in a more detached way if societies were to control, or at least not be dominated by, them – just as they aspired to understand physical laws with the expectation of taming the wildness of nature. The supposition was that societies would continue to be governed by forces that would escape their control if they were left entirely to themselves. But reason would prevail over chance and contingency if human groups could attain a more realistic understanding of the impersonal laws that determined their fate (Gilbert 1943: 23). The fifteenth-century crises led to widespread anxiety about whether humans could significantly influence the social and political world. Many concluded that fortune was 'ultimately in charge' (Skinner 1978: 187ff.). Machiavelli seemed to deny that humans could ever organize their collective existence and steer their future exactly as they pleased but, in the twenty-fifth chapter of *The Prince*, he speculated that fatalism and total capitulation in the face of social forces were unwarranted. His reasoning was that 'fortune is the ruler of half our actions'; 'she allows the other half or thereabouts to be governed by us'.

In the same passage, he commented on the 'impetuous' rivers that run their course unless 'dykes and banks' effectively block their advance. Fortune prevails 'where no measures have been taken to resist her'. So it is with human arrangements (Machiavelli 1950, *The Prince*: ch. 25). It was safe to assume that unpredictable and chaotic events would continue to thwart individual plans and disrupt forms of life. But those were not supernatural forces to which humans must yield; they were like a woman who is susceptible to 'sexual conquest' (Pitkin 1984: ch. 6). Societies might never eliminate the tyranny of fortune but, with the requisite foresight and understanding, they could at least reduce the prospect of being subject to the governance of pure chance (Butterfield 1940: 17ff.). Pivotal to that standpoint was the emphasis on *ragione* – on the dispassionate inquiry into seemingly haphazard and disorderly events that was undertaken with confidence in the human capacity for protecting 'civilized' existence from the forces of necessity that constantly threatened to destroy it.

The idea that necessity knows no law (*necessitas non habet legem*) had been formulated during the final years of the Roman republic (Skinner 1978: 245). It became prominent again around 1300, especially in France, where the concept of *necessitas perpetua* was used to justify occasional suspensions of the conventional restraints on political power (Mastnak 2002: 246ff.). The principle should not be confused with the later doctrine of *raison d'état* which is associated with the conviction that there are irreconcilable tensions between the dictates of responsible statecraft and the absolutist principles of Christian morality (Mastnak 2002: ibid.). Machiavelli's writings were closer to the second position by virtue of stressing that necessity reduced the scope for moral choice in conditions that favoured the strong with the determination to impose their will on others. *Ragione* demanded recognition of the inescapable role of violence in protecting the interests of the city. Machiavelli criticized humanist thinkers who failed to recognize the inescapable clash between ethics and politics – who believed that civility could govern not only princely rule over subjects but also relations between states.

That standpoint was in conflict with the response to the 1494 invasion which held that social catastrophe was the price that had to be paid for straying from Christian virtues. To those who linked *Fortuna* with divine intervention, the only question was how to win God's favour. Savonarola, for example, distinguished between those who groped for 'the counsels of mundane wisdom' by trying to comprehend the patterns of human interaction and those with the deeper knowledge that following the 'counsels of Christianity . . . would please God more' (Gilbert 1965: 42, 138–9, 149–50). Machiavelli's writings, by contrast, represented a major advance to a more detached perspective on the fundamental features of political life – to a more dispassionate analysis of certain 'truths' that were ignored by perspectives that were incapable of providing 'realistic' guidance on how to respond to inescapable threats to security or survival. That development in political theory was part of a larger pattern of development that is captured by the claim that the Renaissance 'set in motion a series of de-centrings' in various interrelated modes of experience – in the natural sciences as well as in history, geography, philosophy and politics – that would have a profound impact on later phases of the European civilizing process (Martin 2007: 24; Elias 2007: 37ff.; Larkins 2010:147ff.).

What united the different spheres was a profound 'change in people's experience of the world in which they lived and their own position within it' (Elias 2007: 37ff.). That transformation marked 'the arrival of societies at a new level of distancing themselves both from the objects and events of this world and from themselves'; they acquired more 'reality-congruent knowledge' as a result of the shift from the dominant egocentric preoccupations with what certain processes 'mean for us' to a more detached inquiry into what they are 'in themselves' (Elias 2007a: 141; Greenblatt 2011: chs. 8–9). Striking changes of orientation towards the world were evident in many domains including such technological breakthroughs as the invention of the first modern terrestrial globe in 1492, at the very beginning of the age of European colonial expansion (Brotton 2006: 35; Larkins 2010: 162ff., 170ff.). Similarly, the discovery of peoples whose existence alarmed the 'interpreters of the Holy Scriptures' who were convinced that the Apostles had spread the faith over the 'entire earth', and who were unaware that 'so vast a part of the world had never before been discovered . . . by men of our hemisphere', had radical social and political consequences (Guicciardini 1969 [1561]: 182). One outcome was the appearance of dichotomies between the dynamic Italian republics and the 'Oriental' despotism of the Ottoman Empire. That dichotomy was muted by the sense of cultural indebtedness to Byzantine civilization and the Arabs, and not least for their access to 'lost' classical writings (Burke 1998: ch. 1). A second consequence – which will be considered in more detail in Chapter 7 – was the emergence of more detached perspectives on human societies that relied on directly observable evidence and displayed scepticism towards, or the outright rejection, of unreflective theological doctrine.[4]

The intellectual impact of the enlargement of the boundaries of social interaction was also evident in the transformation of historical narratives. Guicciardini analysed changes in the larger interstate order to explain the calamity that had consumed Italy as a whole whereas, as noted earlier, the typical chronicler had described in patriotic fashion the parochial history of his city (Burrow 2007: ch. 18). In Guicciardini's writings, and in Machiavelli's, that more detached standpoint was linked with 'the mechanical world picture' that would inform later conceptions of the balance of power that were influenced by changing conceptions of the solar system (Burke 1999: 208; Butterfield 1966). Representations of society as similar to a quasi-physical field of forces emerged in tandem with technical-instrumental conceptions of the world that were geared towards 'rational efficiency' in politics as well as in other spheres of human interaction (Gilbert 1965: 99). Similar transformations were evident in the economic sphere. As in the case of Cosimo de' Medici's 'international interests' that extended well beyond Florentine Tuscany, the relevant strata required a degree of detachment from immediate locations to make rational utilitarian calculations about the value of commercial transactions over long distances (Hale 1981: 207). Lengthening economic webs led to novel forms of orientation and to a new appreciation of the possibilities for exploiting the opportunities that came with them (including, to anticipate reflections on empire in Chapter 6, the practice of importing household slaves in the aftermath of the 1348 plague). Orientations towards the world that embodied higher levels of intellectual detachment promoted significant advances in 'reality-congruent knowledge' that increased collective power over natural and social processes (Elias 2007: 37ff.).

One of the main long-term trends in the history of human societies – namely that the threats that people created for each other increased as the dangers stemming from natural forces decreased – was evident in the Italian city-state system (Elias 2007: 19ff., 65ff.). Renaissance thinkers grappled with the question of whether the Italian city states could break out of cycles of competition and violent conflict – just as they examined how far they could build civility within their respective city walls. For some rulers, as noted above, the answer was found in the 'contrived' balance of power that depended on advances in detachment from parochial interests, and in parallel changes in the level of foresight and self-restraint that, along with the idea of a concert of the great powers and diplomacy, would come to be associated with 'civilization' in a later phase of the European states-system. For Machiavelli, maintaining

---

[4] The reliance on detached empirical observation to achieve more realistic understandings of the world found its greatest expression in the early sixteenth-century Copernican revolution that replaced the geocentric with the heliocentric conception of the universe.

order and civility within the city state rather than developing the basic institutions of international society was the fundamental challenge, one that could not be addressed effectively without confronting inevitable tensions between morality and politics – between the universal principles of Christian ethics and the 'necessities' of statecraft. Critical changes of orientation to the society were set in motion that would have a profound effect on later disputes about the prospects for 'international ethics' in the relations between peoples. Modern standpoints on violence and civilization – on the prospects for, and constraints on, reducing unnecessary suffering in the relations between independent political communities – first emerged in the Italian city-state system.

Civilizing Processes in Renaissance Italy

The first two chapters considered the questions of how different the ancient states-systems were from the modern international order with respect to civilized restraints on violent harm, and what implications can be drawn for the analysis of the preconditions of global civilizing processes. It is important to return to those questions in the light of the discussion of the Renaissance city-state system. There are three similarities with earlier systems of states. First, levels of violence in everyday life were significantly higher than in modern liberal democracies. In common with medieval era, large numbers of people were accustomed to physical violence. Second, Renaissance civilizing processes were also contradictory. One set of social standards governed relations between citizens of the same city; a more permissive code with lower restraints on the use of force applied in the sphere of external relations. Third, 'elimination contests' resulted in a small number of great powers that continued earlier struggles for control of the city-state system. As in the case of the Hellenic system, intra- and intercity conflicts eventually ended in domination by larger, external territorial concentrations of physical power.

Those political dynamics must be understood in connection with assorted endeavours to control violence. There were parallels between earlier attempts to 'tame the warriors' and Renaissance projects of constructing civil urban spaces that restrained the nobility. The emphasis was on creating and maintaining the civil life in the context of violent clashes between political factions that exacerbated tensions and conflicts between rival cities. As in the Hellenic and Hellenistic systems, competing armies were freer to act as they pleased than 'civilized' armies are today and, for long intervals, mercenary forces were largely uncontrolled. The sense of we-feeling was weak and the we–I balance was clearly tilted towards the interests of the city. The level of moral and political unity was too low to underpin lasting collaborative measures to pacify the Italian city-states system.

The great powers were not completely resigned to violence. Their involvement in immediate struggles and their outcomes did not prevent the development of more detached attitudes to relations between cities that under-pinned experiments to maintain the balance of power. Their endeavours were facilitated by restraints on the 'hegemonic principle' that had dominated the Hellenic city-state system. The Italian cities came under pressure to follow a different course. All were locked into strategic rivalries and political inter-dependencies that they could not control. No single city could impose its will on the system. The fledgling diplomatic community facilitated steps to bring some of the restraining principles that were integral to conceptions of the civil life to bear on relations between cities in an attempt to reduce the danger of 'hegemonic wars' and to tame 'hegemonic intoxication'. There was no obvious parallel in the states-systems of classical antiquity.

Renaissance rulers and humanistic thinkers confronted the question of how far they could restrain the unprecedented collective powers at their disposal. Pressures existed in the context of high levels of strategic and political interconnectedness to reflect on how far, or whether, significant advances could occur in the collaborative management of power struggles. Because of the power and influence of the Church, universalistic conceptions of the relationship between ethics and politics – between violence and civilization – were more central to such deliberations than they had been in the ancient states-systems. New tensions between different conceptions of statecraft appeared. They are exemplified by the opposition between Machiavelli's conception of an autonomous 'political ethic' that was emancipated from the dictates of Christian morality, and religious objections to the explicit denial of the supremacy of the divinely sanctioned virtues of mercy and moderation. The Renaissance city-state system was another 'evolutionary dead end' that did not disappear without leaving a cultural legacy that influenced later considera-tions of the principles that should govern the relations between peoples. Important innovations with respect to diplomacy and the balance of power would shape later reflections on principles of restraint in the European society of states, as would the interrelated disputes about how far international cooperation to control unregulated processes could supersede divisive national efforts at overwhelming and outmanoeuvring enemies. The Italian city-state system was a turning point in the history of the European states-systems in bringing those ethical and political considerations to the forefront of the theory and practice of international relations.

5

The European States-System and the Idea of Civilization

> The wars of the seventeenth century were cruel in a somewhat different sense from those of today. The army had, as far as possible, to feed itself when on foreign soil. Plunder and rapine were not merely permitted, but were demanded by military technique. To torment the subjugated inhabitants of occupied territories and to set fire to their houses – all this was, as well as a means of satisfying lust, a deliberate means of collecting war contributions and bringing to light concealed treasure. Soldiers were expected to behave like robbers. It was banditry exacted and organised by the army commanders
>
> (Elias 2006: 101–2)

Elias's comments about seventeenth-century warfare have to be considered in conjunction with his reflections on the longer-term process of state formation that was centred on the dual monopolization of the instruments of violence and taxation. Territorial concentrations of power led to advances in domestic pacification. But the citation at the beginning of this chapter drew attention to the violent character of state formation. The passage was part of a larger discussion about the expulsion of the Huguenots from France that highlighted the use of pliable returning troops to achieve a royal political objective with parallels in many other parts of Europe where emergent states were similarly engaged in rounding out territory, consolidating centralized powers, and subduing recalcitrant subjects (Rae 2002). The wars of that period, Elias argued, were not less cruel than the struggles of the present era; they were cruel in different ways. But what form did cruelty take, and how should later changes be explained? The questions are fundamental to reflections on the distinguishing features of the modern states-system in the following five chapters and to the concluding observations about how key differences are best explained. Those considerations require some observations later in this introduction about the distinctive features of a process-sociological approach to analysing the relationship between violence and civilization in the modern system of states.

Returning to the questions above, part of the reason for the cruelty of seventeenth-century armies is that they had to live off the land; plunder was an essential means of survival. The citation stresses that there was more to their

behaviour than violent self-reliance. Tormenting victims was socially permitted and, for many, a source of pleasure. The age of centrally controlled,
disciplined professional armies that had the logistical capacity to provide
for the basic requirements of their troops lay ahead. In wars between
'civilized peoples', armies would no longer have the same need to compel
the populations of invaded territories to suffer in those ways. As a result of
social and political change over approximately three centuries (Gutmann
1980: 56ff.), plunder and rapine came to be regarded as morally reprehensible and, more recently, as crimes against humanity (Sandholtz 2008).
Those developments are interrelated dimensions of the European civilizing
process. They are a product of the rise of stable monopolies of power that
underpinned a significantly pacified environment in which a more complex
differentiation and integration of social functions could develop. Standards
of self-restraint changed as people responded to external pressures to attune
their behaviour to one another in more peaceful ways. Repugnance towards
violence and suffering appeared that reflected the higher levels of personal
security to which most citizens in contemporary societies have become
accustomed and which are now widely regarded as evidence of radical
differences between 'civilized' and 'barbaric' peoples. More 'impersonal'
forms of 'mechanized struggle' that suppressed the need for aggressive
impulses emerged as part of the same process; they made possible the
unprecedented destructive nature of modern interstate violence (Elias
2012: 196).

Although it was not obvious at the time, a slow crystallization of
monopoly structures had been taking place from around the eleventh
century in areas that the Frankish empire had governed (Elias 2012:
301ff.). The origins of the modern state are to be found in late medieval
'elimination contests'. The analysis of a 'curve of development' stretching
over roughly a millennium stressed the gradual passage from an epoch in
which central political institutions were especially vulnerable to 'refeudali-
zation' to the period in which relatively stable, state monopoly powers
became significantly free from centrifugal influences (Elias 2012: 68,
262–3). Western Europe was the region where absolutist monarchy and
centralized government emerged out of the chaos of the late Middle Ages,
and struck contemporary onlookers as something 'new and extraordinary'
(Elias 2012: 379). Some antecedents of absolutist rule could be found in Italy
during the Renaissance (Elias 2012: appendix 21), but nothing in the previous experience of the two Venetian ambassadors who visited Paris in 1492
prepared them for the impressive achievements of the French state that
they witnessed there. Its enormous strength was the result of success in
monopolizing a right of taxation that underpinned the 'total superiority'
of the centralized powers that were 'revealed nakedly to the eyes of ...
astonished and embittered contemporaries' (Elias 2012: 390ff.).

The Venetian ambassadors observed what would prove to be a turning point in European and indeed in world history. They were themselves a symbol of the increasing political importance of the assiduous gathering of detailed intelligence about French policies and capabilities at the point at which embassies were 'gradually changing from an occasional into a permanent institution' (Elias 2012: 392). The centralization of political functions was different from what had gone before and from what could be found in the majority of non-European regions. The monopolization of state powers, Elias argued, 'is one of the most prominent features of Western history'; moreover, the processes to which those executive capabilities gave rise, namely 'the differentiation and specialization of social functions have attained a higher level in the West than in any other society on earth' (see Elias 2012: 350 and 540 on the earlier taming of 'the warrior class' by a 'strong central authority' in China). The political arrangements that were emerging in France would transform Europe as other societies struggled to match its political and military capacities, and to emulate its standards of 'court rationality'. They were at the centre of a revolution in the history of the Western states-systems that would alter the whole course of human development – first through the overseas empires that modern states alone were able to create and administer and, second, through the politics of imitation in which non-European ruling elites imported Western social ideas and technological and military inventions in order to consolidate their rule and to compete with rivals in the lengthening webs of strategic interaction that radiated outwards from the West (Elias 2012: 423ff.; Ralston 1990). In the 1930s, Elias (2012: 420ff., 470) wrote that the 'incipient transformation of Oriental or African people in the direction of Western standards represents the more recent wave of the continuing civilizing movement that we are able to observe'. The European civilizing process continued to extend outwards from the West that stood at 'the centre of a network of interdependences spreading over wider and wider areas . . . of the rest of the world' (Elias 2012: 420). Such observations, while not anticipating the decolonization process and 'the expansion of international society', foresaw the globalization of interstate struggles (see, however, Elias 2012: 300). In the 1930s, it was possible to detect the 'first outlines of a worldwide system of tensions composed of alliances and supra-state units of various kinds, the prelude of struggles embracing the whole globe, which are the precondition for a worldwide monopoly of physical force' (Elias 2012: 489). That was the most recent phase in the long curve of European social and political development that was summarized by the idea of the civilizing process.

In the course of Western state formation, the gulf increased between (uneven) patterns of domestic pacification and external belligerence that was moderated to some degree by 'civilized' notions of what was permissible and forbidden in wars between states. Earlier outlets for pleasurable killing were steadily closed off. Societies with stable monopolies of power did not encourage as a matter of course the lust for aggression in national populations and armies. The general social trend was one in which public exhibitions of cruelty were regarded as inconsistent with the humane dispositions of 'refined' peoples. But wars continued to be important 'enclaves within civilized society' where 'aggressiveness' was 'allowed freer play' (Elias 2012: 19). It was impossible to conclude that 'civilized' societies were any less likely than their predecessors to unleash devastating violence when national survival was at stake (Elias 2007: 137ff.). Their inhabitants may have convinced themselves that they were less violent than 'savages', but the readiness to use weapons that would lead to the mass incineration of enemies was not qualitatively different from the willingness to use poisoned arrows in 'primitive warfare'. One of the paradoxes of the long process of state formation was that greater controls on violence in the relations between members of the same society were connected with, and made possible, levels of destructive power that less 'civilized' societies could not have begun to imagine.

The fundamental question was how far the nuclear era might lead to a permanent break with the 'hegemonic wars' that had accompanied earlier elimination contests between the great powers in the European states-systems. It was clear that states had become entangled in patterns of interconnectedness that have some formal similarities with the social conditions that existed when early modern European peoples stood on the threshold of the civilizing process. There was a rough – and not entirely 'fortuitous' – analogy between 'the relationships among individual lords in feudal society and among states in the industrial world' [which] has its basis in the developmental curve of Western society itself' (Elias 2012: 266). The parallels raise large questions about the extent to which the modern states-system differs from its predecessors that invite the detailed discussion of the social transformations that accelerated around five centuries ago – specifically the interactions between state formation, domestic pacification, growing human interconnectedness, conceptions of civilization, increases in the collective power to inflict harm on other peoples, and pressures to rein in increasingly dangerous capabilities through serious 'civilizing' initiatives at the global level. An analysis of the interdependencies between those phenomena sheds considerable light on the relationship between violence and civilization in the system of states that emerged in Europe and now embraces the entire world.

As noted earlier, this is a critical chapter in the present work. It is therefore important to pause to consider what is most distinctive about the process-sociological approach to violence and civilization and what is most significant for understanding the development of global harm conventions, whether international or cosmopolitan. The precise nature of the contribution may be obscured by clear parallels between Elias's reflections on world politics and realist or neo-realist theory. Affinities between those perspectives are evident in the shared claim that there is a 'high degree of probability' of violent power struggles and 'elimination contests' whenever a multiplicity of independent political communities depend on themselves for their security and survival (Elias 2012: 296ff.; also Linklater 2009 for further details). The thesis is that states and other 'survival units' have behaved in very similar ways across the centuries and millennia, and that nothing in their history encourages unqualified optimism that they will ever reach a condition in which identification with humanity will be sufficiently strong to control the power to harm that has been vital for survival. But their paths then diverge sharply. From the standpoint of process sociology, it is necessary to consider the most recent illustrations of those recurrent phenomena in conjunction with European state formation and the process of civilization. From the vantage point of neo-realism such an investigation is superfluous. Parsimonious explanation isolates the 'anarchic' system from the totality of social and political life in order to comprehend recurrent properties over the millennia (Waltz 1979: ch. 1). From the standpoint of process sociology, the idea of a social system, while not exactly devoid of value, is criticized for reducing 'everything variable to something invariable', such as supposedly unchanging social structures and associated patterns of behaviour (Elias 2012: 241, 498; Elias 2012: 526). The problem is the supposition that social and political behaviour in different eras is the effect of underlying forces that are identical in all places and all epochs. For Elias, the similarities between the international political dynamics in different eras are profound but extend only so far. As stressed in the introduction to this volume, major differences were noted with respect to the tolerance of mass killing. The standards of self-restraint have not been the same in all eras. They have shifted in tandem with changes in we-feeling and the we–I balance between the state and international society or images of humanity. As the chapters that discussed the earlier Western states-systems have shown, the question of what is permissible and what is forbidden in warfare has not been answered in the same way at all times and in all places. Elias did not examine those variations in the history of the European states-systems in detail. Reflections in the later sections of this work on the relationship between statecraft and civilization will therefore attempt to advance process-sociological inquiry. The importance of the perspective lies elsewhere, namely in the concepts that were employed – principally, but not exclusively – to analyse the changing relationship between violence and civilization in modern societies. The superiority of process sociology over neo-realist systems-theorizing and other mainstream perspectives in International Relations is to be found, first, in the detailed examination of state formation and the civilizing process and, second, in the implications of that analysis for explorations of standards of restraint in world politics in long-term perspective that significantly advance the comparative sociology of states-systems.

The remainder of this chapter begins by summarizing Elias's explanation of the formation of European states as well as interrelated lengthening webs of human interconnectedness and changing conceptions of civilized behaviour. It explains how state-formation developed hand in hand with longer circuits of co-dependence that created strong pressures on people to acquire greater self-control over aggressive impulses and to tame violent tendencies within their respective societies. Such restraints lagged behind in international relations as national monopolies of force were consolidated. The final section considers one of the main responses to the challenges of increasing interstate interdependencies in the period under discussion – the formulation of the idea of *raison d'état* and the conflict with the ethical virtues that were defended by many sixteenth-century humanists such as Erasmus in influential conceptions of civilized statecraft. Such disputes about the relationship between morality and politics (between the imperatives of defending the interests of the state and the incentives to control violent harm) arose at a critical phase in the development of European societies. They were not discussed in Elias's analysis of violence and civilization. It is essential to consider them here in order to understand how the social and political changes that transformed Europe over several centuries led to radical shifts in thinking about the standards of self-restraint that should be embedded in the institutions of the European international society as part of a 'civilized' endeavour to tame struggles between the great powers.

European State Formation

The Venetian envoys who visited Paris in 1492 were clearly aware that they were witnessing something entirely new – a state that possessed extraordinary political powers and military capabilities. Their presence in Paris was evidence of the growing connections between the constituent parts of the European states-system; it demonstrated that the governing elites of the period had come to understand the necessity of monitoring and assessing political developments in other societies (Elias 2012: 392). It was part of a much longer pattern of development. Similar processes had been apparent in the earlier incorporation of 'Franco-English territorial society' within an 'encompassing' European strategic and diplomatic arena in which even the peripheral princes in Germany and Italy tried to affect the outcome of the Hundred Years' War (Elias 2012: 334ff.). 'Growing integration' in that period was the 'first sign' of what would become very much clearer with the Thirty Years' War and the First World War, namely the overall advance in 'worldwide interweaving' that exposed more and more societies to the effects of 'tensions and shifts' in the international distribution of military and political power (Elias 2012: 335). The significance of the Venetian visit to Paris must be understood then in that long-term perspective.

There was no division between 'state' and 'royal household' in the initial stages of European state formation but, in the late fifteenth century, the long-term trend towards their separation was under way (Elias 2012: 393ff.). The Venetian envoys encountered an early phase of the great 'transformation' in which *'the territorial property of one warrior family, its control of certain lands and its claims to tithes or services of various kinds from the people living on this land, was transformed with the advancing division of functions and in the course of numerous struggles, into a centralized control of military power and of regular duties or taxes over a far larger area'* (Elias 2012: 379–80; italics in original). Centralized political structures were an entirely novel departure in societies in which members of the aristocratic warrior class possessed weapons and asserted the right to use them according to their personal inclinations. In a major tilt towards the pacification of the areas that were subject to the monopolization of political and military power, no-one could build fortifications or use weapons without the ruler's express consent (Elias 2012: 380). Even more radical was the right of taxation that allowed the central authorities to preserve their dominion without relying on traditional political strategies that risked dividing the realm (Elias 2012: ibid.). The Venetian ambassadors recognized the contrast with Venice where there were strict limits on central powers of taxation (Elias 2012: 392ff.). Their report expressed astonishment that the French government first calculated its expenditure and only then levied the requisite income through taxes – which was clearly not the practice in Venice (Bonney 1999). The puzzle awaiting solution was: 'How [did] the highly decentralized society of the early Middle Ages, in which numerous greater and smaller warriors were the real rulers of Western territory, become one of the internally more or less pacified but outwardly embattled societies that we call states?' (Elias 2012: 6).

The explanation of how Europe underwent the transition from the medieval order to a system of absolutist states stressed the revolution in the sphere of taxation and the monopolization of force that was linked with the military revolution – specifically the decline of cavalry (and the power of the nobility) as states recruited surplus manpower into infantry armies (Elias 2012: 220–1). The supply of mercenaries broke the state's dependence on the 'war services' of the noble class that gradually lost control of its 'monopoly over weapons' (Elias 2012: 220ff.). As noted earlier, the Venetian envoys were especially struck by the transformative effects of the state's power of taxation (Elias 2012: 392ff.). The two processes drove each other onwards: 'again and again it was the military power concentrated in the hands of the central authority that secured and increased his control of taxes, and it was this concentrated control of taxes that made possible an ever stronger monopolization of physical and military power' (Elias 2012: 390). The emergence of a stronger money economy was fundamentally important because it enabled the governing structures to 'break out of the vicious circle that trapped the rulers of countries with barter economies' (Elias 2012: 396). In those polities, granting ownership of land to indispensable allies was a key instrument in the maintenance of royal power. The practice acted as a check or counterweight to monopolistic tendencies since the recipients acquired local power bases that could be used to mount future challenges to state authority (Elias 2012: 224ff.). The monetarization of economic life made it possible for the centre to pay single fees or permanent salaries to hired officials – neither 'the genesis nor the existence of "states"' could be explained without recognizing the immense political significance of that innovation (Elias 2012: 397). Central power holders were no longer compelled to 'pay for services from (their) own possessions without which expansion would sooner or later be exhausted, but with sums of money from the regular inflow of taxation' (Elias 2012: ibid.). Their power base was strengthened by the capacity to pay for military service and hire armed forces that also removed the dangers inherent in gifts of land. The rise of 'money payment' transformed the possibilities for organizing coercive power – only then were the 'centrifugal tendencies' of the preceding phase 'finally broken'; the way was open for the consolidation of the modern territorial state (Elias 2012: 378).

Elias (2012: 224ff.) stressed how remarkable those developments were, given that they succeeded a prolonged period after the collapse of the Roman empire in which local power groups possessed high levels of political and economic autarky. They were all the more astonishing because feudalization had entrenched the warrior's right to own weapons and use force. The shift from the dominance of centrifugal to centripetal forces was the direct outcome of the 'monopoly mechanism'. Emergent power monopolies competed for the control of territory, material resources and people. Each confronted a straightforward choice between conquering, or in some other way subduing neighbouring populations, and being overtaken by polities that were similarly engaged in military expansion. Free competition between the landed nobles was replaced by state monopolies of power that became entangled in higher-level 'elimination contests' that were waged over larger areas and created longer webs of mutual dependence (Elias 2012: 313, 340–1). The political motives for extending territorial power were often defensive, the intention being to ensure that strategically significant territory did not fall into the hands of actual or potential adversaries. What was true of the later American pioneer applied to the French king and political representatives in that period: '[he] didn't want all the land; he just wanted the land next to his' (Elias 2012: 342). Through competitive struggles, rivals stumbled towards defining their territorial limits. As in the case of France and England at the end of the Hundred Years' War, they could then concentrate on consolidating the monopoly control of military, political and fiscal power (Elias 2012: 321ff.).

There were two main dimensions to that monopolization process: the concentration of power in fewer hands as a result of 'elimination contests', and the 'collectivization of functions' that turned a relatively 'private' monopoly into a 'public one' (Elias 2012: 301ff.). Not least because of the demands of administering the increased wealth that was raised through taxation, central authorities established more specialist institutions staffed by a rising number of trained officials. Slowly at first, and often imperceptibly to people at the time – Elias repeatedly claimed that state building and the process of civilization were largely 'unplanned' – the ruling strata became more 'dependent on [their] dependants' than medieval rulers had ever been, and also less able to indulge their momentary inclinations without regard for the larger network of social restraints (Elias 2012: 304ff., 345ff., 408ff.). The long-term trend was one in which a 'privately owned monopoly in the hands of a single individual or family comes under the control of broader social strata, and transforms itself as the central organ of a state into a public monopoly' (Elias 2012: 305; see Ertman 1997 and Gunn 1999 for more recent discussions of those processes; also Loughlin 2003).

The political role of the king was greatly influenced by the changing balance of power been the nobility and the bourgeoisie. Equipoise suited the interests of kings who tried to ensure that neither class gained the upper hand (Elias 2012: 222–3, 356–7). When the warrior nobility constituted the main challenge to royal authority, urban middle-class interests were protected. In the later phase of the *ancien régime* in France, when the bourgeoisie was an ascendant force, the kings supported the nobility. Rulers responded to the nobles' need for confirmation of their social superiority over the bourgeoisie by appointing them as courtiers, and they skilfully used them to check the power of that ascending class (Elias 2012: 36ff.). At the time, markets were insufficiently developed to function as a major constraint on royal authority; a sharp contrast between the 'economic' and 'political' spheres of social life did not exist (Elias 2012: 338ff.). In short, 'military action and political and economic striving were largely identical, and the urge to increase wealth in the form of land came to the same thing as extending territorial sovereignty and increasing military power' (Elias 2012: 250). But as was the case in the Italian cities, members of the urban classes often gained access to court positions as a result of their knowledge of Roman law and competence in Latin. What Elias (2012:352ff.) described as the 'ambivalence of interests' – a condition in which groups often displayed muted enmity towards each other, but were so interdependent that the main imperative was to learn how to coexist – helped to knit the antagonists together in an integrated social and political whole. As a result of those dynamics, a form of political association emerged that broke free from the recurrent tensions between centralizing and decentralizing tendencies that had characterized earlier feudal polities. In Western Europe, where the balance of social forces was underwritten by what Elias called the 'royal mechanism', 'specialized central organs ... attained a hitherto unknown degree of stability' (Elias 2012: 350). One of the unanticipated consequences was the international states-system that survives to this day.

Civilizing Conduct

The rise of the absolutist state set in motion a fundamental transformation of everyday drives that would define what Europeans came to regard as their condition of civilization (Elias 2012: 218–19). Key features of the relationship between changes in 'the social structure and the structure of affects' could be summarized in the following terms: 'if in this or that region the power of a central authority grows, if over a larger or smaller area the people are forced to live in peace with each other, the moulding of affects and the standards of the drive-economy are very gradually changed as well' in the direction of greater 'reserve' and 'mutual consideration' (Elias 2012: 197–8). In the development of modern European self-images, the idea of civilization grew out of two earlier concepts that had played a central role in moulding the self: *courtoisie* and *civilité*. The three concepts summed up the three stages in the larger pattern of social development. The first was central until, in the course of the sixteenth century, *civilité* began its ascent as the term of choice for members of the social elite. The concept had, 'before the concept civilization was formed and established, practically the same function', namely 'to express the self-image of the European upper class in relation to others whom its members considered simpler or more primitive' – or as 'socially inferior people' (Elias 2012: 47). It gave way in turn to the idea of 'civilization' that found most support amongst the French upper classes in the mid-1770s. The new social idea became linked with the confident assertion of the innate cultural superiority of Europeans. The earlier process of civilization, with all its violence and human misery, was largely forgotten. Elite opinion settled around the conviction that 'civilized' ways had to be disseminated to the lower strata and brought to 'backward' societies in the non-European parts of the world through imperial domination (Elias 2012: 105ff.).

The main chain of events was first evident in the French absolutist court that stood at the hub of a process that would reconfigure Western Europe as a result of the personal ties and channels of communication that bound the royal courts in a larger social figuration. The latter would develop into the 'European court society of the seventeenth and eighteenth centuries' – the great 'supra-national social formation' that was portrayed as the 'last supra-national society of Europe up to the present' day (Elias 2010: 4; Elias 2012: 218–19; also Duindam 1994). 'Martial-military behaviour' was a central feature of 'court civilization' (Elias 2010: 4–5). Repeated wars and geopolitical rivalries did not alter the reality that different European royal households were committed to emulating the style and manners of the court of Louis XIV at Versailles. Most courts identified more closely with the French court than with the lower social strata around them, a 'pre-national' condition that would change when, during the eighteenth century, the rising national bourgeoisie weakened the political influence of the ties between the ruling aristocratic elites in different societies (Elias 2012: 218–19). In the period under discussion, various societies emulated the standards of civilized conduct in the French court as part of a struggle to improve their position in the international hierarchy of power and status (Spierenburg 1981).

Political absolutism was the driving force behind fundamental 'changes in human interweaving and interdependence in conjunction with which people's behaviour and the structuring of their drives were altered in the direction of "civilization"'; it was the key to understanding 'the civilizing of conduct and the corresponding transformation of the structure of mental and emotional life' (Elias 2012: 219, 235). The relevant courts intensified a trend that had already been evident in the earlier feudal royal households where a significant number of nobles had been brought together under the watchful eye of the 'territorial lord'; they had been required to moderate conduct, speech and gestures 'in a somewhat more peaceful atmosphere' given the 'abundance of unwarlike administrative and clerical work' that had to be undertaken to ensure effective government (Elias 2012: 281; Elias 2012: 231, 366–7; also Millet and Moraw 1996). The feudal court was the immediate precursor of modern society because major limits on force, patterns of human interweaving, and the related forms of self-restraint that now distinguish modern 'civilized' peoples from their predecessors first emerged there (Elias 2012: 288–9). In the early modern period, the social distinctions between upper and lower strata were not as sharp as they would become in the absolutist court societies; the behaviour of subordinate groups was not thought to be 'particularly repugnant' whereas, in the later period, greater 'refinement' meant that 'everything reminiscent of lower classes, everything vulgar, was kept at a distance' (Elias 2012: 465). Changing notions of the vulgar and the repugnant – and of the shameful and embarrassing – may not, at first glance, seem to be especially important for understanding the reorganization of state power that occurred with the rise of absolutism (Ranum 1980). The connection is that the continuous refinement of manners was an effective way of consolidating royal power and authority. The 'control of speech', for example, meant that few ministers dared speak their mind to Louis XIV. The whole language of courtesy and civility helped to 'coerce the nobility into obedience, if not subservience' (Ranum 1980: 450–1). The emergent standards of civilization were a critical element then in the configuration of the absolutist system of government.

Some of the political dynamics that led towards such superior, 'civilized' self-images have been noted. But it is valuable to comment further on the importance of the phenomenon that Elias (2012: 355) described as 'one of the most important structural characteristics of more highly developed societies, and a chief factor moulding civilized conduct', namely the impact of the 'ambivalence of interests' on the emergence of new social standards of self-restraint. As discussed above, the concept referred to a condition in which the nobility and the bourgeoisie were joined together in the courts in relations of mutual dependence that encouraged the joint suppression of open antagonisms and the moderation of mutual enmities. A crucial motivation was the realization that actions that were intended to harm others could rebound on the instigators, triggering a wave of responses and counter-responses that could destroy the social and political order. Neither party had anything to gain in the long-run from endangering stability. Those whose lives were woven together in court society developed a collective awareness of the need for self-restraint in relations with members of the other dominant strata. Throughout the transition to the realization that they were partners as well as adversaries, the two groups tended to 'oscillate between the desire to win major advantages over their social opponents and their fear of ruining the whole social apparatus' on which their position depended (Elias 2012: 354). The ability of the central authorities to increase and exercise their powers was greater when the political resources available to the two strata were more or less in check, and when they did not have common interests and ambitions that could lead them to challenge the king, as had occurred during the English civil war (Elias 2012: 350ff., 360–2). The upper social echelons became more inclined to throw their weight behind the king in order to maintain political stability. Mutual self-restraint contributed to the consolidation and stabilization of new state monopolies of power.

High levels of attunement between the balanced parties were no less important for the fact that modern states defied the pre-eminent trend towards disintegration in feudal polities. The concept of social attunement was important in Elias's explanation of the main long-term patterns of development. It conveyed more than the ordinary-language meaning which states that people are accustomed to certain social practices, as in the observation that people in medieval times were attuned to violence. It referred to the negative and positive elements of the process in which social groups learned how to coexist peacefully. The first of those ideas described the plain reality that different social strata had to understand each other's fears and insecurities, and needs and aspirations, if they were to make headway in taming struggles that had the potential to engulf them in violence. Such patterns of mutual accommodation first developed in 'the circles of court life' in the midst of considerable distrust and enmity (Elias 2012: 442). The positive meaning of attunement involved a shift from the pragmatics of 'reserve and mutual consideration' to a condition in which different groups displayed 'muted affection' as well as 'muted dislike' (Elias 2012: 352). It referred to a condition in which the relevant social strata reached the conclusion that the other party deserved begrudging respect because of the power at its disposal or reluctant admiration because of its achievements. Such moderating influences appeared in and shaped absolutist court societies.

The positive elements of the idea of social attunement are significant for explaining how members of the ruling strata came to identify, tentatively at first, with the hazy notion of France or England, and found meaning and satisfaction in a shared nationality or 'national character' (Elias 2012: appendix 23; Greenfield 1992). The long, overall trend towards identifying with others as equals, irrespective of social origins, was shaped by the patterns of interweaving that drew more people into longer and denser networks, and required them to become more attuned to ways of living together less violently and more amicably. The projection of the civilizing process beyond the narrow realm of the court occurred with the formation of a more complex division of labour: as social roles became 'more differentiated', so did 'the number of functions and thus of people on whom the individual constantly depends' (Elias 2012: 367). In that condition, more and more 'people [had to] attune their conduct to that of others, [and] the web of actions [had to] be organized more and more strictly and accurately, if each individual action [was] to fulfil its social function' (Elias 2012: 406). 'More even' patterns of self-control became critical as the webs of interconnectedness became more extensive; they led to restraints on violence and to levels of personal security that had not existed in preceding social eras (Elias 2012: 413; also Chartier 1997: 140). The expanding web of 'civilized' self-restraints was largely the outcome of attempts by the 'lower orders' to reduce feelings of social inferiority by emulating the more 'civil' and 'polished' manners of the ruling elite. The latter responded to their efforts at 'self-improvement' by inventing ever more 'refined' conduct to emphasize their distinctiveness and joint superiority over the less 'civilized' or 'unruly' social strata (Elias 2012: 472ff.).

The analysis of long-term directions in Western European societies emphasized their unplanned nature – their unforeseen emergence from the constraints and pressures on people who had been forced more closely together by the processes that have been discussed thus far. A central thesis was that the state's role in placing certain external constraints on actors was gradually complemented by more powerful inner restraints that had the compulsive effect of a 'second nature' (Elias 2012: 136). In the course of the civilizing process there was a gradual shift in the relative influence of internal and external constraints as the primary determinants of human behaviour. External controls that had been critical in the early pacification of European societies were at first gradually reinforced, and then partly overtaken, by patterns of self-restraint that developed as people found themselves locked together by social forces that largely operated 'behind their backs' (Elias 2012: 346–7; also 273ff.). The changing threshold of shame and embarrassment (the two human emotions to which most importance was attached in the analysis of the civilizing of conduct) played a key role in the process by which people came to comply with standards of self-restraint because of the compulsions of conscience rather than because of the fear of external sanctions (Elias 2012: 457ff.).

The road to that condition was paved by the influential manners books that appeared between the thirteenth and eighteenth centuries; they were the main source of evidence of changing 'civilizing' sensibilities towards the body and elementary 'natural functions' (Elias 2012: part two; also Curtin 1985; Scaglione 1991: 252ff.; Knox 1991). Erasmus' writings were granted special importance because they discussed – in the more detached manner that was increasingly demanded of people – the emergent standards of civility that reflected changes in how they were bound to one another at the time. They were expressions of the gradual process of social transformation in which 'people moulded themselves and others more deliberately than in the Middle Ages' (Elias 2012: 80ff.). In particular, the pamphlet, *De civilitate morum puerilium,* (On Civility in Boys) that appeared in 1530 gave civility its 'socially accepted' precise meaning in that transitional period (Elias 2012: 60ff.; also Revel 1989; Gillingham 2002). The purpose of analysing such works was to document changing emotional responses across different and seemingly unrelated fields of social interaction. The assumption was that images of refined behaviour in any domain could cast light on the larger structure of 'socially instilled forms of conduct' that included changing attitudes to force amongst 'civilized' people (Elias 2012: 76).

A variety of everyday practices were regarded as providing insights into the dominant social tendencies – even though the custom might seem 'trivial' and to lack general significance, as in the case of the growing use of the knife and fork as eating utensils amongst the ruling elites in the sixteenth century. Principles governing the use of the knife (which had been 'a weapon of attack' and remained a powerful symbol of 'death and danger') were illustrations of a broader trend towards limiting the dangers that threatened people (Elias 2012: 123ff.).[1] In conjunction with changing notions of disgust, the carving of animals – and by implication their slaughter – was '*removed behind the scenes of social life*' (Elias 2012: 121–2, italics in original). The practice was evidence of 'forward thrusts in the threshold of repugnance' with respect to the 'animal'

---

[1] Elias (2012: 126) added that the Chinese regarded the Europeans' use of the knife as barbaric. Repugnance on learning that 'they eat with swords' may have reflected the earlier replacement of a 'warrior class' by a standard-setting 'class of scholarly officials pacified to a particularly high degree'. The removal of the knife from the table, and carving animals behind the scenes, had occurred 'much earlier and more radically' in 'the older civilization of China' (Elias 2012: 122).

dimensions of the self that increasingly had to be suppressed (Elias 2012: ibid.). Other behavioural shifts were evident in changing standards of propriety with respect to spitting and nose-blowing (Elias 2012: 142ff.). They marked the rise of the protective barrier of the 'invisible wall' around the self, at one and the same time 'repelling and separating' one body from another, encouraging revulsion at 'the mere approach of something that has been in contact with the mouth or hands of someone else', and also eliciting shame or embarrassment when 'bodily functions' were 'exposed to the gaze of others' (Elias 2012: 77, 116–17, 126). Changed sensibilities with respect to shame were apparent in the 'ever stricter control' of the sex drive and in the concealment of nakedness (Elias 2012: 160ff., 174ff.). No less important were sensitivities with respect to the sources of social embarrassment that were illustrated by a growing 'conspiracy of silence about sexual matters when in the presence of children lest contact with the vulgar, 'animalic' features of life resulted in the 'soiling of the childish mind' (Elias 2012: 173).

Other manifestations of the 'expanding threshold of repugnance' that are more directly connected with the relationship between violence and civilization in different states-systems were apparent in changing social attitudes to the use of force: to regarding certain practices as cruel and barbaric. Important examples of an earlier greater tolerance of force were the 'visual satisfaction' that was found in witnessing cat-burning on Midsummer day in sixteenth-century Paris, later followed by the pleasure that was found in witnessing pain and torture as instruments of punishment (Elias 2012: 197). The growing pacification of society led to ever stricter internal controls on violence. Using force was no longer an individual entitlement, as it had been for knights in the Middle Ages. As part of the monopolization process, the right to inflict violence on 'wrongdoers' became confined to a specialist cadre of public officials who were expected to comply with the more general civilizing restraints when performing their social functions (Elias 2012: 196). Efforts to pacify society included measures that either restricted or prohibited aristocratic duelling (Elias 2012: 439; Elias 2013: ch. 2). More generally, 'the use of physical violence now receded from human intercourse'; force retreated to the 'barracks' and was only released from that 'storehouse' in the extreme circumstances of 'war or social upheaval' (Elias 2012: 411, 439). All of those transformations reflected the broader movement discussed earlier, specifically the shift away from open contempt for the members of the lower ranks which was endemic in the preceding social order where 'war, rapine, armed attack and plunder constituted a regular form of income for the warriors' (Elias 2012: 203ff., 272). In that period, peasants were at the mercy of lords to a far greater extent than at later stages of social development. The nobility did not have to restrain themselves in their relations with the lower strata. The shift away from such attitudes and behaviour indicated the significant pacification of social interaction, the closer interweaving of peoples' lives and increasing levels of co-dependence, the diminishing contrasts between upper and lower strata, and the lowering of barriers to closer emotional identification between members of the same state-organized society (Elias 2012: 422ff.).

The tilt towards civility would leave its mark on emotional responses to warfare. Individuals would no longer be required to cultivate an appetite for aggression; indeed, such warlike dispositions would come to be regarded as unsuited to the more mechanized forms of military struggle that depended less on the personal lust for killing than on the levels of self-restraint required of all people with specialist tasks within an increasingly complex differentiation of functions (Elias 2012: 196). As part of the process of civilization, the balance of power between military and civilian activities gradually changed. 'Martial fervour' had been 'a necessary precondition of success and prestige for a man of the nobility' but, as human interweaving increased, the relevant attributes would come to be regarded as outmoded; 'profession and money' would become 'the primary source of prestige'; in the longer run, and exemplifying the changing relationship between violence and civilization, peaceful 'middle-class traits' would be regarded as the real measure of individual accomplishment (Elias 2012: 447, 467ff.). As a result of the stabilization of monopolies of power and increasing interconnectedness, physical strength began to lose its critical importance for male identity, personal esteem and social standing. Those were later examples of the overall transformation that had been summarized by Caxton in his late fifteenth-century treatise, *Book on Curtseye*, when he stated that 'thingis somtyme alowed is now repreuid' ('things that were once permitted are now forbidden') – a reflection that could stand, Elias (2012: 89) maintained, as the 'motto for the whole movement' that was clearly underway.

Monopolizing Armed Force

Elias's analysis of European state formation and the emergence of an international states-system sought to explain how inter-group rivalries evolved into worldwide events. The first steps towards larger public monopolies of power in the eleventh and twelfth centuries led to a new phase in the history of 'elimination contests', one that seemed likely to continue until humanity came under the control of a global monopoly of physical force that proceeded to pacify the world (Elias 2012: 287–8, 488ff.). Only then might an equivalent to the European civilizing of conduct emerge. Until that stage was reached, the condition in which private acts of violence were largely forbidden within 'civilized' societies but permitted in relations between societies seemed likely to endure.

Of particular importance for the present inquiry are historical explorations of how the late medieval and early modern 'military revolution' transformed the European states-system (Ayton and Price 1995: introduction). The fiscal demands of the state increased with the establishment of large, professional standing armies that made it possible for the ruling strata to impose public order to a greater extent than before and to wage more destructive warfare over greater areas (Duffy 1980). No less important was the 'nationalization' of chivalric codes that Erasmus and other Northern humanists vigorously opposed. The tensions surrounding that development arose at a critical phase of the civilizing process when the dangerous consequences of the acquisition of ever more destructive monopolies of power were increasingly apparent. The state's growing capacity to inflict harm in more distant areas was resisted by key intellectual figures and social movements that harnessed notions of civility in defence of the establishment of powerful constraints on violence in international relations. It is important to discuss significant shifts in the monopolization of force before turning in the next two sections to how doctrines of restraint in foreign policy addressed the problem of violent harm in the modern states-system.

Early modern states largely eliminated other forms of political association (such as city states and aspiring continental empires) during the seventeenth century by virtue of being sufficiently small to be administered from a central governing point and sufficiently large and powerful to withstand external threats. The most successful relied neither on 'capital-intensive' strategies that failed to convert wealth into effective political and military power nor on 'coercive-intensive' approaches that lacked the fiscal base to support ongoing military-bureaucratic innovation; they followed instead the path of 'capitalized coercion' that combined the effective pacification of society (in the period in which policing agencies had yet to be separated from military forces that specialized in conquest and war) with considerable inventiveness in preparing for and conducting interstate warfare (Tilly 1992: ch. 5). Rather like many Italian city states in the early fifteenth century, they recognized the importance of 'commercialized' economies for the maintenance of permanent armies (Wilson 1999: 181). The consolidation of those capabilities depended not just on the state's monopoly power of taxation but, crucially, on the ability to raise significant reserves of credit (Tilly 1992: 85).

The scale of the fiscal demand that confronted early modern states is evident from the growing size of infantry armies in the period between 1500 and 1700. Larger infantry armies, increasingly trained in using firearms, were essential to resist challenges to (heavily fortified) cities given the widespread use of cannon in artillery bombardment (Wilson 1999). Sharp increases in troop numbers, and in the percentage of the population in arms, occurred in France, Spain, and in England and Wales between 1500 and 1700, and in the Netherlands, Sweden and Russia between 1600 and the end of the following century – though most governments could assume that significant desertion would occur prior to, and during, military campaigns (Hale 1998: 79). Estimates are that during the seventeenth century, an unprecedented 10 to 12 million Europeans enlisted in the armies, resulting in 'problems of recruitment, supply and deployment' that no previous government in Christian Europe had faced (Parker 1996: 45–6). Between 1500 and 1700, the French army increased from 18,000 to 400,000 troops, Spain's from 20,000 to 50,000 and that of England and Wales from 25,000 to 292,000. In the period between 1600 and 1700, the Netherlands' army increased from 20,000 to 100,000 military personnel; Sweden's from 15,000 to 100,000; and Russia's from 35,000 to 170,000 (Tilly 1992: 79). Around 1630, every great power had an army consisting of around 160,000 troops (Parker 1996: 24, 45–6). The overall process was far from inevitable. Before 1530, religious wars ensured that divisions between domestic and international conflicts were blurred; it was not obvious that the emerging 'fiscal-military' monopolies would survive (Wilson 1999: 182ff.). But the long-term effect of the Reformation was the consolidation of territorial concentrations of power (Nexon 2009: ch. 3). Leading schools of Protestantism offered strong support for absolutist state powers over sharply defined borders (Wolin 1960: ch. 5). The revision of the just war doctrine to legitimate the public use of force against the proponents of rival visions of Christianity contributed to the general trend.

The number of mercenaries in early modern European armed forces was invariably high (Tilly 1992: 81ff.). One reason – already noted with respect to the Italian city states – was that governing elites were acutely aware that raising armies from local populations created serious political dangers. The number of army volunteers was usually low. Nobles invariably resisted the state's efforts to monopolize coercive power while the towns tried to preserve traditional local militias (Corvisier 1979: 195–6; Parker 1996: 46–8; Wilson 1999: 186). Nevertheless, the changes that had been unleashed by the gunpowder revolution led inexorably to efforts to establish permanent armies. On one interpretation, it is useful to distinguish between the period between 1450 and 1530 when technological breakthroughs, specifically with respect to gunpowder, altered the composition and tactics of the European forces, and the era between 1660 and 1720 when the emphasis shifted to 'the first sustained expansion of permanent armies' (Wilson 1999). In the intervening years – and specifically in the early part of the seventeenth century – the 'sole permanent form of compulsory military service' existed in Finland and in metropolitan Sweden where parishes were obliged to supply military power under the 'allocation system' (Parker 1996: 52). In an attempt to raise national military units by conscription, several states recruited pardoned criminals and the dispensable 'lowlife' who had been conveniently removed from mainstream society (Corvisier 1979: 64). Many rulers purchased services and loyalties by awarding tax exemptions and related immunities, and by promising the material rewards of plunder. Victorious armies invariably recruited prisoners of war to their ranks – on occasion, as an alternative to execution (Hale 1998: 189ff.; Parker 1996: 46ff.). Many governments discovered that the most cost-effective method was to hire trained mercenary armies, not least the Swiss forces with demonstrated success in employing highly trained and self-disciplined troops. The most powerful states kept their own generals in charge, but the weaker ones hired whole armies from suppliers, such as the Bohemian noble and military entrepreneur, Wallenstein, who were in a direct line of descent from the *condottieri* who were discussed in the last chapter (Parker 1996: 64ff.). Reliance on mercenary forces reduced the burden on states; contractors could often supply credit to governments and, with exceptions, they did not seek or acquire public office or grants of land that created the risk of feudalization; nevertheless, they 'retarded monopolization formation by inhibiting direct control in a key area of state activity'. European states gradually increased their control by appointing 'special commissars' to reduce the wastefulness of the mercenary system (Hintze 1975: chs. 6–7; Ertman 1997: 62ff.). Most states had brought their dependence on mercenaries to an end by the sixteenth century, and their employment more or less ceased entirely after the Thirty Years' War when there had been around one thousand, five hundred active companies in Germany alone (Percy 2007: ch. 3; Wilson 1999: 190ff.).

Supplying large armies not only with weapons but with food and other resources added enormously to the fiscal burden, and that was one reason why some states relied on specialist military entrepreneurs for such purposes (Tilly 1992: 81). The practice of living off the land was standard in the struggle for resources (see Hale 1998: 104 and 179 on the devastation of France in Wars of Religion because of the 'bloodlust killings of civilians' committed by inadequately supplied, undisciplined forces). Civilian communities could purchase immunity from attack and possible devastation through the payment of a tax to passing armies or the provision of supplies in an attempt to reduce the risk of plunder. An example was the German 'fire tax' (*Brandschatzung*), a certificate that villages displayed in the hope of being spared systematic looting (Hale 1998: 185). Many governments issued proclamations forbidding pillage, but enforcement was a different matter since many of those who comprised the marauding armies were simply impossible to control.

As a general rule, the state's interest in restraining the troops had less to do with compassion for their victims than with the advantages of maintaining cordial relations with communities that could supply food, water and other essentials – and with ensuring that the political authorities received their expected share of property that had been seized (Hale 1998: 182–5). But various developments were testimony to the influence of the civilizing process. One example was the demarcation of areas that were separate from the affairs of the battlefield – or what has come to be known as the world inhabited by civilians. Respect for civilian life was low until around the end of the eighteenth century and not least because 'civilians' were frequently involved in the defence of towns (Corvisier 1979: 11, 78). Social attitudes changed with the distinctions between the military and the civilian spheres that developed in tandem with internal pacification. The aristocratic warrior code began to lose its importance in the early modern period as a result of the formation of standing armies and associated state demands for higher levels of military discipline (Thomas 2009: ch. 2; also Lowe 1997: 186ff.) on historical precedents in cities such as London during the late fourteenth and early fifteenth century). The long-term trend towards 'the professionalization of the military' and 'the civilianization of the population' meant that virtues such as courage in warfare became 'more akin to the technical qualifications of an occupational group' (Thomas 2009: 65). It would be erroneous to suggest that atrocities against civilians came to an end although military commanders often decided to conceal them on the grounds that they were 'harmless errors' (Corvisier 1979: 179). The greater restraint shown by aristocratic military leaders after the religious wars did not usually extend beyond the higher military ranks; civilians who were caught up in warfare rarely found that their position had improved markedly (Childs 1982). Moreover, before the eighteenth century, prisoners of war were customarily massacred because of the cost of keeping them alive or standard fears about security. The prevailing attitudes changed as states decided on the value of exchanging prisoners, a custom that largely depended on reciprocity and the fear of violent reprisal.

Prolonged destructive wars with high casualty rates imposed enormous burdens on state structures in the sixteenth and seventeenth centuries. The upshot was that strategic thinking was 'crushed between the sustained growth in army size and the relative scarcity of money, equipment and food' (Parker 1996: 44, 53ff.). Financial weakness was one reason for protracted warfare. Many states could raise sufficient reserves through taxation as well as credit to sustain wars for many years, but they could not acquire the resources that were needed to prevail quickly and decisively (Hale 1998: ch. 9; Parker 1996: 43–4, 80). Early modern states also faced great difficulties because of the rapid disintegration of armies through mutiny and desertion. The question in the light of Elias's broader investigation into the monopolization of coercive power is how the transition to large, centrally controlled standing armies took place. Problems of recruitment and supply had the result that the share of the national budget that was dedicated to defence soared; the costs of supporting state bureaucracies that were also becoming larger had the same consequence towards the end of the seventeenth century (Parker 1996: 62, 147). Resentment at, or outright resistance to, increasing tax burdens meant that often the rising costs of war and defence could only be met through large loans that drove some states to bankruptcy in the sixteenth and seventeenth centuries (Hale 1998:

234ff.; Parker 1996: 63–4). 'Capitalized-coercion states' had a decisive edge over competitors when it came to financing large standing armies, conducting wars and launching imperial ventures (Tilly 1992: 133ff.; also Wilson 1999: 192–3). State monopolies of power emerged through that process, first as private possessions and then as public authorities. The 'economic' and 'political' spheres of social interaction were also gradually separated from each other. In early modern Europe, there was no clear division between state authorities and mercantile power. As in the case of the Britain's reliance on the East India Company, the ruling strata depended on the military and commercial resources of the merchant classes to wield 'extraterritorial power' (Thomson 1994: 32ff.). The consolidation of the state's powers took place by breaking its dependence on such organizations (Thomson 1994: 146ff.). No less important was the state's reduced reliance on mercenaries and greater restraints on foreign enlistment. Those dimensions of the rise of the states' military powers and capabilities illustrate one of the core claims that was advanced in the analysis of the civilizing process, namely the need to regard the divisions between the 'domestic' and the 'international', the 'economic' and the 'political', and between the 'civilian' and the military' as the interdependent parts of one overall pattern of development that can only be explained by analysing the central social dynamics and immanent tendencies of the preceding era (Thomson 1994: conclusion).

The emergence of the state's fiscal and military monopolies as of the fifteenth century transformed Europe. Major wars led to 'the division of the continent into separate sovereign states [each with] a distinct domestic and external sphere characterized by the demilitarization of internal politics and the concentration of armed forced in the hands of a single, largely depersonified agency constituting the state' (Wilson 1999: 203). All governments 'maintained land forces primarily to defend and advance interests that were articulated in a language that transcended the individual and spoke to some real or imagined greater whole' (Wilson 1999: 203). From the 1650s, European wars were waged on the open seas to a greater extent than ever before, a development that was linked with the establishment of substantial national navies and parallel overseas extensions of state power that demonstrated the global significance of the European military revolution (Parker 1996). Estimates are that the main navies quadrupled in size between 1650 and 1700, and enabled states to 'enforce their monopoly on violence in European waters' (Glete 1999: 42). That was the period in which permanent navies replaced the temporary hiring of warships. It was further evidence of how the 'continuing growth of effective, centralizing authority' in the early modern period was extended across the entire gamut of military affairs (Hale 1998: 251). The upshot was that the territorial sovereign state became the dominant 'survival unit' in the modern world. In all regions, societies would be compelled to organize themselves around Western conceptions of statehood that were linked with exclusionary nationalist ideologies that were used to harness mass populations for participation in European-style wars. In that way, the 'split that runs through our [our European] civilization' – the contrast between the principles that apply within and between states – became a division within 'civilization understood as now being that of humanity as a whole' (Elias 2013: 190).

Civility and Statecraft in the Early European System

Elias's explanation of the civilizing process is incomplete without a detailed account of how the division of Europe into sovereign polities raised complex ethical issues about statecraft and civility that have preoccupied analysts of international relations ever since. It is important to connect that point with a central question for the study of harm in world politics which is how far entanglements in longer chains of mutual dependence are accompanied by ethical sensibilities about the new opportunities for causing harm, by political efforts to ensure that such developments are checked by significant efforts to 'civilize' social and political relations, or are shaped instead by satisfaction in, or general indifference, to the increased possibilities for harming people in distant places, including the colonized regions. Worth noting in this context is Elias's observation that Thomas More's utopian reflections on the ideal state were an illuminating example of the late medieval or early modern critical responses to emerging territorial monopolies of power and new modes of warfare (Elias 2009c, 2009d). His political vision was an early reaction to the dangerous dimensions of state formation and a powerful statement about the ideal course the European civilizing process should take. It revealed that moral questions regarding the state and statecraft were distinctive features of the early stages of the civilizing process when strong emotional attachments to Christendom provided the motivation for endeavours to restrain the monopoly powers of the state. The Northern humanists' inquiry into how to 'civilize' and 'rationalize' Christendom by promoting perpetual peace is therefore a useful place to begin (Lowe 1997: 149). Erasmus' ethical reflections on statecraft and civilization demand attention, and not least because of the prominence of his treatise on civility in Elias's investigation of state formation and the process of civilization. That inquiry did not consider his writings on the ethics of statecraft or address the larger debates about the significance of European state formation for the images of human unity and solidarity that had been inherited from various medieval authorities including the irenicist conceptions of peace that had developed in late fourteenth-century English court society (Heath 1995). The analysis did not stress that one of the great influences on modern notions of civility and civilization was also an early critic of what Elias (2013: 190) called the 'curious split [that] runs through our civilization'.

Erasmus lamented the failure to control warfare through forms of 'civilized' statecraft. His writings demonstrated that there was more to the process of civilization than the emergence of state monopolies of power, lengthening webs of co-dependence and changing attitudes to self-restraint between members of the same society – and there was more to that process than the appearance of a multiplicity of states that were locked together in relations of competition and conflict. As part of that civilizing process, important debates arose about the ideal relationship between statecraft and civility – about the relationship between ethics and international politics. The prominence of those controversies in the Italian city-state system has been noted. All that needs to be added is that thinkers such as Erasmus understood that state formation raised important moral questions about how 'civilized' societies should deal with the perils of their common fate.

Early sixteenth-century humanists such as Erasmus proclaimed that 'achieving peace (was) the supreme test of humankind's ability to overcome a disposition toward barbarity' (Lowe 1997: 147). They rejected the enthusiasm for the armed citizen that had been expressed by their Italian precursors; they regarded mercenaries who fought purely for money as enemies of Christendom, and they decried the belief that war justified departures from an ethic of mercy and moderation (Skinner 1978: 244–5). Most were opposed to the compromise with violence that was intrinsic to the idea of just war. In the 1517 oration *The Complaint of Peace*, Erasmus (1989 [1517]: 115) defended the Stoic conviction that all wars were fratricidal, and contended that all who regarded themselves as Christian should 'join wholeheartedly in a conspiracy for peace'. The standpoint had parallels in the early sixteenth-century manuals for princes that turned to Stoic conceptions of 'munificent rule' in a further reminder of how ancient ideas of civility as well as early Christian ideas of *caritas* influenced, and were absorbed within, modern conceptions of 'civilized' rule (H. A. Lloyd 1995).

Reflecting such developments, humanists looked back to the *Pax Romana*, to the writings of Stoics, and particularly to Cicero, for a defence of the virtues of kingly rule, while rejecting the latter's support for the just war doctrine (Lowe 1997: ch. 5). In *Christian Prince*, Erasmus restated the humanist emphasis on governance that worked for the good of the whole commonwealth rather than for 'personal emolument'; it was the responsibility of the prince to recognize that he was 'born for the state' and that it was 'not for his own fancy' (cited in Skinner 1978: 222ff.). Those classical themes were linked with the larger political struggle to tame the nobility by replacing the chivalric zest for war with a pacified aristocratic code. The aim was to blend Stoic and Christian virtues in the 'civil' doctrine that the knight (a concept gradually mutating into the idea of the 'gentleman' or 'gentlemen-bureaucrat') had special duties for promoting peace within the commonwealth. Those ideas were derived from the standard-setting 'Ciceronian ideal of public service' (Lowe 1997: 153, 181ff.). In a related development, English humanists in the early sixteenth century endeavoured to replace personal loyalties to the monarch with a broadened conception of national chivalry – with the abstract idea of serving the nation that was embodied in the person of the king (Lowe 1997: 188; Hale 1998: 37–8). That image underpinned the open condemnation in the mid-sixteenth century of mercenaries who were believed to lack the crucial virtue of 'love for country' (Lowe 1997: 225–6). That pacifying ideal was not an unqualified success. With their greater emphasis on national languages, the humanists helped to give expression to 'national temperaments' and unknowingly paved the way for the later fusion of nation and state (Corvisier 1979: 24). The 'sanctified patriotism' that developed alongside nationalist feelings led to supposedly divinely sanctioned wars against fellow Christians that appalled Erasmus and many other humanists (Housley 2000). His writings condemned such violence on the grounds that all profess 'the same lord'; the interrelated contention was that all people belonged to a universal society that was held together by the natural ties of hospitality and compassion (*concordia*) that reflected the inescapable precariousness of human existence.

Whether it was ever legitimate to injure any fellow human being for the sake of preserving the commonwealth was a central moral issue for Northern humanists. Erasmus maintained that when war was unavoidable, it was imperative that the Christian prince should 'conduct it with as little bloodshed as possible. He will take care that his soldiers have the least possible licence to inflict harm upon innocent victims, and he will try to see that the war spreads over as small an area as possible and that it be not prolonged for any period of time' (cited in Heath 1995: 128). Erasmus (1989 [1517]: 109) was explicit that his abhorrence of violence was specifically directed at wars between Christians but he urged similar restraint in relations with the Turks (Heath 1995). The pacific ideal was more than an intellectual mood or fashion, distant from the harsh realities of court politics (Lowe 1997: 224ff.). The humanist ideal of practical knowledge in the service of the state led many to seek office in the royal courts. Pacific influences on court circles seem to have been strongest in England in the early sixteenth century where the rise of an 'increasingly pacified aristocracy' articulated the collective desire to create a political condition that was especially conducive to trade – and not least by using diplomacy for the purpose of 'taming ... the martial spirit' (Lowe 1997: 191ff.). Wolsey staged court events in 1527 and 1528 that openly celebrated the Christian virtue of peace in the company of foreign ambassadors. The pageants may have been little more than charades; even so, such celebrations of peace 'would have been unthinkable one hundred or even fifty years earlier' (Lowe 1997: 179–81). In the same period, many European jurists who were preoccupied with the relationship between statecraft and civility reflected on how ambassadors should deal with conflicts between obligations to the prince and duties to promote the wider peace that were required by ideals of medieval unity and Christian we-identity (Mattingly 1973: part four, especially chs. 22 and 27).

How far could political action promote a 'civilizing' thrust that was directed towards a world in which force is finally eliminated from human affairs? How far might it always be essential to inflict violent harm and great suffering on adversaries in order to preserve oases of security and civility that could only be found within the territorial state? The proposed answers were often sought through interpretations of the international politics of the ancient world. Several early sixteenth-century English writers explicitly condemned the savagery of Phillip II and Alexander the Great's conquests (Lowe 1997: 223). Many other jurists sought guidance in the reflections on war and international politics that had appeared in the period between the rise of Macedon and the emergence of Rome – a dark and 'ominous' development in Europe that was significantly less violent than that epoch but clearly 'moving in that direction' (Mattingly 1973: 274). Europe had not descended to the excesses of that age, but a marked tendency towards a compromise with utility and prudence was already apparent, especially in France and the Low Countries that had suffered devastating religious warfare (Skinner 1978: 251–3). Against that violent background, Montaigne maintained that it was 'unfortunate', but not unjust, that 'a sudden and unexpected accident of state necessity' led the ruler to 'deviate from his word and his faith' (cited in Skinner 1978: 253). The sixteenth-century Spanish theologian, Luis de Molina, argued that the horrors that were committed in sacking cities were deplorable, but they were 'not unlawful' when it was 'considered necessary for the progress of the war that the soldiers should be given an incentive and the enemy struck with terror' (cited in Hamilton 1963: 154). Again, the ancients provided the relevant political language; many accepted the old proverb, 'necessity knows no law' (*necessitas non habet legem*), a principle that was attributed to Publilius Syrius during the final years of the Roman republic (Skinner 1978: 245). Parallels will be noted with the earlier Machiavellian reaction to the tension between 'otherworldly' Christian virtues and the practical 'imperatives' of statecraft.

Between the ideas of Machiavelli and Erasmus or More there was 'the greatest of ethical divides', notwithstanding their membership of the same humanist tradition (Skinner 1978: 250). Prominent Northern humanists were 'particularly scandalized by the fact that force and violence were coming to be regarded as ordinary adjuncts of statecraft'; they were especially critical of Italian humanists with 'an undue readiness to endorse the morally ambivalent notion of "reason of state"' (Skinner 1978: 245–8). Wedded to the 'project of civilizing Europe's warriors', they abhorred the thesis that 'everything is permissible' for kings at war (Skinner 1978: 247–9). Rejecting the principle that 'necessity knows no law', Erasmus maintained that the dictates of justice should be observed whatever the consequences should be, and not least because he recognized – as Thucydides had in the study of the Peloponnesian Wars – that compromises with violence that set questions about ethical restraint to one side invariably brought 'the worst of men' into positions of power. Great importance was attached to controlling dangerous impulses, displaying restraint, and cultivating foresight and detachment, not just in relations between those who belonged to the same community but also in relations with foreigners, and particularly when it came to decisions about whether or not to wage war. Thomas More distinguished between 'rational judgment' and 'habit' (*consuetudo*) or 'appetite' (*appetitus*) that swept people along with little consideration for morality or regard for the human consequences of political action. Seneca's defence of the 'civilizing' effect of 'patience and tolerance rather than retaliation or anger in the face of injury' was a key influence on the defence of such themes in northern humanist writings – as it had been on earlier medieval treatises (Lowe 1997: 150, 170).

Students of humanist political thought have analysed the civil ideologies that developed in tandem with the fiscal-military power monopolies. Those doctrines with their conception of the levels of restraint that people should observe in their relations with others in the same society – but with their lower expectations of constraints in relations with foreigners – were a central dimension of the civilizing process. Along with the idea of sovereignty, they played a vital role in legitimating state monopoly powers (see Chapter 10). Also important were the neo-Stoic or 'Tacitist' perspectives as defended by Lipsius and others in the late sixteenth century. They provide insights into the socio-psychological or psychogenetic features of the 'disciplinary revolution' that appeared alongside new territorial concentrations of power (Gorski 2003; Kroener 2000; Oestreich 1982). Lipsius' 'advice books' or the 'Mirror of Princes' have commanded particular attention because of the influence of their reflections on the organization of permanent standing armies on European military thinking and practice. Notable was the thesis that civil order depended on a combination of restrained government under the law, tight military discipline, and high levels of emotion management across all social strata (Leira 2008; van Krieken 1990). In the writings on military organization, Lipsius argued that standing armies had to be educated to refrain from rape and plunder, just as rulers had to be adept at taming ambition and capriciousness (Kleinschmidt 2010: 117ff.). The importance of the point is underlined by Grotius's later contention that 'civilized' societies 'do not allow rape' although many judged it permissible in times of war; indeed the 'practice was sufficiently commonplace' that attempts to prohibit pillage and rape could lead to mutiny (Vigarello 2001: 15–16). The significance of the 'civilization' of conduct for military life and capabilities is evident in support for the neo-Stoic goal of regulating 'the behaviour of soldiers outside of service, ensuring moderation in food, drinking and sex, and modesty between soldiers and towards superiors and civilians and abstention from violence, plunder and pillage' (Leira 2008: 680). In an early defence of political absolutism, neo-Stoics tried to integrate 'Senecan/Christian ethics' and Machiavellianism (Leira 2008). Their philosophical standpoint is apparent in the distinctions that Lipsius drew between permissible and impermissible deceit in statecraft. In a revealing response to the tension within the civilizing process (between the pressures to exercise restraint and the temptation to blur the distinction between military necessity and political advantage), he distinguished between three forms of deceit, 'light deceit' that was imperative, 'middle deceit' that was morally acceptable though best avoided, if possible, and excessive duplicity that should be deplored because it was uncoupled from the ethical virtues and motivated by destructive emotions such as malice. The putative ethical middle ground between Machiavelli and More was expressed in the neo-Stoic contention that the exercise of power should be limited by 'military prudence' and by the recognition that the systematic breach of Christian standards of self-restraint in the name of political necessity should be checked because of dangers to the realm. In a standpoint that reflects the Grotian *via media* between the positions of Kant and Machiavelli or Hobbes, prudent statecraft was defined by the willingness to accommodate opposing interests, to avoid disproportionate force, and to eschew expansionist ambitions that could damage the interstate order that all societies had an interest in preserving (Leira 1998; Wight 1991: ch. 1). Those observations about 'civil' statecraft reflected the reality that the civilizing process had engulfed societies in new problems and dilemmas that were a consequence of their capacity to inflict more destructive forms of harm on more people over greater areas. It plunged them into 'entanglements' that people in societies with less force at their disposal had not faced (Elias 2012: 8). It exerted pressures on them to restrain the capacity to cause violent harm by working to create a 'civilized' international society.

   Those conflicting ideas shaped the emerging attitudes to political legitimacy that marked the end of the dream of Christian unity that had inspired Erasmus and More; they would influence articulations of the idea of the 'contrived' balance of power idea in the seventeenth and eighteenth centuries during a period in which various legal theorists were disposed towards 'mechanistic analogies' that attempted to emulate advances in the physical sciences in understanding the equipoise of heavenly bodies (Butterfield 1966: 141). At the close of a period of large-scale violence and cruelty that had been unleashed by the Thirty Years War, the Peace of Westphalia – embracing the Treaties of Münster (between France and the Empire) and Osnabrück (between Sweden and the Empire) – established a constitutional framework for the emergent international society of states. The relevant political units were not sovereign equals in the modern sense; Sweden's attempt to win support for the principle of the equality of monarchs was 'firmly rebuffed' (Reus-Smit 1999: 102). But they were convinced that 'pacification' required decisions based on a union of 'universal consent' and 'collective restraint' (Clark 2005: ch. 3). The principle, *cujus regio ejus religio*, as formulated in the 1555 Peace of Augsburg, had proclaimed the right of sovereigns to deter-mine the dominant religion within the state; Westphalia added the principle of religious toleration in the hope of weaving 'a collective acceptance of Europe's irreducible confessional pluralism' into a lasting 'ecumenical peace' (Phillips 2011: 144–51; also Reus-Smit 2013: 104 on the parallel rise of the principle of sovereignty and a 'nascent' doctrine of individual rights). The third clause of the Treaty of Osnabruck established a responsibility to refrain from supporting or offering sanctuary to dissenting political movements in other states, thereby forbidding the forms of 'subversion and reciprocal destabilization' that had been integral to earlier statecraft in an explicit attempt to restrict interstate conflict to 'tolerable bounds' (Phillips 2011: 143ff.; Davidson 2007).

Weary of the atrocities that had been perpetrated in the name of the true faith, European populations looked to absolutist states to 'civilize' armies, and to maintain order through the 'deconfessionalization' of the political sphere (Parker 2005). Refining Westphalian norms, the Treaty of Utrecht which was agreed in 1713–14 was designed to end conflicts that stemmed from competing dynastic claims for sovereign ownership of specific terri-tories. Following the 1701–13 War of Spanish Succession that resulted from the claims that Louis made on the Spanish Low Countries, the great powers concluded that such 'rights' of succession should be quashed because of the collective interest in maintaining a balance of power (Clark 2005: ch. 4). The Treaties of Utrecht were a critical stage in 'delineating the geographical extension of sovereign rights' and in consolidating 'territorial sovereignty' (Reus-Smit 1999: 116ff.). In the main, states were concerned with rounding out and consolidating control of national territories rather than with 'adventurous expansion' with the result that many sixteenth and eighteenth century wars had a pronounced 'cautious' quality and 'a rational bent' (Hintze 1975: 432–3). A critical advance was 'joint responsibility' for the balance of power, a secularized version of the doctrine of duties to the *respublica Christiana* that helped to preserve respect for international law 'despite all rivalries and conflicts' (Hintze 1975: ibid.). By balancing each other's military strength, states could concentrate on centralizing power which was 'the true character of modern political life' (Hintze 1975: ibid.). The whole process has been described as evidence of Europe's self-proclaimed progress beyond 'barbarism, fanaticism, and conquest' – as its coming of age as a 'republic or confederation of states' with distinctive 'civilized manners' (Pocock 2002: 64–5).

Greater institutionalization has been described as one of the main distinguishing features of the modern states-system – a mark of its unusual complexity when compared to the international systems of classical antiquity (Butterfield 1966; Wight 1977: 73). Representing a marked 'tilt towards civility' was the associated emphasis on what Bolingbroke, reflecting on the Napoleonic Wars, would later call 'reciprocal moderation' – on what can be described as a 'civilized' and 'civilizing' disposition towards foreign affairs that led him to claim that a defeated France should be reintegrated into international society rather than subjected to a humiliating 'Carthaginian' peace (Osiander 1994: 152). That shift was facilitated by the idea of *raison de système* in contrast to the narrow conception of *raison d'état*. It was part of a larger project of pacification based on core institutions (the balance of power, diplomacy and international law) that are more highly developed in the modern society of states than in the earlier Western states-systems (Wight 1977: ch. 1). They are evidence of the 'civilizing' role of distinctive international harm conventions.

At the time, it was a limited 'tilt' not just because the 'civilizing' effect of the principle of sovereign equality had yet to be embedded in the organizing legal principles of the states-system but also because the ruling strata had yet to fuse an expectation of higher standards of self-restraint, greater detachment from immediate conflicts, and higher levels of foresight into an explicit doctrine of great power collective responsibility for managing the international system. Governments were less interested in codifying the 'reciprocally binding rules of international conduct' that could be applied to 'all like cases at all times' than in negotiating the resolution of specific, and invariably bilateral, disputes; in addition, the 'old diplomacy' of the era was largely 'reactive, not anticipatory or preventive', and mainly influenced by what were assumed to be the direct causes of the particular struggles that preceded the diplomatic settlements at Westphalia, Utrecht and later at Vienna (Reus-Smit 1999: 107–8). Only later did states attain greater detachment from specific conflicts and confront the international political dynamics that created a very high probability of permanent power struggles and 'elimination contests' across the system as a whole. The 'old diplomacy' inclined towards secrecy that befitted the world views of absolutist courts that were obsessed with ceremonial rituals that denoted their relative positions within the international status hierarchy; it reflected a condition in which kings regarded foreign policy as 'their private domain' with the consequence that many bilateral agreements were reached without the knowledge – let alone the consent – of other parties (Reus-Smit 1999: 108–9, 115). Such intrigue was endemic in court society; it was the by-product of 'the poisonous vapours of the courtly world within which the rulers acted' (Meinecke 1957: 74).

Early formulations of the doctrine of *raison d'état* were designed to steer rulers away from the pursuit of short-term personal interests and impulsive or arbitrary behaviour and towards the 'higher' goal of advancing the interests of the whole community in an era when the distinction between the royal household and public institutions had yet to be clearly drawn. The relationship between *raison d'état* and civility is therefore more complex than may at first appear. The concept straddled two separate themes: the imperative of acting for the common good, and the necessity of political action that was above customary law, and therefore free from many of the moral restraints that governed the relations between citizens. Early treatises distinguished between 'true and good', or 'false and devilish' *raison d'état;* the former was characterized by the recognition of the duty to observe God's law, the latter was much closer to what has come to be known as the Machiavellian principle that 'the end justifies the means' (Burke 1991). The dictates of *raison d'état* were central elements of the practice of carving out the affairs of state from the great morass of private interests that dominated the preceding social phase, as in the Italian city-state system. Changes of meaning reflected the shift from private monopolies of power centred on the royal household to public monopolies in which people became more 'orientated towards the overall network of interdependencies' that bound them together and made them 'dependent on its optimal functioning' (Elias 2012: 310).

Concepts such as 'state', 'fatherland' and 'public cause' were first employed by opponents of the growing powers of kings (Elias 2012: 392). They were used in the attempt to impose stricter demands on rulers including the commitment to observe 'a high degree of rationality and expediency in political conduct'; they were deployed to promote the control of 'personal inclinations and aversions' as well as the suppression of 'emotions' such as 'hatred and revenge' (which Bismarck would describe as 'bad counsellors in politics'); and they were designed to press rulers to concentrate on the 'practical task of securing the common good' (Meinecke 1957: 6). They reflected the shift from the 'passions' to the 'interests' that would dominate not only theories of economics in the eighteenth century but also twentieth-century realist thought with its emphasis on how the rational calculation of common interests could reduce the number of conflicts that resulted from highly emotive world views and ideological excess (Hirschman 1977). Associated ideas that included the concept of *raison de système* came from the 'same root'; they were part of the overall project in which Calvinism, in particular, sought to curb the 'arbitrariness of leaders' (Hintze 1975: ch. 3, especially pp. 92–3 and 308–9; Gorski 2003; Parker 2002: ch. 10). All of those 'civilized' attributes were central to the idea of the contrived balance of power (Meinecke 1957: 6). They were integral to doctrines of statecraft that renounced the quest for universal domination – an expression of self-restraint that was connected at times with the Italian distinction between 'bad' and 'good' *ragione di stato* (Meinecke 1957: 119). *Raison d'état* was therefore employed to subject rulers to greater restraints in both the domestic and foreign policy domains. Its exponents maintained that the principles that applied to the conduct of foreign policy permitted behaviour that was, in general, forbidden from relations between the citizens of a particular state. It allowed the use of force, treachery and other means for the sake of security and survival, but it did not authorize complete lawlessness. Its other side was that societies have common interests in preserving international society, and should moderate their foreign policy accordingly.

Key psychogenetic dimensions of the civilizing process – specifically those pertaining to greater, all-round emotion control – were central to the thesis that the balance of power had a vital role to play in taming the monarchs and in pacifying international relations. They included a commitment to 'the principle of self-limitation' and an appreciation of the need for foresight so that succumbing to the temptation to press home a short-term national advantage was constrained by an appreciation that such action could unleash a chain of events that could inflict lasting damage on international society as a whole. A degree of detachment from immediate strategic concerns and an ability to think long-term about the international system as a whole (*raison de système*) were as important as 'self-limitation' for the politics of restraining aspiring hegemons (Butterfield 1966: 140–1). The balance of power has enjoyed a preeminent place in analyses of international society as the foundation on which the other institutions and practices of that society ultimately depend – the duty of non-intervention that has long been connected with the principle of equal sovereignty, the belief that diplomacy and international law are indispensable restraints on national egoism, and the conviction, that was added in the nineteenth century, that the great powers have special collective responsibilities for preserving international order (Bull 1977: part 2; Dunne 2003; Bukovansky *et al.* 2012). The restraints that are intrinsic to the operation of international society have been at the heart of a distinctive, European civilizing process.

Court Society, Civilization and Diplomacy

The 'contrived' balance of power is a modern European invention that represented a break with the 'hegemonic wars' that dominated international relations in the ancient world. Although, as Hume (1875) [1777] observed, particular cities clearly acted to balance the power of specific rivals, there was no exact counterpart to that institution in the states-systems of classical antiquity. As discussed in chapters one and two, city states gravitated towards the idea of the equality of city states relatively late in the development of the Hellenic international system. The 'scaled up' forms of social and political organization that succeeded the classical polis did not organize their relations around the principle of equality but also aimed for military and political dominance in accordance with the hegemonic principle. The modern idea of cooperating to uphold the balance of power reflected the plain reality that a relatively even distribution of military power made it difficult, but not impossible, for any state to impose its will on all of the others. Diplomatic collaboration to check the power of any would-be hegemon was testimony to the appearance of more rational – or less emotive – political responses to strategic interdependencies. Close co-operation to that end may have been facilitated, as Morgenthau (1973: 217–18) argued, by the reality that the ruling elites believed they were part of the same civilization. The images of civility and civilization that appeared within the European courts (as warriors were turned into courtiers) influenced standards of restraint in relations between the great powers. According to Gibbon, Europe formed 'one great republic' with shared standards of 'politeness and cultivation' and a common 'system of arts, and laws, and manners' that 'imposed moderation', preserved 'the mutual influence of fear and shame' and instilled 'a sense of honour and justice' (cited in Morgenthau 1973: ibid.). The link between court society, civility or civilization and the moderate conduct of foreign policy is most evident in the rise of modern diplomacy.

The writings of the leading French ambassador, Francois de Callières [1645–1717] provide a window onto early eighteenth-century conceptions of diplomacy in which 'power politics and civilized behaviour [were] considered in unison' (Keens-Soper and Schweizer 1983: 41).[2] The function of the ambassador was to strive to reconcile statecraft and civility – to defend the honour of the prince and to promote greater all-round self-restraint in the context of increasingly dangerous political and military interconnectedness (Keens-Soper and Schweizer 1983: 39ff.). Acknowledging that the two objectives were not always compatible, Callières (1983 [1716]: 122–3) maintained that the ambassador had to stand by the principle that 'obedience has its bounds' and should not countenance actions such as encouraging political rebellion in another state since that violated 'the laws of God and justice'. The ambassador had to advise the Prince when foreign policy transgressed higher principles and, if rebuffed, had to request to be recalled while honouring the duty not to divulge 'his master's secret'

---

[2] Late in life, Callières was appointed to the court of Louis XIV, and became *secretaire du cabinet* at Versailles, an office that involved supplying the Secretary of State with responsibility for foreign affairs with memoranda on the conditions of peace. He may have been influenced by Abraham de Wicquefort (1606–82), who served under Richelieu at the French court, and by Bernard du Rosier (1404–75), who is usually regarded as the author of the first treatise on the art of negotiation (see Behrens 1936; Keens-Soper 1997, and Keens-Soper and Schweizer 1983a). Also important for understanding the relationship between court society, the civilizing process and diplomacy is Dolet's mid-sixteenth -century treatise on the offices of the ambassador (Dolet 1933 [1541]). Frigo (2008) provides an important overview of diplomatic theories of the sixteenth and seventeenth centuries (see also Mastenbroek 1999).

(Callières 1983 [1716]: 123). One of the main responsibilities of the diplomat was to reach for a degree of detachment from 'national' standpoints that assisted the search for mutual advantages in interstate relations. It was understood that no higher political authority could direct princes in the international system that had replaced the *respublica Christiana*. However, European court societies were the 'parts of a civilization' that could work together to promote 'order and adjustment by civilized means' – that is, agree on essential standards of self-restraint (Keens-Soper and Schweizer 1983: 35). Callières' perspective was a manifestation of the larger social dynamic in which the French absolutist court became the model of civility that other European courts endeavoured to emulate (Elias 2006b; Frigo 2000; Burke 1992: 158ff.). His treatise on diplomacy revealed that the court was 'standard-setting' not only with respect to manners and etiquette in the royal centres of power but also with regard to the protocols of diplomacy (McKay and Scott 1983: ch. 7; Scott 2007; Fiedler 2010).

Callières' description of restrained statecraft highlights many of the themes that Elias regarded as illustrative of the 'civilizing' of conduct, and particularly of the influence of 'court rationality' on standards of behaviour within and indeed between societies (Elias 2006b: 101ff.). Court rationality demanded certain protocols in 'the art of dealing with people' – in 'the art of what, with a characteristic narrowing of meaning, we call "diplomacy"' (Elias 2006b: 139). Such 'qualities that are today only required from the external representatives of a country' were 'cultivated in the everyday life of [a] court society' with supranational dimensions (Elias 2006b: ibid.; Henshall 2010: 45ff., 62). In short, court conceptions of diplomatic behaviour developed within a supranational figuration, an observation that warns against the assumption that the relevant social standards emerged within one or more courts and only then migrated to other centres with the result that the different ruling strata became closely bound together. It is conceivable that core dimensions of the civilizing process such as the refinement of physical deportment and gestures that were greatly prized in court society first appeared in ambassadorial circles (Roodenburg 1991:171; Roosen 1980).

Callières' skilful anatomy of the ambassadorial role provides evidence of a degree of 'we-feeling' that existed between those who were socialized into the same estate, a 'solidarity of people ... that found expression in the rituals of their behaviour, whether they encountered one another in war or in peace'; that elite we-identity was stronger than the sense of identification with 'the lower classes' in the same society (Elias 2010: 5; Elias 2013: 156–8). That phenomenon was especially evident in relations between 'military officers on opposite sides in their capacity as gentlemen or noblemen, as members of the same "estate"' (Elias 2013: 157). A crucial feature of the 'dynastic' regimes was that, to some degree, 'the code of honour and civility that ruled relations between nobleman and gentlemen within the dynastic states also ruled the relations between members of the upper classes of different states' (Elias 2013: 152). The 'split' within modern civilization was therefore less sharp than in more recent times. In that period, 'few if any contradictions existed between the code of rules [the ruling strata] observed among themselves within one and the same state and the code they observed in interstate relations' (Elias 2013: ibid.). That reality was evident in the general observance of particular aristocratic standards of self-restraint in warfare as well as in the protocols of diplomacy.

The diplomatic mores of the absolutist state are only intelligible if their relationship with *courtoisie*, the court aristocracy and the civilizing process is understood, and if they are considered in conjunction with the rise of specialist bureaucratic structures with responsibilities for training the diplomatic elite (Der Derian 1987: 89ff.; Fiedler 2010; McKay and Scott 1983: ch. 7; Scott and Storrs 1995: 46ff.). A few examples reveal how Callières understood the links between court society and diplomatic conduct in a period when approximately forty ambassadors represented 'the acutely status-conscious diplomatic society of Europe', and when every gesture, ceremonial trifle, official or unofficial act outwardly reflected the contemporary hierarchy of states' and could give rise to 'tedious disputes and delay' (Keens-Soper and Schweizer 1983a: 11). In that world, it was imperative that the ambassador avoided 'a severe rugged manner' that 'commonly disgusts, and causes aversion' (Callières 1983 [1716]: 75). In a domain in which the observance of court protocol and procedure was often as vital as the substantive business of the day, diplomats had to possess great delicacy and refinement in the use of language (Elias 2012: 111ff.). It was imperative to have a dignified bearing – a 'civil and engaging carriage' – that conveyed moderation and restraint; no less important was the ambassador's capacity to weave himself into other court societies, befriending useful allies, and winning favour through mastery of a court vocabulary that could be used to flatter the prince and the inner circle of influential courtiers (Callières 1983 [1716]: 140ff.). A disputatious manner that emphasized others' faults and deficiencies, and amplified differences, was incompatible with the responsibility for exploring potentials for agreements about 'mutual advantages' (Callières 1983 [1716]:110, 151). The ambassador had to understand other courts in their own terms, setting aside personal antipathy to unfamiliar or alien beliefs and customs (Callières 1983 [1716]: 150). He had to 'divest himself, in some measure, of all his own sentiments, and put himself in the place of a prince with whom he treats; he must as it were transform himself into his person . . . and say thus within himself: *If I were in the place of this prince, with the same power, the same passions, and the same prejudices, what effect would those things produce in me which I have to lay before him*' (Callières 1983 [1716]: 139; emphasis in original). That was the diplomatic parallel to the capacity to think from the standpoint of others that became more central to social and political life in the course of state formation and the civilizing process.

For those reasons, and here Callières (1983 [1716]: 75, 86) followed the writings of de Wicquefort, diplomats could not be recruited from the 'naturally violent and passionate' social strata that had learned their specialist craft in, and been coarsened by, the experience of warfare (Keens-Soper 1997). They had to be drawn from officials that belonged to the lower nobility (the nobility of the robe) rather than from the higher nobility (the nobility of the sword) with its dedication to success in the military sphere (Callières 1983 [1716]: 166ff.; see Roosen 1973 on the standard route to ambassadorial office in that period). A clear preference for recruiting from the nobility of the robe was part of the larger struggle for power and prestige within court society (Elias 2012: 359; Elias 2006b: 76, 183ff., 288ff.; Greenfield 1992: 133ff.). The nobility of the sword that had occupied senior diplomatic positions fought hard to maintain its political privileges when challenged by other noble groups (Elias 2006b: 290; also Roosen 1976: 67 on the higher representation of the nobility of the sword in the later years of Louis XIV's reign). Callières attempted to raise the social standing of specialists in diplomacy and to ensure that they had greater political influence in court circles, an aspiration that was necessarily linked with downgrading the social importance of those with nothing other than a military education and skills in the art of warfare (Elias 2006b: 233ff.). By virtue of being highly attuned to the refined rituals of court society, the nobility of the robe was deemed to be the social stratum that could be trusted to act in the name of the prince (Callières 1983 [1716]: 89). Its members could command respect by earning a reputation for honesty and by displaying their understanding that deceit was often counterproductive because it eroded faith in the ambassador and, more seriously, damaged the honour and reputation of the prince (Callières 1983 [1716]: 80ff.; also Behrens 1936 on the development of diplomatic treatises that considered the rights and wrongs of deception). The celebration of such courtly traits expressed the realization that states had to moderate their ambitions and to behave as 'members of one and the same commonwealth' in a condition of increasingly challenging political and military interdependencies where change in one state was 'capable of disturbing the quiet of all the others' (Callières 1983 [1716]: 68). It was to each state's advantage to become more responsive to each other's circumstances, and to replace impulsive behaviour with the dispassionate assessment of interests and the rational consideration of potentials for promoting shared benefits (Callières 1983 [1716]: 97, 110). The constraints and compulsions of interconnectedness required a break with the traditional ethic of princes that was enshrined in the principle, *sic volo, sic jubeo; stat pro ratione voluntas* – 'let the fact that

I wish this, be sufficient reason' (Callières 1983 [1716]: 62).[3] 'Civilized' diplomatic virtues were pivotal to a vision of a changed we–I balance in international society and to shifts in the social standards of self-restraint so that common dangers could be managed in less destructive ways.

Differences with the court societies in the earlier states-systems in the West will be apparent, and particularly with court rationality in the Macedonian and subsequent periods. They shed considerable light on the changing relationship between violence and civilization in the modern era. Core features of the European civilizing process did not eradicate – nor did Callières expect them to eliminate – power politics, but he stressed that the duties of civility did not cease with the outbreak of war. Warfare provided frequent opportunities for obeying the 'rules of civility' in the interests of the greater good and for the glory of the prince (Callières 1983 [1716]:129). As the discussion has shown, one of the principal functions of the ambassador was to strive to reconcile any tensions between the interests or glory of the prince and the responsibility to act honourably. That 'civilizing' endeavour was the direct descendant of attempts to 'tame the warrior' in the Middle Ages; it was one dimension of the longer-term process – 'the transformation of warriors into courtiers' or 'the courtization of warriors' – that began in the small territorial courts of the eleventh and twelfth centuries and led in the seventeenth and eighteenth centuries to a court aristocracy that replaced the warrior nobility as the social stratum that was assumed to embody the highest social virtues (Elias 2012: 428ff.). The existence of that international 'civilizing' ambition and the diffusion of a diplomatic ethic of self-restraint across Europe were striking illustrations of the standard-setting role of the French absolutist court (Keens-Soper and Schweitzer 1983: 23; Keens-Soper 1997).

The political necessity of moderating drives was a central theme for Callières (1983 [1716]: 69ff., 75ff.) who quoted with approval Richelieu's reflections on how 'affairs in France, and in Christendom' had 'entirely changed' because of the previously neglected commitment to reaping the 'advantages [of] continual negotiations ... managed with prudence' (Callières 1983: 1716]: 70). Callières added that he had become ever more certain during his experience of the 'management of the public affairs' that 'to negotiate without ceasing, openly or secretly, in all places, and that although no

---

[3] Callières may have delayed publishing his work until the death of Louis XIV because his ideas about 'civilized' diplomacy were at odds with the King's position. If true, it shows how difficult the transition that Callières had advocated was for members of the French absolutist court. On his deathbed the King is reported to have confessed that he had 'loved war too much' (Keens-Soper and Schweitzer 1983: 36). See Keens-Soper (1973: 497) on Callières' opposition to wasteful or ruinous wars of conquest or glory, and his marked preference for 'a moderated sense of French interests', and Ertman (1997: 133ff.) on the domestic economic and political costs of Louis XIV's foreign policy ambitions.

present benefit should accrue from it, nor any prospect of future advantage present itself, is what is absolutely necessary for the good and welfare of States' (Callières 1983 [1716]: ibid.). The pressures to acquire greater foresight and detachment that had been evident in the early stages of the European civilizing process became more intensive in the relations between states. They found expression in the contention that 'inferior minds confine their thoughts within the bounds of the country where they are born; but those to whom God has given a greater degree of light, omit nothing that may be of defence to them from afar'; they are also apparent in his observation that 'nature teaches everyone to make much use of his neighbours, because as their neighbourhood puts it in their power to do hurt, so it gives them . . . the power of being serviceable' (Richelieu, cited in Callières 1983 [1716]: 70; see Elias 2006b: 208, 256ff. for an assessment of Richelieu's role in taming the nobility, and Kampmann 2010: 205ff. on his conception of *juste modération* in foreign policy).

Richelieu's defence of the art of diplomacy supports the observation that the sociological analysis of court civilization can shed light on a particular phase in the history of the Western states-systems where pressures mounted to adapt the *habitus* of court society to the realities of growing co-dependencies – and to moderate, as Callières argued, the traditional ethic of the absolutist prince (Elias 2006b: 3). Demands for higher levels of controls over aggressive and violent tendencies had been important elements in the slow transition from the private to the public organization of state monopoly powers. Attempts to change the power balance between the narrowly conceived aspirations of the Prince and the interests of international society – and between the military and diplomatic elements of court society – were interwoven elements of the same process of civilization. The court of Louis XIV was of critical importance for domestic and international reasons. His alleged claim, 'I am the state' – which may have been made by his secretaries if not by the king himself – appears to have been a reaction to critics who invoked ideas of the 'fatherland', public cause' and the 'state' in an attempt to distinguish between public power and the royal household (Elias 2012: 392; also Elias 2010b: 185n40 and Burke 1992: 10). Admirers of Louis portrayed him as the universal peacemaker, but critics condemned his treatment of the Huguenots, and compared the 'cruelty and barbarism' of the invasion of the Palatinate with 'Turkish, Tartar, Barbarian Cruelty', and with what one German pamphlet disparagingly described as 'French reason of state' (Burke 1992: 137ff.). Clearly, certain political tensions within the civilizing process were coming to the surface and were being worked out in tentative form. Callières' analysis of court society, civilization and diplomacy provides unusual insight into that distinctive phase not just in the history of European international society but in the development of the Western states-systems.

Legacies of State Formation and the Civilizing Process

This chapter began by quoting Elias's comment that 'the wars of the seventeenth century were cruel in a somewhat different sense from those of today'. Not the least of the reasons was that armies lived off the land. States lacked the capacity to transport the means of subsistence to distant battlefields in an age when the size of armies had increased substantially and when wars had become protracted and more numerous. Elias stated that 'plunder and rapine were not merely permitted' but 'were demanded by military technique', and he added that the expectation was that soldiers would 'behave like robbers'. The evidence is that military struggle had its customary brutalizing effects, sanctioned in the case of the siege by ancient customs about the rights of victorious armies, and often compounded by religious divisions that denied that apostates and heretics possessed moral rights (Parker 2002: 151ff.).

It is important not to suggest that such atrocities occurred without provoking moral unease or to imply that social attitudes to violent harm were remarkably constant during the period in question (Parker 2002: 159–60). Several examples of shock at atrocities in sixteenth-century wars reflected changing sensibilities and foreshadowed later ethical concerns about excessive force that found expression in the Hague and Geneva Conventions (Parker 2002: 168). Especially during the eighteenth century, repugnance towards merciless violence against civilian communities appears to have increased. Moral condemnation increased more or less in line with extensions of state power and the civilizing process. Ruling elites organized properly equipped, disciplined national armies, and were more capable of preventing their collapse into lawlessness. Simply paying armies on time reduced preying on civilian communities. Moreover, particularly after 1648, states had become unwilling to tolerate the levels of violence that had been widespread during the religious wars. Civilians may have been spared unnecessary violence as a result, but the stable state monopolies of power that made that possible continued to engage in struggles that had the effect of increasing their capacity to inflict more destructive forms of harm over greater distances. The ability to conquer and exploit distant peoples was an integral part of that civilizing process.

It was argued earlier that a central question in the study of harm in world politics is how far the entanglement of societies in longer chains is accompanied by heightened ethical sensibilities about the opportunities for committing acts of violence over greater areas and by major political endeavours to restrain the use of force. Callières' reflections on the importance of diplomacy for taming European power struggles addressed the dangers of increasing interdependencies within the modern states-system. Contrasts with the ancient states-systems will be evident, and especially with the role of struggles for hegemony that demonstrated that states such as Macedon, Alexander's empire, the Hellenistic kingdoms and Rome did not believe that they were answerable to a broader conception of 'we' or to an international society. The clearest parallels are with those phases in the development of the Italian city-state system in which ruling elites agreed to suspend the quest for hegemony and to use the instruments of diplomacy to maintain the balance of power. The sense of we-feeling and the we–I balance, when combined with the break with the hegemonic principle, created the conditions for the emergence of greater institutional complexity that included the further refinement of diplomatic protocols that facilitated the collective management of the states-system. The fledgling diplomatic community that developed in the Italian Renaissance reflected a broader effort to apply some of the restraining principles that were integral to conceptions of the 'civil life' to relations between cities. There are parallels with the impact of court rationality on later conceptions of diplomacy that were also designed to reduce the threat of 'hegemonic wars' and to stifle 'hegemonic intoxication'.

The aristocratic code mitigated the worst effects of the 'split' within modern civilization in the relations between European states, but the gulf between the principles that applied within Europe and in relations with non-European peoples increased with the consolidation of state structures and the development of civilized self-images. Intra-European and colonial wars were not conducted in accordance with the same ethical principles. Standards of self-restraint were more demanding in the case of the former conflicts. The contrast sheds further light on the preconditions of civilizing processes in states-systems. More often than not, the decisive influence on whether societies exercised restraint in foreign policy was the existence of a roughly equal distribution of military power. Any state that wanted to spare its armies unnecessary suffering and to ensure safe return of prisoners of war had to convince others that it would display equivalent self-control and suppress the desire for immediate gratification through acts of revenge (Parker 2002: 161). What was critical was not 'rationality' or 'trust' or 'mutual communication' but 'durability' – the likelihood that the various 'sides [would] meet again', and the probability that previous displays of mercy and moderation would be remembered and that acts of brutality would be repaid in kind (Parker 2002: 167). Major power asymmetries in the relations between Europeans and non-European peoples did not encourage respect for principles of reciprocity or strong commitments to exercise self-restraint. The strong were freer to do what they wanted; the weak had few political resources with which to check their behaviour. The former were even less disposed to constrain their actions when they were sure – as was the case in Europe's relations with non-European peoples – of their civilized superiority. The associated 'split' within civilization underpinned European assumptions that particular forms of violence that were condemned within the 'civilized' world were permissible or necessary in relations with 'savages'. But crucially, imperial cruelties were also challenged as an offense against civility, and later as an assault on civilized values. The critique of colonial violence introduced conceptions of the relationship between violence and civilization that extended earlier discussions of morality, civility and statecraft. Notions of civility that first developed in the ancient states-systems became more central to world politics as a result. Those are matters to discuss in the next chapter.

6

Cruelty and Compassion in the Age of Empire

In 1798, as Napoleon set off for Egypt, he shouted to his troops: 'Soldiers, you are undertaking a conquest with incalculable consequences for civilisation'. Unlike the situation when the concept was formed, from now on nations came to consider the *process* of civilisation as completed within their own societies; they came to see themselves as bearers of an existing or finished civilisation to others, as standard-bearers of expanding civilisation. Of the whole preceding process of civilisation nothing remained in their consciousness except a vague residue. Its outcome was taken simply as an expression of their higher gifts; the fact that, and the question of how, in the course of many centuries, civilised behaviour had been attained was of no interest. And the consciousness of their own superiority, the consciousness of this 'civilisation', from now on served at least those nations which become colonial conquerors, and therefore a kind of upper class to large sections of the non-European world, as a justification of their rule, to the same degree that earlier the ancestors of the concept of civilisation, *politesse* and *civilité*, had served the courtly-aristocratic upper class as a justification of theirs.

(Elias 2012: 57; italics in original)

In the above citation, Elias described a relatively late phase in the process in which first Christian international society and then the members of the European states-system asserted the right to civilize 'backward' peoples. Those attitudes were part of the broader movement towards civility and civilization in Western Europe. As noted in a previous chapter, societies did not first develop the practices of civility within their territorial borders and only then reflect on their significance for relations with other peoples. European feelings of cultural superiority and repugnance towards various non-European social practices were not manifestations of a completed civilizing process: they were critical elements in the formation of 'civilized' self-images. From the beginning, the idea of civilization 'which plays down the national differences between peoples' and stresses 'what is common to all human beings' or 'should be' from the standpoint of its self-appointed 'bearers', gave 'expression to the continuously expansionist tendency of colonizing groups' (Elias 2012: 17). The concept was linked with 'the self-assurance of peoples who ... [had] long expanded outside their borders and colonized beyond them' (Elias 2012: 17, 246ff.). However, too little attention was paid to the relationship between state formation, civilization and imperial expansion in that analysis (van Krieken 1999). A related argument is that the civilizing process was conceived as the result of a largely indigenous 'European genealogy of learning and culture' (Goody 2010: 38ff.). The criticism that it ignored the influence of non-European cultures raises profound questions for the future development of the process-sociological explanation of the civilizing process but there is no space to consider them here (see Hobson 2004, 2012; Liston and Mennell 2009).

European societies did not attempt to make whatever progress they could with respect to civility within their borders and within an emergent international society of states before switching their attention to how to treat less 'advanced' peoples. Those developments occurred in tandem – in relations of mutual dependence. As maintained in the definitive study of the expansion of international society, the 'evolution of the European system of interstate relations and the expansion of Europe across the globe were simultaneous processes ... which influenced and affected each other. Both began at the end of the fifteenth century, and both were concluded by the end of the Second World War, by which time European dominance was clearly at an end and the global international system, while still evolving, was being shaped less by Europeans than by others' (Bull and Watson 1984: 6–7). Not that the states that were at the centre of those processes were already stable and secure power monopolies. For example, the Spanish state in its 'early evolutionary stages' developed as part of the 'nucleus of a rapidly growing and new form of empire' that simultaneously faced the question of how to behave as 'a responsible member of an international community of sovereign states' (Fernandez-Santamaria 1977: 1). In addition, 'when the Spanish conquistadors first encountered the Aztecs and Incas, European states were far from having repudiated the hegemonial principle even in their relations with one another ... the doctrines of the internal and external sovereignty of states had not yet been clearly formulated' (Bull and Watson 1984: 6). It is therefore necessary to locate the 'Napoleonic moment' in a longer-term developmental process that extended over the best part of a millennium, and it is important to recall how various forms of Christian universalism and associated notions of cultural superiority gave rise to a sequence of interlocking 'civilizing' projects that have transformed the modern world (Headley 2002). The consolidation of the sovereign state, the formation of a distinctive international society and the configuration of the overseas colonial empires were part of one overall 'transformation of humanity in a specific direction' that reflected the political dominance of European conceptions of civilization (Elias 2010b: 166).

For analytical purposes, the whole process can be divided as follows: first, the period in which dichotomies between 'civilized' and 'barbarian' groups appeared in tandem with the monopolization of power in emerging state-organized societies; second, the defining epoch in Christian international society in the sixteenth century when Spanish theologians debated the status of 'newly discovered peoples' in the Americas; and third, the era in which Christian international society was superseded by the modern states-system, and in which 'civilization' came to be associated with European society while 'barbarism' or 'savagery' described the prevalent ways of life in the non-European regions. That period reached its apex in the nineteenth century when Europeans incorporated 'the standard of civilization' into a colonial discourse that codified their presumed right to stand in judgment of non-European societies and to reshape them in accordance with their images of human progress. Such assumptions lost favour during the twentieth century, but successor doctrines live on in the transformed standard of civilization of the post-colonial era (Stroikos 2014).

Elias stressed that Napoleon's rallying call marked the beginning of a new phase in the process of civilization in which an international 'upper class' acquired a standard-setting role not unlike the position of French court society in the preceding century. In both cases, the ruling 'establishment' looked down on the 'lower' strata who were expected to internalize feelings of inferiority and who often laboured to emulate their 'superiors'. Analyses of the expansion of the society of states have clarified the central global dynamics. They have explained how, in the first phase of that relationship, the 'lower strata' largely accepted 'upper class' standards of 'civilized' behaviour including Western principles of international relations. They have also shown how the 'cultural revolt against the West' influenced the rapid transition from a European to a universal international society. That challenge to Western dominance did not reject the constitutive principles of that society such as the ideas of sovereignty and non-intervention – indeed many newly independent states would become their keenest exponents (Bull and Watson 1984). But second generation nationalist leaders were more disposed to assert 'indigenous' practices and to reject European colonial assumptions about their right to stand in judgment of them, to stamp out 'erroneous' ways, and to assess their progress in moderniz-ing their societies until they conformed with European understandings of civilization. They paved the way for the 'post-secular' manifestations of the 'cultural revolt against the West' that exist today (Shani 2014).

In short, 'second generation' leaders rejected the European 'standard of civilization' that had been formulated by international lawyers such as James Lorimer in the 1880s, who created a tripartite division between 'civilized', 'barbaric' and 'savage' peoples (Gong 1984). That classification of human types was used to justify excluding the 'uncivilized' from membership of the society of states and to clarify the domestic and international changes that would have to take place before admission into that society – which was regarded as the direct 'product of the special civilization of modern Europe' – could even be contemplated (Hall 1924: 47). As noted in the last chapter, writing in the 1930s, Elias described the diffusion of European values as the most recent observable phase of a civilizing process that had spread outwards and transformed human society as a whole. The transition from a European to a universal society of states that began in the early twentieth century, and which accelerated in the aftermath of the Second World War as a result of decolonization, reveals how that 'civilizing offensive' has continued in modified ways. Of particular interest are various attempts to rework the 'standard of civilization' as part of the ongoing political practice of distinguishing between properly constituted 'civilized' societies and 'lawless' or backward regimes that fail to comply with global standards of propriety. A revised version of the 'standard of civilization' underpins the universal human rights culture (Donnelly 1998). Other illustrations include the discourse of 'civilization' and 'barbarism' that was integral to the 'war against terrorism', and the notion of the 'axis of evil' in the 1980s that can be traced back to the struggle against Fascism, to the demonization of Germany and the Soviet Union at the end of the First World War, and to their initial exclusion from the self-defining democratic, 'civilized' community of states that formed the core of the League of Nations. Those themes have been reworked in recent distinctions between the 'democratic peace' and outlying areas of 'tyranny' and 'lawlessness' (Simpson 2004). Similar contrasts are apparent in Western efforts to export democratic institutions or global 'market civilization' to 'backward' or 'underdeveloped' regions, and to promote state reconstruction in war-torn societies through forms of international trusteeship that are heir to the late nineteenth- and early twentieth-century idea of the 'sacred trust of civilization' (Bain 2003; Bowden and Seabrooke 2006; Fidler 2000; Hobson 2008; Zaum 2007). All of those variations on the 'standard of civilization' are evidence of how the civilizing process has influenced the modern states-system. They also reflect the long established conviction that the modern European sovereign state is the sole foundation and guarantor of 'advanced' ways of life (Bowden 2009: ch. 5).

Those different phases in the recent history of the modern states-system have been linked by a series of debates about the moral and political principles that should apply within Europe or the West and in relations with radically different groups in the other regions of the world. The political context in which those disputes have taken place was astutely summarized by Durkheim [1925] (1973: 192–3) when he referred to the virtual 'law' that states that 'whenever two populations, two groups of people having unequal cultures, come into continuous contact with one another, certain feelings develop that prompt the more cultivated group – or that which deems itself such – to do violence to the other', to those deemed to be 'inferior' by the former which becomes intoxicated by a form of collective 'megalomania' that has the effect that 'nothing restrains [them]'. Amongst those 'feelings' was the belief that 'savages' lacked the self-restraint that distinguished 'advanced' peoples, and the inference that the ethical standards that applied in relations between civilized groups could be set to one side in dealings with supposedly cruel inferiors. European conceptions of the 'civilized' and the 'barbarian' mirrored a more general phenomenon in the relations between human groups which is the marked tendency to contrast the 'minority of the best' in one's own community with the 'minority of the worst' elsewhere (Elias and Scotson 2008: ch. 7). Many societies did not hesitate to behave in 'savage' ways that included genocide in the quest to advance 'civilization' (Powell 2011; van Krieken 1999). However, the idea of civilization had an ambiguous role in that process since it was also used in debates about how to restrain the more powerful groups, and to condemn the violence and exploitation that often accompanied relations with 'inferiors' (Phillips 2012). Theodore Roosevelt gave expression to the tensions within the modern civilizing process when he maintained that 'all civilized mankind' is indebted to the 'settler who drives the savage from the land' but added that a people surrenders the right to call itself 'civilized' when it behaves 'as barbarously as its barbarous foes' (cited in Mennell 2007: 326–7). Such formulations encapsulated the ethical conviction that came to the forefront of European thought in the age of the Enlightenment that 'advanced' peoples forfeit the right to elevate themselves above other groups when they freely ignore 'civilized' restraints on violence in their relations with non-European peoples – when they are nothing other than the practitioners of 'civilized barbarism'.

Precursors of that tension within the idea of civilization and the whole civilizing process were evident in the distinction between the inner circle of Christian international society and the all-inclusive community of humankind that was constructed during the outward expansion of late medieval and early modern peoples. In the middle of the sixteenth century, Vitoria asserted the absolute right of the Church to preach Christianity to the 'newly discovered Indians' and to use force against local rulers who blocked the path of the missionaries. Those orientations to other peoples did not make a sudden appearance with the conquest of the Americas but had arisen in earlier theological deliberations about whether 'infidels' had rights to property or relinquished such entitlements by holding 'false' beliefs. Drawing on those earlier reflections, Vitoria argued that the relations with 'newly discovered Indians' had to comply with 'civilized' standards; they had to respect just war conventions, and they had to be restrained because subject peoples were not 'animals' or 'things' but the members of civil orders that were worthy of respect notwithstanding deviation from the 'true faith' (Vitoria 1917 [1565]: 34ff.). It is important to recall Elias's observations about how state formation in early modern Europe grew out of the preceding social phase, and how the 'monopoly mechanism' accelerated earlier political dynamics and transmitted them to later periods. Concepts of civility and incivility were part of that long-term transformation of human societies. Sixteenth-century debates about the rights of newly discovered peoples were important links in a chain that extended from medieval ideas about Christian civility that were influenced by Graeco-Roman thought to the many variations on the 'standards of civilization' that later generations used to construct images of a globalized 'civilizing offensive' to 'improve' other peoples.

The citation at the beginning of this chapter belonged to the phase that was mentioned earlier in which European conceptions of civilization led to the 'transformation of humanity', but the underlying mentality had unmistakable links with formative Christian doctrines on the right to convert 'barbarous' societies. Elias highlighted the modern ethos where the sense of 'civilization' as a natural condition began to cloud the understanding of the long patterns of development that led to that still unfinished process. But the colonial doctrines that circulated during the Spanish invasion of the Americas anticipated similar conceptions of a permanent civil condition. They regarded that state as a gift of God that had to be shared with less fortunate peoples, and not as the outcome of long-term, reversible social processes. Every society that believes it has undergone a civilizing process – or that is convinced that its condition is a divine gift or a biological endowment – exhibits the same tendency which is to pride itself in its advances beyond 'barbarous' ancestors as well as neighbouring 'backward' social groups (Elias 2008c, 2008d). There is an almost engrained tendency to look down on outsiders with condescension or contempt, to pity them, to be disgusted by what is regarded as vile and reprehensible in their ways of life, to refuse contact for fear of pollution and contamination, to exterminate them, as has been frequent in the West, or to convert derogatory judgments about others' practices, or pity or sympathy for 'backward' peoples, into 'civilizing' efforts to transform them, whether peacefully or by the use of force. As Benjamin (1986: 256) rightly argued, there is 'no document of civilization which is not at the same time a document of barbarism'. Expressed differently, every civilizing process contains its 'decivilizing' tendencies and properties. Each has its internal tensions between, on the hand, the conceivably well-meaning intentions of freeing others from unnecessary suffering, or from perceived ignorance, or from relievable burdens and, on the other hand, the proclivity for domination, exploitation and violence that is anchored in images of cultural superiority and results in an inability to identify emotionally with other peoples or to sympathize with their plight.

'Civilizing processes' at both the national and the global levels acquire much of their momentum from the ways in which powerful groups use distinctions between 'the established and the outsiders' to chart future directions for humanity as a whole. As noted in earlier chapters, those cultural properties have appeared at every stage in the history of the Western states-systems, but they have never been more central than in the period since the European discovery of the Americas. The 'civilizing process' would have unfolded in very different ways if Europeans had constituted the whole of humanity and if they had not entered into relations with other societies where, because of huge inequalities of power, there was little incentive or compulsion to observe the basic principles of reciprocity. The absence of such constraints on European societies is one reason why condescending or derogatory representations of outsiders have had a wholly unprecedented impact in the modern period. Europeans surpassed their predecessors in their astonishing ingenuity in inventing distinctions between 'civilized' and 'uncivilized' peoples that have profoundly influenced global imaginaries (Keal 2003: ch. 2; Bethencourt 2013). Only a few of the variants that were central to the formation of civilized self-images can be described here. Less 'civilized' forms of life were characterized as belonging to the lower rungs of a divinely ordained Great Chain of Being in which all peoples enjoy liberties, including rights of protection, appropriate to their allotted station. Tilting the Chain of Being on its side, 'barbarous' peoples were depicted as 'earlier' rather than 'lower', as the remnants of a distant era in which, to use Locke's phrase, 'all the World was ... America' (Locke 1960 [1698] II: 49). Those evolutionary schemas often replaced the notion that the 'childlike savage' had rights as part of the divine creation with the belief that outsiders should undergo rapid 'modernization' or otherwise give way to the 'juggernaut of civilization'. Other views portrayed 'the other' as the 'noble savage' in possession of levels of freedom, happiness and simplicity that modern peoples lost as they became trapped by the internal and external restraints that are intrinsic to 'civilization'. Such idealized images of 'savages' reflected a growing awareness of the 'neuroses' that come with the 'privations' of civilized life which was linked with the belief that 'happiness' would not be found unless prevailing social 'standards were abolished or greatly relaxed' (Freud 1939: 45–6).

In a clear example of how conceptions of non-European societies have shaped the process of civilization, romanticized images of the 'native' therefore provided a foundation for the philosophical critique of the repressive and stultifying effects of modern society. Their proponents were often more concerned with condemning the social inequalities and excessive controls on the search for satisfaction in 'civilized' ways of life than with protecting outsiders from the violent and non-violent harm that was caused by European imperialists (White 1972). Those images were connected with a new appraisal of the significance and value of other ways of life. Influential strands of thought were expressed in 'perspectivism' that eschewed judging other societies from the standpoint of one's own culture, or with reference to a supposedly trans-cultural perspective, and which, through the acquisition of a measure of critical detachment or self-distancing, concluded that all forms of life are equally valid and worthy of respect (Todorov 1984: 189ff.). From that vantage point, divisions between the 'civilized' and the 'savage' are suspect or wholly false, and not least because, as Montaigne (1993[1580]: 235–6) argued in his essay, *On the Cannibals*, the self-nominating 'civilized' peoples have often surpassed 'savages' in their inventiveness in devising ways of inflicting cruelty. The significance of such ideas for contemporary images of a global civilizing process will be considered later.

All of those colonial mentalities reveal what the Europeans regarded as the standards of self-restraint that should be observed in relations with non-European peoples. The emphasis must be on *self*-restraint since Europeans had considerable liberty in deciding what those constraints were: more often than not, they did not have to establish them through negotiation with out-siders who had the same power to harm them. Elias's writings paid little attention to how such rival conceptions of the relations between Europe and the rest of the world helped to explain the civilizing process and what they disclosed about it; they did not analyse the relationship between that process and colonial genocide, one that many regard as essential for comprehending 'the regression to barbarism' that occurred with the rise of Nazism (Elias 2013: 230; also Chapter 9, p. 354); nor did those writings discuss how 'civilized' attitudes to cruelty and suffering influenced, and were influenced by, contacts with colonized peoples that provided opportunities for violent and non-violent harm that had been largely closed off in the significantly pacified metropolitan centres.

As noted in the previous chapter, modern diplomacy and the contrived balance of power are evidence of how ideas of civility emerged in relations between as well as in relations within societies. Similarly, the main emotional responses to human suffering caused by overseas imperial expansion provide a window onto the changing character of global 'civiliz-ing offensives'. Those aspects of an evolving society of states correct a strong tendency in Elias's writings to depict international relations as a largely unchanging domain where realist dynamics have repeatedly frustrated humanitarian aspirations. As already noted, the civilizing process shaped, and was shaped by, the colonial mentalities described earlier. It was influ-enced from the outset by contacts with the 'non-European other'. More specifically, changing beliefs about what should arouse shame and embar-rassment, and about what was permissible and forbidden, were not only important in relations between the 'established and the outsiders' within the same 'civilized' societies, but ran through notions of 'international ethics' in the colonial era. The idea of savagery, rather like notions of heresy and madness illustrates the 'technique of ostensive self-definition by negation' – the recurrent practice of dignifying a 'specific mode of existence' by contrasting it with other arrangements, whether 'real or imagined' (White 1972: 4–5). It is hardly surprising that the ethnographic record is replete with expressions of disgust at alien practices that conveyed feelings of 'civilized' superiority (Greenblat 1982). Such representations of the habits and physical appearance of other peoples were the means by which established groups documented their supposed supremacy. No less important for the present discussion are the relatively recent orientations to empire and slavery that concluded that 'progress' in the relations between societies depended less on domesticating the 'savage' than on taming the 'civilized' establishment. Here, too, the analyst can identify important connections between social attitudes to non-European peoples and changing configurations of the civilizing process that reflected shifting power balances between European and non-European societies.

Given the sheer volume of literature on colonialism and decolonization, the following discussion is necessarily highly selective. The main organizing theme is how far the conquering powers had an unquestioning faith that the 'civilizing' character of the colonial project gave them unlimited or virtually unlimited rights over subjects, and how far they believed that 'civilized' norms demanded the condemnation of the cruelties and humiliations of imperial domination. The tensions between those perspectives that reflect the two faces of civilization that were discussed earlier first came into sharp opposition in debates during the expansion of medieval Europe on whether the 'infidel' possessed rights. They were refined in sixteenth-century disputes over 'the newly discovered Indians' that introduced the distinction between *civile imperium* (the empire 'brought to bear upon men for their own benefit') and *herile imperium* (the empire in which power is exercised entirely for 'the profit of he who rules' (Fernandez-Santamaria 1997:188ff.). That is the subject of the first part of the following discussion. Later, and with respect to slavery, social opinion divided between those who claimed unqualified rights over 'natural' inferiors and those who maintained that the institution was, or could become, 'civil' – that is, governed by the larger movement within the civilizing process that contended that slaves had the right to be free from cruelty and unnecessary suffering, as demanded by the moral standards of the time. They are discussed in the second and third parts of this chapter. Those tensions were the prelude to practical measures to abolish the Atlantic slave trade, to end the degradations and cruelties of slavery, and to dismantle colonial rule (Anstey 1975: ch. 4). Collective efforts to distinguish between civil and uncivil forms of empire or slavery were part then of a broader endeavour to promote a new phase of the civilizing process in which it was accepted that colonized peoples were entitled to sovereign independence. To analyse the development of those world views is to trace what has been described, albeit controversially, as the 'momentous shift' from ideologies of '"progressive" enslavement' to doctrines of '"progressive" emancipation' (Davis 1984: xvii).

Religious Colonialism

Reference has been made to dichotomies between the 'civilized' and the 'barbaric' that emerged alongside territorial concentrations of physical power. Relations with Europe's internal 'primitives' such as the Basques, the Scots, the Welsh, the Irish and the pagan Scandinavians were suffused with hierarchical representations of social differences (van Krieken 2011). Peoples were graded in accordance with their level of civility; their relative standing was often connected with perceptions of the pleasure they were thought to derive from cruelty. The notion of the barbarian shifted in this period from older associations with paganism to an emphasis on the social 'backwardness' of recently converted groups such as the Scandinavians who were remembered for their traditional 'savagery' (Jones 1971: 394ff.). The medieval image of the barbarian is evident in discourses of internal colonialism that were invented during the early waves of English imperialism which is best regarded as part of a wider European development since various courts and warrior aristocracies were engaged in disseminating 'international norms ... on acceptable social and sexual morality, political organization and relationships, economic structures and forms of exploitation and even on matters such as clothes, food, housing and the forms of settlement' (Davies 1990: 20ff.). Elite groups frequently referred to 'those stubborn, rude and most barbarous peoples' on the periphery who had yet to become attuned to 'sweet civility' based on a combination of public order and assiduous self-restraint (Davies 2000: ch. 5). Around such standards and social hierarchies of difference, social elites constructed their 'civilizing mission' (Davies 1990: 22). Familiar strategies that included not only cultural assimilation but forms of violence that would now be regarded as genocidal were widespread in the period (Fraser 2010; Scales 2010).

Reflecting a move away from the earlier, largely 'neutral' characterization of the Celts, twelfth-century authors such as William of Malmesbury referred to rulers – an example was King David I of Scotland – who had been 'made civilized by (their) upbringing amongst us'; the resulting educative process ensured that 'the rust of his native barbarism was polished away' (Gillingham 1992: 396ff.). Conversion to Christianity had promoted the 'civilization' of the Anglo-Saxons who had been 'barbarians in their look and manners' and 'warlike in their usages' (Jones 1971: 392). William of Malmesbury referred to 'Christian barbarians' such as the Welsh, Scots, Danes and Norwegians who had answered Urban II's call for a crusade (Gillingham 1992: 398). In that way, classical notions of the barbarian were 'rediscovered' and applied to those who lived *in nationibus barbaris*. Especially interesting in terms of a future phase of the civilizing process, David I was portrayed as a 'missionary for civilization' who encouraged subjects to 'live in a more civilized style, dress with more elegance, and learn to eat with more refinement' (Gillingham 1992: 396). English representations of the Scots in the mid-twelfth century referred the 'delight to that inhuman nation, more savage than wild beasts, to cut the throats of old men, to slaughter little children, to rip open the bowels of women' (Gillingham 1992: 397). The treatment of non-combatants and the butchering and decapitating of prisoners of war whom the French normally ransomed were regarded as evidence of the absence of pity and the low regard for the norms of chivalry (Gillingham 1992: 399). Similar views were expressed from the eleventh century onwards in depictions of the 'barbarous' and 'primitive' Irish. The twelfth-century Anglo-Welsh writer, Giraldus Cambrensis (Gerald of Wales) described them as a 'rude people' who had yet to progress beyond 'the primitive habits of pastoral life' and whose conduct demonstrated that they were 'exceedingly averse to civil institutions' (Phillips 1994: 51; Davies 1990; Ohlmeyer 1998). He advanced a progressivist interpretation of history – a precursor of the 'stadial' view of history that is associated with thinkers of the Scottish Enlightenment (Gillingham 2001; Meek 1976) – in which the species moved from 'the forests to the fields and thence to the towns and the conditions of citizens' (cited in Jones 1971: 395ff.). The 'repellent' nature of the Welsh and Scots was especially evident, it was believed, in their continuing attachment to slavery and the slave trade that had virtually disappeared from England in the early twelfth century. Reports of the savagery of war described its function as a 'slave hunt' in which the 'unprofitable' were routinely slaughtered (Gillingham 1992: 401–2; Gillingham 2001). Gradations of civility were linked with different approaches to political succession. They had been bloodthirsty affairs in Celtic societies and in England before the twelfth century, at which point English advances in pacifying power transitions led to stark contrasts between the civility of prosperous towns and money economies and the 'barbaric' and 'crude' ways of rustic Celtic peoples (Gillingham 1992: 403). Such 'civilized' practices were admired because they introduced distinctions between legitimate and illegitimate sons that were designed to tame violent struggles over political succession (Gillingham 1992: 404). No less important were contentions that Celtic sexual behaviour and marriage practices were 'scandalous' when compared to 'civilized' behaviour in twelfth-century England where the Christian idea of monogamy and associated vows and sexual prohibitions had become influential.

More generally, medieval conceptions of 'uncivilized' others drew on diverse sources such as folk beliefs in the existence of 'wild men' (the half man/half beast that represented degeneration) as well as the Aristotelian idea of natural slavery (Bernheimer 1952; Fernandez-Armesto 1987: 225ff.). The 'wild man' of the woodland was the antithesis of the orderly communities of 'civilized' urban dwellers where 'the persuasive power of language' had replaced animal, brute force (Pagden 1982: 20–1).[1] Those ideas would influence the first attempts to account for the inexplicable existence of the peoples of the Americas. The 'ethnographical conundrum' for colonizing groups was how to explain 'the huge variation in the modes of human social organization' (Pagden 1982: 4–5; also Hodgen 1964: ch. 6 and 102 on 'the problem of cultural diversity' for Christian thinkers). The assumed universality of 'civilized' standards made the sheer diversity of alien cultures hard to comprehend. A dominant tendency amongst medieval Christians was to regard difference as 'evidence of species corruption' (White 1972: 9). A prevalent supposition was that 'if there was one, all-powerful, and just God ordering the whole, then how could the differences between men be explained, save by some principle which postulated a more perfect and a less perfect approximation to the ideal form of humanity contained in the mind of God as the paradigm of the species?' (White 1972: ibid.; also Moore 2000 on the link between monotheism and religious persecution). The main contrast was that 'perceived differences . . . had less significance for Greeks and Romans than they had for Hebrews and Christians'; the former regarded them as 'physical and cultural' while the latter perceived them as 'moral and metaphysical', and with devastating results (White 1972: 10). From those standpoints, there was no value in trying to comprehend other ways of life in their own terms, or in imagining how the world was perceived from other perspectives. Some thinkers such as Las Casas tried to balance the focus on essential differences by highlighting similarities between 'the newly discovered Indians' and the ancient Greeks. Immense dangers awaited those who could not be fitted easily into the existing classification of human societies by such favourable analogies and stereotypes.

Cultural reactions to the newly discovered peoples ranged from the suspicion that they were one of the lost tribes of Israel that had somehow become separated from the main course of human development to conjectures that they were the result of a Second Creation as well as speculations about the spontaneous generation of different peoples. In the twelfth century, theological responses to the problem of interpreting mysterious groups drew on classical distinctions between the civility (*civilitas*) of advanced peoples and the 'wildness' or 'irrationality' of 'barbarians', as promulgated by ancient authorities such as Cicero (Jones 1971: 397). Reflections on groups in Central and

---

[1] The previous chapter discussed the importance of court societies for the development of notions of civility and civilization. But it would appear from the evidence of one royal court that images of wildness played an intriguing place in the formation of the 'civilized' habitus. The 'wild-man dances' in the court of Charles VI of France suggested that 'it is a gauge of the pressure of formalized living upon those who were supposed to be its foremost paragons, that it seems to have been necessary at times to open the valves and to let the agonized fury of "natural man" take its unhampered course' (Bernheimer 1952: 67ff.).

South American did not start *ab initio*, notwithstanding biblical silence on their existence, or the absence of an authoritative theological position on their exact place in creation, or clear guidance on how the peoples of Christendom should behave towards them. Long before sixteenth-century debates about 'the Indian', Catholic theologians had wrestled with the 'problem' of the pagan, and they had agonized particularly over the rights and duties that should govern relations with the Muslim world. Unsurprisingly, the idea of the just war was a constant reference in those interwoven deliberations (Hamilton 1963: ch. 8, Russell 1975).

Whether non-believers had legitimate ownership of their lands was a central issue in fourteenth-century debates about duties to pagans. Hostiensis is usually regarded as the main advocate of the thesis that the papacy had both political and spiritual rights over the whole of human creation. That standpoint was coupled with the thesis that a society lost all entitlements to independence if the inhabitants were guilty of 'sins against nature'. On just war foundations, the Church claimed rights of annexation for proselytizing purposes. Innocent IV subscribed to the contrary view, which would prevail in that debate, that Christian society had to recognize that non-believers enjoyed rightful ownership of their lands, although the *ius communicationis* granted Christians unconditional rights of access to convert pagans and to eradicate 'sinful' ways (Hamilton 1963: 119ff.; Ortega 1996). Those discussions gave shape to the 'dual conception of international society' that was later refined by Grotius (Wight 1977: 125ff.). Innocent IV formulated the related doctrine that the Christian realm was part of a universal society that included pagan groups with inalienable rights against the more 'advanced', inner circle. False belief did not cancel rights of ownership or free Christians from sacred responsibilities to respect the humanity of non-Christians. But that construction of social divisions within a universal moral community was no less hierarchical than Hostiensis' opposing view that it was contrary to Christian doctrine to regard pagan societies as the rightful owners of the lands they inhabited.

Significantly, early fourteenth-century portrayals of African political systems such as Mali under Mansa Musa recognized the approximate social equality of affluent societies by the standards of the time (Bull 1984a; Fernandez-Armesto 1987: 147). Greater respect was displayed towards 'regal or noble ambassadors' than to non-royals, but because of certain stereotypes of black Africans that stressed their 'lack of appreciation of the rules of civility and civilization', the level of respect was far from 'equal'. Revealingly, there is no recorded marriage between members of the European and black African ruling families during the Renaissance (Lowe 2005: 9; Lowe 2005a: 25, 43). Prior to the great debates about 'the Indian', the Spanish had reflected on their rights against and duties to the peoples of the Canary Islands, and concluded that paganism did not place them outside the universal community of humankind, although those on the colonial frontier often acted on rather different assumptions that may have been influenced by negative connotations of blackness (Fernandez-Armesto 1987: 227). As already noted, the recognition of common humanity coexisted with the belief in the natural right to enter pagan lands to preach, and to use force if necessary not only for that purpose but to assist persecuted Christians and to eliminate dark practices (often sexual in nature, but including idolatry, cannibalism and other 'barbarous' activities that were deemed 'contrary to nature').

The most famous articulation of that world view was the *Requerimiento* or *Requirement*, the 1513 statement written by Palacios Rubios, which declared that the Christian right of proselytization necessarily qualified 'Indian' title. The *Requirement* stated that submission to the emperor and pope would bring freedom from servitude. But in the case of a refusal to submit, it announced that 'we shall take you and your wives and your children, and shall make slaves of them, and as such shall sell and dispose of them as their Highnesses may command; and we shall take away your goods, *and shall do all the harm and damage that we can*, as to vassals who do not obey' (cited in Hanke 1965: 33, italics added). The clear implication was that death and hardship would be the Indians' own fault (Abulafia 2008: 296–7). Also crucial was the fact that the *Requirement* was principally an exercise in self-justification since it was read in Latin, often miles out to sea (Brown 1988). The absence of the belief that the 'Indian' was the appropriate addressee, and the lack of any obligation to communicate the *Requirement* in a language that the recently discovered peoples understood, illustrates the ethnocentrism of the period (see Abulafia 2008: 294ff. on allusions to the need for communication, on the ritual of 'going through the motions', that led Montaigne and others to regard the Requirement as patently absurd).

With respect to the whole period, the *conquistadores* who treated the Indians like animals, and the clergy who defended them as fellow human beings, did not disagree fundamentally about their joint superiority over subject peoples (Todorov 1984; Seed 1993). Such observations about the Spanish conquerors have been used to correct idealized portraits of celebrated defenders of the 'Indians' including the Dominic friar, Bartolome de Las Casas, the onetime *conquistador* and *encomenderos* who became the foremost champion of the 'newly discovered Indians' (Hanke 1970: ch. 8; Todorov 1984: 165ff., 190–1; also Todorov 1984: 219ff. on the 'generosity of spirit' that led Las Casas to criticize imperial cruelties, to stress the plurality of religious world views and to emphasize the 'relativity' of all notions of barbarism). Despite their condemnation of the cruelties of the conquistadores, attempts to tame the colonial warrior, and genuine compassion for the well-being of the 'Indians', the clergy did not question the legitimacy of Spanish imperial rule. Theological disputes between the followers of Ramon Lull, who favoured peaceful conversion, and those who maintained that force and enslavement were necessary to ensure spiritual transformation, addressed what many regarded as the fundamental questions about the organizing principles of 'civilized' colonial administration. An astute summation states that the colonizers were divided between the likes of Columbus, who thought that the Indians were radically different from the Spanish and must therefore be unequal, and those who concluded that they enjoyed actual or potential equality with their overlords but only because they were essentially the same as Christians – because they demonstrated levels of religious piety that ensured that, with appropriate human kindness, spiritual guidance and discipline, they would become devout Christians (Todorov 1984: 63, 162ff.). Certainly, Las Casas and other defenders of the 'Indians' attempted to widen the scope of emotional identification by stressing parallels with the pious simplicity of true Christians as well as the achievements in civility and artistic creations that ranked alongside those of the much-admired ancients. Their perceived religiosity was used to establish their membership of the larger community of believers, and to support a we–I balance and Christian standards of self-restraint that were intended to tame the sordid ambitions of the *encomenderos*. Nevertheless, there was no strong current of opinion that the 'Indian' could be fundamentally different from the Spanish colonizers and live alongside them as moral and political equals.

Just to survive, the *conquistadores* had to rely on indigenous labour but, reflecting the collective mentality and behaviour of the nobility in the Middle Ages, most saw some form of forced labour as the route to the personal fortune that had previously eluded them, or they trusted that empire would free them from the hardships that had plagued their earlier lives. Bernal Diaz del Castillo, one of Cortes' companions, probably captured the dominant outlook when he stated that 'we came here to serve God, and the king, and also to get rich' (Elliott 1970: 62ff.). Many regarded Indian enslavement as the just reward for the perils and adversities of conquest, or as rightful punishment for the Indians' demonstrable wickedness. But that was not the position taken by the Spanish Crown which prohibited 'Indian' slavery in 1500 following Columbus' transportation of 'natives' for sale in Spain, a decision that had the effect of increasing the number of slaves shipped from Africa (Elliott 1970: 73–4; also Hanke 1965: 125 on the supposition that the latter's greater physical strength equipped them for labour that would cripple more delicate 'Indian' bodies). Exceptions to the principle were permitted if Indians had attacked Spaniards or participated in 'unnatural practices'. For the Church, arguments surrounding labour exploitation could not be divorced from the more fundamental issue of ensuring that colonial rule did not jeopardize the objective of securing the salvation of 'Indian' souls.

Colonial administrators made decisions about labour allocation on the model of the *repartimiento* (after *repartir*, to allot or distribute) that had been pioneered in the West Indies. The *repartimiento* was often interchangeable with *encomienda* (after *encomendar*, to give in trust), which embedded the principle of imperial responsibility for the religious education and spiritual improvement of 'native' peoples (Gibson 1966: 143ff.; Simpson 1950). For the Church, the *encomienda*, which had their origins in the rules governing land that had been seized from the Moors, were key civilizing instruments that could end the perceived idleness of indigenous populations and promote their Christianization (Gibson 1966: 50). Indeed, there was a presumed social compact in which 'Indians' exchanged physical labour for the greater benefits of spiritual enlightenment. From the beginning, the *encomienda* was an unstable compromise between religious imperatives, economic necessities, and elite expectations of permanent labour privileges. For the *encomenderos* who controlled those institutions, personal enrichment through the exploitation of indigenous labour was often far more important than religious enlightenment and conversion. The maltreatment of those that had been entrusted to their care became the central concern of many friars. The abuse of the 'Indian' also troubled the Spanish Crown that was anxious to block the emergence of local landed aristocracies that might escape its political and economic control, and frustrate its desire to extend its power over, and extract wealth from, the remote regions of the empire (Elliott 1970: 74–5; Simpson 1950: 129). The Crown regarded the *encomendia* as temporary social arrangements that were essential for survival in the initial phase of conquest (Gibson 1966: 50). For their part, local aristocracies generally thought that the laws of inheritance should ensure that allocations of land and labour became permanent.[2]

The *encomenderos'* brutal treatment of the Indians and their reduction to chattels led to major disputes about 'international ethics' in the form of deliberations about principles of colonial rule that were unique in the history of the Western states-systems. The Dominican friar, Antonio de Montesinos, was amongst the first to highlight the moral problem of physical harm caused to the 'Indians'. In a sermon in Hispaniola in late 1511, he admonished the congregation for being 'in mortal sin . . . for the cruelty and tyranny' of such practices as forced labour that typified relations with 'these innocent people'. 'Are these not men?', Montesinos continued; 'Have they not rational souls? Are you not bound to love them as you love yourselves? . . . Be certain that, in such a state as this, you can no more be saved than the Moors or Turks' (cited in Hanke 1965: 17). The Laws of Burgos that were promulgated

---

[2] Elias's analysis of the tensions between the centripetal force of the 'monopoly mechanism' and the centrifugal role of 'feudalisation' is relevant to understanding the struggle for imperial control in a period when states were still constructing the political apparatus that would enable them to govern overseas empires and to appropriate the bulk of the wealth for themselves. The objective would have been jeopardized by recognizing permanent property rights that would have allowed local aristocracies to establish an independent power base.

in December 1512 were the first examples of ecclesiastical legislation that had the purpose of restraining the *encomenderos*. The main articles authorized the movement of the 'Indians' to villages where they would receive religious education as well as 'civilizing' instruction in curbing wickedness and eradicating indolence. Core harm conventions that were contained in the Laws were designed to protect indigenous peoples from violence, abuse and overwork. Physical relocation was to be accomplished 'gently', and 'with the least possible harm' – their homes being burned to destroy the possibility of returning to the original settlements. Article 11 forbade the *encomenderos* to use indigenous persons 'as carriers at the mines', and Article 13 insisted that, with the exception of slaves, those who had laboured in the gold mines for five months should be granted forty days' rest. Article 18 held that women over four months pregnant should not be forced to work in the mines but should be confined to 'light household tasks'. Article 21 forbade the 'beating or verbal abuse of Indians', while Article 24 prohibited calling them 'dogs'. The standards of self-restraint that were affirmed by those articles may have had little impact on actual behaviour. In many parts of the Spanish empire, efforts to tame the *encomenderos* provoked resistance or were simply impossible to enforce – but they established the ethical ideals that were robustly defended by clerics such as Las Casas (Simpson 1950: 31ff.; Hanke 1970: ch. 3).

The *encomienda* were abolished by the New Laws of November 1542, which were themselves revoked in October 1545 following the opposition of the *encomederos*. Continuing brutality in the aftermath of the latters' success in repealing the 1512 Laws of Burgos intensified Church efforts to stand up for the 'Indians' (see Elliott 1970: ch. 2; also Gibson 1966: 144ff.) on the effects of the formal abolition of the *repartimiento* in 1632). Charles V suspended further conquest on 16 April 1550 until the leading theologians had debated the ethics of empire. The result was the celebrated exchange between Las Casas and Juan Gines de Sepulveda in Vallodolid in 1550 and 1551 that was principally concerned with whether just war principles authorized conquest in order to spread the faith. At the time, the debate was inconclusive although the general consensus is that Las Casas' views eventually prevailed. Sepulveda's position was that the right to preach was one of four reasons that justified the use of force, the others being repeated sinful practices, 'primitiveness 'that demanded that a people should serve its 'natural' superiors, and obvious failures to protect the weak (Hanke 1970: 41). Conquest was necessary to promote the instruction of wards that were unable to rise above the condition of slaves or serfs. That standpoint should not be conflated with the Aristotelian position that some are born to be slaves. It reflected the belief that people had unequal levels of intelligence and different capacities for self-improvement, and it maintained that the 'Indians', just like the servile people of the Old World, were so deficient in reason and lacking in civility that they had to be subject to paternal authority (Fernandez-Santamaria 1977: 168, 191).

Sepulveda did not defend conversion by brute force or defend cruelty, but he maintained that the subjugation and pacification of colonized territories were essential to ensure that preachers could disseminate the 'true faith'. Against that background, he defended the continuation of the *encomienda*, believing that it was right that the 'Indians' served their 'natural' masters, and self-evident that the loss of gold and other possessions was nothing compared to the possibility of eternal damnation. The route to personal salvation would not have existed but for the Spanish conquest that was explicitly compared with the Roman subjugation of 'barbarian' peoples but with the crucial difference that it was now infused with Christian *caritas* (Fernandez-Santamaria 1977: 213–14). Las Casas was not alone in describing the main cultural differences between the Spaniards and the 'Indians' in broadly evolutionary terms – anticipating in some respects the stadial view of history that was mentioned earlier – and in believing that the latter provided evidence of what early human societies had been (Pagden 1982: 89ff., 166–7). The Indian would become 'civilized' just as Europeans had been elevated through the transformative influence of Greece and Rome.[3]

Las Casas had opposed coercive labour and rejected the belief that conquest was essential to prepare the ground for spiritual conversion. His objective was to ensure that the 'Indians' received correct religious guidance consistent with rights to respect and security to which they were entitled as members of the universal community of humankind. Here, Las Casas drew on Cicero's doctrine of human equality (Nederman 2001: ch. 7). Over roughly five decades, he campaigned for the principle that the means of saving endangered souls should not violate a fundamental ethical obligation to refrain from causing unnecessary suffering or reaping the rewards of unjust enrichment. In Vitoria's words, there was a duty to demonstrate 'in all possible methods that they [the Spanish] do not come to the hurt of the natives, but wish to sojourn as peaceful guests and to travel without doing the natives any harm' (cited in Green and Dickason 1989: 43). Admittedly, as in the ancient empires, humanitarian sentiments were combined with pragmatic considerations – in this case about the most reliable method of securing genuine conversion through the transformation of the inner self. Las Casas favoured peaceful proselytizing, believing that using force to subdue indigenous groups was counterproductive – that it encouraged conversion that had less to do with genuine belief than with the fear of punishment for failing to comply with

---

[3] Developments across time and space that are interconnected parts of long civilizing processes are evident in English state-building and colonial expansion. Direct parallels were drawn between English efforts to tame the 'uncivilized' Irish in the sixteenth century – later exported to efforts to pacify the 'American Indians' – and the Spanish 'civilizing' mission. Crucially, English colonists compared their role to the Romans' earlier, standard-setting endeavour to 'civilize' the native Britons (see Canny 1973; van Krieken 2011).

Christian ideas and rituals. His belief in the essential religiosity of the 'newly discovered Indians' led him to suppose that they would freely accept Christian doctrine as long as the right methods of instruction were deployed. That was not the least of his reasons for rejecting Sepulveda's thesis that the 'Indian' was obliged because of supposed natural inferiority to submit to and serve the colonial overlords.

Such factors must be kept in mind when assessing the contention that Las Casas defended the principle that 'all the peoples of the world are men', and maintained that 'the law of nations and natural law' applied 'to Christian and gentile alike, and to all people of any sect, law, condition, or colour without any distinction whatsoever' (Hanke 1970: 111–13). Las Casas contributed to the 'dual conception of international society' by asserting that the Christian realm was part of a larger human community in which non-Christian societies had basic, but qualified, rights against colonial occupiers. The desire to constrain papal power was one reason for the limited forms of 'self-distancing' that underpinned the late medieval dualistic image of world society (Fernandez-Armesto 1987: 243). As noted earlier, the importance of such ideas at the time of the Vallodolid debates owed much to the Crown's determination to control the landed aristocracies in the distant parts of the empire. Not that it should be supposed that Las Casas believed that the Crown's ability to direct events in those regions would necessarily lead to more civil relations between Spain and the Indies. Renewed concerns about the plight of the 'Indians' appeared as a result of the practice of burdening the subject peoples of Peru with excessive labour (Hemmings 1983: 367ff.). In his later reflections, Las Casas harnessed Innocent IV's support for the principle, *quod omnes tangit debet ab omnibus approbari* (what affects all must be approved by all) to argue that indigenous groups should not be forced to submit to a Christian ruler and to affirm that their consent was crucial to legitimate replacing native with Christian authority. He appears to have argued that the 'Indians' had the right to rise up against Spanish rule since their lands had been unjustly taken, to have their original liberties restored, and to regain the right to determine their future (Muldoon 1979: 151; Green and Dickason 1989: 202; Todorov 1984: 193). It has been said that the court of Charles V was the first in European history to suspend imperial conquest while theologians debated its ethical foundations (Hanke 1970: 36–7). An alternative interpretation is that an unanticipated major advance of human interconnectedness led to new power struggles, to complex discussions about the appropriate powers of different authorities, and to related ethical debates about the rights of colonial subjects. Nothing comparable had occurred in the states-systems of classical antiquity where the 'toil of the spear' was relatively, but not entirely free, from such moral entanglements. Concepts of civility that emerged with state formation and internal colonialism had a double effect. They rationalized the belief that 'simpler' peoples should make way for 'civilization'. They were also used to restrain the 'frontier decivilizing processes' (see Mennell 2007: 201) that had been unleashed by the Spanish conquests, which were latent in Christian doctrines that infidels had no rights, and that would be repeated again and again whenever colonial settlers had no need to depend on indigenous groups and few, if any, external pressures to exercise self-restraint (Muldoon 1979: ch. 6). In the colonial era, states acquired the capacity to project power to the ends of the world but they lacked the ability to restrain violence and ruthlessness along the colonial frontiers where different worlds collided on profoundly unequal terms. In the absence of effective means of enforcement – equivalent to those that states with their monopolies of power could muster closer to home – imperial harm conventions had limited practical effect. A long process was involved in bringing colonial life on the frontier more into line with 'civilized' conceptions of relations between people within the metropolitan societies. There was no more dramatic evidence of how advances in human interconnectedness outpaced the desire or capacity to constrain the power to cause harm in distant regions through the invention of new conceptions of the relationship between violence and civilization.

Race and Slavery

In the minds of the Spanish colonists, the physical seizure and transportation of black Africans was less problematic from an ethical-religious point of view than the enslavement of 'Indians'. 'Civilizing offensives' to ensure the former's conversion of black Africans to the Christian faith did not have the same urgency. The difference is highlighted by the declaration by Pope Paul III in 1537 that the sacraments should be denied those who enslaved 'Indians' because of their presumed inability to comprehend Christian doctrine (Davis 1970: 192ff.). Not until the end of the eighteenth century did the Anglican Church in Jamaica implement a decision to promote the conversion of black slaves. As a general rule, slaves were not allowed to attend church services, although they did receive instruction in selected parts of the Gospel such as Ecclesiastes 8.6, which conveniently stated that 'whoever obeys a command will come to no harm' (Martin 1999: 67). As for earlier attitudes to black Africans, Las Casas was not alone in supporting the transportation of African slaves to spare the Indians the intolerable burden of relentless physical labour. The number of black slaves increased for such reasons, encouraged by the conviction that enslavement was their natural fate and destination (Davis 1970: 193). The supposition that Africans had known about the Christian faith only to reject it for Islam may help to explain why enslaving black Africans did not attract the same moral opprobrium as Indian slavery.

By the fifteenth century, when the first serious contacts with African societies took place, the Church simultaneously condemned the enslavement of fellow Christians and legitimated the seizure of 'infidels' as a punitive measure or as a method of gaining new converts. In 1452, Pope Nicholas V granted the Portuguese king the right to own Moors and pagans; in 1488 Pope Innocent VIII distributed around one hundred Moor slaves that had arrived as a gift from Ferdinand of Spain to members of the nobility and cardinals (Davis 1970: 118–19). Demeaning representations of blackness became increasingly prominent from the start of Portugal's imperial expansion in the late fifteenth century (Fernandez-Armesto 1987: 227). The royal chronicler, Zuzara, had previously described the first slaves to arrive in Portugal – at Lagos in the Algarve – on 8 August 1444. He expressed some sympathy with their plight while representing it as their 'fate', and he stated in his chronicle that it was not only permissible 'to capture and enslave black Africans', but legitimate 'to treat them in an inhuman way' (Lowe 2005: 10–11). Significantly, around that time, the black slave was frequently described In Italy as *moro nero*, the black Moor (Davis 1970: 119n20). It is important to recall that Christian views of the non-Christian world were influenced by the belief that all peoples were equally part of the divine creation. That conviction distinguished the early modern world from the states-systems of classical antiquity, and it promoted ethical reflections about the rights and entitlements of 'backward' peoples that had hardly been central to the political theory and practice of the ancient world. But the outlook had highly ambiguous implications for non-believers, as has been noted. The non-observance of the Christian faith demanded interrogation, specifically of how the very existence of 'heathen' societies could be explained and, depending on the answer, how their inhabitants should be treated. Cultural differences acquired a profound moral significance that they did not have in the ancient world; so did differences of skin colour. The whole direction of the modern 'civilizing process' was shaped by racial attitudes that had no counterpart or equal in the earlier states-systems of the West.

Throughout history, slave-owners have had diverse accounts of their social distance from slaves, and many different justifications have been offered for the absence of concern for, or outright contempt for, their welfare. However, the Atlantic slave trade seems to have been unique in relying on racial characteristics to justify the ownership of, and traffic in, slaves (Davis 1970: 69). The reasons for attaching such moral importance to racial differences have long been debated, and almost certainly elude any simplistic mono-causal explanation. As previously noted, early encounters between white European and black African elites appeared to revolve around mutual respect, often anchored in the evidence of material equalities. Certainly, race did not have any particular moral and political salience. European attitudes displayed admiration for societies with substantial power and wealth. As late as the final part of the fifteenth century, racial prejudice seems not to have featured in the more prominent artistic depictions of blackness (Mark 1974).

Slavery may have been the main reason for attributing moral and political significance to racial differences (Green 1987), but blackness had long been an enigmatic phenomenon for those who believed that all humans had initially been white. Many Christian thinkers had argued that departure from the norm could only be explained as the product of sin or moral decline (Jordan 1969: 248). Accounts of the stigmatization of blackness in the early stages of Iberian expansion have stressed the influence of the biblical claim that the curse that was placed on Ham and his descendants meant that 'Ham was smitten in his skin' and his offspring were 'ugly and dark-skinned'. Even so, blackness seems to have been relatively free of derogatory connotations in the early Christian period (Mark 1974: 11). Blacks appeared in Italy as captives or as Muslim prisoners of war in the early part of the thirteenth century, but even then blackness does not seem to have denoted 'servile status'; if anything, attitudes were neutral if not broadly 'positive' (Mark 1974: 22ff.). The negative connotations of blackness may have enjoyed most support amongst Jewish scholars prior to the sixteenth century, at which point the revival of interest in Jewish works in the Christian world coincided with Spanish colonial expansion. On some accounts, speculations by Jewish writers in the period between AD 200 and 600 that Ham's crime had been to castrate Noah may have established the link between blackness and sexual deviance that Christian thinkers latched onto during the sixteenth-century overseas expansion (Jordan 1969: 36). References to the biblical curse of Canaan were part of a larger trend of 'merging blackness of skin with a variety of derogatory physical and characterological traits' that had appeared in Islamic regions during the eighth and ninth centuries (Davis 1984: 42–3). Additional factors were the association of blackness with the devil, death and black magic. The reduction of Africans to animal nature was clearly pronounced in derogatory references to an 'apelike' character, an alleged 'beastliness' and supposedly unbridled instincts (such as engrained lasciviousness) that signified the supposed gulf between 'civilized', white humanity and black 'savagery'. Direct parallels were drawn between conceptions of savages who were under the control of 'immediate desire, without discipline, without constraint, without real morality', and the insane that were similarly beyond the reach of 'civilization' (Foucault 1973: 193).

Representations of black African sexuality that reflected changing European assumptions about the body, natural functions and nakedness that were core parts of the 'civilizing process' made their distinctive contribution to the invention of racial hierarchies. The first Europeans to reach West Africa were seemingly baffled by behaviour that combined some familiar social restraints with unusual levels of freedom or 'licentiousness' that included sexual abandon and public nakedness that were not restrained by the 'civilizing' emotions of shame and embarrassment (Davis 1970: 504–5;

Bush 1990: 94ff.). No doubt, many envied the absence of sexual shame that was a reminder of the price that Europeans paid in the form of sexual repression for 'civilization'. For them, colonization provided opportunities for erotic experiences (whether real or vicarious) that were largely closed off in their own societies; the provided an escape route from the constraints that were imposed by dominant conceptions of respectability. Representations of the 'sexual other' with their high 'fantasy-content' provide insights into the course of the 'civilizing process'; they invite further analysis of how far European ideas about shame and embarrassment did not develop within the continent first of all and only then shape attitudes to black 'outsiders', but were forged in relations between European and African societies as part of a lengthening of interconnections in which Europeans became assured of their right to impose 'civilized' values and social interpretations on the rest of the world. Crucially, as far as relations between Europe and black Africans were concerned, 'civilized' images of the governance of 'animal' impulses and libidinous forces helped to justify the physical seizure and exploitation of slaves (Davis 1970: 505; Jordan 1969: 30ff., 150ff.).

Blackness in itself did not explain slavery but, for many, black slavery was not exactly hard to justify. Various cultural resources lay to hand. The negative connotations of blackness made it easier for the interested parties to justify the practice, and such racist attitudes became more prevalent once black slavery had become widespread, each apparently reinforcing the other in an upward spiral. But there is still much to be said for the observation that 'there is simply not enough evidence (and very little chance of more to come) to show precisely when and how and why Negroes [sic] came to be treated so differently from white men, though there is just enough to make historians differ as to its meaning' (Jordan 1969: 44; also Davis 1984: 36ff.). What is clear is that slavery was linked with infidel or heathen status, with evil and God's punishment, with the possession of 'animal' or 'uncivilized' characteristics, and with the traditional rights of conquerors in war. Black Africans 'qualified' for slavery on each and every score (Jordan 1969: 56). Crucially, as in many other periods, 'racial' or 'ethnic' differences were emphasized in the context of rapidly increasing power disparities that developed alongside widening divisions between the 'established' and the 'outsiders' (Elias 2008c: 16).

The rise of the Atlantic slave trade cannot be considered in isolation from the Western African wars that often led to the enslavement of the vanquished; indeed states such as Dahomey and the Ashanti specialized in supplying slaves for Western traffickers (Davis 1970: 205). The indigenous roots of slavery meant that Western slavers could sidestep criticisms that they had forced an alien and 'barbarous' institution on innocent peoples. Such beliefs – or rationalizations – became deeply embedded in negative images of Africa that replaced earlier perspectives that portrayed African and European societies as 'near equals' (Davis 1970: 204ff.). Whether

Western slave organizations were directly or indirectly responsible for encouraging slave wars is another matter. In any event, many were quick to plead that slavery had the indisputable merit of protecting Africans from almost certain death; transportation to the Americas would promote their spiritual welfare, and was entirely consistent with the Golden Rule (Davis 1970: 206ff.). The ordeals of the 'middle passage' told a very different story. Moreover, the possibility of physical death was exchanged for the certainties of 'social death' (the loss of membership of one's community and the existence of few, if any, rights against the slave-owning society) as well as 'natal alienation' – the non-recognition of sexual union as marriage, the denial of rights over offspring who were simply added to the slave owners' account, the lack of secure kinship ties given the brutal realities of sale and physical separation, and sexual ownership of the body (Patterson 1982). Not that all slaves were rendered completely subservient and absolutely powerless. Resistance and rebellion, and the resilience of traditional cultural practices in slave communities, require a more complex narrative. However, the modes of transportation to the Americas were characterized by forms of cruelty and violence that were designed to break and remake personality structures – to forge the 'docile' and disciplined self that would command greater monetary value as a commodity to be traded in the slave markets (hooks 1982: 19–20).

The institution of slavery had been a feature of Christian wars against the Moors as well as a central dimension of Portuguese expansion into Africa in the fifteenth century, and a critical element of the Iberian conquest of America. But the Atlantic slave trade is often regarded as the internationalization of a Spanish and Portuguese practice that resulted in new levels of mental and physical cruelty. English reports of Portuguese behaviour noted that they marked the body of slaves 'as we doe Sheepe with a hot Iron', and did so with guile, duping the slaves into thinking that those without 'the marke' were of no 'account in Brasil or in Portugall' (Jordan 1969: 60). Distinctions between more and less 'civilized' slavery emerged around a general consensus about the legitimacy of the institution. The degree of brutalization to which slaves were subjected does not seem to have varied greatly according to the nationality of the slave-owners. Branding slaves 'as a form of identification' seems to have been routine throughout the Americas up to the second half of the eighteenth century (Patterson 1982: 59). Changing the slave's name (and using generic terms such as 'Samboe' in the American South and 'Quashee' in the West Indies) was a central weapon in the combined harm of cultural deracination and degradation that underpinned 'social death' (Patterson 1982: 54ff.; Bush 1990: 52ff.). From the late seventeenth century, the pronounced trend in European societies was 'to treat Negroes (sic) more like property and less like men, to send them to the fields at younger ages, to deny them automatic existence as inherent members of the community, to tighten the bonds on their personal and civil freedom, and correspondingly to loosen the traditional restraints on the master's freedom to deal with his human property as he saw fit' (Jordan 1969: 82). Again, the contrast with earlier encounters with admired African principalities is striking. The development occurred alongside further increases in the state's monopoly powers and the pronounced shift from a Christian international society to a European states-system with a sharp sense of 'cultural differentiation' from the 'uncivilized' world (Wight 1977: 34ff.). Crucial to that transition was the belief that state-organized societies were the cradles and custodians of 'civilization'. Social groups that were acephalous or lacked equivalents to modern, sovereign legal and political institutions were 'semi-civilized' at best. Sharp contrasts between different forms of social and political organization that developed in tandem with the European civilizing process were a manifestation of a steepening of the gradient between the 'established' and the 'outsiders', of a widening of power inequalities that had the consequence of contracting the scope of emotional identification, and of an associated tendency amongst the stronger groups to act as they wished with little regard for the welfare of their human possessions.

However, civilized self-images had long underpinned distinctions between civil and uncivil slavery that ran parallel to the conceptual division between civil and herile empire. An important illustration was *Las Siete Partidas* – the legal code including the Spanish slave laws of 1563 that has been described as one of the most 'humane' documents in the West Indies until the reversals that occurred with the Atlantic slave trade (Goveia 2000: 581). As a violation of natural liberty, slavery was described as 'the most evil and the most despicable thing which can be found among men, because man, who is the most noble, and free creature . . . is placed in the power of another' (cited in Klein 1971: 142). By enjoying legal personality, the slave could not be subject to the unlimited powers of the master, hence the principle enshrined in Part IV, Tit. XXI that although 'a master has complete authority over his slave to dispose of him as he pleases', he should 'not kill or wound him, although he may give cause for it, except by order of the judge of the district, nor should he strike him in a way contrary to natural reason, or put him to death by starvation'. It was assumed that enslavement did not annul original rights to security and property, or to Christian communion, marriage and parenthood. At best, enforcement was uneven, but the law did at least proclaim that a master could lose the right to own a slave as a result of serious abuses including excessive labour, the sexual abuse of female slaves, and enforced prostitution (Goveia 2000; Bush 1990: 28).

Similar conceptions of civility were also enshrined in the French slave laws, the *Code Noir* which was established by the Royal Edict of 1685. The Code limited the slave owners' punitive rights while nevertheless asserting the state's authority to punish slaves by burning alive, breaking on the wheel ('a favourite punishment'), branding and dismembering (Goveia 2000: 588ff.). It contained articles that opposed breaking up slave families for the purpose of sale, and it penalized 'the concubinage of free men with slaves, except in cases where the union was converted into legal marriage' (Bush 1990: 28). The code imposed legal obligations on slave-owners to provide food, shelter and clothing, but there was large-scale resistance to such encroachments on established property rights that were hard to enforce in any case.

By comparison with the Spanish and French codes, which at least recognized the slave's legal personality, British practice in the West Indies tended to regard the black African slave as little different from other kinds of property. Laws such as the Leeward Islands Act of 1798 imposed a fine of £100 on any white found guilty of 'having criminal commerce' with married slaves (Bush 1990: 30). The Laws of Jamaica of 1826 imposed the death penalty 'without benefit of the clergy' for 'any person committing a rape on a female slave'. The same penalty applied to men who were convicted of abusing slave girls under the age of ten. Such legislation was rare and, again, may have been enforced infrequently. Crucially, slaves were not allowed to testify in court against free persons. Ameliorative measures were introduced in the late eighteenth century in response to growing public opposition to the slave trade. The rape of a slave woman was not a criminal offence in the British Caribbean until the final years of slavery. However, slave-owners who were found guilty of rape faced no more than the inconvenience of 'a small monetary fine' (Beckles 1989: 43; also Beckles 2000 on rape and female slave prostitution). The slave's conversion to Christianity could not undo the dominant forms of social distance or 'emotional disidentification' (de Swaan 1995, 1997). By the end of the seventeenth century, several US states had passed legislation against manumission on the assumption that religious conversion mattered less than past heathenism and the economic utility of slavery (Jordan 1969: 92–3; Davis 1970: 119ff.). Perceptions of the difficulty of reconciling the slave's acceptance of Christian beliefs with continuing labour subjection were countered by the argument that blacks were congenitally incapable of intellectual progress, as accounts of their humble place in the Great Chain of Being contended (Jordan 1969: ch. 6).

Campaigns Against the Slave Trade and Slavery

Prior to the end of the eighteenth century, there was little organized political opposition to slavery. Various religious associations reflected broader social opinion about its economic usefulness, or they defended enslavement as punishment for sin, or insisted that temporary suffering was nothing compared with the possibility of salvation. Stoic moral ideas which, as noted earlier, had shaped earlier European attitudes to civility were galvanized to support the contention that with slavery the body was in chains, but the soul was free.

The enslavement of the body could be portrayed as a peculiar form of spiritual liberation, as a partial release from what the Bishop of London in 1727 called 'the Bondage of Sin and Satan', and 'the Dominion of Mens Lusts and Passions and inordinate Desires' (Davis 1970: 234–5). The ambiguities of Christian doctrine which were apparent during the Spanish conquest persisted during the era of the Atlantic slave trade. Whatever their supposed intellectual and other deficiencies, slaves had been created after all in the image of God, and religious groups were often troubled by acts of cruelty that breached the 'civilized' harm conventions of the time. Although its motives have long been debated, Britain's direct involvement in the slave trade led to the 1807 Abolition Act whereas its determination to end the Atlantic slave trade was expressed in the 1833 Abolition of Slavery Act. As far as the present discussion is concerned, the key question is how resistance to slavery and the slave trade reflected distinguishing features of the course of the 'civilizing process' in the eighteenth and nineteenth centuries. They included heightened sensitivity to violence, and the interrelated trend towards identifying with other people, irrespective of social origins, and with sympathizing with their suffering. Those orientations were projected 'outwards' in the effort to end practices that had come to be regarded as the hallmarks of 'savages', as an stain on 'civilized' peoples that led to collective guilt, and as a symbol of the 'moral backwardness of international society' (Quirk 2011: ch. 2; Keal 2003; also Demos 1996; Hurwitz 1973: ch. 2; Foreman 1996). It is also necessary to consider how far public opposition to the Atlantic slave trade and slavery reflected not only an existing 'civilizing process' but also new 'civilized' self-images that linked British domestic and foreign policy with the idea of 'moral progress' that was encapsulated in the self-flattering claim that the British antislavery crusade was 'among the three or four perfectly virtuous pages comprised in the history of nations' (Lecky 1913 [1869]: vol. 1, 153).

The cruelties endured by slaves from the point of capture, through the whole process of transportation to the fate that awaited them in the Americas need not be related here. It is instructive however to consider methods of punishment that shed light on changing emotional attitudes to violence in that particular phase of the civilizing process. The evidence is that punitive methods such as castration declined in several American colonies because of increased public antipathy towards the most 'cruel' forms of physical violence. The first slave code in Georgia (in 1755) prohibited maiming and emascula-tion – punishments that British colonial officials had regarded as 'uncivilized' when they were first introduced to the Americas (Jordan 1969: 154ff.) – but the process was uneven so that in North Carolina, until 1764, jailers were paid for castrating slaves, and slave-owners could expect compensation for the deaths of those who failed to survive the ordeal. In line with evolving moral sentiments, Virginia abolished the law permitting castration with an exception made for the rape of white females by black slaves. The belief that there was no such thing as rape in relations between slaves was simply taken for granted (Jordan 1969: 157). Many Quakers and other religious groups owned slaves and participated in the slave trade. However, the leading critics of the cruelty of the slave trade, and later of slavery, were religious groups, and particularly Quaker and Methodist organizations that were motivated by Christian ideas of humanity as embodied in the principle, 'do to others as you will be done by' (Jordan 1969: 193ff.; Abruzzo 2011: ch. 1). Humanitarian convictions informed their protests against cruelty to slaves; one outcome was a raft of legislative measures that prohibited physical abuse and that equated murdering a slave with killing a white person (see Davis 1970: 74 for further examples of developments in the United States; also Crawford 2002: 187–8). It may be that such changes had the paradoxical effect of making slavery more palatable to many critics at the very time when ethical concerns about the Atlantic slave trade were increasing (Jordan 1969: 365ff.). In any event, the period revealed significant progress in curtailing the sovereign powers that slave-owners regarded as their birthright. It marked a stage in redrawing the moral and legal boundaries between private privilege and public authority, and in the hardening of expectations that slave-owners were answerable to the larger community and expected to comply, as a result of the changing we–I balance, with 'civilized' restraints. With respect to the process of civilization, the movement signified the growing influence of a 'middle class masculinity' that regarded physical brutality as the shameful residue of a violent past in 'a rational and enlightened age'; public levels of support for the emancipation of slaves increased as part of a larger rise in ethical concern for the plight of 'weak and dependent' human beings (Hall 2002: 27ff.).

Similar sentiments to those that had been expressed in the earlier Spanish and French slave codes informed the new measures to 'civilize' slavery. Violence against enslaved women that included the use of the whip troubled many who were unconvinced by the case for emancipation. As part of shifts in emotional attitudes to violence and suffering, cruelty to women came to be regarded as the single most 'barbaric' feature of slavery – as the offence that demanded urgent prohibition. That standpoint reflected broader assumptions about gender and, specifically, an emerging social consensus about how men should treat the 'gentler sex' that was central to evolving understandings about core 'civilized values' (Beckles 1989: 38–9). But many who were engaged in that particular struggle denied that civility and slavery (however reformed) could ever be compatible. 'Doubtless', wrote the author of *A View of the Past and Present State of Jamaica*, first published in 1823, 'there is in the very nature of slavery, in its mildest form, something unfavourable to the cultivation of moral feeling. Men may be restrained . . . by very good and well-intentioned laws, from exercising acts of cruelty and oppression on the slaves, but still harsh ideas and arbitrary habits, which may find innumerable petty occasions of venting themselves, grow up, whenever slavery exists, in minds where principle has not taken a strong hold' (Stewart 1823: 181–2). Those comments about the relative importance of external and internal restraints on cruelty and capriciousness encapsulated social attitudes to slavery in that pivotal phase of the European civilizing process. They stressed that steep power gradients provided opportunities for cruelty and indifference that clashed with the requirement for self-mastery and self-restraint that was grounded in the official ethical standards of 'civilization' (Abruzzo 2011: ch. 2).

From the 1820s onwards, abolitionists attempted to harvest support for their cause by drawing public attention to the particular brutalities suffered by female slaves whereas many plantation owners continued to argue that coercion was necessary to restrain the 'aggressive' impulses that slaves, in contrast with rational, self-disciplined, 'civilized' subjects, were powerless to control (Beckles 1989: 39ff.). That was the period in which 'abolitionists used the treatment of slave women as a yardstick to measure how far slave societies were removed from their idea of a civilized and moral society' (Altink 2002: 110). Their campaigns led to the first British colonial legislation to outlaw the use of the whip against black slave women which was introduced in Trinidad in 1826 in the face of the vehement resistance of the plantation owners (Bush 1990: 42; also Beckles 1989: 42). Female opposition to slavery was often grounded in a sense of emotional identification or we-feeling with enslaved women who were cruelly denied the shared intimacies of family life – as well as in anxieties about the threats to slave-owning families that were the inevitable consequence of the power that white males wielded over female slaves (Hurwitz 1973: 88ff.; also Ferguson 1992). It was widely believed that white women had a capacity for sympathizing with female slaves that could 'civilize' male attitudes to slavery in the metropolitan and colonial societies, beginning in the home (Altink 2002). Empathy for slave women was often linked with the belief in a 'civilizing mission' to improve the circumstances of those who had been denied the right to speak for themselves. The upshot was a mode of 'imperial feminism' or 'white woman's burden' (Midgley 1998). Emotional identification with female slaves had much to do with the desire to universalize the enjoyment of domesticity at a time when the ascending bourgeoisie attached great importance to the comforting sanctuary of family life – one that confined women to traditional social roles. Domesticity provided emotional warmth in societies that were increasingly at the mercy of cold and impersonal market relations (Ashworth 1987; Altink 2002; Ware 1992). The critical role that women played in social movements that had organized to improve the conditions of slaves and to abolish slavery and the slave trade was interconnected with, and almost certainly influenced the development of 'enlightened' conceptions of masculinity.

There was a world of difference between opposing cruelty to slaves and wishing to see the abolition of the Atlantic slave trade, although opponents of forced transportation such as Wilberforce were involved in the interim step of 'civilizing' slavery – with ensuring that owners honoured the responsibility for the physical and spiritual welfare of those in their care. Many opponents of the slave trade hoped that ending human trafficking would force slave-owners to treat existing slaves more humanely. Regarding the Atlantic trade, in the early eighteenth century, organizations including the Royal African Company asked agents to ensure that slaves were genuine prisoners of war. Since the law of nations allowed enslavement in war, their transportation to the Americas would then be entirely permissible. The reality was that slave traders were perfectly aware that captives were seized in other ways – for example, by raiding parties that followed the instructions of African rulers – although it may be that some believed they were helping to save lives (Davis 1970: 206). In the sixteenth century, critics of the slave trade including Domingo de Soto (a friend of Las Casas) had argued that it would be morally wrong to continue owning people who might well have been purchased in good faith if the subsequent evidence revealed – as he suspected was usually the case with African slavery – that they had lost their liberty as punishment for trivial offences or through unlawful seizure (Davis 1970: 210). Towards the end of that century, the Spanish theologian, Tomas de Mercado, maintained that slave traders sinned by transporting Africans who had been taken illicitly – and since it could be presumed that many women and children had been acquired in precisely that way, no slave trader could engage in the commerce with 'a clear conscience'. Like the purchasers of stolen goods, they were complicit in the harm of immoral slavery rather than the saviours of 'victims of oppression' (Davis 1970: 210–2). Wesley (1958–9 [1872]: 78) made the same point when drawing a direct parallel between someone who has paid for goods, but is 'not concerned to know how they are come by', and the person who, taking possession of goods that are known to be stolen, is 'a partaker with a thief, and . . . not a jot honester than him'. Indeed, unjust enrichment from slavery was the greater evil because it was 'procured by means nothing near so innocent as picking of pockets, housebreaking, or robbery upon the highway'; the beneficiaries were 'the spring that puts all the rest in motion' (Wesley 1958–9 [1872]: 78).

The political significance of such sentiments is worth considering in more detail. They are best regarded as evidence of how people came under greater pressure to display 'complex responsibility'. That orientation involved the conviction that privileged positions within global economic and social chains should raise serious questions not just about the legality of injuries that people deliberately inflicted on others but also about the morality of the benefits that came their way, however unintentionally, because of harmful social practices (Linklater 2011: 101). In the late eighteenth and early nineteenth centuries, an ethical concern with unjust enrichment that was the product of deformed social institutions led British and American Quakers to organize public boycotts of slave products. The core issue was expressed in the contention that 'to live in ease and plenty by the toil of those, whom violence and cruelty have put in our power, is neither consistent with Christianity nor common justice'; the related duty to 'avoid being any way concerned in reaping the unrighteous profits arising from the iniquitous practice of dealing in negro or other slaves' also featured prominently in later English Quaker resolutions. The organizations later decided to exclude 'anyone concerned in the unchristian traffic in negroes' (cited in Sherrard 1959: 101–2).

What began as an exercise in personal abstention in the 1760s – often influenced by a sense of religious guilt associated with commercial profits – evolved into systematic campaigns to boycott the valuable commodity of sugar that had a major impact on the British struggle for emancipation (Crawford 2002: 178). Organized boycotts were an example of the quest to 'civilize' or 'moralize consumption' that was taken forward in many subsequent campaigns of compassion (Hall 2002: 315). An influential example of the more general trend was William Fox's 1791 pamphlet, *Address to the People of Great Britain*, which attempted to extend the sense of personal culpability for the evil consequences of the slave trade by proclaiming this ethical principle: 'let us not think, that the crime rests alone with those who conduct the traffic ... If we purchase the commodity we participate in the crime. The slave-dealer, the slave-holder, and the slave-driver, are virtually the agents of the consumer ... [the consumer] is the original cause, the first mover in the horrid process' (cited in Muthu 2012: 217). The mere existence of such sentiments supports the thesis that the 'humanitarian sensibility' influenced political mobilization to abolish the slave trade and slavery (Crawford 2002: 4, 104, 115). That perspective rejects materialist explanations of abolitionism that maintain that slave labour simply became unprofitable as Britain underwent the transition from mercantilism to industrial capitalism (Williams 1964); see the critical overview in Davis 2006, Haskell 1985 and Ashworth 1987). The argument is that a new ethic encouraged and inspired many people to deal with the remote consequences of their actions, and to feel not just 'passive sympathy' for distant strangers but an inner compulsion to take practical measures to alleviate or eliminate unacceptable suffering (Linklater 2011: 189). Those formulations of the moral questions that arose as people became entangled in lengthening commercial webs were the precursors of recent concerns about the opportunities for unjust enrichment that the affluent enjoy as a result of their privileged place within global relations of dominance and dependence (Pogge 2002). They were indicative of a changing we–I balance in which sympathy for others was interwoven with a strong sense of personal culpability and guilt. As the next chapter will show, such orientations to distant suffering are one of the central legacies of the Enlightenment.

Public sympathy for slaves moved to the centre of religious and philosophical thought towards the end of the eighteenth century. The absence of that elementary moral emotion amongst the captains of slave ships was lamented in the writings of critics such as John Wesley who asked in his 1774 work, *Thoughts Upon Slavery*, 'What is your heart made of? Is there no such principle as compassion there? Do you never feel another's pain? Have you no sympathy, no sense of human woe, no pity for the miserable? When you saw the flowing eyes, the heaving breasts, or the bleeding sides and tortured limbs of your fellow-creatures, was you a stone, or a brute? Did not one tear drop from your eye? . . . And is your conscience quite reconciled to this? Does it never reproach you at all? . . . Can you see, can you feel, no harm therein? Is it doing as you would be done to? . . . Have no more any part in this detestable business' (Wesley 1958–9 [1872]: 77–8).[4] For Wesley and for many others, it was incumbent on all those who were involved in the slave trade to display remorse for a life so thoroughly 'stained with blood', and to seek purification and redemption through slave emancipation (Kaufmann and Pape 1999; also Wood 2000; Anstey 1975; Cell 1979). Those moral pleas were part of a broad 'civilizing offensive' to bridge the emotional gulf between the pro-slavery strata in European societies and the largely invisible world of the slave.

The social impact of the conviction that slavery and the slave trade were not just 'barbaric' rather than 'civilized', but 'barbarizing' rather than 'civilizing', was strengthened by slave testimonials by Cugoano and Equiano in Britain, and by Frederick Douglass, Nat Turner and others in the United States (Crawford 2002: 179ff.). Cugoano's essay on slavery was especially significant because of its inversion of 'civilization' and 'barbarism'. Cruelties to slaves had demonstrated that 'civilized' societies were guilty of the 'barbarous' violation of the moral principles that lay at the heart of Christianity.[5] Such slave narratives helped to widen the scope of emotional identification by encouraging sympathy and solidarity that were anchored in the universal vulnerabilities of the body (Hall 2002: 314). Complementing them was the literary genre that provided sympathetic representations of the slave's aversion to suffering, and attempted to communicate the inner world of his or her

---

[4] Changing attitudes to the slave trade were heightened by public responses to the legal case involving the slave ship, the Zong, whose crew in 1783 threw more than one hundred and thirty sick slaves overboard allegedly to conserve water but, in reality, to prevent the spread of disease, and to protect the monetary value of the remaining human cargo. The cost of the lost slaves was to be recovered through an insurance claim. The legal representative maintained that the action was entirely legitimate because 'the Blacks were property', the case of slaves being no different from casting horses overboard (for further details, see Walvin 1992: 16ff.).

[5] Around the age of 13, Cugoano had been captured from a settlement in what is now Ghana and transported to Grenada. His essay on slavery appeared in 1787. Amongst his correspondents were Edmund Burke and Granville Sharpe (Gates and Andrews 1998: 13–19).

thoughts and feelings to the 'civilized' inhabitants of distant metropolitan societies. Despite the 'artificial sentimentality' that ran through many images of the 'noble savage', various slave testimonials contributed to enlarging the circles of solidarity to include blacks who 'had been cut off from the normal mechanisms of sympathy and identification' by 'the weight of ancient fears' associated with colour, by 'the consequences of an immense cultural barrier', by 'the European's sensitivity to unrepressed sexuality', by various vices that were the direct consequence of enslavement, and by 'the very spirit of secular science which brought emancipation to the European mind' while blacks were consigned to a condition of 'natural inferiority' (Davis 1970: 514ff.).

Changing emotional attitudes to slavery and the slave trade led to new cosmopolitan harm conventions that were embedded in domestic and international law. The 1815 Declaration of the Eight Powers proclaimed that the slave trade was 'repugnant to the principles of humanity and universal morality', and added that 'the public voice, in all civilized countries, calls aloud for its prompt suppression' (Clark 2007: 55). Amongst those legal developments were the courts that Britain established through bilateral treaties with Brazil, the Netherlands, Norway, Portugal, Spain and Sweden. Slave traders were tried in various locations extending from Cape Town and Sierra Leone to New York and Havana (Crawford 2002: 185–6). International agreements and political pressures to abolish the slave trade were far from effective in the Caribbean, notwithstanding Britain's use of its naval power to secure compliance with the new 'standards of civilization'. Estimates are that the number of slaves that were transported annually across the Atlantic each year immediately after the end of the Napoleonic Wars was not much lower than the annual average through the 1780s (Blackburn 1988: 413–14).

Collective measures to bring about the emancipation of slaves did not bring an end to forced labour in many colonies. Earlier arguments that praised coerced labour as the key to progress from engrained indolence to useful industriousness were refashioned to stress its indispensable role in promoting the self-discipline that would equip former slaves for the life of the diligent wage labourer. The distinctively bourgeois elements of abolitionism in the late eighteenth century emphasized the virtues of hard work and thrift. Typical of the bourgeois emphasis on discipline is an extract from the British Colonial Office memorandum in the period before emancipation that expressed the fear of a major labour shortage if the 'negro escaped the necessity ... for labour [which] would be as bad for him as for his owner. He would be cut off from civilizing influences, would have no incentive to better his condition or to impose any but the slightest degree of discipline upon himself. Thus he might well become a more degraded being than his ancestors in Africa' (cited in Blackburn 1988: 441). Those social ideas were at the heart of an emerging middle-class identity that found the slave trade and slavery abominable but did not question the 'civilizing' effects of the workplace or the role of religion in checking the 'native's' ingrained disposition to pursue 'sensual gratifications' (Hall 2002: 297).

National self-images that were interwoven with domestic political struggles to secure the hegemony of bourgeois values were no less important. Abolitionism was integral to the construction of a distinctive vision of British civilization in which the nation was portrayed as the indispensable agent of social progress (Davis 1984: 109; Elias 2013: 149). It was a core element of images of a free nation that prided itself in having defeated French despotism and believed that it was uniquely dedicated to the fusion of religious virtue and the protection of liberty, while failing to take a clear stand on the social and political problems that resulted from the industrial revolution (Altink 2002; Hurwitz 1973: ch. 2; Quirk 2011: chs. 1–2; Davis 1987: 803). The 'anti-slavery project' was a clear example of how the European civilizing process transformed international society – of how a 'civilizing offensive' influenced the development of global harm conventions. But significant continuities with preceding eras must be noted. Opposition to the Atlantic slave trade and slavery should not be mistaken for a major advance in support for the principle of human equality (Quirk 2011: chs. 1–2; Quirk and Richardson 2009). Abolitionism was tied to 'benevolent paternalism'; it was connected with long-established hierarchical conceptions of peoples that were expressed in the doctrine that colonialism was justified to end the 'uncivilized' practice of human enslavement in 'backward' societies (Quirk 2011: chs. 1–2). Other continuities included the British 'apprentice' scheme that was introduced in 1834, hard on the heels of legislation to secure the emancipation of all slaves in Britain's colonies within the following six years. It required former slaves to work ten-hour days and as many as forty-five hours each week on plantations. The system authorized imprisonment for absenteeism and permitted the flogging of female 'apprentices' (Green 1976: ch. 5). The defence of systems of tutelage because of their supposed civilizing function is clearly hard to reconcile with the thesis that humanitarian motives drove the movement towards slave emancipation. It would seem to lend support to the contention that societies swing from one mode of domination to another as opposed to following an upward curve towards higher levels of freedom, as proclaimed by nineteenth-century discourses of progressive modernity.[6] However, abolitionists were generally appalled by a scheme that was widely condemned as 'slavery by another name'. Efforts to dismantle it succeeded in 1838, the year

---

[6] Support for that interpretation can be derived from the reality that humanitarianism led not to financial compensation for the 780,000 former slaves in the British West Indies colonies but to the plantation owners. In 1834 alone, the British government made around 20 million pounds available for that purpose. The apprenticeship scheme was established to ensure that plantation owners had an adequate labour supply, to instruct slaves for a life of wage labour, and to avoid the social disorder that many feared would be the outcome of emancipation. Many abolitionists opposed all of those measures.

that many regard as marking the 'real victory' of the abolitionist movement (Porter 1999: 206).

Political struggles over the apprenticeship scheme were part of a broader debate about the nature and direction of an imperial 'civilizing process'. At its core was a tension between two social forces. One side embraced the belief that forced labour, ably assisted by what Carlyle called the 'beneficent whip', was essential if 'civilized' self-constraints were to be instilled in 'backward' social groups. The other side mobilized public campaigns of compassion against the apprenticeship scheme in the belief that grinding servitude was a variation on slavery that prolonged the gross disfigurement of the 'civilized' world (Blackburn 1988: 456ff., also Abruzzo 2011: chs. 4 and 6; Crawford 2002: 190ff.; Hall 2002: 109–10). Revealing was the stance of the leading abolitionist, Thomas Clarkson, who, while not opposed to 'coerced labour' as such, was 'outraged' by 'the claim of personal proprietorship that justified arbitrary and unlimited authority' (Davis 1987: 805). What have been described as the 'moderate abolitionists' had hoped that slave-owners would humanize slavery, but the latter's stubborn opposition to restrictions on, *inter alia*, flogging women, convinced them that the institution was simply impossible to reform (Davis 1987: 805). Those who belonged to what has been called the 'immediatist' camp were shocked by persistent violence against female slaves that was increasingly regarded as 'unmanly', and as wholly incompatible with the ethical virtues of 'the man of feeling' (Altink 2002; Elias 2012: 467).

The 'apprentice scheme' was dismantled in 1838 as a result of successful campaigns by the Anti-Slavery Society. Forced labour, on the other hand, survived until well into the twentieth century in, for example, the French and Portuguese colonial territories albeit in the context of the new principles of international legitimacy that were enshrined in the articles of the Covenant of the League of Nations that established the Mandate System (Bain 2003: ch. 4; Crawford 2002: 197n156). Slavery was adapted to circumvent those global standards with the result that contemporary anti-slave movements have focused less on the physical seizure and sale of persons than on systems of human exploitation such as indebted labour that formerly existed alongside 'classical' chattel slavery but have now largely displaced it. The greater reliance on indentured migration schemes in the aftermath of the legal abolition of chattel slavery demonstrated that abolition was a first step towards eliminating a specific form of human exploitation rather than a historical endpoint (Quirk 2011: ch. 4).

More will be said about international trusteeship at a later stage but, as a prior step, it is important to turn to the relationship between changing conceptions of permissible and forbidden methods of suppressing slave revolts and conducting colonial wars. A version of the doctrine that 'might is right' was prevalent in relations with rebellious or unruly slaves. It was exemplified by the notorious comments by General Lothar von Trotha, German military commander in South West Africa, and a veteran of wars in China and East Africa, who defended the unrestrained use of force when dealing with rebellion or unrest in the colonies in the following terms: 'I know enough tribes in Africa. They all have the same mentality insofar as they yield only to force. It was and remains my policy to apply this force with unmitigated terrorism and even cruelty. I shall destroy the rebellious tribes by shedding rivers of blood ...' (Crawford 2002: 229). Widespread resistance to imperial rule was often repressed with a ferocity that reflected the desire to be unhindered by international harm conventions that were thought to apply only in relations between state-organized, 'civilized' groups (Kiernan 1998). One reason for the dual standard of morality was the concern that complying with the laws of war would disadvantage 'civilized' forces in conflicts with 'cruel savages' that observed no such restraints (Linklater 2011: 130). The anthropology of pain reinforced that ethic. At the 1899 Hague Peace Conference, Sir John Ardaugh opposed outlawing the dumdum bullet on the grounds that 'civilized man is much more susceptible to injury than savages ... The savage, like the tiger, is not so impressionable', and fights on 'even when desperately wounded' (O'Connell 1995: 265; Kiernan 1998: ch. 10). Reflecting the larger European civilizing process, colonial discourses stressed the differences between 'savage' peoples who were highly attuned to violence and suffering, and 'civilized' societies that had a lower tolerance of pain and a greater capacity for human sympathy because of cultural 'refinement' (Bending 2000: 123ff.). Those attitudes did not go unchallenged. The brutal suppression of the Jamaican rebellion of December 1831 intensified demands in Britain for the immediate emancipation of slaves (Porter 1999: 204). Although destructive impulses were not easily restrained in the colonial wars of the late eighteenth and nineteenth century, there was an important shift towards the view that 'advanced' peoples should behave in a 'civilized' way in relations with 'social inferiors', including in conflicts with anti-colonial movements. The desire to publicize colonial violence increased, and not least because of the propaganda value of portraying competitors in the international struggle for power and security as lax in observing 'civilized' standards. What emerged was the conviction that the 'civilized' should not only observe such constraints but prepare colonial peoples for a painless transition to forms of self-government that were closely modelled on idealized European images of social and political development. As an example, French colonial thought during the Third Republic developed the idea of the *mission civilisatrice* to defend the objective of sharing the material and spiritual advantages of progress with peoples whose ways of life lacked intrinsic worth (Conklin 1997).

International trusteeship carried forward the 'standard of civilization' which was one of the main expressions of evolving orientations towards non-European peoples. It was a primary example of how the civilizing process shaped international society in the transition from the period in which the Europeans regarded the colonies as permanent possessions that they could treat as they saw fit to the era in which they accepted global legal and moral obligations to equip them for eventual sovereign independence. Evidence of the effects of the civilizing process on changing attitudes to the colonies can be found in Burke's earlier conception of trusteeship (the ancestor of the idea of the 'sacred trust of civilization') that advanced a political theory of imperial responsibility in opposition to traditional conceptions of absolute sovereign rights over 'inferior' peoples (Bain 2003: chs. 1–2; Crawford 2002: ch. 6). Its most influential formulation can be found in the contribution to the December 1783 Parliamentary debate on the East India Bill. In his speech, Burke asserted that 'all political power which is set over men, and all ... privilege claimed ... in exclusion of them, being wholly artificial, and ... a derogation from the natural equality of mankind at large, ought to be some way or other exercised ultimately for their benefit'. 'Such rights, or privileges', he added, should be regarded 'in the strictest sense a *trust*; and it is of the very essence of every trust to be rendered *accountable*; and even totally to *cease*, when it substantially varies from the purposes for which alone it could have a lawful existence' (Burke 1899 [1783]: 172–3, italics in original). The standpoint revived many of the ethical anxieties about cruelty and unnecessary suffering that had been central to the Spanish debates about imperial rule in the first wave of European overseas expansion. Official reports of settler brutality along the lawless colonial frontier during British expansion in the 1830s led the relevant House of Commons' Committee to observe in 1836–7 that 'the effect of European intercourse ... has been, upon the whole, hitherto a calamity upon the native and savage nations' (Porter 1999: 207–8). The extension of metropolitan sovereign powers over colonial authorities was regarded as the main remedy for the absence of 'civil' rule in frontier regions and as the prerequisite for ensuring that conquered peoples shared in the benefits of 'civilization', as required by the emergent international ethic of trusteeship.

The level of support for trusteeship increased because of failures to establish effective ways of granting colonial subjects the freedom from the cruelty, violence and exploitation that the citizens of 'civilized' societies had come to regard as their birthright. Two notorious examples of colonial abuses that revealed the difficulty, if not the impossibility, of reconciling empire with civility were the actions of the East India Company (which resulted in the impeachment of Warren Hastings), and the cruelties committed in the Belgian Congo in the latter part of the nineteenth century that were widely condemned as a 'standing disgrace to Christian civilization' (Bellamy 2012: 88ff.).

In response to such events, abolitionists 'harnessed the emotions of embarrassment and shame' (emotions that had been central to the whole civilizing process) to condemn the cruelties of empire and to encourage emotional identification with, and compassion for, the victims of imperial rule (Crawford 2002: 387ff.; Nadelmann 1990). By appealing to 'emotion' as much to 'reason', reformist organizations persuaded significant sections of the population in Britain and elsewhere that the colonial empires that had been a source of collective pride were in need of urgent reform. Expressing changing attitudes to colonized peoples, Article VI of the 1885 Berlin Act required the signatories to 'watch over the preservation of the native tribes, and to care for the improvement of the conditions of their moral and material well-being, and to help in suppressing slavery, and especially the Slave Trade' (Bain 2003: 63–74; Porter 1999: 218). The League of Nations Mandates System denied the legitimacy of colonial rule that was geared simply to maximizing metropolitan wealth; its organizing principles stated that the governance of peoples who were 'not yet able to stand by themselves' had to comply with the principle that the 'wellbeing and development of the (colonial) peoples form a sacred trust of civilization', an idea that revealed the precise impact of the civilizing process on evolving notions of permissible and impermissible behaviour in international society (cited in Bain 2003: 101; Gong 1984: 76ff.). The system created the international legal obligation to assist the colonies in learning how to combine self-government with good government, a process that would take, it was generally assumed, many decades (and in the case of the more 'primitive' societies, several centuries) to complete.

But the political course followed by many colonies would not be the one that was envisaged by their imperial overlords. Of critical importance was the assault on the Western principle that self-government had to wait until the newly independent states had satisfied an external test of their capacity for good government. Self-government was prioritized over good government in the United Nations General Assembly Resolution 1514 that was passed on 14 December 1960. Now familiar questions about the responsibilities of Western liberal-democracies to peoples in 'failed states' or to the victims of regimes that have no compunction in violating human rights emerged in its wake. A new 'standard of civilization' with respect to former colonies that did not follow the anticipated path of 'modernization' and 'development' has led to state-building projects and great power interventions that have created concerns about the re-imposition of imperial governance and the re-emergence of colonial mentalities. The idea of the 'responsibility to protect' is an illustration of the standards of self-restraint that are now expected of sovereign rulers in international society (see also Chapter 10, p. 403 below). The troubled question has emerged in the recent period of whether humanitarian intervention is permissible or indeed obligatory, as some argue, for 'civilized' people who cannot take pride in their social and political accomplishments while remaining inactive in the face of serious human rights violations. Elias argued that European societies were unprepared for the 'regression to barbarism' in their own continent (see Chapter 9). They were no more ready for the political challenges that would emerge with the failures of 'modernization theory' – because the transition to Western-type states and the acceptance of the 'civilized' principles that accompanied their formation has not been as smooth and automatic as many assumed they would be when the process of decolonization gathered pace after the Second World War.

Moral Progress, Civilization and World Politics

Earlier chapters addressed the questions of how different the ancient states-systems were from the modern international order with respect to the relationship between violence and civilization, and they asked what implications can be drawn for the analysis of the preconditions of global civilizing processes. They stressed the common ground between the ancient and the early modern states-systems. Restraints on violence within political communities were invariably greater than the restraints on force in their external relations. The constitutive parts displayed low levels of sympathy for 'outsiders'; an exploitative orientation towards social 'inferiors' pervaded everyday life. In the ancient world, the practice of human enslavement was rarely called into question. No great public debate considered the rights and wrongs of colonialism and human enslavement; no social movement emerged to secure the emancipation of slaves. So it was with slavery and the slave trade in the modern states-system until recently.

It has been argued that a central question in the study of harm in world politics is how far the entanglement of societies in longer chains is accompanied by heightened ethical sensibilities about violence and by major political endeavours to restrain the use of force. The formation of modern European territorial monopolies of power with global reach represented a major advance in the capacity to cause suffering in distant places. The gulf between the principles that applied within Europe and in relations with non-European peoples widened with the consolidation of state structures and the formation of civilized self-images. The resulting 'split' within modern civilization underpinned European assumptions that particular forms of violence that were forbidden within the 'civilized' world were permissible in relations with 'savages'. For long intervals, the modern states-system echoed central political features of the ancient world. But 'civilizing' efforts to control the use of force also developed. From the earliest periods of European colonial expansion, imperial cruelties were challenged as an offense against the laws of reason and, later, as an assault on civilized values. The critique of colonial violence rested initially on religious conceptions of the relationship between violence and civilization that extended the political and philosophical discussions of civility in the Roman period and in the early Middle Ages. What was revolutionary about the later modern period was the employment of conceptions of civilization and images of a universal human community to challenge the slave trade and chattel slavery followed by the institution of empire itself. A stronger sense of we-feeling and identification with fellow-humans and their suffering was connected with a changing we–I balance so that colonists became answerable to principles of humanity that were embedded in a more 'civilized' international society.

The abolition of the Atlantic slave trade and African slavery stands out as one of the more remarkable examples of 'moral progress' in the sense of institutionalizing a 'principle of humaneness' in which the 'laws, customs, institutions, and practices' of a 'culture, society, or historical era' display greater 'sensitivity to', and 'less tolerance' of, 'the pain and suffering of human beings' (Macklin 1977: 371–2). Similar themes were evident in religious condemnations of the unnecessary suffering that was caused in the first wave of European overseas expansion. They were linked with the idea that the main purpose of empire was to liberate others from ignorance and sin that could lead to everlasting torment. Empire was regarded as the indispensable instrument of a civilizing process that was infused with sacred purposes. Religious conceptions of the principles governing imperial administration and the governance of slaves remained influential in the nineteenth century. The medieval international system turned out to be an 'evolutionary dead end but it left an important 'civilizing' legacy that influenced later understandings of what is permissible and forbidden in relations between the colonized and colonizing peoples. The idea of the 'sacred trust of civilization' established the radical principle that independent colonies could eventually be admitted into European international society on equal terms with the foundational, 'civilized' members, but only as long as they demonstrated the capacity to organize their affairs in accordance with 'modern' principles of society and politics.

Those changing Western standpoints were examples of a broader shift in the relations between 'the established and the outsiders': between governments and citizens, men and women, adults and children, as well as between imperial rulers and their subjects (Elias 2013: 28). The social gradient between European and other peoples became less steep because of increased support for the idea of human equality that came to be regarded as fundamental to civilized existence. The moral conviction that every human being has the right to be free from mental degradation and physical abuse acquired unprecedented importance in the history of the Western states-systems. Whether that was the dominant influence on the main patterns of development remains a contested issue. Debates about the reasons for abolition of the Atlantic slave trade have highlighted one of the central questions which is whether the altruistic concern with the wellbeing of other humans was more important than an interest in removing the burden of guilt or in establishing moral superiority over others through claims to embody civilized values.

From the vantage point of process sociology, the tendency to inquire into whether 'ideals' or 'interests' are ultimately determining with respect to any sphere of human interaction is unprofitable. The examination of the European civilizing process altered the terms of the debate by analysing the social compulsions that led to the 'relative autonomy' of particular 'civilized' sensibilities towards violence and suffering (Elias 2008b: 132–3, Elias 2008e: 136–7). As discussed in the previous chapter, the explanation stressed that the widening of the scope of emotional identification between members of the same society and the reduced tolerance of violent harm and social degradation have to be understood in connection with state formation and internal pacification, changing patterns of human interweaving, and the associated pressures on people to become attuned to the interests of others in more 'humane' or considerate ways. Progressions in the shape of changing moral attitudes to the permissible and the forbidden took place in the period under consideration. But they did not occur because moral ideas developed independently of other social forces, or because the people involved were inherently more 'humane' or 'compassionate' than their ancestors. The relevant moral dispositions could not be explained, the argument was, without understanding the social and political forces that pushed people in the direction where they felt a stronger inner compulsion to comply with the expectations of self-restraint that were intrinsic to their 'civilization'.

The point then was to understand the social and political conditions that have favoured 'enlightened' moralities of that kind. Explaining normative change in the recent period can be furthered by recognizing the importance of the changing balance of power between social groups. The increasing power capabilities of the bourgeoisie in relation to the traditional aristocracy led to the growing importance of universal and egalitarian moral sensibilities. The latter were used, as in the case of abolitionism, to forge an interwoven class and national identity that opposed forms of exploitation and suffering that had not caused widespread outrage or led to the clamour for reform in the earlier Western states-systems. That development helped to check the results of major power asymmetries in the relations between Europeans and non-European peoples that did not favour respect for principles of reciprocity. The strong had few incentives to exercise self-restraint in their relations with colonized peoples; the latter had few resources that could be used to extract political concessions from the dominant strata or to encourage greater controls on physical violence. Universalistic and egalitarian principles were the bridge between shifting power balances within 'civilized' societies and public demands for new conceptions of the permissible and the forbidden in imperial encounters. Disgust with the 'savagery' of colonial wars was one manifestation of the attempt to tame the colonists that extended the earlier process of 'taming the warriors'. Such an approach explains how such notions as 'the sacred trust of civilization' emerged as a link between the civilizing process and new prohibitions of harm in European international society. Therein lies one of the main explanations of core differences between the ancient and the modern states-systems.

7

Enlightenment Thought and Global Civilization

> The concept underlying this enlightened, socially critical reform movement was always the same: that the improvement of institutions, education and law will be brought about by the advance of knowledge ... Progress would be achieved, therefore, first by the enlightenment of kings and rulers in conformity with 'reason' or 'nature', which comes to the same thing, and then by placing in leading positions enlightened (that is, reform-minded) men. A certain aspect of this whole progressive process of reform came to be designated by a fixed concept: *civilisation* ... Society, from this point of view, had reached a particular stage on the road to civilisation. But it was insufficient. Society could not stand still there. The process was continuing and ought to be pushed further: 'the civilisation of peoples is not yet complete.'
>
> (Elias 2012: 55, italics in original)

'Civilization' was incomplete, Holbach argued in the late eighteenth century, because human reason had yet to be employed intelligently to improve society. Numerous obstacles delayed 'the progress of useful knowledge' that could be applied to ensure the perfection of government, social institutions and morals, but nothing did more to block advances in 'public happiness', or the 'progress of human reason', or 'the entire civilization of men' than 'the continual wars into which thoughtless princes are drawn at every moment' (Holbach, cited in Elias 2012: 54–5). Central features of the so-called Enlightenment project are contained in that observation: the belief in reason as an instrument not only of social reform but of indefinite progress, and the vision of a cosmopolitan future in which all peoples are bound together by universal moral principles that demonstrate the unique accomplishments of European civilization (Schlereth 1977). Whether the so-called Enlightenment project is a caricature of the dominant ideas of the period is a matter to come back to later. The main issues are best approached by stating that the Enlightenment was a crucial phase in the long-term development of a civilizing process that was profoundly influenced by court rationality (Elias 2012: ch. 2) That process led to ideals of civility and visions of the 'polite nation' that combined cosmopolitan aspirations with confidence in the superiority of French standards of behaviour (Zurbuchen 2003; Gordon 1994, especially ch. 3;

Gay 1969: 41ff.). On that interpretation, progressivist ideals were a radical extension of earlier notions of civilité, but with the crucial twist that elite political orientations shifted away from constructing more subtle, refined social distinctions that distinguished them from the lower orders towards efforts to free the masses and other societies from 'barbaric or irrational' conditions. From that standpoint, Voltaire and Condorcet's aspirations for humanity were an attempt to build on the advances in internal pacification and in the interrelated softening of manners that had already taken place under the governance of 'benevolent' kings.

Elias's statement about the connections between civilization and court society raises large questions about the relationship between the Enlightenment and political absolutism (Gagliardo 1968; Hellmuth 2004; Scott 1990; Krieger 1970: part 3). The pressures to rationalize state structures in response to the increasing costs of war led to domestic programmes of reform coupled with the active promotion of commerce. One consequence was that several absolutist states became more open to Enlightenment political ideals. They increased the significance of bourgeois elements in courts that had come to recognize the need for a discourse of government in the public interest that superseded earlier conceptions of the state as a private realm – as a royal household that was distinct from, and not answerable to, the larger society. Frederick II's decision to describe himself as 'the first servant of the state' was designed to alter negative perceptions of an unbreakable alliance with the nobility; it emphasized the distinction between the monarch and the state, and signified the tilt towards constitutional governance based on a 'confraternity' of citizens (Gagliardo 1968: ch. 4). Support for the thesis that absolutist rule was essential to restrain 'naturally evil' human impulses declined in that period. The monarchs' greater reliance on expert elites to consolidate state power lent an increasingly 'bourgeois tone to government' (Gagliardo 1968: ibid.). The main course of development included a greater stress on the importance of the ruler's clemency in dealing with adversaries, and a shift towards the social imperative of self-control that reflected the influence of Roman imperial conceptions of mercy towards social 'inferiors' (Noyes 2014: 214). That feature of divine kingship, which Montesquieu described as the 'distinguishing characteristic of monarchs', was contrasted with the increasingly obsolete 'feudal code of honour and revenge' (Noyes 2014: 211ff.).

The statement that reformist elements such as the Physiocrats functioned 'entirely within the framework of the existing social system' appears to clash with common assumptions about the Enlightenment faith in human perfectibility (Elias 2012: 48). That claim seems hard to reconcile with interpretations of the Enlightenment which contend that leading thinkers had what is now widely regarded as a naïve and dangerous faith in the human ability to bring society under the dominion of pure reason, to eradicate myth and religious superstition, and to rely on social engineering to sweep away archaic social and political institutions that contradicted the natural right to freedom and equality. Elias (2012: 52–3) referred to Mirabeau's melancholic remark that civilization was a phase in the cyclical movement in which progressive epochs were followed by an apparently inevitable collapse into barbarism. Mirabeau had argued that 'we have deluded ourselves that there are differences between civilized and barbarian nations when all are barbaric in different ways since none has adhered to the natural order or learned how to perpetuate our species safely' (cited in Vardi 2012: 167–8). As far as the rhythms of history are concerned, the most prominent Enlightenment thinkers doubted that they could be broken once and for all. The more pessimistic French theorists inclined towards the view that the use of reason could improve social arrangements for a limited period and defer the seemingly inevitable destiny of every form of life (Vyverberg 1958; Gay 1964: ch. 9; Hampson 1968: 149ff.). Expressing that standpoint, Diderot observed that 'the fate which rules the world decrees that everything should pass away ... Everything carries within itself a hidden germ of destruction' (cited in Vyverberg 1958:199; also Diderot 1992 [1772]: 40). Reservations about the limited power of human reason did not shake confidence in the belief that the purpose of social inquiry was to understand the laws or probabilities of human interaction in order to reform the system of 'arbitrary' or 'irrational' government where 'rulers are almighty and can regulate all human affairs as they think fit'; the political objective of the reformists was 'to guide social processes in a more enlightened and rational way than hitherto' (Elias 2012: 52–3; Baker 1975: ch. 3). Exemplifying that trend, the Physiocrats expressed the radical standpoint that public order was governed by social laws that existed independently of, and did not derive their legitimacy from, secular or religious authorities. That position represented a challenge to the dominant conceptions of traditional institutions, although the Physiocrats aimed not to overthrow the ruling strata but to steer court society towards enlightened rule that was informed by a deeper comprehension of social and political dynamics (Elias 2009e).

Representative of the new attitudes to society and politics was Bishop Berkeley's statement that such advances could increase the levels of foresight and restraint (central features of the European civilizing process, as discussed in Chapter 5) that were essential for taming capricious social forces. By understanding 'the settled laws of nature', humans could acquire 'a sort of foresight, which enables us to regulate our actions for the benefit of life', and achieve greater freedom from the 'uncertainty and confusion' that characterizes a world that is significantly beyond human control (Berkeley 1988 [1710]: para 31). Declining support amongst the intelligentsia for the doctrine of original sin – and challenges to that idea have solid claims to be regarded as the single development that most unified the diverse patterns of Enlightenment thought – was linked with enthusiastic support for Locke's critique of the doctrine of innate ideas that underpinned the conviction that the social environment was the chief determinant of individual and collective behaviour (Robertson 2005: 28ff.). With appropriate changes in social and political organization, it was assumed, human conduct could be significantly improved. With enlightened government, the effects of malevolent conditions could be ameliorated.

Enlightened thinkers were far from unanimous in believing that people could realize a utopian vision of the perfect society through the exercise of pure reason, but they rejected theories of politics that were dependent on revealed religion, and they concluded that societies would be improved if public institutions were guided by a more realistic understanding of the universal or recurrent features of human existence. Such orientations to the social world reflected admiration for the remarkable progress of the natural sciences in the period since Newton discovered the laws governing physical reality, an advance beyond slavish obedience to the decrees of established religion that demonstrated how rational inquiry could explain what had once seemed incomprehensible (Porter 2000). Confidence in the benefits of linking scientific thought to exercises in radical social engineering was especially evident in Hume's argument for distinguishing between what belongs to the realm of pure chance and what can be explained in the language of 'cause and effect' with positive consequences for the ideal of the governance of laws in the 'civilized monarchy' (Hume 1875b [1777]: 186). The enormous diversity of customs did not alter the fact that human nature is more or less everywhere the same, and subject to similar pressures and dynamics (Hume 1975 [1748]: 8.1.65). Especially because of advances in scientific reasoning and the demonstrated achievements of the modern experimental method, Enlightenment thinkers believed that their age surpassed all previous epochs. But, as emphasized above, progress in that sphere and in the enlargement of human possibilities did not mean that the modern age was presumed to stand on the threshold of the 'end of history' and to become immune from the processes of decline and decay that had destroyed earlier civilizations (Bronner 2006: ch. 2). Providential history in its secularized form did not enjoy support amongst, inter alia, thinkers of the Scottish Enlightenment who believed that it was legitimate to look forward to 'gradual' social advances but erroneous to think that progress was 'guaranteed' (Berry 2003: 249).

An acute awareness of the complexities of social and political is evident in Kant's observation that humanity is a 'coalition' that faces the permanent threat of 'dissension' and dissolution, but is nevertheless 'destined by nature to develop, through mutual compulsion and laws written by them, into a cosmopolitan society' that ensures 'peaceful coexistence' (Kant 1978 [1798]: 249). The process could be expected to unfold in a largely unplanned manner for, as Shaftesbury had earlier argued, 'we polish one another, and rub off our Corners and rough Sides by a sort of amicable collision'

(Shaftesbury 1978 [1711]: 64). A core assumption in Kant's writings – indicative of a shift in the civilizing process towards political visions of planned social directions at the national and global levels – was that compliance with the ethical imperative of managing such conflicts would lead to freely chosen internal controls on violent tendencies that would transform world politics. The necessary advances could take many centuries. Kant contended that it was often only through the bitter experience of conflict that the species learned what would have seemed perfectly evident had it been accustomed to using its rational faculties all along. Nevertheless, confidence in employing reason and scientific knowledge to improve social life extended earlier Renaissance breakthroughs in reflecting on the prospects for taming necessity and for reducing human vulnerability to the tyranny of fortune.

Too many interpretations of the Enlightenment have assumed that the leading thinkers were committed to radical, simplistic notions of human perfectibility. Distorted readings have maintained that the seeds of political domination were inherent in the naïvety of regarding science as the privileged pathway to grasping universal truths about society and nature, in a corresponding determination to free the oppressed from ignorance and superstition, and in assumptions that Europeans had access to moral truths that entitled them to liberate other peoples from stagnation and barbarism (Horkheimer and Adorno 1973: 4; but see Bronner 2006: 3–4). It is true that some thinkers such as Condorcet (1965 [1794]: 57–8) believed that there was good reason to think that the time will come when free individuals will rely on rationality alone to eradicate 'misery and folly'. He maintained that 'nature has set no term to the perfection of human faculties; that the perfectibility of man is truly indefinite; and that the progress of this perfectibility ... has no other limit than the duration of the globe upon which nature has cast us' (Condorcet 1965 [1794]: 52). However, such expressions of optimism were usually qualified by darker references to the fragility of human existence (Condorcet 1965 [1794]: ibid.). The image of a generalized commitment to a totalizing, universal political mission to subject all human relations to the governance of reason is largely a myth that ignores the reality of multiple Enlightenments and the absence of a single unifying 'teleology of civility' (Pittock 2003: 262–3).

The modest political ambitions of most thinkers of the Enlightenment had less to do with realizing some utopian end-state than with responding to the challenges of a turning point in human history given that the rapid extension of the social division of labour and associated increases in global interconnect-edness had compounded the moral and political problems of the 'unintended consequences' of human action (Berry 1997: 144ff.; Gay 1969: 98ff.). Reason created the prospect of increasing human power over social forces. It equipped societies with a deeper comprehension of the limits on such endeavours and a more profound appreciation of the very real possibility of failure and decline.

That was not because humans were intrinsically corrupt or evil but because they were often so preoccupied with short-term objectives that the main patterns of development were largely the product of chance rather than rational deliberation (Jackson 2004). That is the 'project of Enlightenment' that informs the discussion in this chapter.

Critics of totalizing images of the Enlightenment therefore deny that there was one 'project of modernity' to which all leading thinkers subscribed. They emphasize 'multiple enlightenments' that were loosely tied together by a critical stance on society and politics that anticipated the gradual accumulation of reliable, socially useful evidence about human prospects. To explain the diversity of opinion, distinctions have been drawn between the 'mainstream moderate Enlightenment' in Britain and the 'radical Enlightenment' that became the dominant voice in France from around the 1740s. Influenced by Locke and Newton, and defended by Voltaire and Hume in different ways, the moderate Enlightenment argued that religious belief was valuable, if not essential, for the preservation of a harmonious social order (Hume 1821 [1775]: 300; Smith 1982 [1759]: III.2.33). Religious belief was what Lord Chesterfield described as 'collateral security ... to virtue' (cited in Hampson 1968: 158; Becker 1959: 49ff.; Cassirer 1951: 137ff.). Its exponents thought that popular belief in divine punishment was one of the crucial foundations on which widespread compliance with laws and morals ultimately rested. They were inclined to the view that social hierarchy was no less valuable. They regarded the intelligentsia as part of a broader ruling elite comprising the monarchy, aristocracy and the holders of ecclesiastical office that had curbed religious fanaticism and intolerance in a 'long civilizing process' that extended the aristocratic modes of civility within European court society (Israel 2006: 360ff.). Particular emphasis was placed on the role of moral sentiments such as sympathy in binding people together in civilized communities (Himmelfarb 2005).

Exponents of the radical Enlightenment criticized what they regarded as the submissive social conservatism of British moral and political thought. They protested that the 1688 Glorious Revolution had led to a political compromise between the intelligentsia, the monarchy and the church, and to support for patriotism and empire, that entrenched traditional privileges and betrayed the 'principles of popular sovereignty and natural equality' (Israel 2006: 368–9, 361–2; Himmelfarb 2005). Radical Enlightenment thinkers believed that the masses could be improved by education and they were optimistic about the potentials for equality and emancipation, but they were nevertheless generally suspicious of the great mass of society and disposed to delay political emancipation until the populace was clearly more 'civilized' (Hampson 1968: 154). The dominant strand of political thought in the British Enlightenment had supported the notion of a divinely ordered universe and a religiously sanctioned social order anchored in the rule of law, but it was opposed to conferring democratic freedoms on all people. It supported political tolerance with exceptions for, amongst others, atheists and Jews; and it was comfortable with empire or slavery. Radical Enlightenment thinkers were committed to different social objectives in the light of the conviction that appeals to divine authority and supernatural agency should be abandoned and morality based entirely on secular foundations; they maintained that human equality demanded an end to racial and gender hierarchies, support for comprehensive tolerance, maximum levels of personal liberty and democratic republicanism, and the condemnation of colonial domination and enslavement. All such ideas were linked with the often rhetorical conviction that the use of reason could remove the worst social and political imperfections (Israel 2006: 866; Porter 2000: 10ff.). But even the more radical of Enlightenment thinkers were wary of grand designs to reorganize society. Most were comfortable with incremental reform in the light of Montesquieu's warnings about the dangers of tampering with tried and tested social and political institutions and advice about the need to embark on far-reaching programmes of change with a 'trembling hand' (cited in Hampson 1968: 112).

Significantly for the course the European civilizing process was about to take, many Enlightenment figures believed that a major advance in gender relations was observable in their epoch (Barker-Benfield 1992; Garrett 2003: 85–6). Belief in progress in relations between the sexes was not always bound up with the idea of the equality of men and women, however. Hume believed that natural gender differences existed, and that men had sought to dom-inate women from the earliest times, but different eras could be compared to establish how far the male drive for dominance had undergone 'refinement' (Garrett 2003:86; Vogel 2000: 12). When considered in long-term perspec-tive, it seemed abundantly clear that the exercise of male power had changed from the coercive modes that were the norm in earlier historical eras to the 'gentler', more civil forms that had come to the forefront in the commercial societies of the era (Porter 2000: 285ff., 325; Fletcher 1995: ch. 16). For many thinkers, progress in relations between men and women was the real test of how far a civilizing process had eliminated violence within and between societies (Porter 2000: ch. 14; Goodman 1994: introduction; Towns 2009). As discussed in the earlier chapters, those conceptions of civility had been defended in the earlier Western states-systems as part of the effort to 'tame the warriors' but, with the radical Enlightenment, the moral imperative of placing universal and egalitarian principles at the centre of social and political life moved to the forefront of reflections on global prospects for the first time.

For those reasons, the most influential thinkers of the period believed that they were living in what Kant (1991 [1784]: 58) called an '*enlightened* age' (but not an 'age of *enlightenment*') in which humans were more aware of the possibility, and indeed of the urgency, of exercising greater control over their collective fate through the exercise of public reason (italics in original). Kant (1991 [1798]: 182–3) observed that moral progress was evident in the 'sympathy' that 'spectators' felt for the ideals of the French Revolution. The same long-term trend encouraged confidence in the possibility of gradual advancement towards a world of republican states that renounced 'wars of aggression' once and for all and cooperated to protect universal human rights. The awareness of participating in an ongoing historical 'process' which is apparent in the writings of Kant and Mendelssohn was linked with a realistic conviction that there was a great deal to struggle for and much that could go wrong in the quest to reduce unnecessary suffering and to dismantle unjustifiable constraints on human liberty (Outram 1995: ch. 1). The intrinsic value of that collective search for social improvement was linked explicitly with the imperative of exercising freedom responsibly. Those orientations stressed the uncertainties that were inherent in possessing a free will but envisaged a condition in which humanity exercised greater control over social processes in a new balance of power between 'civilizing' internal and external restraints (Carter 2000: 85ff.; Passmore 1965).

It has been contended that the 'project of the Enlightenment' cannot be reduced to a single political programme but should be regarded as promoting a critical spirit – a distinctive 'tone of voice' and new moral 'sensibility' (Goldie, cited in Porter 2000: xxi). An emphasis on that *ethos* is central to 'pluralizing the Enlightenment', to highlighting the various tensions as well as the family resemblances between leading perspectives (Schmidt 2000). On that argument, two errors need to be expunged from the exegesis of the principal writings: the belief that the 'Enlightenment project' has been responsible for a great deal of suffering in the world – not least because of the 'civilizing missions' that were unleashed in its name – and the antithetical claim that the violence of modern wars and genocide represent a total abandonment of its 'civilizing' aspirations for humanity (Muthu 2003: 260ff.). From that standpoint, it is essential to resist the temptation of being either unreservedly for or against the Enlightenment; it is necessary to embrace instead its 'philosophical ethos that could be described as a permanent critique of our historical era' through which it may become possible to ascertain with greater precision what is – and is not – 'indispensable for the constitution of ourselves as autonomous subjects' (Foucault 1991: 42–3).

Similar sensibilities underpinned the claim that social and political developments usually take place in unplanned ways and with unpredicted and often adverse consequences. The ensuing challenge was to develop more advanced explanations of social processes in order to distinguish between the restraints that are necessary 'for complicated societies to function' and the restraints that do little more than preserve the dominance 'of certain ruling groups', and to steer society accordingly (Elias 2013b: 164). Contentions such as those echo

Kant's conviction that 'no one can or ought to decide what the highest degree may be at which mankind may have to stop progressing', and Diderot's statement that no-one knows how far progress can advance if it is not 'brought to a halt' (Kant 1991 [1781]: 191); Diderot 1992 [1775]: 24). The confidence that societies have yet to discover the limits of their power to organize their collective affairs around principles of humanity, and the belief that they should not be deterred from testing their potential through planned exercises in social reform by the darker interpretations of history and human nature, continue to define the 'political' for contemporary thinkers who have kept faith with the ethos of the Enlightenment (Geras 2000; Pagden 2013; Todorov 2009). That theme has special importance for the study of international relations where two flawed ideas – the belief that the desire for power that is embedded in human nature and the conviction that anarchy compels states to compete for security – have been used repeatedly in the critique of philosophical visions of 'perpetual peace'. The crucial breakthrough to a superior perspective was first made by Enlightenment thinkers. They applied the realization that social existence is a 'process' with immanent progressive potentials to the realm of world politics that was often regarded – as it is in many circles today – as unchanging and unchangeable in fundamental respects (Elias 2012: 52ff.).

The themes that have been raised in this introduction are explored in the following pages by first considering Enlightenment responses to the 'enlarge-ment' of the human world in the late eighteenth century, and by focusing on the main conceptions of 'civilized' politics in a period of heightened sensitivity to the question of how the diverse human groups that had been forced together in the age of imperial expansion can learn to coexist amicably. The discussion then turns to leading accounts of the paradoxes and ambiguities of rising levels of human interconnectedness, and to efforts to defend 'compassionate cosmo-politanism' that were central to 'sentimentalist Enlightenments' that have been overshadowed by discussions of the rationalist dispositions that supposedly characterized the 'Age of Reason' (Frazer 2010: introduction). An account of the emergence of modern grand narratives that harnessed 'universal history' to a 'civilizing', cosmopolitan political project is then provided. One of the central features of Enlightenment thought was the commitment to more detached, processual thinking about the physical and social worlds that involved the 'relativization' of thought coupled with an increased awareness of the problem of ethnocentrism – of the problems that 'civilized' peoples simultaneously created for themselves and others. A major part of the 'civilizing' legacy of the Enlightenment was its globalism – specifically its inquiry into long-term patterns of social change that had transformed the species as a whole and urgently required the transition from provincial, national horizons to cosmopolitan politics that would herald the emergence of a new phase of the European civilizing process.

Widening Worlds and the Question of Difference

Nothing, according to Raynal's *Histoire Philosophique* (parts of which were written by Diderot), had done more to transform the history of the species than the discovery of the route to the Indies *via* the Cape of Good Hope and the unexpected encounters with the peoples of the New World (Outram 1995: 73–4). Those twin discoveries initiated a 'commercial revolution'. Previously isolated people 'in the most distant lands [became] linked by new relationships and new needs': the 'industrial products of the north were transported to the south'; 'the textiles of the Orient became the luxuries of Westerners; and everywhere men mutually exchanged their opinions, their laws, their customs, their illnesses, and their medicines, their virtues and their vices'; as a result, 'everything changed' and would 'go on changing'; those interwoven developments raised the question of whether humanity would one day enjoy 'more peace, more happiness, or more pleasure' or face only a condition of unedifying 'constant change' (Outram 1995: 73). Burke observed that in the new phase of human history, 'the Great Map of Mankind is unrolld at once; and there is no state or Gradation of barbarism, and no mode of refinement which we have not at the same instant under our View'; the map encompassed 'the very different Civility of Europe and of China; The barbarism of Persia and Abyssinia; the erratick manners of Tartary, and of Arabia [and] The Savage State of North America, and of New Zealand' (Correspondence with William Robertson, 9 June 1777 cited in Mansfield 1984: 102).

The discovery of the peoples of Central and South America had led to the enlargement of 'the sphere of contemplation' (Locke, cited in Marshall and Williams 1982: 258). As noted in Chapter 6, European responses to the initial phases of the expansion of human horizons were influenced by a peculiar combination of wonder or bemusement and remarkable self-certainty about how the 'civilized' peoples of Christendom and then Europe should conduct relations with the rest of the world. The 'newly discovered' peoples in the late fifteenth and early sixteenth centuries had raised perplexing questions for the Christian world. Their very existence was the source of astonishment; the reasons for their departure from Christian norms called out for explanation; the protocols of ensuring their conversion and securing their salvation had to be determined so that they could be set on the correct evolutionary path. The second wave of discovery in the late eighteenth century had rather different social and political consequences. Deviance from Christianity was no longer bewildering. Just and unjust means of spreading the 'true' faith were no longer a central puzzle and preoccupation. Innovative responses to contacts with newly discovered peoples stressed the remarkably varied ways in which societies had reacted to specific environmental challenges in the universal struggle to survive. Burke's 'great map of mankind' did more than lay out the great diversity of the ways of life that had developed under such circumstances, or encourage curiosity and respect for the diversity of human types. It fuelled the historical imagination. By analysing other peoples, human societies could gain a deeper understanding of themselves; they could acquire an enriched appreciation of how their predecessors had lived in the distant past as well as a more rounded comprehension of what the human species had once been, of its varied accomplishments during the rise to 'civilization', and of what it might become through the exercise of reason in the centuries to come.

At the heart of various philosophical and literary engagements with the exotic 'other' was a high level of certainty about a long-term movement from 'barbarism' to 'civilization'. Critics of Enlightenment thought have linked that discourse with the commitment to a 'totalizing' universal project and with the tyrannical desire to remake other societies in the image of Europe. There is certainly no doubt that many Enlightenment thinkers, including Hume and Kant, held views about other peoples that are now regarded as profoundly unenlightened. Hume (1875c) [1777]: 252) remarked that he was inclined 'to suspect the Negroes . . . to be naturally inferior to the whites', adding that there never was a 'civilized nation' or a person 'eminent either in action or speculation' of 'any other complexion than white'. There were, he contended, 'no ingenious manufactures amongst them, no arts, no sciences' (see also Immerwahr 1992). Kant observed that nature had given the African little intelligence although pernicious references to fundamental differences between whites and blacks did not feature in the later writings (Muthu 2003: 183–4; see also Bernasconi 2011 and Kleingeld 2004).

Romanticized notions of the 'noble savage' did not have such pejorative connotations, although the perception that they lacked any significant cultural accomplishments helped to drive a major wedge between 'civilized' Europeans and 'simpler' societies (Muthu 2003: ch. 2). As noted earlier, those images were largely self-referential and highlighted the innocence and simplicity that modern peoples had supposedly lost in the course of becoming overly 'refined' and 'civilized' (Hampson 1968: 106–7; White 1972). Idealizing simpler and supposedly happier conditions was a key element of the 'primitivist' critique of 'civilization' that celebrated amongst, other things, the apparently 'natural' state of sexual freedom in societies such as Tahiti which, in reality, had more to do with patriarchy and prostitution than emancipation from the repressive qualities of 'civilized' societies (Vogel 2000). 'Primitivists' projected their aspirations for greater freedom and authenticity onto idealized or fantasy-ridden conceptions of distant societies and channelled their frustrated hopes into related utopian images that expressed discontent with civilization (Elias 2009c). A related aspect of what has been called the 'painful Enlightenment' cast doubt on distinctions between the 'civilized' and the 'savage', and asked how the belief in the former's alleged superiority could be justified given the high level of internal decadence and external destructiveness (Vogel 2000:5; Marshall and Williams 1982: ch. 9). One example was Georg Forster's observation – Foster was a German naturalist and ethnologist who accompanied Cook on his second Pacific voyage – about the hypocrisy of 'civilized' societies that condemned 'savages' for acts of cannibalism while not only tolerating the slaughter of thousands of fellow-Europeans in interstate wars but regarding such violence as entirely 'natural' and honourable (Vogel 2000: 19).

Distorted portraits of other groups were more than a convenient method of condemning social and political trends within European societies. Diderot (1992 [1772]: 67) contended that the inhabitants of Tahiti surpassed the Europeans by keeping 'strictly to the law of nature', thereby being 'nearer to having good laws than any civilized people'. Running through such interpretations was the positive contention that humanity found expression in diverse ways of life by wrestling with specific environmental challenges. The emphasis on cultural variations on shared struggles to satisfy elementary needs bred respect for radically different social systems. Admiration for other peoples that was intrinsic to that standpoint questioned the value of locating societies on a spectrum that extended from 'barbarism' to 'civilization', although that way of thinking was indeed central to the 'stadial' conception of history that is rightly associated with the Scottish Enlightenment. Others assumed at least a degree of incommensurability between the organizing principles of different cultures, and regarded 'imperialist cross-cultural judgments' of the kind that had been found in Christian enterprises to bring 'civilization' to 'newly discovered peoples' with immense suspicion (Muthu 2003: 275ff.).

Montesquieu (1973 [1721]: Letter 59) has one of the Persian visitors to Europe observe that 'if triangles had a god, they would give him three sides', the point being that most societies have lacked critical distance from their own values when judging other peoples, and have been strongly disposed to judge alien practices in self-flattering ways. To promote greater detachment or decentration, *The Persian Letters* constructed an account of the outsiders' perspective on unfamiliar European social practices. Montesquieu's exercise in thinking from the standpoint of others, in 'relativizing' his own ethnocentric standpoint and cultural identity, was a major influence on later anthropological thought. An example was Forster's aspiration to understand humanity 'from as many different perspectives as possible' and to strive for the most 'comprehensive' of views of social diversity and human development; the standpoint should not be conflated with recent 'conceptions of transcultural dialogue' (Vogel 2000: 15, 21) but there are similarities with contemporary versions of Enlightenment cosmopolitanism that support greater detachment from 'shared identities' in conjunction with 'reciprocal and transformative encounters between strangers' (Anderson 2001: 21–2). The exercise in self-distancing was not confined to the search for an external standpoint from which to launch a critique of the internal deficiencies of European societies.

The emphasis shifted to the moral condemnation of European attitudes and violent behaviour towards 'less advanced' peoples. The conviction that no way of life should be dismissed out of hand as plainly barbaric or as self-evidently flawed because of its immorality and false beliefs was intertwined with an ethical defence of the universal sympathies that befitted the 'friend of humanity' – which was the perspective that Forster embraced when announcing that 'all peoples of the world have the same claim on my good will' (Vogel 2000: 15–16). At the heart of that 'cultural cosmopolitan' idea was the recognition, as noted earlier, that all societies have undergone complex patterns of development in response to the difficulties and challenges that human beings confront more or less everywhere. A degree of emotional identification with people in other societies – based on the recognition that each had undergone its distinctive civilizing process – represented a major shift from condescending ideas about 'unrefined' savages towards the sympathies and solidarities of modern secular humanism (Kleingeld 1999; Muthu 2003). Diderot's writings are especially instructive in this regard because they combined respect for other forms of life with a critical detachment from European values that was encapsulated in the belief that 'civilized' societies will, in all probability, suffer the same fate as all ways of life and perish eventually. Underscoring the theme, Diderot referred to the possibility that in an isolated region in some future period, a more 'civilized' condition might emerge that avoided the 'childhood of the savage' and the 'decrepitude' of 'our' era (cited in Vyverberg 1958: 200).

Critical self-distancing led to robust opposition to the European colonial practice of imposing alien values on peoples who should be left free to devise their own responses to the trials of human existence (Muthu 2003: 58–9). Diderot believed that it was in the nature of things that, if left to themselves, 'savage' peoples would rise to 'civilization' just as it was more or less inevitable that 'civilized' societies would at some point revert to 'barbarism' (Muthu 2003: 84). More seriously, 'irreversible destruction' and colonial cruelties including slavery had been caused by waves of European expansion; they demonstrated how the process of civilization had brought unrelieved misery to many other parts of the world, and not least because the modern equivalents of ancient warriors could ransack societies in the distant regions of the empire free from the social controls and self-restraints that were the hallmarks of a 'civilized' existence (Vogel 2000: 5; Barker-Benfield 1992: 105). In Diderot's writings, the very idea of the possibility of 'civil' empire or 'civilized' slavery was rejected out of hand. The large-scale monopolies of power that were widely admired in Europe were unable to create civility in remote parts. Their indifference to the fate of the victims of the 1769–70 Bengal famine was plain evidence of the corrupting effect of absolute imperial power (Muthu 2003: 87ff.). Far from the reach of the restraining hand of state institutions, colonists could readily succumb to the greed and rapaciousness that was checked or punished in 'civilized', metropolitan centres. Settlers often came from the marginal, less 'civilized', sectors of society and were inclined to think that the hardships of oceanic travel entitled them to seize whatever they could from less 'advanced' and often defenceless peoples. The absence of reciprocal ties between those groups meant that there were few restrictions on 'frontier decivilizing processes' – that is, limited external restraints on appetite and impulse, and weak internal controls based on shame, guilt, embarrassment or self-reproach with respect to misconduct that had been fundamental to the whole process of civilization. Ethical concern for the victims of violent and non-violent harm that might be expected of 'civilized' peoples was weak, and often completely absent, in the outlying colonized regions (Diderot 1992a).

Political opposition to colonialism and slavery undermines claims that there was a single, overarching 'Enlightenment project' that aimed to establish European power over other societies on a presumed right to promote a global civilizing offensive (Muthu 2003; Vogel 2000; see, however, Hall and Hobson 2010). In one important strand of thought, advances in self-distancing or critical detachment from the claims of 'civilization' were used to support cosmopolitanism – not the version that proposes remaking the rest of humanity in the image of its most 'advanced' representatives but the form that is encapsulated by the idea of the 'cosmophile' or 'friend of humanity' mentioned earlier who is motivated by the Stoic belief that all peoples should be bound together by relations of mutual respect and shared sympathies. The purpose of that Enlightenment project was to replace 'pathological loyalties' that bred fanaticism and intolerance with a plurality of overlapping emotional attachments that befitted world citizens (Vogel 2003). It has been stated that those who travelled to the Americas in the late fifteenth and early sixteenth centuries can be divided into two main camps – those who were convinced that 'the other' was different and therefore unequal, and those who thought that 'the other' was equal but essentially the same. What was missing was a glimmer of recognition that 'the other' could be radically different and equal (Todorov 1984: 42). No such accusation can be levelled at members of the radical Enlightenment (Muthu 2003: 282, also 80, 116–17). As already noted, those attitudes towards indigenous peoples often sowed doubts in the minds of colonizers about the validity of their claims to be the custodians of civilized values. Unease or disquiet prepared the way for the transition from an egocentric belief in a single civilization that was surrounded by 'inferior' forms of life to a more detached standpoint in which multiple cultures or civilizations of equal value were regarded more sympathetically as facing similar challenges to prosper and survive. That questioning of the belief that 'civilization' was the mono-poly of European societies would have far-reaching consequences for the structure of international society in the twentieth century.

The Ambiguities of Global Interconnectedness

Significant advances in detachment that were exemplified by changing conceptions of the planet and the cosmos, by the rise of anatomy and by the emergence of self-portraiture in the Italian Renaissance were taken further during the European Enlightenment. Immediately after his remark about the gods that triangles would be inclined to worship, Montesquieu (1973: [1721]: Letter 59) referred to the Persian correspondent's observation that the region humans inhabit 'is merely a point in the universe'; although they flatter themselves that they are 'the direct models of Providence', it was impossible to reconcile their 'extravagant pretensions with such tininess'; the earth, like the 'heavens themselves', was not 'immune from decay'; furthermore, the precariousness of the natural environment exposed the species to 'a hundred thousand factors [that are] capable of destroying it' (Montesquieu 1973 [1721]: Letter 113). Reflecting the trend towards greater detachment, Fontenelle speculated in his 1686 work, *Dialogue sur la pluralite des mondes*, that the earth might not be the only heavenly body that was capable of supporting intelligent life (Hampson 1999: 266). Changing conceptions of the place of humanity in the cosmos were also evident in the fictional representation of the visitor from Sirius, far more intelligent than any human being, who left behind a work explaining the meaning of life that turned out, confirming the suspicions of its first reader, Fontenelle, to be entirely blank (Hampson 1968: 122).

Greater detachment in the emergent natural sciences was connected with similar orientations to the social forces that had brought diverse societies together in longer webs of interdependence and subjected them to universalizing processes. The former did not constitute a mode of discovery that developed autonomously, untouched by broader societal changes. The natural sciences did not make breakthroughs to higher levels of detachment that then spread outwards to other areas of cultural endeavour. Rather, the emergence of modern scientific inquiry belonged to the larger process in which people had come under pressure to think of themselves, as it were, from a distance, and to consider longer interdependencies as impersonal phenomena that existed independently of, and that appeared to be external to, them. The radical Cartesian distinction between the 'knowing subject' and a supposedly 'objective reality' was a bridge between cognitive changes in investigations into society and politics and experimental natural-scientific inquiries (Elias 2007: 58ff.). Raynal expressed the social value of greater detachment when he observed that to contemplate human prospects it was necessary to rise 'above all human considerations' and even to 'soar above the atmosphere, and behold the globe beneath us' (Pocock 2005: 236). Gibbon was attracted to analysing human parallels to the interdependent structures that biologists had found in non-human, animal species (Hampson 1968: 107–8).

Orientations of that kind supported systematic endeavours to understand the interdependent nature of social and political institutions in a fast-changing era – a focus that shifted attention from history as a product of the actions of individual kings and queens, and heroic leaders, to the interwoven impact of climate, industry, government, morals and manners on the *longue durée*. The movement towards new conceptions of the social totality was linked with attempts to locate modern social relations in the larger universe of human interconnections that had developed over greater expanses of space, and which could be traced back over much longer tracts of time than had been imagined in biblical chronology that asserted that the world had been created around six millennia ago (Hampson 1968: 107–8). From some perspectives, societies had formed separately in different regions, and had been gradually drawn together by conquest and commerce. As a result, one of the great challenges of the age was to comprehend the significance of the Europeans' role in unfolding the 'Great Map of Mankind' for the future of the species. In the course of describing 'the revolution in commerce' that had produced 'new connections' between 'the inhabitants of the most distant regions, for the supply of wants they had never before experienced', Raynal asked whether recent events and revolutions had 'any utility to the human race'. 'Will they ever add', he inquired, 'to the tranquillity, the happiness, and the pleasures of mankind? Can they improve our present state, or do they only change it?' (cited in Pocock 2005: 235).

Kant argued that the enlargement of the social world had led to major advances in commerce that extended beyond the material benefits of economic exchange to the assorted gains in human understanding that stemmed from greater inter-societal contact, as exemplified by the idea of 'epistolary commerce' in the cosmopolitan republic of letters (Muthu 2003: 98; Goodman 1984: 17). Cultural breakthroughs to more realistic views of the scale of the *oecumene* were linked with the belief that, in the beginning, the world had been owned in common (Kant 1991 [1795]: 106). The broadening of inter-societal contact represented a symbolic return to the *status quo ante*: the recovery of a more unified, distant age before societies began to evolve in separate and diverse directions that made it difficult for them to understand and identify with each other. Kant famously argued that the incorporation of diverse societies in the *oecumene* brought significant moral advances. With the flourish of the pen, the enlightened social strata could bring violations of the dignity of persons in any place to the attention of morally concerned publics everywhere. They were invited to contemplate the other side of the enlargement of human contact, namely the reality that the technologies that brought human societies into mutually advantageous contact also allowed the more powerful societies to surpass all earlier peoples in the capacity to bring 'evil and violence' to the inhabitants of the most remote areas (Kant 1991 [1797]: 172).

Recognition of the ambiguities of global interconnectedness was not confined to Kant's writings. The authors of the *Histoire Philosophique* observed that 'our voyages on every ocean ... have strengthened the chain of our initial brotherhood; inculcated the true principles of a universal morality based on the identity of needs, pains, pleasures ... encouraged the practice of benevolence towards every individual who claims it, whatever his customs, country, laws, or religion. But at the same time our minds have been turned towards profitable speculations ... Long voyages and expeditions have engendered a new species of nomad savages ... in whom the mastery of a terrible element has begotten ferocity of character' (cited in Pocock 2005: 326–7). On that account, the real savage who was heir to those who had once lived in wild regions was the 'unmasked human' on the colonial frontier – the unrestrained, 'civilized' individual whose behaviour refuted any assumption that compassion was natural and destined to prevail whenever strangers came into contact (Muthu 2003: 74). Diderot and others recognized the absence of we-feeling between the colonizing and the colonized peoples as well as the former's unwillingness to comply with the 'civilized' standards of self-restraint in the societies from which they came. Moral condemnation of the 'barbarism of civilization' in a period when more and more people were being thrust together by imperial conquest was a core element of the radical Enlightenment. The critique is especially evident in the opposition that was noted earlier between contented 'savages' who happily remain in their place of birth, and the 'civil man' who 'for centuries allowed his restlessness, his inability ... to remain still in a room, to drive him continually overseas' (Pagden 1995: 132–4; see Chapter 2, p. 69 on the critique of Alexander's desire for imperial conquest). Diderot observed that 'all travellers are suspect' because they carry with them various vices including the potentiality for enslaving others. With some exceptions, he added, they were removed from the constraints and controls of the public gaze and free to reverse the civilizing process that had led from the state of nature to civil society; they were all too willing to take the path that led 'from civility to savagery' (Pagden 1995: 132–4). The worst product of their 'insatiable thirst for gold' was 'the most infamous and atrocious of all forms of commerce, that is slaves'; to those who defended human enslavement on the grounds that valuable land would otherwise be 'uncultivated' and wasted, it was necessary to reply: 'Wilderness let them remain, if to render them productive, men must be reduced to a brutal condition, be it that of the buyer, the seller, or the sold' (cited in Pocock 2005: 327). Those ethical sentiments illustrated what have been described as 'Enlightenment anxieties about global interconnections' that included the deformed institution of slavery (Muthu 2012).

Slavery violated the basic ethic of true commerce – most evidently in the case of monopolistic trading companies – but a future in which non-exploitative economic exchange prevailed could at least be envisaged.

Diderot reflected at length on the right principles of contact and communication between the overseas empires and the vulnerable groups who were at their mercy. He maintained that using unoccupied land was entirely permissible, as were the traveller's requests for sustenance: so much could be claimed in accordance with the rules of cosmopolitan hospitality that were basic to humanity. Annexing inhabited land, on the other hand, was morally unacceptable. The establishment of fortified settlements near indigenous groups required considerable care and sensitivity. The peoples who were most affected were within their rights to ask for an explanation. Observance of the rules of hospitality could be demanded of them, but they could not be expected to acquiesce in the development of threatening settlements, and they could not be reprimanded if they exercised their entitlement, as had occurred in China, to ban those who wished to live alongside them (Diderot 1992 [1783]: 175-6). Kant 1991[1795]: 106-7) reached similar conclusions about Chinese and Japanese decisions to restrict contact with the encroaching European powers.

Whether European imperialism was ever defensible and whether it brought tangible benefits to conquered societies were keenly debated issues. Some, such as Forster, appear to have concluded that contact with Europeans had brought tangible advantages to distant peoples. For that reason, 'voyages of discovery ... given to benevolent and truly useful purposes, should be continued in future' (cited in Vogel 2000: 19–20). Diderot condemned 'outrageous land-grabbing' in colonized regions and the 'violent contempt for those of a different colour or faith' but maintained that Europeans could be the 'benevolent liberators' of peoples who were 'crying out for civilization' (cited in Keller 2006: 38). Condorcet argued that the Europeans had at the very least a duty of restitution to compensate the rest of world for their shameless avarice (Carter 2000: 96). Many other Enlightenment figures shared Cook's position on the miseries of European imperialism. Cook (1969 [1773]: 175) referred to the 'shame' of 'Civilized Christians' who 'debauch their Morals already too prone to vice, and we interduce among them wants and perhaps disease which they never before knew and which serve only to disturb that happy tranquillity they and their fore Fathers injoy'd. If anyone denies the truth of this assertion let him tell me what the Natives of the whole extent of America have gained by the commerce they have had with Europeans'. Whether non-exploitative commerce was at all feasible given unequal power relations was the central question. Forster concluded that if some groups could only profit by imposing costs on subject peoples, such as the South Seas' populations, then it would have been better if they had never been discovered. The conditions of such societies would be greatly improved if colonial domination came to a halt before 'the corrupt manners of the civilized nations can contaminate these innocent peoples' and further demonstrate that 'philanthropy and the political systems of Europe do not accord with each other' (cited in Vogel 2000: 3, 17–18). The question of 'Europe's special responsibility for the future of global relationships' became fundamental at this juncture when all peoples were being forced into a single stream of universal history – and all the more urgently because of the suspicion that the overseas expansion of the 'civilized' world might already have passed the stage where it was plausible to suppose that advances in human knowledge would bring happiness to all peoples (Vogel 2000: 21).

It is useful to return to the point that several Enlightenment thinkers were keen to stress Europe's achievement in establishing stable territorial mono-polies of power and they were disposed towards gradual social reform rather than revolutionary transformation. Ideally, reconstituted, 'enlightened' politi-cal arrangements would stand at the hub of a worldwide economic and political system that was dedicated to 'non-exploitative commercial relations' and mutually advantageous communication (Muthu 2003: 103). Imperial cruelties led Diderot and others to state that the civilizing process was reversed or suspended whenever European colonists escaped the reach of the political authorities. Here is Raynal: 'In proportion as the distance from the capital increases, this mask detaches itself; it falls off on the frontiers; and, between one hemisphere and another, is totally lost. When a man hath crossed the line, he is neither an Englishman, a Dutchman, a Frenchman, a Spaniard, or a Portuguese. He preserves nothing of his country, except the principles and prejudices which give a sanction to his conduct and . . . [becomes] . . . capable of all the enormities which can contribute most speedily to the completion of his designs; he is a domestic tiger again let loose in the woods . . . ' (cited in Pocock 2005: 279). Geographical remoteness liberated those who were pre-pared 'to expose themselves to infinite dangers and labours, upon the precar-ious hope of making a rapid fortune' free from the shackles of 'civilization'; crucially, it lifted the guiding hand of 'shame or fear' in remote places where those who were 'dissatisfied with their lot', and disposed to exhibit 'contempt for life', were 'no longer awed by the presence of their fellow-citizens' (cited in Pocock 2005: 281). The decadence of empire was evident in indifference to the suffering of colonized peoples, and in the brutal exploitation that resulted from freedom from the restraints of law as well as liberation from the moral emotions that prevented violence and avarice when in the company of 'civilized' others (Muthu 2003: 96ff.). Regarding moral indifference, as noted earlier, Diderot condemned the passive stance of the British East India Company when millions of Bengalis were dying of famine (Muthu 2003: 88). Propagandists would later succeed in describing the catastrophe as proof that Indians were incapable of satisfying their basic needs without the helping hand of paternalistic British imperialists (Arnold 1999). But at the time, many thinkers including Diderot condemned the Company for the 'negligence and insensibility' that led to the focus on protecting financial interests rather than on how to use existing reserves of grain to help the starving (Muthu 2003: 88).

The moral and political corruption of European empires was especially apparent in the use of slavery to acquire luxuries. On asking a maimed slave whether his master was responsible for his condition, Candide was informed that mutilation and disfigurement are 'the price at which you eat sugar in Europe'; the slave added that if the preachers were right that all peoples are 'children of Adam, blacks as well as whites', and 'second cousins', then 'it is impossible to treat one's relations in a more barbarous manner' (Voltaire 1918 [1759]: 51). In condemning slavery in the *Histoire*, Voltaire denied the 'civilizing' role of commerce. His preferred narrative described the formation of 'a world-system which began as plunder and proceeded through slavery and monopoly, and may never become a global partnership in active commerce' – at least not until European societies acknowledged that the 'crossing of blue water' had been 'the ultimate decivilizing act' (Pocock 2005: 237, 280). Major doubts about Europe's legacy to the rest of the world were raised not only by the violence of those who, in traversing the oceans, escaped the restraining hand of the modern state, but also by the nature of everyday life in the metropolitan societies – specifically, because the inhabitants of 'civilized' societies were entangled in global relations of production and exchange that brought them riches at immense cost to the powerless. What is evident in those observations is the vision of a global civilizing process that protects all peoples, and especially the weak and most vulnerable, from the assorted forms of violent and non-violent harm that modern societies could inflict. Especially striking was the moral conviction that such a transformation must start not with the elevation of 'savages' but with taming or 'civilizing' Europeans – with restraining the dominant and most destructive groups in the world political and economic system. That was to envisage a long-term, intergenerational civilizing process – one of very few of its kind in the history of the Western states-systems – in which 'advanced' societies removed violence and exploitation from interdependencies with other peoples.

Compassionate Cosmopolitanism

In the conclusion to the previous chapter the question was raised of how far the entanglement of human societies in longer social and political chains is accompanied by ethical and political concerns about acts of violence in distant areas. Raynal's examination of the world-historical significance of the new wave of European expansion described the negative consequences of the greater integration of human societies including the brutality or indifference of adventurers and colonial administrators. Lengthening social webs had not been attended by significant changes of ethical orientation. The evisceration of sympathy was exemplified by the peculiar contradictions of European mentalities. The same people who abhorred the cruel traits of previous generations, and who were driven to tears by theatrical representations of distress, could listen to accounts of the suffering of slaves 'coolly and without emotion'; the 'torments of a people to whom we owe our luxuries' seemed to be incapable of reaching 'our hearts' (Diderot, cited in Muthu 2003: 109). Many Enlightenment thinkers responded incredulously to the idea that the 'discourse of sentiment' could inspire Europeans to organize to eradicate 'the contradictions of history' that included indifference to the realities of distant suffering (Pocock 2005: 237).

In so doing, they considered a central issue for thinkers of the Scottish Enlightenment which was how the moral imagination that attuned people to living with others in the same society could be reconfigured in response to rising levels of global interconnectedness and the governance of increasingly impersonal social forces (Berry 1997; Mazlish 1989). Explorations of the problem of distance – of the duties that were appropriate given that strangers had become entangled in longer social relations – some limited to their society, others stretching over vast areas – reflected the changing contours of the European civilizing process. Contributors to the discussion emphasized the tensions between Stoic ethical ideals and the absence of concern for those with whom there was no emotional as opposed to material connection. Referring to 'the first law of Nature', Lord Kames highlighted the gulf between the local or bounded qualities of conventional social moralities and the widening circles of interaction and spheres of contemplation. The most fundamental of all human duties demanded 'abstaining from injuring others [which] is enforced by the most efficacious sanctions', but resentment towards those who violated the law of humanity was governed by 'different degrees'. As he observed, 'an injury done to a man himself, provokes resentment in its highest degree. An injury of the same kind done to a friend or relation, raises resentment in a lower degree; and the passion becomes gradually fainter, in proportion to the slightness of the connection' (cited in Reibman 1987: 63–4). Those philosophical reflections about gradations of sympathy and obligation were central to the political theory of the Scottish Enlightenment. As noted elsewhere, they were most compellingly formulated in a passage in Smith's writings which stated that a person who cannot sleep at night, knowing that he will lose his 'little finger' the following day, can 'snore with the most profound security over the ruin of a hundred million of his brethren' – provided, in an important caveat, that 'he never [sees] them' (Linklater 2011: 219–20; Smith 1982 [1759]: III.3.4; also Hume 1975 [1751]: 5.2.186). Smith, Kames, Hume and others registered the simple reality that personal pain, fear and anxiety tend to contract individual moral horizons; people can become so absorbed in the immediate disturbances that befall them, or close friends and family members, that the predicaments of other people fade from view. Moreover, feelings of compassion and injustice were more likely to be awakened by an injury that was inflicted on co-nationals than by the suffering of those who existed at some distant point along the global webs of interconnectedness. Knowledge of such remote suffering might foster melancholic reflections on the precariousness and cruelties of human affairs, but those moral emotions only became deeply felt and provided the spur to action when a person's energies were consumed by his or her 'paltry misfortune' or by the distressing suffering of close associates (Smith 1982 [1759]: III.3.4).

Such gradients of moral concern did not augur well for the just organization of relations between strangers that had been drawn together by universalizing processes. The issue was where the solution to the problem of 'limited altruism' could be found (Linklater 2011: 83). Drawing on earlier analyses of sentiment and sociability, including Shaftesbury's reflections on the modes of 'disciplined self-expression' that befitted 'post-courtly European culture' (Klein 1994: 3ff., 193), Smith focused his attention on the natural human capacity for sympathy. So did Hume (1969 [1739/40]: Bk II, sec 11), who argued that 'no quality of human nature is more remarkable, both in itself and in its consequences, than that propensity we have to sympathize with others'. It was to such emotions (rather than reason), the contention was, that philosophers should turn if they were to understand the latent potentials for extending civility and sociability and for combating malevolent factionalism. However, it is important to ask how much Smith – the greatest theorist of sympathy – invested in the thesis that the emotion was critical for forming new solidarities that bridged the social divide between increasingly individuated and privatized people in complex, globalizing commercial societies. The question arises because of Smith's 'unsentimental' conception of human behaviour and clear recognition of self-interested motivation in the context of a changing we–I balance. 'Nobody', he professed, 'but a beggar chuses to depend chiefly upon the benevolence of his fellow-citizens'; 'it is not from the benevolence of the butcher, the brewer or the baker, that we expect our dinner, but from their regard to their own interest'; he added that 'we address ourselves, not to their humanity, but to their self-love' (Smith 1910 [1776]: 13).

Significantly, Smith did not suppose that there was a fatal contradiction between the generalized pursuit of self-interest and the existence of a just public order. Crucial was the relationship between sympathy or fellow-feeling and the social bond between increasingly individuated modern subjects. It was obvious, Smith argued, that people cannot directly experience the suffering of others, but they are capable of identifying with them through a process of imaginative reconstruction in which they reflect on how they would deal with similar trials or afflictions (Smith 1982 [1759]: I.i.1.2). That empathic capacity could provide a link between peoples who were scattered over large areas. As noted at an earlier stage of the discussion, the intensity of sympathy – the strength of we-feeling – was rarely as powerful as a person's emotional response to his or her own setbacks (Smith 1982 [1759]: I.i.4.7). Self-love created a barrier to close identification, but it also made an imagined community of sentiment possible. Those who were crippled by one or other form of suffering knew that they could not expect strangers to share their mental anguish, however much they might hope that they would sympathize with their plight. A sense of proportion in social relations led them to reduce their claims on, and expectations of, others – to 'flatten ... the sharpness of [their] natural tone' until the point was reached where the perspectives of victim and spectator are more perfectly attuned to one another; symmetry of that kind rather than perfect 'unisons' was all that was essential for the 'harmony of society' (Smith 1982 [1759]: I. i.4.7; also Forman-Barzilai 2010). To a far greater extent than in slave or feudal societies, the inhabitants of commercial societies had to learn how to 'grasp the other's situation' and how to 'calibrate' their respective demands non-violently; 'non-coercive speech' had come to have a fundamental 'civilizing' role in promoting mutual attune-ment with the rise of more complex human arrangements (Griswold 1999: 296ff.). The stranger's benevolence might delight the victim by revealing a high level of sensitivity to his or her welfare, but excessive demands on the gener-osity of others went beyond the requirements of social justice. That was the main foundation of the bond between people who were not connected by powerful emotional solidarities. So Smith argued in reflections on the challenges that result from the increased differentiation of functions in 'civilized' societies.

Under such conditions, the argument was, selfless generosity was less important for the maintenance of public order than respect for principles of justice which protect commercial society from the dangers of excessive self-love, confined sympathies and poisonous factionalism (Smith 1982 [1759]: I. iv.7, II.ii.3.3). The most fundamental principle of all that has been central to liberal conceptions of civilized existence ever since was the 'negative' obliga-tion to avoid harming others (Smith 1982 [1759]: III.2.15). As already noted, people could not expect more from one another as a matter of right. The standpoint might seem to envisage a society in which the cold-hearted engaged in the mechanical calculation of the minimum requirements of justice. But regard for that principle required a level of thoughtfulness and foresight that reduced the dangers of causing harm inadvertently or as a result of negligence (Smith 1982 [1759]: II.iii.7–10). Sensitivity to those dangers required 'great humanity and great benevolence' which were no less funda-mental for social harmony (Smith 1982 [1759]: VI.ii. intro.2). The supposition was that those of high moral character should attach immense value to being free from the shame that can result from falling short of social standards, and to being immune from the 'inner disgrace' or 'indelible stain' that results from failing to heed the dictates of conscience (Smith 1982 [1759]: III.3.4–6). In short, it was not 'the love of our neighbour', or 'the love of mankind' that required that people refrain from securing minor gains by imposing serious costs on others, but 'a stronger love, a more powerful affection', namely, 'the love of what is honourable and noble, of the grandeur, and dignity, and superiority of our characters' (Smith 1982 [1759]: III.3.4). Those personality traits had been the preserve of social elites with their honour code in European court societies. Smith imagined the extension and democratization of such features of the civilizing process by arguing that the claims that 'self-love' made on others could be constrained by the recognition that each person is 'but one of the multitude', and 'in no respect better than any other' (Smith 1982 [1759]: II.ii.2.1).

The political problem that arose starkly in commercial societies (but had clear global ramifications which will be considered later) was that individuals are strongly inclined to favour their particular interests as a result of the 'self-deceit' that is the 'fatal weakness of mankind' and 'the source of half the disorders of human life' (Smith 1982 [1759]: III.4.6). Smith stressed the need for higher levels of individual self-monitoring and self-regulation that have already been noted in the discussion of the psychogenetic dimensions of the European civilizing process. To encourage higher levels of reflectiveness, he urged taking the position of the spectator who considered personal conditions in a 'candid and impartial light' (Smith 1982 [1759]: I.i.4.8). The contention was that 'we can never survey our own sentiments and motives [and] form any judgment concerning them, unless we remove ourselves, as it were, from our own natural station', and view personal traits and behaviour 'at a certain distance from us' (Smith 1982 [1759]: III.1.2). It was important to divide the self into two parts, one taking the standpoint of an 'impartial spectator' that enables people to see the other partial side as if in a 'mirror' (Smith 1982 [1759]: III.1.2–3). Such self-distancing was deemed to be crucial for learning how to live together in complex societies that had lost the solidarities of 'traditional' communities. It was a means of organizing relations between strangers over great distances where people had to balance their special responsibilities to close associates with obligations to those 'with whom [they] have no particular connexion' (Smith 1982 [1759]: II.ii.2.1).

Similar psychogenetic dispositions were necessary at the global level given the greater interweaving of human societies. Societies were not obligated to make sacrifices of interest so that others would benefit, but they were required to engage in self-distancing to ensure that relations between peoples complied with elementary principles of justice such as the primary duty to avoid and minimize harm (Griswold 1999: 129ff.). Smith described, as Montesquieu (1973 [1721]: Letter 94) did in the *Persian Letters*, the familiar gulf between the standards that apply in relations within and in relations between societies, and lamented the reality that efforts to disadvantage other societies often received public acclaim rather than the 'dishonour' they deserved (Smith 1982 [1759]: III.3.42; also 1982 [1759]: VI.i.16). Professing that Europe was a single community or civilization, Montesquieu asserted that he was 'a human being of necessity and a Frenchman by accident' (cited in Hampson 1999: 281). Echoes of that perspective are evident in Smith's observation that national affinities have intrinsic worth, but are enriched when combined with 'civilized' restraint in foreign policy – just as the responsibilities that individuals have to close associates in the same society must be reconciled with their obligation to act justly in relations with strangers.

In his perspective on balancing local and global attachments, Smith (1982 [1759]: III.3.11) revealed the influence of the Stoic thesis that individuals should not regard themselves as 'separated and detached' monads but rather as citizens of the world who imagined how their actions can affect 'any other equally important part of this immense system' (Smith 1982 [1759]: III.3.11). That was not just an ethical ideal. Smith believed that structural changes created new incentives to curb the single-minded pursuit of self-interest and to enlarge the circle of human sympathy. The concept of the 'invisible hand' was employed to explain how a proper balance between individual and collective, and between national and international objectives, could be struck (Smith 1982 [1759]: II.ii.3.1–3). The precise meaning of the term continues to be debated, but it is perhaps best regarded as running parallel to the idea of the 'ambivalence of interests' that was discussed earlier (see above, Chapter 5, p. 197. The realization that the promotion of selfish ends could destroy the larger political order on which all social strata depended was, according to Elias, one of the factors that prevented the dissolution of state monopolies of power. A similar thesis was noted in Callières' reflections on the importance of courtly diplomacy for the relations between increasingly interconnected states. A related theme is evident in Smith's remark that societies should endeavour to preserve the balance of military power and to promote 'peace and general tranquillity . . . within the circle of their negotiations' with a view to maintaining the order on which their security and welfare was clearly dependent (Smith 1982 [1759]: VI.ii.2.6). The extension of global commerce created similar incentives to act with restraint and to exercise foresight and not least because of the increased danger of unmanageable conflicts and tensions over greater areas (van de Haar 2010).

There is an unmistakeable parallel with Callières' deliberations on the crucial role of the 'refined' nobility of the robe as against the 'warlike' nobility of the sword for successful diplomacy. Confidence in the 'civilizing' potential of commercial relations rested on a similar belief that new forms of masculinity were eroding traditional aristocratic notions of male honour (Barker-Benfield 1992: 141ff.). The standpoint reflected Shaftesbury's image of 'post-courtly European culture' which was an important link between Castiglione's six-teenth-century analysis of the courtier and nineteenth-century conceptions of the 'man of feeling' whose orientation to the world could be softened by the company of women (Barker-Benfield 1992:23, ch. 3; Klein 1994; Elias 2012: 281–2). Contrasts between 'savage' warrior societies where males were attuned to torture – to inflicting it without remorse and also to enduring great pain with dignity – were designed to underline the distinctive qualities of modern commercial societies where personal courage and prowess in warfare are no longer the main routes to social esteem (Smith 1982 [1759]: V.2.8–9; also Elias 2007a: 125ff.). Smith stressed that the general refinement of manners required ever stronger efforts to 'civilize' warfare and to ensure that victorious armies did not ride roughshod over the interests of adversaries (Buchan 2006, 2011). Hume maintained that interstate warfare had already been tamed to some extent as a result of new patterns of conscience-formation amongst the male population (Porter (2000:249). But in an important caveat, he observed that the taming of violent inclinations lagged behind in relations with 'unrest-rained' savages who failed to observe the rules of warfare (Hume 1975 [1751]: 3.1.148).

Comparisons between Smith's standpoint on sympathy, justice and perso-nal honour and Kant's writings on duty and compassion are important for understanding the general direction in which 'enlightened' European attitudes to violence and civilization were heading. His major works contained a more comprehensive analysis of how the ambivalence of interests exerted a 'civilizing' role on sovereign communities, and a more sophisticated discussion of how modern warfare could destroy the indisputable benefits of commercial exchange. Kant (1991) [1784a]: 44) emphasized that 'unsocial sociability' – the wish to be one's own master and the necessity of living with others in society – was evident in the tension between destructive tendencies and shared interests in controlling aggressive impulses in civil society. Advances in civility in the form of 'a law-governed social order' had not been consciously planned but had been driven along by the compulsions of interconnectedness. Recognition of the effects of war on commerce – rather than 'motives of morality' – had begun to exercise a disciplining role on ruling elites (Kant 1991 [1784a]: 48ff., Kant 1991 [1795]: 114). As in the case of Smith's writings, Kant's standpoint reflected the influence of *The Spirit of the Laws* where Montesquieu (1989 [1748]: Bk 20.ch.2) had argued that 'the natural effect of commerce is to lead to peace'; by exchanging goods, societies became 'reciprocally dependent' with the effect of increasing the social value of self-restraint. Both believed that Stoic conceptions of world citizenship had a vital role to play in taming the struggles between sovereign states (Kant 1991 [1792]: 90).

Despite those basic similarities, Kant and Smith are usually thought to hold antithetical philosophical standpoints. Smith is associated with the doctrine that ethics rest on emotional foundations – and Kant with the preference for cold-blooded reason over fleeting, unreliable human emotions. They would appear to be substantially at odds over whether sympathy or reason was central to the social bond but it is unwise to press the contrast too far – especially but not only with regard to Kant's 'pre-critical' studies that were written before the

1780s. In that period, Kant embraced the 'sentimentalism' that was rejected in his later works on the metaphysical foundation of ethics, but he would continue to regard human 'sensitivity' as a crucial part of moral motivation and as central to binding strangers together over greater distances (Frazer 2010: ch. 5). Kant argued that people should not strive to avoid sites of suffering. Efforts to protect the self from unsettling images could deprive the individual of invaluable sympathies that might not develop if people looked to reason alone for instruction on how to behave (see Linklater 2011: 95). Kant's image of the world citizen did not deny that transnational sympathies can play an important role in taming the sovereigns. His vision of a cosmopolitan political order should not be regarded as one in which peoples are tied together by nothing other than the rational, mechanical compliance with categorical imperatives. Kant's support for humanity (*Humanitat*) was bound up with the belief that world citizens had to undergo a cosmopolitan education with respect to fundamental moral emotions such as compassion. The idea of humanity referred to 'the universal feeling of sympathy' that was intrinsic to the forms of sociability that distinguished 'civilized' humans from 'lower animals' (Kant 1952 [1790]: Part One, second section: 226). Identification with humanity could underpin a global civilizing process in which each person recognized the importance of 'an all-encompassing sphere of cosmopolitan sentiment, not so much in order to promote the good of the world as to cultivate the means that lead indirectly to it, namely, the agreeableness of society, sociability, mutual love and respect' (Kant 1964 [1797]: 140). Those passages should dispel the myth that Kant did not attach much significance to moral emotions at either the national or international level (Muthu 2003: 150–1). Although Kant (1964 [1797]: 125) insisted that philosophical ethics are ultimately grounded in rational principles rather than in 'sympathetic sadness' and associated moral dispositions, he stressed that actual social moralities ultimately depend on the sympathetic engagement with the 'joy and sadness' of others.

In his reflections on the moral and political challenges of lengthening socials webs, Kant emphasized that there was more to the transformation of world politics than simply extending the governance of rational principles over larger areas. He stressed – even more than Smith had done – that changes in the emotional life were vital psychogenetic dimensions of a cosmopolitan ethic. The relevant moral sensibilities could counteract the indifference of people to the interests of those who did not belong to their bounded community (Muthu 2003: 153). Whether such orientations would ever become the driving force behind a future global civilizing' process was the question. The issue barely arose in the earlier Western states-systems or in the present international order before the Enlightenment. Kant recognized that the condition that prompted that question, namely the sharp rise in global connectedness, is a highly ambiguous one. The argument for extending human sympathies stemmed from the observable reality that the material connections between distant strangers had increased whereas emotional ties seriously lagged behind. The latter continued to be centred on family ties or on shared nationality. But there was more to the case for widening the scope of emotional identification than support for moral values with intrinsic worth. Of great importance was the practical need to organize global relations around principles of mutual respect given that the power to export harm to, and to cause evil, in distant areas had greatly increased in the era of European overseas expansion. Kant's cosmopolitanism owed a great deal to the Stoic principle that the duty to refrain from harm is the least that each person owes all others – and has the right to expect in turn – as equal members of the same species. His support for that doctrine which has been noted in Smith's writings can be regarded as an attempt to adapt the habitus of those who belong to specific sovereign states to changing global political realities. His cosmopolitanism was not at odds with national or other parochial or confined loyalties. Quite the contrary – the two had to be combined in novel ways to overcome the inherent limitations of parochial bounded communities and to avoid the dangers of cosmopolitan standpoints that were indifferent to the wellbeing of particular persons because of some distorted conception of caring for humanity that ignored the wellbeing of the constituent individual parts (Muthu 2003: 153).

Like Diderot, Kant judged that Chinese and the Japanese political authorities had reasonable grounds for fearing European encroachment and for restricting contact. He shared the former's position that European penetration of new territories should proceed not by conquest but by 'treaty' that refrained from exploiting the 'ignorance of the inhabitants' (Kant 1991[1797]: 172–3). However, the 'appallingly great' abuses that had occurred during the age of discovery did not annul the right to seek out other peoples and to establish community with them (Kant 1991 [1795]: 106). But all those who were encountered in this way owed the travellers who had 'discovered' them nothing more than assistance in accordance with the basic duties of hospitality. Foreigners who behaved peacefully were 'not to be treated with hostility' (Kant 1991 [1795]: ibid.). The right to restrict contact was itself grounded in the cosmopolitan moral principle that no society should have to suffer the effects of distorted commerce in its authentic sense that, 'reflecting common semantic origins', included economic interaction and sympathetic communication with other members of humanity (Pagden 1994). Those that were exposed to such abuses were entitled to turn strangers away as long as they did not leave them helpless (Kant 1991 [1795]: 105–6).

It is well known that Kant thought that one of the defining features of the enlightened age was the reality that a violation of right in any part of the world had become a matter of global concern. Colonial violence was not the least of the reasons for the defence of the significant enlargement of moral horizons. Travel to foreign lands and 'attempts to settle on them with a view to linking them with the motherland, [could] also occasion evil and acts of violence in one part of the globe with ensuing repercussions which are felt everywhere else' (Kant 1991 [1797]: 172). Kant was adamant that the project of taming sovereign rulers with their 'barbaric' custom of resorting to war was one element of a larger project of global transformation to bring all worldwide connections, whether initiated by private or public actors, under the 'civilizing' rule of law. The defence of cosmopolitan law (*ius cosmopoliticum*) was a response to rising levels of human interconnectedness that escaped the regulatory domains of existing civil law (*ius civitatis*) and the traditional law of nations (*ius gentium*) (Kant 1991[1795]: 98–9; Kant 1991 [1797]: 165). The reality was that the global interdependencies that distinguished the modern era required a revolution in moral and political thinking as well as parallel changes in the relative power of national, international and cosmopolitan legal and moral responsibilities (which is a matter to come back to in Chapter 10). As Kant well knew, the prospects for moving in that direction depended largely on levels of co-dependence that existed between many European societies but were largely absent from their relations with the world's vulnerable peoples. In the latter sphere, the need for higher levels of self-restraint that depended on ethical conceptions of what was just or right was evidently so much greater.

The observation that individuals (and by extension, political associations) in the state of nature expose each other to permanent insecurity underpinned Kant's argument about the ethical imperative to reduce the fears that were inherent in that condition and to curb the aggressive impulses that could thrive in those circumstances. None of the parties involved might harm each other intentionally, but mere contiguity in a state of 'lawless freedom' gave each person the right to demand that all become associated in a 'civil' condition where disputes could be settled 'in a civilized manner by legal proceedings, not in a barbaric manner (like that of the savages) by acts of war' (Kant 1991 [1795]: 102ff.; Kant 1991 [1797]: 171). The argument highlighted the danger that 'radical evil' can flourish whenever individuals or societies face the uncertainties that are intrinsic to the state of nature (Kant 1991 [1795]: 101; also Bernstein 2002). Kant's cosmopolitan orientation was not naïvely optimistic about human prospects but preserved elements of the 'realism' that can be traced back to Augustinian pessimism. Within sovereign states, the 'depravity of human nature' was contained by 'governmental constraints' that created the civil condition in which respect for the moral law – and the greater importance of internal as against external restraints on action – could develop; but human 'wickedness' was especially obvious in the relations between societies where no higher political authority could check egoistical behaviour and where humanity had made little progress beyond its original wild and lawless state (Kant 1991 [1795]: 103, 121).

The contention that Enlightenment thinkers were the first to regard 'social existence' as a 'process' (Elias 2012:52ff.) does not take account of similar breakthroughs during the Italian Renaissance or 'first Enlightenment' (see ch. 4, p. 152 above, especially note 1). However, because of the European Enlightenment, the conviction that process-thinking is applicable to international relations, the belief that world politics are not governed by immutable laws, and the confidence that societies can do more than simply preserve a precarious balance of power for limited intervals became more central to the theory and practice of the modern states-system than they had been in its predecessors. Kant argued that the 'affected by principle' should be at the heart of a planned global civilizing process that established cosmopolitan structures and accompanying changes in the emotional lives of people so that all persons could be free from indefensible violent harm (Fraser 2007; Linklater 2007). There was of course no complete rupture with the past. The 'affected by principle' had been transmitted from classical antiquity to the medieval and modern eras *via* Stoic philosophy and Roman law. But the utopian elements of the traditions of thought did not become pivotal to images of a global civilizing process until the late eighteenth century, at which point it becomes legitimate to refer to a significant new departure in the history of the Western states-systems. Kant and Smith's writings were at one and the same time reflections of that general trend and examples of how the salient moral and political issues were theorized in highly sophisticated ways.

Kant's defence of the cosmopolitan duty to refrain from causing unnecessary harm was a compelling response to the 'problem of distance' (Kant 1991 [1797]: 172). The central puzzle anticipated contemporary reasoning about how far the capacity for ethical responsibility depends on the physical proximity of others, how far the ability to extend social relations across space leaves the victims and the vulnerable inaudible, and how far the willingness to restrain the power to harm decreases proportionally (Bauman 2000: 184ff.; Forman-Barzilai 2005). The Kantian solution provides an effective response to the advocates of communitarian or republican perspectives who deny that cosmopolitan principles can compete with 'local' attachments that give people emotional satisfaction and define their sense of self and primary moral responsibilities. The contention was that a global civilizing process does not depend on a pre-existent sense of belonging to a surrogate for the nation, or on nothing other than an idealistic vision of a worldwide moral and political community. The important precondition was the desire to create arrangements that protected people everywhere from unnecessary harm in the context of increasing global interdependencies, and to graft the requisite civilizing ethical and emotional commitments onto the relevant governing structures. As previously argued, the argument resonates with more recent cosmopolitan standpoints which maintain that those who are closest to 'us' emotionally are especially vulnerable to 'our' actions, but those who are placed further along the global chains are often no less affected [and may indeed be even more adversely affected] by what 'we' do or do not do (Linklater 2011: 147–8). For that reason, they have inalienable rights to be included within the scope of moral consideration and to enjoy the forms of legal and political protection that have been established through the practices of citizenship in 'civilized', national communities. Globalizing those achievements was at the heart of Kant's ethical vision of the union of cosmopolitanism and compassion in a new phase of the European civilizing process.

Universal History and Cosmopolitan Ideals

Universal history which was one of the great achievements of the European Enlightenment represented a limited advance in detachment from national perspectives in the context of rising levels of human interconnectedness. The focus on the development of humanity and on the prospects for a cosmopolitan political future reflected the prevalent European civilized self-images. Collective pride was accompanied by moral anxieties about the dangers that 'civilized' societies posed to each other and to weaker, less 'advanced' groups. Those ethical concerns were critical for the emergence of more universal orientations to the world that were concerned with the fate of all peoples and with the future of humanity.

The dominant narratives provided an extended conception of time that was in harmony with the broadened comprehension of space in the 'age of discovery'. Hume's writings illustrated the point when asserting that it was not difficult to understand the reasons for the 'peculiar force and vivacity' with which people respond to events in their proximity: 'ourself is intimately present to us' (Hume 1969 [1739/40]: II, vii–viii). Exactly the same reasoning – the same obstacle to 'breaking the action of the mind' – explained human indifference to any occurrence that is not 'contiguous to us either in space or time'; everywhere in 'common life', one could observe an appetite for 'enjoying the present' and for 'leaving what is afar off to the care of chance and fortune'; indeed, Hume (1969 [1739/40]: II, vii–viii) argued, 'the consequence of a removal in space are [sic] much inferior to those of a removal in time'. However, the human species was clearly divorced from the animal kingdom because its 'thoughts are not limited by any narrow bounds, either of place or time'; the imagination stretched out not only to 'the most distant regions of this globe' but beyond the world itself, 'to the planets and heavenly bodies'; the mind looked backward in time to consider the origins of the species; it looked forward by reflecting on how present actions might affect 'posterity', and by speculating about 'the judgments which will be formed of [its] character a thousand years hence' (Hume 1875d [1777]: 152). Those points exemplified the striking movement towards more detached, universal standpoints that were noted earlier.

As in the Italian Renaissance, the growth of detachment was evident in several spheres of experience including reflections on the origins and development of the species. Breaking with Christian conceptions of time, thinkers such as Erasmus Darwin speculated that many millions of years may have passed before 'the commencement of the history of mankind' (cited in Hampson 1968: 221). The growing realization that nature had a history, that human groups had emerged from the natural world, and that societies had undergone long developmental processes broke with biblical chronology and providential history. New perspectives on time were required to understand the origins of language, the long process of taming nature, the evolution of different forms of societies and modes of government, and the role of conquest and commerce in forging various interdependencies between social groups that had been dispersed across the world. The ascent to greater detachment with respect to those phenomena was linked with the realization that Europeans were a minority – albeit the most powerful minority – of the human population (Marshall and Williams 1982: 98). Changing European self-images were bound up with the interlinked realization that Christian history had focused on one of many patterns of social development (Rossi 1984: ch.19; Marshall and Williams 1982: 91ff.). It is hardly surprising that humanity became the principal object of inquiry in response to the greater interweaving of diverse social groups with radically unequal life-chances and power capabilities.

Those dimensions of the 'enlargement of the sphere of contemplation' shaped the cosmological background to social and political thought: they were powerful forces behind the process of self-distancing that was critical for what would later be described as the 'disenchantment of the world'. Increasing awareness of long-term processes of change was combined with a humbling appreciation of the insignificance of human life in the larger cosmos and with the sense of the indifference of the universe to the wellbeing or indeed survival of the species. 'Suns encrust themselves, and are extinguished, planets perish and disperse themselves in the vast plains of air', Holbach argued, 'and man, an infinitely small portion of the globe, which is itself but an imperceptible point in the immensity of space, vainly believes it is for himself this universe is made'; the fallacy was to suppose that 'nature is governed by a cause, whose intelligence is conformable to his own', and to assume that there is some higher guarantee that the 'species can never disappear' (Holbach 1999 [1770]: 51, 65). He further stressed the need for humanity to look down on itself as if from above – in the manner in which it analysed the physical environment – and to confront the dangerous 'illusion' that gave the species a greatly 'exalted opinion' of itself (Holbach 1999 [1770]: 66). Though fiercely resisted by those who were convinced that language and reason were divine endowments, those ideas signified the 'slow death' of the 'Adam myth' and the demise of associated narcissistic, collective self-images (Rossi 1984: ch. 36). Hume (1875e [1777]: 226–7) observed that the apprehension of those realities is 'evidently too distant ever to have any effect' but, if it did, it would almost certainly 'destroy patriotism as well as ambition'. For many thinkers, that was precisely what was at stake in forging a new temporality. That was fundamental for constructing a 'we identity' that was centred on radical political projects that embodied the sense of human responsibility for the fate of the species. A major part of that orientation was the vision of a cosmopolitan endeavour to create the conditions in which the most positive human capacities and talents could flourish (Hampson 1968: 218ff.; Rossi 1984).

Broadening the scope of historical inquiry to encompass the evolution of the whole species necessarily came up against the problem of the scarcity of evidence about the nature of early societies. Such lacunae could be overcome, it was supposed, by conjectures (that were grounded in supposedly invariable human drives and behaviour) about the missing links in a continuous pattern of development (Berry 1997: 63ff.). As a step in the direction of more recent sociological analysis of long processes that have affected humanity as a whole, the 'stadial' approach of the Scottish Enlightenment contended that the species had gone through the four principal phases of hunting, pasturage, agriculture and commerce (Meek 1976). Through each historical epochs, Smith argued, society 'grew closer to civility' (Pittock 2003: 262ff.); Skinner (2003: 178). Representative approaches recognized that highly sophisticated societies including China had succeeded in establishing a lasting civil order but they celebrated the unique accomplishments of modernity; they contrasted a dynamic European states-system with the bland uniformity and cultural stagnation of 'civilized', non-European peoples (Israel 2006: ch. 25; Dew 2009; Marshall and Williams 1982: 133ff., 176ff.). Societies such as China were understood to possess sophisticated ways of satisfying complex human needs that were the hallmarks of civil 'refinement'. Savage groups were thought to be consumed as a result of physical necessities by an endless quest to satisfy immediate needs and desires; they were portrayed as displaying low levels of self-restraint and the weak inhibitions on aggressive or warlike impulses that reflected the condition of humanity in a lower stage of civilization.

Scottish Enlightenment thinkers considered their epoch in a long-term perspective that highlighted the revolutionary effects of what Montesquieu (1989 [1748]: Bk. 5. ch. 6) had called the *doux commerce* that replaced the violent inclinations of the nobility and war between autocratic rulers with peaceful cooperation geared towards the acquisition of wealth and luxuries (Berry 1997: 95ff.; Hirschman 1977: 56ff.; Terjanian 2013). Montesquieu's reflections on the civilizing of manners influenced philosophers such as Hume (1875f [1777]: 291ff.) who described the transition from militaristic states, such as Sparta, where the delights of fighting had outweighed the interest in welfare, to commercial societies where the 'pleasures of luxury' had replaced the appetite for war with the result that a return to ancient statecraft was virtually inconceivable. With the decline of 'feudal aristocratic heroism', Kant, Smith and others stated, military courage and valour had steadily lost their importance as the preferred route to individual success and social esteem (Pittock 2003: 271). Commercial society reduced the appeal of the life spent in what Hume called the 'fortified camp' (Porter 2000: 250). It weakened the passions and 'prejudices' that fuelled 'animosity between nations', 'soften[ed] and polishe[d] the manners of men', 'unite[d] them by one of the strongest of all ties, the desire of supplying their mutual wants', and 'dispose[d] them to peace' (Robertson, cited in Berry 1997: 141). Not every Enlightenment thinker regarded that transformation as an unqualified good. For some, the declining importance of military values in commercial societies raised serious doubts about the national resolution to wage war against enemies. But the broad consensus was that major wars would become less frequent and less brutal. Those were not dreamy aspirations. Economic trans-formations and cultural changes that owed a great deal to Enlightenment ideals contributed to the gradual decline of warrior society (Corvisier 1979: ch. 1, 123, 183). As part of that development, the armed forces retreated to the barracks (Corvisier 1979: 123–4, ch. 9). In that context, the older doctrine of 'bellicism' that stressed the inevitability of war gave way to 'pacific-ism' which was the belief that the complete eradication of war rather than the mitigation of its effects should be at the heart of a new global civilizing offensive (Dawson 1996: introduction; Ceadel 1989: ch. 6).

The nature of the analysis of long-term historical developments provides insights into Enlightenment conceptions of moral and political progress. Given the centrality of the ideal of perpetual peace in his writings, Kant's standpoint deserves most attention. When contemplating the unfolding of history, he maintained, it was hard to avoid feelings of dis-appointment and distaste. Displays of wisdom were apparent from time to time, but the human past appeared to have been the product of folly and vanity, of hatred and the love of destruction. With such comments, Kant seemed to agree with Condorcet's observation in a manuscript note that 'history is man's confession' (cited in Baker 1975: 343, ch. 6). The question was what to make of a species that took great pride in its alleged superiority (Linklater 2011: 253).

A survey of the history of human species therefore demonstrated the error of investing too much faith in human capabilities. As creatures of impulse, humans required a master that had, in turn, to be controlled (Kant 1991 [1784a]: 46). Only the power of the state had originally stood between citizens and the collapse into 'barbarism', but with the advancement of 'civilization', the importance of self-restraint relative to external controls had changed, though not in the relations between states to the same extent as in the relations within civil society. Violence at the international level continued to lag behind the general trend towards the internal pacification of civilized societies. Support for the judgment that global progress was impossible could rely on the seemingly ingrained disposition to use force and on countless examples of the power of 'radical evil' (Bernstein 2002). But to deny the possibility that societies could live in peace was to assume that humanity was condemned forever like animal species to remain subject to a 'law-governed nature' (Kant 1991 [1784a]: 42). It was to deny the existence of the capacity for moral freedom. Kant's standpoint on the significance of long-term tendencies for the concept of progress explicitly rejected three rival conceptions of history that reflected broader social controversies about the relationship between violence and civilization: that there had been steady decline from an original state of pure innocence ('moral terrorism'); that history is nothing other than endless recurrence and repetition ('abderitism') and that the past inspires confidence in inevitable progress that will be driven along by the emancipatory power of reason ('eudaemonism') (Kant 1991 [1798]: 178ff.).

The alternative approach rejected Rousseau's portrait of history as the loss of an original condition of innocence where no-one stood 'in need of his fellow-creatures' or possessed 'any desire to hurt them' (Rousseau 1968 [1754]: 188); but it recognized the force of his argument that societies had acquired the capacity to cause ever more destructive forms of harm; human groups had become 'the scourge' of other species and their history displayed an appetite for 'subduing and enslaving their neighbours' or massacring 'their fellow-creatures by thousands' (Rousseau 1968 [1754]: 192ff.). Kant also placed the evolution of the power to harm at the centre of a grand narrative that rejected theories of human decline and eternal recurrence, and emphasized the limited moral advances that had occurred in the context of increasing global interconnections. Unqualified protestations about the shortcomings of modern political life ignored the reality that societies had 'reached a higher level of morality' that made it possible to find fault with existing social arrangements and to envisage alternative paths of development (Kant 1991 [1792]: 89). Signs of progress could be discerned in the 'greater agreement over ... principles' that underpin 'mutual understanding and peace' (Kant 1991 [1795]: 114). The reality that a violation of human rights in any part of the world was increasingly regarded as an offence everywhere was a case in point. But above all else, Kant believed that the contours of a future world order that realized the ideal of perpetual peace were already evident in the free association of European republicans that could be progressively enlarged by admitting new members through mutual consent.

The objective of such an international association would be to narrow the gulf between the standards of self-restraint that were deemed vital for preserving orderly and humane relations between citizens of the same state and the significantly weaker and less demanding expectations of self-control at the global level (Elias 2013: 150–2, 169ff.). Universal history was central to that cosmopolitan political vision. As more recent scholars have argued, world history has a vital role to play in orientating people to the longer social and economic webs that have formed over the centuries and millennia; its 'post-national' temporal horizons are critical for understanding the unique but flawed achievements of the human societies, for promoting stronger identification with the species as a whole, and for facilitating the development of new forms of conscience-formation that alter the relationship between the individual, the sovereign state and humanity (McNeill 1986: 16). For Kant, universal history encouraged levels of detachment and foresight that were essential for advancing a global civilizing process that already existed in broad outline. It was a way of encouraging 'concern as to how our remote descendants will manage to cope with the burden of history which we shall bequeath to them a few centuries from now' (Kant 1991 [1784a]: 53). It was a means of promoting careful reflection about how particular societies and epochs could be 'honourably remembered in the most distant ages' (Kant 1991 [1784a]: ibid.). In the language of the *Encyclopedie*, it had become possible in a more enlightened age 'to assemble knowledge scattered across the earth, to reveal its overall structure to our contemporaries and to pass it on to those will come after us; so that the achievements of past ages do not become worthless for the centuries to come, so that our descendants, in becoming better informed, may at the same time become more virtuous and content, and so that we do not leave this earth without having earned the respect of the human race' (Diderot 1992 [1775]: 21–2). The purpose of universal history was to help orientate humans to the realities and the consequences of the greater interweaving of their lives; it was to foster the willingness to cooperate globally to advance towards an ideal condition in which societies would be as *'wise as serpents'* and as *'harmless as doves'* (Kant 1991 [1795]: 116, italics in original). That long-term 'pacific-ist' objective was supported by universal history that highlighted the contradictions between the violent potentials of 'civilized' societies and the social ideals that had developed with their internal pacification and which provided the foundation for an international order that broke decisively with the 'barbaric' arrangements of the past.

The Global 'Civilizing' Legacy of the Enlightenment

Assessing the historical legacy of the Enlightenment has long been the subject of debate. Critics such as Burke (1968 [1790]: 183ff.) maintained that the intoxication of reason, the fanatical defence of individual rights that were drastically uncoupled from correlative social responsibilities, and the rejection of monarchy and religion in a supposedly 'enlightened age' explained the regression to 'barbarism' that was unleashed by the French

Revolution. Horkheimer and Adorno (1973) argued that the zest for promoting the 'rational' reconstruction of society led to the despotism of instrumental reason. Foucault (1973) famously contended that humanitarian reform led to forms of power and control that were more effective than their predecessors because they were embedded more deeply in the recesses of the self-regulating, individual mind. But the latter argument was linked with support for the critical ethos of the Enlightenment that analysed more carefully than ever before the differences between the social conditions that were necessary for the existence of a decent society that endeavoured to eliminate indefensible harm and unnecessary suffering, and political arrangements that had no other purpose than perpetuating the dominance of sectional interests (Elias 2013b: 164).

From that standpoint, what was most important about the (radical) Enlightenment was the humanitarian impulse that aimed to eliminate 'obvious and pointless physical suffering' that included 'the cruel treatment of animals, the mistreatment of children, of the sick, and the insane; the corporal punishments of public flogging and executions; imprisonment for debt; duelling, war, and imperialism; the abuse of the poor, their economic exploitation unrelieved by charity, the press-gang and injustice generally; political corruption; and the slave trade and slavery' (Barker-Benfield 1992: 224; Hampson 1968: 150ff.). At its heart of that conception of civilization was the rejection of theological discourses that used the doctrine of original sin to reconcile people to pain and misery. At its centre was 'the affirmation of ordinary life', the positive evaluation of the everyday activities in which people find happiness and meaning (Taylor 1989; Porter 2000). The upshot was political support for a range of government measures that ranged from large-scale social reform to end cruelty and suffering to the defence of specific individual entitlements in 'civilized' arrangements such as the right to commit suicide to end personal unhappiness or despair (Hume 1875g [1777]; Montesquieu 1973 [1721]: Letter 76); also Minois 1999).

The emergence of the universal human rights culture and the humanitarian laws of war are part of the same development. They are examples of major differences between the 'international ethics' of classical antiquity – where low levels of sympathy for 'outsiders' existed alongside the harshly exploitative nature of everyday life – and modern ethical sensibilities that became central to society and politics as a result of the European Enlightenment. The most important movements reflected core features of the civilizing process that were discussed in Chapter 5, and specifically the reduced tolerance of physical violence that developed as part of the gradual internal pacification of society. Changing attitudes to violence, exploitation and humiliation also shaped orientations to relations between societies. It was noted earlier that one of the main questions in the study of harm is how far the incorporation of societies in longer webs of mutual dependence is attended by anxieties about the increased possibility of committing acts of violence over greater areas. The 'split within civilization' became a major moral problem for Enlightenment thinkers. The division between the standards that generally governed relations between 'civilized' European peoples and the norms that were thought to be appropriate in relations with 'savage', non-European peoples aroused particular moral concern. Ancient and modern colonizing armies had assumed that they could behave as they so wished in relations with 'uncivilized' peoples. Such licentiousness had often been opposed on either prudential or moral grounds in earlier epochs. But the ethical problem of colonialism and slavery acquired unprecedented importance as a result of core aspects of the European civilizing process. Taming the imperialists was part of the same pattern of development that began with 'taming the warriors' in the late medieval and early modern court societies. So was the endeavour to tame the sovereigns.

Related to the critique of original sin that was mentioned earlier was the belief that humans had to take collective responsibility for their social and political conditions. The contrast was with the notion of fate that had been central to classical antiquity (Williams 1993), and with parallel medieval conceptions of the irresistible force of the 'wheel of fortune'. An obvious parallel with Renaissance thought is evident in Smith's reference to fortune 'which governs the world, [and] has some influence where we should be least willing to allow her any' (Smith 1982 [1759]: II.iii.3.1). What especially distinguished Enlightenment thinking was greater confidence in using the rational investigation of social laws or tendencies to improve human arrangements. That development was testimony to the existence of stable state-organized societies that had been rare for long periods in Renaissance Italy and that had confined collective action to attempts to limit struggles between cities by using diplomacy to preserve the balance of power. Domestic pacification and 'civilization' made the imagination of more radical global transformations possible. Enlightenment thinkers were well aware of the dangers that accompanied the emergence of state monopolies of power. They had an acute sense of the destructive nature of modern warfare and of imperial cruelties that clashed with 'civilized' self-images and that had to be brought under control in accordance with the moral sensibilities of world citizens. For reasons that will be discussed in the next chapter, such confidence in human possibilities would prove to be short-lived. In recent times, the balance of opinion has changed once again, and many thinkers argue that some of the dominant themes in eighteenth-century analyses of overall long-term trends in world politics have turned out to be broadly correct – at least with respect to the most recent phase in the history of the modern states-system.

8

Total Warfare and Decivilizing Processes

It is true that people no longer hunt each other for food. Cannibalism, as well as slavery, has become rarer. But the way in which people maim, kill and torture each other in the course of their power struggles, their wars, revolutions and other violent conflicts, is different mainly in terms of the techniques used and the numbers of people concerned.

(Elias 2007: 175)

Kant's vision of perpetual peace was the high point of Enlightenment cosmopolitanism. It anticipated a world in which states display unusually high levels of self-restraint, guided by universal moral principles that attuned them to the realities of the closer interweaving of societies. Kant broadly agreed with Condorcet's belief that the species had reached the shores of a great revolution in history. Because of his confidence in the liberating power of scientific elites, Condorcet (1965 [1794]: 53–4) was more optimistic that the present stage of human development promised a future in which 'all enlightened men, from then on onwards . . . will be the friends of humanity [and] will work together for its perfection and its happiness'. Kant would not have disagreed with Concordet's hope that, in the future, all peoples would regard war as the greatest of all evils (Hampson 1968: 244). Such visions that located traditional reflections on 'the good society' within a more fundamental discussion of the ideal global order represented a significant extension of earlier critiques of the double standard of morality in social and political life. The conviction that the two moralities were problematical or 'contradictory' reflected the growing influence of post-aristocratic, bourgeois universalistic norms in European societies. Support increased for the belief that more onerous ethical expectations should apply in the relations between states, that there should be greater accountability to the members of other societies, and that substantially higher levels of self-monitoring and self-restraint should govern the conduct of foreign policy.

Enlightenment cosmopolitanism underpinned the assault on colonialism and slavery, and it informed the critique of a civilization that condemned the cruelty and unrestrained lives of 'savages' while despatching thousands to violent death in modern warfare. It represented a radical shift in thinking about the possibilities of a civilizing process that extended beyond national borders. The rise of universalistic thinking was accompanied in the late eighteenth century by a pronounced shift towards the more humane treatment of prisoners of war. That development reflected the realignment of social forces as the nobility lost power and influence to the rising commercial sectors who believed that the greatest opportunities for personal success existed in the peaceful 'economic' domain (Corvisier 1979: 12ff.).

Such 'civilizing' objectives were often defended in the early stages of the French Revolution by leading critics of the aristocratic mode of warfare. But that period is usually regarded as sounding the death-knell for Enlightenment cosmopolitanism – as introducing universal conscription and virulent nationalism, and edging ever closer towards 'total war'. The Revolution has spawned numerous accounts of how a naïve Enlightenment confidence in an imminent global civilizing process was shattered, and of how the dual standard of morality was reinvented as part of a larger transformation of European society that would have disastrous global consequences. It fostered discussions of how civility could only be secured within sovereign states, each unified by strong national ties that separated peoples from each other more sharply than before, and each unified by emotionally charged images of the 'nationalization' of suffering that would have been made little sense in the preceding era. Various standpoints also tracked parallel or interlocking tendencies in which the trend towards total warfare altered moral sensitivities, and not least because of the rise of new grand narratives that focused on the following trinity: the long-term development of the human capacity to cause more devastating forms of harm to more and more people over greater distances; the need for new levels of detachment and foresight in an era of rapidly increasing human interconnectedness in conjunction with the requirement for parallel advances in global cooperation so that societies could acquire greater leverage over social and political processes that were in danger of spiralling out of control; and the renewed emphasis on Enlightenment visions of limited war or perpetual peace that could be realized through an appropriate widening of the scope of emotional identification and extension of sympathies and solidarities. The paradox of the emergent age of total warfare is clear. Increasingly, destructive harm has done much to promote the realization that most people have similar aversions to pain and suffering (that can be at least as central to the organization of society and politics as the cultural and other phenomena that have traditionally divided them from each other); it has fostered the belief that efforts to create new forms of political community that keep pace with advances in destructive power and that contain the use of force can be firmly based on such universalities of experience. Two processes were therefore inextricably locked together. No advances in the military domain as described, no steps forward in collective learning as in the case of the rise of the Concert of Europe in response to the turmoil of the revolutionary wars, and no parallel rise of the first modern peace associations. The question is which movement has the upper hand at any historical juncture.

The first part of this chapter briefly considers the effects of the French revolutionary wars on the dominant attitudes to the state and nation, and to war and masculinity. It discusses the rise of mass armies and total warfare, the public exaltation of potent national symbols of sacrifice and suffering, and the collapse of the Enlightenment hope of universal concord as societies became more attuned to impersonal violence and long-distance warfare. It considers how those transformations promoted major shifts in cultural attitudes to war and suffering that were accompanied by diplomatic measures to promote international law as the 'gentle civilizer of nations' (Koskenniemi 2001). In short, three overlapping 'civilizing' dimensions of world politics that have continued down to the present day were set in motion by the unprecedented violence that followed the French Revolution: the attempt to exercise greater control over international political interaction that began with the Concert system; the emphasis on reducing suffering in warfare that was pioneered by the first peace movements and by such non-governmental organizations as the International Red Cross; and related developments in the laws of war that created interstate obligations to spare combatants (and in due course non-combatants) 'unnecessary suffering' or 'superfluous injury' (Linklater 2011: 37). In the aftermath of the revolutionary and Napoleonic wars, specific strata in different societies became linked by support for a global civilizing process that built shared human sympathies around the urgency of taming the sovereign power to inflict unprecedented levels of violent harm.

Revolutionary Warfare

It is important to begin with how military conflict changed with the French Revolution. The wars of the European aristocracies were simultaneously seemingly unlimited and highly regulated affairs – unlimited because of their frequency, but constrained because economic resources prohibited raising large standing armies or engaging in protracted warfare (Strachan 1983: ch. 2). Violent struggle was governed by an aristocratic honour code which demonstrated that the European nobility would not have been entirely bewildered by the idea of an interstate civilizing process – if not the version that was defended by many *philosophes* then the vision that was a direct offshoot of traditional 'court rationality'. That ethic encouraged the belief that 'aristocratic ritual and *politesse* could even extend onto the battlefield' with the result that European warfare was often compared to a duel, albeit with high casualty rates (Bell 2007: 34ff.; Rothenberg 1977: 90ff.). The idea of 'civilized' warfare was anchored in contrasts with the 'Turkish' way of war that involved fighting to the last as against accepting an honourable surrender; Western Europeans who imported the more brutal practices of wars in regions to the East were condemned for transgressing the restraints that distinguished a higher civilization (Anderson 1988: 191ff.).

Late eighteenth-century society witnessed the separation of military professionals from the rest of the population. In the same period, many states broke with the earlier practice of encouraging the general populace to rise up against occupying forces. The upshot was that armies were less inclined to wage war against civilian strata in a period when the meaning of 'civilian' shifted from denoting technical expertise in civil law to involvement in non-military pursuits (Bell 2007: 11). In the course of becoming more disciplined, several armies had less need to prey on vulnerable populations (Howard 1978: 73; Howard 1994: 4; Parker 1994). As part of the general moderating of warfare in the eighteenth century, societies moved from the earlier convention of ransoming captives towards formal agreements to exchange prisoners (Anderson 1988: 180ff.; Contamine 2000). What Enlightenment thinkers added was the conviction that war reflected a condition of 'savagery' that Europeans would leave behind with the further progress of 'civilization'. They condemned aristocratic validations of war, and many insisted that the crucial goal was not to restrain military force but to abolish it as part of the larger quest to eliminate violence. Many nobles came to share that way of thinking as a result of the influence of the *philosophes* in late eighteenth-century court society (Swann 1995). The French Revolution would introduce an entirely new mode of warfare. Conscripted forces were mobilized to wage wars of national liberation that would, according to French rhetoric and propaganda, ultimately free Europe of violent conflict. On that conception of history, the 'noncivilized' or 'savage' opponents who blocked the path of 'civilized' peoples – whether domestic or foreign – had few, if any, moral rights (Bell 2007: 49). The nationalist fervour that was released by the revolution therefore resulted in the demonization of political opponents. The associated dichotomies were crucial in bringing 'limited warfare' to an end. Nevertheless, the old restraints on warfare were observed with enough regularity to cast doubt on the notion of a fundamental break with the pre-revolutionary era (Rothenberg 1994). The evidence is that respect for enemies in interstate conflicts did not extend, however, to guerrillas as was clear from the conflict in Spain where 'the rules of civilized warfare were not respected and . . . where any form of reprisals seemed justified' (Forrest 2002: ch. 5). Similarly, total warfare was waged against the people of Vendée (Bell 2007: ch. 5).

The lurch towards ferocity in the struggle with the enemies of liberty was an effect of the disastrous trend towards ever more powerful territorial concentrations of power. The rise of enlightened despotism tamed sovereign rulers to a degree, not least by raising expectations that governments would conform to the laws of nature that had been given constitutional form. For the despots, political concessions to the lower strata were attractive insofar as they increased popular support for the regime. They were not an end in themselves but a way of legitimating and strengthening more efficient, rationalized central authorities. The French Revolution abolished the monarchy and destroyed aristocratic privileges but, in so doing, it accelerated the trend towards greater territorial consolidations of power – not just within France but across the European states-system as a whole, and eventually across the wider world as other societies came to realize that emulating the dominant patterns of state-building in the 'leading edge' region was vital for security and survival (Lefèbvre 1964; Skocpol 1979). No less important was the practice of imitating the new forms of military organization and the innovative methods of waging war (Ralston 1990). In the early phases of the struggle with France, the British ruling class was unwilling to raise a mass army because of the fear that disaffected groups would be better-equipped to turn against it (Bell 2007: 254). Similar suspicions about the loyalties of the people dissuaded the European monarchies from establishing mass armies in the aftermath of the Napoleonic Wars. But the struggle with France forced many ruling elites to recognize that future victories would elude them if they continued to pitch the traditional army against mass forces that were bound tightly together by strong emotional attachments to the nation.

Burke (1968 [1790]: 170–1) abhorred the fact that, with the Revolution, 'the age of chivalry' had come to an abrupt end; the refinement of manners that had 'made power gentle' and 'mitigated ferocity', and that had distinguished modern Europe from Asia and from 'the most brilliant periods of the antique world', had been swept aside by the 'new conquering empire of light and reason'; the calamity was not confined to France but was a disaster for civility across Europe as a whole; unsurprisingly, the war against the Revolution was portrayed as a struggle to defend 'civilization' from the 'savagery' that was exemplified by the large number of wars that broke out in the quarter-century after the Revolution and by the high number of casualties (Freeman 1980: 148–9). The reality is that twenty per cent of all European wars fought between 1490 and 1815 occurred in a twenty-five year period following the Revolution (Bell 2007: 7). Prior to 1790, battles rarely brought together more than 100,000 combatants. The battle of Wagram in 1809 involved around 300,000 combatants; at Leipzig in 1813, the numbers were closer to 500,000, and about 150,000 were either killed or injured (Bell 2007: 7; Parker 2005: 151ff.). Around 1 million French soldiers, and *circa* 5 million Europeans, died during the revolutionary wars. What Burke abhorred was the trend towards what has come to be known as total warfare – the national mobilization of all available social and political resources to inflict maximum destruction on the enemy and to sap the strength and destroy the morale of the larger society, thereby erasing the distinction between the military and civilian spheres that had helped to restrain violent harm in the preceding 'civilized', aristocratic era (Bell 2007: 7–8).

Academic debates about the usefulness of the concept of total warfare which is at the centre of the master narrative of modern military history need not detain us here (see Chickering 1999). There is ample evidence that 'primitive warfare' was no less murderous at times than modern military conflicts (see Linklater 2011: 116ff.). For that reason alone, 'total warfare' usefully describes a shift towards the military engagement of whole peoples that astonished those who had become accustomed to living within significantly more peaceful societies. In longer-term perspective, war between entire societies may have been the norm rather than the exception, or at least it may have been commonplace. Thucydides described how the Peloponnesian War acquired a momentum towards total conflict. The Roman and Macedonian imperial conquests were renowned for ruthlessness towards defeated populations. Crusading warfare had many of the same qualities. Historians have claimed that the concept of total was coined towards the end of the First World War as thinkers envisaged even more violent conflict; it was then hijacked for propaganda purposes by leaders such as Goebbels (Bell 2007: 9). Total war can be regarded as an ideal-type which may be approximated – no more than that – in actual military affairs (Chickering 1999). The concept is described as a modern invention because of social and political capabilities that the preceding, pre-industrial phase societies lacked, namely the power of 'total social mobilization' that was geared towards the 'total destruction' of the enemy and with little regard for moral distinctions between armed forces and 'innocent' civilian strata (Shaw 2005: 42ff.). The term derives much of its power from contrasts with eighteenth-century aristocratic warfare (see Chickering 1999 for a different view), and from the cultural shock that was one consequence of the speed with which Enlightenment visions of progress were dashed by the wars that followed the French Revolution.

It is unnecessary to comment further on whether the term describes the unique nature of modern warfare. Doubts about the explanatory value of that approach have been raised. Its sociological significance is what is of interest here – and specifically how the idea of total war made people more aware of how their lives had become interwoven in the course of successive military revolutions that had increased the state's power to cause harm over greater distances. The European civilizing process had increased levels of personal security, and removed the mercenary threat that had been the scourge of, *inter alia*, the Italian city states. As noted earlier, force had been 'stored in the barracks'; the belief in a secure 'civilian' sphere appeared to more secure. More disciplined armies no longer needed to live off the land. All of those factors help to explain the cultural context that shaped images of total warfare.

The nature of the transformation of modern war was illustrated by the *levée en masse* decree of 23 August 1793 that described mass mobilization in these terms: 'From this moment until the enemy is driven from the territory of the Republic, all the French people are permanently requisitioned for the armies. The young men will go to the front, married men will forge arms and carry supplies, women will make tents and clothing, children will divide old linen into bandages, old men will be carried into the squares to rouse the courage of the soldiers, to teach hatred of kings and the unity of the republic' (cited in Townsend 1997: 5). A crucial factor was the seemingly inexhaustible number of armed men who could be thrown into battle. That capability gave the French state a much greater ability to absorb a higher casualty rate. France was better placed than its adversaries to overwhelm enemies by fighting more often and by using superior numbers to surprise the enemy by quickly changing the main line of attack.

For the purpose of understanding the fate of Enlightenment conceptions of a global civilizing process it is instructive to compare Burke's opinions on violence and civilization with the standpoint taken by Clausewitz. In his 1791 *A Letter to a Member of the National Assembly*, Burke maintained that 'the hellhounds of war, on all sides' would be 'uncoupled and unmuzzled' (Burke 1889 [1791]: 34–5). French military policy that included recourse to assassination had 'destroyed ... all the other manners and principles which have hitherto civilized Europe'; as a result, 'the mode of civilized warfare will not be practised: nor are the French .... entitled to expect it' (Burke 1889 [1791]: ibid.). With the decline of aristocratic we-feeling, traditional restraints on force had been eroded. Clausewitz had been personal witness to the differences between the aristocratic code that had underpinned the 'half-hearted' and 'tame' wars of the eighteenth century ('where we neither want to do much harm to the enemy nor have much to fear from him'), and the lurch towards absolute war that defined the conflict at Jena in 1806 (Clausewitz 1976 [1832]: Book 3, ch. 16). The mobilization of mass armies, whose fighting men could be relied on to sacrifice their lives for the nation and who could be replaced quickly, removed the social constraints that had been part of the aristocratic code. According to Clausewitz, Enlightenment thinkers who regarded recent wars as 'relapses into barbarism' were wholly unprepared for the enemy who, like 'the untamed elements, knows no law other than his own power', and who could deploy military resources to engineer nothing less than the enemy's 'total collapse' (Clausewitz 1976 [1832]: Book 3, ch. 16). Given the impossibility of returning to the limited wars of the previous century where 'no battle had led to the destruction of a defeated army' (Townsend 1997: 5–6), modern states had to adapt quickly to the new forms of armed conflict if they hoped to survive. They had to become attuned to one of the main innovations of Napoleonic warfare which was the concentration of all available resources in what would prove to be the decisive battle; in the era of modern warfare, 'major powers were shattered with virtually a single blow' (Clausewitz 1976 [1832]: Book 3, ch. 17; also Esdaile 1995: ch. 2; Lynn 2000).

In Clausewitz's writings, the precise relationship between revolutionary increases in state power, the metamorphosis of warfare, and Enlightenment confidence in an imminent global civilizing process was not an explicit concern. He did not harness the evidence of recent history, or indeed reflect on the overall course of the human past, to condemn or ridicule the optimism of the Enlightenment. But the analysis clearly rejected the belief that the Age of Enlightenment had begun to secure the victory of the rational self-control of emotional drives and to suppress the immoderate pursuit of egoistical national goals. The aristocratic age had moderated the conduct of war and had elevated the rational calculation of interests over the supposedly collective frenzy of 'savage' peoples. Clausewitz (1976 [1832]: Book 1, ch. 3) echoed broader currents of thought about the 'civilized' nature of his age by stating that 'in any primitive, warlike race the warrior spirit is far more common than among civilized peoples'; attunement to violence was part of the habitus of 'almost every warrior', whereas 'in civilized societies only necessity will stimulate it in the people as a whole, since they lack the natural disposition for it'. Enmity between individuals was not a 'natural' feature of 'civilized' conflict between modern states. But those who had believed that future wars would be confined to the calculated, rational struggle over specific strategic interests had been wrong to think that the main tendencies would differ greatly from those that governed humanity in its 'savage' past. Enlightenment expectations of a significant widening of the scope of emotional identification between peoples, of a new we–I balance involving the state, international society and humanity, and higher standards of self-restraint in international relations as part of the progress of human reason had been shown to be false. Clausewitz emphasized that the Age of Reason had not extinguished such basic emotions as collective anger or the thirst for vengeance – negative emotions that seemed out of place for the reasons that were discussed earlier in the societies that had come to pride themselves on their civilization. Animosity between nations dissolved the earlier constraints on war. Collective hostility that spilled over into hatred between individuals increased as societies became entangled in the decivilizing cycles of 'revenge and retaliation' that are invariably unleashed whenever nations resort to violence in the attempt to settle major political differences (Clausewitz 1976 [1832]: Book 1, ch. 1; Book 2, ch. 2).

It would be fallacious to regard Clausewitz as a miserable apologist for total warfare. He did not dignify mass slaughter or condone the ruthless treatment of civilians – his was an era when the outcome of military struggle was usually decided on the battlefield (Clausewitz 1976 [1832]: Book 5, ch. 14; Heuser 2002: ch. 5). But nor did not he dwell on parallels to the massacres at Melos and the Mycallesus that had featured so prominently in Thucydides' account of the Peloponnesian Wars (Bell 2007: 273ff.; also Keegan 1999: 41ff.; Paret 1976: 169ff.). His main preoccupation was with constructing an essentially clinical analysis of an irresistible 'decivilizing process' that demanded a fundamental revision of strategic thinking. Clausewitz maintained that 'the fact that slaughter is a horrifying spectacle must make us take war more seriously'; no longer was it realistic to hope for generals who could 'win victories without bloodshed'; states would hand the advantage to their adversaries if the violence of modern warfare provided 'an excuse for gradually blunting our swords in the name of humanity' (Clausewitz 1976 [1832]: Book 4, ch. 11). He contrasted aristocratic warfare which was similar to the highly ritualized duel – the 'often boring chess game of soldiers' that was conducted with 'moderation' – with the new 'war of all against all' that released collective passions and frenzies that were typical of the 'savage' condition where wars were waged with few moral restraints (cited in Bell 2007: 241). As a result of advances in the territorial concentration of power, modern war, 'untrammeled by any conventional restraints, had broken loose in all its most elemental fury'; there appeared to be 'no end to the resources mobilized; all limits disappeared in the vigour and enthusiasm shown by governments and their subjects', and by 'the depth of feeling generally aroused'; the 'sole aim of war was to overthrow the opponent' including despised regimes, and 'not until he was prostrate was it considered possible to pause and try to reconcile the opposing interests'; it was as if war was a substitute for prudent diplomacy rather than the restrained and orderly 'continuation of political intercourse, carried on with other means' (Clausewitz 1976 [1832]: Book 1, ch. 1; Book 8, ch. 3). Those seismic changes were due to 'the peoples' new share in these great affairs of states'; 'suddenly war again became the business of the people – a people of thirty millions all of whom considered themselves to be citizens' – with radical consequences for the political organization of European societies; the 'resources and efforts now available for use surpassed all conventional limits; nothing now impeded the vigour with which war could be waged' (Clausewitz 1976 [1832]: Book 8, ch. 3).

Clausewitz's principal work defended the economy of force in the sense of employing whatever violence was needed to break the enemies' willingness to continue to fight. Pre-existing political objectives could and should restrain violence, limiting it to specified ends as against relishing destruction for its own sake. As already noted, for Clausewitz, pleasure in the uninhibited killing of the members of other societies was more typical of 'savages'. Plundering enemy land 'had ceased to be in harmony with the spirit of the times'; behaviour that had been commonplace in classical antiquity, in 'Tartar days and indeed in medieval times', was now condemned as 'unnecessarily barbarous', as harming 'the enemy's subjects rather than their government', as inviting reprisals, and indeed as impeding the 'advance of general civilization'; Europe 'rejoiced at this development' that was regarded (erroneously) 'as a logical outcome of enlightenment' (Clausewitz 1976 [1832]: Book 8, ch. 3). But in the aftermath of the revolutionary wars, efficient armies could no longer be simultaneously 'civilized' and effective – that is, committed to strategies that regarded civilian suffering as morally undesirable as well as unprofitable. Armed forces had to deal with a revolutionary regime that commandeered every resource to destroy its enemies and that freely violated the standards of 'civilized' warfare by licensing troops 'to procure, steal and loot everything they needed' (Clausewitz 1976 [1832]: Book 5, ch. 14). The possibility of 'civilized' conflict had been greatly reduced by a poisonous combination of the greater military and political power that could be deployed in battle and the inescapable feature of all wars which is their tendency to acquire a catastrophic momentum, to become susceptible to unruly chance and unbridled collective emotions and, in the worst of all circumstances, to entirely escape rational control (Clausewitz 1976 [1832]: Book 1, ch. 1, Book 3, ch. 3). Warfare, Clausewitz (1976 [1832]: Book one, ch. 3) argued, is 'the realm of chance. No other human activity gives it greater scope: no other has such incessant and varied dealings with this intruder'. The violence of revolutionary warfare therefore led to the rediscovery or renewed emphasis on the role of *Fortuna* in human affairs. On those grounds, Clausewitz (1976 [1832]: Book 1, ch. 1) stated that the differences between 'civilized' peoples and 'savages' were not as great as many believed, and they had less to do with their 'respective natures' than with their 'attendant circumstances' and key 'institutions'. Certainly, 'the civilized nations do not put their prisoners to death or devastate cities and countries' because 'intelligence plays a larger part in their methods of warfare' and steers them towards 'more effective ways of using force than the crude expression of instinct' Clausewitz (1976 [1832]: Book 1, ch. 1). But 'even the most civilized peoples', Clausewitz (1976 [1832]: ibid) maintained, 'can be fired with passionate hatred for each other' – contrary to Enlightenment conceptions of the changing balance of power between reason and impulse, and related expectations that compassionate cosmopolitanism could provide the basis for unparalleled advances in the collective control of unregulated social processes which, Clausewitz argued, reached their height in periods of interstate warfare.

Clearly, Clausewitz was at odds with those who thought that the 'civilizing' role of commerce had become (or was about to become) the main driving force behind European political development. False predictions and the failure of France's enemies to adapt to the new realities of military conflict allowed the violence of the revolutionary wars to dominate the continent for twenty years (Clausewitz 1976 [1832]: Book 8, ch. 6). However, as already noted, his analysis of absolute war should not be confused with the glorification of violence and national sacrifice that was so pronounced during the revolutionary era. A mode of political realism governed an approach that focused on the necessity of adjusting to the transformation of warfare, and on the indisputable contraction of significant political choice. In an intriguing passage, Clausewitz observed that it was an open question whether future wars will be 'waged with the full resources of the state' or whether a 'gradual separation' between the Government and the people will occur that re-establishes the aristocratic restraints on force that existed in an age when a narrower social base and more limited resources deprived war of 'its tendency towards the extreme and . . . the whole chain of unknown possibilities' that adhered to it (Clausewitz 1976 [1832]: Book 8, ch. 3). It was hard to deny that the 'barriers' that existed because of 'man's ignorance of what is possible', when torn down, 'are not so easily set up again'; as a result, 'when major interests are at stake, mutual hostility will express itself in the same manner as it has in our day' (Clausewitz 1976 [1832]: Book 8, ch. 3). It was equally impossible to ignore the tragic reality that 'the invention of gunpowder' and 'the constant improvement of firearms' revealed that the 'advance of civilization has done nothing practical to alter or deflect the impulse to destroy the enemy, which is central to the very idea of war' (Clausewitz 1976 [1832]: Book 1, ch. 1). Clausewitz's emphasis on the social dynamics that are unleashed in war and that are often impossible to control broke with the Enlightenment notion that Europe stood on the threshold of an age when human reason would reduce the unpredictable dynamics of human interaction. In opposition to Enlightenment thinking, he argued, no future human state of affairs, however 'civilized', was likely to escape the destructive violence and hostility that had been made possible by the interwoven political and military revolutions of the era (Clausewitz 1976 [1832]: Book 8, ch. 3).

Although several Enlightenment thinkers held very complex ideas about how far the species could advance and what the future might hold, none could have predicted the scale of the conflict that was to come. In May 1790, the French National Assembly renounced all 'wars aimed at conquest' and declared that it would 'never employ its forces against the liberty of any people'. On 19 November 1792 the same body declared that it would 'accord fraternity and assistance to all people who shall wish to recover their liberty' (cited in Ceadel 1996: 32), and added one month later that 'the French nation . . . will treat as an enemy any people that refuses to accept liberty and equality and seeks to keep, recall, or compromise with their old princes and privileged orders' (cited in Blanning 2002: 114). On 15 September in the following year, the National Convention declared that the armed forces would no longer be bound by the 'philanthropic idea' that had been previously adopted by the French people in the quest to promote liberty but would 'behave towards the enemies of France in just the same way that the powers of the coalition have behaved towards them' (cited in Blanning 1996: 159). The evidence that other peoples did not share the love of liberty – or particularly welcome having French political ideals thrust upon them – may have bred popular contempt for the communities involved. In any case, in the following years, France was at war with the majority of European states. It unleashed levels of violence without parallel since the Thirty Years' War, and proclaimed the unique virtues of the republic in a xenophobic language that fuelled nationalist feeling across the continent (Blanning 1996: 246–7). An example was Robespierre's claim in the National Assembly in May 1794 that 'the French people seems to have outdistanced the rest of the human race by 2,000 years; one is tempted to regard it as a different species', an arrogance that led opponents to condemn the French for having regressed to 'primitive barbarism' (Blanning 1996: 246). With those declarations, universal convictions declined and the scope of emotional identification contracted; the we–I balance tilted decisively towards an exclusionary and aggressive French nation; aristocratic standards of self-restraint went into decline.

The sense of superiority was translated into unconcealed contempt for enemies that led to the reversal of earlier commitments to refrain from harming innocent civilians. In the conflicts with other European states, civilian communities faced ruthless exploitation (Blanning 2002: 117ff.). As of 1795, French armed forces survived mainly by plunder (Strachan 1983: 41). The regime lurched from the notion of 'war to the chateaux, peace to the cottages' to the practice of confiscating whatever was needed to supply the army and anything (including cultural objects looted from European collections) that would bring wealth and glory to the republic (Blanning 1996: 162). Napoleon was explicit that the strategy was to finance additional wars through conquest. Forced labour was used to fuel such wars, although terrorizing civilians was not official policy (Blanning 2002). Commanders who lamented the cruelty or at least the erosion of military discipline that resulted from living off the land were often powerless to prevent widespread looting (Blanning 1996: 159). Revolutionary ideals that replaced the older aristocratic hierarchy with a system of trial by peers barred the way to punishing the guilty parties. Many military leaders were, in any case, perfectly content to share the spoils of war (Blanning 2002). With respect to Napoleon's armies, exactly how far nationalist loyalties and fervour provided the motivation for mass participation is unclear. What is not disputed is that the promise of personal wealth through looting was no small incentive for those who enlisted. The sheer size of the French armies made living off the land essential; resulting local famines were not uncommon (Best 1998: ch. 7). Those who stood against the regime (in Italy for example) faced calculated ruthlessness. Victorious forces were unleashed on the vanquished. Routed armies did not leave the scene of their defeat without causing as much damage as possible to local communities. Indeed Napoleon maintained that his men had committed acts that 'make one blush to be a member of the human race' but his warning to 'remember Binasco' (where, in May 1796, several hundred members of the peasant army had been slaughtered and the town was set alight) was clearly designed to remind insurrectionists of their likely fate (Blanning 1996: 164ff.). Enlightened thinkers had condemned such atrocities. Only by distorting their core moral and political convictions can the Enlightenment be held responsible for the violence of the revolutionary era.

Towards a New International Political Order

The turmoil of the Napoleonic wars was followed by major collective efforts to stabilize the international system. Three interrelated projects wrestled with the problem of restraining violent harm: the first was the establishment of the Concert system; the second was initiated not by states but by civil society actors that displayed heightened concern about unnecessary suffering in warfare; the third was the appearance of the modern humanitarian laws of war.

Established by the Congress of Vienna in 1815, the Concert of the great powers agreed that they had joint responsibilities for monitoring social and political events with potential systemic significance and for close cooperation to preserve international order. The Concert succeeded in reducing the number of interstate wars as well as the proportion of Europe's population that was killed or injured in military conflicts. The ratio of battlefield deaths to the total population of Europe may have been seven times greater in the eighteenth than in the nineteenth century (Schroeder 1994: vii). The long peace that lasted for forty years – until the outbreak of the Crimean War – was the result of demands for higher levels of self-restraint given the dangerous realities of greater strategic interconnectedness. The pacification of relations between the great powers occurred because of their recognition that any proposed change to the interstate order had to be legitimated by processes of consultation and consent rather than imposed unilaterally by the threat or use of force. More specifically, extended peace rested on a shared conviction that international stability depended on a planned or 'contrived' rather than a 'fortuitous' balance of power (Bull 1977: 104ff.). It relied on joint endeavours to preserve order between the most powerful states but also on the forced suppression of popular democratic and nationalist movements that were believed to have the capacity to destabilize the international system.

The conviction that states had a common interest in working together to preserve the European political order demonstrated the importance of the 'ambivalence of interests' in binding actors together in more complex ways. Enlightened self-interest explained the decision to readmit France into the society of states. Recognition of its importance for the long-term survival of the balance of power prevailed over any desire to seek revenge by imposing punitive measures on a pariah state. (The obvious contrast is with the sanctions against Germany at the end of World War One that fuelled perceptions of national humiliation that had destructive consequences for international order). The consultative mechanism that was placed at the heart of the states-system was based on the recognition that compliance with the 'affected by principle' – a notable shift in the we–I balance – was the key to European political stability. Critics of the Concert arrangements maintained that reactionary governments had restored an obsolescent aristocratic order that suppressed popular liberal and nationalist political aspirations that could not be contained indefinitely. Those who have celebrated its achievements have described the Concert as an instance of a collective social 'learning process' that restored order and brought security to peoples who welcomed relief from the ravages of recent wars (Schroeder 1994: 575ff.). The major accomplishment of the Concert system – and the reason for the long peace – was the great powers' willingness to rely on the art of political accommodation to engineer a workable compromise between divergent strategic interests. In the language of the period, it underpinned a 'just equilibrium' that could be adapted to changing circumstances by relying on the very diplomatic skills that had brought it into being in the first place (Clark 2005: 103ff.). The Concert established the need for special great power responsibilities that can be regarded as a decisive extension of the European civilizing process (Bukovansky et al. 2012). The new doctrine of international responsibility was part of an advance towards a higher level of social and political collaboration in an attempt to pacify an anarchic system. The purpose was to reconcile continued support for territorial sovereignty with the collective adjustment of foreign policy objectives in order to cope with inescapable political and military dangers. The Concert system was an attempt to create a 'global steering mechanism' in recognition of the limitations of the older modalities of foreign policy. 'Taming' the growth of state power was one of 'the principal achievements' of the period, and one of the accomplishments of a joint commitment to 'restrained competition' that was underpinned by an explicit willingness to 'group together' to isolate 'disruptive states' (Mulligan 2008: 402ff.). The architects of the League of Nations and the United Nations would attempt to build on its political achievements in their efforts to restore international order in the aftermath of the twentieth-century's 'total wars'.

The Concert of Europe has been described as a great power condominium that asserted the priority of order over justice, and as 'a benign shared hegemony' that entrenched the dominant states' special rights and responsibilities in international law (Schroeder 1994: 576ff., citing Bull 1977: ch. 9). At the end of the Napoleonic Wars, sovereigns were unwilling to preside over domestic political reforms that would result in the loss of power and privilege. Although they were well aware of the advantages that the revolutionary armies possessed by virtue of fighting as free men, most were convinced that smaller, professional militaries would prove more effective in future wars (Esdaile 1995: ch. 9). Professional forces were kept apart from the civilian sphere in order to reduce the risk of contamination by radical ideas of liberty and equality (French 1997). The principal fear amongst the ruling strata was that with mass armies came the danger of domestic unrest and political revolution although some were troubled that large conscript armies might also increase the possibility of war.

But the Concert system was not entirely blind to larger issues of human justice. The great powers committed themselves in 1815 to the abolition of the Atlantic slave trade (Clark 2007: ch. 2). Although their main objective was to establish a 'just equilibrium' between potential adversaries, success in restoring and maintaining the peace created a stable political environment that also made it easier for civil society actors to organize to promote popular support for the ideal of eradicating war. In that more secure condition, liberals such as Cobden argued that the growth of commerce performed a 'civilizing' role by replacing armed conflict between autocratic governments with peaceful cooperation between free peoples (Schroeder 1994: 575ff.). In 1816 the first modern peace organization – the *Society for the Promotion of Permanent and Universal Peace* – was established in London (Ceadel 1996). Significantly, the Christian-humanitarian sentiments that shaped the British peace movement exhibited the same sense of national pride that influenced other 'civilizing offensives' such as the effort to abolish the Atlantic slave trade and slavery (Ceadel 1996). The long peace would witness an enormous increase of such voluntary internationalist associations.

If the writings of the historian, Francis Buckle, represented an important strand of public opinion then even the Crimean war did not dislodge the belief that the members of the 'civilized' world were steadily advancing towards lasting peace. A period of remarkable stability had not been shattered, he argued, as in the past, 'by a quarrel between two *civilized* nations, but by the encroachment of the *uncivilized* Russians on the still more *uncivilized* Turkey', the two being 'the two most barbarous monarchies now remaining in Europe' (Buckle 1901: 195, italics added). Unrestrained conflict during the American Civil War was not generally regarded as a dark omen of what lay in store for European peoples but was characterized as the unsurprising result of 'local' peculiarities such as the lack of professional, disciplined armed forces in a society that was thought to lag behind the European pattern of state-building and civilization in fundamental respects (French 1997). The long peace had encouraged the conviction that wars had become less numerous and less brutal because of the progress of civilization. It was General Sherman's use of force against civilian populations during the American Civil War, and his contention that 'war is cruelty, and you cannot refine it' – that it is 'simply power unrestricted by constitution or compact' – that captured the general direction in which industrialized military conflicts were heading (Strachan 1983: 75).

The Concert system and a web of peace organizations developed side by side in connection with a general public desire to avoid a repeat of the suffering that had occurred during the Napoleonic era (Ceadel 1996: 220–1). Artistic sensibilities reflected and shaped the changing emotional climate. Visual representations of the deplorable suffering that had been caused by rampaging victorious armies achieved greater cultural prominence and political influence with Goya's *The Disasters of War*, a series of etchings that portrayed the savagery of Napoleon's army in Spain. First published in 1863, thirty-five years after his death, the eighty etchings constituted 'a turning point in the history of moral feelings and of sorrow'; as a result, a 'new standard for responsiveness to suffering' entered the world of art (Sontag 2003: ch. 3). Images of the 'barbarism' of the occupying forces and the 'savagery' of the resistance movement highlighted the insanity of warfare (Hughes 2003: ch. 8). Along with William Howard Russell's dispatches from Crimea, and Roger Fenton's images of suffering in the American Civil War, those artistic representations demonstrated that modern societies had yet to free themselves from such 'barbarities' (Howard 1994: 5–6). They helped to construct the elements of a community of the suffering that transcended emotional identification with any single nation. They clashed with the state's use of carefully contrived propagandist symbols from war zones to shape social attitudes to war and sacrifice and to create or bolster public support for foreign conflicts.

From the first war photography of the Crimean conflict through to more recent media coverage of military conflicts, sanitized images have been employed to encourage the popular belief that one's own society behaves in a restrained and 'civilized' manner, as required by the laws of war, while the enemy resorts to any measure, however 'cruel' and 'barbaric', to promote morally dubious or wholly illegitimate political ends. Time and again, patriotic feelings have been aroused by glorifying the heroic actions of national citizens who are willing to sacrifice their personal wellbeing and survival for the greater good, while concealing evidence of brutalities that would contradict 'civilized' self-images and offend public sensibilities (Paris 2000: chs. 1–2). However, artistic depictions of the human costs of war became sufficiently powerful in the mid-nineteenth century to foster moral sensibilities that were central to two interrelated long-term developments – the rise of international non-governmental organizations such as the International Red Cross, and the emergence of the humanitarian laws of war that together represented a major step forward in globalizing the civilizing process, in remaking international order in the light of a general lowering of the threshold of repugnance towards violence and suffering in war. That dynamic was an unsurprising consequence of the significant pacification of society and of public pressures to democratize increasingly powerful, centralized political institutions in response to the state's demand for conscript armies and for increased taxation (Taithe 1998).

The founders of the Red Cross maintained that the organization had been established to ensure that revolutionary advances in the capacity to inflict violent harm were checked by legal and moral commitments to eliminate 'unnecessary suffering': 'it would be a disgrace to humanity', it was stated, 'if its imagination were less fertile for good than for evil. Murderous refinements of war should have correlative refinements of mercy' in line with the moderate dispositions of the 'human and truly civilized spirit' (cited in Moorehead 1998: 51–2). The 1864 Geneva meeting of the International Red Cross set out rules governing the treatment of wounded soldiers. During the Balkan Wars of 1875–78, the scope of emotional identification was extended to include civilian refugees. In that period, the Christian and 'gentlemanly' values that had inspired Dunant, the founder of the Red Cross, took account of the rights of non-Christian victims of war, hence the establishment of the Red Crescent as an alternative humanitarian symbol (Finnemore 1999). Later, the organization would defend solidarity between strangers that was based on nothing more than the common aversion to pain and suffering. Such solidarity was the 'last bridge' connecting peoples at war whose 'buttresses' should never be allowed to collapse 'under the pressure of passion' when 'the orderly life of nations is shattered' (cited in Moorehead 1998: 373–4).

Similar sentiments informed the first modern military manual – the Lieber Code of 1863 that was compiled during the American Civil War in response to a request from the North for ethical guidelines regarding the conduct of its conflict with the Southern Confederacy.[1] They also influenced the earliest humanitarian laws of war including the St Petersburg Declaration of 1868 which was the first international legal convention to prohibit the use of certain weapons, specifically the explosive bullet that was condemned for causing needless suffering. The use of such instruments of violence was deemed to be impermissible in wars between 'civilized nations'. The Convention emphasized that there comes a point at which the 'necessities of war ought to yield to the requirements of humanity'. The 'progress of civilization', the thesis was, 'should have the effect of alleviating as much as possible the calamities of war'; it dictated that nations should refrain from using weapons that went beyond what was essential to weaken the enemy, and inflicted suffering that was 'contrary to the laws of humanity' (Roberts and Guelff 2001: 53–5). The Lieber Code and the St Petersburg Doctrine both sought to restrain the tendency in war to inflate notions of military necessity and to muddy the crucial moral distinction between what is essential to survive and what is merely convenient or advantageous. The Lieber Code (*General Orders 100*) explicitly defended standards of self-restraint that were designed to deter actions that were based on loose conceptions of strategic necessity: 'Military necessity', it maintained, 'does not admit of cruelty, that is, infliction of suffering for the sake of suffering or for revenge, nor of maiming or wounding

---

[1] A specialist study of military manuals in long-term perspective would provide further insights into the European civilizing process that Elias derived from analysing early manners-books (see Tallett 1992: 122ff. on the Articles of War in the sixteenth and seventeenth centuries; also Contamine 2000: 180ff.).

except in fight, nor of torture to extort confessions ... nor of the wanton devastation of a district ... and in general, ... military necessity does not include any act of hostility which makes the return of peace unnecessarily difficult' (cited in Wells 1992: 35).

Support for the cosmopolitan duty to refrain from causing 'unnecessary suffering' was an advance in defending the 'civilized' principle that solidarity between the suffering is the basis for enlarging the moral and political boundaries of community (Linklater 2011: 122ff.). It was evidence of the 'international ethic' that was thought – and here it is useful to recall Wight's remarks about morality and world politics that were cited at the start of the present investigation – to distinguish modern societies from 'simpler peoples', although it is clear that such 'civilized' sensibilities developed in tandem with the process of state formation that simultaneously promoted internal pacification and exposed more and more people to the destructive effects of ever more violent warfare. It is unsurprising that the idea of civilization that was used to describe the reduced tolerance of violence and increased sensitivity to suffering played a central role in efforts to reduce the gulf between the 'two moralities'. Its significance for changing attitudes to the use of force in international relations extended from the critique of exaggerated conceptions of strategic necessity and acts of cruelty to the proposition that was expressed in the section of the Lieber Code which stated that 'civilized nations look with horror upon offers or rewards for the assassination of enemies as relapses into barbarism' (see Thomas 2001: 57ff.).

The 'civilized' ethical commitments that were embodied in the Lieber Code and the St Petersburg Conventions also shaped the Hague Conventions of 1899 and 1907. An explicit link with civilization was made by the Russian jurist, Feodor Martens, who stated, in the preamble to the second Convention, that its regulations, which declared that 'the right of belligerents to adopt means of injuring the enemy is not unlimited' (Roberts and Guelff 2001: 77), were 'derived from the usage, established among civilized peoples, from the laws of humanity, and the dictates of the public conscience' (Howard 1994: 7–8). The defence of that international ethic owed much to the pressures on European governments to make public concessions to the peace movements while continuing to prepare for future wars (Best 1989). Intriguingly, the important international legal measures to tame sovereign states that appeared in the late nineteenth century asserted the superiority of 'civilization' over *Kultur*, a concept that German thinkers had employed several decades earlier in an attempt to build a distinctive national identity in direct opposition to the universal claims that were central to the French idea of civilization (Koskenniemi 2001: 71ff.; also Elias 2012: 15ff.). As the custodian of 'the legal conscience of the civilized world', the international legal fraternity gave powerful expression to Enlightenment virtues of moderation and self-restraint and set Protestant liberal ideas against the dominant nationalist constructions of male identity that celebrated the personal tests and challenges of warfare (Koskenniemi 2001: ch. 1). The Enlightenment affirmation of 'ordinary life' was embodied in the laws of war in opposition to the 'heroic' ideals of the traditional aristocratic warrior culture. It was a crucial phase in the ongoing 'taming of the warriors' that was required by the dictates of 'civilization'. However, Enlightenment cosmopolitan ideals were already on the defensive by the time those cosmopolitan harm conventions regarding 'unnecessary suffering' were agreed. The Concert system created an international environment in which humanitarian movements were freer to develop but, by the 1860s, an opposing trend – the growing militarization of society – was already apparent (Best 1998).

A central theme in process sociology is that the social habitus – the prevailing everyday attitudes and behaviour – tends to lag behind the unplanned and unexpected interweaving of lives in lengthening chains of mutual dependence. Deeply embedded emotional dispositions invariably change slowly while social interconnections and their attendant dangers forge ahead. Faced with an alarming pace of change that they cannot control, and do not understand, people may look to their existing 'survival units' to protect them. They may become even more emotionally bound to national communities whose past sacrifices and struggles are etched in their collective identities and memories and which are the source of shared pride and feelings of difference from, or superiority over, other peoples. The consolidation of traditional solidarities may give rise to new rivalries at the very time when the greatest challenge is to create a new we–I balance that combines loyalties to established 'survival units' with attachments to untested international associations that represent an advance to a higher level of social and political integration (Elias 2010b: 199ff.). The process-sociological approach therefore highlights the tensions between the dominant sociogenetic and psychogenetic forces in such periods and the changes in orientation towards the social world that are imperative if people are to become attuned to expanding chains of co-dependence and to deal with the associated shared political problems effectively. Notwithstanding their limitations, the three developments surveyed above were important attempts to exercise greater checks on unplanned international processes, to create higher levels of social integration and new forms of political cooperation through the formation of international governmental and non-governmental organizations, and to promote related changes in the social habitus. In their different ways they were illustrations of a growing recognition of the urgency of altering the traditional relationship between national, international and humanitarian responsibilities in the general direction that Kant and other Enlightenment thinkers had advocated.

The Nationalization of Suffering

But as already noted, the future did not belong to the cosmopolitans. The nationalized conceptions of political community that emerged with the French Revolution are often thought to mark the end of the Enlightenment. To document the central change, many scholars have distinguished between 'civic' and 'ethnic' nationalism. The more open and tolerant civic forms of the nation have been contrasted with the ethnic versions that are associated with xenophobic orientations towards other peoples and with weak restraints on violent dispositions (Kohn 1944). In the writings of Hume or Voltaire, the civic mode was thought to be critical for significant achievements in securing fundamental liberties in 'civilized' societies – they did not celebrate the collective identity of the narrowly defined ethnos (Schlereth 1977: 109ff.). Most Enlightenment thinkers believed they were living in a progressive era in which local ties were being modified by cosmopolitan concern for the suffering of other people. However, as is clear from the writings of Rousseau, Burke and Herder, late eighteenth-century social and political thought was far from devoid of sentiments that would influence 'ethnic' nationalism (see Best 1998: 56–9). Those were the strands of political theory that revolutionaries such as Robespierre found most congenial in the struggle against the 'English barbarians' (Bell 2001: ch. 3).

The point was made in the previous section that the wars that followed the French Revolution set particular trends in motion that demonstrated that concerns about suffering were not confined to the community of co-nationals. New and more cosmopolitan sensibilities certainly developed. But those military conflicts also had precisely the opposite effect of generating images of war, nationality and destructive masculinity that became central motifs in the collectivist ideologies of the era. The tension between those standpoints, one envisaging increasingly interconnected societies collaborating to bring pointless suffering to an end, the other celebrating warfare as a test of manliness and as a means of finding personal meaning, was central to the shape of the European civilizing process in the period under discussion. The unstoppable transition from the mercenary to the volunteer army following the French Revolution, and the rise of conscript forces that replaced the earlier 'multinational' forces, created new links between male identity, exclusionary nationalist ideologies and total warfare (Thomson 1994: ch. 2).

Expectations of a more cosmopolitan political future were shattered then by the rise of the modern totalizing nation-state. There is no space here to consider how the change from identification between members of the same ethnos to identification between those who belonged to the same 'imagined nation' took place. Suffice it to note that state-building, rising levels of internal social and economic integration, and persistent geopolitical rivalries combined to generate powerful emotional attachments to potent symbols of sovereign independence. They interacted to give 'conscience formation' a distinctive national colouration that was radically different from what had gone before. New forms of collective conceit and 'self-love' appeared that were linked with a pronounced tendency to demonize enemies that was either shaped by earlier military achievements and imperial conquests or forged in defeat through shared indignation at intolerable injustices (Bell 2001). What is important for the present discussion is how such social processes gave rise to the nationalization of suffering – the trend towards memorializing sacrifices for the nation that developed alongside the commemoration of collective resilience in the face of external threats and the lurch towards 'totalizing' ideologies that diminished the significance of the suffering of other peoples and devalued their struggles with similar ordeals. As noted earlier, the exact influence of nationalism on those that fought for Napoleon or for the revolutionary armies is hard to assess. But the revolution certainly glorified sacrifice for the nation and one of its principal legacies was to bring 'nationalized suffering' to the forefront of European social and political life.

The conversion of 'peasants' into 'citizens' represented a significant widening of the scope of emotional identification between strangers that has been intrinsic to the modern civilizing process (Weber 1977). Heroic status was no longer the preserve of elite noble warriors but was democratized with the rise of nationalism. Men were 'virilized' in the course of identifying more closely with an explicitly 'feminized' national community, constructed through images of an 'alluring female body' (Landes 2004). The egalitarian dimensions of the national ethos conferred a heroic standing on ordinary citizen-soldiers who had volunteered to fight for, and more importantly to die for, their country. It marked a shift towards democratizing the commemoration of sacrifice and suffering that reached its zenith with the 'tombs of the Unknown Soldiers' which were monuments at the end of the First World War to the belief that all were equal – irrespective of rank – in the sacrificial struggle for the nation (Mosse 1990: 92ff.; Anderson 1983: 17ff., 132; Winter 2012). The unifying symbolism of public memorials for fallen soldiers demarcated 'the sacred spaces of a new civic religion' (Mosse 1990: ch. 2).

War-weariness, economic constraints, and the elite fears of large conscript armies that were noted earlier led to the preference for smaller professional armies. But particularly over the last three decades of the nineteenth century, the dominant trend in Prussia and elsewhere was towards coupling short-term conscription with the creation of a large-scale reserve force that could be mobilized and thrown into battle at short notice (French 1997). Although Bismarck's wars had been relatively restrained, any hope that the next major conflict would be anything less than 'total' had all but disappeared by 1900 as a result of the invention of new military technologies (Howard 1983: 63ff.). 'Growing disquiet' emerged *circa* 1899–1907 that states were on a collision course that could lead to unprecedented destruction (Best 1989). However, political and military leaders generally thought that large-scale armies could not be kept in the field for long. Future wars looked certain to be very bloody, but they might have the compensating virtue of being relatively short. In Britain, for instance, death in warfare had come to be regarded as 'noble' and 'heroic' but as increasingly '*unlikely*' (Cannadine 1981, italics in original). From around the end of the 1871 Franco-Prussian War, European societies became suffused with 'a mixture of militarism and bellicose nationalism' (French 1997: 69ff.). In Britain, the resulting ideological cocktail linked masculinity with destructive nationalism and with considerable enthusiasm for participation in military combat. Fuelled by imperialism, racism and social Darwinism, that orientation celebrated the 'pleasures of war' while reinventing medieval notions of chivalry in defence of the thesis that force was indefensible unless it promoted a just and honourable, national cause (Paris 2000: 23ff.). A powerful strand of 'popular militarism' assumed that warfare was natural and legitimate while engagement in conflict was a crucial part of male identity centred on the thrill of foreign adventures, the opportunities for testing personal courage, and the joys of camaraderie that had all but been lost with the coming of the dull routines of bourgeois society (Mosse 1985: ch. 6; Paris 2000: 8). Significantly, some of the most influential proponents of the 'quest for excitement' in war combined the belief in the elevating role of warfare with the critique of Enlightenment thinkers who, in aiming to abolish war, were 'the real pest of *civilization*' which was the word they always had 'on their lips' (Ernst Jünger, cited in Gat 2001: 601, italics added; Kramer 2007: ch. 5; also Elias 2013: appendix x).

It is difficult to comprehend the psychology of the vast number of those who responded so willingly to Kitchener's summons to fight for their country without recalling the influence of 'popular militarism' and patriotic loyalty as well the belief that the war against Germany was a just struggle that was undertaken 'in the name of "civilization"' (Elias 2012: 19). German atrocities in Belgium fuelled the collective belief in undertaking a moral crusade or in fighting, as Asquith put it, 'in defence of principles the maintenance of which is vital to the civilization of the world' (Paris 2000; Kramer 2007: ch. 1; Goebel 2012). Interestingly, in the light of the development of the idea of civilization in the late eighteenth century, the French government, the national press and various public intellectuals described the war as a conflict between German *Kultur* and Western civilization (Kramer 2007: ch. 5). How far powerful nationalist loyalties explained the willingness of 'civilized' people to continue fighting in 'barbarous' conditions is a different matter. Letters from German and British soldiers to family members rarely mentioned sacrifice for the nation (Roper 2004). Military discipline, the fear of punishment, and solidarity with peers appear to have been far more influential in attuning those involved to the appalling conditions on the front. Hatred and fear of the enemy undoubtedly helped 'civilized' people adjust to the brutalities of industrialized trench warfare (Kramer 2007: 238ff.).

Several accounts of the soldier's experience of the First World War invite a brief discussion of the impact of the broader civilizing process. The general assumption that future wars would be fought with restraint, and high levels of confidence in technological progress, meant that 'civilized' peoples were, in the main, wholly unprepared for the ordeal of mechanized slaughter (Cruickshank 1982). Members of the armed forces quickly came to the realization that their 'civilized' condition and taboos against violence were more precarious than they had thought. Sensitivity to violence seems to have increased in the period between 1870 and 1914 with the consequence that soldiers frequently expressed horror at the unfamiliar and disturbing sights and smells of warfare (Hewitson 2007). They became attuned to mass killing although, as the analysis of the European civilizing process would lead one to suppose, post-war personal narratives rarely expressed joy in killing or pleasure in violent destruction (Ferguson 1998: ch. 12). Indeed, some barely mentioned killing at all but focused on the hardships of making the transition from normal civilian life where death was rarely encountered to the unexpected horrors of the front (Hynes 1998: 66ff.).

The sheer scale of the human disaster has encouraged the view that the First World War represented a wholly new point of departure, although whether it was proportionately more catastrophic than earlier wars is far from certain. The percentage of serving soldiers killed in the Franco-Prussian War appears to have been as high as the percentage of those who lost their lives in the First World War (Kramer 2007: introduction). The length of the conflict was clearly different, as was the percentage of the total population that was enlisted in the national militaries. But what was even more significant was the timescale in which mass slaughter took place. As many as one third of the sixty thousand British troops who were killed at the Somme died in the first hour, and possibly in the first few minutes, of the start of the military offensive (Keegan 1991: 255, 305). In the end, the question is not whether the number who died in the First World War was higher than the number who perished in earlier conflicts, either in absolute terms or in proportion to the total populations of the societies involved; it is about assessing its political salience in the light of key features of the civilizing process. The impact of the numbers who were killed or injured on national memory cannot be separated from changing social attitudes to death in that period. It was widely assumed in Britain and in many other European countries from around the 1880s that children would outlive their parents as a result of major improvements in public health and hygiene (Cannadine 1981). The First World War shattered growing optimism about life expectancy. The personal and public significance of death in military conflict was heightened at the very moment when the symbolic importance of 'death in the present in peacetime was markedly diminished' (Cannadine 1981: 232). Arguably, in that context, the feeling that lives had been squandered or pointlessly lost was felt all the more intensely.

It was inevitable that the more general attitudes to life and death in 'civilized' societies would influence popular reactions to the slaughter of the First World War. Millions bore witness to public displays of grief and gratitude in the annual patriotic commemorations of the war dead (Winter 1995). National memorialization reflected the reality that virtually every family shared the same fate of mourning the death of one or more close family members as well as friends and neighbours in the relevant local community whose names are engraved on the war memorials that survive in small rural villages to this day. But it was no less surprising that the European civilizing process at that time was profoundly shaped by the experience of war. 'Civilized' attitudes to war deaths over the last hundred years owe more than a little to the painful memory of unfulfilled lives that were destroyed in what many regarded as meaningless conflict.

The totality of the First World War was the culmination at the time of the dominant European pattern of social and political development since the emergence of the nation-in-arms in the aftermath of the French Revolution. It was exemplified by the greater material and cultural interconnectedness of national citizens, by the state's capacity to mobilize millions of peoples in violent combat, and by increasingly industrialized warfare where advanced technologies were used to break the enemy's will with little regard for legal and moral restraints. Those developments created a heightened sense of the gulf between higher levels of human interconnectedness and the prevalent nationalist orientations that were incapable of bringing such dynamics under some degree of control. Awareness of the catastrophic potential of the main directions of change across Europe had been expressed in liberal analyses of the tensions within the process of civilization. Cobden warned in 1849 against the perilous state of modern industrial societies where 'improvements in science' were brought 'to bear upon the deadly contrivances of war'. Instead of 'making the progress of civilization subservient to the welfare of mankind', the 'discoveries of science' contributed to the 'barbarism of the age' (cited in Pick 1993: 27, see also ch. 9 on the new form of 'cultural critique' that compared industrial civilization and its mode of warfare to a 'driverless train'). Reactions to the First World War stressed the collective disaster that had befallen the peoples of Europe as well as the individual catastrophe for each of the societies involved (Winter 1995). The scale of the conflict promoted recognition of how traditional national solutions to security fears compounded the problems of societies that were locked in struggles that none could control – a problem that the stillborn experiment of the League of Nations was meant to solve. It is hardly surprising that the Great War was portrayed as the last European conflict – 'the war to end all wars' – as more

Europeans, stripped of their innocence, recognized the urgency of dealing with the fatal combination of national forms of emotional identification and the state's capacity to harness unprecedented industrial power in armed struggle. But given the nature of the civilizing process, it is no less surprising that the major powers could not convert a realistic diagnosis of the nature of their predicament and entrapment in the era of industrialized warfare into effective action to build international organizations that upheld new standards of self-restraint as part of a changed we–I balance that extended the scope of emotional identification between peoples who increasingly shared a common fate.

So great was the scale of human suffering that the First World War can be regarded as a 'dividing line' in the history of militarism (Ceadel 1989: 35). The idea of the liberating role of military combat that had been defended by Jünger and others could no longer command much popular support in the stable, liberal democracies after the experience of the First World War. During the 1920s and 1930s, narratives that celebrated the fulfilling role of warfare were confined to fascist movements and regimes. A revitalized peace campaign enjoyed considerable popular support in Britain although influential cinematic portrayals of the conflict typically disseminated patriotic celebrations of courage rather than an internationalist narrative about the larger human tragedy (Paris 2000: ch. 5). The expectation of, and readiness for, violence was already evident elsewhere. In France, the idea of the 'community of suffering' venerated soldiers and abhorred war, but it was largely taken for granted that the number of casualties in any future conflict might exceed even the slaughter of World War One. 'Anti-war sentiment' gave way with the rise of National Socialism to 'widespread pessimism' about the ability of the European great powers to prevent 'self-destructive conflict' (Overy 2012: 185ff.). The post-war pacifist movement in Germany was quickly sidelined by nationalist groups that condemned it for effectively throwing its weight behind the Versailles Settlement, thereby aggravating the sore of collective humiliation that was encapsulated by the idea of the 'stab in the back' (Mosse 1990: ch. 8, 196). Any fear of a return to war was counterbalanced by the conviction that the trinity of war, nationalism and aggressive masculinity formed the gateway to higher levels of human experience (Bartov 2000: 18ff.). The main trends in Germany support the view that the First World War led to the profound brutalization of society and politics, and to the subversion of 'civilized' values. On some accounts, 'industrial killing' in the First World War, the fascistic belief that it was necessary to prepare to inflict equivalent harm in future conflicts, and the Holocaust were part of one overall pattern of development (Bartov 1996: ch. 2). The liberal democracies failed to give political expression to the universal features of human suffering that had been highlighted by the experience of total warfare. They were unable to find a pathway to an advanced combination of the collective management of great power relations, compelling conceptions of human solidarity, and a more powerful body of international law that was designed to tame national egoism and encourage higher levels of foreign policy restraint. That had to await the catastrophic effects of the importation of nationalist racism from Europe's relations with 'colonized inferiors' into the 'civilized' world itself.

Long-Distance Warfare and Impersonal Violence

During the French Revolution, the Hebertists and Girondins believed that there was something inherently immoral and unmanly about fighting from a safe distance as opposed to engaging in traditional hand-to-hand combat that demanded personal courage and heightened the emotional gratifications of warfare (Bell 2007: 140; see Hanson 1989 on parallel themes in classical antiquity). Such orientations to war that compared military conflict to a duel have been detected in the code of chivalry that allegedly governed aerial combat during the First World War (Bourke 1999: 62–3; Robertson 2003: 235ff.). They raise interesting questions about how far a strong element of emotional identification bound together the same strata in different national armies. At Waterloo, infantry were more likely to surrender to enemy counterparts, as did members of the cavalry, thereby reducing the risk of cruelty (Keegan 1991: 321). The general theme has been raised in many other contexts – for example, with respect to snipers who have been compared to cold-blooded murderers rather than authentic warriors who observe the principles of fair play (Bourke 1999: 66–7). Orwell's discussion of the 'naked soldier syndrome' (the reluctance to kill a defenceless opponent) has been noted elsewhere, along with his remarks about the enemy pilot who was the indifferent instrument of impersonal violence – the warrior who would rejoin his family after a bombing mission without giving much thought to the suffering of invisible victims (Linklater 2011: 174, n32; Walzer 1978: 138ff.). Distance shielded the attacker from the devastation. It permitted acts of 'savagery' without the spur of cruel instincts and with a reduced exposure to guilt, shame or self-reproach.

The age of long-distance warfare had been predicted by the Italian thinker, Douhet, in his 1921 work, *The Command of the Air*. The argument was that military conflicts would become shorter and more 'civilized' if they blurred the dividing line between belligerents and non-belligerents so that civilians could not avoid violent harm (Douhet 2003 [1921]:158ff.). The Italian offensive against Abyssinia has been described as the first instance of a deliberate aerial assault on civilians – although during the First World War, it has been argued, the general direction of modern conflict was already evident in the fact that direct physical combat with the enemy was unusual in the context of trench warfare (Coker 2007: 18ff.). The rise of impersonal killing and long-distance violent harm has raised intriguing questions for studies of the relationship between war and the civilizing process. With the development of modern 'civilized' self-images, Elias maintained, death and dying have been concealed 'behind the scenes' along with various practices that also arouse revulsion and disgust. People are less likely to witness public violence. They are less attuned than their medieval forbears were to killing and to death, in peacetime and in war. On that argument, the ability to cause long-distance harm has the obvious merit of protecting those who inflict violence from the traumatic psychological effects of directly witnessing the death, pain and mutilation of others.

Several military historians have reflected on how the 'civilized' dampening of violent and aggressive impulses has affected the modern soldier's willingness to kill. General S. L. A. Marshall's observed in 1947 that the army could not 'unmake' modern man but 'must reckon with the fact that he comes from a civilization in which aggression, connected with the taking of life, is prohibited and unacceptable', or perhaps from a way of life in which 'the fear of aggression has been expressed to him so strongly and absorbed by him so deeply and pervadingly', that it surfaces as the 'greatest handicap when he enters combat. It stays his trigger finger even though he is hardly conscious that it is a restraint upon him' (cited in Keegan 1991: 73–4, 314ff.). Studies of the differences between proximate and remote killing have stated that it is undoubtedly more wicked to destroy ten thousand people by artillery fire than to pommel one person to death with a stone, but the latter act is 'by far the more psychologically difficult act', particularly, it should be added, for those who have been exposed to a civilizing process that establishes, through routine patterns of socialization, expectations that people will refrain from causing violent harm in peaceful circumstances (Milgram 1974: 175). Observations about the restraining effects of 'civilization' have included studies of Vietnam veterans that were amongst the first to show that the violation of 'civilized' social taboos against violence can lead to profound psychological anguish in later life. The evidence suggested that the main reason for personal guilt was 'the ultimate transgression' which was 'joy in killing and mutilating' as well as moral indifference to the fate of children 'whom adults are supposed to nurture and protect' (Lifton 1974: 105, 206). The incidence of 'personal traumatic injury syndrome' amongst Vietnam veterans therefore supports Marshall's view about the relationship between civilization and violence. The customary taboos against killing and wounding in face-to-face settings can be eroded quickly under conditions of heightened insecurity but the actions that follow may produce shock and shame at the unexpected weakening of what were presumed to be the strong internal inhibitions on force that were central to the 'civilized' personal identities of the people involved. Investigations of those issues have highlighted the difficulties that can arise as warriors struggle to resume traditional peaceful roles in the course of their attempted reintegration into the civilian community. The resulting psychological scarring provides a reminder that the transition from peace to war (and back) is more complex for people who have gone through the modern civilizing process than it was for warriors in the earlier states-systems of the West. The latter carried their own weapons and used them on a regular basis; they were more attuned to violence; and they were more accustomed to witnessing death and dying as a result (Elias 2013: 191, 464; Elias 2007: 145–6; Lifton 1974).

The comments that the navigator of the Ebola Gay made about the lack of 'adverse emotional reactions' to the use of the atomic bomb in August 1945 against the inhabitants of Hiroshima seem to confirm the judgment that long-distance violence undermines 'civilized' sensibilities (Lifton 1974: 346ff.). The observations support the contention that social norms have lagged behind technological developments precisely because of the absence of inhibitions on remote killing that are equivalent to the psychological restraints that can deter violence in customary 'face-to-face' settings (Milgram 1974: 175). Reliance on air power in wars over the last few decades has had the effect of protecting military personnel from the direct encounter with enemy and civilian suffering that may have disturbing psychological effects. It has extended one of the core features of the European civilizing process which has been to conceal violence behind the scenes.

A related feature of the social habitus of modern warfare is that the methods do not necessarily require the emotional arousal of warriors to the point where they so hate their adversaries that they relish the opportunity to exterminate them or to maximize their suffering – nor do they depend on publicizing the opportunities for experiencing the joys of killing, or the pleasures of plunder and rape, that were given free rein in many of the pre-industrial massacres that were discussed in previous chapters. Sophisticated technological instruments of war require a level of rational or dispassionate self-discipline – if not the actual suppression of aggressive emotions – that befit office workers or computer operators in the 'civilian' sectors of society (Elias 2007a: 128–9). But the general dampening of such impulses has clearly not had the consequence that warfare is less destructive in its results as opposed to less cruel in the underlying motivations or intentions of the participants. One of the paradoxes of the civilizing process is that it heightened sensitivities to violence and simultaneously constructed disciplined, obedient citizens who could be enlisted to take part in unpre-cedentedly destructive wars. The result of social discipline, linked at times with ideological fervour, is that 'twentieth-century man is potentially a better soldier than he of any other age', despite evidence of the 'deep antipathy to violence and to conflict' that is evident in social attitudes to capital punishment, to physical beatings and so forth (Keegan 1991: 319). The humane and compassionate features of those societies have not pre-vented the invention and use of instruments of violence that are designed to inflict wounds that are 'as terrible and terrifying as possible' (Keegan 1991: 322–3). The civilizing process therefore made modern forms of total warfare possible while generating opposition to 'unnecessary suffering' in the relations within and between societies. Modern states have acquired the capacity to mobilize all human and physical resources that highly pacified societies possess; they have made major advances in providing high levels of personal security for their citizens but, as the nuclear revolution revealed, they also exposed them to unprecedented dangers of mass incineration and destruction. Notwithstanding the impersonal nature of modern military conflicts, it has been argued, there is no radical difference 'between the torment which people threaten to inflict on each other as a result of radiation poisoning – the slow and painful death in the aftermath of an atomic battle – and the torment American Indians in the heyday of their independence continuously threatened to inflict upon each other' (Elias 2007a: 128–9). However, most of the citizens of the societies that can inflict such harm almost certainly think that they are considerably more 'humane' and 'civilized', and they are probably convinced that they would only tolerate such violence if nothing less than the survival of their society was at stake.

Exactly such a process took place during the Second World War as 'civilized' peoples became reconciled to inflicting ever more destructive violence against civilians. Ruling elites came to accept the 'military necessity' of targeting civilian populations in cities such as Dresden (see Harris 1947: 242), but not without first shedding inhibitions against deliberate attacks that expressed either the moral reluctance to break valued taboos or the fear of retaliation (Gat 2001: 789ff.; Legro 1995; Overy 2013: ch. 5). The relevant social inhibitions were weakened in the customary way, as part of the politics of 'tit for tat'. Dissenting groups did not fail to make their protests heard. Opposition to the British bombing campaign on moral and religious grounds was expressed in both Houses of Parliament. However, dominant elite opinion – endorsed by the public for the most part – was closer to Arthur (Bomber) Harris' judgment about how the struggle against Germany should be conducted. It has been argued that Harris believed that the Government should be frank about the bombing campaign, and stressed that 'there was nothing to be ashamed of, except in the sense that everybody might be ashamed of the sort of thing that has to be done in every war, as of war itself' (cited in Probert 2003: 193). His standpoint was influenced by the desire to spare his men the carnage of the First World War. In spite of what occurred in cities such as Hamburg, he argued, 'bombing proved a comparatively humane method', and not least by saving 'the flower of the youth' of Britain and its allies from being 'mown down by the military in the field, as it was in Flanders' (Harris 1947: 176). He maintained that the lives of civilians have always been sacrificed in the history of military conflict, specifically in siege warfare, a practice that continued 'even in the more civilized times of to-day;' he added (erroneously) that with respect to 'the use of aircraft in war, there is, it so happens, no international law at all', and therefore no external constraint on the ancient custom of 'maximum bombardment' whenever a city takes the course of 'continued resistance' (Harris 1947: 177; also Robertson 2003 on similar themes in the development of US strategic thinking).

For its part, the British government prevaricated, privately authorizing the 'terror bombing' of German cities in the hope of destroying the morale of the German people but unwilling to publicize its real military and political objectives and preferring to describe civilian casualties as an unintended consequence of attacks on military targets rather than as official policy (Bellamy 2012: ch. 4). Its purported position was entirely 'consistent with the widely held view in Britain that indiscriminate bombing was the hallmark of barbarism, whereas self-restraint was a feature of being civilized' (Overy 2013: 239). Towards the end of the war, Churchill, in a memorandum to the Chief of Staff, began to distance himself from the strategy he had earlier championed, possibly troubled by public perceptions of how the allies had lost the moral high ground, if not feeling along with many others a sense of shame about the scale of the destruction that a 'civilized' society had caused through 'mere acts of terror and wanton destruction' (Garrett 1993: 18ff.; Taylor 2004: 375–6; Overy 2013: 395–6).

Turning to the conflict with Japan, the fog of war meant that the aerial bombardment of Tokyo in March 1945, and the atomic bomb attacks on Hiroshima and Nagasaki five months later, prevented major public debates about the ethics of attacking civilians – although the American air force had initially opted for 'daylight precision bombing' rather than the saturation bombing that was favoured by the British given the failure to destroy the principal German targets (Crane 2002). The American strategy according to Lieutenant General Doolittle, Commander of the Eighth Air force in 1944–45, was 'the most ethical way to go' (cited in Crane 2002: 229). The inner circle that decided on the atomic bomb attacks did not pause to consider the moral issues that were raised by their course of action – or rather, they believed that the important ethical questions had already been settled. There were many dimensions to their moral certainty, including the conviction that, as public trustees, state officials had the political responsibility to use weapons that others, for reasons of personal conscience, might not wish to deploy. The influence of racist assumptions about Japanese inferiority cannot be discounted although they do not seem to have had a significant role in the decision to attack Japanese cities. Three factors appear to have been more important: the belief that Japanese forces would fight to the death for the emperor rather than suffer the dishonour of a humiliating surrender; the supposition that an emphatic victory was needed to prevent the rise of a dangerous parallel to the post-First World War nationalist conviction in Germany that the military had been 'stabbed in the back' rather than truly defeated; and the belief that nothing less than total destruction that brought the horrors of war directly into the lives of every family was necessary to eliminate Japanese militarism (see Dower [1986: 55ff.] on Western beliefs that the Japanese were gripped by a primitive, herd mentality that placed them beyond the pale of 'civilization'). It was widely believed that Japanese aggression, its atrocities in China, including the Rape of Nanking in late 1937, and cruelty towards Allied prisoners of war, justified maximum force. The 'total mobilization of society' in the age of industrial warfare underpinned the contention that 'there (were) no innocent civilians'. Curtis LeMay, Commander of XXI Bomber Command, expressed that view-point when he argued that the 'entire population', including 'men, women and children' were involved in one way or another in supporting the munitions industry (cited in Grayling 2006: 142). As in the case of the British assaults on German cities, there were dissenting voices including scientists such as Niels Bohr who expressed concern not only about the relevant 'humanitarian' issues but also about how any failure to inform Stalin of the proposed atomic bomb attacks would affect future relations between the United States and the Soviet Union (Alperowitz 1996: chs. 12 and 14). Leading military figures such as Admiral William D. Leahy expressed shock that the war had been enlarged to include assaults on women and children with the result that the United States had, in an interesting comparison, 'adopted an ethical standard common to the barbarians of the Dark Ages' (Alperowitz 1996: 3). Evidence that the Japanese war effort was virtually exhausted led some US leaders to argue that surrender could be accomplished by demonstrating the destructive power of the atomic bomb without harming civilians. The Under Secretary of the Navy, Ralph Bard, who resigned over the decision to attack the Japanese cities, had earlier championed such a demonstration of force on the grounds that it was required by the American sense of 'fair play' (Clark 1982: 234–6). But such concerns were outweighed by the belief that the employment of the means of aerial destruction against the 'enemies of civilization' was wholly justified (Overy 2013: 247ff.). Close parallels with earlier perspectives on the rights of 'civilized' peoples against 'barbarians' will be apparent.

Ongoing debates about the morality of bombing German cities such as Dresden and about the rights and wrongs of recognizing Bomber Command through public memorials provide insights into contemporary understandings of violence and civilization, as do continuing controversies about the use of the atomic bomb against Japanese cities (Walzer 1978: 323ff.; Grayling 2006; also Probert 2003: ch. 17, postscript; Garrett 1993: xii–xiv). They have developed in conjunction with widespread support for a new 'bombing norm' (strictly speaking, an anti-bombing norm that affirms the moral duty not to target civilians in order to win wars) that has had a 'civilizing' influence on world politics since the end of the Second World War (Thomas 2001). The principle can be regarded as evidence of how the reduced tolerance of violence that has been one of the main features of the European civilizing process has come to be expressed in greater public concerns about avoidable civilian suffering in warfare (Wheeler 2002).

The belief that war is no longer a rational method of resolving major political differences between the great powers is part of a major shift in Western attitudes towards the use of force that includes the belief that the lives of co-nationals should not be squandered in warfare and the conviction that 'collateral damage' to civilians ought to be minimized. The two goals are not always compatible. Air power has played a prominent role in the wars that Western powers have waged since the end of the bipolar order on the grounds that it can accomplish the rapid dismemberment of the enemy's military and political capabilities while greatly minimizing the death and injury of members of the attacking armed forces. Critics have argued that the effect has been to transfer exposure to death and injury to civilians in the target societies while insisting that they were not deliberately targeted and implying that their suffering was proportionate to strategic objectives. Far from being more 'civilized' than earlier warfare, it has been contended, modern wars remain 'fundamentally degenerate' not just because of inevitable civilian deaths and injury caused by 'small massacres', but also because of the 'indirect, less visible and less quantifiable', as well as the 'more acceptable', injuries that result from deliberate assaults on the social and economic infrastructure (Shaw 2005: 82–89; Thomas 2001: ch. 5). For their part, military leaders and government officials have described efforts to 'humanize' Western wars by deploying 'nonlethal weapons' that demonstrate 'reverence for life' and the 'commitment to the use of minimum force'; they have been described as 'kinder, gentler operations' that provide 'proof of our civility and restraint' (US Colonel Martin Stanton, cited in Freedman 1998: 16). Disputes over the legality and morality of drone warfare – and about the more general direction of the Western way of warfare – highlight the debate between the claim that modern military technologies unnecessarily harm civilians and the opposing contention that they provide evidence of increased concerns about civilian suffering that distinguish the most recent phase of the civilizing process (Vogel 2011; Crawford 2013; Enemark 2014).

The fact remains that Western publics are uneasy about disproportionate civilian suffering, in part because of sympathy for other peoples, but also because of unease with, or opposition to, violence that contradicts 'civilized' self-images. Opposition to torture in the aftermath of 9/11, and shock at the public disclosure of the atrocities at Abu Ghraib illustrate the latter point, but those reactions do not alter the reality of significant indifference to 'the deaths of others' in war, or undermine confidence that, in 'civilized' societies, atrocities are now rare and extraordinary (Tirman 2011: 302ff.). Resistance to weakening the relevant taboos against unnecessary violent harm is lower when 'civilized', liberal societies face challenges from 'uncivilized', illiberal political movements that elicit strong feelings of hostility and contempt (Coker 2001: ch. 6; Robinson 2006: 176ff.; Tirman 2011: ch. 11). Controversies about the tensions and ambiguities, hypocrisies and inconsistencies, of modern military conflict point to the continuing problem of bringing the conduct of war into line with standards of self-restraint that befit the civilizing process. Ongoing debates revolve around the opposition between the belief that a more humane mode of warfare that complies with higher ethical ideals is not beyond the reach of modern societies and the conviction that there are no grounds for departing from Clausewitzian pessimism about the possibility of ever 'civilizing' warfare. Such disputes are a reminder that 'civilized societies' find themselves in peculiar 'entanglements' that did not exist in earlier societies (Elias 2012: 8).

Advancing Global Civility?

This chapter began by citing Elias's contention that all that changes in the history of warfare are the methods of killing and the number of people involved. The clear implication is that the similarities between states-systems are at least as great as – if not greater than – the differences. That standpoint resonates with statements about patterns of recurrence and repetition in world politics that coexist uneasily with the claim that modern peoples possess conceptions of 'international ethics' that were unknown to 'simpler' civilizations. It is arguable that the modern states-system is at least the equal of its predecessors with respect to massacres. The industrialized slaughters that occurred because of the aerial bombardment of cities during the Second World War are the modern counterparts of pre-industrial mass killings in the earlier states-systems. Such conjectures lend support to Clausewitz's argument that the revolutions in warfare have always run ahead of efforts to impose 'civilized' controls on the state's monopoly control of the instruments of violence.

The first two chapters of this work maintained that ancient Greek, Hellenistic and Roman armies were much freer to act violently than are industrial societies today. They did not face the same need to restrain their behaviour. New levels of violent harm emerged with the industrialization of warfare, but incentives to control the use of force also increased significantly. It was already evident at the end of First World War that advances in the power to harm had to come under greater control, 'so intricately [were] the resources of civilized states interwoven' (Fuller 1923: 75). It had become imperative, assuming that war would not be abolished, to learn how to wage it in a 'manner less injurious to the interwoven fabric of modern civilization' (Liddell Hart 1925: 22, 49ff.; Gat 2001: 531ff.). But such understandings were not converted into effective global steering mechanisms in the interwar period.

At the end of the Second World War, the stable liberal democracies attempted to alter the 'rules of the game' and, in so doing, raised the question of whether they were poised to make substantial progress in 'breaking out of the vicious circle of defining enemies and making victims' that had character- ized so much of the violence of the preceding decades; the relevant states confronted the 'totalizing project' that had fused nationalism, territoriality, citizenship and sovereignty with devastating results (Bartov 2000: 91; Linklater 1998: ch. 1). That did not inaugurate an entirely new phase in the history of the modern states-system or in the development of the Western states-systems more generally. Revolutions in the capacity to inflict violent harm did not come to an end. But the balance of power between different sides of the European civilizing process altered in important respects. Significantly paci- fied states continued to invent more destructive forms of power, but the ethical sensibilities that were part of the same overall pattern of development acquired greater influence on the constitution of international society.

The Second World War altered general attitudes to death and suffering in an even more fundamental way than the First World War had. The 'shadow of death' had been 'lightened at the personal level' as a result of domestic welfare systems, but it was 'intensified at the global level' because civilians had been in the front line of warfare, as images of Hiroshima and Nagasaki, and the first reports of the scale of human suffering at Belsen and the other Nazi death camps, revealed (Cannadine 1981: 235ff.). Diplomatic parallels to the innova- tions that took place at the end of the Napoleonic Wars were evident in the recognition of the need for closer great power cooperation in order to exercise higher levels of control over dangerous strategic interconnections. The nuclear era would create a major paradox of high levels of personal security in the most stable social systems coexisting with the prospect of 'universal death' as a result of superpower conflict (Morgenthau 1971). There was no guarantee that the great powers would avoid a full-scale nuclear war – nor is there a warranty today that they will do so forevermore or long into the future. But the nuclear revolution created new incentives to exercise high levels of foresight and restraint in foreign policy. That trajectory of development was part of the 'long process of pacification and integration of ever larger territories, now encompassing the world as a whole' (van den Bergh 1992: 44). It had to be seen in conjunction with the patterns of state-formation and rising levels of human interconnectedness within societies that resulted in the earlier 'civilizing' of conduct (see Chapter 5).

One example of that process was the post-war effort that had some similarities with the earlier notion of the 'civilization matrice' to bring about the permanent 'demilitarization and democratization' of Germany and 'pre-modern' Japan (Dower 1999: 79ff.; Jackson 2006; Jarausch 2006). A fundamental change in the balance of power would come about between the collective narratives of sacrifice that emerged with the revolutionary wars and the more individualized 'narratives of suffering' that have become especially prominent over the last few decades (Coker 2001: 83ff., 105ff.; Shaw 1991; Hynes 1998: ch. 6; Sontag 2003). The violence that industrialized war inflicted on civilian populations undermined the heroic qualities that the dominant warrior codes in earlier states-systems conferred on personal courage and military prowess. The upshot is that in many parts of the world, the 'militarist [became] extinct' (Ceadel 1989: 42; Mosse 1990: ch. 10; Paris 2000; Coker 2007). The nationalization of suffering has not exactly disappeared with the de-romanticization of warfare, but public commemorations in Britain and elsewhere invariably highlight the 'extraordinary' nature of personal sacrifices in societies where everyday life is governed by non-military pursuits. Co-nationals have little direct connection with foreign wars or personal acquaintance with those who participate in them; their lack of familiarity with, and understanding, of a social stratum that is largely divorced from the larger community is a distinguishing feature of 'post-military' societies.

A second and related example of the process mentioned above reveals that there are major differences between the most recent phase of the modern states-system and the preceding stages, as well as sharp contrasts with the ancient states-systems. As discussed in Chapter 1, the Hellenic civilizing process displayed relatively low degrees of sympathy for the populations of other cities and for 'barbarians'. Social and political institutions were not judged by the extent to which they complied with a 'principle of humaneness' that asserted the importance of reducing 'the pain and suffering of human beings' (see Chapter 6, p. 265). In the recent period, the steady elimination of militarism and the broader enterprise of seeking to bring great power relations under greater control were not simply orientated to the goal of constructing a stable international order. Universal and egalitarian principles that were integral to the quest for justice for individuals were no less important, as the emergence of the universal human rights culture clearly attests.

The development of human rights norms is evidence of a major change of orientation towards the double standard of morality in politics. The wisdom of the 'split within civilization' was largely taken for granted when warfare did not threaten to destroy communities that had become accustomed to higher levels of personal security within state-organized societies. It became a serious moral and political problem as a result of the increasing potential for destructive violence that highly pacified societies and highly disciplined populations had at their disposal. There has been a major shift away from the public endorsement of the Machiavellian conception of an autonomous 'political ethic' which is free from the dictates of 'ordinary morality' that had been celebrated by militaristic regimes and movements in the first half of the twentieth century. The question of what is permissible and forbidden in foreign policy was reopened in the light of particular aversions to violence amongst 'civilized' peoples. They were pushed towards such standpoints as a result of a relatively even distribution of military power that ensured that none of the great powers could escape mass destruction in the event of major war. By contrast, substantial power asymmetries in the relations between Western and non-Western societies did not encourage the same level of respect for principles of reciprocity or create strong incentives to exercise self-restraint. Even so, universal and egalitarian ethical commitments were not confined to discussions about how 'civilized' peoples should conduct their relations with each other. Enlightenment thinkers did not foresee the violent course that international politics would take in the coming decades. But the changes that have taken place over the last few decades demonstrate that they were broadly correct to envisage an overall long-term trend in which the relationship between violence and civilization has been transformed fundamentally.

9

Modernity, Civilization and the Holocaust

Like scientific mass wars, the highly organized and scientifically planned extermination of whole groups of people in specially designed death camps and sealed-off ghettos by starvation, gassing or shooting does not seem entirely out of place in an age of technically advanced mass societies.

(Elias 2013: 225)

The European civilizing process included, as discussed above, the internal pacification of modern societies, the parallel rise of constraints on aggressive impulses that operated through a deep-seated psychological revulsion against violence, and closer emotional bonds between members of the same society. Although largely unplanned, it was transformed into a conscious political project to reform society during the eighteenth and nineteenth centuries. Imperial doctrines most obviously captured the idea of a 'civilizing mission' in that period although many Enlightenment philosophers, in addition to condemning colonial cruelties, insisted that the process of civilization was far from complete within Europe itself. The 'project of modernity' captures the conception of unfinished business with respect to the establishment of social orders that promote human autonomy rather than slavish obedience to authority, that celebrate diversity and pluralism rather than bland uniformity and dogmatism, and that aim to embed ethical commitments to public reason in the rule of law (Devetak 1995). Inextricably connected with that ideal, for Kant at least, was the aspiration to extend the positive side of the civilizing process beyond territorial boundaries in the shape of close cooperation to advance towards perpetual peace. That endeavour was held to be realistic rather than utopian because of what Kant regarded as evidence of growing sympathy between specific social strata whose lives were increasingly intertwined by transnational commercial links and also because of the moral outrage that the 'enlightened' felt on learning about cruelties to colonized peoples.

The most flattering of European self-images held that further advances in civilization were more or less guaranteed although, as noted earlier, philosophers including Kant believed that progress could be reversed and that 'nothing straight [could] be constructed from such warped wood as that which man is made of' (Kant 1991 [1784a]: 46–7). From that perspective, there was nothing in the civilizing process itself that posed a major threat to continuing progress. The lurking threat was the 'animal' within human nature that civilization constantly battled against and might never completely subdue (Freud 1939: ch. 7). It is necessary to turn to the analysis of 'civilized' rationality that was undertaken by Nietzsche, Weber, Horkheimer and Adorno amongst others for the more radical idea that major barriers to progress reside in the structural characteristics of modern societies. More than any other phase in the early twentieth century, the First World War convinced European thinkers that the political problem was 'civilization' rather than dormant 'primitive' instincts (Robertson 2003: ch. 10). In more recent times, the Holocaust has been regarded as evidence that industrialized killing was not a regression to 'barbarism' but the product of modernity itself. An alternative approach which shapes the following discussion is that the Holocaust is best explained by recognizing that 'civilizing' and 'decivilizing processes' always develop in tandem; the important questions are which have the upper hand at any juncture, and what societies can do to alter the balance of power between them (Elias 2013: 230; Fletcher 1997: 82ff.).

Those observations belong to the larger reassessment of European modernity that has combined the examination of the forms of violence that are unique to contemporary societies with deep scepticism about, or direct opposition to, the idea of progress that has been associated with 'the project of the Enlightenment'. The supposed superiority of modern Western civilization fell into disrepute along the way. The Holocaust in particular has been at the heart of recent attempts to understand the complex nature of modern 'civilized' societies. By asking what in their constitution modern societies must permanently guard against, theorists of modernity and post-modernity have developed modes of investigation that are central to understanding the civilizing process (whether or not they have couched their discussions in those terms). They have raised profound questions about whether, or how far, political theory and practice should be attached to the humanitarian project of transforming the internal structure of modern societies as well as promoting cosmopolitan endeavours to modify the principles that have traditionally governed their external relations. Important debates have been centred on how far the period of Nazi rule, and especially the Holocaust, represented the abandonment of European modernity or gave violent expression to its core practices and beliefs. Those reflections on the dangers from which modern societies must protect themselves have also shaped a new phase in the civilizing process in which the rights of individual people have become more central to political communities than ever before in the history of the Western states-systems. Reference has been made to the relationship between the civilizing process, international society and humanity. As will be discussed in the next chapter, the war crimes tribunals at the end of the Second World War placed the idea of civilization at the heart of the project of reconstructing state sovereignty. Collective shock at the Nazi genocides was a major reason for the decisions to embed new cosmopolitan commitments – a cosmopolitan version of the harm principle – in the organizing principles of international society.

To consider those issues in greater detail, this chapter begins with Bauman's argument that the Holocaust was not an aberrant phase of German history but a manifestation of the latent dangers in modernity. Passing references to 'the civilizing process' indicate that his interpretation of the Holocaust was in part a critique of Elias's account of the main social and political directions of the last few centuries. It is therefore important to consider Elias's speculation that the Holocaust flowed from tendencies that are intrinsic to modern industrial societies and unleashed 'decivilizing processes' for which the majority of Europeans were entirely unprepared. A recurrent question in the vast literature on the Holocaust is how far it threw the basic tendencies of the civilizing process such as heightened sensitivity to cruelty and violence into reverse, and how far large-scale industrial killing, the 'banality of evil', and the 'bystander phenomenon' were distinctive manifestations of the social organization and social psychology of ostensibly 'civilized' peoples. Also important is the issue of how far the Nazi genocides combined features of the process of civilization with mass murder that was typical of the wars of classical antiquity and medieval crusading warfare. The question is whether it is useful to portray the Holocaust as 'civilized genocide' – whether that term is as oxymoronic or as distasteful as the idea of 'civilized warfare' or 'civilized torture' or can be usefully employed to describe major differences between modern industrialized slaughter and ancient genocidal killing that occurred during the wars between Athens and Sparta or the destructive violence of Roman imperial expansion (see Levene 2005: ch. 3). The case for using those concepts will be explored in a discussion of 'civilized' euthanasia before considering parallel themes in competing interpretations of the Holocaust. The final section of this chapter discusses one major feature of philosophical ethics in the aftermath of the Holocaust, namely the idea of a cosmopolitanism of the ordinary virtues that was most forcefully articulated in the writings of Primo Levi. The parallel reconfiguration of the relationship between sovereignty, citizenship, nationality and territoriality – the disruption of the nexus that has been fundamental to modern political communities and integral to total war and the physical extermination of other groups – has been a dominant component of a post-Second World War 'civilizing process' that has advanced the principles of the radical Enlightenment (Linklater 1998; van Benthem van den Bergh 2001). That is the subject of discussion in the next chapter.

Modernity and the Holocaust

The supposition that progress in reducing cruelty set Europe apart from other regions was central to several early attempts to come to terms with the incomprehensible violence of the Holocaust. From that standpoint, the Nazi regime could be described as 'an interruption in the normal flow of history, a cancerous growth on the body of civilized society, a momentary madness among sanity' (Bauman 2000: viii; also Elias 2013: 225). The Holocaust could be regarded as the outcome of pathological qualities that were unique to, or at least unusually pronounced in, Germany. Nothing in the German political experience had to be interpreted as issuing a general warning to modern societies about their latent potentialities for enormous violence; nothing demanded a systematic reassessment of core ideological commitments or established practices; nothing required a break with past social trends or the charting of new directions. The combined influence, it was supposed, of distinctive German cultural traits and an economic-political crisis made a largely assimilated Jewish population vulnerable to the first expressions of the anti-Semitism of the Nazi regime, namely sporadic acts of violence and expulsion from public office. By analysing the specifics of that case, it became clear that the coincidence of totalitarian rule and major war gave the Nazi regime the opportunity to launch a project of industrial killing that had seemed entirely inconceivable a few years earlier. Once the war had ended, the victors concentrated on two aims that were entirely consistent with that interpretation: punishing the military and political elite for its 'barbarism' as a step in 'recivilizing' Germany, and aiming to prevent future regressions to 'barbarism' by embedding universal human rights in the legal and political institutions of international society.

The conviction that the Holocaust was a private matter 'between the Jews and their haters' denied that larger questions about the structure of modern societies were at stake (Bauman 2000: 11). For Bauman, the challenge of understanding the Holocaust could not be detached from fundamental questions about the structural defects and limitations of modernity. In an apparent challenge to Elias's approach to longer-term patterns of change that erroneously assumed that it was a variant on the 'Whig view' of history with 'its morally elevating story of humanity emerging from pre-social barbarity', Bauman (2000: 12ff., 89) argued that the Holocaust was 'as much a product, as it was a failure, of modern civilization' (Dunning and Mennell 1998). Recent forms of societal rationalization, as expressed by the growing importance of bureaucratic authority, were a necessary (but not a sufficient) condition of 'mass murder'; to an unprecedented degree, the latter relied on an 'impersonal, well-synchronized co-ordination of autonomous yet complementary actions'; it depended on the rational, disciplined capacity to organize and harness 'skills and habits ... which best grow and thrive in the atmosphere of the office'

(Bauman 2000: 13–15). The perspective is reminiscent of Arendt's reference in the course of witnessing the trial of Adolf Eichmann to the 'banality of evil', a term that was central to the controversial and now superseded conviction that the Nazi genocides were implemented by unremarkable 'ordinary' people who routinely followed the commands of superiors and discharged the mundane, daily responsibilities of specialist bureaucratic functions in a largely detached or disinterested way (Arendt 1994).

State-administered mass killing demonstrated that earlier examples of large-scale slaughter had invariably been 'primitive, wasteful and ineffective by comparison'; in the main, in those eras, only a limited number of people could be mobilized for a limited period to eradicate a limited number of victims (Bauman 2000: 89). By organizing genocide on the model of the production line, the Nazis succeeded in eliminating millions of people without inciting mass hatred or fostering the joy in killing amongst the German population at large. The approach broadly confirms Elias's thesis that the violent, the distressing and the disgusting were gradually pushed behind the scenes and screened from public view in the course of the civilizing process. Significantly, Hitler's secrecy about the plan to eliminate the Jews may have reflected the political judgment that the general population was unprepared for, and not easily attuned to, such 'gross inhumanity' (Kershaw 2000: 522–3). The Nazi regime moved cautiously at first and operated by stealth towards its policy of extermination, alert to the political costs of openly violating 'civilized' restraints on violence and acutely conscious of public fears about where acts of violence would end. But the plain reality was that industrial killing demanded from large numbers of those involved in the organization and implementation of genocide little more than an unquestioning compliance with superior orders and proven reliability in following the directives of public law and bureaucratic codes of conduct. The probability is that fewer people would have been killed had the regime relied on *Angriffslust*, or 'pleasure in attacking' (Mennell 1998: 248–9), or what the Wehrmacht leadership, fearing the break-down of military discipline, called *verwilderung*, or 'running wild' in the form of indiscriminate killing, rape and destruction (Bartov 1994: 121). Moreover, if they so wished, the highly disciplined participants could assuage their conscience by distinguishing between the outer self that was burdened by the harsh duties of public office and the inner self that retained its authenticity and integrity in the face of official demands. It was perhaps easier to divide the self in that way when the consequences of actions were remote, when the people involved were shielded from directly witnessing the suffering they caused, however indirectly, and when the question of culpability could be sidestepped because ultimate responsibility for killing was diffuse.

Bureaucratic rationalization provides a key to understanding how 'mankind, instead of entering into a truly human condition' had relapsed with the 'present collapse of bourgeois civilization' into 'a new kind of barbarism' (Horkheimer and Adorno 1973: xi–xii). That phenomenon high-lights one of the paradoxes of the civilizing process, namely that large sections of the victim population were 'fooled by an apparently peaceful and humane, legalistic and orderly society' into a 'sense of security' that would be instru-mental in 'their downfall' (Bauman 2000: 87–8). The process of civilization explains the widespread belief within Germany and beyond that the society belonged to the 'advanced' family of nations, so that even the September 1935 Nuremberg Laws that deprived Jews of citizenship and outlawed marriage or sexual relations between Jews and non-Jews did not destroy public confidence in the regime's broad support for 'civilized' prohibitions on inflicting violent harm on co-nationals. The Holocaust was possible because the political authorities invented ways of overcoming or circumventing apparently secure 'civilizing' constraints on violence and cruelty. Bureaucratic structures enabled the Nazi regime to pursue its political objectives in the face of such social restraints and associated moral emotions. But as already noted, the exploration of the relationship between modernity and the Holocaust raises as many problems as it solves (Moses 2008). An obvious criticism is that modern, 'civilized' regimes in the first part of the twentieth century did not routinely engage in genocide. The one that embarked on that course promoted its goals not in the full glare of 'civilizing' publicity in a period of peace but in the wartime conditions of fear and secrecy (Elias 2013: 280).

It is no more helpful to regard the Holocaust as the expression of the unique path of German political development – the 'special way' or *Sonderweg* that set it apart from the general European civilizing process. Elias maintained that such an interpretation did more to reassure the members of other 'civi-lized' societies that they were immune from committing similar atrocities than to explain complex social processes. An obvious way of 'coping' with the Holocaust was to portray it as the 'exception', as 'something unique'; it was to characterize the National Socialists as 'a cancerous growth on the body of civilized societies', to regard their actions as the product of 'people who were more or less mentally ill' or 'particularly wicked and immoral', and who were gripped by an 'irrational hatred of Jews' that flowed from specifically German traditions and character traits (Elias 2013: 225). The clear implication was that 'such barbarities cannot take place in the more highly developed societies of the twentieth century' (Elias 2013: ibid.). Analyses that concentrated on the supposedly unique or exceptional protected people from the alarming thought that such things could happen again, that such 'an outbreak of savagery and barbarism . . . may be due to tendencies inherent in the structure of twentieth-century societies'; the resulting challenge was to understand 'the conditions – the social conditions – of twentieth-century civilization, that make [it possible] for barbarities of this kind to recur' (Elias 2013: ibid.). Only by understanding 'common developmental trends' in 'industrializing state societies', including their shared violent history of imperialism, nationalism and war, was it possible to explain what was distinctive about the German case (Elias 2013: 177).

An emphasis on the need to understand the 'social conditions' that led to the Nazi genocides concurred with the argument that bureaucratic domination was a necessary but not sufficient condition for the existence of state-organized group extermination. That was one of several characteristics that Germany shared with other 'civilized' European peoples (Elias 2013: 239ff.). But although genocide relied on 'civilized' forms of rational administration, it was imperative to regard it as a 'breakdown of civilization' (Elias 2013), and not as the product of 'the high stage of our civilization' (Bauman 2000: x). The approach stressed that, because of the civilizing process, the Nazi regime could not impose a 'principle of injury' on society regardless of domestic opinion and political reactions in the wider world (Elias 2013: 234). Fearing that official statements would damage Nazi respectability, Hitler decided in the early to mid-1930s not to publicize his vision of a Europe without Jews. Because of the anticipated opposition of the Catholic Church and other religious organizations, the implementation of the euthanasia policy with respect to 'lives unworthy of living' (a concept advanced by Alfred Hoche and Rudolf Binding in *Release and Destruction of Lives Not Worth Living* published in 1920) was deferred until the outbreak of the Second World War. Government policy was officially reversed in August 1941 because of public anxieties that may have been anchored as much in concerns about 'illegality' and 'deception' as in moral or religious hostility to euthanasia (Burleigh 2002: 158–9). Religious dissent from government policy that over-rode the right to life undoubtedly had some political influence in official circles (Kershaw 1983: 334ff.; also Lewy 1964; Burleigh 1997; Evans 2005: ch. 3). But by the summer of 1941, Aktion T-4, the code name for the euthanasia programme, had already killed at least 70,000 people, many in the care of ecclesiastical institutions (Burleigh 2002: 168ff.; Levy 1964; Proctor 1988: ch. 7). At that point, the regime needed 'T-4s teams of practised murderers' to carry out 'yet greater enormities, where the voices of the Church's respective hierarchies would be conspicuous by their silence' (Burleigh 1997: 141; Browning 1985: ch. 3). Even so, official declarations of a change of direction were not accompanied by a fundamental alteration of policy. The systematic killing of children and adolescents continued until around 1942–43 (Friedlander 1995: ch. 8). The whole process revealed that it was easier for the regime to harness bureaucratic power for some purposes than for others. A great deal depended on the extent to which it could secure public support for a racialized image of political community that undercut common under-standings about what was permissible and forbidden in 'civilized' societies. The contention that Germany was involved in a life-or-death struggle was critical for success in weakening the taboos on violence in relations with the allegedly 'unworthy' and with 'enemies'.

German society was exposed to great dangers because the level of resistance to some forms of violence – and the widespread acceptance of others – demonstrated that 'Enlightenment' values had only limited influence on the political process. For example, in August 1941 Bishop Galen of Münster protested on religious rather than on liberal-humanist grounds against the euthanasia policy (Kershaw 2000: 425ff.; Burleigh 2002: 172–3). From that standpoint, there was no inherent conflict in supporting Germany's war against the Soviet Union and in praying for victory. Others were happy to don Urban II's mantle by describing the invasion of Russia as a 'crusade' or as a 'holy war for homeland and people, for faith and church, for Christ and His most holy Cross'; some compared the war against Bolshevism to the struggle against 'barbarous' Turks in earlier centuries (Lewy 1964: 229ff.). Such political imagery denied that the Soviets could enjoy the rights that were the birthright of Germans or the entitlement of 'civilized' peoples. The consequence was the scorched earth policy of German forces on the Eastern front, and the return to the practice of living off the land that violated the existing humanitarian laws of war and led to widespread pleasure in killing (Burleigh 1997: ch. 3; Neitzel and Welzer 2012).

As part of an orchestrated 'decivilizing process', various groups came to be bracketed along with the Bolsheviks as dangerous 'outsiders' without basic legal and moral entitlements. Some could be placed outside the moral community without having to wear down significant public opposition. The social position of 'Gypsies' is a case in point. They had long been regarded as a poisonous and deviant element in society – as 'in' but not 'of' society. The public appetite for a political solution to the 'gypsy problem' seems to have increased around 1936; the regime's 'anti-Gypsy' policies prior to the Second World War emerged in part in response to growing antipathy towards them (Lewy 2000). Though not always enthusiastically welcomed, discrimination against the 'Gypsies' usually met with public indifference including in the period when the regime defended its policy in the racialized language of the 1935 Nuremberg Laws (Lewy 2000), or when it linked them with the 'Jewish-Bolshevik conspiracy' and transported them to the death camps (Zimmermann 2000).

The position of highly assimilated German Jews was a rather different matter. Almost all accounts reject the contention that public apathy towards the fate of the Jews was grounded in pervasive anti-semitism (Gellately 2001; see, however, Goldhagen 1996). More recent analyses have stated that the level of anti-Semitism was low prior to Hitler's rise to power but increased substantially during the 1930s (Johnson and Reuband 2005). The regime endeavoured to prevent the spread of information about mass killings, precisely because general support was presumed to be lacking (Browning and Matthaus 2004: 388ff.). But resentment of Jewish wealth and influence was not insubstantial during the Depression. Although some members of the clergy protested in the 1930s against the brutal treatment of the Jews, Church hierarchies were often reticent, possibly reflecting wider indifference to discriminatory policies, if not silent approval. In any case, hostility to the power and wealth of Jewish communities does not demonstrate that anti-Semitism explained genocide. What there was in the way of anti-Semitism – in the Catholic Church, for example – was often religious rather than racial, and linked with the ancient stigmatization of the Jews as 'Christ's killers' (Connelly 2012: 169ff.). That is not to suggest that the Church hierarchy feared the consequences of speaking out against Nazi racial ideas or had no sympathy for its racist ideology. There is substantial evidence to suggest that many 'priests colluded in spreading racist ideas'; their opposition was restricted to condemning 'extreme manifestations of racism' rather than 'racism itself' (Connelly 2012: 22ff.).

Moreover, two major sections of society found a separate Jewish community deeply troubling. The first consisted of German nationalists who were hostile to any collective identity that clashed with their demand for the public affirmation of undivided loyalties to the nation; the second comprised liberals who resented 'parochial' strata whose we-identity blocked the assimilation of individuated citizens into 'modern' society (Friedlander 1997: 82). Those instances of 'non-racial anti-Jewish resentment' did not easily translate into public support for intimidation and violence, and they were far removed from the desire to liquidate German or European Jews. The Nazis therefore muted their anti-Semitism in the 1930s precisely because their ideology did not resonate with the dominant strands of public opinion (Bankier 1992: ch. 4). As late as the Posen speech in 1943, Himmler lamented that the extermination programme (not that he referred to the gas chambers directly) had been made more difficult by the fact that every one of 'the 80 million worthy Germans . . . has his own decent Jew' (cited in Dawidowicz 1976: 133). Large numbers of people voiced their disapproval of the deportation in October 1938 of around seventeen thousand Jews with Polish citizenship who had lived in Germany for decades. The following month, they expressed their opposition to the violence that occurred on 9 and 10 November 1938, on what has come to be known as *Kristallnacht* (when around forty Jews were killed and seven thousand businesses were destroyed along with virtually every synagogue in Germany on Goebbels' instruction in retaliation for the shooting of a German official in the Paris embassy). Hitler ordered that there should be no repetition of such violence against the Jews given public suspicion that *Kristallnacht* was not the spontaneous outburst of social rage that the regime claimed it was, but a state-initiated assault on Jewish communities (Longerich 2003: ch. 5). Expressions of 'sympathy, abhorrence and shame', particularly amongst bourgeois social strata, and entirely in line with the larger European civilizing process, could not be simply ignored (Kershaw 1983: 267).

The public did not display the same distaste for the Nuremberg Laws that reduced the Jews from 'citizens' with equal rights to 'state subjects' and out-lawed marriage and sexual contact with 'Aryans' (Kershaw 1983: ch. 6; Bankier 1992: ch. 4). In short, 'negative reactions' to the use of force 'coincided, without any visible contradiction, with a massive and keen approval of the anti-Jewish legislation' with its 'ever-thickening layer of legal discrimination and prohibi-tions' that placed the Jews outside the boundaries of the *Volk* (Bauman 2000: 186–7). Those responses suggest that the larger European civilizing process did not extend as far in Germany as in neighbouring societies – the formation of state monopoly powers, internal pacification and lengthening and deepening chains of interconnectedness had all occurred there but without extending the scope of emotional identification to the same degree to include all co-nationals irrespective of social origins. The development of racist and nationalist 'we-feeling' relaxed 'civilized' standards of self-restraint in relations with the regime's internal and external opponents. Revealingly, sympathy for Jews was often based on fears that Germany would lose respectability in the eyes of other countries, or it was anchored in anxieties about the dramatic spread of insecurity and lawlessness (Bankier 1992: 73ff.). The upshot was that the regime had to construct a 'rational' rather than an 'emotional' anti-Semitism because the latter did not resonate with the prevalent images of a 'civilized *Volk*' (Koonz 2003: 174).

Many of the leading critics of race hatred belonged to social groups that defended 'Christian' or 'liberal-humanist values' (Kershaw 1983: 377). However, the churches' failure to defend 'Enlightenment' principles (and sympathy for the opponents of liberal conceptions of individual rights which was combined with supporting the 'fatherland' in the struggle with Bolshevism) simplified the regime's political task (Lewy 1964). Religious objections to the subordination of the 'divine law' to the nation or race were not insignificant but most fell short of the unambiguous condemnation of Nazism and, as previously noted, they did not prevent Catholic bishops from urging the faithful to support the war against the Soviet Union (Lewy 1964). Promoting regime objectives was made easier because 'expressions of solidarity with the persecuted Jews (were) quite exceptional'; humanitarian opposition to official anti-Semitism was relatively rare (Bankier 1992: 73ff.). Resistance to 'decivilizing processes' would have been stronger had sympathy and solidarity with others flowed automatically from public commitments to Enlightenment principles.

The claim that it is necessary to 'stop viewing the Holocaust as a bizarre and aberrant episode *in* modern history' and to regard it 'as a highly relevant, integral part *of* that history' is therefore only partly correct (Bauman 2000: 223, italics in original). It was indeed the case that bureaucratic domination created unprecedented possibilities for systematic slaughter, especially when there was a major emotional or psychological gulf between the victims and those who were responsible for their destruction. But a standpoint that maintains that industrial killing is entirely possible in modern, 'civilized societies' does not explain how social attitudes to what was forbidden and permissible with respect to violence and public humiliation changed. Only by understanding the fate of liberal-humanist values in German society can one understand how the ruling elite became free to pursue strategies that clashed with 'the standards of civilization' that are defining 'characteristics of advanced contemporary societies' (Elias 2013: 302).

The analysis of the changing power balance between the constituent parts of 'modernity' can usefully begin with the contrasts between the German notion of *Kultur* and French ideas of civilization that were discussed in Chapter 5. In the late eighteenth century, Germany followed the more general European trend in which the rising middle classes threw their weight behind a universal and egalitarian ethic that clashed with the dominant aristocratic values (Elias 2013: 147ff.). In that period, growing support for the bourgeois virtues of commercial society reduced the social standing of the warrior code; however, the broader European tendency in which members of the bourgeoisie were incorporated in the ruling courts did not occur in Germany to the same extent (Elias 2012: 31ff.). One of the political consequences was that only 'a moderate civilizing of the warriors' took place in Prussia that was thought to be encircled by enemies and necessarily in a state of permanent readiness for war (Elias 2013: 72). That was one reason why 'the strategy of compromise had a bad name amongst the German upper classes', and why the idea of fighting to the end, that has long been part of the 'old European warrior tradition' evolved into a 'national tradition' through the co-option of middle-class groups that compromised humanist ideals in the course of identifying ever more closely with exclusionary visions of the state and nation (Elias 2013: 127ff., 145ff.; Tlusty 2011).

The belief in an unacceptable tension between the social standards that applied to relations between people within the state and the principles that governed foreign affairs had come to the forefront of European societies that had undergone the arduous transition from the 'aristocratic-dynastic' to the 'more democratic national state' (Elias 2013: 176). But in Germany, the relatively low level of incorporation of the bourgeoisie into aristocratic court society had the result that there was no lasting tilt towards civility that was grounded in the universal and egalitarian moral commitments of the Enlightenment (Elias 2012: 26ff.). Indeed, throughout Europe as a whole, bourgeois elements had downgraded the importance of humanistic ideals as the idea of the nation ascended in the hierarchy of fundamental social values (Elias 2013: 147, 152ff.). The dominant tendency was to endorse older conceptions of statecraft that enjoyed strong support amongst members of the nobility who retained their grip on, and whose violent dispositions continued to shape, the conduct of foreign policy (Elias 2013: 175–6). Successive military triumphs in the late nineteenth century that propelled Germany into the front rank of the European powers reaffirmed the belief in the superiority of martial virtues, strengthened the conviction that *realpolitik* was critical for success in dealing with adversaries, and devalued the ethic of compassion for the 'underdog' (Elias 2013: ch. 3). At the same time, fears of the 'enemy within' continued to increase. In short, the more powerful groups sought to defend the nation from external enemies while attempting to bolster their position in the face of challenges 'from below' (Elias 2013: 329). In Germany during the latter part of the nineteenth century, large sections of the middle class devalued, and in some cases 'positively despised', conceptions of 'humanity and a generalized morality' (Elias 2013: 129). They accepted the social standards of the warrior code in order to derive collective pride from their association with an increasingly exclusionary nation that was growing in military and political power, even though it granted them little more than second class status (Elias 2013: 192ff.). The changing ethos helps to explain one phenomenon that cut across the nobility and the middle class, namely the strength of support for duelling in Germany, a feature of the aristocratic way of life that upheld and disseminated the positive evaluation of violence and the contempt for weakness (Elias 2013: 54ff.; McAleer 1994; Frevert 1998).

That particular syndrome was reinforced by other distinctive features of Germany's historical experience that led to the 'breakdown of civilization' in a period of major crisis. They included a longstanding collective sense of inferiority given its weakness relative to European states that had experienced political unification much earlier; a counterbalancing sense of group pride and superiority given Germany's rapid rise amongst the great powers, and feelings of national humiliation and disgrace that became more intense as a result of Germany's defeat in the First World War and the perceived travesty of the Versailles settlement. Also important was the belief that strong, centralized leadership was vital for maintaining political order and for ensuring that Germany attained its rightful place amongst the great powers. The same was true of the widespread conviction that individuals should subordinate private interests to the higher goals of the German nation. No less significant was the sudden appearance of parliamentary democracy in a period in which competing groups believed that they were locked in a zero-sum conflict (Elias 2013: ch. 5; Greenfield 1992). Rivals were openly contemptuous of parliamentary 'give and take' and of similar exercises in compromise in the foreign policy domain (Elias 2013: 74, 126–7). Reinforcing and underpinning many of those developments was the hatred and fear of Bolshevism amongst middle-class groups and significant elements of the proletariat (Elias 2013: 207).

That analysis therefore explained Nazism and the Nazi genocides by locating them with long-term patterns of change in Germany while stressing that several social and political dynamics were far from specific to that society.

The approach broadly concurred with the thesis that 'nowhere else in Europe did rapid industrialization confront feudal structures so rapidly and harshly as in Germany' (Herf 1984: 232). In opposition to the contention that the Nazi genocides were '*fully in keeping* with everything we know about our civilization, its guiding principles, its priorities, its immanent vision of the world' (Bauman 2000: 8, italics added), the inquiry was emphatically processual and maintained that large-scale, state-organized violence is only possible in 'civilized' societies as a result of the cumulative effects of 'brutalization and dehumanization' and the steady erosion of the restraining hand of 'conscience' (Elias 2013: 213; Weisbrod 1996). Not only was the Holocaust the greatest regression from 'civilization' in twentieth-century Europe: it was a catastrophe for which 'civilized' Europeans were unprepared. Most assumed that such violence was no longer possible in Europe but had become the monopoly of 'savages' in outlying regions.

European peoples might have been less astonished by genocidal killing in their region – and better placed to prevent it – had they had a clear image in their minds of the violence that had been committed in the name of 'civilization' during the successive waves of European imperial expansion. Pernicious distinctions between 'established' and 'outsider' groups that had been integral to state formation and to modern conceptions of the nation profoundly shaped collective attitudes towards less 'civilized', non-European peoples (Elias 2006; Rae 2002; Levene 2008). The Nazi genocides made the colonial and racist language and practices that had long been evident in relations with imperial subjects central to their conception of a life-or-death struggle for survival against Jews and Bolsheviks within Europe (Moses 2008a; Moses 2010; Stone 2010: ch. 5). Racial doctrines that had shaped Europe's relations with 'barbaric' peoples blew back into the continent.

Unsurprisingly, given the circumstances that were described earlier, many sections of the German population as well as observers in other societies were disinclined to take Nazi ideology at face value. For the overwhelming majority of Europeans, genocide was not remotely on the social horizon – and indeed colonial genocide had come to be regarded as a shameful part of their imperial history. But such orientations did not quash 'the potential for sustained moments of collective psychological over-excitement during periods of . . . war-related national crisis' – particularly in the case of states with a very deep sense of 'grievance against the world' that found solace in a language 'of past grandeur, innocence or purity' through which they expressed 'resentment and anger' at societies that were portrayed as the undeserved beneficiaries of their turmoil or loss (Levene 2005: 188–9). Accustomed to thinking that society and politics were largely governed by the rational pursuit of self-interest, many actors and analysts assumed that the regime's hostility to Jews was no more than a crude instrument that a 'half educated' elite had employed to gain political power; before long, it was widely thought, 'reality' would force the

German state into line with the dominant practices elsewhere (Elias 2013: 234ff.). The collective mistake was to think that support for national ideologies with a high 'fantasy-content' and no obvious long-term political utility would melt away; the misjudgement was to assume that a collective belief-system that ran entirely counter to the liberal-humanist values of the Enlightenment could not gain the upper hand in a technologically advanced, significantly pacified, 'civilized' society (Elias 2013: ibid.). But public commitments to universal, egalitarian principles which have been one of the hallmarks of modernity since the Enlightenment wavered at crucial junctures – on the first occasion when the Nuremberg Laws were passed.

The danger of regression to the ethos of the military-aristocratic code was high in a deeply divided society that faced a serious economic and political crisis; unstable conditions blocked the peaceful transition from autocratic to democratic rule. The struggle to assert German power connected hostility towards external threats and feelings of national humiliation with a profound hatred of internal foes. A central theme in Elias's explanation of the 'breakdown of civilization' was that large sections of the general population invested their hopes and energies in unconditional support for the Nazis and in personal loyalties to Hitler who represented national frustrations and articulated a deep longing for collective salvation (Elias 2013: 313ff.). The reassertion of 'pre-industrial' imperial goals occurred at the very point of their obsolescence – on any realistic assessment of international conditions – as organizing principles of foreign policy (Elias 2013: 288ff.). That was an extreme example of the tendency for the social *habitus* of national citizens to lag behind, and to block more 'reality-congruent' responses to, rising levels of global interconnectedness (Elias 2010b: part 3). In that context, Hitler was the modern counterpart to the 'shaman', 'rainmaker' or 'witch doctor' in 'simpler' societies – the figure that absolved individuals in their 'helplessness' from responsibility for their personal and collective fate in a period of immense danger which no society can be certain it will escape if it is faced with equivalent economic and social challenges, and if state institutions are powerless to prevent the rapid disintegration of society into warring factions (Elias 2013: 314–15).

The social and political conditions that increased the public appeal of an ideology with a high 'fantasy-content' have been noted. Collective fantasies heightened feelings of group admiration amongst the 'chosen' while expelling denigrated adversaries from a racialized vision of political community. Glorification of the Aryan race was secured through pernicious contrasts with Jews and 'Gypsies', 'sexual deviants' and blacks. They were outside the scope of emotional identification and denied protection under the prevalent 'civilized' standards of self-restraint. Exactly how the regime won support for its vision of the racial state remains an intriguing question. A traditional lack of high levels of emotional identification with Jews and other outsiders does not provide the whole answer (see de Swaan 2015 for further discussion). The regime propagated an anti-modernist ethic that portrayed 'sexual degenerates' and 'lower races' as morally defective, as guilty of sexual excess, and as lacking socially required levels of 'civilized' self-discipline (Mosse 1985: 36). It echoed earlier phases in the process of civilization in which distinctions were drawn between the 'pure' and the 'impure', and between the 'normal' and the 'deviant'. In its specific variant on discourses that had long been integral to imperialist projects, the regime constructed images of a racialized, political community that depicted modern forms of life as 'breeding-grounds for immorality and moral sickness'; nostalgia for traditional, organic social relations was strong; the public discourse of a nation surrounded by internal and external enemies celebrated the cult of male toughness that confined women to the domestic sphere and barred the 'feminine' – including an 'unmanly' humanitarian ethic – from a public domain that was transformed by the deliberate 'aestheticization of the white racial body' (Linke 1999: 44ff., Mosse 1985: ch. 8; 126ff.; Todorov 2000: 162ff.).

Nazi attitudes to women were explicitly anti-modern while orientations towards advanced technology were unambiguously modernist. German Fascism has been described as an instance of 'reactionary modernism', a term that refers how the fascination with modern technology was combined with undisguised contempt for Enlightenment liberal-cosmopolitan principles (Herf 1984). Central to a mentality that broke with the ethos of the Enlightenment was the belief that the rules of war that applied to interactions between 'civilized' Europeans had no relevance for relations with Jews and other 'social inferiors'. In his speech to Wehrmacht generals in Sonthofen in May 1944, Himmler raised the question of why the regime had felt compelled to exterminate children. The answer was that in 'this confrontation with Asia we must get used to condemning to oblivion those rules and customs of past European wars to which we have become accustomed and which are more suited to us' (Longerich 2003: 210). In a speech that was delivered a few weeks later, he maintained that no 'pleasure or joy' could be taken in killing women and children, but necessity required firmness rather than compliance with the 'civilized' laws of war if the rise of future avengers was to be prevented (Longerich 2003: 211).

Regarding the more specific matter of the demonization of the German Jews, the evidence is that Nazi propaganda succeeded in increasing levels of anti-Semitism in the 1930s (Kershaw 1983). As noted earlier, physical extermination was not official Nazi policy in that period, and indeed learned debates continue about when precisely the practice of deporting German Jews to Poland and Russia turned into state-administered genocide (Roseman 2002). The Madagascar Plan which envisaged resettling German Jews on that island was under consideration in late 1938, and may have been the regime's preferred 'solution' to the 'Jewish problem' until the middle of 1940 (Browning

and Matthaus (2004: 81ff.; Gerwarth 2011: 178ff.). Seemingly insoluble practical difficulties led to its abandonment and to the search for other relocation
sites. Hitler's shift from the public stance that German Jews were a pestilence
that had to be expelled to the belief that Europe's Jews were a 'sub-human' race
that had to be liquidated seems to have occurred at some point between March
and October 1941 (Gordon 1984: 97ff.). What is certain is that the policy
towards the Jews evolved quickly in wartime conditions. Clearly, 'all those
intricate networks of checks and balances, barriers and hurdles which the
civilizing process has erected', and which were meant to protect human beings
from violence by 'unscrupulous powers', proved to be 'ineffective' (Bauman
2000: 87). But it was not modernity as a process of bureaucratization that
produced that condition. As noted earlier, Bauman did not argue that modern
systems of bureaucratic domination explain the Holocaust; the contention was
that 'the rules of instrumental rationality [were] singularly incapable of preventing such phenomena' (Bauman 2000: 17–18). But to understand the actual
course of events, considerable importance must be attached to the changing
balance of power between competing social forces and to the decisive reality
that 'no political party, interest group, trade union, or Church' was committed
around 1933 to robust public opposition to 'the dangerous growth of anti-
Semitism' (Kershaw 1983: 275).

Checks and balances were weak in the absence of powerful political
elements that vigorously protested against the suspension of quintessentially
modern civil and political rights. The balance of social opinion in Germany in
the early to mid-1930s was incapable of restraining the 'radical dynamism of
the racial fanatics and the deadly bureaucratization of the doctrine of race-
hatred' (Kershaw 1983: 371). From that point on, it became increasingly
'difficult' if not 'impossible' to alter the course of German politics: the emancipation of state monopoly powers from the ineffective constraints of civil
society made it easier for the regime to bully proponents of the humanist,
Enlightenment tradition into submission. The dramatic reversal of the civilizing process and the disfigurement of modernity through the isolation of highly
centralized powers from the countervailing influence of liberal-humanist
values were set in motion. But it is crucial to reiterate that the Nazis
were only able to implement policies that they had been anxious to conceal
from German society and the wider world in the exceptional circumstances
of war. Genocide required more than a combination of anti-Semitic state
structures and a high level of public acquiescence or indifference to the fate
of the Jews. The central importance of the 'cover of wartime conditions'
strongly suggests that modernity was less vulnerable to a 'breakdown of
civilization' than Bauman's interpretation suggests (Gordon 1984: 48). It is
undoubtedly essential to emphasize core features of modernity (particularly
the role of bureaucratic domination) to explain the Nazi genocides; but the
policy of extermination depended on the betrayal of the universalistic and

egalitarian principles that have been no less fundamental to European modernity. That process was more likely in the context of war given 'the split within our civilization' and the specific variant that had long permitted the relaxation of the usual restraints on force in colonial wars against 'savages'. That is where the clearest link between modernity or the civilizing process and the potential for genocide existed. The connection does not by itself account for the Nazis' extermination policies, but it is an important part of the explanation. The different interpretations that Elias and Bauman provided reveal the difficulties in determining the relative influence of specific, and possibly unique, features of long-term processes of change in Germany and various characteristics that were shared by all or most modern, 'civilized' imperial societies. They included the reality all had a 'dualistic' moral code that was integral to the 'split within civilization'. In Germany's case, and to a far greater extent than in Britain, nationalist aspirations were relatively free from the counterbalancing effects of universal moral commitments (Elias 2013: 189ff., 273–4). Various points of overlap or convergence between the two interpretations nevertheless clarify the dangers to which all modern societies are vulnerable and which they must be permanently vigilant in guarding against.

Before proceeding further, it is important to summarize the main reasons for preferring the notion of the civilizing process to the idea of modernity in the following discussion of the Nazi genocides. Bauman made it perfectly clear that modernity was a necessary but not sufficient condition of the Holocaust which could not be understood without analysing specific patterns of social and political change in Germany. But the analysis of the social dynamics in question erred by stating that the civilizing process was one 'of divesting the use and deployment of violence from moral calculus, and of emancipating the desiderata of rationality from interference of ethical norms or moral inhibitions' (Bauman 2000: 28). As earlier chapters have shown, that interpretation of the process of civilization grossly misrepresents Elias's position. His writings stressed how the European civilizing process gave rise to new forms of collective power and made unprecedented levels of destructive harm possible but it could not be reduced to freeing those with monopoly control of the instruments of violence from ethical considerations. The logic of that argument is that it is essential to develop an account of the processes by which specific features of modern societies including the potentials for domination that are inherent in bureaucratic organization were released from the constraining role of the universal and egalitarian principles that have been no less integral to 'civilized' societies since the Enlightenment. It is important to explain how the strategy of physically removing and eliminating 'enemies' prevailed over the 'civilized' prohibitions of violent and non-violent harm between citizens of the same state and, more specifically, it is to show how bureaucratic structures became suffused by a racist ideology that reversed core features of the civilizing process (Stone 2010: 121ff.). Bauman's essentially non-processual approach to modernity does not explain how power struggles within Germany and conflicts with external enemies shaped the outcome of tensions between 'civilizing' and 'decivilizing' processes.

Nor did it recognize how the interplay between domestic and international politics contributed to the 'breakdown of civilization'. Elias's approach has the advantage over Bauman's essentially endogenous perspective precisely because of its attention to the interweaving of intra-state and interstate dynamics that resulted in the drastic shift from a 'humanist-moralist-civilizing' ethos to a 'counter-code with strong anti-humanist, anti-moral, and anti-civilizing tendencies' (Elias 2013: 193; Elias 2013: 460). The close link between warfare and 'decivilizing processes' was a central part of the explanation (Elias 2013: 280). The upshot was an approach that provided a more detailed understanding of changes in the scope of emotional identification between people, in the we–I balance, and in the dominant standards of self-restraint in the period before the Holocaust. Moreover, process sociology can account for a crucial phenomenon that the focus on modernity cannot explain, namely how 'civilized' societies at the end of the Second World War extended the earlier process of civilization by embedding new cosmopolitan harm conventions in international society.

Euthanasia and the Civilizing Process

In a speech to the SS at Posen in October 1943, Himmler declared that it would never be possible to speak frankly and publicly about the systematic destruction of the Jews (the 'never-to-be-written page of glory', the secret best carried to the grave), and he added that, except for a few 'cases of human weakness', members of the SS had discharged their designated responsibilities with unfailing 'integrity' (cited in Dawidowicz 1976: 133). Himmler's speech can be read as recognizing the psychological burden that the regime's extermination policy imposed on those who implemented it. He congratulated his men for controlling their inner feelings and for learning how to remain 'hard' as part of their personal sacrifice for higher collective ideals. There was implicit acknowledgment that a politico-aesthetic struggle to construct 'the hardened male body' had been essential to cancel the psychological inhibitions on violence that were major effects of the European civilizing process. The coarsening of the psyche made it easier to suppress or extinguish shame, guilt and disgust; the key term 'sobriety' referred to the emotional controls that allowed those involved 'to overcome' what has been described as 'the animal pity by which all normal men are affected in the presence of physical suffering' (Arendt 1994: 106; Gerwarth 2011: 72–3; Linke 1999: 129). It was clearly stated in the speech that evil temptations had largely been resisted – that the majority of SS members had not discharged their duties for personal gain, and there was the grotesque insinuation that all had shouldered the burden without succumbing to the pleasures of killing or the satisfaction of witnessing suffering that would have reduced honourable people to 'brute savages' (Hilberg 1985: 131ff.; also Elias 2013: 306ff., Levi 1988: ch. 2; Katz 1993: 84ff.). It is well known that mass shootings in Russia that were part of the *Einsatzgruppen* campaign often produced the psychological effects that the civilizing process would lead one to expect, even in a society that had initiated the programme of 'brutalization and dehumanization' discussed earlier. They included revulsion and disgust, and assorted psychological disorders that may have led to persistent guilt and remorse. Hitler lamented that it was necessary to weaken the pernicious influence of Christianity with its advocacy of compassion for the underdog (Steigmann-Gall 2003: ch. 1). The regime devised means of liquidating its enemies that were meant to remove the traumatic effects of killing, particularly women and children. The gas vans, followed by the extermination camps, were justified as more 'humane' methods of destruction precisely because they made it simpler for the killers to combine 'greater efficiency' with 'psychological detachment' (Browning and Matthaus 2004: 353ff.). A principal aim was to reduce the level of unnecessary suffering for members of the SS by minimizing contact with the victims, while organizing slaughter on a scale that mass shootings could not have achieved (Lifton 2000: 159).

As previously stated, the social taboos against killing that are central to the civilizing process cannot be torn down overnight, although the 'armour of civilized conduct' can crumble quickly when groups are anxious about their security or survival (see Chapter 11, p. 433). At other times, the weakening of restraints to the point where large numbers of people who had shown no previous appetite for violence become compliant or willing participants in mass slaughter depends on a specific 'decivilizing process' – on 'the gradual hardening of a particular moral climate' and the coarsening of individual moral sensibilities through 'disidentification' or 'dissociation' that entails withdrawing sympathy for other persons; in particular, growing indifference towards distress can be the prelude to the willingness to inflict suffering (Lifton and Markusen 1991: ch. 7). The development of the euthanasia policy in the 1930s was made possible by the changing emotional attitudes towards those who were under the care of medical professionals. It revealed how the social habitus was transformed by deliberate policies of 'brutalization and dehumanization'. The political consequences of those changes extended well beyond the hospital ward. Many who took part in the programme moved with apparent ease into key positions in the death camps (Burleigh 2001: ch. 5).

Under normal circumstances, a medical corps that was obliged by the Hippocratic Oath to 'do no harm' to the vulnerable in its care would be expected to resist government efforts to harness them to administering a state-organized programme of cruelty. Analyses of the reasons for involvement in the euthanasia programme have shown that participants were not forced to take part and could usually secure transfer to other duties, had they so wished (Friedlander 1995: ch. 11). Many chose to become involved for ideological reasons, others for career advancement. By those means, professional commitments to those in distress were eroded. Between 1939 and 1941, around seventy thousand Germans were the first to be killed by carbon monoxide poisoning in gas chambers, a policy that Hitler is reputed to have favoured on the grounds that it was more 'humane' than the alternatives (Friedlander 1995: 86). Defenders of the euthanasia policy argued that hardness should replace feelings of sympathy that were deemed to clash with the ultimate wellbeing of patients. To reshape public attitudes to euthanasia, the captions of one propaganda film contended that 'the prevention of hereditarily ill progeny' was 'a moral imperative' that expressed 'practical love for one's neighbour' (Burleigh 2002: 181–2). It is therefore legitimate to refer to a programme of 'civilized' euthanasia in which many perpetrators concluded that they were engaged in 'mercy killing' to prevent pointless human suffering. Many 'mental patients' had unknowingly passed on 'their suffering to their descendants' prior to committal to an asylum; those miseries, it was argued, should not be 'perpetuated in the bodies of their children' (Burleigh 2002: 179ff.). 'Healthy people' had 'to perform arduous, often disgusting tasks, to ease the lives of these innocent persons', whenever possible (Burleigh 2002: 183). Several methods were used to 'erode instinctive sympathies with the disturbed or distressed'; appeals to compassion were employed to overcome initial feelings of repugnance towards such a programme (Burleigh 2002: 186ff., also Burleigh 1997: ch. 4).

The euthanasia project was also regarded as critical for the long-term interests of the Reich. Immediately after the outbreak of the Second World War, Hitler maintained that 'the food supply does not allow for the incurably ill to be dragged through the war' (Proctor 1999: 170ff.). Taking up the language of 'lives not worth living', Nazi ideology emphasized the social cost of providing for 'useless eaters' (a term that would later be used to describe Jews imprisoned in the East). Others defended taking the lives of psychiatric patients in anticipation of the burden of supporting war casualties. Humanitarian reasons were offered in defence of the euthanasia policy, but economic and military calculations were the main driving-force (Proctor 1988: 182ff.). A core assumption was that the unhealthy should not be protected from the sacrifices that the healthy had to make in the interests of the Reich. The changing nature of the emotional climate was exemplified by official support for the argument that the benefits of human experimentation should not be deferred because of outdated beliefs in the sanctity of human life. At the Doctors' Trial at Nuremberg, some of the defendants argued that military necessity had provided the 'moral' justification for sacrificing a few 'useless' lives in order to promote a higher social good, while others invoked the standard defence of obeying superior orders (Grodin 1992). On such grounds, the Hippocratic Oath was racialized (Burleigh 2002: 263).

The euthanasia policy revealed how the regime used propagandist techniques to alter the moral-emotional climate in medical institutions and in the larger society. But secrecy was paramount. The programme never had legal authorization and it constituted murder even by the standards of the regime. Many explanations have been advanced of how state institutions succeeded in persuading medical staff who took the Hippocratic Oath seriously, and who had no prior 'history of cruelty', to become directly involved in killing or to comply, and without apparent ethical qualms, with commands to contribute to implementing the programme (McFarland-Icke 1999: 218). Attempts to minimize feelings of personal responsibility for involvement (and to suppress predictable feelings of shame or guilt) were significant factors (Bauman 2000: 163). The psychological cover provided by the claim that subordinates were simply obeying instructions helped to secure compliance. In a hierarchical medical order that stressed the duty of obedience, many nurses may have assumed that the euthanasia programme had legal authorization, and indeed had been ordered by Hitler (McFarland-Icke 1999: 8–9, 228). In fact, a law that was drafted in October 1940 did not reach the statute books. The regime avoided the political controversies that would have arisen had it placed the details of the programme full-square in the public domain. But assumptions about legality gave the programme legitimacy, and many appear to have thought that the political authorities would have intervened if improprieties were involved. Undoubtedly, many feared that non-compliance would result in sanctions given the trend towards 'increasingly draconian punishment for politically nonconformist behaviour' (Kershaw 1983: 360). Inevitably, the programme degraded relations between medical staff and patients as the former attuned themselves to 'medicalized killing' wrapped in the discourse of humanitarianism (McFarland-Icke 1999: 215ff.). But the programme did not require generalized cruelty; it depended instead on 'the assistance not only of those who could kill without a guilty conscience but also of those who killed *with*, or more accurately, *in spite of* a guilty conscience' (McFarland-Icke 1999: 257, italics in original). It may have been important that participants could 'bring forth a self that could adapt to killing without ... feeling oneself a murderer' (Lifton 2000: 425). The contention is that the daily retreat into the solace of the private sphere made it easier for medical staff to maintain psychological equilibrium. Outward conformity with official demands could coexist with inward faithfulness to higher ideals that may have preserved the individual's self-respect and sense of moral worth (Todorov 2000: 128ff.).

Genocide and the Civilizing Process

The euthanasia programme demonstrated how the Hippocratic duty to 'do no harm' was redefined in order to establish the social responsibility to free individual patients and their families from relievable suffering, and how a culture of compliance secured widespread acquiescence with superior instructions. The quasi-medical language that legitimated that programme also informed the regime's attitudes to 'Gypsies', criminals, homosexuals and Jews. Its strategies were suffused with notions of eradicating a 'bacillus' and ending a 'plague'. No doubt, the National Socialist regime saw itself as eliminating those who failed to live up to its vision of a utopian social order. There were several links between the general course of the European civilizing process with its emphasis on hygiene, the overall trajectory of social development that harnessed scientific knowledge to tame or eliminate the unruly or 'harmful', and the Nazi doctrine of racial purification (Bauman 2000: 70ff.). The Nazis were hardly alone in aiming to breed out 'inferior' elements that had no place in the official policy of progressive modernization. Support for the biological improvement of national populations through eugenics existed on both the Left and the Right of the political spectrum in the major liberal democracies in the early part of the twentieth century. The Nazis regarded the practice of sterilization in the United States as standard-setting, and feared that German military power would lag behind such societies unless similar methods were adopted (Proctor 1988: 97ff.). Moreover, their opposition to alcohol and tobacco, and advocacy of healthy eating, cannot be divorced from the larger European civilizing process (Proctor 1999; Corbin 1996). It is peculiar nevertheless to claim that the Holocaust did not 'depart from the main track of the civilizing process' but demonstrated its inner spirit and clearly revealed what it was capable of (Bauman 2000: 93).

The dominant strata have often secured their power and privileges, and the sense of social superiority by representing outsiders as polluting or unclean. The Nazi 'sanitary utopia' varied an ancient theme in the 'civilized' stigmatization of inferiors by portraying them as a cancerous growth in society. It demanded what Hitler called 'cleanliness' in all realms of 'culture' and 'public life' (Koonz 2003: 22; Proctor 1999; Weikart 2009: ch. 2). As part of the ideology of racial hygiene, various groups were identified as a serious danger to the health of society: gypsies because their 'migrant lifestyle' allegedly posed a major 'health risk' (Proctor 1988: 214ff.), and Jews because a supposedly higher susceptibility to certain diseases would endanger the *Volk* but for laws that prevented racial intermarriage. The 'medicalization of anti-Semitism' required 'quarantine' in the interests of 'hygienic necessity' (Proctor 1988: 194ff.). The regime argued that all such measures were the essential parts of one unified public health policy (Proctor 1988). As already noted, some aspects of the Nazi image of social improvement were not so far removed from efforts to plan the future course of civilization that members of the regime could be universally condemned as utter 'cranks'. The sterilization programme, for example, could not be classified as a war crime at Nuremberg precisely because similar measures had been lawful in the United States (Proctor 1988: 97ff.). But the 'sanitary' ideal of cleansing a 'racialized' political community was such a departure from the broader civilizing process that the regime was compelled to invent ways of circumventing its inconvenient ethical prohibitions.

The significance of the civilizing process even when mass killing is involved is made clear by the fact that the Holocaust was conducted, as noted earlier, in absolute secrecy in wartime conditions, without arousing public hostility and rage, although in various speeches and newspaper articles the regime left little to the public's imagination (Bankier 1994). How much the general population knew about the mass killings has been the subject of considerable debate. Knowledge of atrocities and shootings committed by the *Einsatzgruppen* was widespread as a result of 'unspecific' rumours circulated by soldiers returning from leave; killing in the mobile gas-units and in extermination camps was 'carried out much more secretly, and found little echo inside Germany' (Kershaw 1983: 364ff.). The evidence suggests that many Germans discounted rumours about mass killings at Auschwitz and in other death camps because such behaviour clashed with prevailing 'civilized' self-images or were presumed to be 'atrocity propaganda'. On some interpretations, significant numbers of Germans, civilians as well as soldiers, became aware of mass murder during 1943 with the consequence that some church sermons late that year and in the early part of 1944, as well as correspondence with the regime, specifically condemned racial killing (Bankier 1992). Some assessments speculate that a third of the German population was quite well informed about the Holocaust, and about a half knew something about it (Johnson and Reuband 2005). A significant proportion chose to ignore the reports, preferring simply to get on with their lives. It appears that many first heard about the scale of the atrocities as a result of the disclosures at the Nuremberg trials. But had they made the effort, it has been argued, most people could have acquired accurate information about what was taking place in the camps.

Though 'built by hate', it has been argued, the road to Auschwitz was 'paved with indifference' combined with at least 'silent disapproval' of the Jews as well as 'active engagement' in genocide (Kershaw 1983: 277; Burleigh 1997: 168). From the first deportations to the mass killings, anti-Semitism does not explain the motivation of perhaps the majority of those who were involved in implementing (as opposed to designing) the programme of extermination. On some interpretations, the immense brutality of the war against Russia provides an important clue to the disposition of large numbers of ordinary people who were actively or passively involved in genocide. The 'Barbarossa decree' of 13 May 1941 instructed the Army to ignore all moral scruples in the quest for military success. Collective reprisals against civilians (including women and children) were legitimated. The 'shooting license' stated that military courts would not punish German soldiers for acts of violence against civilian populations (Browning 2001: 11). At least 2 million Russian prisoners of war had died because of starvation, disease and execution by early 1942 when 'the final solution' was under way (see Browning 1985: 6 for further details). That the war in the East was a crucial stage in the move towards the Holocaust is evident from calculations that between one and a half million and 2 million Jews were eliminated during that phase of the conflict. The brutality transformed the ordinary soldier's habitus or emotional world and encouraged 'decivilized' dispositions that might not have developed under different circumstances (Cesarani 1994). Of particular significance was the conviction that violent actions were necessary in the struggle against a totally alien civilization rather than a heinous crime against fellow human beings. However attenuated, a sense of affinity with the enemy in the West was contrasted with complete dissociation from the eastern 'Jewish-Bolshevik *Untermenschen* 'that resulted in brutalities that troubled several army commanders but mainly because of the threat to army discipline (Bartov 2001: 114–15). Breakdowns of military discipline that led to plunder and rape were not only rarer on the Western front but more likely to be punished, no doubt because of a degree of emotional identification with other members of the same civilization and respect for the relevant 'civilized' standards of self-restraint survived there (Bartov 1994; Bartov 1992: 65ff.; Elias 2013: 231). On the other hand, official attitudes to sexual violence against Soviet women indicate that such behaviour was not categorized as the unacceptably 'serious' product of the 'lack of self-restraint' (Muhlhauser 2008: 202). The Barbarossa Decree in which that expression is found stated that criminal offenses against Soviet civilians would not be punished. Revealingly, official standpoints on sexual encounters between Germans and 'racial inferiors' in the East were divided between those who believed that military brothels should not be tolerated and those who saw them as a method of satisfying the irrepressible needs of 'impulse-driven human beings', however civilized (Muhlhauser 2008: 205ff.).

Deeper insights into the social processes that transformed 'ordinary men' into mass killers were provided by the detailed study of the role of Reserve Peace Battalion 101 in the massacre of Jews in Poland in 1942. Its members were ordered to liquidate the Jewish population of Jozefow. The commander, Major Wilhelm Trapp, had the responsibility for implementing orders to shoot all civilians including women and children. In the course of explaining their duties to those under his command, Trapp, who displayed signs of physical distress in discharging the obligations that had been conferred on him, made it clear that those who had no wish to take part in the killings would be assigned other responsibilities (Browning 2001: 57ff.). Of the five hundred in the battalion, around a dozen asked to be transferred to other roles, a number that might have been higher had more realized what lay ahead, but the desire to avoid personal isolation and stigmatization for exhibiting cowardice rather than male hardness appears to have preserved group solidarity. As noted earlier, some asked to be relieved from tasks that they found impossible to bear; others found avoidance strategies; but many freely participated in the killings. Later reports of shooting women and children stressed the 'shame and horror' that resulted from transgressing social taboos against killing the weak (Browning 2001: 69). The taboo was broken not, it seems, because of powerful anti-Semitic beliefs but, because in the course of the war, Jews were bracketed with other enemies who had been placed outside the circle of emotional identification, so cementing the distinction between 'us' and 'them' that is absolutely 'standard in war' (Browning 2001: 73). Racial indoctrination may have been a key factor in placing Jews outside the 'moral community', but perceptions of a beleaguered Germany may have been at least as important in overriding deep-seated taboos against harming women and children. Certainly, the inhibitions against killing women and children weakened over time, though not uniformly since some personnel limited their involvement in killing 'when they could do so without great cost or inconvenience'; but only a 'minority of nonconformists managed to preserve a beleaguered sense of moral autonomy that emboldened them to employ patterns of behaviour and stratagems of evasion that kept them from becoming killers' (Browning 2001: 102, 127).

Volunteers for such killings were not hard to find, and many who took part in mass slaughter undoubtedly derived immense pleasure and satisfaction from humiliating, torturing and liquidating adversaries. The psychological changes that the members of Reserve Police Battalion 101 underwent have wider implications because they had not been sent to Poland to murder Jews following official rulings about their obvious suitability for the task (Browning 2001: 164). With the exception of those who had served in the First World War, most 'had not seen battle or encountered a deadly enemy ... Thus, wartime brutalization through prior combat was not an immediate experience directly influencing the policemen's behaviour at Jozefow' (Browning 2001:161ff.). It is probable that many had joined the police force to avoid being conscripted into the armed forces but, once the killing began, they became 'increasingly brutalized' and slaughter became 'progressively easier' (Browning 2001: ibid.). Milgram's influential psychological study of 'obedience to authority' was designed to explain precisely such rapid changes in individual orientations towards inflicting pain and suffering that explain involvement in 'socially organized evil' (Milgram 1974: 29; Browning 2001: 167ff.; also Bauman 2000: ch. 6 who also refers to Zimbardo's influential Stanford police experiments, and Blass 2000). The experiment revealed that 'ordinary people' with no pronounced inclination to behave violently towards others would override the 'deeply ingrained disposition not to harm others' in order to please authority figures who maintained that such behaviour was crucial in order to complete valuable scientific experiments (Milgram 1974: 59).

The study of Battalion 101 suggests that decisive leadership was indispensable for securing obedience and that vacillation or displays of significant reservations created the risk of defection (Browning 2001; Milgram 1979). The Nazi elite was well aware of the absolute importance of firm and uncompromising leadership. The route to securing compliance was a central theme in Himmler's Posen speech. He emphasized the need for the unquestioning obedience of superior orders by men of 'low rank', and added that as 'a matter of course . . . all high-ranking leaders of the SS (should be) models of unconditional obedience'. Enforcing orders in Germany might be relatively easy, but problems would emerge 'the larger our territory grows' – or with the further 'scaling up' of social and political organization. Upholding their 'sacredness' would depend increasingly on the devotion of senior ranks to the twin imperatives of 'duty' and 'loyalty' (cited in Dawidowicz 1976: 136–7). As Commandant of Auschwitz, Hoess (2000: 150ff.), maintained that it was necessary to obey the will of the Führer even if 'tormented by serious doubts'; it was 'psychologically essential' to 'appear convinced of the necessity for this gruesomely harsh order' to liquidate the Jews so that subordinates would carry out their tasks. It was necessary, he added, to 'exercise intense self-control in order to prevent my innermost doubts and feelings of oppression from becoming apparent' and, in a reference to the need for hardness given the effects of the civilizing process, to 'appear cold and indifferent to events that must have wrung the heart of anyone possessed of human feelings' (see Levi in Hoess 2000: 19–20 for an assessment).

It nevertheless seems that the desire to conform with group norms may have been at least as important as the pressure to obey authority in eroding 'civilizing' restraints on violence (Browning 2001: 184ff.). In the case of Battalion 101, where the entire group was ordered to liquidate Jews, non-compliance on the part of any individual immediately shifted the burden onto others, risking perceptions of 'shirking' or of assuming moral superiority over those who chose to obey. Whatever the motivation, the compulsion to step outside the standard 'civilized' harm conventions led many perpetrators to feel not so much sorrow for the victims as self-pity given the enormity of the 'unpleasant' tasks that were expected of them (Browning 2001: 215).

Reference was made earlier to the complex psychological passage from peace to war that people had to go through when the right to bear arms and to use force had been eliminated from highly pacified societies, and when the majority rarely witnessed death and dying. Milgram's experiments continue to command interest because they appeared to explain how 'normal' humans can be drawn into forms of evil that confound expectations of 'civilized' behaviour. Shorn of its ancient theological roots, the concept of evil has been integral to studies of the Holocaust and subsequent genocides ever since Arendt used the idea of the 'banality of evil', borrowed from Karl Jaspers, to describe the gulf between the unmistakable ordinariness of Eichmann's physical appearance and his extraordinary crimes (Arendt 1994; Fine 2001). On that argument, the implementation of the Nazi genocides owed as much to indifference to suffering or the 'sheer thoughtlessness' of the likes of Eichmann as to the pathological traits that are usually associated with innate wickedness, pleasure in inflicting or witnessing suffering, and a reassuringly demonic outward appearance that clearly separates those with cruel dispositions from 'civilized' people (Arendt 1994: 288; see the critique in Amery 1980: 25ff.). The central point is that the extermination of Europe's Jews could not have been taken place without the involvement of a substantial cohort of people that behaved not like the 'free companies' that had plagued local communities in early modern Europe (or like rabid anti-Semites) but in the manner of orderly civil servants that had all the passionless, routinized qualities of Weber's ideal-typical public official. That was the official whose 'honour' is 'vested in his ability to execute conscientiously the order of the superior authorities, exactly as if the order agreed with his own conviction', and 'even if the order appears wrong to him' (see Weber 1948 [1919]: 95) who added that, without such 'moral discipline and self-denial', the entire political apparatus would collapse). A similar point was made by Levi (2000: 477) when he stated that 'monsters exist, but they are too few in number to be truly dangerous. More dangerous are the common men, the functionaries ready to believe and to act without asking questions'. It was crucial to understand that the likes of Baer, Hoess' successor at Auschwitz, and 'the thousands of other faithful and blind executors of orders' belonged to 'the century's most dangerous human type' (Levi 1997: 103; also the discussion of Eichmann's trial in Elias 2013: 226).

As discussed earlier, numerous references by members of the Nazi elite to the importance of unwavering leadership indicate that they fully understood the political significance and practical utility of that phenomenon. However, critiques of earlier assumptions about the 'typical perpetrator' and about the crucial role of an army of impartial administrators faithfully following the letter of the law and dutifully complying with the orders of superiors have grown in recent years. The political importance of such a social stratum is not disputed, but investigations that stress the ordinariness of the majority of perpetrators are accused of failing to recognize the diversity of types of participants including the radical nationalists who were prepared in the 1920s to use violence to promote their cause, who had an anti-Semitic 'Nazi pedigree' in the early 1930s, and who supported ever more extreme forms of violence as the decade unfolded (Roseman 2007; Stone 2010: ch. 2). Recent studies of Eichmann have described the shift from initial revulsion towards scenes of suffering and bloodshed, and discomfort with the goal of physical annihilation, to the radical anti-Semitism that led to the destruction of all feelings of compassion for the 'enemy' (Cesarani 2004: chs. 4–5). Those detailed examinations of the interplay between 'decivilizing processes' and changing personality traits highlight the dynamics of 'total moral collapse' that were largely obscured by earlier studies of bureaucratized violence (Cesarani 2004: chs. 6 and 9).

Central dimensions of the European civilizing process – including the greater importance of internal restraints relative to external compulsion as a result of domestic pacification and the growth of interdependencies between people – are important for understanding the administration of the Nazi genocides. One of the consequences has been that the citizens of modern states are less likely than their medieval forebears were to swing between the emotional extremes of pity and cruelty, and also less prone to outbursts of anger and threats of violence (Elias 2012: 186ff.). Those realities do not mean that they are necessarily less dangerous to each other. They can be harnessed to industrial killing precisely because they are inclined to comply with higher authorities and the demands of bureaucratic organizations, but only after a general weakening of the social taboos against killing that depends on political turmoil and invariably 'requires considerable time' (Elias 2013: 213).

It is hardly surprising then that many Germans were disgusted by 'old-fashioned spontaneous pogroms' in Romania, and that some in the SS felt the need to act to prevent the slaughter of Jews. Clearly, such moral responses that are 'second nature' as a result of conscience formation in 'civilized' societies can be overridden under the social conditions that were discussed above. But it is difficult to eradicate them entirely even amongst populations that have been brutalized by the experience of high levels of violence – which was one reason why the regime tried to minimize direct personal involvement in genocidal killing while diffusing responsibility for violence. Eichmann maintained that his technical expertise spared Jews unnecessary suffering by ensuring that killing took place not through 'sheer butchery' in the manner of savages but in a 'civilized way' (Arendt 1994: 190). For his part, Hoess (2000: 147) argued that the gas chambers released the guards from distress caused by mass shootings while delaying the suffering of the victims 'until their last moment came'. As with the earlier euthanasia programme, humanitarian language was a veil that was used to conceal the real motives. Industrial-style killing was designed to protect the sensitivities, such as they were, of those who controlled the technologies of mass slaughter. The Holocaust was an obvious assault on the humanist values of Western civilization, but the decision to place mass killing behind the scenes in remote locations revealed that one dimension of the process of civilization – namely, strong personal inclinations to avoid the offensive, the disgusting or the unsettling – had not exactly disappeared from view (de Swaan 2003: 140). In addition, at least the pretence of civilization had to be maintained even in the death camps. Himmler, Hoess and others congratulated themselves on their 'civilized' revulsion against brutality but boasted that they possessed the moral strength to ensure that they were not immobilized by 'civilized' feelings of disgust or remorse (Katz 1993: 96–7). Nazi leaders such as Goebbels did not deny, at least privately, that the genocides were anything other than 'barbaric' but they were quick to add that the regime could have 'no truck with senti-mentality' in its 'life-or-death struggle' against the 'Jewish bacillus' (Longerich 2003: 172–3).

The implementation of genocide depended on a gradient of evil that stretched from fanatical anti-semitism, pleasure in killing or satisfaction that mass slaughter had been implemented, the tacit consent of the removal of enemies, opportunistic involvement in the extermination programme, and the indifference of Weberian-style officials who dutifully performed specialist tasks within hierarchical bureaucratic organizations. The gradient of personal involvement raised complex questions about moral responsibility and blame during the Nuremberg trials, and specifically about whether, in the higher echelons of the Nazi regime, a 'Speer' was as guilty as a 'Himmler', whether the churches should be condemned because of the failure to organize resistance to the treatment of the Jews, whether business corporations should be prosecuted for profiting from the exploitation of slave labour in the camps, and whether it was reasonable to impute 'moral guilt' to all those who 'went right on with their activities, undisturbed in their social life and amusements, as if nothing had happened' (Jaspers 1947: 73).

Related issues about the apportionment of blame have run through reflec-tions on the potential for resistance under totalitarian rule, and specifically on the rights and wrongs of attributing blame and responsibility to individuals and institutions. They were interwoven with inquiries into the degree to which reparation for injustice demanded not only the punishment of those who had committed atrocities but also apology, contrition and restitution from society at large. The most important lines of investigation have centred on the problem of complicity in violent harm and the bystander's indifference to the fate of others.

It is useful to begin the following brief discussion of how 'civilized' peoples deal with the question of moral and political responsibility by considering the idea of prosecuting business corporations – or 'economic war criminals' – that had first been raised by the Frankfurt School theorist, Franz Neuman (Salter 2000). Leaders of business associations such as Flick, IG Farben and Krupp were tried and convicted for using slave labour. In the pursuit of its commer-cial interests, IG Farben became gradually entangled in Nazi rule and complicit in, and co-responsible for, amongst other things, the atrocities at Auschwitz

(Hayes 1987: epilogue). External constraints, political opportunism, and the preoccupation with economic self-interest removed ethical considerations. When dealing with the regime, there was always a reluctance to 'draw the line' (Kobrak and Schneider 2004). The widespread belief that the Nazis' period in office would be short-lived may explain decisions on the part of business as well as religious organizations to adopt a strategy of appeasement. Although big business was invariably unwilling to condone 'the penetration of anti-Semitism into economic life', it offered little 'adamant resistance', preferring instead to 'hold out until sanity' returned (Hayes 1995: 59). However, 'personal ambition and corporate competition produced a striking decline in human sympathy once the Nazi regime made its determination to dispossess Germany's remaining Jews unmistakable' (Hayes 1995: 61).

The question of the bystander has been a core theme in Holocaust narratives, but perhaps no more emphatically than in Jaspers' work and in Elie Wiesel's writings where the following claim is made: 'This, this was the thing I had wanted to understand ever since the war. Nothing else. How a human being can remain indifferent. The executioners I understood; also the victims, though with more difficulty. For the others, all the others, those who were neither for nor against, those who sprawled in passive patience, those who told themselves, "The storm will blow over and everything will be normal again", those who thought themselves above the battle, those who were permanently and merely spectators – all those were closed to me, incomprehensible' (cited in R. M. Brown 1990: 54). In the first major study of responsibility and the Holocaust, Jaspers (1947) argued that elementary human solidarity demands that every person accepts some accountability for the wrongs that are committed with his or her knowledge. The failure to prevent harm should generate moral guilt. In a rough parallel with Solon's argument in ancient Greece that the injuries of the world would disappear if bystanders experienced the same sense of resentment as those who had been wronged (Bowker 1975: 39), Jaspers maintained that everyone has a moral duty to take some risks to prevent wrongdoing, though not to the point of endangering their lives. Business corporations that were implicated in Nazi domination in the manner noted earlier prompted similar reactions, although there is no moral equivalence between opportunistic enterprises and powerless bystanders. If the exercise in apportioning blame should take account of power asymmetries and unequal capacities to influence political outcomes, then the acquiescence of those who were close to the regime and/or able to have some impact on its decisions is more alarming than the indifference of the individual citizen who could have no such impact (Linklater 2011: 70–1). As is widely known, many of the issues that arose during the Nuremberg trials continue to surface in discussions about the relative silence of the Vatican and raise important ethical questions about the problem of omissive harm in the sense of failing to warn endangered people of impending danger and endeavouring to help them (Goldhagen 2002: 172–3; Linklater 2011: chs. 1–2).

Discussions of omissive harm have relied on valuable distinctions between actions that 'civilized' people are expected to perform, and behaviour that has a heroic or supererogatory character (Linklater 2011: 77ff.). The upshot is that no blame should be attached to those who did not take a public stance against a tyrannical regime because they had good reason to fear violent death. The question then is what form the Lutheran moment as expressed in the claim, 'Here I stand, I can do no other', could or should have taken for those who were neither enemies of, nor threatened by, the regime. Philosophical questions about the moral responsibilities of people to one another in ostensibly 'civilized' societies go beyond the parameters of the present discussion. They are compounded by the fact that most Germans could not have foreseen the lengths to which the regime would go under the cover of war or because many did believe that 'everything would become normal again' if the regime collapsed or as a result of compromises with moderate political forces. That would appear to have been a widely shared position amongst conservatives such as Franz von Papen, the Reich Chancellor who facilitated Hitler's ascent to power. More complex and controversial is the case of the Catholic Church that has been accused of having attached more importance to dealing with threats to its political influence, and to concerns about the fate of Catholics under Nazi rule, than to taking a principled stance against the regression to 'barbarism' (Evans 2005: ch. 3). All that need be added is that disputes about the choices that were made revolve around the question of what individuals and organizations could have done to challenge the regime's assault on 'civilized' values. Apart from revealing how 'civilized' peoples have debated the issue of apportioning blame, the relevant deliberations have shown how, in the light of the Holocaust, societies have discussed how to organize themselves so that they are not at the mercy of disparate, uncoordinated and therefore ineffectual responses if or when similar dangers emerge in the future. Those are unprecedented developments in the history of the Western states-systems.

Central issues about moral and political responsibility were considered in several in-depth interviews at the end of the war with, for example, von Papen on his role as Chancellor during Hitler's rise to power, and on his subsequent conduct as German ambassador to Austria and Turkey towards the end of the conflict. They were also explored in the late 1970s in famous interviews with Albert Speer who rose from 'Hitler's Architect' to become Minister of Armaments in 1942 (Sereny 1995). During the Nuremberg Trials, the judge, Thomas Dodd, questioned von Papen on the issue of responsibility in politics, and stated 'that when any institution, whether it be an institution of government, or any other kind of institution, embarks upon an evil course, a man has a moral responsibility to completely disassociate himself from it, at least that, and a greater responsibility not to assist it in any way ... to carry out any part of its program (Overy 2002: 435–7). Similarly, at the trial of Karl Brandt, the former Reich Commissioner for Health and Sanitation, Judge Sebring asked whether it is not obviously 'true that in any military organization, even one of an authoritarian State, there comes a point beyond which the officer receiving an order subjects himself to individual responsibility, at least in the eyes of civilized society', for executing military orders that are 'unlawful' or exceed what might seem to be justified by 'extreme military necessity' (cited in Schmidt 2007: 373).

Von Papen's answer has been described as typical of 'the complicity of a wide circle of conservative Germans, who were slowly disabused of their early illusions about Hitler, but too patriotic and too prudent to pull away from the system' (Overy 2002: 423). Part of his explanation for his behaviour was that, prior to the Munich Agreement, the Western powers had assumed that a diplomatic agreement with Hitler was entirely conceivable, a judgement that it was also perfectly reasonable for the 'German patriot' to make (Overy 2002: 440). With respect to the camps, he admitted to knowledge of their existence but not of the brutalities that occurred there. Von Papen suggested that deaths were caused by food shortages following the destruction of the railways and, in the language of moral equivalence, he compared them to the British aerial bombardment of Dresden that had similarly illustrated the 'mental disease of humanity' that concludes that 'everything is allowed in war' (Overy 2002: 433).

Von Papen, who had never joined the Nazi party (but was associated with the regime in an ambassadorial capacity), was acquitted at Nuremberg, unlike Speer, who was accused of having 'authorized, directed and participated' in war crimes and crimes against humanity – and 'particularly the abuse and exploitation of human beings for forced labour in the conduct of aggressive war' (cited in Sereny 1995: 143). In 1941, Speer may not have known about the construction of camps to liquidate the Jews (Sereny 1995: 228ff.). Indeed, some leading Nazis may have been sincere when they pleaded that the number of reported deaths appeared to them to be exaggerated, and when they maintained that they would have been horrified to learn of the nature of the killings, although most 'would have tried to put it out of their minds' (Sereny 1995: 248). The question remains for 'civilized' societies of when a threshold was reached that 'civilized' people should not have crossed – in short, when those with significant political roles and responsibilities must be judged guilty of condoning or ignoring policies that drove the civilizing process into reverse.

Dodd suggested that, in von Papen's case, the tipping point should have been reached in the 1930s given the regime's use of political murder, the burning of the Reichstag on 27 February 1933, and the 'infamous laws'

(Overy 2002: 436). Sereny (1995: 266) maintained that, with respect to Speer, the 'watershed' was reached when he became aware of the killings in the Ukraine in 1941 (Fest 1979: 234ff.). By realizing around the time of Himmler's Posen speech that mass murder was taking place in the camps (but possibly only discovering the exact truth about the gas chambers during the Nuremberg trials), he became 'an active participant in the crime' of genocide (Sereny 1995: 401, 704; Fest 2001: 184ff.). Of the twenty-one Nazi leaders who were indicted at Nuremberg, Speer alone accepted responsibility for his involvement in the atrocities (Sereny 1995: 703–4); Fest 2001: 329ff.). He acknowledged what he described as 'tacit acceptance of the persecution and the murder of millions of Jews', and stressed that he suspected atrocities were taking place but lacked proof, and in any event, had not taken part in planning genocide (Sereny 1995: 707). He has been described as typical of the social stratum that knew enough about the killings to conclude that it was wise not to attempt to know more (Fest 2001: 329).

What is most important for the present discussion is not whether the defence that leaders such as Papen or Speer advanced was credible but what lessons follow for the political project of restraining the state's monopoly powers when they become the driving force behind a major 'decivilizing' process. Speer's crimes highlighted the ease with which 'relatively civilized' persons (including highly trained technical experts that have little appreciation of, or appetite for, the rituals of political debate and public accountability) can become complicit in evil (Fest 2001: 339ff.). Those processes have been emphasized to underline the need for legal and political arrangements that hold those who commit or condone acts of violence to account – and also serve as a future deterrent. Such institutional innovations are incomplete without a supporting civil culture that recognizes the critical importance of the distinction between 'simple responsibility' where obligations are fulfilled by complying with official rules or obeying superiors' decisions about what is permissible and what is forbidden in 'civilized' societies, and 'complex respon- sibility' where the social expectation is that obligations will be shaped by greater reflectiveness about the possible consequences of individual and collective actions, by greater foresight, and by higher levels of self-restraint (Linklater 2011: 101–2). Suffice it to add that, as discussed in the previous chapter, the critical importance of complex responsibility for 'civilized' inter- action was recognized by Smith and Hume in the context of lengthening webs of interconnectedness. Similar beliefs about the obligations of military and political leaders and their subordinates have been central to developments in international criminal law.

Discussions of the 'bystander phenomenon' – of failures to take a stand against state-organized violence and intimidation – have also been central to the literature on the Holocaust. Again, what is most important for the present discussion are the political lessons that many have derived from the analysis of the Nazi genocides, and specifically for collective enterprises to embed 'civilized' sensitivities in everyday life. It is clear from discussions of *Kristallnacht* that authoritarian regimes that are concerned with cultivating an image of respectability at home and abroad cannot easily ignore domestic or international criticisms of violence. The question is how far moral and other sanctions are enforced. Hitler's reported observation that European societies no longer gave any thought to 'the destruction of the Armenians' (see Dadrian 1998: 117), as well as the relative silence of the German people with respect to the Nuremberg Laws, and the indifference of the Churches to discrimination against the Jews are worth noting in this context. They reveal that violent groups can be emboldened by a general unwillingness to challenge or resist government policies. How far public criticism would have altered the course of events in Germany cannot be determined with any precision, but significant protest might have made all the difference when the regime seemed to be 'testing the water' to ascertain what it might be able to achieve (Staub 2003: ch. 22).

Investigations of those dynamics have raised the question of how far it is appropriate to apportion guilt to bystanders as well as perpetrators, and to conclude that an entire people has a duty of collective restitution to those who suffered at the hands of a regime that enjoyed significant electoral support (Jaspers 1947; also Levi 1988). In the German case, the issue of collective guilt and apology has been inseparable from discussions about how far anti-Semitic views were prevalent – that is, about how far attitudes to the Jews reflected not just indifference but 'passive complicity' in their humiliation, or malevolent or vicious dispositions (Barnett 1999: ch. 7). The issue of how 'civilized' societies should deal with the 'bystander problem' is further complicated by the reality that the people involved can occupy very different positions on a spectrum of attitudes to suffering. Some may be understandably anxious about the personal consequences of making even a small stand against official policy; for pragmatic reasons, they may acquiesce in policies that they privately regard as shameful and wrong; they may experience quiet satisfaction at the misery of others or pleasure at the final settling of old scores.

But what is not in dispute is that modern societies – and not only autocratic ones although the following condition is heightened there – provide a fertile breeding ground for large numbers of 'privatized persons' with little sense of connectedness with others and, especially, with low levels of emotional identification with members of stigmatized groups (Elias 2013: 327; Barnett 1999). The argument which has important nineteenth-century antecedents (see Mazlish 1989) is that the sense of responsibility for, and accountability to, others declines as they are rendered less visible and less audible by lengthening social webs (Bauman 2000: 24ff., 192ff.). In Germany, it has been argued, the trend towards 'privatization' was the 'counterpart' of the inability of people who were 'docile and numbed', and highly dependent on authority figures, to 'organize themselves and to take any initiative towards a concerted action independently of or against the official state agencies' (Elias 2013: 262ff., 308ff., 327ff., 400). Debates about whether those who assisted Jewish victims of Nazi oppression were inspired to act by their emotional bonds with specific people or by respect for universal ethical imperatives are worth noting at this point (see Rorty 1989: ch. 9; Geras 1995). One influential study has maintained that rescuers had a strong sense of personal connectedness with, and a feeling of responsibility for, victims who were outside their immediate social circles, precisely the emotional ties that bystanders in the main did not have (Oliner and Oliner 1988; Geras 1998: 64). The latter could take the path of 'internal emigration' into the private sphere where, through care for family and friends, they could assure themselves that their intrinsic goodness had not been compromised by, for example, the burdens of office (see, however, Waller 2002: 111ff.). Those were amongst the main features of the 'social conditions' that made the Nazi atrocities possible. Various steps have been taken since the end of the Second World War to promote normative and institutional changes in 'civilized' societies to cope with and reduce such dangers. They include the global prohibition of genocide in conjunction with the promotion of universal human rights and, when all else fails, recourse to judicial institutions that have the responsibility for enforcing international criminal law.

The Cosmopolitanism of Ordinary Virtues

What is the political significance of the Holocaust for the so-called project of modernity? The Nazi genocides have been interpreted as marking the demise of Enlightenment optimism and as demonstrating the calamitous consequences of utopian projects of social engineering that looked to science and technology to perfect society. Various theological discussions discussed whether the Holocaust was God's punishment for past sins, a test of 'faithfulness', or in some other way suffused with sacred meaning (Katz 2005). By contrast, several 'modern' and 'postmodern' reflections have kept faith with Enlightenment values and restated the defence of ordinary virtues in order to protect the achievements of 'civilized' societies from their dangerous structural features. The principles in question have an intriguing relationship with the lessons that have been drawn from studies of the bystander phenomenon and from analyses of the social processes that can lead ordinary people to become complicit in evil. As noted earlier, those lessons include the awareness of the need to foster collective sensitivities to the vulnerability of groups that have long been victims of discrimination, stigmatization and violence (not least through forms of public education that are designed to ensure that the Nazi and other genocides are not forgotten). Such innovations along with the international legal mechanisms that have the function of securing justice for victims of human rights abuse have been central to a global 'civilizing' offensive that has reacted against the disastrous fusion of sovereignty, territoriality, citizenship and national-ity by encouraging cosmopolitan socio- and psycho-genetic forces that alter the relationship between the individual citizen, the state, and humanity. What is therefore critical in addition to global institutional change is the development of a cosmopolitan habitus or what has been called 'cosmopo-litan subjectivity' (Vandekerckhove and van Hooft 2010).

Core ethical dimensions of that 'civilizing' project were encapsulated by Adorno (2000: 167ff.) when he observed that people may not know what is 'good' but, in the aftermath of the Nazi atrocities, they can have no doubt about what is 'bad' and what should be resisted. Auschwitz, he argued, demanded the affirmation of an ethic that took the 'injurable animal' as its starting point (Bernstein 2000). The inescapable vulnerability of people and the precarious-ness of social and political institutions generated the need for a 'new catego-rical imperative' that orientated 'thoughts and actions so that Auschwitz will not repeat itself, so that nothing similar will happen' again (Adorno 1973: 365). As discussed in Chapter 7, that perspective was central to Enlightenment quests to replace the 'heroism' of the warrior code that has been central to the history of the Western states-systems with the humanistic 'affirmation of ordinary life' (Taylor 1989: 12ff., part 3). In short, everyday peaceful pleasures organized around the family, the workplace and so forth became valued as the principal source of personal meaning as opposed to being portrayed as the mundane backdrop to supposedly higher collective ideals.

The rise to prominence of the personal testimony since the end of the Second World War has played no small part in placing 'the affirmation of ordinary life' and the ideal of combating unnecessary pain and suffering at the heart of cosmopolitan visions of the future course of the civilizing process. That development found its most brilliant advocate in Levi's reflections on the ethical principle that 'cruelty is the worst thing we do' (Gordon 2001: 26ff.). Levi's variant on that maxim emphasized the duty 'not to create pain, neither in ourselves nor in any other creature capable of perceiving it', unless necessary in order to avoid 'greater suffering to oneself or others' (Levi 1997: 214; Levi 2001:71). That was 'a simple rule' with very 'complex' ramifications that different religious and secular perspectives had converged towards from 'radically different presuppositions' (Levi 1989: 183–4).

One of the distinguishing features of that humanistic approach was its emphasis on how that ethical injunction is violated not only by inflicting physical harm but also by calculated acts of humiliation that withhold basic forms of respect and recognition. Levi's writings stressed the violence of refusals to grant others even the bare minimum of consideration, communica-tion and accountability in the death camps. They emphasized 'the look' and 'the look denied' that conveyed unambiguously the unspoken assumption that the other was worthless and irrelevant (Levi 1988: 138, 148; Levi 2000: 52–4). The same sentiment is evident in several recent conceptions of an ethic of responsibility to 'otherness' that may be regarded as intrinsic to the most recent phase of the civilizing process (see Gordon 2001: ch. 1). That orientation is central to efforts to strengthen cultural and psychological in addition to institutional or legal barriers against any future attempts to reverse the civilizing process. Their function is to support a social habitus that extends earlier features of that process including the widening of the scope of emotional identification between people and the interrelated critique of open displays of undisguised contempt for 'social inferiors' (Wouters 1998).

Of particular significance in the light of Elias's discussion of the place of the privatization of bodily functions in the European civilizing process, and of feelings of shame and embarrassment at their public exposure, were Levi's comments on the 'useless cruelty of violated modesty' during the transportation to the death camps and on the 'coercion of nudity' (Levi 1988: 66, ch. 5). No less important and for the same reasons, were his observations about feelings of disgust at being forced to urinate and defecate in the presence of others. The removal of natural functions behind the scenes, that has been central to the civilizing process (Elias 2012: 129ff.), exposed those in the camps to 'deliberate and gratuitous viciousness'; the result was, in an intriguing formulation, the 'trauma for which civilization does not prepare us' (Levi 1988: 88ff.). In response to 'excremental coercion', efforts were made to salvage a modicum of privacy by erecting screens; they offered 'symbolic' resistance to total reduction to 'animals' (Levi 1988: 88ff.). Those references to the particular sensitivities of 'civilized' people further demonstrate that the Nazi genocides were not a natural outgrowth of the civilizing process. The abandonment of basic taboos on implementing strategies of humiliation was unmistakeable evidence of the 'breakdown of civilization' (Weitzman 2010).

Levi's observations conveyed the shock at the collapse of 'civilized' standards in the 'Hobbesian' condition of the camps that was especially 'painful for the cultivated man' (Levi 1998: 108). But a certain faith in humanity and in the potential for future conditions that were in line with Enlightenment values explained the contention that 'ordinary virtues' did not disappear entirely in the camps (Levi 2001: 25). Several testimonies argued that many prisoners tried to live by the morality of avoiding harm to others, but requests for Good Samaritanism were invariably regarded as 'excessive' and were usually declined (Todorov 2000: 36). Levi (1998: 59) described the constant pleading of the 'weaker, or less cunning, or older, or too young, hounding you with … demands for help'. Resources were not squandered on those who were doomed to die and who could offer nothing in return; yet, crucially, most felt ashamed at failing to help (Levi 1998: 59–62; Levi 2001: 39; also Todorov 2000: 71ff.). Significantly, women's narratives have often stressed the distinctive social bonds that were anchored in their particular vulnerability to sexual humiliation and exploitation as well as rape (Ofer and Weitzman 1998; also Sommer 2008; Muhlhauser 2008; Shik 2008; Todorov 2000: 71ff.; Monroe 2004; Weitzman 2010).

The humanist defence of ordinary virtues is therefore linked with the empirical argument that they survived even in the death camps and must be embedded in social and political institutions where they can form a powerful barrier against any future efforts to weaken or reverse the civilizing process. The more radical statements of that position hope for major transformations of the scope of emotional identification so that societies willingly accept cosmopolitan obligations to rescue the victims of genocide. The aim is to combat powerful tendencies within liberalism that place negative moral duties to avoid injury at the heart of social life but remain largely indifferent to distant suffering. The alternative ethical vision states that 'our shared vulnerability or common capacity to suffer, is sufficient to establish between us bonds of mutual obligation' that do not 'stop at some regional or national boundary' (Geras 1998: 58ff.). The aspiration is that the relevant dispositions and sensitivities become entrenched in individual psyches so that emotions such as 'shame' and the 'foretaste of it' become major 'mobilizing' forces in a 'world overpopulated with bystanders' (Geras 1998: 57, 120).

Whether societies will develop in that direction in the course of a future global civilizing process is a speculative matter. But it can be stated with confidence that it will not occur unless the basic ethical responsibilities that were discussed by Levi are embedded in everyday life. Associated changes in personality traits and psychological dispositions are no less important for a global civilizing process than are the structural changes that are exemplified by legal institutions with responsibility for the enforcement of international criminal law. Without question, one of the most important political responses to the Holocaust has been the establishment of precisely those legal institutions that can bring sovereign leaders and their representatives to account. But there is more to the ideals behind those innovations than imposing external restraints on those who are prepared to unleash indefensible violent harm. The aim is to encourage individual self-restraint that is anchored not in the fear of external sanctions but in supporting cosmopolitan ethical principles as a matter of conscience. A similar emphasis on the dual character of 'civilized' restraints can be found in Levi's argument for the combined role of 'the cushioning effect' of the law and 'the moral sense that constitutes a self-imposed law' (Levi 2000: 103). That intricate web of socio- and psycho-genetic forces was missing from German society in the years preceding the Nazi genocides but it has never been particularly strong in many societies that have described themselves as highly civilized. Not least because of the Holocaust it has become more central than ever before to visions of a 'civilized' condition in which the ordinary virtues are central to the constitution of international society.

Towards a Planned Global Civilizing Process

The Nazi genocides and the total warfare of which they were part can be cited as conclusive evidence of the lack of moral progress in world politics over the decades or centuries – as a demonstration of how little has changed in the history of the Western states-systems. If there is a key difference between the present and the past it is that the modern equivalents of the ancient massacres could only have occurred in highly advanced industrial societies with the capacity to mobilize the technical expertise of large numbers of highly disciplined specialists in the implementation of state-directed, bureaucratized mass murder. Modern 'civilized' societies permit large-scale indifference to suffering in that the members of hierarchically organized structures can be shielded from experiencing the distress that is caused by the routine perfor-mance of administrative tasks; they can be protected from the shame and guilt that would ordinarily affect 'civilized' people by the comforting thought that ultimate responsibility for violent harm belongs rests with superiors. Therein lies one of the important links between modernity or the Holocaust and the civilizing process.

Other connections between those phenomena were the result of the long history of European imperial doctrines that became integrated within power struggles within the continent. The Nazi regime combined that dimension of the more general 'split' within modern civilization with the conviction that various kinds of violence that had been forbidden in relations between 'advanced' peoples were permissible and indeed necessary in 'life-or-death' struggles with internal and external enemies who were depicted as racial inferiors. The Nazis drew on core elements of the European civilizing process during the age of imperial expansion when the colonizing powers assumed that they could behave more or less as they pleased in conflicts with 'lesser' peoples; the Enlightenment critique of colonial cruelties that had transformed attitudes to civilization in neighbouring societies was rejected. Returning to the question of differences between the ancient and modern states-systems, Greek, Hellenistic and Roman armies had combined low levels of sympathy for 'outsiders' with modes of exploitation that included the enslavement of the inhabitants of defeated cities. The National Socialists represented a return to a tolerance of suffering that was not blocked or restrained by the 'civilizing' influence of Stoic and Christian conceptions of mercy. The suspension of such forces was linked with the recovery of 'hegemonic intoxication' and the reappearance of the 'hegemonic wars' that had dominated the earlier states-systems and were increasingly out of place in relations between 'civilized', industrialized societies. The entitlement to use whatever force was presumed to be essential to overwhelm adversaries constituted a regression to 'barbaric' practices by a people who had reached a higher level of 'civilization'.

But it is misleading to claim that the Nazi genocides revealed the essential nature of the process of civilization or the character of European modernity. 'Barbarism' occurred in the context of a profound economic and political crisis that bred widespread feelings of helplessness in a society where public support for 'enlightenment' values had been limited. Mass killing was the outcome of a systematic offensive against the social prohibitions and inhibitions on violence in a society in which major sections of the dominant social strata remained firmly wedded to a 'pre-modern', aristocratic warrior code. Even then, the worst atrocities occurred in wartime conditions of secrecy. A regime that had promoted 'disidentification' with the Jews and other 'enemies' of the Reich still found it necessary to conceal evidence of mass slaughter from the great majority of the German people, and from the wider world. That much was testimony to the continued importance of 'civilized' values. Nazi mass murder was a form of 'civilized' genocide.

Efforts to link the Holocaust with modernity are correct that industrial societies have unprecedented means of organizing large-scale killing but they fail to examine the complex processes by which 'civilized' restraints are weakened. An important connection with the civilizing process was captured by the observation that Europeans were largely unprepared for genocidal killing because of the belief that their civilized state was a 'natural' attribute of 'advanced' peoples rather a largely unplanned process that could be reversed (Elias 2013: 231). The naïve supposition that European societies enjoyed permanent immunity from future regression helps to explain the expectation in Germany and elsewhere that political realities would compel the regime to abandon its crude, ideological posturing and to comply with standard understandings of the relationship between violence and civilization.

Greater awareness of the need for domestic and international institutions and practices that defend 'civilized' values led to the extension of the social and political dynamics that were discussed in Chapter 5. Increased support for the universal and egalitarian values that distinguished 'civilized' peoples had not taken place because of autonomous patterns of moral learning however. It had not occurred because the people involved were intrinsically more humane than their predecessors; rather it was inextricably linked with major advances in the state's violent capabilities and with attendant political struggles. Total warfare and the Nazi genocides led to major extensions of the process of civilization. They revealed that the capacity to inflict harm over greater distances had greatly exceeded moral and political restraints on violence, and they demonstrated that it had become imperative to control the unprecedented powers that modern industrial societies have at their disposal. Progressions in the form of changing moral attitudes to the permissible and the forbidden took place in the era under consideration. They represented a major collective endeavour to address the dangerous imbalance between violent capabilities and 'civilized' restraints in the international states-system. The experience of industrialized killing was followed by new understandings of the radical changes that had to be implemented to protect the civilizing process and to prevent future regressions. Greater planning that has been a central feature of the recent phase of the civilizing process also distinguishes the contemporary stage of world politics (Elias 2007: 13; Elias 2013d: 192–3). The objective has been to rediscover the path that societies had seemed to be following during the age of Enlightenment.

Perhaps it is still generally assumed that 'civilized' societies are immune from the dangers that led to the rise of Nazism; perhaps the risks are widely believed to be confined to societies that are undergoing the difficult transition from autocracy to democracy that Germany had failed to make in the 1930s (Elias 2013: 175–6). On that interpretation, one of the main political responsibilities of 'civilized' societies is facilitating the establishment of stable democratic arrangements and promoting respect for human rights in other regions. Especially with the removal of the threat of nuclear war between the superpowers, secure 'civilized' societies may think that they face no more than 'localized' reversals of 'civilized' practices and need not dwell any longer on the danger of a wholescale regression to 'barbarism'. However, the question remains of whether 'civilized' societies could deceive themselves once again into thinking that they will escape major 'decivilizing processes' that can befall people as a result of unforeseen political or economic crises. No-one can be absolutely certain that support for 'civilized' principles is so deep-seated, and that the scope of emotional identification between people has widened so considerably and permanently, that the dangers can be ruled out in perpetuity.

The political responses to the Nazi genocides aimed to develop in a conscious and planned way a global counterpart to the combination of 'civilizing' socio- and psycho-genetic forces that had developed earlier at the national level. Earlier states-systems lacked sufficient institutional complexity to attempt to steer international society in that direction. Not least because of their 'civilized' self-images, modern societies have made unprecedented advances in establishing global mechanisms for publicizing and condemning violations of human rights. No parallel development in 'international ethics' can be found amongst 'simpler' peoples in the ancient states-systems. That they exist at all has a great deal do with the personal narratives of suffering that democratized core features of the conceptions of aristocratic civility that were inherited from earlier periods in the history of the Western states-systems. In an unparalleled change in the relationship between violence and civilization in world politics, national governments, international organizations and non-state actors have in their different but complementary ways created the outlines of a cosmopolitan legal and political sphere that links two interrelated principles – the Stoic value that every human being has a *prima facie* duty to refrain from harming all others, and the Kantian conviction that all people should unite to ensure that assaults on human rights in any part of the world are universally condemned and prevented wherever possible. Those twin normative standpoints that have affirmed the values of 'ordinary life' have their institutional counterpart in global agencies with responsibility for promoting compliance with international humanitarian law. They have given expression to the most recent phase of a civilizing process that is inspired by core Enlightenment principles. Far from disclosing the essence of the civilizing process, the Holocaust has had the long-term effect of deepening public commitments to such global values in the societies involved. The upshot is a global civilizing process that has extended the earlier dynamic of 'taming of the warriors' and the imperialists by striving to 'tame the sovereigns'.

10

Sovereignty, Citizenship and Humanity in the Global Civilizing Process

> The peoples of the earth are now confronted by [the] task ... of contributing gradually to a renunciation of the traditional warlike institutions through voluntary self-limitation, and perhaps even through voluntary submission to the arbitration of humanity. The mass of human beings, and in particular the leading strata of states, may perhaps gradually advance towards that stage of civilisation. But ... the task of achieving a pacification of humanity which is not enforced externally but is based on voluntary decisions remains for the present insoluble.
>
> (Elias 2010c: 145)

The principle of sovereignty has been central to European state formation and the process of civilization, and fundamental to the development of the modern society of states from its emergence in Europe to its subsequent enlargement to embrace the entire inhabited world. It was important in legitimating state monopoly powers and in the construction of a unique we–I balance in the international states-system. Indeed, to write a history of sovereignty is effectively to document the development of that balance in the relations between territorial states. Modern conceptions of sovereignty became linked with the principle that states are obliged to comply only with international legal obligations that they have freely imposed on themselves. The general understanding was that acts of self-limitation could be reversed when sovereign states decided that they had become incompatible with core objectives, and when they assumed – as they were legally entitled to do – that it was necessary to use force to protect vital security interests. But that was not how sovereignty was constructed in the early history of the modern states-system and, because of the influence of the European civilizing process, it is not how it is understood today.

The first part of the following discussion notes that political theories that defined sovereignty in terms of absolute rights rather than responsibilities were the product of a long process in which Christian ethical constraints on state power were weakened. They were the outcome of a changing we–I balance that reflected a particular phase in the development of relationships between sovereign powers, international society and humanity. The dominant conceptions of territorial sovereignty shifted in the light of lengthening and more dangerous human webs that created pressures to restrain the sovereign right to use force to settle major political differences. The industrialization of war and the Nazi genocides were followed by concerted efforts to rework the relationship between sovereign rights and international and humanitarian legal and moral responsibilities – in short, to change the we–I balance in the modern society of states.

The second section traces important developments with respect to the humanitarian laws of war. They were evidence of new legal principles with respect to avoiding 'unnecessary suffering' in European military conflicts that represented the internationalization of the dominant attitudes to violence and civilization in the leading sovereign states. The core international responsibilities that were constructed between 1814 and 1914 revealed how 'the international law of the civilized nations' replaced the earlier conceptions of Christian international society (Steiger 2001: 66ff.; also Keene 2002: 126ff. on the 'internationalization of civilization'). The law pertaining to 'civilized' peoples addressed the 'Janus-faced' nature of state formation and sovereignty, namely the coexistence of high levels of internal pacification with the high probability or certainty of destructive warfare. Systematic political efforts to deal with 'the split within civilization' were intricately linked with new understandings of the relationship between sovereignty and violence that stemmed from the larger civilizing process.

The analysis of those developments describes one of the principal outcomes of the European civilizing process, namely the establishment of new international criminal legal principles and procedures at the end of the Second World War which are discussed in the second section. That 'civilizing' initiative was designed to supersede the classical doctrine of sovereign immunity from prosecution while creating new legal responsibilities for all military personnel. The whole movement was interwoven with the extension of the universal human rights culture – with interlinked claims that sovereign states have fundamental moral responsibilities for protecting the rights of their citizens or subjects while the 'international community' has legal and moral obligations to act to prevent serious human rights violations, conceivably by using force in accordance with the principle of humanitarian intervention. That is the subject of the third section.

Those legal and political developments have often clashed with a second long-term trend in the modern society of states. Late nineteenth- and early twentieth-century experiments in embedding Western claims about 'civilized' restraints on force in international law coincided with the emerging 'revolt against the West' that was exemplified by Chinese and Japanese demands for an end to 'unequal treaties' and to the related principle of 'extraterritoriality' that dictated that disputes involving Europeans had to be resolved in accordance with the principles of European law. The long-term significance of that challenge to the global establishment was far from obvious to European peoples at the time. The architects of the nineteenth-century 'standard of civilization' and those who presided over the later transition from colonized territory to sovereign state were almost unanimous in believing that non-European peoples would adopt the dominant Western forms of political community and accept the core principles of European international society, including the principles of sovereign equality and non-intervention, diplomatic immunity and the doctrine of *pacta sunt servanda*. The imperial powers made the idea of civilization central to attempts to justify political controls over non-European peoples and to proclaim their 'natural entitlement' to elevate them to the heights that had been reached by 'advanced' Europeans. The concept was central to the imperial strategy of persuading other societies to internalize European images of their cultural inferiority and to overcome 'backwardness' by emulating the social standards and political institutions of the global establishment. The broad consensus was that a global political order would emerge in which sovereign nation-states were closely bound together by commitments to universalized, Western 'civilized' values.

That image of the future would turn out to be fundamentally mistaken. The smooth transition of many newly independent states to stable liberal democracies failed to take place in an era in which the Western powers became increasingly obliged by their conceptions of civilized existence to take an active stand against serious human rights violations in other societies. Two images of international society with their competing ideas about sovereignty came into conflict. The 'pluralist' conception in which territorial sovereignty and the principle of non-intervention that are regarded as crucial for maintaining order and stability between the great powers clashed with the 'solidarist' perspective in which individual human beings rather than states are the ultimate members of international society, external recognition of sovereign status is dependent on compliance with human rights principles, and the 'international community' may be entitled to intervene militarily in the internal affairs of a sovereign state to prevent or end a humanitarian emergency (Bull 1966). The solidarist elements of the international humanitarian laws of war that commanded significant support within Western liberal democracies came into conflict with the pluralist conception of international society that has enjoyed strong support amongst peoples that regard sovereignty as the most potent and meaningful symbol of their hard-won political struggle for independence. The rise of new international legal tests of the legitimacy of national governments became intertwined with major disputes about fundamental universal human rights and with related fears that the dominant powers would use their self-appointed role as guardians of 'civilized' values to resurrect colonial and neo-colonial political arrangements. Recent controversies about international criminal law or about the notion of 'the responsibility to protect' are descended from those earlier tensions over

Western efforts to reconstruct sovereignty in the light of a specific 'standard of civilization'. At their core lie competing images of the appropriate we–I balance in international society.

The next two sections of this chapter consider assorted efforts to refashion traditional conceptions of sovereign rights and responsibilities in response to the challenges of current levels of global interconnectedness. The fourth section discusses various interlocked political problems that are the outcome of the lengthening webs of economic and social interdependence that the pacification of dominant states and regions have made possible; they are also the product of changing power balances between public and private authorities in 'global market civilization'. The resulting poorly regulated social processes have the capacity not only to lead to economic or ecological crises but to generate social and political instability and violent conflict in affected regions. Whether they will create conflict in the more affluent societies is unclear, but they may influence future configurations of violence and civilization – specifically whether the more privileged societies and social strata believe that they are obliged to use force to assist those who may be caught up in violent struggle or decide instead that 'civilized' societies should not become involved in attempting to end violence in what may be regarded as 'uncivilized' societies that are consumed by 'tribalism'.

The final section considers recent efforts to develop conceptions of global ethical responsibility in response to longer chains of mutual dependence. Attempts to reconstruct state sovereignty by devising images of world or cosmopolitan citizenship, or global environmental citizenship, are important examples of that development. Those political concepts have been used to criticize traditional conceptions of the relationship between the duties that national citizens have to each other and the obligations that states have to one another as well as to international society, humanity and the 'global commons'. They reflect a growing awareness of the urgency of creating new we-identities, a transformed we–I balance and reconfigured standards of self-restraint that address the disjuncture between traditional images of political community and international society and inadequately controlled patterns of co-dependence. There are rough parallels between the dangers that societies face today as a result of higher levels of social and economic integration and the challenges that confronted the peoples of early modern Europe – and indeed societies in the earlier Western states-systems – as they became forced together in longer social webs. There are broad similarities between the conditions in which state formation took place and the process of civilization developed and the contemporary phase of human interconnectedness in which societies are obliged to consider whether they can agree on transcultural standards of self-restraint that enable people to become attuned to the interests of others over great distances. Tensions between the pluralist and solidarist conceptions of international society are reinforced by political responses to those challenges.

For some participants in contemporary debates about the future of sovereignty, cosmopolitanism has an indispensable contribution to make to defending principles of justice that can orientate people to current realities. For others, the language of global ethical responsibilities must be understood in conjunction with the history of unequal power relations; it cannot be separated from fundamental questions about the current and future distribution of political resources, life chances and meaningful opportunities. To rephrase the point, for some social and political groups, cosmopolitanism is critical for moving beyond a pluralist society of sovereign states that has run its course; it is the key to a new we–I balance. But for others, national sovereignty is central to resisting political strategies that may only ensure the continuing domination of Western conceptions of civilization that are unwelcome reminders of the imperial era. Those disputes are distinguishing features of deliberations on the rights and responsibilities of sovereign political authorities in contemporary international society.

Sovereign Rights and Responsibilities

The concept of sovereignty emerged alongside the dual monopoly powers of the modern state that were discussed in Chapter 5. From the outset it was a crucial theme in the defence of the legitimacy of the state and its legal rights in the face of diverse, and at times interlocked, internal and external challenges (Hinsley 1986; Spruyt 1994). As previously noted, Elias stressed the state's monopoly control of the instruments of violence and the right of taxation. But the idea of sovereignty underpinned two other monopoly powers that reflect the linkages between state formation, the process of civilization and the emergence of European international society: the legal right to represent the community in diplomatic negotiations and the associated authority to bind it in international law. Those monopoly powers have been linked with the doctrine of the supremacy of domestic law and with the rejection of any supposedly higher external court of appeal (Linklater 1998: 27ff.). The idea of sovereignty was at the hub then of the development and legitimation of the state monopoly powers that have been fundamental to the whole process of civilization and its expression in 'pluralist' international society.

The Peace of Augsburg has special importance for understanding the evolution of the sovereign principle. In 1555, after three decades of religious conflict, the central articles affirmed the principle, *cuius regio, eius religio*, which established the sovereign's right to determine the official religion within the domestic domain. It was assumed that the dominant religion would vary from state to each state, but important links with the medieval notion of a unified Christian international society survived in the principle that the rights of the sovereign were not absolute. Augsburg enshrined the doctrine that rulers had the obligation to tolerate minority religious views. The main fear was that intolerance would risk intervention by an external power that sympathized with a persecuted kindred minority, or might lead to its violent retaliation against devotees of the opposing faith within its borders. It was understood that such responses and counter-responses could quickly embroil the different parties in interrelated civil and interstate wars (Krasner 1999: ch. 3; Hinsley 1986: 175).

The qualifications of sovereign rights that were established at Augsburg and again at Westphalia in 1648 were distant antecedents of recent measures to make the external recognition of sovereignty conditional on compliance with international standards of restraint with respect to minority and individual human rights (Krasner 1999: ch. 3). States found it valuable to quality 'Westphalian sovereignty' – the exclusion of external authorities from their domestic jurisdiction – in return for 'international legal sovereignty' – recognition of appropriateness for membership of the society of states (Krasner 1999: 237–8). The changing relationship between the two sides of sovereignty sheds considerable light on the evolution of modern international society.

Levels of compliance with the normative expectations that were associated with membership of that society reflected the usual power asymmetries; they depended on the extent to which states could disregard the relevant standards of restraint with little cost to themselves. The existence of certain restrictions on sovereign rights from as early as the mid-sixteenth century does not alter the plain reality that, over the following three centuries, the 'monopoly mechanism' curtailed the powers and liberties of religious and political institutions both 'above 'and 'below' centralizing state institutions. Most regimes regarded alternative sites of political authority with considerable suspicion and as a potential source of internal instability. With the spread of the more virulent forms of nationalism from the end of late eighteenth century, domestic opponents of sovereign expressions of collective pride were often portrayed as dangerous or disloyal. Those developments broke with earlier notions of Christian international society by tilting the we–I balance decisively in favour of autonomous sovereign nation-states (Hinsley 1986).

Significantly, the early modern philosophical defence of the sovereign's supreme law-making power did not support political absolutism. Bodin argued that rulers should govern in accordance with local laws and customs and should be restrained by the law of nature and by ultimate answerability to God. On that basis, he maintained that 'no prince of this world' could claim to be truly sovereign; it was false to think that 'to have absolute power is not to be subject to any law at all' (Bodin 1992 [1583]: 10). The idea of sovereignty referred to the functional need for a final legal court of appeal in state-organized societies, but that structural necessity was clearly bound up with the ethical conviction that 'the law of God or nature' should constrain the exercise of state power (Bodin 1992 [1583]: 110ff.). The doctrine that sovereignty was essential for the internal pacification of society was compatible, and was indeed derived from, the medieval doctrine that natural law was the ultimate foundation of the positive law (Pemberton 2009: ch. 3). Revealingly, Bodin did not defend modern conceptions of the state's monopoly control of the instruments of force, but argued that 'aristocratic violence' could play a vital role in supporting the sovereign's responsibility for maintaining public order (Phillips 2011: 125–6). Using Bodin's standpoint to support absolute sovereign power was a later development.

The corollary of domestic sovereignty was the principle that no external authority had the right to impose its national laws on the territory in question, to hold a ruler accountable for matters that came within the sphere of domestic jurisdiction, to intervene militarily in the internal affairs of other societies, or to claim an entitlement to represent another government in international society or to commit it to international legal obligations without its express consent. But there was a long process in developing those aspects of modern ideas of constitutional separateness and political autonomy that initially clashed with theological doctrines that proclaimed that rulers were answerable to a more inclusive Christian society. It is instructive that Bodin rejected Machiavelli's assertion that the prince should be prepared to cast aside religious restraints in the interests of the state under conditions of conflict. Early modern political theories of sovereignty contended that the rights of separate political communities were circumscribed by natural law and the *ius gentium*. External sovereignty understood as 'constitutional independence' (James 1986) did not release foreign policymakers from fundamental moral restraints, just as internal sovereignty, understood as the final court of legal appeal, did not support a doctrine of absolute political power and unqualified rights over subjects.

Bodin's differences with Machiavelli provide a useful reminder that early discourses of sovereignty did not insist that there were irreconcilable tensions between Christian ethics and statecraft. Over time, sovereignty would become associated with the freedom to do whatever was required to protect the 'national interest'. But there have long been conflicts between the defence of unqualified state's rights and the conviction that sovereign rulers have fundamental responsibilities for maintaining international order and preserving the society of states. Diplomats such as Lord Bolingbroke – one of the architects of the 1713 Treaty of Utrecht that entrenched the principle of the sovereign equality of states in modern international society – referred to 'the constitution of Europe' to defend the precept that sovereigns were not free to behave as they wished but were to be judged by the extent to which they observed the 'civilizing' virtues of foresight and self-restraint that were essential for 'repose' or 'tranquillity' in interstate relations (Osiander 1994: 110ff.). The 'civilizing' constitutive principles and practices of the European society of states – including the notion of the special responsibilities of the great powers that was formulated with greater precision in the post-Napoleonic Concert system – addressed the problem of order between increasingly interconnected states that insisted on absolute sovereign rights. There is an important parallel with the emerging conceptions of 'civilized' diplomacy in the early eighteenth century French court that also envisaged a we–I balance in which sovereign rights were harmonized with obligations to the larger European society of states.

Only in the nineteenth century as modern nationalism weakened the importance of aristocratic we-identity within international society did sovereignty acquire its 'absolute' form. Only then did particular political and intellectual groups link it with the 'Social Darwinian' contention that the essence of the state was expressed in aggressive national self-assertion, in international struggles and in overseas conquest (Hinsley 1986: 208ff.). The broad movement towards legal positivism legitimated the pernicious doctrine that states had unqualified rights to withdraw from international agreements whenever they believed that they clashed with vital interests. States did not gravitate towards that view as one. As discussed in the previous chapter, the practice of emphasizing the gulf between the principles that should apply within the state and the standards that should be observed in their external relations was stronger in Germany where *Kultur* was set against 'civilization' with drastic consequences for the European political order. But because of the violence unleashed by 'totalizing' conceptions of political community, the pendulum has swung back in recent times to the position where sovereign rights are far more conditional on compliance with duties to international society and interrelated obligations to humanity than they were in the period when Bodin discussed the idea of sovereignty or when Bolingbroke reflected on the foundations of the tranquillity of Europe. As previously discussed, the tension between civilization and *Kultur* was important for the late nineteenth-century international legal analyses of the correct balance between sovereign rights and responsibilities. It was a central part of a tradition of reflection on the relationship between sovereignty, civilization and international society that would be extended in later discussions of international criminal law.

Several recent analyses of state sovereignty have shown that the concept has not had a fixed meaning but has been constantly reworked in response to changing social and political conditions (Bartelson 1995, Biersteker and Weber 1996; Kalmo and Skinner 2010). Shifts in the relationship between sovereign rights and responsibilities that reflected the need for greater self-restraint as a result of increasingly destructive warfare illustrate the point. Bolingbroke's conception of 'civilized' foreign policy in the early eighteenth century was restated a few decades later by Vattel who commended the great powers' foresight in preserving the balance of power for reasons of high 'principle' rather than national 'expediency' (Hinsley 1986:199). A core contention was that states were no longer a 'confused heap of detached pieces, each of which thought herself very little concerned in the fate of the others, and seldom regarded things that did not immediately concern her'; they were so 'closely connected' that all had come to depend on the close monitoring of political developments to ensure that the balance of military power thwarted any state that aspired to 'predominate, and prescribe laws to the others' (Vattel [1758] 1863: III, iii.47). As the century drew to a close, it was even more evident to thinkers such as Kant that the 'risks of uncontrolled behaviour' demanded not the supersession of national sovereignty – an impossible task in any case – but its 'self-imposed improvement' through a deeper sense of 'responsibility' to international society and the inclusive community of humankind (Hinsley 1986: 212–13). Various post-war international conferences to rebuild the interstate order gave practical expression to those aspirations for taming sovereignty (Hinsley 1986: 200, 226ff.; Clark 2005; Holsti 2004). In the relevant deliberations at the end of the Napoleonic wars and at the end of the two major wars of the twentieth century, societies worked out their tentative compromises between cherished national rights and international or cosmopolitan responsibilities. They were significant attempts to tame sovereign powers by embedding the ethical obligation to refrain from causing unnecessary harm – a core element of the liberal dimension of the civilizing process since the mid-nineteenth century – in the organizing principles of international society (Donelan 1990: ch. 4; Jackson 2000: ch. 1).

The pivotal role of the idea of civilization in the reconceptualization of sovereign rights and responsibilities from the nineteenth century is exemplified by the sections of the 1863 Lieber Code that addressed the question of military necessity – a code that its author maintained was derived not from any existing authoritative legal text but from the core beliefs and practices of 'civilization'. Even strategic necessity, Lieber maintained, did not excuse 'suffering for the sake of suffering or for revenge', or permit 'the employment of weapons that uselessly aggravate the sufferings of disabled men, or render their death inevitable'; it was important to respect the principle that those 'who take up arms against one another in public war do not cease on this account to be moral beings, responsible to one another and to God' (cited in Meron 1998a: 135ff.; Best 1994: 42–3). In a similar spirit, the preamble to the Fourth Hague Convention (the so-called Martens clause) maintained that civilians and combatants 'remain under the protection and the rule of the principles of the law of nations, as they result from the usages established among civilized peoples, from the laws of humanity and the dictates of the public conscience'; the articles defended the principle that 'the right of belligerents to adopt means of injuring the enemy is not unlimited' (cited in Best 1994: 76). The idea of civilization is therefore crucial for understanding how the moral boundaries between permissible and impermissible violent harm, and between acceptable and unacceptable levels and forms of human suffering, have shifted in conjunction with the transformation of warfare in the modern states-system. In particular, the international legal obligation to avoid causing 'unnecessary suffering' and 'superfluous injury' has been part of the diplomatic endeavour to question justifications for violence that rest on standard doctrines of military necessity (Detter 2000: 395; Linklater 2011: 122ff.).

The Martens clause promoted the 'self-limitation' of sovereignty but the great majority of states continued to support the premise that the principle expressed an inalienable right to decide when force was essential to defend vital interests. On that argument, the core meaning of sovereignty is evident in the reserve powers that can be employed in an 'extreme emergency', as encapsulated by the renowned thesis that 'the sovereign is he who decides on the exception' (Schmitt 1985 [1934]: ch. 1). But the status of that political claim is precisely what has been at stake in reflections on sovereignty and civilization over the past few decades. The opening speech by Shawcross at the Nuremberg trials stated that 'modern civilization puts unlimited weapons of destruction in the hands of men. It cannot tolerate so vast an area of legal irresponsibility' (quoted in Kelman and Hamilton 1989: 73). The significance of that claim for the development of international criminal law will be considered later. The key point at this stage of the discussion is that the prosecution at the Nuremberg trials argued that the defendants did not possess the unqualified sovereign right to decide what constituted strategic necessity. By stating that the legitimacy of such deliberations was a matter for courts of law, they established the basic legal principle that the burden of proof regarding allegations about the strategic impossibility of observing with humanitarian norms rested with the relevant military and political leadership (see Detter 2000: 398 who refers to the subsequent general decline of appeals to strategic necessity in the justification of military action; also Best 1994: 328ff.). Those legal considerations of sovereignty, civilization and international society led to the significant reconfiguration of the relationship between national rights and responsibilities. They constituted an unprecedented assault on the most pernicious consequences of 'the duality of normative codes within the nation-state' (Elias 2013: 169ff.). Such efforts to tame the exercise of national sovereignty by embedding new conceptions of personal responsibility in international criminal law have been critical elements of the 'civilizing' endeavour to bridge the two spheres of domestic and international politics.

War Crimes and Civilization

The idea of punishable 'crimes against humanity' and the notion of 'crimes against the peace' have been central concepts in the attempt to ensure support for universal ethical responsibilities that demonstrate the impact of the

European civilizing process on contemporary international society. The whole movement with respect to 'international ethics' is unprecedented in the history of the Western states-systems. The link between the idea of civilization and the humanitarian laws of war goes back at least as far as the 1868 St Petersburg Declaration which contended that in the relations between 'civilized nations', it was essential to identify the moment at which 'the necessities of war ought to yield to the requirement of humanity'; the 1907 Hague Conventions defended 'the interests of humanity and the ever progressive needs of civilization'; with the 1977 Geneva Protocols, similar legal principles were derived from 'established custom, from the principles of humanity and from the dictates of public conscience' (Roberts and Guelff 2001: 54, 69, 423). By that time, the idea of civilization was tarnished because of its association with Western cultural supremacy. But in the latter part of the nineteenth and well into the twentieth century, the concept was at the heart of international law which expressed, according to many legal scholars and diplomats, the moral 'conscience' of the civilized world. Interestingly in the light of the early course of the European civilizing process, it was supported precisely because it transcended *Kultur* or parochial national traditions (Koskenniemi 2001: chs. 1–2). The idea of civilization was regarded as having a 'transcendent' quality that provided an image of a future political condition in which European peoples reached a higher state of civilization by eradicating unnecessary suffering in warfare. That was the period between the end of the Napoleonic Wars and the end of the First World War when 'the international law of the civilized nations' that was mentioned earlier formed a bridge between earlier Christian images of the society of states and what has been described as the recent period in which the 'international law of the world citizen' and common humanity have acquired greater political significance (Steiger 2001; Teitel 2011).

The 'civilizing' initiative recognized the importance of creating not only standard-setting legal conventions that exerted external pressures on states but also internal restraints that ensured that compliance was a matter of obeying the dictates of conscience. It was recognized that the modern laws of war would accomplish little unless combined with significant changes in psychological attitudes to principles of self-restraint. In a notable statement of the need for changes at the level of 'conscience formation', Moynier (who was a central figure in the first four decades of the International Committee of the Red Cross) argued that 'what is called "the law of war" is, essentially, a bastion against the abuse of force, a brake put on the unleashing of bestial passions aroused by the heat of battle; it is therefore necessary, after proclaiming this law, to take special measures to get it into the mind (ésprit) and the conscience of any society willing to pursue its end by war ... It is an illusion to believe that last-minute preachings of moderation to men already excited by the smell of powder, will bring any worthwhile result' (cited in Best 1983: 286).

That standpoint emphasized that a global civilizing process depended on a novel combination of 'sociogenetic' and 'psychogenetic' changes – on a rough parallel to the earlier transformations in European societies that were discussed in Chapter 5.

A major trend in international legal thinking was taken further at the end of the First World War when certain antecedents of the idea of crimes against humanity appeared in diplomatic deliberations about whether to prosecute the Kaiser and other German war leaders as well as Turkish perpetrators of alleged atrocities against the Armenians (Articles 227–30 of the Versailles Treaty addressed the central issues). A 'High Tribunal' with the responsibility for prosecuting those who had committed 'violations of the laws and customs of war and of the laws of humanity' might have been established at the end of the First World War had the United States not blocked the way (Marrus 1997: 2ff.; Willis 1982: ch. 5). Specific concerns about charges of 'Victor's Justice' led the American delegation to argue initially for relying on existing legal mechanisms, namely domestic courts. Anything else, the contention was, would assume 'a degree of responsibility hitherto unknown to municipal or international law' (Willis 1982: 75–6). The US Secretary of State, Lansing, expressed the Administration's official position when stating, in an intriguing formulation, that 'the essence of sovereignty (is) the absence of responsibility. When the people confided it to a monarch or other head of State, it was legally speaking to them only that he was responsible, although there might be a moral obligation to mankind. Legally however, there was no super-sovereignty' (cited in Willis 1982: 74).

One can only speculate about the short-term effects of introducing new international legal restraints on the exercise of sovereign powers in that period. It is a matter of conjecture, for example, whether it would have influenced Hitler's policies towards the Jews. His remark that was cited earlier about the state of indifference to the fate of the Armenians displayed the confidence that the European powers might well stand by while the Nazi regime pursued its violent objectives. Only twenty-five years after the decision not to create international legal machinery to prosecute those who might be guilty of war crimes, the victorious great powers invoked the idea of 'civilization' to defend the establishment of such judicial procedures. The discourse of civilization that had shaped the development of international humanitarian laws of war filled an obvious legal gap in the Allies' argument. The Nazi and Japanese leaders could not be accused of violating positive international law at least as far as crimes against humanity were concerned. As the Nuremberg Tribunal observed in its final judgment, none of the established international conventions had established the principle of individual criminal responsibility for offences against the law of nations. Moreover, given that appealing to the immutable tenets of the law of reason raised obvious difficulties, it was convenient to claim that the Nazi leadership had violated the standards of 'civilized nations' (see Best 1994: 180ff.). At the Tokyo Tribunal, the accused were charged with contradicting Japan's claim prior to 1930 to have taken its 'place among the civilized communities of the world'; the implication was that it had 'voluntarily incurred ... obligations designed to further the cause of peace, to outlaw aggressive war, and to mitigate the horrors of war' (see the Majority Judgment in Boister and Cryer 2008: 110). The Nuremberg Tribunal clarified what was at stake when it referred to treaties such as the Kellogg–Briand Pact to which Germany was signatory. The point was that the Axis powers must have realized that they were violating 'civilized' principles that defined the we–I balance between the sovereign state and an international society with pronounced solidarist dimensions.

At the Nuremberg trial, Justice Robert Jackson argued that 'the wrongs which we seek to condemn and punish have been so calculated, so malignant, and so devastating, that civilization cannot tolerate their being ignored because it cannot survive their being repeated' (cited in Schmidt 2007: 341; also Tusa and Tusa 1983: 154ff.; Douglas 2001). Crucial was the exhibition at Nuremberg of the head of a Polish prisoner of war (the so-called shrunken head of Buchenwald) which produced feelings of revulsion that were expressed in terms of the conflict between 'civilization' and 'barbarism'. Only 'savages' engaged in headhunting; museum exhibits provided material evidence of the incontrovertible superiority of 'civilized' peoples over 'barbarians' (see Douglas 2001a: 83ff. who cites the French prosecutor, François de Menthon, on the Nazi's regression to the 'primitive barbarity of ancient Germany'). The idea of civilization was used to move such violent actions from the sphere of sovereign domestic jurisdiction and to classify them as punishable offences under international criminal law. The concept was employed to transform the conventional understandings about the relationship between political and military leaders and those who were subject to their command. The chief British prosecutor at Nuremberg, Sir Hartley Shawcross, was explicit that it was 'in the interest of civilization' to regard actions that might have been 'in accordance with the laws of the German state' as 'crimes against the laws of nations' and clearly not as 'matters of domestic concern' (cited in Marrus 1997: 188–9).

The language used in the official indictment of the German war leaders contained several references to the 'general principles ... derived from the criminal law of all civilized nations' that could be used to identity actions from which there could be no dispensation even in warfare; the relevant principles were deemed to override classical notions of sovereign rights and associated conceptions of the personality of the state that had been used to absolve individuals of responsibility for supposed violations of 'civilized' standards and to establish the absolute right to immunity from prosecution (Marrus 1997: 57ff.). The two principal legal developments declared, first, that their 'official position' as Heads of State or high-ranking officials in Government 'shall not be considered as freeing them from responsibility or mitigating punishment' (Article 7 of the Charter of the International Military Tribunal signed on 8 August 1945); and, second, as stated in Article 8, that anyone acting 'pursuant to order of his Government or of a superior shall not free him from responsibility, but may be considered in mitigation of punishment' (Marrus 1997: 51ff.). The latter innovation specifically addressed the political problem that although modern societies had made advances in dampening cruel and aggressive dispositions, they had not made significant progress in combating forms of violence 'that have their origin in authority' (Milgram 1974: 164). The key issue with respect to 'superior orders' was the scope for moral choice in military organizations that demanded high levels of obedience and could ruthlessly punish non-compliance. The Tribunal stated that the 'true test, which is found in varying degrees in the criminal law of most nations, is not the existence of the order, but whether moral choice was in fact possible . . . A soldier could be relieved of personal responsibility for the soldier's acts only if the soldier could show that he or she did not have a moral choice to disobey his or her superior's orders' (cited in May 2005: 181; also Kelman and Hamilton 1989: 70ff.).

The Nuremberg Trials were a turning point in the development of a Western-initiated global civilizing process – albeit an unlikely one because the Allies had initially favoured 'summary proceedings followed by speedy punishment – in all likelihood death' (Marrus 1997: 242; also Overy 2002: 6–7). At the *Inter-Allied Conference on the Punishment of War Crimes* in January 1942, they declared that 'the sense of justice of the civilized world' demanded recourse to the 'channels of organized justice' rather than 'acts of vengeance on the part of the general public' that might result in domestic instability and sow the seeds of a future nationalist revival (Taylor 1971: 26–7). The legal revolution of Nuremberg was no more evident than in the establishment under Article 6(c) of the Charter of the principle that war leaders could be prosecuted for crimes against humanity – for committing acts of violence against civilian populations. The charge of prosecuting 'total war' – or causing 'the murder and ill-treatment' of prisoners of war and civilian populations that included genocide, torture, medical experimentation on living subjects, the use of slave labour, the confiscation of public and private property and, specifically the persecution and extermination of the Jews on 'political, racial and religious grounds' – extended a very long-term 'civilizing' trend in European societies. More than any other provision, the Article redrew the legal and moral boundary between the domestic and the international political domains just as the dividing line between 'public' and 'private' has been redrawn within societies in the course of the civilizing process in conjunction with changing conceptions of permissible and forbidden harm. Across all of the social and public institutions involved, support for 'civilized' standards led to higher levels of external accountability coupled with new standards of criminal responsibility.

As far as the international criminal prosecutions were concerned, legal proceedings had to overcome the standard defence of state sovereignty which was expressed by American delegates at the meetings that led to the 8 August 1945 London Charter on the trial of German war leaders. They referred to 'the general principle of foreign policy of our Government from time immemorial that the internal affairs of another government are not ordinarily our business; that is to say, the way Germany treats its inhabitants, or any other country treats its inhabitants, is not our affair any more than it is the affair of some other government to interpose itself in our problems' (cited in Forsythe 2009: 297). That standpoint was overridden by the ethical principle that was defended by the Nuremberg prosecutor, Justice Benjamin B. Ferencz, who stated that 'the true sovereign in international law, that becomes more and more clear, is the human being' since only 'his or her protection matters' (cited in Schmidt 2006: 17). Almost inevitably, with total warfare acting as the catalyst, social standards that embodied the conviction that cruelty and unnecessary suffering should be forbidden from 'civilized' societies intruded into the traditionally resistant enclave of international politics. It was one of the last bastions to hold out against the infiltration of higher standards of external scrutiny and accountability because of the continuing influence of territorial sovereignty, geopolitical rivalries that led to appeals to strategic necessity, and the duality of nation-state moral codes. The globalization of the liberal harm principle was at the heart of legal action against war criminals (Linklater 2011: ch. 1; May 2005: ch. 5). The emergence of international criminal law in accordance with the 'solidarist' principle that was defended by Ferencz and others was a critical step in the 'civilizing' process of embedding cosmopolitan harm conventions in international society, albeit in selective ways. For example, the list of war crimes 'included most violations of the laws or customs of war, such as murder, pillage, and destruction of towns', but one form of violence that was missing from the Nuremberg indictment was rape which was only added to the list of crimes against humanity following the use of sexual violence as an instrument of warfare in the Yugoslav conflicts (Askins 1997: 136ff.; also Meron 1998a: ch. 11 on the Tokyo Tribunal).

For Judge Jackson, the decision to prosecute at Nuremberg constituted the triumph of reason and justice over power and vengeance; it was not just a reaction to Nazi 'barbarism' but a major advance beyond the 'primitivism' of international relations more generally, as illustrated by national propaganda during the two world wars that had used the imagery of a struggle to defeat the 'Hun' or the 'Japs' to mobilize public opinion. The Nuremberg and Tokyo trials exercised a 'civilizing' role of distinguishing between the regime and the subject people, recognizing that however intertwined they were in practice, and however much the former depended on at least the latter's tacit consent, they were not one and the same. The decision to hold entire political organizations culpable for mass killing – the Gestapo and the SS, for example – was predicated on the supposition that it would prepare the way for individual prosecutions in accordance with established liberal conceptions of criminal responsibility.

The legal process was therefore targeted at state officials and those with command responsibilities who had inflicted serious harm or who had failed to make serious attempts to prevent it. The whole process was far from uncontroversial. Criticisms of the legitimacy of the trials were made at an early stage by German Protestant church leaders who protested against 'Victor's Justice' that neglected the Soviet Union's crimes in Poland. Some defendants were quick to advance a similar point. At his trial, Karl Brandt stated that it was 'not surprising that the nation which in the face of the history of humanity will forever have to bear the guilt for Hiroshima and Nagasaki . . . attempts to hide behind moral superlatives'; he added, *contra* Jackson, that 'what dictates is power' rather than justice, and proceeded to described himself as a victim of an 'act of political vengeance' and 'political murder' (cited in Schmidt 2007: 396). That there were double standards that are intrinsic to Victors' Justice is not in doubt. Revealingly, in the summer of 1945, the Allies considered including the bombing of cities in the indictment of the Nazi leaders, but decided against doing so on the advice of the British Foreign Office that German defence lawyers would almost certainly use that argument against them (Overy 2013: 650). It is perhaps unsurprising that the concept of civilization which was so central to the indictments at Nuremberg and Tokyo was also deployed in the case for the defence. In the concluding statement at Nuremberg, the defence argued that the tribunal breached the convention that there can be no punishment without a previous law (*nullum crimen sine lege, nulla poena sine lege*). The allegation was 'that *ex post facto* punishment is abhorrent to the law of all civilized nations' (Marrus 1997: 228ff.). In a dissenting statement at the Tokyo military tribunal, the Indian representative, Justice Pal, argued that the decision to prosecute and punish without demonstrable evidence of the violation of existing principles of law 'obliterated the centuries of civilization which stretch between us and the summary slaying of the defeated in a war' (cited in Boister and Cryer 2008: 827).

Important questions about how far law is a means of securing justice or an instrument of revenge arose in conjunction with the trial of General Yamashita, the commander of Japanese forces in the Philippines towards the end of the Second World War, a trial that raised complex issues about the specific issue of command responsibility. Yamashita was found guilty and hanged for failing to prevent atrocities in the months prior to Japan's surrender. That atrocities took place is not in question. How much Yamashita knew about them is less clear. Whether he could have prevented them is questionable, according to many, because the American assault on Japan had seriously damaged the military command structure. The judgment against Yamashita established a principle of responsibility according to which senior officers were obliged to do everything in their power to ensure that those under their command complied with the laws of war; they could be found guilty for having 'deliberately and recklessly' disregarded the duty 'to take adequate steps' to prevent their violation (Best 1994: 191–2; Dower 1999: 444ff.; Meron 1998a: 82ff.; Walzer 1978: 319ff.). Whether justified or not – and some have claimed that Yamashita was judged in accordance with wholly inappropriate notions of 'strict liability' (Walzer 1978: 320) – the verdict established the principal of commander responsibility to exercise 'due diligence' to ensure that subordinates respected the laws of war (Meron 1998a: 82ff.). As for later developments with respect to international criminal law, the 'Yamashita doctrine' was not incorporated into the 1949 Geneva Conventions, although the 1977 Additional Protocol I established a principle of due diligence, as did the statutes governing the tribunals for investigating war crimes and crimes against humanity in the former Yugoslavia and Rwanda (Meron 1998a: 85–6; Roberts and Guelff 2001: 565ff., 615ff.). Such provisions have upheld the principle that the 'burden of proof' falls on officers; as the 'presumptively guilty' parties, the onus is on them to demonstrate that all reasonable measures were taken to ensure that those under their command complied with the humanitarian laws of war (Walzer 1978: 322). Those are central dimensions of how the 'process of civilization' has been extended to include international legal measures that are designed to tame state sovereignty.

Enlarging the Scope of Sovereign Responsibility

The Nuremberg and Tokyo war crimes tribunals inaugurated a new phase in the relationship between state sovereignty, citizenship and humanity. What followed by way of the universal human rights culture and with respect to international criminal law can be conveniently summarized by recalling Kant's distinction between *ius civile* (civil law), *ius gentium* (the law of nations) and *ius cosmopolitum* (the law of world citizenship) (see Chapter 7, p. 296). As a result of the war crimes tribunals, the balance of power between those spheres of law changed fundamentally. Obligations under cosmopolitan harm conventions that had the function of protecting individuals in their own right were added to traditional sovereign responsibilities under international harm conventions in order to place additional restraints on the use of force. States that violate the rights of individual citizens can no longer claim that other powers violate the constitutive principles of international society by interfering in matters that fall exclusively within their sovereign jurisdiction.

The overall but uneven trend in which the international recognition of sovereignty has become conditional on compliance with global conventions regarding human rights has to be understood in the long-term perspective that is provided by the examination of the European civilizing process. It represents the global extension of 'civilized' attitudes to violence, cruelty and suffering that have shaped political struggles to curtail the traditional entitlements of various private associations within many sovereign states and to subject them to more demanding public standards of legal and moral accountability. A major example is the suspension of previously unrestrained male rights to use violence against women and children in 'civilized' societies (Perrot 1990). In most of the societies involved, the traditional male 'right' to demand sexual favours has been outlawed; as a result, marital rape is now a criminal offence in many legal systems (Vigarello 2001: ch. 15). Similar shifts are apparent in changing orientations towards the use of physical punishment in schools and towards the traditional rights of private sporting associations to hunt and kill non-human species. The criminalization of 'cruelty to animals' is an additional manifestation of the ongoing transformation of emotional attitudes to suffering (Elias and Dunning 2008a: introduction). New social standards of restraint with respect to violent and non-violent harm – novel understandings of what is permissible and forbidden on the part of private associations – therefore spread across most realms of social interaction. They are important dimensions of interwoven political struggles against traditional systems of exclusion that were made possible by the increasing power of universal and egalitarian moral principles in societies that had undergone the transition from monarchical rule to popular sovereignty (Linklater 1998: chs. 1–2; also Elias 2012: 304ff.). Public awareness of the tensions or contradictions between actual social practices and such ethical commitments became sharper as a result.

But it is only in the last few decades that 'civilized' orientations to violence and human suffering have led to parallel global attempts to constrain the exercise of sovereign power in relations with citizens. They led to various social and political initiatives to promote the outward extension of salient features of the European civilizing process that were far from inevitable but hard to resist. They included the belief that societies had to support international principles that outlawed genocide, notwithstanding major reservations about policy implications (Smith 2010). The grounds for preferring the wellbeing of co-nationals to the welfare of other human beings with equal moral rights have become less secure as a result. With the partial democratization of international society (in the sense that the individual has come to enjoy a degree of equality with the sovereign state in international law) came stronger pressures to hold regimes globally accountable for the protection of human rights and to provide humanitarian assistance to victims, irrespective of class, ethnicity, citizenship, gender, sexuality and race.

In reality, the governments that have transgressed such norms have often been protected from moral condemnation and punitive action whenever allies, and the great powers, in particular, have decided that their strategic interests are best served by ignoring their violent behaviour. Support for human rights often clashes with political realism; there is clearly much to be said for the argument that the human rights culture is riddled with double standards. Nevertheless, the power balance between the three types of law in the Kantian triptych has shifted dramatically, as is clear from recent shifts in Western attitudes to humanitarian intervention. The contrast with interventions in the bipolar era is instructive. Indian intervention in Bangladesh in 1971, Tanzanian action in Uganda in 1979 and Vietnamese intervention in Cambodia in 1978 demonstrated that states preferred to invoke the classical right of self-defence rather than invoke a principle of humanitarian intervention to justify the use of force against regimes that were held responsible for major violations of human rights (Bull 1984b; Wheeler 2000). With the end of the bipolar era, many liberal analysts and political leaders argued for embedding a principle of humanitarian intervention in international society in order to deal effectively with human rights emergencies (Wheeler 2000). The controversial thesis was that with respect to the most violent tyrannical regimes, serious national and global commitments to the prevention of human suffering demanded rather more than public condemnation or private diplomacy, namely the use of force. The dominant 'practice of sovereignty' had long blocked movement in that direction, and its supporters warned against eroding classical understandings, but the liberal standpoints under discussion have held that transformed conceptions of sovereignty could become inextricably linked with global support for an ethic of humanitarian intervention (Suganami 2007: 523ff.). Notwithstanding dominant views to the contrary, the idea of sovereignty and the use of force to protect human rights are, at least in principle, entirely compatible (Suganami 2007).

But the current phase of international society is characterized by the tension between the two dominant conceptions that were discussed earlier – between the pluralist standpoint that defends the primacy of sovereign responsibilities that are the key to an ethic of coexistence and the solidarist perspective in which those international obligations are suffused with the cosmopolitan commitment to assist the victims of humanitarian emergencies. Its transitional character is evident in the improbability of either an imminent restoration of a classical, pluralist order in which human rights violations no longer arouse widespread concern or a decisive shift towards an unambiguously solidarist framework in which there is a universal consensus about the principle and the practice of humanitarian intervention (Hurrell 2007; Wheeler 2000). Competing conceptions of the necessary we–I balance exist, and not least because of the expansion of international society. However, important advances in embedding solidarist values in an international society that remains pluralist at core (see Dunne 1998: ch. 8) are evident in two areas – in the convergence of humanitarian legal principles governing intra-state and interstate conflicts (Detter 2000: 37), and in the emergence of the doctrine of 'universal jurisdiction' with respect to the prosecution of war criminals (Best 1994: 396).

No less important in seeking to balance the two conceptions of international society – and raising its own distinctive controversies – has been the idea of the 'responsibility to protect' which was first proposed by the 2001 report of the International Commission on Intervention and State Sovereignty that had been established by the UN General Assembly. According to the doctrine, the state's duty to safeguard its citizens' security is linked with the principle that 'where a population is suffering serious harm, as a result of internal war, insurgency, repression or state failure, and the state in question is unwilling or unable to halt or avert it, the principle of non-intervention yields to the international responsibility to protect' (*International Commission on Intervention and State Sovereignty* 2001: xii). Original formulations of the doctrine added that if the United Nations 'fails to discharge its responsibility to protect in conscience-shocking situations crying out for action', then 'concerned states' may decide on 'collectively authorized international intervention' (*International Commission on Intervention and State Sovereignty* 2001: xiii, 49; see Bellamy 2008 on the weaker position endorsed by the United Nations in 2005). It is too early to know whether such ideas will become a stepping stone to a more solidarist international society where the sense of cosmopolitan duty underpins more extensive political programmes to protect vulnerable people in world society. Whether or not radical change occurs, 'civilizing' pressures and influences have clearly swept over a range of domestic and international political institutions, creating pressures to transform organizing principles in the light of contemporary social attitudes to harm and suffering. The successful pacification of national territories and entire regions leads many to think that 'civilized' peoples ought to do more to help the victims of human rights abuses. Their supposition is that the societies in question should not only assume the responsibility for assisting those who are denied the personal security that is largely taken for granted in 'civilized' societies but accept that failures to act should generate collective shame or guilt – just as the Atlantic slave trade and slavery did in an earlier phase of the European civilizing process.

Those emotional responses to inactivity in the face of distant suffering remain weak. Ethical commitments to protect human rights are embedded in international humanitarian law but they have not been internalized in the personality structures of people to the extent that they feel compelled by the dictates of conscience to support the use of force to assist distant strangers.

Considerable uncertainty about the effectiveness of military involvement is undoubtedly one reason for the desire to minimize such commitments, as are public concerns about placing military personnel in harm's way in what may seem to be intractable civil conflicts. Obligations to co-nationals remain in tension with obligations to fellow human beings; when they openly clash the former continue to take priority. For those reasons, the traditional 'split' within civilization endures.

Also important is how the controversial doctrine of the responsibility to protect was constructed to serve national security interests in the aftermath of 9/11. The 2002 *National Security Strategy of the United States of America* advanced 'a stricter standard of sovereign responsibility' by claiming that states have a fundamental international obligation not to harbour terrorist groups within their sovereign territories. The failure to honour that responsibility entitled 'injured states' to override the sovereignty of any 'outlaw' state by exercising the right to military intervention. The doctrine sought to embed a new standard of civilization in a 'hegemonic' system of international law by describing target states as the 'enemies of civilization' (see Reinold 2013: 99ff.; Collet 2009; Rengger 2013). The ethical controversies that surround such claims need not detain us here. What is most significant for the present discussion is the incorporation of the idea of civilization in public discourse in order to legitimate military action in non-Western societies. It has been argued that national claims to be the custodian of civilized values pose a major threat to 'civility' in international relations (Jackson 2000: 287ff., 412ff.). The implication is that the contention that the state represents civilized standards of conduct endangers the taboos against violence that govern relations between 'advanced' peoples, specifically where the dominant political discourse mimics the language employed in the older colonial wars. For the critics, it is as if 'civilization' has become indistinguishable from a liberal hegemonic culture that sacrifices universal and egalitarian commitments in order to protect the interests of the global political establishment. Traditional conceptions of sovereignty and the associated 'pluralist' we–I balance have clashed with efforts to use the idea of civilization to construct universal ethical ideals that many regard as a cloak for particularistic values and interests with divisive results in 'post-European' international society.

Private Power and Global Responsibility

Previous sections have considered how the aspirations for a global civilizing process that is orientated towards taming relations between the great powers have been enlarged in recent times to include support for the universal human right to be free from unnecessary violence. Preserving achievements in those domains depends to a greater extent than in the earlier Western states-systems on global economic stability and on coordinated approaches to environmental management. Longer social and economic webs have contributed to those problems that would not have existed at all but for major advances in territorial pacification. They demonstrate that various economic and ecological problems exemplify the reality that most people have little control over, or understanding of, the social forces that push them 'involuntarily in one direction or another' (Elias 2010c: 84ff.). In a significant break with the past, the great majority of those who live in the most stable regions do not expect to take up arms for the state. Not only are they free from the danger of being killed or maimed in interstate wars, but they have good reason to believe that their immediate successors will also enjoy equally high levels of physical security. But the global webs that have led to that unusual condition in the history of the Western states-systems have exposed them to vulnerabilities of a different sort that include the unpredictable consequences of climate change. One of the major challenges of the era is addressing the paradox of successful pacification which is the potential for major intra- and interstate conflict in many areas that can only be reduced if states assume greater collective responsibility for controlling the unstable dynamics of current patterns of global interconnectedness – if they further transform the concept of sovereignty and change the we–I balance accordingly.

Several developments in international law have broadened the idea of sovereign responsibility in response to the need for greater accountability to the members of other societies. The shift is evident in the differences between the 1895 Harmon Doctrine and the 1941 Trail Smelter decision with respect to sovereign obligations to avoid harm to the environment. The former held that sovereignty freed national governments from the legal responsibility to consider the interests of outsiders; the latter endorsed the idea of sovereign accountability to others as required by the principle, *sic utere tuo ut alienum non laedas* ('one must use one's property so as not to injure others'). Critics have argued that the Trail Smelter arbitration was a limited achievement because of the important caveat that sovereign rights could only be restrained when there was clear and incontrovertible evidence of serious injury to others. Complex questions arise about what counts as indisputable evidence of major harm, and about where the ultimate authority to adjudicate between competing interpretations should lie. But the historical significance of the Trail Smelter arbitration is the recognition that traditional conceptions of sovereign rights had to be revised as a result of lengthening and deepening social ties that create distant or 'transnational harm' while public systems of accountability that could ensure justice for the victims lag behind (Linklater 2011: 66; Mason 2005). Many international non-governmental organizations have supported a cosmopolitan version of the 'affected by' or 'harm principle' that, in the language of critical social theory, asserts that all people have the right to be consulted about deliberations and decisions that may damage their interests, wherever they may take place and wherever they live (Fraser 2007; Linklater 2007). As the 'gentle civilizer of nations', international law has made some progress in embedding that ethical principle in the constitution of international society. That is an important step, as is the part that various non-governmental organizations have played not only in supporting new transnational public spheres that run parallel to the global reorganization of political and economic power but also in advocating notions of the 'connected self' who recognizes how everyday acts affect, and are affected by the actions of, distant strangers (see Chapter 11, p. 420). Those developments reflect increasing demands for modern counterparts to the individual and collective self-restraint and self-regulation that were intrinsic features of earlier phases of the European civilizing process. They identify the need for new conceptions of solidarity or 'we-feeling', and for parallel changes in the we–I balance.

Traditional attachments to sovereign nation-states constrain efforts to create powerful international organizations that are less susceptible to the current reality of significant colonization by corporate interests (Mattli and Woods 2009). An additional obstacle has its foundation in global structures, organizations and ideologies that, in various alliances with the more powerful state institutions, protect markets from far-reaching government controls. For their political supporters, the emergence of such instruments of transnational governance is evidence of social and political progress; it provides the basis for a new 'standard of civilization' that sets out the ideals that societies should aim for by developing 'free market' economies, increasing personal liberties, and encouraging new social interdependencies that promote global peace. For the critics, the long-term challenge is to devise global coordinating mechanisms that can protect people in all societies from, *inter alia*, the dangers of environmental degradation and economic insecurity. The related concern is that the continued dominance of neo-liberal international institutions and supporting ideologies will intensify vulnerability and insecurity in several countries and further underline the biases and distortions of the dominant liberal visions of a global civilizing process that in, opposing violent harm, neglect the forms of non-violent or 'structural' harm that are the product of transnational social and economic processes of integration (Linklater 2011: ch. 2).

Marx's writings were prescient in identifying the emerging global problem but they failed to explain its origins and development or to propose a feasible political solution. They described an emerging epoch in which 'abstract harm' – non-violent harm that spreads haphazardly across borders through the operation of invisible global capitalist forces – would replace 'concrete harm' – violent harm that, for example, societies deliberately inflict on each other in military conflict. As many have argued, those writings underestimated the power of nationalism and the potential for interstate violence, but it is entirely feasible that a long-term change in the relative influence of abstract and concrete harm will prove to be the most fundamental feature of the contemporary era. One of the weaknesses of Marx's approach was the failure to understand how the transformation of the dominant forms of harm resulted from the interplay between state-formation, geopolitics and war, and capitalist forces and relations of production. It regarded the latter as the main pacemaker of social and political change but, as the analysis of the European civilizing process maintained, capitalist social relations would not have developed so extensively but for the emergence of state monopoly powers and internal pacification. At the heart of the argument, as discussed in Chapter 5, was the analysis of two interrelated dynamics – the separation of public monopolies from the royal court or household, and the division between state institutions and a relatively autonomous commercial sphere that sovereigns actively encouraged not least to finance standing arms and to wage major interstate wars.

Chapter 5 discussed how the process-sociological analysis of European state-formation highlighted alliances between absolutist rulers and the emergent bourgeoisie that were intended to balance the power of the traditional aristocracy. Moreover, support for the bourgeoisie as the agent of capitalist development was essential to finance state bureaucracies and to organize large conscript armies. The fiscal costs of successive military revolutions increased the state's dependence on that social class given its fundamental role in the promotion of economic growth (Tilly 1992). Modern societies became increasingly bound together in an interrelated international states-system and in a global capitalist economy as a result. Assuming the causal primacy of the latter domain, Marx's analysis of European modernity stressed the growing importance of capitalist crises, and failed to anticipate or allow for the significantly autonomous military and political clashes that lay ahead, and their catastrophic fusion during the so-called twenty years' crisis (Carr 2001 [1939]). Interestingly, one proposed political solution to that crisis that involved global planning to ensure human security in the sense of freedom from violent harm and economic hardship appealed to the feelings of obligation to other people that are 'implicit in our conception of civilization' and that had already been embedded in the laws of war that affirmed the duty 'not to inflict *unnecessary* death or suffering on other human beings' (Carr 2001 [1939]: 141, italics in original). Similar views of the relationship between 'civilized' values, international solidarity or 'we-feeling', and global economic planning will be noted later.

There have been important parallels between the pressures within modern states to create powerful, central institutions to deal with the problems that result from interdependencies between members of the same society, and the incentives for sovereign states to create global 'steering mechanisms' that address the challenges that stem from recent universalizing processes (Mennell 2007: ch. 9, 320). But the parallels extend only so far.

Supranational authorities that pool sovereign powers remain relatively weak (Kahler and Lake 2009). The argument for global economic planning that was integral to 'Third World' demands in the mid-1970s for a New International Economic Order clashed with the emergent neo-liberal assault on the perceived irrationalities of state interference in market-determined, resource allocation (Richardson 2001). Since then, liberal capitalist states and associated global business corporations have spearheaded the deregulation of markets on the grounds that it promotes international competitiveness and efficiencies that increase global wealth. The defence is not simply about 'economics' since the standpoint has been implicitly linked with powerful liberal civilizational claims that celebrate the 'free market' as an indispensable constraint on sovereign power and as a necessary guarantor of fundamental personal liberties (McDonald 2009).

The counterargument which has been advanced by green political theorists and ecological movements, has maintained that liberal capitalist states are implicated in the consolidation of inadequately regulated global market arrangements that lead to potentially irreversible environmental harm. In the critique of the global hegemony of neo-liberal ideology, some have argued for 'ecologically responsible statehood' – for the transformation of political communities through major advances with respect to sovereign responsibilities for the protection of the global commons (Eckersley 2004). A related argument supports 'ecological citizenship' that transcends traditional conceptions of sovereign rights and obligations (Dobson 2003). Those critiques of classical images of 'Westphalian sovereignty' and national citizenship are important challenges to one of the peculiar paradoxes of the most recent phase of the civilizing process. Changing attitudes to violent harm have led to the erosion of the rights that sovereign states and private associations had long regarded as their natural entitlement. What was once permissible has been forbidden as a result. The deregulation of markets is associated with a reverse process in which many earlier restraints on business enterprises have been lifted. Demands for corporate social responsibility are a response to the reality that such associations have become much freer to behave as they wish without, it is often argued, a proportionate increase in concern for the human and environmental consequences of commercial activity. Those are recent versions of the global ethic that was developed by Enlightenment thinkers in response to the closer interweaving of societies on profoundly unequal terms. They raise similar questions about the appropriate contemporary we–I balance where 'I' refers not to the sovereign state – as in earlier parts of this discussion – but to corporate associations.

Struggles between sovereigns led ruling elites to throw their weight behind bourgeois class forces in order to benefit from capitalist development. Unplanned relations were integral to 'elimination struggles' between states and to the monopolization of coercive power in a smaller number of great powers. The retreat of the liberal state from market intervention also led to equalled unplanned monopolization processes in the economic sphere (van Benthem van den Bergh 2012). The compulsions of competition in the world of liberalized economies led to parallel 'elimination contests' that have resulted in the condition that Marx foresaw in which an increasing proportion of the world's population is at the mercy of global capitalist forces that escape the levels of democratic accountability that 'civilized' populations have come to expect in their relations with sovereign political authorities. One of the consequences is the contradiction between the privatization of the material benefits of largely unregulated transnational economic forces and the socialization or collectivization of attendant risks (Mattli and Woods 2009). The interpenetration of the public and private domains, and accompanying changes in the balance of power between social forces, compound the political problem of resolving that distinctive tension (Hall and Biersteker 2002). In the course of the nineteenth and twentieth centuries, the ruling strata in liberal capitalist societies were compelled to make significant concessions to subordinate groups in order to secure their loyalty or to foster their acceptance of the prevailing social and political arrangements. But from the early 1980s, there has been a substantial shift in the balance of power between state structures and transnational capitalist organizations, and other social groups. A new global political 'establishment' has emerged that is based in complex networks between neo-liberal state structures, international organizations and transnational business enterprises. Its rise has been inextricably connected with the erosion of the power resources that were once available to traditional outsider groups.

The significance of those developments for the relationship between violence and civilization in the modern states-system is best explored by considering the potential ramifications of the profoundly unequal distribution of the capacity to influence the dominant social and political structures and the main global trajectories of development. Analyses of 'governance beyond the state' (whether it comprises 'private authority structures' that oversee relatively autonomous economic organizations or collaborative arrangements between sovereign authorities and non-state actors to regulate specific sectors of transnational social and economic activity) have stressed the absence of significant democratic accountability (Hurrell 2007: ch. 4; Mattli and Woods 2009). Far from underpinning political freedoms, the argument is, free market ideologies insulate the 'economic' domain from the structures of 'democratic deliberation' that are vital for preserving the ethical ideal of ensuring the public accountability of the dominant strata as well as the collective management of global social and political forces in order to achieve a more just distribution of capacities and resources (Robinson and Harris 2000). Competing interpretations have emphasized the contrast between the vision of a 'global constitutional project' that has the objective of securing genuine democracy '*within, between*, and *beyond* the world of sovereign states' and the current forms of 'hegemonic global law' that protect powerful economic and political interests (Brunkhorst 2005: 84ff., 127ff., 151, italics in original). They have contended that 'disciplinary neoliberalism' has weakened counter-hegemonic political organizations and social movements through a combination of power structures and ideologies that portray prevailing arrangements as 'natural' and dismiss ethical visions of alternative global trajectories on the grounds that they are demonstrably unworkable (Gill 1995). Sovereign responsibilities and wider solidarities have contracted in the process.

The idea of global 'market civilization' captures the normative claims that underpin the belief in the progressive outcomes of longer and deeper capitalist social relations (Bowden and Seabrooke 2006). The criticism that global capitalist structures preside over dangerous levels of 'organized irresponsibility' (see Chapter 11, p. 451ff.) highlights the tensions within neo-liberal conceptions of a universal 'civilizing process'. Earlier parts of the discussion referred to the 'split' within modern civilization regarding attitudes to permissible and forbidden force. A more recent variant on that tension is apparent in the disjuncture between the expectations of restraint that apply with respect to sovereign political authorities and everyday conduct in 'civilized' societies and the less demanding pressures and incentives to exercise self-restraint and foresight that are intrinsic to the habitus of many corporate actors (Faro 2014). The unevenness of the development of the standards of self-restraint in different social spheres underpins the argument for 'taming the financial aristocracies', an expression that alludes to an earlier phase in European state formation and the civilizing process that is encapsulated in the notion of 'taming the warriors' (Blomert 2012; also Mennell 2014).

Although various forms of violence are often condemned as 'barbaric' in the contemporary world, it is rare for unfettered economic activity to be described in similar terms. But as stated earlier, it was not unusual only a few decades ago for critics of unrestrained capitalist activity to wrap their critique in the language of civilization. Examples include the contention that the unequal condition in which the rich can exploit market power by buying from those with little choice but to sell their products at unfavourable rates was 'a monstrous parasite upon civilization itself' (Collingwood 1999: 504ff.). A similar argument that was employed in defence of sovereign political responsibilities to promote global economic planning after the Second World War stressed the Kantian theme that 'the circle of interests directly regulated by law expands with the growth of civilization' (Lauterpacht, cited in Carr 2001 [1939]: 202n13). The plain reality that the concept has come to be viewed with considerable suspicion is part of the explanation for the abandonment of an earlier discourse. However, dominant civilized self-images have narrowed the meaning of the uses of 'civilization' in current interpretations of politics with major implications for the critical analysis of the problematical effects of capitalism on the 'civilizing process' and for attendant reflections on sovereign responsibilities. One consequence is the narrowing of what people have the right to expect as citizens of 'civilized' societies or as members of the world society that has been shaped by them. The central question is what the language of civilization condemns and ignores, and whether a crucial moral resource can be mobilized in support of alternative political visions of sovereign responsibilities and future social directions that are influenced by, *inter alia*, Enlightenment conceptions of ethical conduct in the context of unequal power relations in expanding global webs of interdependence.

The last point is best explored by returning to one of the themes that was discussed in connection with the Enlightenment, namely the balance of power between short and long-term perspectives. One of the perceived shortcomings of global 'market civilization' is the considerable shortening of time-horizons that is the product of corporate elimination contests and monopolistic objectives that expose societies to various immediate and longer-term structural dangers. Concerns about intergenerational justice highlight the central issue that failures to address the problem of climate change may unfairly transfer social and economic burdens to future generations. It is interesting to speculate about whether coming generations will regard current failures to impose sufficient self-restraint on demands on the natural environment and to act with requisite foresight as evidence that the so-called civilized societies of the present era existed in a more 'primitive' time – in a 'Middle Ages' that were populated by 'late barbarians' (Elias 2011: 174; Elias 2013a: 252–3; Elias 2012: 67; Elias 2007: 140–1). The observation invites greater detachment from the currently dominant conceptions of civilization as well as interrelated reflections on alternative conceptualizations that support stronger cosmopolitan long-term orientations.

The earlier discussion of Enlightenment universal history referred to a parallel issue that was illustrated by Kant's emphasis on the potentially restraining effect of reflecting on how the coming generations will cope with the inherited burdens of history, and on whether modern peoples will be 'honourably remembered' for the munificence of their bequest (see Chapter 7, p. 303). Efforts to promote the long-term perspective and not least with regard to the question of intergenerational equity are evident in support for the 'precautionary principle' which states that potentially hazardous government policies and corporate strategies should be suspended until the balance of scientific opinion removes any reasonable doubt that they will leave behind a legacy of significant harm. Opponents have protested at what is perceived as excessive aversion to risk that imposes unacceptable restraints on commercial activity and associated costs for business enterprises and those they employ (Bratspies 2006; Mason 2005: ch. 6; Linklater 2011: 66). It is also important to recall one of the core arguments in the Trail Smelter decision which was that sovereign rights should only be limited when there is incontrovertible evidence of significant harm. Complex legal and philosophical disputes about the definition of serious harm are intrinsically connected with debates about the correct balance of power between short- and long-term time horizons (Linklater 2011: chs. 1–2). The issues are relatively straightforward in the case of concrete harm where there is clear evidence that particular individuals or groups are responsible for deliberate mental or physical harm to specific individuals; they are immensely complicated with respect to abstract harm where causal links can be opaque and where ultimate responsibility is diffuse and dispersed.

For those reasons, the liberal harm principle remains central to current controversies about the relationship between individual liberties and social obligations that have direct significance for reflections about 'civilized' sovereign rights and responsibilities in the current era. Those who defend the principle often argue for strict definitions of harm that restrict the scope of the criminal law and avoid burdening individuals with excessive duties. The critics deny that the concept of harm has a precise meaning so that the state's coercive powers must necessarily be limited; they contend that its interpretation is open to indefinite expansion and that governments can claim the right to interfere in ever more areas on the argument that they are protecting citizens from avoidable harm. Related problems revolve around the question of whether the liberal harm principle requires only compliance with negative obligations to refrain from causing physical injury and other 'serious' harms to other persons. For many liberals, assisting others is, depending on the circumstances of those involved, an exercise in charity or an example of heroic or supererogatory action that deserves special commendation because it exceeds standard expectations about obligations between people.

That distinction between necessary social obligations and voluntary acts of kindness has important implications for sovereign rights and duties as well as corporate responsibilities. The standard economic liberal argument is that the burden of moral proof falls on those who argue for curtailing property rights and related entitlements including the right to maximize wealth (Cutler 2002). From that perspective, sovereign authorities have the responsibility to prevent and punish the most 'serious' forms of violent and non-violent harm but they abuse their powers if they burden corporate enterprises with obligations that inhibit competitiveness and reduce autonomy. The standpoint clearly rests on a specific normative image of the we–I balance. Critics of that conception of the harm principle have argued that such constructions of negative obligations fail to address forms of harm that are the outcome – often unintended and unforeseen – of how societies are organized or structured as opposed to the product of individual wrongdoing. They maintain that harm is often defined so narrowly that vulnerable groups are denied the forms of legal and political protection to which they are entitled as citizens of 'civilized' societies. A parallel line of argument with respect to the current world order is that the belief in the primacy of negative obligations that is associated with the liberal harm principle has more far-reaching consequences than is usually realized. The logic of the argument is that sovereign states and other actors have a non-optional responsibility to dismantle global regimes that adversely affect the interests of the world's poorest and most vulnerable peoples. The political reforms in question do not depend on charity or benevolence, it is argued, but follow from the ancient Stoic contention that every human being has a duty as a matter of justice not to harm the interests of others (Pogge 2002). The standpoint links a specific normative image of the we–I balance with conceptions of sovereign global responsibilities that go well beyond those that are associated with narrower interpretations of the significance of the liberal harm principle for the organization of international society.

Rival ethical standpoints on the meaning and significance of the liberal harm principle therefore contain different conceptions of the rights and responsibilities of 'civilized' sovereign communities. They provide different political visions of the ideal future direction of a Western-initiated global civilizing process. Crucially, as far as the comparative analysis of violence and civilization in the Western states-systems is concerned, they include moral claims that international order is to be judged ultimately by the extent to which the constituent parts are committed to global reforms that protect the vulnerable in world society. Philosophical disagreements about the moral standing of 'global market civilization' do not of themselves shed empirical light on issues regarding the relationship between civilization and violence. But they provide a reminder of how specific biases within classical liberalism towards the problem of violence have resulted in large-scale indifference to 'structural harm'.

The Western powers may believe that geopolitical crises have finally come to an end in the liberal regions and not least because of the achievements of 'market civilization', and the majority of Western peoples may think that the potentials for violence are confined to less 'civilized' societies. They may prove to be entirely correct in their judgments about the relationship between violence and civilization in the current world order. It is impossible to predict whether those are permanent changes or whether such confidence will lead to the forms of self-deception that led many to believe that the late nineteenth-century liberal world order would eradicate interstate violence (see Carr 2001 [1939]) and that led many to think that the genocide was no longer possible in Europe. It may seem farfetched to suppose that a counterpart to the violence of the 'twenty years' crisis' could erupt in 'civilized' societies in the foreseeable future. However, increasing economic inequalities, social marginalization and political exclusion can have precisely that affect in other regions that affluent societies are not powerless to influence. The inhabitants of the most stable and pacified liberal democracies may remain immune from the violence that exists in many other societies but they cannot escape many of the direct consequences that include the exodus of refugees; nor can they avoid the effect of anti-Western ideologies that fuel terrorist struggles against societies that may further compromise 'civilized' restraints on force in the quest for security. The 'economic' and the 'political' cannot be divorced, and the potential direction of the relationship between violence and civilization must be understood holistically. Controversies about the ideal balance between public authority and corporate power, and between global regulation and free markets, must be considered in that context. They pose important political questions about sovereign rights and responsibilities that are inextricably connected with ethical issues about the nature of a just world order and the meaning of 'civilized' coexistence.

Ethical Responsibility and the Global Civilizing Process

Unlike most of the constitutive political units in the earlier Western states-systems, modern 'civilized' societies possess a range of cosmopolitan visions of a more just world order. Struggles over the importance of cosmopolitanism for global order have become important features of the contemporary political battleground. The proponents of universal moral principles invariably struggle to convince others that they are not engaged in an attempt to globalize culturally specific preferences that have little or no appeal to other peoples that may dismiss them as instruments of domination. The controversies are unsurprising dimensions of the struggle to discover new ways in which diverse and distant peoples can become attuned to one another and live together amicably and in a 'civilized' way; they are an inevitable accompaniment to endeavours to develop an 'ethic of responsibility' that addresses global political problems that are the product of longer and thicker webs of mutual dependence (Jonas 1984).

It is important to briefly consider those developments in long-term perspective. In the modern states-system as in its predecessors, the great powers have had a stranglehold on the configuration of the dominant global harm conventions. They have assiduously defended their sovereign rights while acquiring various international responsibilities in the course of adapting, in the recent period, to the dangers of unprecedented violent warfare. Their objectives have not been confined to placing restraints on the sovereign entitlement to use force simply for the sake of preserving international order. As discussed above, they have had to respond to political pressures to redefine sovereign responsibilities in the light of moral arguments for preventing 'superfluous injury' and 'unnecessary suffering' to individuals in their own right. The development of the humanitarian laws of war and international criminal law are monuments to those major shifts in the 'practice of sovereignty'.

Those transformations reflect the ethic of affirming everyday life which has been a core dimension of the most recent phase of the European civilizing process. They are part of larger patterns of social and political change that have led to the partial liberalization and democratization of international society. Traditionally, great power deliberations about the judicious balance between sovereign rights and responsibilities were designed to construct an international order that displayed substantial indifference to the interests to traditional 'outsiders' – small states, national minorities and individual persons. The upshot was that international harm convention had pride of place in the modern states-system, as was the case in the earlier systems of states in the West. In that phase of the civilizing process, sovereign responsibilities were not constructed in accordance with strong ethical commitments to the establishment of cosmopolitan harm conventions.

As a result of liberalizing and democratizing forces in international society, entitlements to participate in deliberations about global harm conventions have come to be shared not only with small states but, in recent times, with international non-governmental organizations or 'transnational advocacy networks' that include the political representatives of minority nations and indigenous peoples' movements (Keck and Sikkink 1998). Across the spectrum of international non-governmental organizations, agencies have applied pressures on states to enlarge the scope of moral consideration and to assume more extensive, cosmopolitan sovereign responsibilities in the light of broadened 'we-feelings'. The result has been a substantial advance in extending rights to protection from violence that were once monopolized by the dominant social strata. But larger issues are at now at stake because of the global chains that bind distant strangers together. As discussed earlier, a central question in the comparative study of states-systems is how far the growth of such global entanglements is accompanied by serious moral and political initiatives to restrain the use of force, and by national and international commitments to extend social standards of self-restraint over greater distances. In the contemporary era – though the issue had already been addressed by several Enlightenment thinkers – that question has had to address the possibilities for exploiting the vulnerable, for unjust enrichment, and for other forms of non-violent harm to other peoples. Political opposition to those forms of power and dominance restate core features of struggles that occurred earlier within 'civilized' societies and within international society. The participants have advanced demands for protection from unnecessary suffering and they have insisted on rights of representation in global decision-making processes to protect core interests and to influence broader social and political directions.

Crucially, those claims are addressed to a global establishment that does not consist only of the great powers or the larger power blocs that include global business enterprises and international regulatory bodies; they are also directed at the affluent social strata in the powerful societies that are the beneficiaries of current global political and economic arrangements and who are urged to display higher levels of self-restraint and to accept greater personal responsibility for conduct that may contribute inadvertently to environmental harm. A recurrent ethical theme is that, contrary to the standard double standard of morality in world politics, many of the 'civilized' principles that govern relations between citizens of the same political community should automatically govern transnational connections between distant strangers in different societies. Idealized sovereign obligations to promote global justice in accordance with that envisaged we–I balance are constructed accordingly.

Compelling theoretical reflections on moral and political responsibility have emphasized the shortcomings of conventional moralities that concentrate on the visible and the 'proximate' – and specifically on issues that affect co-nationals first and foremost. Those perspectives now seem deficient because of the failure to respond to the 'cumulative' negative effects of the ways in which peoples have become tied together. The challenges result from the gradual and unforeseen accumulation of political problems that affect not only the interests of those who belong to the same society or the welfare of distant strangers but also the wellbeing of the entire species as well as generations that have yet to be born. Again, there are unmistakeable parallels with Enlightenment concep-tions of the ethical imperative to rethink traditional orientations to time and space in the context of the 'great unfolding' of the map of mankind – in short, with earlier influential philosophical writings that responded to marked social trends that have become even more pronounced in the last few decades. The most recent variations on the theme have been developed in reaction to the challenges of environmental degradation. They have focused on how a global 'ethic of responsibility' can enable different peoples to orientate themselves to the unforeseen consequences of the closer interweaving of societies and to attune themselves to the necessity for cooperation at a higher level in order to bring social processes under significant collective control. Although not directly concerned with sovereign responsibilities, *per se*, such analyses provide major insights into the social dynamics that create strong pressures to embed more radical harm conventions in interna-tional society. They reflect intriguing shifts within the civilizing process and immanent potentials, specifically by considering the tensions between social forces and conventional moralities that can only be resolved by embracing a new global ethic of responsibility that applies to sovereign authorities, corporate and other actors and individual people in their own right.

A central premise is that customary social moralities have been 'geared' to the 'proximate range of action' while 'traditional ethics reckoned only with noncumulative behaviour'; there were no obvious reasons to suspect that the dominant forms of political organization and everyday actions could have long-term environmental consequences that now raise serious questions about their long-term legitimacy and sustainability (Jonas 1984: 5–7). Social moralities that have enabled the citizens of many sovereign communities to coexist relatively amicably provide very few clues as to how sovereign states should deal with the dangers that have emerged with unprecedented collective power over the biosphere. Only a global moral code that places new principles of responsibility at the 'centre of the ethical stage' in both the private and public domains can meet the contemporary challenge. What is specifically required is 'a new ethics of long-range responsibility, coextensive with the range of our power' that now exceeds the capacity 'to foresee . . . to evaluate and to judge'; what is needed are broadened conceptions of individual and collective responsibility that respond to the 'excess of causal reach over . . . prescience', and address the problems that arise because various organizations and institutions can take initiatives for which they are only minimally accountable, particularly at the global level (Jonas 1984: 21–2, 117).

New conceptions of social responsibility – and, by implication, more radical extensions of sovereign responsibilities and a novel we–I balance – are therefore deemed to be central to a desirable future condition in which peoples are become more attuned to the moral and political significance of contemporary global transformations. Two ethical maxims regarding the widening of ethical horizons that command limited, but not insubstantial, support in modern societies have been formulated in this context. The first is to 'act so that the effects of your action are not destructive of the future possibility of [human] life'; the second is 'do not compromise the conditions for an indefinite continuation of humanity on earth' (Jonas 1984: 11). Those twin imperatives are designed to globalize two fundamental personality traits that were pivotal to the European civilizing process, specifically, the internalization of social standards of self-restraint that are appropriate for the conditions in which peoples now find themselves, and the related capacity for, and commitment to, greater foresight regarding the possible long-term consequences of current social practices and generalized modes of behaviour. In a parallel with early modern Europe, the two maxims address growing pressures and compulsions to consider how actions may adversely affect those who are placed farther along the global chains of mutual dependence.

The emphasis on the need for greater reflectiveness about moral responsibilities explicitly recognizes that political movements and institutions that attempt to escape the limitations of conventional moralities will have very limited success unless there are significant changes in personality structures – or at the level of individual conscience (Jonas 1984: 85ff.). The authors of *The Federalist Papers* had earlier highlighted the importance of the connection between the private and public spheres when they maintained that democratic governance depends on a society that consists of individuals who are committed to, and adept at, bringing one another to account, and fully cognizant, as John Adams put it, of the potential political importance of matters that seem remote from everyday life (Lerner 2001: 38ff.). The contemporary counterpart emphasizes the importance of the *education sentimentale*; its purpose is to foster cosmopolitan feelings of responsibility to others in a period in which the long-term effects of social action are immensely difficult to assess (Jonas 1984: 28). The main contention is that the shared fears, vulnerabilities and insecurities that have been intrinsic to moralities that have affirmed the 'virtues of ordinary life' are even more significant for global responsibilities, particularly given the realities of profound cultural differences and the deeply contested nature of universal visions of the good society or good life. Concerns about the negative consequences of global interconnections have demonstrated that 'the perception of the *malum* is infinitely easier to us than the perception of the *bonum*; it is more direct, more compelling, less given to differences of opinion or taste, and, most of all, obtruding itself without our looking for it' (Jonas 1984: 27). Similar notions of human vulnerability and 'injurability' have shaped societal commitments to the ethical imperative to 'do no harm' that have been integral to the most recent phase of the 'civilizing process' at national levels and with respect to the organizing principles of international society (Linklater 2011: 105ff.). The upshot as far as state sovereignty is concerned is that a cosmopolitan ethic that is linked with the sophisticated interpretation of the obligations that follow from the harm principle is the key to specific images of moral and political responsibility that can drive 'the process of civilization' beyond the confines of the nation-state.

Even such a humanistic response to the power of 'proximity' and challenge to short-term horizons may seem utopian, and not least because of the continuing value of nineteenth-century analyses of how urbanization and industrialization had reduced traditional relations between people to the bare 'cash nexus' (Mazlish 1989). *The Federalist Papers* highlighted the dangers of widespread indifference to public affairs that was inherent in a society consisting of individual maximizers orientated towards short-term goals (Lerner 2001: 38ff.). Tocqueville (1945 [1840]: 99) diagnosed the challenge confronting modern societies in striking fashion when stating that, with the supersession of 'aristocratic communities', the 'bond of human affection is extended, but it is relaxed ... the woof of time is every instant broken, and the track of generations effaced. Those who went before are soon forgotten; of those who will come after no one has any idea'; in a condition of growing individual self-reliance, people had become increasingly 'strangers to one another', 'the interest of man is confined to those in close propinquity to himself ... It throws him back for ever on himself alone and threatens in the end to confine him entirely within the solitude of his own heart'. Those reflections on highly-individuated subjects who are ignorant of their ancestors and disinterested in their descendants have clear implications for analyses of societal potentials for an extended sense of moral and political responsibility in the current era. It stretches credulity to think that individuals who are 'isolated from their contemporaries' in the same society will agonize about the well-being of distant others with whom they have no emotional as opposed to material connections, or to make major personal sacrifices for the sake of future generations. Such a conception of the we–I balance is in conflict with core aspects of their life experience in contemporary 'civilized' societies.

As for the question of whether or not the awareness of unexpected possibilities for harming other people is followed by more cosmopolitan ethical convictions and the related widening of sovereign responsibilities, the reality of close proximity is that the consequences of actions are often clearly visible. Demands for accountability can be issued directly, often more or less immediately, and those who are adversely affected by the actions of others may be able to mobilize public opinion by appealing to shared understandings of what is irresponsible or reprehensible conduct – and perhaps of what is tolerated and forbidden by their conceptions of 'civilized' existence. As the relations between peoples become more impersonal and more attenuated, causal responsibility for harm is obscured and the fair distribution of moral obligations to correct injustices is harder to allocate (Bauman 2000: 184ff.). Then the central question is whether conventional understandings of social obligation can be superseded by strong transnational solidarities and parallel structures of legal and political accountability as opposed to increasing levels of moral indifference.

What dictates that 'even the daily exercise of our powers ... becomes an ethical problem' when it affects, and has implications for, people in other societies, and for unborn generations? (Jonas 1996: 103). Part of the answer can be found in explanations of the process by which particular European groups came to challenge the cruelties of empire. Many opposed colonial violence because of inner rather than external compulsions – because it clashed with their cherished identity as civilized people. Such considerations may be crucial for similar breakthroughs in the contemporary era where the question is what can motivate powerful groups to become more assiduous in protecting weaker groups from harm, including future harm that is the unintended consequence of global political and economic structures and processes. The analysis of the ethic of responsibility accords particular causal importance to the political role that specific moral emotions can play in shaping initiatives to prevent, *inter alia*, environmental harm that burdens future generations. It highlights the contribution that 'anticipatory remorse' as well as 'anticipatory pity' and 'shame' can make to creating necessary standards of self-restraint grounded in a more cosmopolitan form of 'we-feeling' (Jonas 1996: 108–9). Some empirical confirmation for the approach may be found in studies of 'transnational advocacy networks' that contend that moral concerns about distant suffering are more easily aroused when people are not in doubt that others have been harmed, and when there is a cogent explanation of their own causal role in the misery of others (Keck and Sikkink 1998: 27; Heins 2008). Those investigations point to the significance of the 'connected self' who acknowledges that others have the right to expect that they will address the injustices that are inherent in their material interconnectedness with other peoples and display the 'great humanity and great benevolence' that was central to Adam Smith's liberal ethic (Dobson 2003: ch. 1; Linklater 2011: 82, 228–9). That is the context in which political demands for more cosmopolitan individual and sovereign responsibilities to distant, but interconnected peoples have been advanced, not least by many civil society actors that build their 'moral authority' on those foundations (Hall and Biersteker 2002; Vogel 2009).

Some rough parallels between the early phases of the European civilizing process and contemporary global conditions were noted earlier. In both cases more and more people were forced together by processes that they did not understand and could not control. In European societies, those involved became subject to pressures to become attuned to changing social realities, to moderate behaviour so as not to harm, insult or offend others, and to acquire greater foresight about how their actions might adversely affect other people, albeit unintentionally or inadvertently. Compulsions to attune 'individual conduct to some larger entity remote in time and space, [spread] to ever-broader sections of society' in tandem with 'the extension of interdependence' (Elias 2012: 419). Increasing interconnectedness in the context of state formation led to new 'social constraints towards self-restraint' and to conditions in which the scope of emotional identification between members of the same society widened. Conflicts between groups did not disappear but were often the result of the ways in which people were drawn together in unequal power relations. What changed in the course of the civilizing process were the means by which such intra-societal, 'integration conflicts' and 'quarrels' were resolved (Elias 2008f: 136–7). What did not alter was the practice of resolving major interstate differences violently.

The defence of a new global 'ethic of responsibility' rests on a broadly similar analysis of how transnational dynamics can transform relations between closely interwoven societies. Demands have arisen to accept that 'the span of foresight should equal the span of the chain of consequences' and to moderate behaviour that adversely affects those who are at the 'mercy of [our] power' (Jonas 1996: 101–2). In their relations with each other, modern societies now face greater pressures than did their predecessors to develop moral and political commitments that resemble the 'civilizing' of conduct in early modern Europe. Demands to extend sovereign responsibilities as part of a new we–balance encompassing state structures, international society and humanity – understood to include future generations – are a central part of that process. It is important to add that familiar constraints on the replication of earlier domestic patterns of change at the global level have clearly not disappeared. Insider–outsider dualisms remain powerful; the long-term trend towards individualism that corrodes traditional solidarities and weakens restraints on the pursuit of short-term interests may not have run its course; increasing asymmetries of power and wealth stand in the way of closer parallels between the domestic and the global domains. However, the analysis of global responsibilities identifies immanent potentials for closer approximations between the course of the civilizing process within European states and an international counterpart that combines the ethos of compassionate cosmopolitanism with a realistic understanding of the relationship between intra- and interstate violence and instability and global inequalities of power, status and wealth.

Sovereignty, Civilization and International Society

The idea of sovereignty was a pivotal element of European state formation and the larger civilizing process. It was inextricably connected with the emergence and consolidation of state monopoly powers. The concept refers to ultimate authority in the judicial sphere that was fundamental to dispute-settlement and the earlier pacification of state-organized socie-ties. Constitutional independence is the corollary of the notion of the final court of appeal. It has come to be linked with one of the distinctive principles of modern international society which is the doctrine of the legal equality of states that has exercised a restraining influence in world politics by denying that the great powers have the right to extinguish the constitutional independence of others at will. The right to equal sovereignty has offered small powers a degree of protection from predatory powers. Although the latter have often curtailed the autonomy of others to the point where their constitutional independence has lost much of its meaning, they have invariably felt obliged to pay at least lip service to the principle that great and small powers are on the same legal plane (Krasner 1999).

It is erroneous to think that sovereignty has licensed states to behave exactly as they choose in their external relations. Sovereign rights have been linked with the legal responsibility to respect the constitutional separateness of others. Moving from legalities to the political context, sovereignty has come to symbolize the boundary between the 'inside' and the 'outside' that are governed by different ethical principles. That reality is not the consequence of sovereignty as such but the result of power struggles that have shaped the dominant understandings of the relationship between sovereign rights and international or humanitarian responsibilities at every historical juncture. The 'Janus-faced' nature of state formation in which internal pacification coexists with preparation for war has led ruling elites to claim various liberties of action to protect their security and survival. But what sovereigns are legally obliged to do apart from respecting one another's constitutional independence is an open question. The range of sovereign responsibilities has depended in large part on the extent to which the ruling strata have been bound together by aristocratic ties or the bonds of civilization, or sharply divided by the fear of generalized warfare. From the concept of sovereignty itself, no particular we–I balance or web of social restraints automatically follows. Its precise meaning which altered as 'aristocratic internationalism' gave way to bourgeois nationalism will almost certainly change again during the future development of the society of states. Strong commitments to cosmopolitan responsibilities are, at least in principle, entirely consistent with the idea of territorial sovereignty.

The contribution of sovereignty to internal pacification that was followed by closer emotional identification with the nation ensured the 'split' within civilization. Modern states acquired increasingly destructive forms of military power; reduced tolerance of violence in everyday life coexisted with the high expectation and acceptance of the use of force in international relations. The balance between sovereign rights and responsibilities reflected the political reality that the 'social constraints towards self-restraint' were much lower in relations between states than in relations between members of the same 'survival unit'. Nevertheless, the notions of civilization that developed alongside domestic pacification had a profound influence on attitudes to human suffering in other societies, as is clear from the revised conceptions of imperial sovereignty that appeared from the time of the Enlightenment. The establishment of the humanitarian laws of war in the nineteenth century and the subsequent rise of the universal human rights culture and international criminal law are all part of the same long-term development. They reflected the growing influence of universal and egalitarian principles in European societies as a result of the transformations in the relations between 'established' and outsider' groups that were described earlier (see Pemberton 2009: 212 on the 'downward thrust' of sovereignty in the recent period).

The moral conviction that every human being has the right to be free from physical harm and degradation has led to changing constructions of sovereign responsibilities that are unprecedented in the history of the Western states-systems. The changes illustrate the shifting power balance between the pluralist and solidarist images of international society that are evident in prevalent Western definitions of 'legitimate statehood' – of the political communities that are fit to belong to 'the international civil order' and that can be trusted to uphold its core values by supporting strategies to establish 'civilized internal orders' (Taylor 1999: 138ff.; Sorensen 1999). Those core features of contemporary 'international ethics' have qualified state sovereignty in important areas. They are manifestations of the impact of the civilizing process on the dominant, but profoundly contested, Western conceptions of the boundaries between the permissible and impermissible exercise of sovereign power.

The rise of nationalism and growing demands for popular sovereignty from the end of the eighteenth century reconfigured political communities in Europe. A dramatic shift in emphasis towards sovereign rights and away from sovereign responsibilities took place as part of the drift towards total warfare. But societies that underwent the transition to democratic rule became more aware of the tensions between professed commitments to universal, egalitarian principles and *realpolitik* in foreign policy. Those internal dynamics interacted in crucial ways with the gradual incorporation of modern societies in dangerous strategic entanglements. The levels of violence that accompanied that development created new external pressures to place restraints on the exercise of state autonomy. The transformation of the 'practices of sovereignty' over the last few decades is the result of the interplay between those internal and external forces that combined to give rise to the humanitarian laws of war in the nineteenth century that prohibited cruelty and 'unnecessary suffering'. Certain parallels emerged between the earlier 'courtization of the warriors' and the more recent taming of the sovereigns with their increasingly violent interdependencies.

Their 'civilized' character is not only evident in social attitudes to suffering and in broad support for universal moral principles. The liberal defence of the 'civilizing' role of free markets is a crucial part of the equation, as are associated doctrines of 'legitimate statehood' in the era of 'global market civilization'. The interconnections between geopolitical struggle and the state's promotion of capitalist development led to poorly managed transnational economic and social relations that encouraged the critics to argue for new conceptions of international ethics and sovereign responsibilities. Again, there is nothing in the concept of sovereignty itself that prevents the development of more cosmopolitan orientations to the welfare of distant others, to the wellbeing of coming generations and to the future of humanity. The political conditions in which sovereignty now functions have created a variant on the long-established 'split' within modern civilization. Powerful economic interests that are engaged in short-term 'elimination contests' and struggles for dominance clash with various social movements that combine the ethical concern with the immediate plight of the vulnerable with longer-term perspectives on the relationship between 'society' and 'nature'. Those tensions have created moral and political challenges for 'civilized' peoples with respect to the relationship between state sovereignty and the scope of emotional identification, the we–I balance, and global social standards of restraint that did not exist in the earlier Western states-systems.

11

Process Sociology, Civilization and International Society

> The fact that we have not yet learned how to curb wars, the reciprocal mass destructions of members of different states, and other forms of behaviour that one cannot help calling barbarous, lends support to the assumption that in the overall context of the possible development of humankind what we call modern times represents a very early rather than a late stage of development ... We have not yet learned to cope with the obvious contradictions of our age. We know already *that* human beings are able to live in a much more civilised manner with each other ... We know already that much depends on achieving a better balance between self-restraint and self-fulfilment, but a stable social order that warrants such a balance still eludes us. It should not be beyond the reach of humankind in the thousands of years ahead of us
>
> (Elias 2011: 174, italics in original)

Elias maintained that Caxton's comment that 'things that were permitted are now forbidden' could stand as the 'motto' for the civilizing process that was to come (see Chapter 5, p. 201). The European path of social and development shaped diverse and interrelated spheres of social interaction including the standards that governed bodily functions, changes in table manners and (of particular importance for the present discussion) shifts in emotional responses to cruelty and violence. Elias was less consistent on the subject of whether things that were once permitted in the relations between states are now forbidden. His reflections of world politics raised, but did not answer, important questions about whether, or how far, the modern global system is different from its predecessors. One of the aims of this chapter is to consider how the process-sociological analysis of violence and civilization contributes to a comparative analysis of the Western states-systems that attempts to answer the question of how far distinctive under-standings of what is permissible and forbidden have developed in contem-porary international society.

The first part of the chapter explains the relationship between Elias's reflections on world politics and his larger inquiry into violence and civiliza-tion in modern European societies that has shaped the discussion of the last six chapters. Some points that were introduced at specific points in this inquiry are brought together and extended in order to show that they formed a coherent perspective on world politics. The discussion highlights the respects in which the investigation gives shape and direction to a sociology of states-systems that assesses the extent to which long-term developments in the modern society of states represent a major break with the past. The second section turns to English School reflections on international society. They lack the depth and breadth of process-sociological reflections on violence and civilization, but by analysing global civilizing processes they fill an important gap in that investigation. Societies of states are domains of interaction in which independent political communities establish, insofar as they can, crucial distinctions between permissible and forbidden conduct in the relations between peoples. Forging closer connections between English School analysis and process sociology which has neglected the realm of international society is key to developing a more synoptic account of violence and civilization in the Western states-systems.

The following discussion considers four distinctive features of the most recent phase in the development of the modern society of states which are all connected with the European civilizing process. It draws together some earlier observations to construct a brief overview of the relationship between violence and civilization in the most recent phase of the modern states-system. The phenomena of principal interest are the taming of the great powers, the expansion of international society from Europe to the rest of the world, the impact of cosmopolitan standards of social restraint on the construction of sovereign authority, and 'organized irresponsibility' in global 'market civilization'. Analysing those phenomena is essential for understanding the extent to which influential conceptions of 'international ethics' that did not exist amongst 'simpler civilizations' have become influential in the modern period. The final section turns to the question of the social conditions that have favoured the emergence of moral standpoints that have challenged conceptions of what is permissible in foreign policy that were largely taken for granted in the earlier Western states-systems. The aim is to correct one of the biases of Elias's analysis which was to explain why there has been so little in the way of a counterpart to the European civilizing process in international relations. It is to understand the particular forces that have led to a global equivalent that is linked with the process of civilization that shaped the European continent and relations with other societies over approximately five centuries.

Violence, Civilization and World Politics

Some sections of Elias's writings described international relations as the 'realm of recurrence and repetition' (see Wight 1966a); others maintained that the modern states-system may be poised to follow a radically new course of development. Four main points are worth making in this context. First, over and again, Elias's reflections are unambiguously pessimistic precisely because no higher monopoly of power is capable of restraining independent political communities where self-reliance for security and survival has bred similar patterns of distrust and suspicion over the millennia. Their behaviour in the heat of particular conflicts has often been dominated by highly emotive short-term views that led to unrestrained violence against demonized adversaries. Relations between states in recent times were described as displaying many of the same characteristics as relations between 'survival units' in the age of humanity's alleged 'barbarism' (Elias 2013: 190). As noted above, there were no obvious differences between the use of poisoned arrows to kill or main enemies in early warfare and the preparation to employ the technology of 'mass incineration' against adversaries in the nuclear era. If there was any substantial difference it is that the members of (internally) highly pacified modern societies almost certainly regard themselves as considerably more 'civilized' and restrained than their 'barbaric', war-prone ancestors.

Modern 'civilized' peoples are not wholly mistaken about some fundamental differences between their own ways of life and those of 'savages'. The historical evidence is that young males in early societies were attuned from an early age to carrying and using weapons to hunt their prey, to defend themselves from external attack, and to appropriate people and goods from neighbouring groups. The inhabitants of highly pacified societies today, on the other hand, do not in the main carry weapons or expect to use them. In everyday life, they are unlikely to witness the death or dying of other people. Military specialists who are responsible within a complex differentiation of functions for inflicting violence on behalf of the survival unit have to undergo extensive, expert training in the art of warfare in specially constructed military barracks that have been separated from the larger civilian society. 'Behind the scenes', as Elias stated, they undergo prolonged and intensive preparation for the difficult transition from peace to war where they are free (but not unreservedly so) to break the 'civilized' taboos against taking life.

The pleasure in killing and torturing enemies that was characteristic of many earlier warrior societies declined in the modern era with the civilizing process. Stable 'civilized' societies offer inhabitants few opportunities for experiencing 'the joy in killing and destruction'; such appetites have 'been suppressed from everyday life' (Elias 2012: 196). Wars became 'more impersonal' in the process (Elias 2012: ibid.). The 'direct physical combat between a man and his hated adversary [has] given way to a mechanized struggle which requires a strict control of the affects'; as a result, 'in the civilized world, even in war individuals can no longer give free rein to their pleasure, spurred on by the sight of the enemy, but must fight, no matter how they may feel, according to the commands of invisible or only indirectly visible leaders, against a frequently invisible or only indirectly visible enemy' (Elias 2012: ibid.).

The 'necessary restraint and transformation of aggression cultivated in the everyday life of civilized society' is not easily reversed 'even in these enclaves' (Elias 2012: ibid.). Indeed, nothing less than an 'immense social upheaval' and 'carefully concerted propaganda' could 'reawaken and legitimize in large masses of people the socially outlawed drives, the joy in killing and destruction that have been repressed from everyday civilized life' (Elias 2012: ibid.). Such is the impact of 'civilizing' taboos on the individual psyche that a significant number of former combatants have experienced the prolonged traumatic psychological effects of warfare on re-entering society and in endeavouring to become attuned once again to the peaceful routines of everyday life. The contention is that warriors in earlier groups did not undergo such a complex transition from peace to war or confront similar psychological challenges on rejoining society. The condition of post-traumatic stress disorder is evidence of changes in the inner moral life – of transformations at the level of the individual's conscience formation – that have been integral to the European civilizing process.

Modern societies have acquired the capacity to inflict unprecedented violence over ever greater distances by enlisting skilled specialists who are trained to discharge military responsibilities without necessarily having to display the hatred and anger that often typified the behaviour of ancient warriors in the 'heat of battle'. That is one reason why 'civilized' societies have an extraordinary ability to kill and injure over larger areas that nevertheless exists alongside the moral sensitivities about violence and suffering that distinguish them from 'savage' peoples. One of the paradoxes of the bipolar era was that people who enjoyed relatively low expectations of suffering violent harm in daily life faced the danger of instantaneous mass extermination because of relations between 'annihilation units' (Elias 2007a: 129; Elias 2010b: 186ff.). Those peculiarities are a modern variant on the traditional 'Janus-faced' nature of the civilizing process. For Elias, they demonstrated that the similarities between different phases in the history of the relations between groups are greater than the differences; they revealed the improbability of a future global counterpart to the civilizing process as long as 'survival units' escape subjection to a higher monopoly of physical power.

The second point is that Elias provided an interesting variant on what International Relations scholars will identify as an essentially realist explanation of interstate rivalries. The main contrast was the former's greater emphasis on the role of collective emotions in fuelling international conflict. The analysis was an important contribution to efforts to go beyond the dominant materialist modes of explanation in International Relations that have reduced behaviour to struggles over raw interests and ignored the social and political role of collective emotions that has been central to process-sociological inquiry (see Chapter 5; also Bleiker and Hutchison

2014). But the analysis of the emotional dimensions of international conflict broadly converged with realist or neo-realist contentions about the gulf between stable state-organized societies where civilizing processes have developed and the unchanging international political realm where few, if any, counterparts are to be found.

Elias borrowed the concept of the 'double-bind process' to explain recurrent features of relations between states. The term was employed to analyse the dynamics that unfold as societies respond in 'highly emotive' ways to the actions of adversaries; it was designed to explain how their behaviour can provoke similar affects in their opponents with the result that all become more tightly locked together in spiralling competition and conflict that they cannot control (Elias 2007: 162ff.). Emotionally charged struggles over short-term strategic advantages blocked the more detached analysis of the conditions in which the parties found themselves that holds the key to political solutions to a shared predicament (Elias 2010b: 195; Elias 2007: 162ff., 171ff.). Collective fantasies associated with 'group love' linked with demonizing images of enemies prevented a 'realistic assessment' of the political dynamics in which they were entangled and blocked the way to a correspondingly more 'realistic practice' (Elias 2007: 112ff.). Blind to their role in creating feelings of insecurity in others, peoples who were gripped by world views with a high 'fantasy content' compounded the political difficulties that confronted them while convincing themselves that they acted defensively and reasonably in circumstances for which their malevolent adversaries were entirely to blame. Actions and reactions that led states to rely on ever more violent measures confirmed their respective 'negative image' of others (Elias 2013: 368). Such emotive attachments have dominated political life whenever societies believed that they were denied the respect they believed they deserved, as was the case in post-First World War Germany where the idea of the 'stab in the back' was linked with 'idealized' self-images and distorted views of other societies that revealed how societies can succumb to a form of 'collective illness' that results in their downfall though not before they have inflicted terrible harm on other societies (Elias 2008c: 28–9).

From that standpoint, the bridge to more stable, cooperative relations depends on whether rivals can comprehend the social processes that bind them together, and on how far opposing groups can reach beyond their respective immediate fears and think in a more detached way from the perspective of others. What is crucial, but often hard to attain, is an orientation to conflict that focuses less on what every policy and manoeuvre that is initiated by an opponent 'means for me' and more on what every action and response means for 'us' (all of the affected parties) and what the relevant social dynamics are 'in themselves' (see Chapter 4, p. 182). In short, they must undergo a sophisticated collective learning process in which the highly emotive involvement in the outcome of immediate struggles is counterbalanced by a degree of detachment from, and a realistic understanding of, the web of constraints in which all are entangled (Elias 2007: 160ff., 171–2; Elias 2010c: 156ff.). Armed with more 'reality-congruent knowledge', foreign policy elites can engage in the politics of compromise and mutual accommodation that is necessary for reaching agreements about basic principles of self-restraint (Kilminster 2007: 120). The balance of power between those more positive forms of attunement to others and negative images of adversaries may then shift radically although serious doubts about the others' ultimate intentions and objectives do not leave the scene. There is implicit recognition in Elias's writings that such uncertainties can foster the suspicion that adversaries may be quick to exploit another's willingness to compromise or a unilateral display of restraint that is designed to communicate good faith and to elicit a reciprocated response. The political legitimacy of elements of the ruling strata that have endeavoured to deal peacefully with adversaries can be undermined by domestic opponents; the latter may gather support by portraying the former as weak and ineffective; they may accuse them of being unfit to hold public office and, in extreme cases, condemn them as traitors.

A third point revolves around an important division within process sociology on whether the nuclear revolution had the effect of taming or 'civilizing' the superpowers. At the height of the Second Cold War, Elias (2010c: 123ff.) displayed little confidence that the superpowers would avoid nuclear war. Parallels were drawn between ancient and modern great power struggles. In classical antiquity, conflicts between the few remaining great powers that had survived earlier 'elimination contests' had descended into 'hegemonic wars' that were fuelled by 'hegemonic intoxication' (Elias 2010c: 101). In the modern states-system, the danger of nuclear war demonstrated that the long-term trend towards the accumulation of ever more destructive military power had reached the 'end of the road' and that humanity faced the very real possibility of a return to the 'caves' (Elias (2010c: 78, 120, 128). But the danger of nuclear war, Elias added, might not be enough to produce major changes of behaviour. A full-scale conflict between the superpowers might have to occur before the surviving societies realized that the hour had come to embark on an entirely new course of development in which the link between security and hegemony is finally broken (van Benthem van den Bergh 2012).

The opposing standpoint within process sociology maintained that the balance of terror had exercised a broadly pacifying effect. As the 'functional equivalent' of a stable monopoly of physical power, nuclear bipolarity created unprecedented pressures to exercise extreme caution, to exercise foresight and to think from the standpoint of the other – in short, to display levels of 'reciprocal restraint' that mirrored features of the earlier European, intrastate civilizing process (van den Bergh 1992: ch. 2). The risk of nuclear annihilation had introduced unparalleled incentives in great power relations to develop a more 'realistic' assessment of the other's motives and objectives in tandem with a more 'realistic practice' that limited the damaging effects of high 'fantasy content' world views (see the parallel discussion in Waltz 1981, 2012). Crucially, the route to a worldwide monopoly of force through imperial conquest had now been closed off (van den Bergh 1992: ch. 6).

Elias's reflections on the nuclear era are consistent with his position in the late 1930s that there is a high probability that elimination contests between larger territorial monopolies of power will continue until humanity comes under the control of a world state (Elias 2010b: 202ff.; Elias 2010c: 134–5). The argument was that competition for the control of 'larger and larger areas' was already 'in full swing' (Elias 2012: 479–80). But as a result of the nuclear revolution, the phenomenon of 'hegemonic intoxication' that had dominated the European states-systems since the classical era appeared to be drawing to an end (Elias 2010c: 101, 123–5, 144ff.). Larger numbers of people had come to the realization that societies faced the entirely novel political problem of replacing 'hegemonic wars' with a collective quest to pacify the world as a whole (Elias 2010c: 144ff.). The idea of humanity no longer referred simply to ethical aspirations that have long been dismissed as utopian. Although the 'undertones of sentimental idealism' still clung to it (Elias 2011: 206), the concept reflected the observable reality that societies now had an increasingly interdependent fate (Elias 2008: 87).

Elias's analysis of European state formation explained the complex processes by which centrifugal forces were replaced by political compromises between social strata that led to the slow pacification of society and to the 'civilizing' of conduct in which the relative power of internal and external restraints on behaviour gradually changed. The other side of that course of development was the continuation of elimination contests at the international level that led to the danger of nuclear war and to the possible annihilation of 'civilized' societies. But the fourth point in this discussion is that it would be curious if the ethical dimensions of the ways in which people have become bound together within those social groups had no impact whatsoever on their external relations. As discussed earlier, Elias maintained that societies that have undergone the transition from autocratic to democratic systems of rule have often been troubled by foreign policy that clashes with 'civilized' standards of behaviour. The modern ethical sensibilities that had shaped responses to the Nazi genocide revealed the differences, he argued, between the greater tolerance of violence in classical antiquity and the widespread feelings of shock and disgust at serious human rights violations in the present era. Various international non-governmental organizations such as Amnesty International were testimony to 'the spread of a sense of responsibility among individuals for the fate of others far beyond the frontiers of their own country or continent' (Elias 2010b: 151). The 'worldwide interweaving' of societies meant that more and more people were aware of distant suffering and felt 'a duty to do something about the misery of other human groups'; the overall level of commitment to eradicating poverty was still limited when considered in 'absolute terms'; nevertheless, 'conscience formation [had] changed in the course of the twentieth century' (Elias 2013: 29). None of those changes altered the reality that the highly disciplined members of industrializing and bureaucratizing societies had acquired levels of destructive power that made them more dangerous to each other. The important sociological questions were how far the balance of influence between those two faces of the civilizing process has changed over time, and whether there is reason to suppose that, in the near future, the more restrained and humanitarian side will prevail over the more violent face of civilization.

Elias's last writings in the 1980s stressed that modern peoples are now clearly interconnected in economic and social as well as in geopolitical ways that have some parallels with the socio- and psycho-genetic processes that accompanied the emergence of larger monopolies of physical power in early modern Europe (Elias 2007a: 128–9; Elias 2007: 175). As with the intensification of the division of labour within societies, rising levels of global interconnectedness have introduced some similar compulsions and pressures to tame selfish ambitions, to co-operate to manage certain shared problems and to become more closely attuned to the interests of other groups. With the incorporation of people in longer webs of mutual dependence, 'the effective survival unit [was] now visibly shifting . . . from the level of the nation-states to the post-national unions of states, and beyond them, to humanity' itself (Elias 2010b: 195ff.). However, the argument was, the development of stronger post-national emotional orientations is far from certain. For many people, surrendering sovereign powers to regional or global political associations is tantamount to sacrificing all that earlier generations had fought for; it involves a loss of collective pride in past national achievements that the living should be eager to pass on to their successors (Elias 2008c; Elias 2007: introduction). For many people, humanity remains little more than a 'beautiful ideal' or a 'blank space on the map of the emotions' (Elias 2010b: 181). As a result of the continuing influence of 'natio-centric socialization', they remain hostile to 'higher' political arrangements that are deemed to clash with 'traditional national self-images' or they recognize the instrumental value of unions of states but confess that they derive little emotional warmth from them (Elias 2012: 508n13; Elias 2010b: 188ff.). National attachments and ossified 'we images' that are 'among the most dangerous structural features of the transitional stage at which we now find ourselves' continued to exercise a 'drag effect' on the development of stronger international associations that are necessary if unplanned social processes are to be brought under greater collective control (Elias 2010b: 198, 207; Elias 2011: 165ff.).

Those comments suggest that the modern states-system is uniquely and perhaps very finely balanced between opposing social and political tendencies.

Elias did not rule out the possibility that societies will learn to live together non-violently in the course of long intergenerational learning processes over centuries or millennia. It was not beyond the ingenuity of the human species to solve the problem of violent harm in the remaining period in which life can be sustained on the planet, assuming that it does not destroy itself first (Elias 2011: 173). But what is true of 'civilized' groups would also be true of any future global civilizing process that succeeded in pacifying humanity. In those societies, the 'armour of civilized conduct would crumble very rapidly' if the 'degree of insecurity that existed earlier were to break in upon us again, and if danger became as incalculable as it once was. Corresponding fears would soon burst the limits set to them today' (Elias 2012: 576, also 484–5). The risks could be expected to remain high in international politics as long as one of the preconditions of the modern European civilizing process – the existence of a monopoly of power that can compel compliance and punish transgressions of the dominant standards of restraint – was missing (Elias 2010b: 199ff.). There had been an unmistakeable overall trend towards the social and political integration of the species. The process could be at an early stage of development; still greater increases in the interweaving of societies might take place in the future. But it was prudent to suppose that the 'integration–disintegration' tensions that had existed throughout human history would now be played out at the global level. The 'immense process of integration' that the species has undergone has often developed in tandem with 'counter-thrusts' that eventually gained the upper hand. It was essential to be realize that a 'dominant disintegration process' that undermines precarious achievements in extending 'civilized' restraints into the troubled domain of international politics could lie ahead (Elias 2010b: 148, 202).

The Civilizing Process and International Society

The analysis of the European civilizing process explained how the 'monopoly mechanism' had ended the localized power struggles that followed the collapse of the Roman imperial system of government and the short-lived reassertions of centralized power in the Carolingian and Merovingian empires. It analysed parallel changes in the pacification of society, higher levels of interconnectedness and new forms of attunement between people. But elimination contests did not cease; they were transferred to the distinctive sphere of international politics where the restraints of the 'civilized' life were either absent or significantly weaker (Elias 2012: 296–7). In that analysis there was no conception of what Bull (1977) famously described as 'the anarchical society'. There are clear tensions between the realist dimensions of Elias's inquiry and the English School analysis of the surprisingly high level of order that exists between modern states in the absence of a higher monopoly of control of the instruments of force. The latter approach maintains that state formation is

not as 'Janus-faced' as Elias believed, and it denies that the 'duality of normative codes within the nation-state' is quite as stark and unrelieved as he
supposed (Elias 2013: 169ff.). It asserts that 'outward preparation' for war
is often linked with common interests in preserving international order that
have been connected with the invention of sophisticated institutional and
diplomatic methods of reaching agreements on standards of restraint that
are embodied in international law and largely followed by mutual consent
but vulnerable to familiar power struggles and inequalities.

Despite some references to 'supranational court society', the neglect of the
'civilizing' role of international society is a major lacuna in Elias's writings.
As noted earlier, the latter did not recognize that the institutions of the society
of states are the product of the larger European civilizing process. They did not
discuss major illustrations of their inseparability that include such interrelated
phenomena as the 'standard of civilization', the 'sacred trust of civilization' and
the 'civilized', humanitarian laws of war. For their part, members of the
English School have not developed Wight's contention that every international
society emerged in a region where there was a powerful sense of cultural or
civilizational we-identity that was formed in opposition to the outer regions
inhabited by 'savages'. The former have not analysed the connections between
what some have described as the 'civilizing' role of international society and
the larger European process of civilization (Linklater and Suganami 2006:
121–2). In short, neither perspective has considered state-building, the waves
of European colonial expansion and the evolution of international society as
three interrelated parts of one single trajectory of development. Process
sociology provides the foundations for the necessary synthesis because of the
breakthrough in regarding the overall direction of change as one that was
characterized by the emergence of specific conceptions of civilization that were
connected with European state formation.

Sociological inquiry can seek to explain changing conceptions of what is
permissible and what is forbidden at each of the three levels just noted.
The society of states has priority in this part of the discussion because it is
the domain where sovereign communities discover whether or not they can
agree on international (or cosmopolitan) harm conventions that rest on shared
understandings of indefensible harm and unacceptable suffering. That
has been a central theme in English School inquiry as is evident from the
contention that the universal society of states is 'the most encompassing
normative framework that humans have fashioned thus far' for combining
the objective of maintaining political independence with shared interests in
coexisting 'on a finite planetary space' that underpin cooperation to tackle
'mutual hostility, conflict, war, oppression, subjugation [and] slavery' (Jackson
2000: 11–13, 181, 425). Those transformations, it has been argued, are best
explained not by using the tarnished idea of civilization with its connotations
of Western cultural superiority but by referring to advances in global civility.

The latter concept is used to describe commitments to prudence, moderation and self-restraint that no single culture or civilization has monopolized; it refers to shared capacities that make it possible for societies that are radically different in many respects to coexist in a multicultural international society (Jackson 2000: 408).

Core features of any society of states can be regarded as outcomes of the civil dispositions that exist in most of the constitutive political parts. They include the partial shift in the relative power of the fear of coercion and the internal restraints that societies impose on themselves because of the willingness to comply with agreed conceptions of correct behaviour. No less important are the forms of self-restraint that arise in conjunction with the acceptance of the need to think from the standpoint of others and to view one's actions 'from a greater distance' (Elias 2012: 484). But the idea of civility has limited value for understanding the development of such characteristics in the modern states-system. Earlier illustrations of the 'inseparability' of key organizing principles of international society and the European civilizing process highlight the importance of global power relations that the idea of civility obscures. Moreover, as earlier chapters have shown, basic institutions of international society such as diplomacy are only explicable by understanding the relationship between court society and the development of 'civilized' codes of conduct. It is instructive that the idea of civility was gradually replaced in the late eighteenth century by the idea of civilization that reflected the spirit of reform that was promoted by the ascending middle-class groups and expressed in the moral conviction that civilization was a condition that had to be brought to 'backward' non-European peoples (Elias 2012: 52ff., 105ff.). Wight's contention that every society of states has emerged in a cultural zone that distinguished itself from the world of the 'barbarians' draws attention to the civilizational dimensions of modern international society though not to the idea of the European civilizing process itself. That concept provides the bridge between the English School analysis of international society and the process-sociological explanation of long-term patterns of intra- and inter-societal development. It is the key to incorporating their strengths in a more synoptic framework of inquiry that contributes to realising the Eliasian vision of 'higher-level synthesis' in social-scientific inquiry.

Things That Were Once Permitted Are Now Forbidden?

One of the purposes of the comparative study of states-systems is to ascertain how far actions that were permitted in earlier times are forbidden in contemporary international society. The following four areas of discussion provide preliminary observations about what is most distinctive about standards of self-restraint, the forms of we-feeling and the we–I balance in the most recent phase of the modern states-system. They are designed to reveal the changes of 'personality structures and especially of structures of conscience or self-control which represent a standard of humaneness going far beyond that of antiquity', and indeed all of the earlier states-systems in the West (Elias 2013: 446).

The Taming of the Great Powers

It is necessary to begin with the struggles between the great powers and the extent to which they have been tamed by the 'civilizing' institutions of international society. One of the central themes in the study of the civilizing process is that the main patterns of change evolve 'behind the backs' of people who are pulled along in unexpected ways by social forces that are beyond their control (Elias 2007: 77). There are few better examples as far as the great powers are concerned than the processes that led to the nuclear era. But that was part of a broader chain of events. In earlier stages of the modern states-system, the great powers found themselves locked together in 'the production line of the same machinery' and forced to realize that 'sudden and radical change in one sector' could have disruptive consequences for all (Elias 2012: 353). They were aware of the immense dangers that accompanied the 'worldwide interweaving' of peoples and the rise of 'an interdependent system of countries' where every 'shift of power directly or indirectly' affected every country (Elias 2012: 335). Competition for power and security, and 'inevitable conflicts', had become 'increasingly risky' for the 'precarious system of nations' (Elias 2012: ibid). Pressures mounted to work out how to resolve 'future interstate conflicts by less dangerous means' (Elias 2012: 488).

The behaviour of the victorious powers at the end of the Second World War provided an example of patterns of self-restraint and foresight that had been integral to the 'civilizing' of conduct within the major European societies. No matter how much they might have wanted to destroy their industrial capabilities and to prevent future re-armament, pragmatism dictated read-mitting Germany and Japan into the international system of states. There was an obvious contrast with the policy towards a defeated Germany approxi-mately twenty-five years earlier and a clear parallel with Bismarck's policy towards the defeated Austrians (Elias 2013: 20; Elias 2010c: 114). An earlier diplomatic agreement not to impose a humiliating settlement on France at the end of the Napoleonic Wars has also been noted in this context (Clark 2005: 85ff.). Those foreign policy standpoints were evidence that pressures to take a more detached perspective on one's place in the human chain were not confined to social relations within national frontiers; worldwide networks of strategic interconnections and diplomatic entanglements also created incentives to learn how to see oneself 'from a greater distance' that had already shaped intra-societal developments within 'civilized' states (Elias 2012: 440; Elias 2012: 287–8).

There have long been tensions between the longer-term, more detached considerations of the foundations of international order and the shorter-term, more involved national quest for military and political advantage. Recognition that international order could not be left to chance but had to be constructed through diplomatic consultation and collective action in the attempt to avert increasingly destructive warfare has often clashed with the pursuit of immediate national security goals in the context of fear and distrust. As discussed in Chapter 4, the awareness of the importance of great power restraint and co-operation to preserve the balance of power goes back at least as far as the Italian Renaissance. That shift was part of an overall trend in which, in response to incentives to settle their differences peacefully, the major powers found it prudent to rely on and refine 'civilizing' practices such as diplomacy. Elements of we-feeling developed as part of the struggle to control violent harm; but the we–I balance was profoundly influenced by strong and divisive attachments to particular city states. The international society of the time was shaped by 'integration–disintegration tensions' that have existed in all phases in the development of the modern society of states and in all of the Western states-systems. As noted above, Elias did not believe that those tensions were about to be resolved by a global civilizing offensive that pacified the relations between the superpowers while van Benthem van den Bergh (1992) maintained that the balance of terror had introduced new levels of reciprocal restraint. The latter were part of a longer process of international political development that has been investigated by English School as well as constructivist scholars.

Detailed historical studies have shown how peace settlements at the end of major great power conflicts influenced the pronounced trend towards the increased collective management of the international system (Clark 2005: 65, 84; Osiander 1994). Following the violence of the Thirty Years' War, the dominant powers resolved at Westphalia to proceed as far as possible on the basis of mutual consent. The Treaties of Utrecht (1713–15) institutionalized the idea of the balance of power (Reus-Smit 1999: 116ff.). That was a period in which the European states recognized that they were no longer 'a confused heap of detached pieces' with little reason to look beyond immediate objectives or to consider 'the fate of others', but were the interdependent parts of an international system with a common interest in attuning their respective foreign policies to prevent hegemonic wars (see Chapter 10, p. 392). Modern diplomatic practices that enable states to exercise greater control over 'the same production line' were refined in that era. Crucially, following the Napoleonic wars, the dominant powers supported the principle that they should use their combined authority as 'great responsibles' to steer the international system through its inevitable political crises. In a sequence of postwar settlements, they constructed constitutional frameworks that embedded expectations of 'strategic restraint'; they attempted to reach shared understandings of the levels of national self-limitation that were essential if international order was to survive and if the society of states was to function smoothly (Ikenberry 2001; van Benthem van den Bergh 1992: 30ff.).

There is a clear parallel with the general trend within modern states in which new steering mechanisms have been created in response to the problems associated with higher levels of social and economic integration. Increasingly destructive warfare in relations between highly interdependent peoples introduced similar pressures to create international institutions that explored the possibility of agreements on essential foreign policy constraints. The challenge was to deal with one of the side effects of the civilizing process, namely the increased capacity to inflict violent harm that was a direct product of achievements in pacifying state-organized societies. What has been described as the 'obsolescence of force' in the relations between the great powers is a phase in a continuous civilizing process in which larger territorial monopolies of power became more dangerous to each other; they were pushed towards recognition of the need to act in concert to moderate the struggles for power and security that tied them together. Various peace conferences and permanent international institutions are, in the language of process sociology, important examples of how parallels to intra-societal developments in the realm of 'social constraints towards self-constraint' appeared in the modern society of states; they are instances of the 'spread of foresight and restraint' over much greater distances (Elias 2012: 418ff.). The relevant institutional innovations exemplify the crucial role of 'meeting regimes' in taming international struggles for power and in controlling or suppressing violent or aggressive dispositions (van Vree 1999). They have been critical in promoting higher levels of mutual attunement and in developing principles of self-restraint that partly reconcile different understandings of what is permissible and what is forbidden in relations between peoples. They are evidence of the principal 'direction' of any civilizing process, namely 'resolving conflicts and disagreements on the basis of jointly acknowledged rules, instead of by violence' (Elias 2013d: 268).

The emergence of global steering arrangements was part of an overall social trend that connects the taming or 'courtization' of the warriors with the taming of great power rivalries through the political initiatives that were taken at the end of the Second World War to eliminate militarism. A major 'civilizing' offensive was undertaken to liberate state structures in the defeated Axis powers from warrior cultures that glorified violence (Jackson 2006; Jarausch 2006). The twentieth century is often described as one of the most violent in the whole of human history, but the Second World War represented a turning point in the evolution of international society for those reasons.

The subsequent 'long peace' between the great powers represents the renewal of an earlier movement towards a 'civilianization' or 'civilizing' of the military domain that had been interrupted by short-lived, failed experiments in totalitarian rule that were undertaken by regimes that had an ambivalent relationship with, if not outright contempt for, Enlightenment values and European standards of civilization (Kershaw 2005). In the industrial regions of the world, the past few decades have witnessed the re-emergence of the social trend that was celebrated by Enlightenment thinkers for whom glorifying war and cherishing military values were the hallmarks of an 'obsolete' and 'barbaric' age that commercial society was poised to eradicate (van Doorn 1984: 44–5).

Those sentiments only moved to the centre of the study of international relations in the very recent period. They were especially evident in studies of the general trend in which the traditional 'military-political system' lost its appeal for 'trading states' that severed the link between military conquest and economic growth, preferring instead to pursue financial and commercial success by assuming specialist roles within a complex global division of labour. The states in question pointed the way forward by breaking with the central trend between 1500 and 1900 that was dominated by the formation of larger – but fewer – territorial concentrations of physical violence with increased powers over national populations and weak international allegiances (Rosecrance 1986: 67). Their commitment to global commerce was an instance of an overall tendency to sever the traditional link between military conquest and national wealth that is the bridge between the earlier liberal critique of mercantilism and the more recent idea of the 'liberal peace' with its specific we-identity, we–I balance and shared standards of self-restraint that reflect the 'liberal conscience' (Doyle 1983).

Echoing earlier themes in the British liberal tradition, several analysts in the late 1980s argued that warfare was about to suffer the same fate as slavery and duelling, and to fall out of favour as part of changing understandings of what it means to belong to 'civilized' societies (Ray 1989). On that argument war is 'immoral, repulsive and uncivilized' as well as 'ineffective' and 'futile' in conflicts between highly interdependent, industrialized societies (Mueller 1989: 217; also Jervis 2011 and Lebow 2010, 2010a). Those standpoints have partially rehabilitated earlier liberal standpoints on world politics that seemed to have been largely swept aside by the triumph of realist or neo-realist pessimism in the aftermath of two world wars. Some of the classic formulations are worth noting because they maintained that a new phase in the civilizing process was within reach in which public antipathy to war would grow in response to the combined effect of external compulsions and profound structural and psychological changes in the societies involved. The writings of Sir Norman Angell remain important because of broad parallels with process-sociological analysis of civilizing processes. As a result of the growth of closer economic ties, Angell argued, 'the possibility of one part injuring another without injury to itself has been diminished' (Angell 1912: 20ff., 272–3). A general dampening of the 'impulses to injury' and a weakening of national attachments were underway as part of the more general 'civilizing' of drives that had previously led to the abolition of forms of violence including the aristocratic duel and the use of torture that had once provided 'public amusement' (Angell 1912: 209–10). The increased costliness of war encouraged the view that interstate force would be eradicated as part of the same European civilizing process.

Unsurprisingly, given the scale of the great power conflicts that lay ahead, such images of the future of international society were dismissed on the grounds of their utopianism. But given the post-Second World War 'long peace' as well as the continuing growth of human interconnectedness and progressions in the area of human rights, such writings remain important precisely because of the attempt to identify distinctive historical trends and potentials in the most recent phase of the modern states-system. Wight speculated – and Elias broadly concurred – that, if the past is any guide, then states-systems appear to be destined to end in violence because of elimination contests that culminate in empire. The modern society of states may yet prove to be the exception – it may not be the 'evolutionary dead end' that the earlier states-systems in the West turned out to be.

Recent developments suggest that there is a very high probability that 'the frequency of war will sharply decline' at least with respect to relations between the major powers, although there is no guarantee that it will disappear forever (Lebow 2010: 268; Lebow 2010a; also Buzan 2011; Jervis 2011 and Mearsheimer 2006). The nuclear revolution had a 'civilizing effect' by pushing the superpowers to settle their differences non-violently. The idea that industrial states can resolve major differences by force is now patently absurd (Buzan 2011), which is not to deny the probability that the great powers will continue to use force in the outlying areas in perceived similarities with earlier colonial wars (Feichtinger, Malinowski and Richards 2012). Unprecedented changes in the relative power of economic as opposed to traditional forms of strategic interdependencies have had a pronounced pacifying effect (Buzan and Little 2000). But their effect has not been confined to changing the external pressures and incentives to act with greater restraint. They have brought to the surface of world politics major transformations within industrial societies that succeeded in making the transition to liberal-democratic government. As part of the civilizing process, 'middle class traits gradually (moved) into the foreground' while aristocratic norms lost much of their significance as 'the primary sources of 'prestige' and self-esteem; greater importance came to be attached to 'money-earning functions' and to other peaceful activities as opposed to the displays of military prowess and courage that were highly valued attributes in the traditional male warrior codes (Elias 2012: 4267ff.; Elias 2013: 182ff.).

In many of those societies, bourgeois values coexisted without any apparent contradiction with the frequent use of force in conflicts between the great powers. The current reality is that the great majority of people in highly pacified societies find personal meaning in commercial, administrative and in other peaceful forms of employment (Lebow 2010: 268). In the present phase of the civilizing process, they have no direct acquaintance with warfare, no expectation of risking their lives for the good of the nation, and few social ties with a separate caste of military specialists. Rousing national representations of the elevating individual and collective experience of participating in warfare that existed only a few decades ago have virtually disappeared from the public discourse in 'post-military society', and now seem wholly alien or absurd (Shaw 1991).

With the taming of the great powers, the earlier civilizing process that included the reduction of levels of interpersonal violence within stable, state-organized societies was extended into the domain of international politics. Unprecedented global social standards of self-restraint are part of a broader pacification process that effectively began with the 'taming of the warriors' in court societies. The relationship between violence and civilization has changed as patterns of social interconnectedness that were integral to the earlier civilizing process have been replicated at the international level. The ancient 'split' within civilization is significantly less profound as a result.

The Expansion of International Society

The 'civilizing' of relations between the great powers is a major revolution in the history of the Western states-systems. A second fundamental reconfiguration is the expansion of the society of states that has been a crucial dimension of the globalization of the European civilizing process. The point has been made that the analysis of the 'civilizing' institutions of international society was missing from Elias's major study – so was the investigation of their globalization as non-European peoples were incorporated as independent states within the 'global covenant' that originated in Europe. That transformation of world politics is one example of how the rise of the sovereign state and the interrelated conceptions of civilization from the 1500s onwards led to profound socio- and psycho-genetic changes that would affect humanity as a whole in unplanned and unpredicted ways. Expansionist territorial states, and strategic and economic rivalries that came to be conducted on a worldwide scale, forced all peoples into a single stream of world history with European civilization at its core. Only in the last few decades did non-European peoples win the political struggle to join international society as formally equal sovereign states. Notwithstanding the 'numerous back-eddies and local breakdowns of civilized complexity', it has been maintained, there has been 'an ineluctable expansion of the portions of the globe subjected to or incorporated within civilized social structures' (McNeill 1983a: 10). Such claims are riddled with controversial ambiguities and can be interpreted as contending that humanity as a whole has progressed in the recent period. But it is entirely valid to describe the expansion of international society as evidence of how almost all peoples have been incorporated in a society of states that is governed by standards of self-restraint that can only be understood as direct offshoots of the European civilizing process. The point is not that non-European peoples have become more 'civilized' in some normative sense but that they became entangled in a global civilizing process that originated in Europe.

Those peoples were incorporated in global 'civilized social structures' that were suffused with imperialist assumptions about European racial and cultural inferiority. The formal rejection of the Japanese demand for racial equality at Versailles in 1919 was one illustration of initial European hostility to admitting non-European peoples into the society of states as moral and political equals (Clark 2009: ch. 4). As noted in Chapter 6, the conviction that international society was an exclusive 'European club' was defended on the grounds that other peoples were less 'civilized' or barbarous 'outcasts' (Zarakol 2011). Their gradual acceptance as social equals – a process that is far from complete – was part of a profound alteration of the course of the European civilizing process. Parallel changes occurred in the Chinese and Ottoman civilizing processes where a 'hegemonial conception of international society' that was antithetical to the idea of the sovereign equality of states had existed for centuries (Bull and Watson 1984: introduction). With respect to its membership, international society has outgrown Europe or the West although core political and economic institutions are far from 'post-European' or 'post-Western' but remain heavily biased towards Western values and interests that reflect the continuing influence of the dominant civilization. That condition seems certain to change because of shifts in the balance of military, political and economic power that may give rise to new interstate tensions and rivalries. The question is whether the participants will succeed in agreeing on universal legal and moral standards of self-restraint that bridge the differences between the peoples that were forced together by European colonial expansion.

Elias's observation that what changes in the course of history are the 'social standards of self-control' invites discussion of how far major shifts that have affected humanity as a whole are reflected in the organizing practices of international society. There are two points to make in this context. First, during the waves of colonial expansion, European societies had little compunction in violating 'civilized' standards of self-restraint in relations with 'savages'. As discussed in Chapter 6, the double standard of morality existed in a more dramatic or extreme form in relations with Europe's outsiders where violence, humiliation and exploitation were widespread. The level of self-control of violent and destructive inclinations that 'civilized' peoples observed within their respective borders, and to some degree in relations with each other, did not have the same influence on relations with 'barbarians'. The colonial strata advanced many reasons for observing less demanding restraints in that sphere including the variant on the doctrine of military necessity which stated that European interests would suffer if 'civilized' standards were observed in conflicts with 'cruel' savages who did not recognize constraints in the form of the laws of war. So great were the power disparities between imperial overlords and colonial peoples that the former could often behave as they wanted, ignoring the imperatives of conscience that were influential in other social spheres. There was little or no incentive to think from the standpoint of others or to make political concessions to people who could offer little in return. The process of civilization licensed lifting many taboos against violence between peoples, but it also provided the moral resources for condemning those who cast aside 'civilized' ethical constraints as they proceeded to dominate, exterminate, displace, exploit, enslave and in other ways harm subjugated peoples. The countervailing standpoint was that imperial cruelties clashed with the normative ideals that were integral to the collective identities of supposedly civilized peoples.

The nineteenth-century European 'standard of civilization' embodied the peculiar ambiguities of the civilizing process. The doctrine reasserted a right to colonize, judge and transform colonized societies while holding out the distant promise, on the assumption that imperial rule would bring civilization to 'backward' regions, of membership of the society of states (Gong 1984; Suzuki 2009). From the early to mid-nineteenth century, the dominant principles of domestic and international legitimacy were shaped by the moral conviction that the overseas empires should be governed, to a greater extent than ever before, by constraints on violent and non-violent harm that were hallmarks of a 'civilized' existence (Crawford 2002). The social gradient between the colonizers and the colonized became less steep as a result of an ethos that would be linked with conceptions of international trusteeship and with the idea of 'the sacred trust of civilization that were key steps in the transition from an exclusively European to a universal society of states (Bain 2003). The prevailing understandings about permissible and forbidden forms of colonial administration shifted radically with the consequence that the constituent parts of international society no longer thought that it was morally acceptable to take colonial territories by force or to seize, transport and sell other peoples who had been reduced to mere commodities. The 'toil of the spear' that had been central to the states-systems of classical antiquity became impermissible as part of the larger transformation of Western understandings about violence and civilization.

One of the key distinguishing features of the modern states-system is the notable, if incomplete, achievement in weakening pernicious contrasts between the 'civilized' and the 'barbaric' that blocked the development of images of an international society of nominal equals in the earlier Western states-systems. Such demeaning distinctions are no longer regarded as legitimate reasons for excluding the great majority of the world's peoples from membership of the society of states. For 'civilized' peoples, it is unacceptable to invoke differences of race or civilization to justify various traditional forms of violent harm against 'natural inferiors' as well as public forms of humiliation and stigmatization and other actions that deny others the equal respect that has come to be regarded as part of the birthright of all human beings. The usual caveats apply. The speed with which contrasts between the 'civilized' and the 'savage' emerged in the aftermath of 9/11 provided a reminder of how quickly colonial imaginaries can be rekindled under conditions of insecurity (Pasha 2009). The tenacity of pernicious contrasts between peoples must be understood in long-term perspective. They are relics of earlier phases of the process of civilization that included the divisions between the 'civil' and 'uncivil' in the first stages of European state formation, in successive waves of 'medieval' and 'modern' outward expansion, and in the colonial phase of the modern society of states with its distinctive assumptions about 'less advanced' peoples who stood in the way of 'civilized humanity'.

One of the legacies is the temptation to characterize the violent resistance to Western political, economic and cultural dominance that has been initiated by, *inter alia*, radical Islamist groups as a 'pre-modern', 'external' assault on Western values. Their anger may be regarded as symptomatic of the absence of the rational, self-disciplined habitus that distinguishes more peaceful, 'civilized' peoples (Linklater 2014). The groups in question may seem to draw on 'indigenous values' that are opposed to extraneous Western images of 'modernity' but, on many interpretations, it is necessary to understood such reactions relationally and processually, as the outcome of the social and cultural changes that were set in motion by traumatic encounters with European invaders (Mishra 2012). The catastrophic 'loss of meaning' led to 'deep mourning' and the collective distress and 'depression' from which the peoples involved have not recovered, and which are still only partly understood (Elias 2013: 83–4). The whole process is part of a broader complex of collective responses to the history of pressures on colonial subjects to acknowledge their 'inferiority' and to recognize their complete dependence on Europeans for access to civilization and progress. 'Anti-Western' social movements that proclaim the superiority of 'traditional' belief-systems are hardly a surprising reaction to a European civilizing process that legitimized, and was shaped by, colonial violence and calculated strategies of humiliation (Kull 2011). They are the most recent manifestations of the 'cultural revolt against the West' that revolutionized the society of states. The challenges to the dominant global economic and political structures are not explicable in terms of social 'pathologies' that demonstrate, as stated in the 'new barbarian thesis', an inability to adapt to 'modern' social structures and belief-systems; they are the product of historical struggles by non-Western movements to win respect for 'traditional' customs and values (Jacoby 2011; Pasha 2012; Phillips 2011: conclusion). As noted earlier, the ensuing foreign policy challenges for the 'civilized' powers will not be solved by concentrating on the systemic imperatives that neo-realists regard as the decisive influence on all states-systems. Major political challenges result from the invalidation of earlier predictions of the voluntary acceptance of European 'civilized' standards in all non-European regions. The quest for a global agreement on standards of self-restrain must now start from different premises – with a deeper awareness of the need to promote cultural justice in the context of widening social differences (Shapcott 2001).

The second main point is that the changes that have taken place in weakening pernicious distinctions between peoples clearly cannot be explained simply in terms of 'moral progress' within Western societies. They were brought about by global 'emancipation struggles' that have, in interrelated ways, reduced the social gradient between the former colonial and colonized peoples as well as between rulers and ruled, men and women, and adults and children within many societies (Elias 2013: 28, also Reus-Smit 2011; Reus-Smit 2013: ch. 5). As integral parts of that process, anti-colonial struggles to win membership of the society of states were influenced by multiple forces including the reality that many 'first generation' national leaders were educated in European universities and attracted by, or at least exposed to, moral claims that freedom and equality were central to the civilization to which those institutions belonged. A deep awareness of contradictions between imperial domination and European social and political ideals – and of the paradoxical expectation that colonized peoples would defend 'civilization' in the two world wars – developed in that environment. Counter-hegemonic movements illustrated how the participants in emancipation struggles can accumulate significant power resources and secure moral and political legitimacy by turning the dominant ideologies against those who claim to live in accordance with more 'civilized' principles. Those modes of resistance also demonstrate how the ethical sensitivities that emerged with the rise of state monopolies of power acquired relative autonomy from other spheres of society and influenced directions of change within Europe and in the wider world. Political and ideological competition between superpowers that were anxious to flourish their anti-colonial credentials in the struggle to win Third World support was no less important. Changing principles of legitimacy – new conceptions of what was permissible and what was forbidden – increased the reputational costs of attempting to preserve the overseas empires in an era when the political resolve and material capabilities of European governments were considerably weakened (Crawford 2002). Anti-imperial emancipation struggles prevailed because major changes in the power balance between Europe and its colonies – and between the traditional

European great powers and the superpowers – coincided with the collapse of the moral defence of empire that had been at the heart of the European civilizing process.

In the 1950s and 1960s it was generally assumed in the West that anti-colonial leaders were (or would become) committed to liberal-democratic principles although it was understood that many may have used Western political discourse strategically to ensure that their claims found a sympathetic hearing in the former colonial societies (Bull 1984c). In any case, successor nationalist elites in post-colonial states became more inclined to advance their interests by drawing on 'traditional' or 'indigenous' values. Associated emancipation struggles spearheaded the 'cultural revolt against the West' that has become more closely linked with a religious revolt against secular modernization (Bull 1984c; Shani 2014). The upshot is that the society of states is not underpinned any more by a widespread belief that the constituent parts belong to a single civilization or can be reasonably governed by an alien 'standard of civilization'. English School analysis of that development has often combined expressions of relief that non-Western societies have accepted the basic principles and practices of European international society with an explicit recognition of the need for major political endeavours to reduce global injustices (Bull 1977: ch. 4). The political reality is that a significant number of powerful non-Western ruling elites accept the pluralist image of international society that emerged in Europe and reject the solidarism that is associated, *inter alia*, with Western conceptions of human rights (Bull and Watson 1984). Earlier endeavours to free their societies from the effects of Western assumptions about their racial and cultural superiority live on in the contemporary resistance to the solidarist values that arouse memories of the older European 'standard of civilization'.

Process sociology provides invaluable resources for understanding the present situation which can be described as an unfinished transition from a condition in which different civilizations – whether European, Chinese, Japanese and so on – believed that they were surrounded by 'inferior' human groups to one in which multiple cultures or civilizations (effectively civilizing processes) now face each other as moral equals. To the English School analysis of the relationship between 'the revolt against the West' and the expansion of international society, process sociology can add a deeper awareness of the challenges involved in promoting a global civilizing process in the technical sense of that term – an appreciation that draws on Elias's investigation of the European civilizing process in order to understand comparable patterns of socio- and psychogenetic change in the non-European world (Mennell 1996). Central to that orientation is the awareness that different peoples are still at an early stage in comprehending how they developed through diverse but often, interlinked civilizing processes that have become more closely interwoven in recent centuries (Hobson 2004, 2012). Part of the challenge that faces the societies involved is acquiring greater detachment from their respective conceptions of civilized behaviour as well as an improved capacity to think from the standpoint of others. It is to develop capacities that were intrinsic to the ways in which people became attuned to living with others within their diverse 'civilized' communities so that their political representatives can make parallel moral and cultural advances in the first universal international society. Crucial here is promotion of 'effective political dialogue and cooperation' given that societies or regions have different conceptions of the standards of self-restraint that define 'civilized' interaction. They have divergent understandings of the desirable constraints on conduct within separate societies and in their external relations. In process-sociological terms, the problem confronting international society is how to bring those diverse under-standings of the political world into closer alignment as part of the broader endeavour to achieve higher levels of attunement between the constituent parts (Elias 2012: 453). That standpoint rests on the supposition that no civilization is a 'pinnacle' or culminating point (Elias 2012: 488) and that only when the 'tensions between and within states have been mastered' will humanity earn the right to regard itself as 'more truly civilized' (Elias 2012: 488ff.). The purpose of 'effective dialogue and cooperation' is to create transnational solidarities that facilitate clear movement in that direction.

Cosmopolitan Standards of Restraint

Given its association with notions of cultural superiority, the idea of civiliza-tion, which was central to the formulation of the humanitarian laws of war only a few decades ago, has lost its prominent role in the public defence of global ethical projects. But the idea of a Western-driven global civilizing process certainly does identify central features of recent changes in social standards of self-restraint that are outgrowths of earlier developmental trends in Europe. They are important dimensions of the latest phase. Many Western political initiatives are reminders of the continuing influence of nineteenth-century liberal moral convictions that assumed that the spread of liberalism would result in world peace. Empirical support for the contention that liberal states have a special relationship with each other that has included breaking with the practice of using force to resolve major conflicts has been linked with the belief that it is possible to transform international society as a whole by globalizing human rights, undertaking democracy promotion, and extending commitments to free trade. The supposition that there no insurmountable barriers to organizing the international system around such principles has been at the heart of global 'civilizing offensives' to extend liberal progress in forbidding actions that were once permitted (Gat 2006: ch. 16).

Whether or not that conjecture about human prospects proves to be naïvely optimistic, Enlightenment suppositions about the moderating effect of commerce, and related anticipations of the positive evaluation of 'ordinary life', are closer to being realized in the liberal sphere of peace due to a distinctive 'civilized' we-identity and associated developments at the level of the we–I balance and social standards of restraint. Those changes reflect what has been described as the shift from the *summum bonum* that was (and remains central) to many religious perspectives (and to some secular ideologies) to the celebration of ordinary virtues and pleasures. They reveal how the question of 'how can I be happy?' replaced the earlier preoccupation with 'how can I be saved?' (Porter 2000: 21–2). Liberal optimism about the possibility of reforming world politics so that all peoples can live together non-violently rests on the assumption that, despite their cultural and other differences, most people want to prolong life as long as possible without the burden of pain and suffering, and look to domestic and international institutions to help them, insofar as they can, in the quest for personal satisfaction and happiness. The universal human rights culture and international criminal law represent a victory for the liberal belief that, in certain respects, most people are broadly united in the hope of living in freedom from unjustifiable harm and relievable suffering.

The innovations that have just been described express collective sensitivities that are clearly linked with the liberal conviction that 'cruelty is the worst thing we do'. Moreover, collective endeavours to disseminate liberal principles demonstrate the part that the associated 'harm principle' has played in shaping interwoven domestic and international principles of legitimacy. There are few better examples of the limitations of the thesis that little of substance has changed in the relations between states over the centuries or millennia. Realism provides the essential reminder that 'military necessity' can lead to a weakening of support for global harm conventions that are designed to minimize suffering in war. Its warnings do not alter the reality that new and more demanding standards of self-restraint have been embedded in contemporary international society. The upshot is that states are less free than they once were to behave as they wish even though the foreign policy domain often seems to be one of the surviving bastions of 'princely' rule in liberal-democratic societies (Elias 2010b: 205–6). The state's ability to escape domestic and international accountability for violations of basic cosmopolitan values has been reduced. That development cannot be reversed without overcoming significant antipathy to 'superfluous injury' that is part of the habitus of large numbers of 'civilized' people. Over the last few decades, an expanding web of international non-governmental organizations that make the case for more extensive humanitarian responsibilities before the court of 'world opinion' has played a vital role in pressing states to conform with global legal and ethical standards (Stearns 2005). Various international regimes have been important in encouraging compliance with new global norms in the uncongenial context of anarchy (Keohane 1984). Those associations have provided a vital counterweight to 'decivilizing' tendencies in the relations between states by drawing public attention to excessive violence and by attempting to shame governments that breach harm conventions that embody cosmopolitan principles of legitimacy (van Benthem van den Bergh 2001).

Contemporary international society has turned an important corner because of the related standards of self-restraint are integral to the principal global harm conventions. That shift reflects the moral belief that international society is be judged not only by how far it contributes to order but also by the extent to which it protects the vulnerable (Clark 2013). The whole movement demonstrates the unprecedented influence of the idea of human equality on international relations (Buzan and Little 2000: 340). Cosmopolitan harm conventions that affirm the equal right of every person to be free from cruelty, unnecessary violence, and degrading and humiliating treatment irrespective of social differences are core elements of an 'international ethic' with universalistic and egalitarian underpinnings that had significantly less political impact in all earlier periods in the history of the Western states-systems.

The liberal peace and efforts to promote liberal-democratic values are evidence of how the ethical sensibilities that distinguish highly pacified, 'civilized' societies from male warrior cultures has given rise to an international society that is substantially different from the earlier states-systems in the West. Various international legal conventions that have been discussed attest to its influence. They include the humanitarian laws of warfare that were established to reduce 'superfluous injury' and 'unnecessary suffering', the universal human rights culture, international criminal law and the recent notion of the 'responsibility to protect'. Those revisions to the structure of international society mark the 'transition to a new position of the individual vis-à-vis his or her society' as part of the gravitation towards 'a new, higher level of integration' between people; they exemplify changing orientations towards the desirable balance between sovereign rights and international and humanitarian responsibilities (Elias 2010b: 180ff., 207–8).

One of the purposes of the analysis of civilizing processes is to explain how certain values come to seem 'natural' and 'self-evident' to some peoples – but not to others – with what can be contradictory and controversial effects. Analyses of liberal pacification have not been connected with the examination of the European civilizing process; nor have they considered how 'civilized' attitudes to violent harm that shaped, *inter alia*, campaigns to abolish public execution and the death penalty as well as other forms of cruel punishment have influenced the international society of states. It is important to recall that the examination of the civilizing process maintains that 'civilized' attitudes to violent harm must be seen in conjunction with the shifts in the ways in which people came to been bound together in earlier European societies. State formation, the shifting balance of power between external and inner constraints, and increasing levels of repugnance towards cruelty and violence were different sides of one pattern of development. Normative shifts did not precede those other transformations, and they were not the driving force behind them, but nor were they mere garlands thrown over, and designed to conceal, the self-interested behaviour of ruling social strata. Moral concerns about how 'civilized' societies should conduct their foreign policy are an outgrowth of the processes that forced peoples together and confronted them with the challenge of learning how to coexist peacefully in longer chains that came to include the dangerous interconnections of the era of 'total warfare'. The major powers' involvement in embedding a 'principle of huma- neness' in international society has taken place not because modern peoples are 'better people' than their ancestors – and far less disposed because of 'innate' qualities to commit acts of violence than, for example, the societies of classical antiquity – but because they have different sensibilities that reflect, amongst other things, the peculiar compulsions of modern interdependencies. Moreover, as in the case of Britain's role in the abolition of the Atlantic slave trade or the United States' defence of human rights in the bipolar era, liberal 'civilizing offensives' cannot be divorced from power struggles within and between societies. One of the clear outcomes of those social dynamics is that 'revulsion against the use of violence' increased in Western societies (Elias 2013e: 226), as did human 'sensitivity to forms of oppression and inequality in the interactions between humans both as groups and individuals' more generally (Elias 2013: 367; Elias 2013a: 253). No less important is the attendant trend in which 'civilized' societies now find themselves in peculiar 'entangle- ments' that earlier societies did not face (Elias 2012: 8). Those difficulties are no more apparent than in unexpected deliberations about the rights and wrongs of Western military intervention in other regions.

It was noted earlier that only a few decades ago, the dominant strands of thought in the West held that the newly independent societies would, in all probability, follow the path to 'modernity', at one and the same time emulating the Western process of state formation and embracing related conceptions of civilization. The reality has turned out to be rather different. Many peoples in several formerly colonized regions now face the crisis of the state because different groups that were thrown together in the imperial era do not trust each other with the monopoly control of the instruments of violence (Elias 2013: 241ff.). Western responses to the human costs of such political crises provide a window onto the current phase of the civilizing process. Unremarkably, many governments have promoted state-building or rebuilding projects that include democracy promotion and support for human rights that clearly reflect their earlier civilizing process and continuing desire to promote its globalization. More generally, modern societies cannot lay a claim to a 'civilized' status while doing nothing to help those whose lives are in danger – hence the emergence in recent years of moral arguments for embedding a principle of humanitarian intervention in international society (Wheeler 2000). The latter have shed interesting light on the tensions between the pluralist and solidarist conceptions of international society that are inherent in the current phase of the process of civilization and in the divided nature of international society.

Parallels have been drawn between earlier colonial, 'civilizing' missions and recent wars of 'modernization' or 'transformative invasions' that have combined 'humanitarian', liberal-democratic projects with the standard objective of securing social and political outcomes that suit great power interests (Feichtinger, Malinowski and Richards 2012; Peterson 2013). Certain inherent tensions within the relevant societies are mirrored in selective public support for intervention as well as in inconsistencies regarding human suffering that is caused by the Western use of force. Increased public concern about the plight of the civilian is a major dimension of the current phase of the civilizing process (Bellamy 2012; Thomas 2001). It is nevertheless the case that the tolerance of civilian casualties remains high when 'advanced' peoples believe that they are engaged in a struggle with groups that are deemed to be incapable of restraining violent impulses and consumed by hatred for others and the thirst for vengeance. Societies that find gratuitous violence disturbing and distasteful, and that do not regard warfare as central to their collective identity, may find it difficult to understand peoples that apparently 'lag behind' because of 'pre-modern' attachments to the violent resolution of conflict. It is a short step to collective exasperation with groups that seemingly cannot be assisted and who are – for many 'civilized' peoples – not worth trying to help (Sadowski 1996). The 'new barbarism thesis' refers to supposedly intractable cultural traits that have replaced earlier biological explanations of how 'simpler' peoples are prepared to commit acts of violence that have been eliminated from – and are often represented as an inexplicable assault on – 'civilized' societies (Jacoby 2011). The inhabitants of 'civilized' societies may feel some compulsion to act to end human rights violations, but running through the same communities are perceptions that the lives of military personnel should not be wasted in trying to protect 'savages' from their presumed 'atavism'. One side of the civilizing process urges serious commitments to assist desperate strangers; the other reflects earlier cultural and indeed racist, colonial imaginaries and reassuring cultural stereotypes of unbridgeable differences between 'civilized' and 'uncivilized' peoples. The tensions between opposing standpoints that reveal the distinctive 'entanglements' of the civilizing process are not about to be resolved.

Organized Irresponsibility

A final distinguishing feature of the contemporary society of states is captured by the concept of organized irresponsibility, an idea that describes permissive legal frameworks that protect the 'non-liability' of actors with respect to unintended harm to others or negligent damage to the physical environment (Veitch 2007: 114ff.). Analyses of the phenomenon resonate with a recurrent critique of the liberal harm principle which is that a highly restricted definition of harm tolerates indifference to conduct that imposes serious costs on the vulnerable. A related argument highlights the limitations of the utilitarian law on harm – tort – and maintains that enforcing 'strict liability' risks the overall social benefits of individual and collective freedom of action. To the question, 'who is my neighbour?', the unambiguous answer is 'no-one' (Brion 2001: 80). The idea of organized responsibility can be usefully linked with changes in the relative power of 'I-identity' and 'we-identity' – to radical shifts in the we–I balance that can be traced back at least as far as the Renaissance and which are central to European or Western 'civilized' self-images (Elias 2010b: 176). The belief that the individual has a 'natural right' to be free from violent harm is a major part of that transformation; the later defence of the economic freedoms that have been central to market civilization is no less important. Critics argue that a basic tension exists within a specific liberal civilizing process that condemns the savagery of violent illiberal regimes and political movements but is relatively silent about the less tangible, unintended or cumulative forms of non-violent harm to those with limited power resources. On some accounts, the 'liberalism of restraint' that was designed to curtail the powers of sovereign governments has given way to a 'liberalism of imposition' of free market ideologies and practices (Sorenson 2007). For some, the proposed solution is a version of welfare liberalism that maintains that global political and economic institutions should play a central role in protecting the weak from the destructive effects of 'market civilization' (Richardson 2001; Clark 2013).

The emphasis in that literature on the problem of non-violent harm in world politics would seem to point to questions about global justice that are, at best, only indirectly connected with the analysis of the relationship between violence and civilization in the Western states-systems. But the link is evident in the implication that changes in the organization of modern societies do not augur well for the future of a world order in which the inhabitants of affluent societies are largely insulated from the lives of the most vulnerable communities, where they have little in common with them and little cause to identity with them, where they do not depend on them for the satisfaction of their basic needs and wants, and have, as a result, little incentive to grant their representatives a significant stake in global decision-making processes that determine, amongst other things, the distribution of global wealth and unequal levels of protection from environmental harm. Influential developments in recent writings on the questions of international justice reflect the awareness of the growing importance of non-violent harm in world society. Through the use of such concepts as 'transnational exploitation' and 'transnational justice', they have contributed to exploring different types of harm that raise moral questions about the responsibilities of the most powerful strata in the global economic and political system (see below, p. 457ff.). They mirror the contemporary condition in which, for once, restraining violent harm in relations between independent political communities is not the absolutely pre-eminent question for societies that are bound together in an international system. The focus has shifted emphatically to the problem of non-violent harm that has grown in importance because of the advances in global social and economic interconnectedness that were made possible by major advances in territorial pacification.

Reflections on welfare internationalism and the deficiencies of the post-Western society of states that have referred in passing to the idea of civilization have tended to focus on the problem of legitimacy rather than on the question of violence, but the two are closely connected and lead the inquiry back to earlier considerations of tensions within the current phase of the civilizing process. An interesting point of departure is the contention that Western societies should spearhead a 'civilizing' initiative to eradicate global starvation and malnutrition that stands comparison with nineteenth-century campaigns to abolish the Atlantic slave trade (Vincent 1986: 138, 151). The moral case for assisting the suffering was combined with the consequentialist thesis that it could strengthen international society in the long run. The burden was on the affluent to develop the capacity to think from the standpoint of the more vulnerable members of world society and to introduce the changes that were necessary to ensure that the institutions of international society acquire greater moral legitimacy in their eyes (Vincent 1986).

The reference to civilization invites comment on one of the main features of the European civilizing process which was the widening of the scope of emotional identification between different social strata within the same state-organized societies. The argument for global action to end starvation and malnutrition called for a further enlargement of horizons on the part of 'civilized' peoples who do not confront the same political pressures to make concessions to less powerful groups that the ruling strata in European societies faced during the nineteenth and twentieth centuries. The emphasis therefore shifted to the enlightened self-interest of the most privileged strata in interna-tional society and to moral responsibilities that are required by 'civilized' self-images and considerations of humanity. More recent philosophical writings have also addressed the question of how to bridge the emotional gulf between the affluent and the vulnerable in the modern world. As discussed in the earlier work on the problem of harm, the stress on the 'connected self' is one such response to that moral and political challenge, as is the idea of 'complex responsibility' that was discussed earlier. New ethical discourses that revolve around concepts such as 'transnational exploitation' and 'transnational justice' reflect a deepening social awareness of how different groups are bound together in the world-system, and a more profound understanding of the diverse ways in which people harm, and are harmed by, others in the context of 'organized irresponsibility'; those discourses are attempts to give greater specificity to visions of cosmopolitan obligation and responsibility in an era in which the limitations of traditional moral and political discourses that focus on the 'proximate range of action' and on 'noncumulative behaviour' have been exposed (Linklater 2011: ch. 1). What can be described as the cosmopolitan turn can be understood in that context as the quest to create a political theory and practice that can enable human beings to organize their lives together at a significantly higher level of social and political integration in accordance with the principles of justice that were defended by Smith and Kant in the age of enlightenment.

Various images of the global 'civilizing' role of cosmopolitanism are more central to the political theory of international relations today than in the earlier states-systems in the West. Their significance is not restricted to what is most obvious about them, namely the attempt to develop ethical yardsticks for assessing the degree of global economic justice. From the standpoint of process sociology, their importance is evident in an implicit recognition of the problem of emotional identification in international relations. The plain reality is that ethical concerns about distant suffering that have emerged in 'civilized' socie- ties do not automatically translate into strong public support for global assistance programmes – 'passive' sympathy that is in harmony with 'civilizing' sensibilities does not easily mutate into 'active' sympathy that takes the form of transformative campaigns of compassion or, more radically, for a general clamour for major global institutional reform that breaks with the principle of 'organized responsibility' and the practices of 'market civilization' (Linklater 2011: 222ff.). It is not inconceivable that levels of public support for 'welfare internationalism' will increase in future. But in the absence of major changes in the dominant structures and in the global balance of political forces, it is unsurprising that cosmopolitan political theorists have focused on ethical tenets that they believe the members of affluent societies should observe as a matter of principle. Their efforts have been concentrated on convincing others to act differently as a matter of conscience given that no higher political authority or system of external restraints can bring about fundamental changes of behaviour. Cosmopolitan theorists are engaged in the promotion of new patterns of 'conscience formation' at a time when widening global inequalities have the effect that the most affluent social strata have even fewer incentives to calculate the political costs of indifference to distant suffering; in that context, the capacity for emotional identification with those who are most seriously exposed to the adverse effects of 'organized irresponsibility' is further weakened (Mennell 2007: 305ff.).

As for the significance of organized irresponsibility for overall trends regarding the relationship between violence and civilization in world politics – the significant pacification of major regions of world society and the taming of the great powers in particular that made the development of higher levels of human integration possible is not in obvious danger. The political initiatives that were taken at the end of the Second World War to ensure higher levels of international economic cooperation, and to eradicate militarism through a major 'civilizing offensive', have protected affluent societies from a recurrence of the interlocking economic instabilities and rising geopolitical tensions that characterized the 'twenty years' crisis'. The political architecture may prove to be sufficiently robust and resilient to ensure that future global economic crises and instabilities do not endanger unusual achievements in taming the great powers. They may prove to be sufficiently adaptable to ensure that significant concessions are made to discontented groups and their political representatives, particularly where changing power balances improve the position of traditional outsiders in relations with the global establishment (Bieler and Morton 2006). But the indefinite preservation and global extension of a highly pacified 'market civilization' cannot be taken for granted. Historical analyses of the rise and fall of international orders strongly advise against complacency regarding the stability of political institutions and the durability of restraints on force (Philips 2011: conclusion). Social and political arrangements have often contained immanent dynamics that seemed to have marginal importance to most people at the time, and to be unlikely to determine the future course of development; only later did those processes gather pace in entirely unexpected ways and bring about the violent transformation of the societies in question. The long view perspective cannot discount the possibility of the emergence of violent counter-hegemonic movements against 'organized irresponsibility' in the more stable Western societies or the rise of similar political challenges to the global order in non-Western parts of the world. Not least because of the uncertainties of climate change – conceivably the Achilles' heel of the modern international system – it cannot exclude the potential for additional crises of the state in post-colonial societies that combine domestic upheaval with regional conflict.

The link between the possible political consequences of organized irresponsibility and the relationship between violence and civilization will be clear. The prospect of further examples of state collapse that results in internal wars and regional political instability and interstate violence raises again the question of whether 'civilized' people will be prepared to assist others or if the perceived savagery of non-Western conflicts will result in decisions to stand aside. Furthermore, and with respect to any future counter-hegemonic political challenges to the Western-dominated international order, violent reaction and suppression will in all probability raise complex questions about the collective identity of 'civilized' peoples that stretch back to the age of European empire. Familiar questions can be expected to arise about the extent to which 'civilized' principles should be observed in military conflict or put to one side in relations with 'savages' who fail to reciprocate. The final point is that such questions reveal how the four distinguishing features of the current phase in the history of the Western states-systems are interconnected parts of one social and political dynamic that was set in motion by the European civilizing process. The taming of the great powers has facilitated the development of longer social and economic webs that are subject to the consequences of organized responsibility. Questions about the cosmopolitan standards of restraint that 'civilized' people should follow in the 'economic' as well as in the 'political' domain arise most acutely because achievements with regard to the global expansion of the core principles and practices of European international society have been accompanied by the unexpected phenomenon of several crises of the state in non-European regions. A more detailed analysis of the interplay between those four features of the modern states-system that draws together the particular strengths of process sociology and English School inquiry can provide a deeper understanding of the changing contours of violence and civilization in world politics.

Towards an Explanation of the Global 'Civilizing Process'

This work began with specific questions about the extent to which there are major differences between the international politics of classical antiquity and the most recent phase of the modern states-system. The inquiry has analysed the relationship between violence and what have come to be known as 'civilized' values in the Western states-systems. Basic similarities between the modern states-system and its Western precursors – and between the most recent phase of the modern society of states and its immediate predecessors – have been stressed. Crucial differences have been noted in the dominant standards of self-restraint in relations between the great powers and in the relations between 'civilized' and 'savage' peoples. Related shifts in cosmopolitan harm conventions that impose obligations on national governments in the area of human rights have been emphasized. The question is how those differences are best explained.

The comments that were made in earlier chapters about some of the conditions that favoured the development of civilizing processes in previous states-systems provide the basis for the following explanation of how those developmental patterns have been extended further in contemporary international society. The dominant tendency in Elias's writings to focus on explaining the absence of such patterns of development in international relations has been emphasized. The contrast with the argument that the balance of terror was the functional equivalent of the state's monopoly of power was highlighted because it shifted the focus towards understanding the political conditions under which global civilizing processes have developed. The argument has been that forging closer connections between process sociological and the English School analysis of international society corrects a major imbalance in the former's perspective and provides the means of advancing the argument about the taming or civilizing effects of nuclear bipolarity. The principal objective of this section is to take some preliminary steps towards explaining the achievements of the modern society of states that integrate and build on earlier observations about the limited 'civilizing' of conduct in the earlier Western states-systems.

The following discussion is framed by the argument that 'in the course of a civilizing process the self-control apparatus becomes stronger relative to external restraints' (Elias 2013: 35ff.). But 'living together in a civilized way', it is argued, 'includes very much more than just non-violence', namely a range of 'positive characteristics' that only emerge 'when the threat that people will attack each other physically . . . has been banished from their social relations' (Elias 2013: 186). The inquiry begins with the preconditions of major shifts in the relationship between the 'self-control apparatus' and the realm of 'external restraints' in conditions in which societies struggle to tame violence; it considers the social forces that have encouraged the emergence of the more 'positive characteristics' of a civilizing process that include the widening of the scope of emotional identification between different peoples as well as the development of moral concerns for the future of humanity. It combines the three core themes in process sociology that have been used at various stages in this work with an English School analysis of the distinctions between national responsibilities (the duties of governments to their citizens), international responsibilities (the obligations that states have to international society), humanitarian responsibilities (duties that all people owe each other) and 'global commons' responsibilities (duties to protect the global environment). (Jackson 2000: 170–8). That taxonomy is important for understanding changes in the we–I balance that stretch from advances in 'non-violent' coexistence to the more 'positive characteristics' of a global civilizing process in which humanitarian and global commons responsibilities have greater significance than they had in the past.

The link between state formation and the process of civilization is the starting point for understanding interlinked patterns of change within the societies involved and in their external relations. Stable, state monopolies of power were crucial for achieving relatively high levels of personal security in complex societies; they have been the *sine qua non* of the most elementary international civilizing processes. Stable political conditions were often lacking in the Hellenic and Italian city-states systems, and they have not always been the norm in modern international society. For long intervals, the constitutive 'survival units' in all three systems were susceptible to violent internal struggles with a pronounced 'transnational' dimension. The recurrent political problem was how to pacify domestic space rather than how to bring civility to the international system, conceived as a separate domain. The modern state contributed to a global civilizing process by replacing mercenary forces that caused misery by living off the land with more disciplined, professional militaries that became answerable to 'civilized' standards of self-restraint in the metropolitan centres. Only when sovereign territory had been significantly pacified could states devote their energies to the challenges that are part of the 'Janus-faced' character of state formation. Only when they were free from 'internal' disorder could they turn to promoting 'civilizing' restraints in what had come to be regarded as the relatively autonomous sphere of international politics. Then they could they ask what 'civilized' principles and practices meant for foreign policy conduct and for collective approaches to managing the problems of rising levels of human interconnectedness.

Similar themes are evident in English School arguments about 'the state's positive role in world affairs' as well as in the recognition that state formation simultaneously solved some problems that people had in living together and created new dangers of comparable gravity (Bull 1979). The monopolization of coercive power in early modern Europe removed some of the risks that people faced when they relied on their own instruments of violence for their security or survival. It disarmed and disabled violent factions; it imposed external constraints on rival groups that were followed by a degree of detachment from short-term sectional objectives and by a shared recognition and internalization of the value of political compromise if public order was to survive. The Eliasian analysis of state formation demonstrated that the relationship between centrifugal and centripetal forces was long in the balance. Whether a sense of we-feeling would emerge between the dominant social strata was in doubt. Where it developed in France and elsewhere, it was invariably linked with violence towards internal adversaries and with their physical expulsion (Elias 2006; Rae 2002).

That dimension of state formation and consolidation created the risk of intervention by external powers that sympathized with persecuted minorities. Early modern European states addressed the problem by embedding a principle of religious toleration in the Westphalian settlement. They recognized the need to reduce the fragility of arrangements that could reconcile sovereign demands for political independence with international responsibilities to act in concert to preserve the society of states. The 'supranational' court society contributed to a sense of we-feeling and to a we–I balance that enabled the ruling elites to find some common ground in basic principles of non-violent coexistence through the tools of diplomacy. It provided evidence for the larger claim that societies that regard themselves as part of the same civilization possess a common political vocabulary that facilitates reaching such agreements (Wight 1977: ch. 1). In the case of early modern Europe, the civilizing process was evident not only in state-building and in domestic political transformations but in the interrelated evolution of the complex institutions of international society.

The existence of multiple power monopolies created a high probability of struggles for power and security fuelled by mutual distrust, and attendant dangers that major political disputes would be resolved violently. The dynamics entrenched the contrast between the civil principles that governed domestic politics and the presumed necessity of the use of force and duplicity in international politics. Simply being part of the same civilization was no guarantee that states would break free from highly emotive world views that accompanied double-bind processes; it offered no warranty that they would abide by 'civilized' standards in relations with enemies. As various agreements to exchange prisoners of war revealed – and as later developments with respect to chemical, biological and nuclear weapons also demonstrated – the fragile reed of reciprocity has often been the indispensable foundation of the general observance of critical standards of self-restraint. The durability of social encounters – the virtual certainty that rivals would encounter each other again – underpinned the 'civilizing' practice of prisoner exchange. Each side understood that the return of captives depended on mutual restraint, and that the slaughter of prisoners risked immediate retaliation. Such reciprocity almost always depended on a relatively even distribution of power between interdependent groups. The corollary was exemplified by the relations between European colonizers and indigenous communities. Where there were serious power inequalities, and where weaker societies could not retaliate when they were harmed, the strong groups had little incentive to act with the same self-restraint (Cell 1979; Keohane 1986).

Prisoner exchange depended on restraints on violent behaviour that sprang from anger and the desire for revenge. The practice was heavily reliant on the ability to replace highly emotive behaviour that underpinned the immediate gratification of such impulses with a more detached, longer-term approach to solving shared problems. The development of an international society in which the great powers agreed on basic pluralist principles was an illustration of a comparable breakthrough on a larger scale. For the relevant agreements to exist, states had to transcend to some extent emotive 'involvement' in external threats and challenges. They had to acquire a degree of 'detachment' that was evident in advances in asking what certain fundamental political dynamics were in themselves. Self-restraint, foresight with respect to the conduct of foreign policy, and the willingness to think from the standpoint of others – all central to the process-sociological analysis of state formation and the rise of 'civilized' mentalities – rested on such cognitive breakthroughs. Above all else, the gradual realization that states were part of the same 'production line', and that they could not exercise their sovereign right to make foreign policy decisions without the probability of retaliation, injected a 'civilizing' dynamic into international relations. The process was especially evident in the emergence of higher levels of consultation and cooperation between the great powers in the aftermath of the Napoleonic wars. The sheer scale of the destruction that could be inflicted exercised a taming effect on states. As English School analysts have argued, global harm conventions that embody shared understandings about how to reconcile national and international responsibilities have invariably depended on the constraining effects of an inherently precarious and unstable balance of power (Dunne 2003). The latter has often encouraged a generalized willingness to forgo minor political advantages for the sake of preserving arrangements that can bring long-lasting benefits by taming struggles for security and power. It has contributed to the development of agreements about the desirable we–I balance and about associated understandings about what is permissible and what is forbidden in foreign policy. Underlying fears and anxieties with respect to security constrained the development of we-feeling and the degree to which sovereign states have been restrained by internal rather than external compulsions. But the 'contrived' balance of power demonstrated how enlightened self-interest could result in a high level of self-regulation and self-restraint. In particular, unprecedented destructive power increased 'the social constraints towards self-constraint' that were at the heart of superpower efforts to manage the 'balance of terror'. A further point is that the latter constituted the 'functional equivalent' of a 'civilizing' worldwide monopoly of force by pacifying great power struggles and permitting extensive webs of interdependence that created additional incentives to enlarge the scope of reciprocal restraint in world politics. Shared interests in using international organizations to manage the challenges of 'complex interdependence' have led to global agreements that endure in large part because states must (in a parallel with the forces that underpinned the rules of prisoner exchange) face each again and again in the relevant diplomatic forums (Keohane 1984). Societies can often restrain each other by collective efforts at shaming actual or potential defectors and by imposing tangible reputational costs. The balance between internal and external restraints has altered in the relations between the most stable industrial powers as a result of the relevant pressures to conform to global understandings of the necessary relationship between different types of sovereign responsibility.

What states have accomplished in that domain, and how far they have succeeded in creating international or cosmopolitan harm conventions that embody support for humanitarian responsibilities have depended on the extent of their identification with the same civilization. As the discussion of the Greek city states and the European states-system showed, a we-identity that was linked with the sense of belonging to the 'civilized' world had a restraining role on acts of violence such as killing or mutilating captured enemies in the manner of 'savages'. But social identities that were anchored in a sense of membership of the same civilization rested on cultural dichotomies that exposed outsiders to the risk of great violence. 'Civilized' identities supported forms of we-feeling, a we–I balance and social standards of restraint that encouraged evenly balanced societies to place controls on violence; the other side was not just the absence of we-feeling with outsiders but derogatory representations of them that licensed or authorized levels of force that were prohibited or widely condemned within the 'civilized' world. By way of example, compliance with the rules of war in the eighteenth century owed a great deal to the reality that military elites believed that they constituted a transnational social stratum that was the chief custodian of 'civilized' values. Warfare was understood as a contest between similar regime-types that were expected to observe similar restraints to those that defined the aristocratic duel (van Crefeld 1989: ch. 19). Such conceptions of the laws of war did not apply in relations with 'barbarians'.

The civilizing process that was common to the interdependent parts of the European society of states influenced the dominant global harm conventions. The same was true of the honour code that united hoplite warriors in the classical Greek city states and underpinned restraints on intercity violence as well as the international code of chivalry which meant that medieval knights departed for battle in the belief that, if captured, they would be ransomed rather than summarily executed. In both cases, the relevant harm conventions that were integral to a specific civilizing process restricted certain rights to the male warrior elite. Medieval knights did not believe that they had to share their collective privileges with the lower strata or observe chivalric restraints in relations with them. They formed an international establishment that looked down on outsiders without such rights, just as European states formed an international 'ruling class' that did not believe that the 'civilized' laws of war should govern relations with 'savages'. Those examples indicate once again that ideas of civilization have prohibited some forms of violence and permitted or even demanded others. They are a reminder that, in the main, global civilizing processes have not rested on shared commitments to universal and egalitarian values. The belief in the equality of all human beings had little political significance in the earlier states-systems in the West or, indeed, in the modern system until recently. The main restraints on harm functioned without that ethical commitment but that is no longer the case. A unique global civilizing process is now in place that is suffused with universal and egalitarian values that reflect what many regard as the essence of Western civilization. Their main expression is the web of cosmopolitan standards of self-restraint that was discussed earlier. One consequence is the existence of powerful strands of public opinion which insist that societies must honour their humanitarian responsibilities for the welfare of prisoners of war as a matter of principle and because of the associated international legal responsibilities. They should do so, the argument is, not because they live in fear of retaliation if they behave differently – and not just because of regard for the principle of reciprocity – but because that is how 'civilized' peoples should understand their humanitarian responsibilities even in conflicts with adversaries with little respect for 'civilized reciprocity' (Holmes 2007: 276-7; Neocleous 2011).

Those pressures to demonstrate that foreign policy behaviour complies with, or does not openly contradict, the principle of human equality represent a major change in the relationship between external restraints that increased as a result of higher levels of destructive power and internal controls that are associated with the more 'positive characteristics' of the European civilizing process. The overall shift explains why sovereign states are expected to balance their national and international responsibilities with humanitarian obligations that include support for the laws of war and the human rights culture. A new power balance between the military and civilian sectors in the process of European state formation was a basic precondition for the emergence of global harm conventions that were designed to spare the innocent unnecessary suffering in war. Collective measures to address the problem of violent harm were the outcome of changing sensitivities to needless pain and injury in 'civilized' societies where, for the overwhelming majority of people, personal meaning and satisfaction were increasingly found not in the military but in the civilian sphere.

As part of the civilizing process, the idea that the civilian should be spared unnecessary suffering has acquired a moral significance that it did not possess in earlier times (Slim 2008; Bellamy 2012: introduction, ch. 1). Profound shifts in social attitudes in this domain occurred between the French Revolution and the post-Second World War era. As with the principles governing the treatment of prisoners of war, support for civilian immunity was initially anchored in principles of reciprocity, but it has become 'internalized' in the world views of many societies, or is at least 'embedded' in international law with the result that blatant violations now provoke widespread public condemnation (Thomas 2001: ch. 2). That development was a response to the peculiar paradox that was mentioned earlier, namely that modern peoples who are orientated towards peaceful preoccupations, and accustomed to low levels of violence in relations with other members of the same state-organized society, acquired destructive capabilities that jeopardized domestic political achievements. Their response to that condition reflected the influence of attachments to human equality that became central to the politics of 'civilized' societies as a result of assorted 'emancipation struggles' that were part of major internal shifts in the power balance between the dominant and subordinate social strata. Humanitarian projects that reflect sympathy for the victims of war are part of that legacy, as are the many international governmental and non-governmental organizations that have been involved in the global protection of 'inalienable' human rights. They are evidence of changing power relations between the sovereign state, international non-governmental organizations and individual rights – and between international responsibilities to the society of states and humanitarian responsibilities to the members of world society.

Nevertheless, universal and egalitarian values that have been pivotal to the development of humanitarian responsibilities remain weak relative to national and international responsibilities, but the very fact that the members of the society of states accept that there are such moral obligations deserves comment. Those human concerns were not priorities in the earlier Western states-systems or in most of their constitutive parts until recently. Various normative images now exist of how the idea of equality can give shape and direction to a global civilizing process with 'positive characteristics'. They address the insecurities of those who are especially exposed to the negative effects of rising levels of human interconnectedness including vulnerability to economic exploitation, unjust enrichment and other forms of non-violent harm. They are evidence of a partial widening of the scope of emotional identification so that duties to co-nationals do not exhaust the sense of moral responsibility for other people. Those cultural resources demonstrate the immanent potential for more radical shifts in the relative power of national, international and humanitarian responsibilities; they are also invaluable social reserves that can be harnessed to resist efforts to contract the scope of moral consideration in the context of international power struggles. That is one reason why current endeavours to give concrete meaning to conceptions of world citizenship are so important. All such concepts are critical to political efforts to promote new forms of cosmopolitan 'conscience formation'.

The related question is how far those who identify with a specific civilization confront the harm that their ways of life have caused by virtue of pernicious distinctions between the 'advanced' and the 'backward'. The issue is whether they think of civilization in the singular – as a set of traits that they monopolize – or recognize that different peoples have undergone distinctive civilizing processes with their own intrinsic value. Significant progressions occurred in this area in the recent phase of the modern states-system as different peoples became tied together in relations of co-dependence that provided subordinate groups with new opportunities to launch 'emancipation struggles' that asserted the right to be treated with equal respect. Compliance with the relevant global principles is evidence of a 'civilizing' shift in which the 'self-control apparatus' that was weak in relations with colonized peoples became 'stronger relative to external restraints'. Key features of the 'radical Enlightenment' highlighted the ambiguities of 'civilization' and promoted greater detachment from modern ways of life. They revealed that 'civilization' was a barrier to transformed relations between European and non-European peoples that ended imperial cruelties, if not colonialism itself. A political course was mapped out that led to the doctrine of international trusteeship and to the period in which Europeans began to regard empire with feelings of collective shame rather than national pride. The chief monument to those transformations is the expansion of international society.

The contemporary phase of world politics is one in which sovereign states are 'consciously working out, for the first time, a set of transcultural values and ethical standards' (Watson 1987: 152). The implication is that societies that have been forced together face the unique challenge of creating universal moral principles that enable peoples to become attuned to one another over greater distances. As noted earlier, there is a rough parallel with the social conditions that led to the European civilizing process where lengthening webs of interconnectedness created pressures on people to think in a more detached way from the standpoint of others and to modify behaviour accordingly. The modern global context differs not just because there is no equivalent to earlier patterns of state formation but because various peoples have been incorporated in an international society that has been profoundly influenced at every stage by European ideas of civilization. Despite earlier assumptions about 'modernization', the constitutive political units of international society do not identify with a single civilization. They are faced with a far greater challenge than their European predecessors were in agreeing on global stan-dards of self-restraint. The existence of very different civilizing processes has compounded the traditional problem of establishing the principles that should be observed in their relations with each other and within their national boundaries. The expansion of international society is testimony to consider-able success in constructing principles that bridge substantial political and cultural differences. The societies in question – not only European societies but also China, Japan and the Ottoman Empire – made significant advances in freeing themselves from the 'hegemonial conceptions of international society' in which they placed themselves at the centre of a 'civilized' core and regarded others as 'social inferiors' that should submit to their 'standard of civilization' (Bull and Watson 1984: 3ff.). But there is clearly a great deal to do to 'promote effective dialogue and cooperation' between societies with different concep-tions of the standards of self-restraint that should be observed in both domestic and international politics (Elias 2012: 453). The challenge exists in part because of competing perspectives on sovereign rights and responsibilities that reflect the tension between the pluralist and solidarist conceptions of international society.

Various efforts to construct new conceptions of global responsibility and international justice and to defend images of cosmopolitan citizenship are united in the quest to promote agreements on 'transcultural values and ethical standards'. Discussions of world citizenship reflect the need for a new political vocabulary that attunes societies and their political representatives to the realities of the present phase of human integration. Similarly, notions of environmental citizenship which have been linked with the defence of far-reaching responsibilities for the global commons are designed to orientate people to challenges that now confront humanity. The success of such endeavours will depend to a significant extent on how far different peoples come to know more about the different civilizing processes they have undergone, about how they have shaped each other, and about how they were drawn together and became ever more closely interwoven in the modern era. A central theme in process sociology is that a deeper comprehension of such long processes is necessary if peoples are to achieve a higher level of mutual understanding that enables them to become more attuned to each other. The relevant grand narratives that are still under construction are crucial for promoting global 'civilizing' offensives that take forward recent achievements in acquiring detachment from provincial perspectives. They are vital for developing more cosmopolitan orientations between people and interlinked principles of mutual restraint that counteract the 'drag effect' that national loyalties continue to exert on efforts to enlarge sovereign responsibilities (Linklater 2010).

It is scarcely surprising that the material interconnections that have drawn peoples together forged ahead of human loyalties that remain attached to traditional 'survival units'. Those social bonds have become a major cultural liability in an era in which human lives are interwoven in increasingly elaborate ways; they hold back 'post-national' political associations that can deal with the negative effects of rising levels of global interconnectedness. Many doubt that circumstances are likely to change so that human societies come to have common political symbols that underpin feelings of emotional identification with the species as a whole. Aware of the constraints, Elias and several world historians have argued that grand narratives that locate the contemporary era in very long-term patterns of biological evolution and cultural development have a valuable role to play in promoting identification with the species as a whole. Large issues arise here which will be the starting point for the final volume of this trilogy on the problem of harm in world politics. Suffice it to add that they involve the further extension of the advances in detachment that were evident in earlier historical narratives that were not confined to describing the development of a specific 'survival unit' but which attempted to explain patterns of change on a larger canvass – with respect to the Hellenic civilizing process as in the case of Thucydides' grand narrative, or with regard to the gradual unification of the inhabited world that Polybius analysed in his account of the rise of Rome. Parallel shifts of orientation were evident in Guiccardini's study of the history of Italy that went beyond classical accounts of the evolution of a particular city and in Enlightenment universal histories that attempted to explain the development of human societies from the earliest times to the modern period. Those examples of the broadening of temporal and geographical horizons were linked with the consciousness of lengthening of human connections; they were experiments in moving to a higher level of detachment in an attempt to make the latter intelligible, and to promote new forms of orientation to the rapidly changing social and political world.

The final point is that more recent grand narratives are part of the same general trend. They are also attempts to orientate people to the realities of global interdependencies. In Elias's writings, their function is not limited to increasing knowledge of the human world but is directly linked with the practical need to alter the balance of power between obligations to specific states and to responsibilities for humanity. One implication is that the relevant grand narratives are crucial for 'locking in' recent achievements with respect to global civilizing processes and for erecting cultural barriers to their reversal. Another is that broadened and more detached narratives that address the formation and development of humanity are a crucial counterpart to political efforts to alter the relationship between national, international, humanitarian and 'global commons' responsibilities. The former are a vital accompaniment to an envisaged planned global civilizing process that would represent a new stage in the history of the Western states-systems. The latter may not survive or develop further unless such changes in orientation – that are captured by the idea of a 'cosmopolitan education' (Nussbaum 2002) – become deeply embedded in the social habitus of contemporary peoples.

Conclusion

This chapter began with Elias's comment that Caxton's observation that 'things that were once permitted are now forbidden' could stand for the motto for what was to come – at least with respect to the relations between members of the same state-organized societies. Relations between states, on the other hand, remained remarkably constant throughout this period and reflected the dominant patterns across earlier eras. No political authority could force sovereign states to observe the 'civilized' harm conventions that developed in tandem with state formation. Elias was generally pessimistic about the prospects for ending the 'split within civilization'. All past struggles between the great powers that survived elimination contests descended into hegemonic warfare. There were no guarantees that the modern states-system would escape a similar final struggle for dominance between the last few remaining major powers.

At least the scale of the destruction that the superpowers could inflict on one another created pressures to display some of the self-restraint and foresight that had been typical of the civilizing process. Moreover, the species was undergoing a major new phase of social and economic integration which, though not immune from reversal, created additional pressures and incentives to develop global standards of self-restraint. But Elias's writings were often directed at explaining the double-bind processes that perpetuated the 'split within civilization' rather than with discussing the prospects for a global civilizing process. The argument of this chapter has been that English School interpretations of the 'civilizing' role of international society overcome some of the limitations of that analysis. When combined, the two perspectives provide the resources for exploring the changing relationship between the permissible and the forbidden in international societies, and for investigating the extent to which the most recent phase of the states-system differs from earlier periods. Four distinguishing aspects of the changing relationship between violence and civilization in contemporary international society have been discussed. Core themes in process sociology and English School inquiry have been used to explain significant patterns of change that demonstrate that the modern states-system has turned a corner in some respects, most obviously with regard to the taming of the great powers, the dismantling of the barriers between the 'civilized' members of international society and the 'barbarian' peoples who were incorporated within the European empires, the development of cosmopolitan harm conventions and associated standards of self-restraint, and the lifting of many traditional constraints on economic activity within global 'market civilization'. The first three achievements are not bound to survive indefinitely but it is probable that they will be hard to reverse for the foreseeable future. The permanent problem remains of powerful attachments to survival units with historical narratives and shared symbols that celebrate local achievements and recall collective ordeals and challenges. Global narratives that offer long-term perspectives on the development of human societies can play a vital role in addressing the disjuncture between traditional patterns of emotional identification with 'survival units' and levels of global integration that require new levels of international cooperation to address the multiple challenges facing humanity.

~

Conclusion

The speculation that the ancient Greeks and Romans did not possess the equivalent of modern ethical sensitivities to violent harm and the contention that they did not condemn what has come to be known as genocide have framed this inquiry. A central objective has been to assess those empirical contentions about the differences between the dominant harm conventions in the ancient and modern states-systems. The investigation has specifically engaged with Wight's observation that all international societies appear to have developed within a bounded cultural region where sharp distinctions were presumed to exist between the 'advanced' and the 'backward' peoples, and by his claim – which has a direct parallel in Elias's writings – that modern ethical sensibilities to violence and suffering in warfare may have been absent in the 'simpler civilizations'. Those observations were in competition with the proposition that international relations have barely changed in some fundamental respects over the millennia.

The relationship between civilizations and international societies and, particularly, the issue of how far 'civilized' values have influenced relations between independent political communities in the modern era have been fundamental to this approach to the sociology of states-systems. Wight's foundational essay on that subject was largely silent on how the two phenomena were related. There was no discussion of how civilizations – or civilizing processes – shaped, and were influenced by, the development of international societies. The argument in these pages has been that understanding the distinctive moral sensitivities to which Wight referred, requires an examination of the process which was central to Elias's exploration of long-term trends over approximately the last five centuries. As the last few chapters have argued, the process-sociological analysis of the development of civilized self-images has to be modified to show how state formation was the hub of a triad of interrelated developments that included the rise of the overseas empires and the emergence of a distinctive European international society. How far emotional attitudes to violence and suffering changed at each of those levels, and in interconnected ways, has been a central question in this inquiry. The emergence of what have been come to be known as individual human rights within

468

state-organized societies was one transformation of moral sensitivities that was linked with efforts to eradicate imperial violence and to embed the rights of individual persons to be protected from unnecessary suffering in military conflicts in the humanitarian laws of war. Those are fundamental examples of how ethical values that developed in the course of state-formation and the civilizing process have configured the international society that developed in Europe.

No similar triad of social transformations existed in the earlier Western states-systems. As the analysis of the European civilizing process argued, the tolerance of violence in everyday life and in the relations between peoples was much higher in classical antiquity and in the medieval world than it is in 'civilized' societies today. There were lower levels of restraint on the physical exploitation of other people. The ruling strata were much less dependent on subordinate groups for the satisfaction of their interests than the dominant groups in European societies were from around the start of the nineteenth century. They had little incentive to make major political concessions to the lower strata or to take account of demands from below to alleviate suffering. Restraints on force were often respected in relations between elite groups in the warrior societies of those earlier periods but they invariably existed alongside the absence of equivalent constraints on violence in dealings with 'social inferiors' and in relations with 'savages'. To understand core dimensions of the European civilizing process and its relationship with the modern society of states, it is important to understand unprecedented changes in the balance of power between the dominant and subordinate social strata that were bound up with the increased influence of universal and egalitarian norms on modern social and political life.

The central dimensions of the relationship between state formation and the civilizing process were therefore connected with distinctive relations between violence and civilization in European international society. Rising levels of collective power and the invention of more destructive instruments of force were made possible by state monopolies and domestic pacification. That transformation existed alongside the changing sensitivities to violence and cruelty that have distinguished 'civilized' ways of life from the 'survival units' that were bound together in earlier states-systems. For long periods, the 'split within civilization' was as profound in the modern society of states as it had been in the preceding international orders. Restraints on the use of force in the relations between members of the same society – and between the elite strata specifically – coexisted with the high tolerance of violence in relations between societies. Warfare was not just the accepted means of resolving major differences between 'survival units'; it was central to the identity of the male warrior in those eras. Nevertheless, increasingly destructive capabilities that were intrinsic to total warfare created pressures to tame relations between the great powers. They interacted with changing social attitudes to violence and cruelty in 'civilized' societies to give rise to a wholly new phase in the history of the Western states-systems.

Process sociology contains a battery of concepts – 'we identity' and 'the scope of emotional identification', the 'we–I balance' and the idea of 'social standards of self-restraint' – that can be used to explain shifting conceptions of what is permissible and forbidden within states and in their relations with each other. The idea of the we–I balance is of particular interest for reflecting on how closer linkages between process sociology and the English School analysis of international society can be developed in future. There is an important link between that concept and English School reflections on the relationship between several types of sovereign responsibility that include the obligations of states to their citizens and to international society as well as their responsibilities to humanity and for the global commons. Understanding changes in the relative importance of those levels of responsibility – and comprehending their interdependence with shifts in orientation to 'we' and 'I' – is central to the investigation of changing conceptions of the permissible and the forbidden in international societies.

The analysis of four other shifts in balances of power between competing social dynamics is also significant for understanding those phenomena. It is crucial to investigate shifting power balances between political strategies that have been designed to increase destructive power and moral sensitivities to suffering that are integral to the conceptions of civility and civilization that developed as people became bound together in more complex societies. A second and related issue is how far ethical restraints on the use of force, and on the conquest and exploitation of people, kept pace with advances in the capacity to cause greater harm to more and more people over ever larger distances. A third question concerns the balance of power between external and internal restraints on violent harm. It is how far restraints on foreign policy were the result of the fear of retaliation or the direct product of internalized ethical commitments or 'conscience'. A fourth issue involves the balance of power between the individual, the state and humanity, or the relative influence of responsibilities for citizens and the wider obligations mentioned earlier that include respect for the international harm conventions that are intrinsic to the society of states and the cosmopolitan harm conventions that uphold the rights of individual persons to be spared unnecessary suffering.

An exploration of the tensions between those phenomena is essential for deciding 'whether the development of humanity ... has already reached a stage – or can ever reach a stage – where a more stable equilibrium of the we–I balance will prevail' (Elias 2010b: 180). The comparative sociology of states-systems is fundamental to such an inquiry. Those are critical levels of social and political integration where narrower and wider conceptions of 'we' come into conflict. As this volume has argued, the Western states-systems have not been hermetically sealed forms of world political organization but have been part of a long chain of social and political development in which societies in later historical eras reflected on the experience of earlier states-systems on whether to learn how to make advances in the art of war or to attempt to construct ethical restraints on force. Elias argued that it would be a very 'advanced civilization' where people comply with standards of restraint as a matter of conscience and not because of the fear of external sanctions. That observation was connected with the observation that such a social condition may seem to be unattainable and with the normative contention that it is vital to strive to make progress in that direction. There is much to be said for developing the comparative sociology of states-systems in that sober but cautiously optimistic spirit.

BIBLIOGRAPHY

Abruzzo, M. (2011) *Polemical Pain: Slavery, Cruelty and the Rise of Humanitarianism*. Baltimore: The Johns Hopkins University Press.

Abulafia, D. (2008) *The Discovery of Mankind: Atlantic Encounters in the Age of Columbus*. New Haven: Yale University Press.

Adams, C. (2007) 'War and Society'. In Sabin, van Wees and Whitby (2007a).

Adler, E. and Barnett, M. (eds.) (1998) *Security Communities*. Cambridge: Cambridge University Press.

Adler, E. and Pouliot, V. (eds.) (2011) *International Practices*. Cambridge: Cambridge University Press.

Adcock, F. E. (1957) *The Greek and Macedonian Art of War*. Berkeley: University of California Press.

Adorno, T. W. (1973) *Negative Dialectics*. London: Routledge and Kegan Paul.

Adorno, T. W. (2000) *Problems of Moral Philosophy*. Cambridge: Polity Press.

Aeschylus, *Seven Against Thebes* (1963 edition translated by H. W. Smyth). London: William Heinemann.

Ager, S. L. (1996) *Interstate Arbitrations in the Greek World, 337–90 BC*. Berkeley: University of California Press.

Alford, C. F. (1993) 'Greek Tragedy and Civilization: The Cultivation of Pity', *Political Research Quarterly*, 46 (2), 259–80.

Allan P. and Keller, A. (eds.) (2006) *What Is a Just Peace?* Oxford: Oxford University Press.

Allmand, C. (ed.) (1976) *War, Literature, and Politics in the Late Middle Ages*. Liverpool: Liverpool University Press.

Allmand, C. (ed.) (1998) *Society at War: The Experience of England and France during the Hundred Years War*. Woodbridge: Boydell Press.

Allmand, C. (1999) 'War and the Non-Combatant in the Middle Ages'. In Keen (1999).

Alperowitz, G. (1996) *The Decision to Use the Atomic Bomb*. New York: Vintage Books.

Althoff, G. (1998) 'Ira Regis: Prolegomena to a History of Royal Anger'. In Rosenwein (1998).

Altink, H. (2002) '"An Outrage on all Decency": Abolitionist Reactions to Flogging Jamaican Slave Women, 1780–1834'. In Wiedemann and Gardner (2002).

Amery, J. (1980) *At The Mind's Limits: Contemplations by a Survivor on Auschwitz and Its Realities*. Bloomington: Indiana University Press.

Anderson, A. (2001) *The Powers of Distance: Cosmopolitanism and the Cultivation of Detachment*. Princeton: Princeton University Press.

Anderson, B. (1983) *Imagined Communities: Reflections on the Origin and Spread of Nationalism*. London: Verso.

Anderson, M. S. (1988) *War and Society in Europe of the Ancien Regime: 1618–1789*. London: Fontana.

Anderson, P. (1983) *Imagined Communities: Reflections on the Origin and Spread of Nationalism*. London: Verso.

Angell, N. (1912) *The Great Illusion: A Study of the Relation of Military Power to National Advantage*. London: William Heinemann.

Anglo, S. (1977) 'The Courtier: The Renaissance and Changing Ideals'. In Dickens (1977).

Annas, G. J. and Grodin, M. A. (eds.) (1992) *The Nazi Doctors and the Nuremberg Code: Human Rights in Human Experimentation*. Oxford: Oxford University Press.

Anstey, R. (1975) *The Atlantic Slave Trade and British Abolition, 1760–1810*. London: MacMillan.

Arendt, H. (1994) *Eichmann in Jerusalem: A Report on the Banality of Evil*. Harmondsworth: Penguin.

Aristotle, *The Politics* (1948 edition translated by E. Barker). Oxford: Clarendon Press.

Arnold, D. (1999) 'Hunger in the Garden of Plenty: The Bengal Famine of 1770'. In Johns (1999).

Arnold, J. H. and Brady, S. (eds.) (2011) *What Is Masculinity? Historical Dynamics from Antiquity to the Contemporary World*. Basingstoke: Palgrave Macmillan.

Arrian, *The Campaigns of Alexander* (1971 edition translated by A. de Selicourt). Harmondsworth: Penguin.

Asbach, O. and Schröder, P. (eds.) (2010) *War, the State and International Law in Seventeenth-Century Europe*. London: Ashgate.

Asbridge, T. (2004) *The First Crusade: A New History*. London: Free Press.

Ashworth, J. (1987) 'The Relationship between Capitalism and Humanitarianism', *American Historical Review*, 92 (4), 813–28.

Askins, K. D. (1997) *War Crimes against Women: Prosecution in International War Crimes Tribunals*. The Hague: Martinus Nijhoff Publishers.

Atkins, E. M. (2000) 'Cicero'. In Rowe and Schofield (2000).

Austin, M. M. (1986) 'Hellenistic Kings, War, and the Economy', *The Classical Quarterly*, 36 (2), 450–66.

Austin, M. (1993) 'Alexander and the Macedonian Invasion of Asia: Aspects of the Historiography of War and Empire in Antiquity'. In Rich and Shipley (1993).

Austin, M., Harries, J. and Smith, C. (eds.) (1998) *Modus Operandi: Essays in Honour of Geoffrey Rickman*. London: Institute of Classical Studies.

Ayton, A. and Price, J. L. (eds.) (1995) *The Medieval Military Revolution: State, Society and Military Change in Medieval and Early Modern Europe*. London: I. B. Tauris.

Bachrach, B. S. (1999) 'Early Medieval Europe'. In Raaflaub and Rosenstein (1999).

Badian, E. (1958) 'Alexander the Great and the Unity of Mankind', *Historia*, (7), 425–44.

Bain, W. (2003) *Between Anarchy and Society: Trusteeship and the Obligations of Power*. Oxford: Oxford University Press.

Baker, K. M. (1975) *Condorcet: From Natural Philosophy to Social Mathematics*. Chicago: The University of Chicago Press.

Baker, P. (2005) 'Warfare'. In Erskine (2005).

Baldry, H. C. (1965) *The Unity of Mankind in Greek Thought*. Cambridge: Cambridge University Press.

Bankier, D. (1992) *The Germans and the Final Solution: Public Opinion under Nazism*. Oxford: Basil Blackwell.

Bankier, D. (1994) 'German Public Awareness of the Final Solution'. In Cesarani (1994).

Baraz, D. (2003) *Medieval Cruelty: Changing Perceptions, Late Antiquity to the Early Modern Period*. Ithaca: Cornell University Press.

Barber, M. (1992) *The Two Cities: Medieval Europe, 1050–1320*. London: Routledge.

Barker-Benfield, G. J. (1992) *The Culture of Sensibility: Sex and Society in Eighteenth-Century Britain*. Chicago: The University of Chicago Press.

Barnett, V. J. (1999) *Bystanders: Conscience and Complicity During the Holocaust*. London: Praeger.

Barnie, J. (1974) *War in Medieval Society: Social Values and the Hundred Years War, 1337–99*. London: Weidenfeld and Nicolson.

Barnwell, P. S. (1997) *Kings, Courtiers and Imperium: The Barbarian West, 565–725*. London: Duckworth.

Barraclough, G. (1956) *History in a Changing World*. Oxford: Basil Blackwell.

Bartelson, J. (1995) *A Genealogy of Sovereignty*. Cambridge: Cambridge University Press.

Bartlett, R. (1986) *Trial by Fire and Water: The Medieval Judicial Ideal*. Oxford: Clarendon Press.

Bartlett, R. (1993) *The Making of Europe: Conquest, Colonialism and Cultural Change, 950–1350*. London: Allen Lane.

Bartlett, R. (2000) *England under the Norman and Angevin Kings, 1075–1225*. Oxford: Clarendon Press.

Bartlett, R. and Mackay, A. (eds.) (1989) *Medieval Frontier Societies*. Oxford: Clarendon Press.

Barton, R. E. (1998) '"Zealous Anger" and the Renegotiation of Aristocratic Relationships in Eleventh- and Twelfth-Century France'. In Rosenwein (1998).

Barton, C. A. (2001) *Roman Honor: The Fire in the Bones*. Berkeley: University of California Press.

Barton, C. A. (2007) 'The Price of Peace in Ancient Rome'. In Raaflaub (2007).

Bartov, O. (1992) *Hitler's Army: Soldiers, Nazis, and War in the Third Reich*. Oxford: Oxford University Press.

Bartov, O. (1994) 'Operation Barbarossa and the Origins of the Final Solution'. In Cesarini (1994).

Bartov, O. (1996) *Murder in Our Midst: The Holocaust, Industrial Killing, and Representation*. Oxford: Oxford University Press.

Bartov, O. (2000) *Mirrors of Destruction: War, Genocide, and Modern Identity*. Oxford: Oxford University Press.

Bartov, O. (2001) *The Eastern Front, 1941–45: German Troops and the Barbarisation of Warfare*. Basingstoke: Palgrave.

Bauman, R. A. (1996) *Crime and Punishment in Ancient Rome*. London: Routledge.

Bauman, Z. (2000) *Modernity and the Holocaust*. Cambridge: Polity Press.

Baumeister, R. F. (1997) *Evil: Inside Human Violence and Cruelty*. New York: W. W. Freeman.

Bauslaugh, R. A. (1991) *The Concept of Neutrality in Classical Greece*. Berkeley: University of California Press.

Bax, M. (1987) 'Religious Regimes and State Formation: Towards a Research Perspective', *Anthropological Quarterly*, 60 (1), 1–11.

Becker, C. L. (1959) *The Heavenly City of the Eighteenth-Century Philosophers*. New Haven: Yale University Press.

Becker, M. B. (1967) *Florence in Transition, Volume one: The Decline of the Commune*. Baltimore: The Johns Hopkins Press.

Becker, M. B. (1968) *Florence in Transition, Volume two: Studies in the Rise of the Territorial State*. Baltimore: The Johns Hopkins Press.

Becker, M. B. (1976) 'Changing Patterns of Violence and Justice in Fourteenth- and Fifteenth-Century Florence', *Comparative Studies in Society and History*, 18, 281–96.

Becker, M. B. (1988) *Civility and Society in Western Europe, 1300–1600*. Bloomington: Indiana University Press.

Beckles, H. McD. (1989) *Natural Rebels: A Social History of Enslaved Black Women in Barbados*. London: Zed Books.

Beckles, H. McD. (2000) 'Property Rights in Pleasure: The Marketing of Enslaved Women's Sexuality'. In Shepherd and Beckles (2000).

Bederman, D. J. (2001) *International Law in Antiquity*. Cambridge: Cambridge University Press.

Bedford, D. and Workman, P. (2001) 'The Tragic Reading of the Thucydidean Tragedy', *Review of International Studies*, 27 (1), 51–67.

Behrens, B. (1936) 'Treatises on the Ambassador Written in the Fifteenth and Sixteenth Centuries', *English Historical Review*, 51 (204), 616–27.

Beiss, F., Roseman, M. and Schissler, H. (eds.) (2007) *Conflict, Cooperation and Continuity: Essays on Modern German History*. Oxford: Berghahn Books.

Bell, D. A. (2001) *The Cult of the Nation in France: Inventing Nationalism, 1680–1800*. Cambridge, MA: Harvard University Press.

Bell, D. A. (2007) *The First Total War: Napoleon's Europe and the Birth of Modern Warfare*. London: Bloomsbury.

Bellamy, A. J. (2008) 'The Responsibility to Protect and the Problem of Military Intervention', *International Affairs*, 84 (4), 615–39.

Bellamy, A. J. (2012) *Massacres and Morality: Mass Atrocities in an Age of Civilian Immunity*. Oxford: Oxford University Press.

Bending, L. (2000) *The Representation of Bodily Pain in Late Nineteenth Century English Culture*. Oxford: Oxford University Press.

Benjamin, W. (1986) *Illuminations*. New York: Schocken Books.

Bennett, M. (1999) 'Military Masculinity in England and Northern France, c.1050–c.1225'. In Hadley (1999).

Benthem van den Bergh, G. van (1992) *The Nuclear Revolution and the End of the Cold War: Forced Restraint*. Basingstoke: MacMillan.

Benthem van den Bergh, G. van (2001) 'Decivilising Processes?'. *Figurations: Newsletter of the Norbert Elias Foundation*, 16, available at http://norbertelias foundation.nl/figurations.php.

Benthem van den Bergh, G. van (2012) 'Norbert Elias and the Human Condition', *Human Figurations: Long-Term Perspectives on the Human Condition*, 1 (2) available at http://hdl.handle.net/2027/spo/11217607.0001.207.

Bentley, M. (ed.) (1997) *Companion to Historiography*. London: Routledge.

Berger S. (ed.) (2008) *A Companion to Nineteenth-Century Europe, 1789–1914*. Oxford: Blackwell.

Berkeley, G. (1988) [1710] *Principles of Human Knowledge*. London: Penguin.

Bernasconi, R. (2011) 'Kant's Third Thoughts on Race'. In Elden and Mendieta (2011).

Bernheimer, R. (1952) *Wild Men in the Middle Ages: A Study in Art, Sentiment, and Demonology*. Cambridge: Harvard University Press.

Bernstein, J. M. (2000) '"After Auschwitz": Trauma and the Grammar of Ethics'. In Fine and Turner (2000).

Bernstein, R. J. (2002) *Radical Evil: A Philosophical Interrogation*. Cambridge: Polity Press.

Berry, C. J. (1997) *Social Theory of the Scottish Enlightenment*. Edinburgh: Edinburgh University Press.

Berry, C. J. (2003) 'Sociality and Socialisation'. In Broadie (2003).

Bessel, R. (ed.) (1996) *Fascist Italy and Nazi Germany: Comparisons and Contrasts*. Cambridge: Cambridge University Press.

Best, G. (1983) *Humanity in Warfare: The Modern History of the International Law of Armed Conflicts*. London: Methuen.

Best, G. (1994) *War and Law since 1945*. Oxford: Clarendon Press.

Best, G. (1998) *War and Society in Revolutionary Europe, 1770–1870*. Stroud: Sutton Publishing.

Best, G. (1989) 'The Militarization of European Society, 1870–1914'. In Gillis (1989).

Beston, P. (2000) 'Hellenistic Military Leadership'. In van Wees (2000).

Bethencourt, F. (2013) *Racisms: From the Crusades to the Twentieth Century*. Princeton: Princeton University Press.

Bieler, A. and Morton, A. (eds.) (2006) *Images of Gramsci: Connections and Contentions in Political Theory and International Relations*. London: Routledge.

Biersteker, T. J. and Weber, C. (eds.) (1996) *State Sovereignty as Social Construct*. Cambridge: Cambridge University Press.

Billows, R. A. (2007) 'International Relations'. In Sabin, van Wees, and Whitby (2007).

Biow, D. (2002) *Doctors, Ambassadors, Secretaries: Humanism and Professions in Renaissance Italy*. Chicago: Chicago University Press.

Bisson, T. N. (2009) *The Crisis of the Twelfth-Century: Power, Lordship, and the Origins of European Government*. Princeton: Princeton University Press.

Bix, H. P. (2000) *Hirohito and the Making of Modern Japan*. London: Duckworth.

Black, J. (ed.) (1999) *War in the Early Modern World, 1450–1815*. London: Routledge.

Blackburn, R. (1988) *The Overthrow of Colonial Slavery, 1776–1848*. London: Verso.

Blake, E. O. (1970) 'The Formation of the "Crusade Idea"', *Journal of Ecclesiastical History*, 21 (1), 11–31.

Blanning, T. C. W. (1996) *The French Revolutionary Wars, 1787–1802*. London: Arnold.

Blanning, T. C. W. (ed.) (2000) *The Eighteenth Century: Europe 1688–1815*. Oxford: Oxford University Press.

Blanning, T. C. W. (2002) 'Liberation or Occupation: Theory and Practice in the French Revolutionaries' Treatment of Civilians outside France'. In Grimsley and Rogers (2002).

Blanning, T. C. W. (2008) *The Pursuit of Glory: Europe 1648–1815*. London: Penguin.

Blass, T. (ed.) (2000) *Obedience to Authority: Current Perspectives on the Milgram Paradigm*. Mahwah, NJ: Lawrence Erlbaum.

Bleiker, R. and Hutchison, E. (eds.) (2014) 'Forum on Emotions and World Politics', *International Theory*, 6 (3).

Bliese, J. R. E. (1989) 'Rhetoric and Morale: A Study of Battle Orations from the Central Middle Ages', *Journal of Medieval History*, 15 (3), 201–26.

Bloch, M. (1962) *Feudal Society*. London: Routledge and Kegan Paul.

Blomert, R. (2002) 'Re-Civilizing Processes as a Mission of the International Community', *Figurations: Newsletter of the Norbert Elias Foundation*, 17, available at http://norberteliasfoundation.nl/figurations.php.

Blomert, R. (2012) 'The Taming of Economic Aristocracies', *Human Figurations: Long-Term Perspectives on the Human Condition*, 1(2), available at http://elias-i.nsfhost.com/elias/figs.htm.

Bloxham, D. and Moses, A. D. (eds.) (2010) *The Oxford Handbook of Genocide Studies*. Oxford: Oxford University Press.

Blundell, M. W. (1989) *Helping Friends and Harming Enemies: A Study in Sophocles and Greek Ethics*. Cambridge: Cambridge University Press.

Blythe, J. M. (2000) '"Civil Humanism" and Medieval Political Thought'. In Hankins (2000).

Bock, G., Skinner Q. and Viroli, M. (eds.) (1990) *Machiavelli and Republicanism*. Cambridge: Cambridge University Press.

Bodin, J. (1992) [1583] *On Sovereignty*. Cambridge: Cambridge University Press.

Boemeke, M. F., Chickering, R. and Forster, S. (eds.) (1999) *Anticipating Total War: The German and American Experiences, 1871–1914*. Cambridge: Cambridge University Press.

Bohman, J. and Lutz-Bachmann, M. (eds.) (1997) *Perpetual Peace: Essays on Kant's Cosmopolitan Ideal*. Cambridge, MA: MIT Press.

Boister, N. and Cryer, R. (eds.) (2008) *Documents on the Tokyo International Military Tribunal: Charter, Indictments and Judgments*. Oxford: Oxford University Press.

Boli, J. and Thomas, G. M. (eds.) (1999) *Constructing World Culture: International Nongovernmental Organizations since 1875*. Stanford: Stanford University Press.

Bonney, R. (ed.) (1999) *The Rise of the Fiscal State in Europe, c. 1200–1815*. Oxford: Oxford University Press.

Booth, K. (ed.) (2011) *Realism and World Politics*. Abingdon: Routledge.

Bosworth, A. B. (1988) *Conquest and Empire: The Reign of Alexander the Great*. Cambridge: Cambridge University Press.

Bosworth, A. B. (1996) *Alexander and the East: The Tragedy of Triumph*. Clarendon: Oxford University Press.

Bourke, J. (1999) *An Intimate History of Killing: Face–to–Face Killing in Twentieth Century Warfare*. London: Granta.

Bowden, B. (2009) *The Empire of Civilization: The Evolution of an Imperial Idea*. Chicago: The University of Chicago Press.

Bowden, B. and Seabrooke, L. (eds.) (2006) *Global Standards of Market Civilization*. Abingdon: Routledge.

Bowker, J. (1975) *Problems of Suffering in Religions of the World*. Cambridge: Cambridge University Press.

Bowsky, M. (1967) 'The Medieval Commune and Internal Violence: Police Power and Public Safety in Siena, 1287–1355', *American Historical Review*, 73 (1), 1–17.

Bozeman, A. B. (1960) *Politics and Culture in International History*. Princeton: Princeton University Press.

Bradbury, J. (1992) *The Medieval Siege*. Woodbridge: The Boydell Press.

Bratspies, R. M. (2006) 'Trail Smelter's (Semi) Precautionary Legacy'. In Bratspies and Miller (2006).

Bratspies, R. M. and Miller, R. A. (eds.) (2006) *Transboundary Harm in International Law: Lessons from the Trail Smelter Arbitration*. Cambridge: Cambridge University Press.

Braund, D. (1995) 'Piracy under the Principate and the Ideology of Imperial Eradication'. In Rich and Shipley (1995).

Bredero, A. H. (1994) *Christendom and Christianity in the Middle Ages*. Grand Rapid, Michigan: Eerdmans Publishing Company.

Bremmer, J. and Roodenburg, H. (eds.) (1991) *A Cultural History of Gestures*. Ithaca, NY: Cornell University Press.

Bridges, E., Hall, E. and Rhodes, P. J. (eds.) (2007) *Cultural Responses to the Persian Wars: Antiquity to the Third Millennium*. Oxford: Oxford University Press.

Bringmann, K. (1993) 'The King as Benefactor: Some Remarks on Ideal Kingship in the Age of Hellenism'. In Bulloch, Gruen, Long and Stewart (1993).

Brion, D. J. (2001) 'Torts and Gods: Idolatry in the Law'. In Davis (2001a).

Broadie, A. (ed.) (2003) *The Cambridge Companion to the Scottish Enlightenment*. Cambridge: Cambridge University Press.

Brock, G. and Brighouse, H. (eds.) (2005) *The Political Philosophy of Cosmopolitanism*. Cambridge: Cambridge University Press.

Bronner, S. E. (2006) *Reclaiming the Enlightenment: Toward a Politics of Radical Engagement*. New York: Columbia University Press.

Brosius, M. (2006) *The Persians: An Introduction*. Abingdon: Routledge.

Brotton, J. (2006) *The Renaissance: A Very Short Introduction*. Oxford: Oxford University Press.

Brown, C. (1988) 'The Modern Requirement? Reflections on Normative International Theory in a Post Western World', *Millennium*, 17(2), 339–48.

Brown, J. C. (1982) *In the Shadow of Florence: Provincial Society in Renaissance Pescia*. Oxford: Oxford University Press.

Brown, J. C. and Davis, R. C. (eds.) (1998) *Gender and Society in Renaissance Italy*. London: Longman.

Brown, P. (1990) *The Body and Society: Men, Women and Sexual Renunciation in Early Christianity*. London: Faber and Faber.

Brown, R. M. (1990) 'The Holocaust as a Problem in Moral Choice'. In Lefkovitz (1990).

Browning, C. R. (1985) *Fateful Months: Essays on the Emergence of the Final Solution*. New York: Holmes and Meier.

Browning, C. R. (2001) *Ordinary Men: Reserve Police Battalion 101 and the Final Solution in Poland*. London: Penguin.

Browning, C. R. with J. Matthaus (2004) *The Origins of the Final Solution: The Evolution of Nazi Jewish Policy, September 1939–March 1942*. Lincoln: University of Nebraska Press.

Brundage, J. A. (1987) *Law, Sex, and Christian Society in Medieval Europe.* Chicago: University of Chicago Press.

Brunkhorst, H. (2005) *Solidarity: From Civic Friendship to a Global Legal Community.* Cambridge, MA: MIT Press.

Brunt, P. A. (1977) 'From Epictetus to Arrian', *Athenaeum*, 19–48.

Brunt, P. A. (1978) 'Laus Imperii'. In Garnsey and Whittaker (1978).

Brunt, P. (1998) 'Marcus Aurelius and Slavery'. In Austin, Harries and Smith (1998).

Buchan, B. (2006) 'Civilisation, Sovereignty and War: The Scottish Enlightenment and International Relations', *International Relations*, 20 (2), 175–92.

Buchan, B. (2011) 'Civilized Fictions: Warfare and Civilization in Enlightenment Thought'. *Alternatives: Global, Local, Political*, 36 (1), 64–71.

Buckle, F. (1901) *History of Civilization in England, volume one.* London: Longmans Green and Co.

Buhrer-Thierry, G. (1998) '"Just Anger" or "Vengeful Anger": The Punishment of Blinding in the Early Medieval West'. In Rosenwein (1998).

Bukovansky, M., Clark, I., Eckersley, R., Price, R. Reus-Smit, C. and Wheeler, N. (2012) *Special Responsibilities: Global Problems and American Power.* Cambridge: Cambridge University Press.

Bull, H. (1966) 'The Grotian Conception of International Society'. In Butterfield and Wight (1966).

Bull, H. (1977) *The Anarchical Society: A Study of Order in World Politics.* London: MacMillan.

Bull, H. (1979) The State's Positive Role in World Affairs', *Daedalus*, 108 (4), 111–23.

Bull, H. (1984) 'The Emergence of Universal International Society'. In Bull and Watson (1984).

Bull, H. (1984a) 'European States and African Political Communities'. In Bull and Watson (1984).

Bull, H. (ed.) (1984b) *Intervention in World Politics.* Oxford: Clarendon Press.

Bull, H. (1984c) 'The Revolt against the West'. In Bull and Watson (1984).

Bull, H. (1990) 'The Importance of Grotius in the Study of International Relations'. In Bull, Kingsbury and Roberts (1990).

Bull, H., Kingsbury, B. and Roberts, A. (eds.) (1990) *Hugo Grotius and International Relations.* Oxford: Clarendon Press.

Bull, H. and Watson, A. (eds.) (1984) *The Expansion of International Society.* Oxford: Clarendon Press.

Bulloch, A. W., Gruen, E. S., Long, A. A. and Stewart, A. (eds.) (1993) *Images and Ideologies: Self-Definition in the Hellenistic World.* Berkeley: University of California Press.

Bullock, A. (1985) *The Humanist Tradition in the West.* London: Thames and Hudson.

Bullough, V. L. and Brundage, J. (eds.) (1996) *Handbook of Medieval Sexuality.* London: Garland.

Bumke, J. (2000) *Courtly Culture: Literature and Society in the High Middle Ages.* New York: Overlook Press.

Burchill, S. and Linklater, A. (eds.) (2013) *Theories of International Relations.* Basingstoke: Palgrave.

Burckhardt, J. (1944) [1860] *The Civilization of the Renaissance in Italy* (translated by S. G. C. Middlemore). Oxford: Phaidon Press.

Burke, E. (1899) [1791] 'A Letter to a Member of the National Assembly'. In Burke (1899a), volume 4.

Burke, E. (1899) [1793] 'Ninth Report of the Select Committee of the House of Commons on the Affairs of India'. In Burke (1899a), volume 8.

Burke, E. (1899a) *The Works of the Right Honourable Edmund Burke.* London: John C. Nimmo.

Burke, E. (1968) [1790] *Reflections on the Revolution in France.* Harmondsworth: Pelican.

Burke, E. (1999) [1783] 'Speech on Fox's India Bill'. In Fidler and Welsh (1999).

Burke, P. (1969) *The Renaissance Sense of the Past.* London: Edward Arnold.

Burke, P. (ed.) (1973) *A New Kind of History from the Writings of Lucien Febvre.* London: Routledge and Kegan Paul.

Burke, P. (1986) 'City-States'. In Hall (1986).

Burke, P. (1987) *The Renaissance.* Houndmills, Basingstoke: MacMillan.

Burke, P. (1991) 'Tacitus, Scepticism, and Reason of State'. In Burns and Goldie (1991).

Burke, P. (1992) *The Fabrication of Louis XIV.* New Haven: Yale University Press.

Burke, P. (1993) *The Art of Conversation.* Cambridge: Polity Press.

Burke, P. (1995) *The Fortunes of the Courtier: The European Reception of Castiglione's Cortegiana.* Cambridge: Polity Press.

Burke, P. (1997) *The Renaissance.* Basingstoke: Macmillan.

Burke, P. (1998) *The European Renaissance: Centres and Peripheries.* Oxford: Blackwell.

Burke, P. (1999) *The Italian Renaissance: Culture and Society in Italy.* Cambridge: Polity Press.

Burke. P. (2002) 'The Historical Geography of the Renaissance'. In Ruggiero (2002).

Burke, P. (2003) 'The Annales, Braudel and Historical Sociology'. In Delanty and Isin (2003).

Burleigh, M. (1997) *Ethics and Extermination: Reflections on Nazi Genocide.* Cambridge: Cambridge University Press.

Burleigh, M. (2001) *The Third Reich: A History.* London: Pan Books.

Burleigh, M. (2002) *Death and Deliverance: Euthanasia in Germany, 1900-1945.* London: Pan.

Burns, J. H. and Goldie, M. (eds.) (1991) *The Cambridge History of Political Thought, 1450-1700.* Cambridge: Cambridge University Press.

Burrow, J. (2007) *A History of Histories: Epics, Chronicles, Romances and Inquiries from Herodotus and Thucydides to the Twentieth Century.* London: Allen Lane.

Bush, B. (1990) *Slave Women in Caribbean Slave Society, 1650–1838*. Oxford: James Currey.

Butterfield, H. (1940) *The Statecraft of Machiavelli*. London: G. Bell and Sons.

Butterfield, H. (1966) 'The Balance of Power'. In Butterfield and Wight (1966).

Butterfield, H. and Wight, M. (eds.) (1966) *Diplomatic Investigations: Essays in the Theory of International Politics*. London: George Allen and Unwin.

Buzan, B. (2011) 'A World without Superpowers: Decentred Globalism', *International Relations*, 25 (1), 3–25.

Buzan, B. and Little, R. (2000) *International Systems in World History: Remaking the Study of International Relations*. Oxford: Oxford University Press.

Caferro, W. (1998) *Mercenary Companies and the Decline of Siena*. Baltimore: The Johns Hopkins University Press.

Caferro, W. (2006) *John Hawkwood: An English Mercenary in Fourteenth-Century Italy*. Baltimore: The Johns Hopkins University Press.

Caferro, W. (2011) *Contesting the Renaissance*. Oxford: Wiley-Blackwell.

Cairns, D. L. (1993) *Aidos: The Psychology and Ethics of Honour and Shame in Ancient Greek Literature*. Oxford: Clarendon Press.

Callières, F. de (1983) [1716] *The Art of Diplomacy* (edited by H. M. A. Keens-Soper and K. W. Schweizer). Leicester: Leicester University Press.

Cameron, A. (1993) *The Later Roman Empire, AD 284–430*. London: Fontana.

Cameron, E. (ed.) (1999) *Early Modern Europe: An Oxford History*. Oxford: Oxford University Press.

Campbell, B. (1995) 'War and Diplomacy: Rome and Parthia, 31 BC–AD 235'. In Rich and Shipley (1995).

Campbell, B. (2001) 'Diplomacy in the Roman World (c. 500 BC–AD 235)', *Diplomacy and Statecraft*, 12 (1), 1–22.

Campbell, B. (2002) *War and Society in Imperial Rome, 31 BC–AD 284*. London: Routledge.

Cannadine, D. (1981) 'War and Death, Grief and Mourning in Modern Britain'. In Whaley (1981).

Canny, N. P. (1973) 'The Ideology of English Colonization: From Ireland to America', *William and Mary Quarterly*, 30 (4), 575–98.

Canny, N. (ed.) (1998) *The Oxford History of the British Empire, Volume One: The Origins of Empire*. Oxford: Oxford University Press.

Cardini, F. (1990) 'The Warrior and the Knight'. In Le Goff (1990).

Carman, J. and Harding, A. (eds.) (1999) *Ancient Warfare: Archaeological Perspectives*. Stroud: Sutton Publishing.

Carr, E. H. (2001) [1939] *The Twenty Years' Crisis, 1919–1939: An Introduction to the Study of International Relations*. Basingstoke: Palgrave.

Carter, I. (2000) 'Can Enlightenment Morality Be Justified Teleologically?'. In Geras and Wokler (2000).

Carter, J. J. and Pittock, J. H. (eds.) (1987) *Aberdeen and the Enlightenment*. Aberdeen: Aberdeen University Press.

Cartledge, P., Garnsey, P. and Greun, E. (eds.) (1997) *Hellenistic Constructs: Essays in Culture, History, and Historiography*. Berkeley: University of California Press.

Cary, M. (1956) *The Medieval Alexander*. Cambridge: Cambridge University Press.

Cassirer, E. (1951) *The Philosophy of the Enlightenment*. Princeton: Princeton University Press.

Castiglione, B. (1959) [1528] *The Book of the Courtier* (translated by C. S. Singleton). New York: Anchor Books.

Ceadel, M. (1989) *Thinking about Peace and War*. Oxford: Oxford University Press.

Ceadel, M. (1996) *The Origins of War Prevention: The British Peace Movement and International Relations, 1730–1854*. Oxford: Clarendon Press.

Cell, J. (1979) 'The Imperial Conscience'. In Marsh (1979).

Cesarani, D. (ed.) (1994) *The Final Solution: Origins and Implementation*. London: Routledge.

Cesarani, D. (2004) *Eichmann: His Life and Crimes*. London: William Heinemann.

Chabod, F. (1964) 'Was There a Renaissance State?' In Lubasz (1964).

Chambers, D. S. and Dean, T. (1997) *Clean Hands and Rough Justice: An Investigating Magistrate in Renaissance Italy*. Ann Arbor: The University of Michigan Press.

Chaniotis, A. (2005) *War in the Hellenistic World: A Social and Cultural History*. Oxford: Blackwell.

Chartier, R. (ed.) (1989) *A History of Private Life, Volume 3: Passions of the Renaissance*. Cambridge, MA: Harvard University Press.

Chartier, R. (1997) *On the Edge of the Cliff: History, Language, and Practices*. Baltimore: The Johns Hopkins University Press.

Chickering, R. (1999) 'Total War: The Use and Abuse of a Concept'. In Boemeke, Chickering and Forster (1999).

Chickering, R. and Forster, S. (eds.) (2000) *Great War, Total War: Combat and Mobilization on the Western Front, 1914–1918*. Cambridge: Cambridge University Press.

Chickering, R., Showalter, D. and van de Ven, H. (eds.) (2012) *The Cambridge History of War, Volume Four: War and the Modern World*. Cambridge: Cambridge University Press.

Childs, J. (1982) *Armies and Warfare in Europe, 1648–1789*. Manchester: Manchester University Press.

Chojnacki, S. (1972) 'Crime, Punishment and the Trecento Venetian State'. In Martines (1972).

Chrysos, E. (1997) 'The Empire in East and West'. In Webster and Brown (1997).

Cicero, *De Officiis* (1947 edition translated by W. Miller). London: William Heinemann.

Clark, A. M. (2001) *Diplomacy of Conscience: Amnesty International and Changing Human Rights Norms*. Princeton: Princeton University Press.

Clark, I. (1982) *Limited Nuclear War*. Oxford: Martin Robertson.

Clark. I. (1990) *Waging War: A Philosophical Introduction*. Oxford: Clarendon Press.

Clark, I. (2005) *Legitimacy in International Society*. Oxford: Oxford University Press.

Clark, I. (2007) *International Legitimacy and World Society*. Oxford: Oxford University Press.

Clark, I. (2009) 'Bringing Hegemony Back in: the United States and International Order' *International Affairs*, 85 (1), 23–36.

Clark, I. (2013) *The Vulnerable and International Society*. Oxford: Oxford University Press.

Clark, I. and Neumann, I. B. (eds.) (1996) *Classical Theories of International Relations*. Basingstoke: MacMillan.

Clausewitz, C, von (1976) [1832] *On War* (edited by M. Howard and P. Paret). Princeton: Princeton University Press.

Cobban, A. (1960) *In Search for Humanity: The Role of the Enlightenment in Modern History*. London: Jonathan Cape.

Cobban, A. (1965) 'The Enlightenment and the French Revolution'. In Wasserman (1965).

Cohen, D. (1995) *Law, Violence and Community in Classical Athens*. Cambridge: Cambridge University Press.

Cohen, J. (ed.) 2002) *For Love of Country*. Boston: Beacon Press.

Cohn, N. (1993) *Europe's Inner Demons: The Demonization of Christians in Medieval Christendom*. London: Chatto, Heinemann for Sussex University Press.

Coker, C. (2001) *Humane Warfare*. London: Routledge.

Coker, C. (2007) *The Warrior Ethos: Military Culture and the War on Terror*. Abingdon: Routledge.

Cole, S. G. (1984) 'Greek Sanctions against Sexual Assault', *Classical Philology*, 79 (2), 97–113.

Collet, T. (2009) 'Civilization and Civilized in post-9/11 US Presidential Speeches', *Discourse and Society*, 20 (4), 455–75.

Collingwood, R. G. (1999) 'What Civilization Means'. In Collingwood (1999a).

Collingwood, R. G. (1999a) *The New Leviathan: Or Man, Society, Civilization and Barbarism*. Oxford: Clarendon Press.

Condorcet, Marquis de (1965) [1794] 'Sketch for a Historical Picture of the Progress of the Human Mind'. In Gardiner (1978).

Conklin, A. (1997) *A Mission to Civilize: The Republican Idea of Empire in France and West Africa, 1895–1939*. Stanford: Stanford University Press.

Connelly, J. (2012) *From Enemy to Brother: The Revolution in Catholic Teaching on the Jews, 1933–1965*. Cambridge, MA: Harvard University Press.

Connor, W. R. (1988) 'Early Greek Land Warfare as Symbolic Expression', *Past and Present*, 119, 3–29.

Contamine, P. (1984) *War in the Middle Ages*. London: Guild Publishing.

Contamine, P. (2000) 'The Growth of State Control. Practices of War, 1300–1800: Ransom and Booty'. In Contamine (2000a).

Contamine, P. (ed.) (2000a) *War and Competition Between States*. Oxford: Clarendon University Press.

Cook, J. (1969) [1775] *The Journals of Captain Cook on his Voyages of Discovery, volume 2, The Voyage of the Resolution and Adventure, 1772–1775*. Cambridge: Cambridge University Press.

Cooter, R., Harrison, M. and Sturdy, S. (eds.) (1998) *War, Medicine and Modernity*. Stroud: Sutton Publishing.

Corbin, A. (1996) *The Foul and the Flagrant: Odour and the Social Imagination*. London: MacMillan.

Cornell, T. J. (1991) 'Rome: The History of an Anachronism'. In Molho, Raaflaub and Emlen (1991).

Cornell, T. (1995) 'The End of Roman Imperial Expansion'. In Rich and Shipley (1995).

Corvisier, A. (1979) *Armies and Societies in Europe, 1494–1789*. Bloomington: Indiana University Press.

Covini, M. N. (2000) 'Political and Military Bonds in the Italian State-System, Thirteenth to Sixteenth Centuries'. In Contamine (2000a).

Cowdrey, H. E. J. (1970) 'The Peace and the Truce of God in the Eleventh Century', *Past and Present*, 46, 42–67.

Cowdrey, H. (2002) 'Pope Urban II's Preaching of the First Crusade'. In Madden (2002a).

Cox, R. W. (1983) 'Gramsci, Hegemony and International Relations: An Essay in Method', *Millennium*, 12 (2), 162–75.

Crane, C. C. (2002) '"Contrary to Our National Ideals": American Strategic Bombing of Civilians in World War II'. In Grimsley and Rogers (2002).

Crawford, N. C. (2002) *Argument and Change in World Politics: Ethics, Decolonization, and Humanitarian Intervention*. Cambridge: Cambridge University Press.

Crawford, N. C. (2013) *Accountability for Killing: Moral Responsibility for Collateral Damage in America's Post-9/11 Wars*. Oxford: Oxford University Press.

Crefeld, M. van (1989) *Technology and War: From 2000 BC to the Present*. London: Free Press.

Crook, T., Gill, R. and Taithe, B. (eds.) (2011) *Evil, Barbarism and Empire: Britain and Abroad, c. 1830–2000*. Basingstoke: Palgrave.

Cruickshank, J. (1982) *Variations on Catastrophe: Some French Responses to the Great War*. Oxford: Clarendon Press.

Cugoano, O. (1998) [1787] 'Thoughts and Sentiments on the Evil and Wicked Traffic of the Slavery and Commerce of the Human Species'. In Gates and Andrews (1998).

Curtin, M. (1985) 'A Question of Manners: Status and Gender in Etiquette and Courtesy', *Journal of Modern History*, 57 (3), 395–423.

Curtius (Quintus Curtius Rufus) *The History of Alexander the Great* (1962 edition translated by J. C. Rolfe). London: William Heinemann.

Cutler, A. C. (2002) 'Private International Regimes and Interfirm Cooperation'. In Hall and Biersteker (2002).

Dadrian, V. N. (1998) 'The Comparative Aspects of the Armenian and Jewish Cases of Genocide: A Sociohistorical Perspective'. In Rosenbaum (1998).

Davidson, N. S. (2007) 'Religious Minorities'. In Martin (2007a).

Davies, R. R. (1990) *Domination and Conquest: The Experience of Ireland, Scotland and Wales, 1100–1300*. Cambridge: Cambridge University Press.

Davies, R. R. (2000) *The First English Empire: Power and Identities in the British Isles, 1093–1343*. Oxford: Oxford University Press.

Davies, R. R. (2003) 'The Medieval State: The Tyranny of a Concept?', *Journal of Historical Sociology*, 16 (2), 280–300.

Davies, W. and Fouracre, P. (eds.) (1986) *The Settlement of Disputes in Early Medieval Europe*. Cambridge: Cambridge University Press.

Davis, D. B. (1970) *The Problem of Slavery in Western Culture*. Harmondsworth: Penguin.

Davis, D. B. (1984) *Slavery and Human Progress*. Oxford: Oxford University Press.

Davis, D. B. (1987) 'Reflections on Abolitionism and Hegemonic Ideology', *American Historical Review*, 92 (4), 797–812.

Davis, D. B. (2006) *Inhuman Bondage: The Rise and Fall of Slavery in the New World*. Oxford: Oxford University Press.

Davis, R. C. (2007) 'The Renaissance Goes up in Smoke'. In Martin (2007).

Davis, W. (2001) 'Introduction: The Dimensions and Dilemmas of a Modern Virtue'. In Davis (2001a).

Davis, W. (ed.) (2001a) *Taking Responsibility: Comparative Perspectives*. Charlottesville: University Press of Virginia.

Davis, N. and Kraay, C. M. (1973) *The Hellenistic Kingdoms: Portraits, Coins and History*. London: Thames and Hudson.

Dawidowicz, L. S. (ed.) (1976) *A Holocaust Reader*. New York: Behrman House.

Dawson, D. (1996) *The Origins of Western Warfare: Militarism and Morality in the Ancient World*. Boulder, CO: Westview Press.

De Romilly, J. (1958) 'Eunoia in Isocrates or the Political Importance of Creating Good Will', *Journal of Hellenic Studies*, 78, 92–101.

De Romilly, J. (1974) 'Fairness and Kindness in Thucydides', *Phoenix*, 28 (1), 95–100.

De Romilly, J. (1977) *The Rise and Fall of States According to Greek Authors*. Ann Arbor: The University of Michigan Press.

De Souza, P. (1999) *Piracy in the Graeco-Roman World*. Cambridge: Cambridge University Press.

De Souza, P. (2007) 'Battle'. In Sabin, van Wees and Whitby (2007).

De Souza, P. (2008) 'Parta Victoriis Pax: Roman Emperors as Peacemakers'. In De Souza and France (2008).

De-Souza, P. and France, J. (eds.) (2008) *War and Peace in Ancient and Medieval History*. Cambridge: Cambridge University Press.

Der Derian, J. (1987) *On Diplomacy: A Genealogy of Western Estrangement*. Oxford: Basil Blackwell.

Dean, T. (1994) 'Criminal Justice in Mid-Fifteenth Century Bologna'. In Dean and Lowe (1994a).

Dean, T. and Lowe, K. J. P. (1994) 'Writing the History of Crime in the Italian Renaissance'. In Dean and Lowe (1994a).

Dean, T. and Lowe, K. J. P. (eds.) (1994a) *Crime, Society and the Law in Renaissance Italy*. Cambridge: Cambridge University Press.

Dean, T. (2001) *Crime in Medieval Europe, 1200–1550*. London: Longman.

Delanty, G. (ed.) (2012) *The Routledge Handbook of Cosmopolitan Studies*. Abingdon: Routledge.

Delanty, G. and Isin, E. (eds.) (2003) *Handbook of Historical Sociology*. London: Sage.

Delogu, P. (2002) *An Introduction to Medieval History*. London: Duckworth.

Demos, J. (1996) 'Shame and Guilt in Early New England'. In Harre and Parrott (1996).

Denley, P. (1988) 'The Mediterranean in the Age of the Renaissance, 1200–1500'. In Holmes (1988).

Detter, I. (2000) *The Law of War*. Cambridge: Cambridge University Press.

Deutsch, K. (1970) *Political Community in the North Atlantic Area*. London: Archon Books.

Devetak, R. (1995) 'The Project of Modernity and International Relations Theory', *Millennium*, 24 (1), 27–51.

Dew, N. (2009) *Orientalism in Louis XIV's France*. Oxford: Oxford University Press.

Dickens, A. G. (ed.) (1977) *The Courts of Europe: Politics, Patronage and Royalty, 1400–1800*. London: Thames and Hudson.

Diderot, D. (1992) [1772] 'The Supplement au Voyage de Bougainville'. In Diderot (1992a).

Diderot, D. (1992 [1775] 'Articles in the Encyclopedie'. In Diderot (1992a).

Diderot, D. (1992) [1783] 'Extracts from the Histoire des Deux Indes'. In Diderot (1992a).

Diderot, D. (1992a) *Political Writings*. Cambridge: Cambridge University Press.

Dillon, S. (2006) 'Women on the Columns of Trajan and Marcus Aurelius and the Visual Language of Roman Victory'. In Dillon and Welch (2006).

Dillon, S. and Welch, K. E. (eds.) (2006) *Representations of War in Ancient Rome*. Cambridge: Cambridge University Press.

Diodorus of Sicily, *The Library of History: volume 10*. The Loeb Classical Library (1954 edition translated by R. M. Gear). Cambridge, MA: Harvard University Press.

Diodorus of Sicily, *The Library of History: volume 11*. The Loeb Classical Library (1957 edition translated by F. R. Walton). Cambridge, MA: Harvard University Press.

Dobson, A. (2003) *Citizenship and the Environment*. Oxford: Oxford University Press

Dobson, A. and Eckersley, R. (eds.) (2006) *Political Theory and the Ecological Challenge*. Cambridge: Cambridge University Press.

Dodds, E. R. (1973) *The Ancient Idea of Progress and Other Essays on Greek Literature and Belief*. Oxford: Clarendon Press.

Dolet, E. (1933) [1541] 'Etienne Dolet on the Functions of the Ambassador', *The American Journal of International Law*, (27), 82–95.

Donelan, M. D. (1990) *Elements of International Political Theory*. Oxford: Clarendon Press.

Donnelly, J. (1998) 'Human Rights: A New Standard of Civilization?', *International Affairs*, 74 (1), 1–23.

Donnelly, J. (2013) 'Realism'. In Burchill and Linklater (2013).

Doorn, J. van (1984) 'Continuity and Discontinuity in Civil-Military Relations'. In Martin and McCrate (1984).

Douglas, L. (2001) 'The Shrunken Head of Buchenwald: Icons of Atrocity at Nuremberg'. In Zelizer (2001).

Douglas, L. (2001a) *The Memory of Judgment: Making Law and History in the Trials of the Holocaust*. New Haven: Yale University Press.

Douhet, G. (2003) [1921] *The Command of the Air*. Dehradun: Natraj Publishers.

Dover, K. J. (1974) *Greek Popular Morality in the Time of Plato and Aristotle*. Oxford: Basil Blackwell.

Dower, J. (1986) *War without Mercy: Race and Power in the Pacific War*. London: Faber and Faber.

Dower, J. (1999) *Embracing Defeat: Japan in the Wake of World War II*. New York: W. W. Norton.

Downey, G. (1955) 'Philanthropia in Religion and Statecraft in the Fourth Century after Christ', *Historia*, 4 (2–3), 199–208.

Doyle, M. (1983) 'Kant, Liberal Legacies, and Foreign Affairs, Parts I and II', *Philosophy and Public Affairs*, 12 (3), 205–35 and 12 (4):323–53.

Drake, H. A. (ed.) (2006) *Violence in Late Antiquity: Perceptions and Practices*. Aldershot: Ashgate.

Dudink, S., Hagemann, K. and Tosh, J. (eds.) (2004) *Masculinities in Politics and War: Gendering Modern History*. Manchester: Manchester University Press.

Dudley, E. and Novak, M. E. (eds.) (1972) *The Wild Man Within: An Image in Western Thought from the Renaissance to Romanticism*. Pittsburgh: University of Pittsburgh Press.

Duffy, M. (ed.) (1980) 'Introduction'. In Duffy (1980a).

Duffy, M. (ed.) (1980a) *The Military Revolution and the State, 1500–1800*. University of Exeter Studies in History, no. 1. Exeter: University of Exeter Press.

Duindam, J. (1994) *Myths of Power: Norbert Elias and the Early Modern European Court*. Amsterdam: Amsterdam University Press.

Duncalf. F. (1969) 'The Councils of Piacenza and Clermont'. In Setton (1969).

Dunne, T. (1998) *Inventing International Society: A History of the English School*. Basingstoke: MacMillan.

Dunne, T. (2003) 'Society and Hierarchy in International Relations', *International Relations*, 17 (3), 303–20.

Dunning, E. and Hughes, J. (2013) *Norbert Elias and Modern Sociology: Knowledge, Interdependence, Power, Process*. London: Bloomsbury.

Dunning, E. and Mennell, S. (1998) 'Elias on Germany, Nazism and the Holocaust: On the Balance between "Civilizing" and "Decivilizing" Trends in the Social Development of Western Europe', *British Journal of Sociology*, 49 (3), 339–57.

Dunning, E. and Mennell, S. (eds.) (2003) *Norbert Elias, volume 2*. London: Sage.

Durkheim, E. [1925] (1973) *Moral Education: A Study in the Theory and Application of the Sociology of Education*. New York: The Free Press.

Earle, E. M. (ed.) (1943) *Makers of Modern Strategy: Military Thought from Machiavelli to Hitler*. Princeton: Princeton University Press.

Earle, T. F. and Lowe, K. J. P. (eds.) (2005) *Black Africans in Renaissance Europe*. Cambridge: Cambridge University Press.

Eckersley, R. (2004) *The Green State: Rethinking Democracy and Sovereignty*. Cambridge, MA: MIT Press.

Eckstein, A. M. (1995) *Moral Vision in the Histories of Polybius*. Berkeley: University of California Press.

Eckstein, A. M. (2006) *Mediterranean Anarchy, Interstate War, and the Rise of Rome*. Berkeley: University of California Press.

Eckstein, A. M. (2006a) 'Conceptualising Roman Imperial Expansion under the Republic: An Introduction'. In Rosenstein and Morstein-Marx (2006).

Eckstein, A. M. (2007) 'Intra-Greek Balancing, the Mediterranean Crisis of c. 201–200 BCE, and the Rise of Rome'. In Kaufman, Little and Wohlforth (2007).

Eckstein, A. M. (2008) *Rome Enters the East: From Anarchy to Hierarchy in the Hellenistic Mediterranean, 230–170BC*. Oxford: Blackwell.

Edgington, S. B. and Lambert, S. (eds.) (2001) *Gendering the Crusades*. Cardiff: University of Wales Press.

Eisenstadt, S. (1963) *The Political System of Empires*. Glencoe: Free Press.

Eksteins, M. (1989) *Rites of Spring: The Great War and the Birth of the Modern Age*. London: Bantam.

Edgerton, S. Y. (1985) *Pictures and Punishment: Art and Criminal Prosecution During the Florentine Renaissance*. Ithaca: Cornell University Press.

Elden, S. and Mendieta, E. (eds.) (2011) *Reading Kant's Geography*. Albany: State University of Press.

Elias, N. (2006) 'The Expulsion of the Huguenots from France'. In Elias (2006a).

Elias, N. (2006a) *Early Writings*. Dublin: University College Dublin Press. [Collected Works, volume 1].

Elias, N. (2006b) *The Court Society*. Dublin: University College Dublin Press. [Collected Works, volume 2].

Elias, N. (2007) *Involvement and Detachment*. Dublin: University College Dublin Press. [Collected Works, volume 8].

Elias, N. (2007a) *An Essay on Time*. Dublin: University College Dublin Press. [Collected Works volume 9].

Elias, N. (2008) 'Technisation and Civilisation'. In Elias (2008h).

Elias, N. (2008a) 'Fear of Death'. In Elias (2008h).

Elias, N. (2008b) 'The Genesis of Sport as a Sociological Problem, Part 1'. In Elias and Dunning (2008a).

Elias, N. (2008c) 'Towards a Theory of Established-Outsider Relations'. In Elias and Scotson (2008).

Elias, N. (2008d) 'Further Aspects of Established-Outsider Relations: The Maycomb Model'. In Elias and Scotson (2008).

Elias, N. (2008e) 'The Genesis of Sport as a Sociological Problem, Part 2'. In Elias and Dunning (2008a).

Elias, N. (2008f) 'Towards a Theory of Communities'. In Elias (2008h).

Elias, N. (2008g) 'National Peculiarities of British Public Opinion'. In Elias (2008h).

Elias, N. (2008h) *On Civilising Processes, State Formation and National Identity (Essays II)*. Dublin: University College Dublin Press. [Collected Works, vol.15].

Elias, N. (2009) 'Figuration'. In Elias (2009f).

Elias, N. (2009a) 'Scientific Establishments'. In Elias (2009g).

Elias, N. (2009b) 'The Changing Balance of Power between the Sexes – a Process-Sociological Study: The Example of the Ancient Roman State'. In Elias (2009f).

Elias, N. (2009c) 'Thomas More and "Utopia"'. In Elias (2009g).

Elias, N. (2009d) 'Thomas More's Critique of the State: With Some Thoughts on a Definition of the Concept of Utopia'. In Elias (2009g).

Elias, N. (2009e) 'On the Sociogenesis of Sociology'. In Elias (2009f).

Elias, N. (2009f) *On Sociology and Humanities (Essays III)*. Dublin: University College Dublin Press [Collected Works, vol.16].

Elias, N. (2009g) *On The Sociology of Knowledge and the Sciences (Essays I)*. Dublin: University College Dublin Press. [Collected Works, volume 14].

Elias, N. (2010) 'The Fate of German Baroque Poetry: Between the Traditions of Court and Middle Class'. In Elias (2010a).

Elias, N. (2010a) *Mozart and Other Essays on Courtly Art*. Dublin: University College Dublin Press. [Collected Works, volume 12].

Elias, N. (2010b) *The Society of Individuals*. Dublin. University College Dublin Press. [Collected Works, volume. 10].

Elias, N. (2010c) *The Loneliness of the Dying and Humana Conditio*. Dublin: University College Dublin Press. [Collected Works, volume 6].

Elias, N. (2011) *The Symbol Theory*. Dublin: University College Dublin Press. [Collected Works, volume 13].

Elias, N. (2012) [1939] *On the Process of Civilization: Sociogenetic and Psychogenetic Investigations*. Dublin: University College Dublin Press. [Collected Works, volume 3].

Elias, N. (2013) *Studies on the Germans: Power Struggles and the Development of Habitus in the Nineteenth and Twentieth Centuries*. Dublin: University College Dublin Press. [Collected Works, volume 11].

Elias, N. (2013a) 'The Janus Face of States'. In Elias (2013f).

Elias, N. (2013b) 'An Interview in Amsterdam'. In Elias (2013f).

Elias, N. (2013c) 'Sociology as the History of Manners'. In Elias (2013f).

Elias, N. (2013d) 'We Need more Empathy for the Human Difficulties of the Process of Civilization'. In Elias (2013f).

Elias, N. (2013e) 'Knowledge and Power'. In Elias (2013f).

Elias, N. (2013f) *Interviews and Autobiographical Reflections*. Dublin: University College Dublin Press. [Collected Works, volume 17].

Elias, N. and Dunning, E. (2008) 'Leisure in the Sparetime Spectrum'. In Elias and Dunning (2008a).

Elias, N. and Dunning, E. (2008a) *Quest for Excitement: Sport and Leisure in the Civilising Process*. Dublin: University College Dublin Press. [Collected Works, volume 7].

Elias, N. and Scotson, J. (2008) *The Established and the Outsiders*. Dublin: University College Dublin Press. [Collected Works, volume 4].

Eliav-Feldon, M., Isaac, B. and Ziegler, J. (eds.) (2009) *The Origins of Racism in the West*. Cambridge: Cambridge University Press.

Elliott, J. H. (1970) *Imperial Spain 1469–1716*. Harmondsworth: Pelican.

Elshtain, J. B. (1987) *Women and War*. New York: Basic Books.

Emlyn-Jones, C., Hardwick, L. and Purkis, J. (eds.) (1992) *Homer: Readings and Images*. London: Duckworth.

Enemark, C. (2014) *Armed Drones and the Ethics of War: Military Virtue in a post-Heroic Age*. Abingdon: Routledge.

Epictetus, *The Discourses* (1959 edition translated by W. A. Oldfather). London: William Heinemann.

Erasmus, D. (1936) [1516] *The Education of a Christian Prince*. New York: Columbia University Press.

Erasmus, D. (1989) [1517] 'The Complaint of Peace'. In Erasmus (1989a).

Erasmus, D. (1989a) *The Praise of Folly and Other Writings* (translated by R. M. Adams). New York: W. W. Norton.

Erdkamp, P. (ed.) (2007) *A Companion to the Roman Army*. Oxford: Blackwell.

Erdmann, C. (1977) *The Origin of the Idea of Crusade*. Princeton: Princeton University Press.

Erskine, A. (1995) 'Rome in the Greek World: The Significance of a Name'. In Powell (1995).

Erskine, A. (ed.) (2005) *A Companion to the Hellenistic World*. Oxford: Blackwell.

Ertman, T. (1997) *Birth of the Leviathan: Building States and Regimes in Medieval and Early Modern Europe*. Cambridge: Cambridge University Press.

Esdaile, C. J. (1995) *The Wars of Napoleon*. London: Longman.

Evans, R. (1997) *Rituals of Retribution: Capital Punishment in Germany, 1600–1987*. Harmondsworth: Penguin.

Evans, R. J. (2003) *The Coming of the Third Reich*. London: Allen Lane.

Evans, R. J. (2005) *The Third Reich in Power: 1933–1939*. London: Allen Lane.

Faro, F. (2014) 'An Eliasian Approach to the Financial Crisis', paper presented at the conference, *Plunging into Turmoil: Social Sciences and the Crisis*, Superior Institute for Social and Political Sciences of the University of Lisbon, 16th–17th October.

Fear, A. (2007) 'War and Society'. In Sabin, van Wees and Whitby (2007a).

Feinberg, J. (1985) *Offence to Others: The Moral Limits of the Criminal Law*. Oxford: Oxford University Press.

Feichtinger, M., Malinowski, S. and Richards, C. (2012) 'Transformative Invasions: Western Post-9/11 Counterinsurgency and the Lessons of Colonialism', *Humanity: An International Journal of Human Rights, Humanitarianism, and Development*, 3 (1), 35–63.

Ferguson, J. (1958) *Moral Values in the Ancient World*. London: Methuen.

Ferguson, M. (1992) *Subject to Others: British Women Writers and Colonial Slavery, 1670–1834*. London: Routledge.

Ferguson, N. (1998) *The Pity of War*. London: Penguin Books.

Fernandez-Armesto, F. (1987) *Before Columbus: Exploration and Colonisation from the Mediterranean to the Atlantic, 1229–1492*. London: MacMillan.

Fernandez-Santamaria, J. A. (1977) *The State, War and Peace: Spanish Political Thought in the Renaissance, 1516–1559*. Cambridge: Cambridge University Press.

Fest, J. (1979) *The Face of the Third Reich*. London: Penguin.

Fest, J. (2001) *Speer: The Final Verdict*. London: Weidenfeld and Nicolson.

Fidler, D. P. (2000) 'A Kinder, Gentler System of Capitulations? International Law, Structural Adjustment Policies and the Standard of Liberal, Globalized Civilization', *Texas International Law Journal*, 35 (3), 387–414.

Fidler, D. P. and Welsh, J. M. (eds.) (1999) *Empire and Community: Edmund Burke's Writings and Speeches on International Relations*. Boulder, CO: Westview Press.

Fiedler, D. (2010) 'The Courtization of Ambassadors: The Figuration of Diplomacy in the Time of Jean Hotman, Marquis de Villiers-St. Paul, 1552–1636', accessed 3 March 2013 at www.jforward.org/June 2010.

Findlen, P. (2007) 'The Sun at the Center of the World'. In Martin (2007).

Fine R. (2001) 'Understanding Evil: Arendt and the Final Solution'. In Lara (2001).

Fine, R. and Turner, C. (eds.) (2000) *Social Theory after the Holocaust*. Liverpool: Liverpool University Press.

Finley, M. I. (1974) (ed.) *Studies in Ancient Society*. London: Routledge and Kegan Paul.

Finley, M. I. (1980) *Ancient Slavery and Modern Ideology*. London: Chatto and Windus.

Finnemore, M. (1999) 'Rules of War and Wars of Rules: The International Red Cross and the Restraint of State Violence'. In Boli and Thomas (1999).

Fischer, M. (1992) 'Feudal Europe, 800–1300: Communal Discourse and Conflictual Practices', *International Organization*, 46 (2), 427–66.

Fischer, M. (1993) 'On Contexts, Facts, and Norms: Response to Hall and Kratochwil', *International Organization*, 47 (3), 493–500.

Fisher, N. R. E. (1992) *Hybris: A Study in the Values of Honour and Shame in Ancient Greece*. Warminster: Aris and Philips.

Fisher, N. R. E. (1998) 'Violence, Masculinity and the Law in Athens'. In Foxhall and Salmon (1998).

Fitzpatrick, M., Jones, P. Knellwolf, C. and McCalman, I. (eds.) (2004) *The Enlightenment World*. Abingdon: Routledge.

Fletcher, A. (1995) *Gender, Sex and Subordination in England 1500–1800*. New Haven: Yale University Press.

Fletcher, J. (1997) *Violence and Civilisation: An Introduction to the Work of Norbert Elias*. Cambridge: Polity Press.

Flikschuh, K. and Ypi, L. (eds.) (2014) *Kant and Colonialism: Historical and Critical Perspectives*. Oxford: Oxford University Press.

Flower, H. I. (2004) 'Spectacle and Political Culture in the Roman Republic'. In Flower (2004a).

Flower, H. I. (ed.) (2004a) *The Cambridge Companion to the Roman Republic*. Cambridge: Cambridge University Press.

Foreman, P. G. (1996) *Criticism and the Color Line: Race and Revisionism in American Literary Studies*. New Brunswick: Rutgers University Press.

Forman-Barzilai, F. (2005) 'Sympathy in Space(s): Adam Smith on Proximity', *Political Theory*, 33 (2), 189–217.

Forman-Barzilai, F. (2010) *Adam Smith and the Circles of Sympathy: Cosmopolitanism and Moral Theory*. Cambridge: Cambridge University Press.

Forrest, A. (1997) 'The Nation in Arms I: The French Wars'. In Townsend (1997a).

Forrest, A. (2002) *Napoleon's Men: The Soldiers of the Revolution and Empire*. London: Hambledon and London.

Forrest, A., Haggeman, K. and Rendall, J. (eds.) (2009) *Soldiers, Citizens and Civilians: Experiences and Perceptions of the Revolutionary and Napoleonic Wars, 1790–1820*. Basingstoke: Palgrave MacMillan.

Forrest, W. G. (1968) *A History of Sparta: 950-192BC*. London: Hutchison.

Forsythe, D. P. (2009) *Encyclopaedia of Human Rights, volume one*. Oxford: Oxford University Press.

Foucault, M. (1973) *Madness and Civilization: A History of Insanity in the Age of Reason.* New York: Vintage Books.

Foucault, M. (1991) 'What Is Enlightenment?' In Rabinow (1991).

Foxhall, L. and Salmon, J. (eds.) (1998) *When Men Were Men: Masculinity, Power and Identity in Classical Antiquity.* London: Routledge.

France, J. (1999) *Western Warfare in Age of Crusades, 1000–1300.* Ithaca: Cornell University Press.

France, J. (2008) 'Siege Conventions in Western Europe and the Latin East'. In De Souza and France (2002).

Fraser, J. E. (2010) 'Early Medieval Europe: The Case of Britain and Ireland'. In Bloxham and Moses (2010).

Fraser, N. (2007) 'Transnationalizing the Public Sphere: On the Legitimacy and Efficacy of Public Opinion in a Post-Westphalian World', *Theory, Culture and Society,* 24 (4), 7–31.

Frassetto, M. (1998) 'Violence, Knightly Piety and the Peace of God Movement in Aquitaine'. In Kagay and Villalon (1998).

Frazer, M. L. (2010) *The Enlightenment of Sympathy: Justice and the Moral Sentiments in the Eighteenth Century and Today.* Oxford: Oxford University Press.

Freedman, L. (1998) 'The Revolution in Strategic Affairs'. *Adelphi Papers,* Issue 318.

Freedman, P. (1998) 'Peasant Anger in the Late Middle Ages'. In Rosenwein (1998).

Freeman, M. (1980) *Edmund Burke and the Critique of Political Radicalism.* Oxford: Basil Blackwell.

French, D. (1997) 'The Nation in Arms II: The Nineteenth Century'. In Townsend (1997a).

Freud, S. (1939) *Civilization and Its Discontents.* London: The Hogarth Press.

Freud, S. (2001) [1915] 'Thoughts for the Times on War and Death'. In Freud (2001a).

Freud, S. (2001a) *The Standard Edition of the Complete Psychological Works of Sigmund Freud,* volume 14. London: Vintage.

Frevert, U. (1998) 'The Taming of the Noble Ruffian: Male Violence and Duelling in Early Modern and Modern Germany'. In Spierenburg (1998a).

Friedlander, H. (1995) *The Origins of Nazi Genocide: From Euthanasia to the Final Solution.* Chapel Hill: The University of North Carolina Press.

Friedlander, S. (1997) *Nazi Germany and the Jews, Volume One: The Years of Persecution 1933–39.* London: Weidenfeld and Nicolson.

Friedman, Y. (1995) 'Women in Captivity and Their Ransom during the Crusader Period'. In Goodich, Menache and Schein (1995).

Friedman, Y. (2001) 'Captivity and Ransom: The Experience of Women'. In Edgington and Lambert (2001).

Frigo, D. (2000) '"Small States" and Diplomacy: Mantua and Montena'. In Frigo (2000a).

Frigo, D. (ed.) 2000a) *Politics and Diplomacy in Early Modern Italy: The Structure of Diplomatic Practice, 1450–1800.* Cambridge: Cambridge University Press.

Frigo, D. (2008) 'Prudence and Experience: Ambassadors and Political Culture in Early Modern Italy', *Journal of Medieval and Early Modern Studies*, 38 (1), 15–34.

Fronto, Marcellus Cornelius, *Correspondence* (1955 edition translated by C. R. Haines). London: William Heinemann.

Fubini, R. (1995) 'The Italian League and the Policy of the Balance of Power at the Accession of Lorenzo de' Medici', *Journal of Modern History*, 67 (supplement), 166–99.

Fulbrook, M. (ed.) (2007) *Un-Civilizing Processes? Excess and Transgression in German Society and Culture: Perspectives Debating with Norbert Elias.* Amsterdam: Rodopi.

Fuller, J. F. C. (1923) *The Reformation of War.* London: Hutchinson and co.

Fuller, J. F. C. (1972) *The Conduct of War.* London: Eyre Methuen.

Gabriel, N. and Mennell, S. (eds.) (2011) *Norbert Elias and Figurational Research: Processual Thinking in Sociology.* Oxford: Wiley-Blackwell.

Gagliardo, J. G. (1968) *Enlightened Despotism.* London: Routledge.

Gardiner, P. (ed.) (1965) *Theories of History.* New York: Free Press.

Garlan, Y. (1976) *War in the Ancient World: A Social History.* London: Chatto and Windus.

Garland, R. (1995) *The Eye of the Beholder: Deformity and Disability in the Graeco-Roman World.* Ithaca, NY: Cornell University Press.

Garnsey, P. (1974) 'Legal Privilege in the Roman Empire'. In Finley (1974).

Garnsey, P. (2004) 'Roman Citizenship and Roman Law in the Late Empire'. In Swain and Edwards (2004).

Garnsey, P. D. A. and Whittaker, C. R. (eds.) (1978) *Imperialism in the Ancient World.* Cambridge: Cambridge University Press.

Garrett, A. (2003) 'Anthropology: The "Original" of Human Nature'. In Broadie (2003).

Garrett, S. A. (1993) *Ethics and Airpower in World War II: The British Bombing of German Cities.* New York: St. Martin's Press.

Gat, A. (2001) *A History of Military Thought: From the Enlightenment to the Cold War.* Oxford: Oxford University Press.

Gat, A. (2006) *War in Human Civilization.* Oxford: Oxford University Press.

Gates, H. L. and Andrews, W. L. (eds.) (1998) *Pioneers of the Black Atlantic: Five Slave Narratives from the Enlightenment 1772–1815.* Washington: Civitas.

Gay, P. (1964) *The Party of Humanity: Studies in the French Enlightenment.* London: Weidenfeld and Nicolson.

Gay, P. (1967) *The Enlightenment: An Interpretation. Volume 1: The Rise of Modern Paganism.* London: Weidenfeld and Nicolson.

Gay, P. (1969) *The Enlightenment: An Interpretation. Volume 2: The Science of Freedom.* London: Weidenfeld and Nicholson.

Geary, P. J. (1994) 'Living with Conflicts in Stateless France: A Typology of Conflict Management Mechanisms, 1050–1200'. In Geary (1994a).

Geary, P. J. (1994a) *Living with the Dead in the Middle Ages*. Ithaca: Cornell University Press.

Gellately, R. (2001) *Backing Hitler: Consent and Coercion in Nazi Germany*. Oxford: Oxford University Press.

Geras, N. (1995) *Solidarity in the Conversation of Humankind: The Ungroundable Liberalism of Richard Rorty*. London: Verso.

Geras, N. (1998) *The Contract of Mutual Indifference: Political Philosophy after the Holocaust*. London: Verso.

Geras, N. (2000) 'Four Assumptions about Human Nature'. In Geras and Wokler (2000).

Geras, N. and Wokler, R. (eds.) (2000) *The Enlightenment and Modernity*. Basingstoke: Macmillan.

Geremek, B. (1990) 'The Marginal Man'. In Le Goff (1990).

Gerth, H. H. and Mills, C. W. (eds.) (1948) *From Max Weber: Essays in Sociology*. London: Routledge and Kegan Paul.

Gerwarth, R. (2011) *Hitler's Hangman: The Life of Heydrich*. London: Yale University Press.

Giardina, A. (ed.) (1993) *The Romans*. Chicago: University of Chicago Press.

Gibson, C. (1966) *Spain in America*. New York: Harper.

Gilbert, F. (1943) 'Machiavelli: The Renaissance of the Art of War'. In Earle (1943).

Gilbert, F. (1965) *Machiavelli and Guicciardini: Politics and History in Sixteenth Century Florence*. Princeton: Princeton University Press.

Gill, S. (1995) 'Globalisation, Market Civilisation and Disciplinary Neoliberalism', *Millennium*, 24 (3), 399–423.

Gill, S. (ed.) (2012) *Global Crises and the Crisis of Global Leadership*. Cambridge: Cambridge University Press.

Gillingham, J. (1992) 'The Beginnings of English Imperialism', *Journal of Historical Sociology*, 5 (4), 392–409.

Gillingham, J. (2001) 'Civilizing the English: The English Histories of William of Malmesbury and David Hume', *Historical Research*, 74 (183), 17–43.

Gillingham, J. (2002) 'From *Civilitas* to Civility: Codes of Manners in Medieval and Early Modern Europe', *Transactions of the Royal Historical Society, Sixth Series*, 12, 267–89.

Gillis, J. R. (ed.) (1989) *The Militarization of the Western World*. New Brunswick: Rutgers University Press.

Gilliver, C. M. (1996) 'The Roman Army and Morality in War'. In Lloyd (1996).

Gilliver, C. M. (1999) *The Roman Art of War*. Stroud: Tempus.

Gilliver, C. M. (2007) 'Battle'. In Sabin, van Wees and Whitby (2007a).

Glanville, L. (2013) 'The Myth of "Traditional" Sovereignty', *International Studies Quarterly*, 55 (1), 79–90.

Glete, J. (1999) 'Warfare at Sea, 1450–1815'. In Black (1999).

Goebel, S. (2012) 'Britain's "Last Crusade": From War Propaganda to War Commemoration, c. 1914–1930'. In Welch and Fox (2012).

Goetz, H.-W. (1992) 'Protection of the Church, Defense of the Law, and Reform: On the Purposes and Character of the Peace of God, 989–1038'. In Head and Landes (1992).

Goffman, D. (2007) 'The Ottoman Empire'. In Martin (2007).

Goldhagen, D. J. (1996) *Hitler's Willing Executioners: Ordinary Germans and the Holocaust*. London: Little, Brown.

Goldhagen, D. J. (2002) *A Moral Reckoning: The Role of the Catholic Church in the Holocaust and Its Unfulfilled Duty of Repair*. London: Little, Brown.

Goldsworthy, A. (2007) 'War'. In Sabin, van Wees and Whitby (2007a).

Gong, G. W. (1984) *The Standard of 'Civilization' in International Society*. Oxford: Clarendon Press.

Goodich, M., Menache, S. and Schein, S. (eds.) (1995) *Cross-Cultural Convergences in the Crusader Period*. New York: Peter Lang.

Goodman, D. (1994) *The Republic of Letters: A Cultural History of the French Enlightenment*. Ithaca: Cornell University Press.

Goodman, M. D. and Holladay, A. J. (1986) 'Religious Scruples in Ancient Warfare', *The Classical Quarterly*, 36 (1), 151–71.

Goody, J. (2010) *Renaissances: The One or the Many?* Cambridge: Cambridge University Press.

Gordon, S. A. (1984) *Hitler, Germans and the 'Jewish Question'*. Princeton: Princeton University Press.

Gordon, D. (1994) *Citizens without Sovereignty: Equality and Sociability in French Thought, 1670–1789*. Princeton: Princeton University Press.

Gordon, R. S. C. (2001) *Primo Levi's Ordinary Virtues: From Testimony to Ethics*. Oxford: Oxford University Press.

Gorski, P. S. (2003) *The Disciplinary Revolution: Calvinism and the Rise of the State in Early Modern Europe*. Chicago: Chicago University Press.

Goudsblom, J. (2004) 'Christian Religion and the European Civilizing Process: The Views of Norbert Elias and Max Weber Compared in the Context of the Augustinian and Lucretian Traditions'. In Loyal and Quilley (2004).

Goudsblom, J., Jones, E. and Mennell, S. (1996) *The Course of Human History: Economic Growth, Social Process, and Civilization*. London: M. E. Sharpe.

Goveia, E. V. (2000) 'The West Indian Slave Laws of the Eighteenth Century'. In Shepherd and Beckles (2000).

Grafton, A. (1991) 'Humanism and Political Theory'. In Burns and Goldie (1991).

Grayling, A. C. (2006) *Among the Dead Cities: Was the Allied Bombing of Civilians in WWII a Necessity or a Crime?* London: Bloomsbury.

Green, L. C. and Dickason, O. P. (1989) *The Law of Nations and the New World*. Edmonton: The University of Alberta Press.

Green, P. (1990) *Alexander to Actium: The Historical Evolution of the Hellenistic Age*. Berkeley: University of California Press.

Green, P. (ed.) (1993) *Hellenistic History and Culture*. Berkeley: University of California Press.

Green, W. A. (1976) *British Slave Emancipation: The Sugar Colonies and the Great Experiment, 1830–1865*. Oxford: Clarendon Press.

Green, W. A. (1987) 'Race and Slavery: Considerations on the Williams Thesis'. In Solow and Engerman (1987).

Greenblatt, S. (1982) 'Filthy Rites', *Daedalus*, 111 (3), 1–16.

Greenblatt, S. (2011) *The Swerve: How the Renaissance Began*. London: Bodley Head.

Greenfield, L. (1992) *Nationalism: Five Roads to Modernity*. Cambridge, MA: Harvard University Press.

Greenstein, F. I. and Polsby, N. W. (eds.) (1975) *Handbook of Political Science, volume 3, Macropolitical Theory*. Reading, MA: Addison-Wesley.

Griffin, M. (2000) 'Seneca and Pliny'. In Rowe and Schofield (2000).

Grimsley, M. and Rogers, C. J. (eds.) (2002) *Civilians in the Path of War*. Lincoln: University of Nebraska Press.

Griswold, C. L. (1999) *Adam Smith and the Virtues of Enlightenment*. Cambridge: Cambridge University Press.

Grodin, M. A. (1992) 'Historical Origins of the Nuremberg Code'. In Annas and Grodin (1992).

Grubb, J. S. (1991) 'Diplomacy in the Italian City-State'. In Molho, Raaflaub and Emlen (1991).

Gruen, E. S. (1984) *The Hellenistic World and Coming of Rome: volumes one and two*. Berkeley: University of California Press.

Guicciardini, F. (1969) [1561] *A History of Italy*. London: Collier-Macmillan.

Gunn, S. (1999) 'War, Religion, and the State'. In Cameron (1999).

Gutmann, M. P. (1980) *War and Rural Life in the Early Modern Low Countries*. Princeton: Princeton University Press.

Haar, E. van de (2009) *Classical Liberalism and International Relations Theory: Hume, Smith, Mises, and Hayek*. Basingstoke: Palgrave MacMillan.

Haar, E. van de (2010) 'The Liberal Divide over Trade, Peace and War', *International Relations*, 24 (2), 132–54.

Hadley, D. M. (ed.) (1999) *Masculinity in Medieval Europe*. London: Longman.

Hagemann, K. (2009) '"Unimaginable Horror and Misery": The Battle of Leipzig in October 1813 in Civilian Experience and Perception'. In Forrest, Hagemann and Rendall (2009).

Hahm, D. E. (2000) 'Kings and Constitutions: Hellenistic Theories'. In Rowe and Schofield (2000).

Hale, J. R. (1960) 'War and Public Opinion in Renaissance Italy'. In Jacob (1960).

Hale, J. R. (ed.) (1973) *Renaissance Venice*. London: Faber and Faber.

Hale, J. R. (ed.) (1981) *A Concise Encyclopaedia of the Italian Renaissance*. London: Thames and Hudson.

Hale, J. R. (1993) *The Civilization of Europe in the Renaissance*. London: HarperCollins.

Hale, J. R. (1998) *War and Society in Renaissance Europe, 1450–1620*. Stroud: Sutton Publishing.

Hall, C. (2002) *Civilising Subjects: Metropole and Colony in the English Imagination 1830–1867*. Cambridge: Polity Press.

Hall, E. (1989) *Inventing the Barbarian: Greek Self-Definition through Tragedy*. Oxford: Clarendon Press.

Hall, E. (1993) 'Asia Unmanned: Images of Victory in Classical Athens'. In Rich and Shipley (1993).

Hall, E. (2010) *Greek Tragedy: Suffering under the Sun*. Oxford: Oxford University Press.

Hall, J. A. (ed.) (1986) *States in History*. Oxford: Basil Blackwell.

Hall, J. M. (1997) *Ethnic Identity in Greek Antiquity*. Cambridge: Cambridge University Press.

Hall, M and Hobson, J. (ed.) (2010) 'Liberal International Theory: Eurocentric But Not Always Imperialist', *International Theory*, 2 (2), 210–45.

Hall, R. B. and Biersteker, T. J. (eds.) (2002) *The Emergence of Private Authority in Global Governance*. Cambridge: Cambridge University Press.

Hall, R. B. and Kratochwil, F. V. (1993) 'Medieval Tales: Neorealist "Science" and the Abuse of History', *International Organization*, 47 (3), 479–91.

Hall, W. E. (1924) *A Treatise on International Law*. Oxford: Clarendon Press.

Halsall, G. (1998) 'Violence and Society in the Early Medieval West: An Introductory Survey'. In Halsall (1998a).

Halsall, G. (ed.) (1998a) *Violence and Society in the Early Medieval West*. London: Boydell Press.

Hamilton, B. (1963) *Political Thought in Sixteenth Century Spain: A Study of the Political Ideas of Vitoria, Soto, Suarez and Molina*. Oxford: Clarendon Press.

Hamilton, C. D. (1999) 'The Hellenistic World'. In Raaflaub and Rosenwein (1999).

Hamilton, J. R. (1973) *Alexander the Great*. London: Hutchinson.

Hammond, N. G. L (1967) *A History of Greece to 322BC*. Oxford: Clarendon Press.

Hammond, N. G. L. (1989) *The Macedonian State: The Origins, Institutions and History*. Oxford: Clarendon Press.

Hammond, N. G. L. (1993) 'The Macedonian Imprint on the Hellenistic World'. In Green (1993).

Hammond, N. G. L. and Griffith, G. T. (1979) *A History of Macedonia: Volume Two, 550–336 BC*. Oxford: Clarendon Press.

Hampson, N. (1968) *The Enlightenment: The Pelican History of European Thought 4*. Harmondsworth: Penguin.

Hampson, N. (1981) 'The Enlightenment in France'. In Porter and Teich (1981).

Hampson, N. (1999) 'The Enlightenment'. In Cameron (1999).

Hanke, L. (1965) *The Spanish Struggle for Justice in the Conquest of America*. Boston: Little, Brown.

Hanke, L. (1970) *Aristotle and the American Indians: A Study in Race Prejudice in the Modern World*. Bloomington: Indiana University Press.

Hankins, J. (1996) 'Humanism and the Origins of Modern Political Thought'. In Kraye (1996).

Hankins, J. (ed.) (2000) *Renaissance Civic Humanism: Reappraisals and Reflections*. Cambridge: Cambridge University Press.

Hanley, R. P. (2009) *Adam Smith and the Character of Virtue*. Cambridge: Cambridge University Press.

Hannaford, I. (1996) *Race: The History of an Idea in the West*. Baltimore: The Johns Hopkins University Press.

Hanson, V. D. (1989) *The Western Way of War: Infantry Battle in Classical Greece*. New York: Hodder and Stoughton.

Hanson, V. D. (ed.) (1991) *Hoplites: The Classical Greek Battle Experience*. London: Routledge.

Hanson, V. D. (1995) *The Other Greeks: The Family Farm and the Agrarian Roots of Western Civilization*. London: The Free Press.

Hanson, V. D. (1998) *Warfare and Agriculture in Classical Greece*. Berkeley: University of California Press.

Hanson, V. D. (1999) 'Hoplite Obliteration: The Case of the Town of Thespiae'. In Carman and Harding (1999).

Hanson, V. D. (2001) *Why the West Has Won: Carnage and Culture from Salamis to Vietnam*. London: Faber and Faber.

Hardie, P. (2007) 'Images of the Persian Wars in Rome'. In Bridges, Hall and Rhodes (2007).

Hardwick, L. (1992) 'Convergence and Divergence in Reading Homer'. In Emlyn-Jones, Hardwick and Purkis (1992).

Harre, R. and Parrott, W. G. (eds.) (1996) *The Emotions: Social, Cultural and Biological Dimensions*. London: Sage.

Harris, A. (1947) *Bomber Offensive*. London: Collins.

Harris, W. V. (1979) *War and Imperialism in Republican Rome, 327–70 BC*. Oxford: Clarendon Press.

Harris, W. V. (1982) 'The Theoretical Possibility of Extensive Infanticide in the Graeco-Roman World', *Classical Quarterly*, 32 (1), 114–16.

Harris, W. V. (2001) *Restraining Rage: The Ideology of Anger Control in Classical Antiquity*. Cambridge, MA: Harvard University Press.

Hartmann, A. V. and Heuser, B. (eds.) (2001) *War, Peace and World Orders in European History*. London: Routledge.

Hartog, F. (1988) *The Mirror of Herodotus: The Representation of the Other in the Writing of History*. Berkeley: University of California Press.

Haskell, T. L. (1985) 'Capitalism and the Origins of the Humanitarian Sensibility', *American Historical Review*, 90 (2), 339–61 and 547–66.

Hay, D. (1977) *The Italian Renaissance in Its Historical Background*. Cambridge: Cambridge University Press.

Hay, D. and Law, J. (1989) *Italy in the Age of the Renaissance, 1380–1530*. London: Longman.

Hayes, P. (1987) *Industry and Ideology: IG Farben in the Nazi Era*. Cambridge: Cambridge University Press.

Hayes, P. (1995) 'Profits and Persecution: Corporate Involvement in the Holocaust'. In Pacy and Wertheimer (1995).

Hayes, P. and Roth, J. K. (eds.) (2010) *The Oxford Handbook of Holocaust Studies*. Oxford: Oxford University Press.

Head, T. and Landes, R. (eds.) (1992) *The Peace of God: Social Violence and Religious Response in France around the Year 1000*. Ithaca: Cornell University Press.

Headley, J. (2002) 'The Universalizing Principle and Process: On the West's Intrinsic Commitment to a Global Context', *Journal of World History*, 13 (2), 291–321.

Heath, P. (1995) 'War and Peace in the Works of Erasmus: A Medieval Perspective'. In Ayton and Price (1995).

Heins, V. (2008) *NonGovernmental Organisations in International Society: Struggles over Recognition*. Basingstoke: Palgrave MacMillan.

Hellmuth, E. (2004) 'Enlightenment and Government'. In Fitzpatrick, Jones, Knellwolf and McCalman (2004).

Hemming, J. (1983) *The Conquest of the Incas*. Harmondsworth: Penguin.

Hen, Y. (2011) *Roman Barbarians: The Royal Court and Culture in the Early Medieval West*. Basingstoke: Palgrave Macmillan.

Henshall, N. (2010) *The Zenith of European Monarchy and Its Elites: The Politics of Culture, 1650–1750*. Basingstoke: Palgrave Macmillan.

Herbert, U. (ed.) (2000) *National Socialist Extermination Policies: Contemporary Perspectives and Controversies*. Oxford: Berghahn Books.

Herf, J. (1984) *Reactionary Modernism: Technology, Culture, and Politics in Weimar and the Third Reich*. Cambridge: Cambridge University Press.

Herman, G. (1987) *Ritualised Friendship and the Greek City*. Cambridge: Cambridge University Press.

Herman, G. (1997) 'The Court Society of the Hellenistic Age'. In Cartledge, Garnsey and Gruen (1997).

Herman, G. (2006) *Morality and Behaviour in Democratic Athens: A Social History*. Cambridge: Cambridge University Press.

Herodotus, *The Persian Wars* (1950 edition translated by A. D. Godley). Cambridge, MA: Harvard University Press.

Herzog, D. (ed.) (2008) *Brutality and Desire: War and Sexuality in Europe's Twentieth Century*. Basingstoke: Palgrave MacMillan.

Heskel, J. (1997) 'Macedonia and the North, 400–336'. In Tritle (1997).

Heuser, B. (2002) *Reading Clausewitz*. London: Pimlico.

Heuser, B., and Hartmann, A. V. (2001) 'Conclusions'. In Hartmann and Heuser (2001).

Hewitson, M. (2007) 'Violence and Civilization: Transgression in Modern Wars'. In Fulbrook (2007).

Hilberg, R. (1985) *The Destruction of the European Jews*. New York: Holmes and Meier.

Himmelfarb, G. (2005) *The Roads to Modernity: The British, French, and American Enlightenments*. New York: Alfred A. Knopf.

Himmelfarb, G. (2007) *Victorian Essays*. Yale: Sheridan Press.

Hingley, R. (2005) *Globalizing Roman Culture: Unity, Diversity and Empire*. Abingdon: Routledge.

Hinnells, J. R. and Porter, R. (eds.) (1999) *Religion, Health and Suffering*. London: Kegan Paul International.

Hinsley, F. H. (1986) *Sovereignty*. Cambridge: Cambridge University Press.

Hintze, O. (1975) *Historical Essays* (edited with an introduction by Felix Gilbert). New York: Oxford University Press.

Hirschman, A. O. (1977) *The Passions and the Interests: Political Arguments for Capitalism Before Its Triumph*. Princeton: Princeton University Press.

Hobson, C. (2008) 'Democracy as "Civilization"', *Global Society*, 22 (1), 75–95.

Hobson, J. M. (2004) *The Eastern Origins of Western Civilization*. Cambridge: Cambridge University Press.

Hobson, J. M. (2012) *The Eurocentric Conception of World Politics: Western International Theory, 1760–2010*. Cambridge: Cambridge University Press.

Hochstrasser, T. J. and Schröder, P. (eds.) (2003) *Early Modern Natural Law Theories: Contexts and Strategies in the Early Enlightenment*. Dordrecht: Kluwer Academic Publications

Hodgen, M. T. (1964) *Early Anthropology in the Sixteenth and Seventeenth Centuries*. Philadelphia: University of Pennsylvania Press.

Hoess, R. (2000) *Commandant of Auschwitz: The Autobiography of Rudolf Hoess*. London: Phoenix.

Holbach, Baron d' (1999) [1770] *The System of Nature, volume one*. Manchester: Clinamen Press.

Holmes, G. (ed.) (1998) *The Oxford Illustrated History of Medieval Europe*. Oxford: Oxford University Press.

Holmes, S. (2007) *The Matador's Cape: America's Reckless Response to Terror*. Cambridge: Cambridge University Press.

Holsti, K. (2004) *Taming the Sovereigns: Institutional Change in International Politics*. Cambridge: Cambridge University Press.

Homer, *The Iliad* (1950 edition translated by E. V. Rieu). Harmondsworth: Penguin.

Honig, J. W. (2001) 'Warfare in the Middle Ages'. In Hartmann and Heuser (2001).

Hooft, S. van and Vandekerckhove, W. (eds.) (2010) *Questioning Cosmopolitanism*. Dordrecht: Springer.

Hook, J. (2004) *The Sack of Rome, 1527*. London: Palgrave Macmillan.

hooks, b. (1982) *Ain't I a Woman: Black Women and Feminism*. London: Pluto Press.

Hopkins, K. (1978) *Conquerors and Slaves: Sociological Studies in Roman History: volume 1*. Cambridge: Cambridge University Press.

Hopkins, K. (1983) *Death and Renewal: Sociological Studies in Roman History: volume 2*. Cambridge: Cambridge University Press.

Horkheimer, M. and Adorno, T. W. (1973) *Dialectic of Enlightenment*. London: Allen Lane.

Hornblower, S. (1987) *Thucydides*. London: Duckworth.

Hörnqvist, M. (2000) 'The Two Myths of Civic Humanism'. In Hankins (2000).

Hörnqvist, M. (2012) 'Machiavelli's Three Desires: Florentine Republicans on Liberty, Empire and Justice'. In Muthu (2012).

Housley, N. (2000) 'Pro Deo et Patria Mori: Sanctified Patriotism in Europe, 1400–1600'. In Contamine (2000).

Housley, N. (2002) *The Crusaders*. Stroud: Tempus.

Housley, N. (2002a) 'Crusades against Christians: Their Origins and Early Development, c. 1000–1216'. In Madden (2002).

Howard, M. (1978) *War and the Liberal Conscience*. London: Temple Smith.

Howard. M. (1983) *Clausewitz*. Oxford: Oxford University Press.

Howard, M. (1994) 'Constraints on Warfare'. In Howard, Andreopoulos and Shulman (1994).

Howard, M., Andreopoulos, G. J. and Shulman, M. R. (eds.) (1994) *The Laws of War: Constraints on Warfare in the Western World*. New Haven: Yale University Press.

Hughes, R. (2003) *Goya*. London: Harvill.

Huizinga, J. (1955) *The Waning of the Middle Ages: A Study of the Forms of Life, Thought, and Art in France and the Netherlands in the Fourteenth and Fifteenth Centuries*. Harmondsworth: Penguin.

Hume, D. (1821) [1775] *The History of England from the Invasion of Caesar to the Revolution in 1688*. Philadelphia: Edward Parker.

Hume, D. (1875) [1777] 'The Balance of Power'. In Hume (1875a).

Hume, D. (1875a) [1777] *Essays: Moral, Political and Literary* (edited by T. H. Green and T. H. Grose). London: Longmans, Green.

Hume, D. (1875b) [1777] 'Of the Rise and Progress of the Arts and Sciences'. In Hume (1875a).

Hume, D. (1875c) [1777] 'Of National Characters'. In Hume (1875a).

Hume, D. (1875d) [1777] 'Of the Dignity or Meanness of Human Nature'. In Hume (1875a).

Hume, D. (1875e) [1777] 'The Sceptic'. In Hume (1875a).

Hume, D. (1875f) [1777] 'Of Commerce'. In Hume (1875a).

Hume, D. (1875g) [1777] 'Of Suicide'. In Hume (1882).

Hume, D. (1969) [1739/40] *A Treatise of Human Nature*. Harmondsworth: Penguin.

Hume, D. (1975) [1748] 'An Enquiry Concerning Human Understanding'. In Hume (1975a).

Hume, D. (1975) [1751] 'An Enquiry Concerning the Principles of Morals'. In Hume (1975a).

Hume, D. (1975a) *Enquiries Concerning Human Understanding and Concerning the Principles of Morals*. Oxford: Clarendon Press.

Humphries, M. (2007) 'International Relations'. In Sabin, van Wees and Whitby (2007a).

Hunt, P. (2010) *War, Peace, and Alliance in Demosthenes' Athens*. Cambridge: Cambridge University Press.

Hunting, C. (1978) 'The *Philosophes* and Black Slavery, 1748–1765', *Journal of the History of Ideas*, 39 (3), 405–18.

Hurrell, A. (2007) *On Global Order: Power, Values and the Constitution of International Society*. Oxford: Oxford University Press.

Hurwitz, E. F. (1973) *Politics and the Public Conscience: Slave Emancipation and the Abolitionist Movement in Britain*. London: George Allen and Unwin.

Hyams, P. (1998) 'What Did Henry III of England Think in Bed and in French about Kingship and Anger?' In Rosenwein (1998).

Hynes, S. (1998) *The Soldiers' Tale: Bearing Witness to Modern War*. London: Pimlico.

Ikenberry, G. J. (2001) *After Victory: Institutions, Strategic Restraint, and the Rebuilding of Order after Major Wars*. Princeton: Princeton University Press.

Ilardi, V. (1986) 'The Italian League, Francesco Sforza, and Charles VII (1454–1461)'. In Ilardi (1986a).

Ilardi, V. (1986a) *Studies in Italian Renaissance Diplomatic History*. London: Variorum Reprints.

Immerwahr, J. (1992) 'Hume's Revised Racism', *Journal of the History of Ideas*, 53 (3), 481–6.

International Commission on Intervention and State Sovereignty (2001) *The Responsibility to Protect*. Ottawa: International Development Research Centre.

Isaac, B. H. (2004) *The Invention of Racism in Classical Antiquity*. Princeton: Princeton University Press.

Isocrates, *Oration to Philip*. The Loeb Classical Library (vol. 1, 1928 edition translated by G. Norlin). London: William Heinemann.

Isocrates, *Panegyricus*. The Loeb Classical Library (vol. 1. 1928a edition translated by G. Norlin). London: William Heinemann.

Israel, J. I. (2006) *Enlightenment Contested: Philosophy, Modernity, and the Emancipation of Man 1670–1752*. Oxford: Oxford University Press.

Jackson, A. (1993) 'War and Raids for Booty in the World of Odysseus'. In Rich and Shipley (1993).

Jackson, C. (2004) 'Progress and Optimism'. In Fitzpatrick, Jones, Knellwolf and McCalman (2004).

Jackson, P. T. (2006) *Civilizing the Enemy: German Reconstruction and the Invention of the West*. Michigan: University of Michigan.

Jackson, R. (ed.) (1999) *Sovereignty at the Millennium*. Oxford: Blackwell.

Jackson, R. (2000) *The Global Covenant: Human Conduct in a World of States*. Oxford: Oxford University Press.

Jacob, E. F. (ed.) (1960) *Italian Renaissance Studies*. London: Faber and Faber.

Jacoby, T. (2011) 'Islam, Violence and the New Barbarism'. In Crook, Gill and Taithe (2011).

Jaeger, C. S. (1985) *The Origins of Courtliness: Civilizing Trends and the Formation of Courtly Ideas, 939–1210*. Philadelphia: University of Pennsylvania Press.

James, A. (1986) *Sovereign Statehood: The Basis of International Society*. London: Allen and Unwin.

Jarausch, K. H. (2006) *After Hitler: Recivilizing Germans, 1945–95*. Oxford: Oxford University Press.

Jaspers, K. (1947) *The Question of German Guilt*. New York: Dial Press.

Jervis, R. (2011) 'Force in Our Times', *International Relations*, 25 (4): 403–25.

Johns, A. (ed.) (1999) *Dreadful Visitations: Confronting Natural Catastrophe in the Age of Enlightenment*. London: Routledge.

Johnson, E. and Reuband, K-H. (2005) *What We Knew: Terror, Mass Murder and Everyday Life in Nazi Germany*. London: John Murray.

Johnson, E. N. (1975) 'The German Crusade on the Baltic'. In Setton (1975).

Johnson, J. T. (1981) *Just War Tradition and the Restraint of War: A Moral and Historical Inquiry*. Princeton: Princeton University Press.

Johnson, J. T. (1987) *The Quest for Peace: Three Moral Traditions in Western Cultural History*. Princeton: Princeton University Press.

Jonas, H. (1984) *The Imperative of Responsibility: In Search of an Ethics for the Technological Age*. London: University of Chicago Press.

Jonas, H. (1996) *Mortality and Morality: A Search for the Good after Auschwitz*. Evanston, IL: Northwestern University Press.

Jones, L. (ed.) (2005) *Encyclopaedia of Religion, volume 6*. Detroit: Thomson Gale.

Jones, W. R. (1971) 'The Image of the Barbarian in Medieval Europe', *Comparative Studies in Society and History*, 13 (4), 376–407.

Jordan, W. D. (1969) *White over Black: American Attitudes toward the Negro, 1550–1812*. Baltimore: Penguin.

Jouanna, J. (1999) *Hippocrates*. Baltimore: The Johns Hopkins University Press.

Kaeuper, R. W. (1999) *Chivalry and Violence in Medieval Europe*. Oxford: Oxford University Press.

Kaeuper, R. W. (2000) 'Chivalry and the "Civilizing Process"'. In Kaeuper (2000a).

Kaeuper, R. W. (ed.) (2000a) *Violence in Medieval Society*. Woodbridge: The Boydell Press.

Kagan, D. (ed.) (1975) *Studies in the Greek Historians, volume 24 of Yale Classical Studies*. Cambridge: Cambridge University Press.

Kagan, D. (2003) *The Peloponnesian War*. New York: Viking.

Kagay, D. J. (1998) 'The Iberian Diffidamentum: From Vassalic Defiance to the Code Duello'. In Kagay and Villalon (1998).

Kagay, D. J. and Villalon, L. J. A. (eds.) (1998) *The Final Argument: The Imprint of Violence on Society in Medieval and Early Modern Europe*. Woodbridge: Boydell Press.

Kahler, M. and Lake, D. A. (2009) 'Economic Integration and Global Governance: Why so Little Supranationalism?' In Mattli and Woods (2009).

Kaimio, M. (1992) 'Violence in Greek Tragedy'. In Viljamaa, Timonen and Krotzl (1992).

Kalmo, H. and Skinner, Q. (eds.) (2010) *Sovereignty in Fragments: The Past, Present and Future of a Contested Concept*. Cambridge: Cambridge University Press.

Kampmann, C. (2010) 'Peace Impossible? The Holy Roman Empire and the European State-System in the Seventeenth Century'. In Asbach and Schröder (2010).

Kant, I. (1952) [1790] *The Critique of Judgment*. Oxford: Clarendon Press.

Kant, I. (1964) [1797] *The Doctrine of Virtue: Part Two of the Metaphysic of Morals*. Philadelphia: University of Pennsylvania Press.

Kant, I. (1978) [1798] *Anthropology from a Pragmatic Point of View*. London: Feffer and Simons.

Kant, I. (1991) [1781] 'Appendix from "The Critique of Pure Reason"'. In Reiss (1991).

Kant, I. (1991) [1784] 'An Answer to the Question, What Is Enlightenment?' In Reiss (1991).

Kant, I. (1991) [1784a] 'Idea for a Universal History with a Cosmopolitan Purpose'. In Reiss (1991).

Kant. I. (1991) [1792] 'On the Common Saying: "This May Be True in Theory, But It Does Not Apply in Practice"'. In Reiss (1991).

Kant, I. (1991) [1795] 'Perpetual Peace: A Philosophical Sketch'. In Reiss (1991).

Kant, I. (1991) [1797] 'The Metaphysics of Morals'. In Reiss (1991).

Kant. I. (1991) [1798] 'The Contest of Faculties: A Renewed Attempt to Answer the Question: "Is the Human Race Continually Improving?"'. In Reiss (1991).

Karavites, P. (1992) *Promise-Giving and Treaty-Making: Homer and the Near East*. Leiden: E. J. Brill.

Karras, R. M. (2003) *From Boys to Men: Formations of Masculinity in Late Medieval Europe*. Philadelphia: University of Pennsylvania Press.

Kaspersen, L. B. and Gabriel, N. (2008) 'The Importance of Survival Units for Norbert Elias's Figurational Perspective', *Sociological Review*, 56 (3), 370–83.

Kaster, R. A. (2005) *Emotion, Restraint and Community in Ancient Rome*. Oxford: Oxford University Press.

Katz, F. E. (1993) *Ordinary People and Extraordinary Evil: A Report on the Beguilings of Evil*. Albany: State University of New York Press.

Katz, S. T. (1994) *The Holocaust in Historical Context, Volume One: The Holocaust and Mass Death Before the Modern Age*. Oxford: Oxford University Press.

Katz, S. T. (2005) 'Holocaust: The Jewish Theological Responses'. In Jones (2005).

Kaufmann, C. D. and Pape, R. A. (1999) 'Explaining Costly International Moral Action: Britain's Sixty-Year Campaign against the Atlantic Slave Trade', *International Organization*, 53 (4), 631–68.

Kaufman, S. J., Little, R. and Wohlforth, W. C. (eds.) (2007) *The Balance of Power in World History*. Basingstoke: Palgrave Macmillan.

Keal, P. (2003) *European Conquest and the Rights of Indigenous Peoples: The Moral Backwardness of International Society*. Cambridge: Cambridge University Press.

Keck, M. and Sikkink, K. (1998) *Activists Beyond Borders: Advocacy Networks in International Politics*. Cornell: Cornell University Press.

Kedar, B. Z. (2002) 'The Subjected Muslims of the Frankish Levant'. In Madden (2002a).

Keegan, J. (1991) *The Face of Battle: A Study of Agincourt, Waterloo and the Somme*. London: Pimlico.

Keegan, J. (1994) *A History of Warfare*. London: Pimlico.

Keegan, J. (1999) *War and Our World*. London: Pimlico.

Keen, M. (1965) *The Laws of War in the Late Middle Ages*. London: Routledge and Kegan Paul.

Keen, M. (1976) 'Chivalry, Nobility, and the Man-at-Arms'. In Allmand (1976).

Keen, M. (1984) *Chivalry*. New Haven: Yale University Press.

Keen, M. (ed.) (1999) *Medieval Warfare: A History*. Oxford: Oxford University Press.

Keene, E. (2002) *Beyond the Anarchical Society: Grotius, Colonialism and Order in World Politics*. Cambridge: Cambridge University Press.

Keens-Soper, H. M. A. (1973) 'Francois de Callières and Diplomatic Theory', *Historical Journal*, 16 (3), 485–508.

Keens-Soper, H. M. A. (1997) 'Abraham de Wicquefort and Diplomatic Theory', *Diplomacy and Statecraft*, 8 (2), 16–30.

Keens-Soper, H. M. A. and Schweizer, K. W. (1983) 'Diplomatic Theory in the Ancien Regime'. In Callières (1983) [1716].

Keens-Soper, H. M. A. and Schweizer, K. W. (1983a) 'The Life and Work of Francois de Callières'. In Callières (1983) [1716].

Keller, A. (2006) 'Justice, Peace, and History: A Reappraisal'. In Allan and Keller (2006).

Kelman, H. C. and Hamilton, V. L. (1989) *Crimes of Obedience: Toward a Social Psychology of Authority and Responsibility*. New Haven: Yale University Press.

Kempers, B. (1992) *Painting, Power and Patronage: The Rise of the Professional Artist in the Italian Renaissance*. London: Allen Lane.

Keohane, R.O. (1984) *After Hegemony: Cooperation and Discord in the World Political Economy*. Princeton: Princeton University Press.

Keohane, R. O. (1986) 'Reciprocity in International Relations', *International Organization*, 40 (1), 1–27.

Keohane, R. O. (1989) *International Institutions and State Power: Essays in International Relations Theory*. Boulder, CO: Westview Press.

Kern, P. B. (1999) *Ancient Siege Warfare*. London: Souvenir Press.

Kershaw, I. (1983) *Popular Opinion and Political Dissent in the Third Reich: Bavaria 1933-1945*. Oxford: Clarendon Press.

Kershaw, I. (2000) *Hitler 1936-1945: Nemesis*. London: Allen Lane.

Kershaw, I. (2005) 'War and Political Violence in Twentieth-Century Europe', *Contemporary European History*, 14 (1), 107-23.

Kiernan, B. (2007) *Blood and Soil: A World History of Genocide and Extermination from Sparta to Darfur*. New Haven: Yale University Press.

Kiernan, V. (1998) *Colonial Empires and Armies, 1815-1960*. Stroud: Sutton Publishing.

Kilminster, R. (2007) *Norbert Elias: Post-Philosophical Sociology*. Abingdon: Routledge.

King, J. R. (1998) 'The Friar Tuck Syndrome: Clerical Violence and the Barons' War'. In Kagay and Villalon (1998).

Kingsbury, B. and Strauman, B. (2010) 'Introduction: The Roman Foundations of the Law of Nations'. In Kingsbury and Strauman (2010a).

Kingsbury, B. and Strauman, B. (eds.) (2010a) *The Roman Foundations of the Law of Nations: Alberico Gentili and the Justice of Empire*. Oxford: Oxford University Press.

Kinsman, R. S. (ed.) (1974) *The Darker Side of the Renaissance: Beyond the Fields of Reason*. Berkeley: University of California Press.

Klapisch-Zuber, C. (1990) 'Women and the Family'. In Le Goff (1990).

Klein, L. E. (1994) *Shaftesbury and the Culture of Politeness: Moral Discourse and Cultural Politics in Early Eighteenth Century England*. Cambridge: Cambridge University Press.

Klein, H. S. (1971) 'Anglicism, Catholicism and the Negro Slave'. In Lane (1971).

Kleingeld, P. (1999) 'Six Varieties of Cosmopolitanism in Late Eighteenth Century Germany', *Journal of the History of Ideas*, 60 (3), 505-24.

Kleingeld, P. (2014) 'Kant's Second Thoughts on Colonialism'. In Flikschuh and Ypi (2014).

Kleinschmidt, H. (2010) 'War, Diplomacy and the Ethics of Self-Constraint in the Age of Grotius'. In Asbach and Schroder (2010).

Knox, D. (1991) 'Disciplina: The Monastic and Clerical Origins of European Civility'. In Monsafani and Musto (1991).

Kobrak, C. and Schneider, A. H. (2004) 'Big Business and the Third Reich: An Appraisal of the Historical Arguments'. In Stone (2004).

Kohn, H. (1944) *The Idea of Nationalism*. New York: Macmillan.

Kokaz, N. (2001) 'Moderating Power: A Thucydidean Perspective', *Review of International Studies*, 27 (1), 27-49.

Kokaz, N. (2001a) 'Between Anarchy and Tyranny: Excellence and the Pursuit of Power and Peace in Ancient Greece', *Review of International Studies*, 27 (special issue), 91-118.

Konstan, D. (2001) *Pity Transformed*. London: Duckworth.

Konstan, D. (2005) 'Clemency as a Virtue', *Classical Philology*, 100 (4), 337–46.

Koonz, C. (2003) *The Nazi Conscience*. Cambridge, MA: Belknap Press.

Koskenniemi, M. (2001) *The Gentle Civilizer of Nations: The Rise and Fall of International Law, 1870–1960*. Cambridge: Cambridge University Press.

Kramer, A. (2007) *Dynamic of Destruction: Culture and Mass Killing in the First World War*. Oxford: Oxford University Press.

Krasner, S. D. (1999) *Sovereignty: Organized Hypocrisy*. Princeton: Princeton University Press.

Kraye, J. (ed.) (1996) *The Cambridge Companion to Renaissance Humanism*. Cambridge: Cambridge University Press.

Krentz, P. (1985) 'Casualties in Hoplite Battles', *Greek Roman and Byzantine Studies*, 26 (1), 13–20.

Krieger, L. (1970) *Kings and Philosophers, 1689–1789*. London: Weidenfeld and Nicolson.

Krieken, R. van (1990) 'Social Discipline and State Formation: Weber and Oestreich on the Historical Sociology of Subjectivity', *Amsterdams Sociologisch Tijdschrift*, 17 (1), 3–28.

Krieken, R. van (1998) *Norbert Elias*. London: Routledge.

Krieken, R. van (1999) 'The Barbarism of Civilization: Cultural Genocide and the "Stolen Generation"', *British Journal of Sociology*, 50 (2), 297–315.

Krieken, R. van (2011) 'Three Faces of Civilization: "In the Beginning All Was Ireland"'. In Gabriel and Mennell (2011).

Kristeller, P. (1972) *Renaissance Concepts of Man, and Other Essays*. New York: Harper and Row.

Kroener, B. R. (2000) 'The Modern State and Military Society in the Eighteenth Century'. In Contamine (2000a).

Kull, S. (2011) *Feeling Betrayed: The Roots of Muslim Anger at America*. Washington, DC: The Brookings Institution.

Kyle, D. G. (1998) *Spectacles of Death in Ancient Rome*. London: Routledge.

Laiou, A. E. (ed.) (1993) *Consent and Coercion to Sex and Marriage in Ancient and Medieval Societies*. Washington, DC: Dumbarton Oaks Research Library.

Landes, J. B. (2004) 'Republic Citizenship and Heterosocial Desire: Concepts of Masculinity in Revolutionary France'. In Dudink, Hagemann and Tosh (2004).

Lane, A. J. (ed.) (1971) *The Debate over Slavery: Stanley Elkins and His Critics*. Chicago: University of Illinois Press.

Lane, F. C. (1973) *Venice: A Maritime Republic*. Baltimore: The Johns Hopkins University Press.

Lara, M. P. (ed.) (2001) *Rethinking Evil: Contemporary Perspectives*. Berkeley: University of California Press.

Larkins, J. (2010) *From Hierarchy to Anarchy: Territory and Politics before Westphalia*. Basingstoke: Palgrave MacMillan.

Lateiner, D. (1977) 'Heralds and Corpses in Thucydides', *The Classical World*, 71 (2), 97–106.

Latham A. A. (2012) *Theorizing Medieval Geopolitics: War and World Order in the Age of the Crusades*. Abingdon: Routledge.

Lawrence, J. (2003) 'Forging a Peaceable Kingdom: War, Violence, and Fear of Brutalization in Post-First World Britain', *Journal of Modern History*, 75 (3), 557–89.

Lebow, R. N. (2003) *The Tragic Vision of Politics: Ethics, Interests and Orders*. Cambridge: Cambridge University Press.

Lebow, R. N. (2008) *A Cultural Theory of International Relations*. Cambridge: Cambridge University Press.

Lebow, R. N. (2010) 'The Past and Future of War', *International Relations*, 24 (3), 243–70.

Lebow, R. N. (2010a) *Why Nations Fight: Past and Future Motives for War*. Cambridge: Cambridge University Press.

Lefebvre, G. (1964) 'Enlightened Despotism'. In Lubasz (1964).

Le Goff, J. (1988) *Medieval Civilisation*. Oxford: Basil Blackwell.

Le Goff, J. (ed.) (1990) *Medieval Callings*. Chicago: The University of Chicago Press.

Lecky, W. E. H. (1913) [1869] *A History of European Morals: From Augustus to Charlemagne*. London: Longmans, Green and co.

Lefkovitz, E. (ed.) (1990) *Dimensions of the Holocaust*. Evanston, Illinois: Northwestern University Press.

Legro, J. W. (1995) *Cooperation under Fire: Anglo-American Restraint During World War II*. Ithaca: Cornell University Press.

Leira, H. (2008) 'Justus Lipsius, Political Humanism and the Disciplining of 17th Century Statecraft', *Review of International Studies*, 34 (4), 669–692.

Lendon, J. E. (1997) *Empire of Honour: The Art of Government in the Roman World*. Oxford: Oxford University Press.

Lendon, J. E. (2000) 'Homeric Vengeance and the Outbreak of Greek Wars'. In van Wees (2000).

Lendon, J. E. (2007) 'War and Society'. In Sabin, van Wees, and Whitby (2007a).

Lerner, R. (2001) 'The American Founders' Responsibility'. In Davis (2001a).

Lesaffer, R. (2002) '*Amicitia* in Renaissance Peace and Alliance Treaties, 1450–1530', *Journal of the History of International Law*, 4: 77–99.

Levene, M. (2005) *Genocide in the Age of the Nation-State, volume one: The Meaning of Genocide*. London: I. B. Tauris.

Levene, M. (2008) 'Empires, Native Peoples, and Genocides'. In Moses (2008b).

Levi, P. (1988) *The Drowned and the Saved*. London: Michael Joseph.

Levi, P. (1989) 'Against Pain'. In Levi (1989a).

Levi, P. (1989a) *Other People's Trades*. London: Michael Joseph.

Levi, P. (1997) *The Mirror Maker*. London: Abacus.

Levi, P. (2000) *If This Is a Man; The Truce*. London: Everyman.

Levi, P. (2001) *The Voice of Memory. Primo Levi: Interviews 1961–87*, edited by M. Belpoliti and R. Gordon. Cambridge: Polity Press.

Lewis, G. (2000) 'Pro-Slavery Ideology'. In Sherene and Beckles (2000).

Lewy, G. (1964) *The Catholic Church and Nazi Germany*. London: Weidenfeld and Nicolson.

Lewy, G. (2000) *The Nazi Persecution of the Gypsies*. Oxford: Oxford University Press.

Leyser, K. (1994) *Communications and Power in Medieval Europe: The Ottonian and Carolingian Empires*. London: Hambledon Press.

Liddell Hart. B. H. (1925) *Paris or the Future of War*. New York: E. P. Dutton.

Liebeschuetz, W. (1995) 'The End of the Roman Army in the Western Empire'. In Rich and Shipley (1995).

Liebeschuetz, W. (2007) 'Warlords and Landlords'. In Erdkamp (2007).

Lifton, R. J. (1974) *Home From the War, Vietnam Veterans: Neither Victims nor Executioners*. London: Wildwood House.

Lifton, R.J. (2000) *The Nazi Doctors: Medical Killing and the Psychology of Genocide*. New York: Basic Books.

Lifton, R. J. and Markusen, E. (1991) *The Genocidal Mentality: Nazi Holocaust and Nazi Threat*. London: Macmillan.

Linke, U. (1999) *German Bodies: Race and Representation after Hitler*. London: Routledge.

Linklater, A. (1982/1990) *Men and Citizens in the Theory of International Relations*. London: Macmillan.

Linklater, A. (1990) *Beyond Realism and Marxism: Critical Theory and International Relations*. Basingstoke: Macmillan.

Linklater, A. (1998) *The Transformation of Political Community: Ethical Foundations of the Post-Westphalian Era*. Cambridge: Polity Press.

Linklater, A. (2006) 'Cosmopolitanism'. In Dobson and Eckersley (2006).

Linklater, A. (2007) 'Public Spheres and Civilizing Processes', *Theory, Culture and Society*, 24 (4), 31–7.

Linklater, A. (2009) 'Human Interconnectedness', *International Relations*, 23 (3), 481–97.

Linklater, A. (2010) 'The Global Civilizing Process and the Ambiguities of Human Interconnectedness', *European Journal of International Relations*, 16 (2), 155–78.

Linklater, A. (2011) *The Problem of Harm in World Politics: Theoretical Investigations*. Cambridge: Cambridge University Press.

Linklater, A. (2012) 'The Global Civilizing Role of Cosmopolitanism'. In Delanty (2012).

Linklater, A. (2014) 'Anger and World Politics: How Collective Emotions Change over Time', *International Theory*, 6 (3), 574–8.

Linklater, A. and Suganami, H. (2006) *The English School of International Relations: A Contemporary Reassessment*. Cambridge: Cambridge University Press.

Lintott, A. W. (1968) *Violence in Republican Rome*. Oxford: Clarendon Press.

Lintott, A. W. (1982) *Violence, Civil Strife and Revolution in the Ancient City, 750–330 BC*. London: Croom Helm.

Lintott, A. W. (1992) 'Cruelty in the Political Life of the Ancient World'. In Viljamaa, Timonen and Krotzl (1992).

Liston, K. and Mennell, S. (2009) 'Ill Met in Ghana: Progress and Process in Goody and Elias', *Theory, Culture and Society*, 26 (7–8), 52–70.

Little, R. (2007) *The Balance of Power in International Relations: Metaphors, Myths and Models*. Cambridge: Cambridge University Press.

Livy, *The War with Hannibal (History of Rome from Its Foundations)*, 1976 edition translation by H. Bettenson. Harmondsworth: Penguin.

Lloyd, A. B. (ed.) (1996) *Battle in Antiquity*. London: Duckworth.

Lloyd, H. A. (1995) 'Josse Clichtove and the Just War'. In Ayton and Price (1995).

Lloyd, S. (1995) 'The Crusading Movement, 1096–1274'. In Riley-Smith (1995).

Locke, J. (1960) [1698] *Two Treatises on Government*. Cambridge: Cambridge University Press.

Lomas, K. (1995) 'The Greeks in the West and the Hellenization of Italy'. In Powell (1995).

Lomas, K. (2004) 'Italy during the Roman Republic, 338–331 BC'. In Flower (2004).

Long, A. A. (1993) 'Hellenistic Ethics and Philosophical Power'. In Green (1993).

Longerich, P. (2003) *The Unwritten Order: Hitler's Role in the Final Solution*. Tempus: Stroud.

Lotter, F. (1989) 'The Crusading Idea and the Conquest of the Region East of the Elbe'. In Bartlett and Mackay (1989).

Loughlin, M. (2003) 'Ten Tenets of Sovereignty'. In Walker (2003).

Low, P. (2007) *Interstate Relations in Classical Greece: Morality and Power*. Cambridge: Cambridge University Press.

Lowe, B. (1997) *Imagining Peace: A History of Early English Pacifist Ideas: 1340–1560*. Pennsylvania: The Pennsylvania State University Press.

Lowe, K. (2005) 'Introduction: The Black African Presence in Renaissance Europe'. In Earle and Lowe (2005).

Lowe, K. (2005a) 'The Stereotyping of Black Africans in Renaissance Europe'. In Earle and Lowe (2005).

Loyal, S. and Quilley, S. (eds.) (2004) *The Sociology of Norbert Elias*. Cambridge: Cambridge University Press.

Luard, E. (1976) *Types of International Society*. London: Collier Macmillan.

Lubasz, H. (ed.) (1964) *The Development of the Modern State*. London: Collier MacMillan.

Lynn, J. A. (2000) 'International Rivalry and Warfare'. In Blanning (2000).

MacMullen, R. (1990) 'Judicial Savagery in the Roman Empire'. In MacMullen (1990a).

MacMullen, R. (1990a) *Changes in the Roman Empire: Essays in the Ordinary*. Princeton: Princeton University Press.

McAleer, K. (1994) *Dueling: The Cult of Honor in Fin-de-Siècle Germany*. Princeton: Princeton University Press.

McDonald, P. J. (2009) *The Invisible Hand of Peace: Capitalism, the War Machine, and International Relations Theory*. Cambridge: Cambridge University Press.

McDonnell, M. (2006) *Roman Manliness: Virtus and the Roman Republic*. Cambridge: Cambridge University Press.

McFarland-Icke, B. R. (1999) *Nurses in Nazi Germany: Moral Choice in History*. Princeton: Princeton University Press.

McKay, D. and Scott, H. M. (1983) *The Rise of the Great Powers, 1648–1815*. London: Longman.

McLellan, D. (ed.) *Karl Marx: Selected Writings*. Oxford: Oxford University Press.

McNeill, W. H. (1963) *The Rise of the West: A History of the Human Community*. Chicago: University of Chicago Press.

McNeill, W. H. (1983) *The Pursuit of Power: Technology, Armed Force, and Society since AD 1000*. Oxford: Basil Blackwell.

McNeill, W. H. (1983a) *The Great Frontier: Freedom and Hierarchy in Modern Times*. Princeton: Princeton University Press.

McNeill, W. H. (1986) *Mythistory and Other Essays*. Chicago: The University of Chicago Press.

McQueen, E. (1995) 'Why Philip Won'. In Powell (1995).

Machiavelli, N. (1950) *The Prince and the Discourses*. New York: Random House.

Macklin, R. (1977) 'Moral Progress', *Ethics*, 87 (4), 370–82.

Madden, T. F. (2002) 'Editor's Introduction'. In Madden (2002a).

Madden, T. F. (ed.) (2002a) *The Crusades: The Essential Readings*. Oxford: Blackwell.

Malkin, I., Constantakopoulou, C. and Panagopoulou, K. (eds.) (2009) *Greek and Roman Networks in the Mediterranean*. Abingdon: Routledge.

Mallett, M. (1974) *Mercenaries and Their Masters: Warfare in Renaissance Italy*. London: Bodley Head.

Mann, M. (1986) *The Sources of Social Power, volume 1: A History of Power from the Beginning to AD1760*. Cambridge: Cambridge University Press.

Mansfield, H. C. (1984) *Selected Letters of Edmund Burke*. Chicago: The University of Chicago Press.

Mark, P. (1974) *Africans in European Eyes: The Portrayal of Black Africans in Fourteenth and Fifteenth Century Europe*. Syracuse, NY: Syracuse University Press.

Marrus, M. R. (1997) *The Nuremberg War Crimes Trial, 1945–46: A Documentary History*. Boston: Bedford.

Marsak, L. M. (ed.) (1972) *The Enlightenment*. New York: John Wiley and Sons.

Marsh P. (ed.) (1979) *The Conscience of the Victorian State*. Hassocks, Sussex: Harvester.

Marshall, P. and Williams, G. (1982) *The Great Map of Mankind: British Perceptions of the World in the Age of Enlightenment*. London: J. M. Dent and Sons.

Martin, J. J. (2007) 'The Renaissance: A World in Motion'. In Martin (2007a).

Martin, J. J. (ed.) (2007a) *The Renaissance World*. Abingdon: Routledge.

Martin, M. L. and McCrate, E. S. (eds.) (1984) *The Military, Militarism, and the Polity: Essays in Honor of Morris Janowitz*. New York: Free Press.

Martin, S. I. (1999) *Britain's Slave Trade*. London: Macmillan.

Martines, L. (ed.) (1972) *Violence and Civil Disorder in Italian Cities, 1200–1500*. Berkeley: University of California Press.

Martines, L. (1974) 'The Gentleman in Renaissance Italy: Strains of Isolation in the Body Politic'. In Kinsman (1974).

Martines, L. (1979) *Power and Imagination: City-States in Renaissance Italy*. London: Alfred A. Knopf.

Mason, M. R. (2005) *The New Accountability: Environmental Responsibility Across Borders*. London: Earthscan.

Mastenbroek, W. (1999) 'Negotiating as Emotion Management' *Theory, Culture and Society*, 16 (4), 49–73.

Mastnak, T. (2002) *Crusading Peace: Christendom, the Muslim World, and Western Political Order*. Berkeley: University of California Press.

Mattern, S. P. (1999) *Rome and the Enemy: Imperial Strategy in the Principate*. Berkeley: University of California Press.

Mattingly, G. (1973) *Renaissance Diplomacy*. Harmondsworth: Penguin.

Mattli, W. and Woods, N. (2009) 'In Whose Benefit? Explaining Regulatory Change in Global Politics'. In Mattli and Woods (2009a).

Mattli, W. and Woods, N. (eds.) (2009a) *The Politics of Global Regulation*. Princeton: Princeton University Press.

May, L. (2005) *Crimes against Humanity: A Normative Account*. Cambridge: Cambridge University Press.

Mazlish, B. (1989) *A New Science: The Breakdown of Connections and the Birth of Sociology*. Oxford: Oxford University Press.

Mazower, M. (2006) 'An International Civilization? Empire, Internationalism and the Crisis of the Mid-Twentieth Century', *International Affairs*, 82 (3), 553–56.

Mearsheimer, J. (2006) 'China's Unpeaceful Rise', *Current History*, (105), 160–2.

Meek, R. L. (1973) 'Introduction' to *Turgot on Progress, Sociology and Economics*, Cambridge: Cambridge University Press.

Meek, R. (1976) *Social Science and the Ignoble Savage*. Cambridge: Cambridge University Press.

Meinecke, F. (1957) *Machiavellism: The Doctrine of Raison d'Etat and Its Place in Modern History*. London: Routledge and Kegan Paul.

Mennell, S. (1990) 'Decivilizing Processes: Theoretical Significance and Some Lines of Research', *International Sociology*, 5 (2), 205–23.

Mennell, S. (1996) 'Asia and Europe: Comparing Civilizing Processes'. In Goudsblom, Jones and Mennell (1996).

Mennell, S. (1998) *Norbert Elias: An Introduction*. Dublin: University College Dublin Press.

Mennell, S. (2007) *The American Civilizing Process*. Cambridge: Polity Press.

Mennell, S. (2014) 'What Economists Forgot (and What Wall Street and the City Never Learned): A Sociological Perspective on the Crisis in Economics', *History of the Human Sciences*, 27 (3), 20–37.

Merback, M. B. (1999) *The Thief, the Cross and the Wheel: Pain and the Spectacle of Punishment in Medieval and Renaissance Europe*. London: Reaktion Books.

Meron, T. (1998) *Bloody Constraint: War and Chivalry in Shakespeare*. Oxford: Oxford University Press.

Meron, T. (1998a) *War Crimes Law Come of Age: Essays*. Oxford: Oxford University Press.

Milgram, S. (1974) *Obedience to Authority: An Experimental View*. London: Pinter and Martin.

Midgley, C. (1998) 'Anti-Slavery and the Roots of "Imperial Feminism"'. In Midgley (1998a).

Midgley, C. (ed.) (1998a) *Gender and Imperialism*. Manchester: Manchester University Press.

Miller. R. J. (2010) 'The Doctrine of Discovery'. In Miller, Ruru, Behrendt and Lindberg (2010).

Miller, R. J., Ruru, J. Behrendt, L. and Lindberg, T. (eds.) (2010) *Discovering Indigenous Lands: The Doctrine of Discovery in the English Colonies*. Oxford: Oxford University Press.

Millet, H. and Moraw, P. (1996) 'Clerics in the State'. In Reinhard (1996).

Minois, G. (1999) *History of Suicide: Voluntary Death in Western Culture*. Baltimore: The Johns Hopkins University Press.

Mishra, P. (2012) *From the Ruins of Empire: The Revolt against the West and the Making of Asia*. London: Allen Lane.

Mitchell, L. G. (1997) *Greeks Bearing Gifts: The Public Use of Private Relationships in the Greek World, 435–323 BC*. Cambridge: Cambridge University Press.

Moles, J. (2000) 'The Cynics'. In Rowe and Schofield (2000).

Molho, A., Raaflaub, K. and Emlen, J. (eds.) (1991) *City States in Classical Antiquity and Medieval Italy*. Ann Arbor: The University of Michigan Press.

Monroe, K. R. (2004) *The Hand of Compassion: Portraits of Moral Choice During the Holocaust*. Princeton: Princeton University Press.

Monsafani, J. and Musto, R. G. (eds.) (1991) *Renaissance Society and Culture: Essays in Honour of Eugene F. Rice Jnr*. New York: Italica Press.

Montaigne, M. de (1993) [1580] 'On the Cannibals'. In Montaigne (1993a).

Montaigne, M. de (1993a) *The Complete Essays* (translated by M. A. Screech). London: Penguin.

Montesquieu (1973) [1721] *The Persian Letters*. Harmondsworth: Penguin.

Montesquieu (1989) [1748] *The Spirit of Laws*. Cambridge: Cambridge University Press.

Moore, B. (2000) *Moral Purity and Persecution in History*. Princeton: Princeton University Press.

Morgenthau, H. J. (1971) 'Death in the Nuclear Age'. In Morgenthau (1971a).

Morgenthau, H. J. (1971a) *Politics in the Twentieth Century*. Chicago: University of Chicago Press.

Morgenthau, H. (1973) *Politics Among Nations: The Struggle for Power and Peace*. New York: Alfred Knopf.

Moorehead, C. (1998) *Dunant's Dream: War, Switzerland and the History of the Red Cross*. New York: Carroll and Graf.

Morris, N. and Rothman, D. J. (eds.) (1995) *The Oxford History of the Prison: The Practice of Punishment in Western Society*. Oxford: Oxford University Press.

Moses, A. D. (2008) 'Genocide and Modernity'. In Stone (2008).

Moses, A. D. (2008a) 'Empire, Colony, Genocide: Keywords and the Philosophy of History'. In Moses (2008b).

Moses, A. D. (ed.) (2008b) *Empire, Colony, Genocide: Conquest, Occupation, and Subaltern Resistance in World History*. Oxford: Berghahn Books.

Moses, A. D. (2010) 'Colonialism'. In Hayes and Roth (2010).

Mosse, G. L. (1985) *Nationalism and Sexuality: Middle Class Morality and Sexual Norms in Modern Europe*. Madison: University of Wisconsin Press.

Mosse, G. L. (1990) *Fallen Soldiers: Reshaping the Memory of the World Wars*. Oxford: Oxford University Press.

Moxon, I. S., Smart, J. D. and Woodman, A. J. (eds.) (1986) *Past Perspectives: Studies in Greek and Roman Historical Writing*. Cambridge: Cambridge University Press.

Muchembled, R. (2002) 'Manners, Courts, and Civility'. In Ruggiero (2002).

Mueller, J. (1989) *Retreat from Doomsday: The Obsolescence of Major War*. New York: BasicBooks.

Muhlhauser, R. (2008) 'Between "Racial Awareness" and Fantasies of Potency: Nazi Sexual Politics in the Occupied Territories of the Soviet Union, 1942–1945'. In Herzog (2008).

Muir, E. (1994) 'The Double Binds of Manly Revenge in Renaissance Italy'. In Trexler (1994).

Muir, E. (1998) *Mad Blood Stirring: Vendetta in Renaissance Italy*. Baltimore: The Johns Hopkins Press.

Muldoon, J. (1979) *Popes, Lawyers, and Infidels: The Church and the Non-Christian World 1250–1550*. Liverpool: Liverpool University Press.

Mulligan, W. (2008) 'Restrained Competition: International Relations'. In Berger (2008).

Murray, A. C. (2006) '"Pax et Disciplina": Roman Public Law and the Merovingian State'. In Noble (2006).

Murray, J. (1996) 'Hiding Behind the Universal Man: Male Sexuality in the Middle Ages'. In Bullough and Brundage (1996).

Murray, J. (ed.) (1999) *Conflicted Identities and Multiple Masculinities: Men in the Medieval West*. London: Garland Publishing.

Murray, O. and Price, S. (eds.) (1990) *The Greek City from Homer to Alexander.* Oxford: Clarendon Press.

Muthu, S. (2003) *Enlightenment Against Empire.* Princeton: Princeton University Press.

Muthu, S. (2012) 'Conquest, Commerce and Cosmopolitanism in Enlightenment Political Thought'. In Muthu (2012a).

Muthu, S. (ed.) (2012a) *Empire and Modern Political Thought.* Cambridge: Cambridge University Press.

Nadelmann, E. A. (1990) 'Global Prohibition Regimes: The Evolution of Norms in International Society', *International Organization,* 44 (4), 479–526.

Nauert, C. G. (2006) *Humanism and the Culture of Renaissance Europe.* Cambridge: Cambridge University Press.

Nederman, C. J. (2000) *Worlds of Difference: European Discourses of Toleration, c.1110–c.1550.* Pennsylvania: The Pennsylvania State University Press.

Neitzer, S. and Welzer, H. (2012) *Soldaten: On Fighting, Killing, and Dying: The Secret World War II Transcripts of German POWs.* New York: Alfred A. Knopf.

Nelson, B. (1973) 'Civilizational Complexes and Inter-Civilizational Relations', *Sociological Analysis,* 34 (2), 79–105.

Neocleous, M. (2011) 'The Police of Civilization: The War on Terror as Civilizing Offensive', *International Political Sociology,* 5, 144–59.

Nexon, D. H. (2009) *The Struggle for Power in Early Modern Europe: Religious Conflict: Dynastic Empires and International Change.* Princeton: Princeton University Press.

Nicholls, J. (1985) *The Matter of Courtesy: Medieval Courtesy Books and the Gawain-Poet.* Woodbridge: D. S. Brewer.

Nirenberg, D. (1996) *Communities of Violence: Persecution of Minorities in the Middle Ages.* Princeton: Princeton University Press.

Noble, T. F. X. (ed.) (2006) *From Roman Provinces to Medieval Kingdoms.* Abingdon: Routledge.

North, H. (1966) *Sophrosyne: Self-Knowledge and Self-Restraint in Greek Literature.* Ithaca, NY: Cornell University Press.

Noyes, D. (2014) 'The Theatre of Clemency'. In Ure and Frost (2014).

Nussbaum, M. C. (2001) *Upheavals of Thought: The Intelligence of the Emotions.* Cambridge: Cambridge University Press.

Nussbaum, M. C. (2002) 'Cosmopolitan Education'. In Cohen (2002).

Oakley, S. P. (1985) 'Single Combat in the Roman Republic', *The Classical Quarterly,* 35 (2), 392–410.

Oakley, S. (1995) 'The Roman Conquest of Italy'. In Rich and Shipley (1995).

Ober, J. (1985) *Fortress Attica: Defence of the Athenian Land Frontier, 404–322 B.C.* Leiden: E. J. Brill.

Ober, J. (1994) 'The Rules of War in Classical Greece'. In Howard, Andreopoulos and Shulman (1994).

O'Connell, R. L. (1995) *Ride of the Second Horseman: The Birth and Death of War*. Oxford: Oxford University Press.

Oestreich, B. (1982) *Neo-Stoicism and the Early Modern State*. Cambridge: Cambridge University Press.

Ofer, D. and Weitzman, L. J. (eds.) (1998) *Women in the Holocaust*. New Haven: Yale University Press.

Ohlmeyer, J. C. (1998) '"Civilizinge of those Rude Partes": Colonization within Britain and Ireland, 1580s–1640s'. In Canny (1998).

Oliners, S. P. and Oliner, P. M. (1988) *The Altruistic Personality: Rescuers of Jews in Nazi Europe*. New York: Free Press.

Ormerod, H. A. (1978) *Piracy in the Ancient World: An Essay on Mediterranean History*. Liverpool: Liverpool University Press.

Ortega, M. C. (1996) 'Vitoria and the Universalist Conception of International Relations'. In Clark and Neumann (1996).

Orwin, C. (1994) *The Humanity of Thucydides*. Princeton: Princeton University Press.

Osiander, A. (1994) *The States-System of Europe, 1640–1990: Peacemaking and the Conditions of International Stability*. Oxford: Clarendon Press.

Osiander, A. (2007) *Before the State: Systemic Political Change in the West from the Greeks to the French Revolution*. Oxford: Oxford University Press.

Outram, D. (1995) *The Enlightenment*. Cambridge: Cambridge University Press.

Overy, R. (2002) *Interrogations: Inside the Minds of the Nazi Elite*. London: Penguin.

Overy, R. (2012) 'Saving Civilization: British Public Opinion and the Coming of War in 1939'. In Welch and Fox (2012).

Overy, R. (2013) *The Bombing War: Europe 1939–1945*. London: Allen Lane.

Pacy, J. S. and Wertheimer, A. P. (eds.) (1995) *Perspectives on the Holocaust: Essays in Honor of Raul Hilberg*. Boulder: Westview Press.

Pagden, A. (1982) *The Fall of Natural Man: The American Indian and the Origins of Comparative Ethnology*. Cambridge: Cambridge University Press.

Pagden, A. (1994) '"The Defence of Civilization" in Eighteenth-Century Social Theory'. In Pagden (1994a).

Pagden, A. (ed.) (1994a) *The Uncertainties of Empire: Essays on Iberian and Ibero-American Intellectual History*. Aldershot: Variorum.

Pagden, A. (1995a) *Lords of All The World: Ideologies of Empire in Spain, Britain and France, c. 1500–c.1800*. New Haven: Yale University Press.

Pagden, A. (1995b) 'The Effacement of Difference: Colonialism and the Origins of Nationalism in Diderot and Herder'. In Prakash (1995).

Pagden, A. (ed.) (2002) *The Idea of Europe: From Antiquity to the European Union*. Cambridge: Cambridge University Press.

Pagden, A. (2013) *The Enlightenment: Why It Still Matters*. Oxford: Oxford University Press.

Panagopoulos, A. (1978) *Captives and Hostages in the Peloponnesian War*. Athens: Grigoris Publications.

Paret, P. (1976) *Clausewitz and the State.* Oxford: Clarendon Press.

Paris, M. (2000) *Warrior Nation: Images of War in British Popular Culture, 1850–2000.* London: Reaktion Books.

Parker, G. (1994) 'Early Modern Europe'. In Howard, Andreopoulos and Shulman (1994).

Parker, G. (1996) *The Military Revolution: Military Innovation and the Rise of the West, 1500–1800.* Cambridge: Cambridge University Press.

Parker, G. (2002) 'The Etiquette of Atrocity: The Laws of War in Early Modern Europe'. In Parker (2002a).

Parker, G. (2002a) *Empire, War and Faith in Early Modern Europe.* London: Allen Lane.

Parker, G. (2005) 'Dynastic War, 1494–1660'. In Parker (2005a).

Parker, G. (ed.) (2005a) *The Cambridge History of Warfare.* Cambridge: Cambridge University Press.

Parry, A. M. (1989) 'Thucydides' Historical Perspective'. In Parry (1989a).

Parry, A. M. (1989a) *The Language of Achilles and Other Papers.* Oxford: Clarendon Press.

Pascua, E. (2008) 'Peace Among Equals: War and Treaties in Twelfth-Century Europe'. In De Souza and France (2008).

Pasha, M. (2009) 'Global Exception and Islamic Exceptionalism', *International Politics*, 46 (5), 527–49.

Pasha, M. (2012) 'Global Leadership and the Islamic World: Crisis, Contention and Challenge'. In Gill (2012).

Passmore, J. A. (1965) 'The Malleability of Man in Eighteenth-Century Thought'. In Wasserman (1965).

Patterson, O. (1982) *Slavery and Social Death: A Comparative Study.* Cambridge, MA: Harvard University Press.

Pemberton, J.-A. (2009) *Sovereignty: Interpretations.* Basingstoke: Palgrave Macmillan.

Percy, S. (2007) *Mercenaries: The History of a Norm in International Relations.* Oxford: Oxford University Press.

Perlman, S. (1976) 'Panhellenism, the Polis and Imperialism', *Historia*, 25 (1), 1–30.

Perrot, M. (1990) 'Roles and Characters'. In Perrot (1990a).

Perrot, M. (ed.) (1990a) *A History of Private Life, volume 4: From the Fires of Revolution to the Great War.* Cambridge, MA: Harvard University Press.

Peters, E. M. (1995) 'Prison Before the Prison: The Ancient and Medieval Worlds'. In Morris and Rothman (1995).

Peterson, J. H. (2013) 'Creating Space for Emancipatory Human Security: Liberal Obstructions and the Potential of Agonism, *International Studies Quarterly*, 57 (2), 318–28.

Peyroux, C. (1998) 'Gertrude's Furor: Reading Anger in an Early Medieval Saint's Life'. In Rosenwein (1998).

Phillips, A. (2011) *War, Religion and Empire: The Transformation of International Orders.* Cambridge: Cambridge University Press.

Phillips, A. (2012) 'Saving Civilization from Empire: Belligerency, Pacificism and the Two Faces of Civilization during the Second Opium War', *European Journal of International Relations*, 18 (1), 5–27.

Phillips, J. (1995) 'The Latin East, 1098–1291'. In Riley-Smith (1995).

Phillips, J. (ed.) (1997) *The First Crusade: Origins and Impact*. Manchester: Manchester University Press.

Phillips, J. (2004) *The Fourth Crusade and the Sack of Constantinople*. London: Viking.

Phillips, M. M. (1964) *The 'Adages' of Erasmus: A Study with Translations*. Cambridge: Cambridge University Press.

Phillips, S. (1994) 'The Outer World of the European Middle Ages'. In Schwartz (1994).

Philpott, D. (2001) *Revolutions in Sovereignty: How Ideas Shaped Modern International Relations*. Princeton: Princeton University Press.

Pick, D. (1993) *War Machine: The Rationalisation of Suffering in the Modern Age*. New Haven: Yale University Press.

Pitkin, H. F. (1984) *Fortune Is a Woman: Gender and Politics in the Thought of Niccolo Machiavelli*. Berkeley: University of California Press.

Pittock, M. G. H. (2003) 'Historiography'. In Broadie (2003).

Pitts, L. F. (1989) 'Relations between Rome and the German "Kings" on the Middle Danube in the First to Four Centuries', *Journal of Roman Studies*, 79 (1), 45–58.

Plato, *The Republic* (1955 edited by H. D. P. Lee). Harmondsworth: Penguin.

Plato, *Menexenus* (1966 edition translated by R. G. Bury). Cambridge, MA: Harvard University Press.

Pliny, *Natural History*, volume 2, Books 3–7, (translated by H. Rackham). London: William Heinemann.

Plutarch, *Lives, volume 7* (1919 edition translated by B. Perrin of Alexander). London: William Heinemann.

Pocock, J. G. A. (2002) 'Some Europes in Their History'. In Pagden (2002).

Pocock, J. G. A. (2005) *Barbarism and Religion: Volume 4, Barbarians, Savages and Empires*. Cambridge: Cambridge University Press.

Pogge, T. (2002) *World Poverty and Human Rights*. Cambridge: Polity Press.

Pohl, W. (1997) 'The Barbarian Successor States'. In Webster and Brown (1997).

Poliakoff, M. B. (1987) *Combat Sports in the Ancient World: Competition, Violence, and Culture*. New Haven: Yale University Press.

Polybius, *The Rise of the Roman Empire* (1979 edition translated by I. Scott-Kilvert). Harmondsworth: Penguin.

Porter, A. (1999) 'Trusteeship, Anti-Slavery, and Humanitarianism'. In Porter (1999a).

Porter, A. (ed.) (1999a) *The Oxford History of the British Empire, Volume Three: The Nineteenth Century*. Oxford: Oxford University Press.

Porter, R. (2000) *Enlightenment: Britain and the Creation of the Modern World*. London: Allen Lane.

Porter, R. and Teich, M. (eds.) (1981) *The Enlightenment in National Context*. Cambridge: Cambridge University Press.

Pouncey, P. R. (1980) *The Necessities of War: A Study of Thucydides' Pessimism*. New York: Columbia University Press.

Powell, A. (ed.) (1995) *The Greek World*. London: Routledge.

Powell, C. (2011) *Barbaric Civilization: A Critical Sociology of Genocide*. London: McGill-Queen's University Press.

Powell, R. (2013) 'The Theoretical Concept of the Civilizing Offensive: (Beschavingsoffensief): Notes on Its Origins and Use', *Human Figurations: Long-Term Perspectives on the Human Condition*, available at http://quod.lib .umich.edu/h/humfig/11217607.0002.2.

Prakash, G. (ed.) (1995) *After Colonialism: Imperial Histories and Postcolonial Displacements*. Princeton: Princeton University Press.

Prawer, J. (1985) 'Social Classes in the Crusader States: The "Minorities"'. In Setton (1985).

Prawer, J. (1985a) 'Social Classes in the Latin Kingdom: The Franks'. In Setton (1985).

Price, J. J. (2001) *Thucydides and Internal War*. Cambridge: Cambridge University Press.

Pritchard, D. M. (2013) *Sport, Democracy and War in Classical Athens*. Cambridge: Cambridge University Press.

Pritchett, W. K. (1971) *The Greek State at War, Part 1*. Berkeley: University of California Press.

Pritchett, W. K. (1974) *The Greek State at War, Part 2*. Berkeley: University of California Press.

Pritchett, W. K. (1985) *The Greek State at War, Part 4*. Berkeley: University of California Press.

Pritchett, W. K. (1991) *The Greek State at War, Part 5*. Berkeley: University of California Press.

Probert, H. (2003) *Bomber Harris: His Life and Times*. London: Greenhill Books.

Proctor, R. N. (1988) *Racial Hygiene: Medicine under the Nazis*. Cambridge, MA: Harvard University Press.

Proctor, R. N. (1999) *The Nazi War on Cancer*. Princeton: Princeton University Press.

Quilley, S (2011) 'Entropy, the Anthroposphere and the Ecology of Civilization: An Essay on the Problem of "Liberalism in One Village" in the Long View', *The Sociological Review*, 59 (supplement), 65–90.

Quinn, T. J. (1995) 'Thucydides and the Massacre at Mycallesus', *Mnemosyne*, 48 (5), 571–4.

Quirk, J. (2011) *The Anti-Slavery Project: From the Slave Trade to Human Trafficking*. Pennsylvania: University of Philadelphia Press.

Quirk, J. and Richardson, D. (2009) 'Anti-Slavery, European Identity and International Society: A Macro-Historical Perspective', *Journal of Modern European History*, 7 (1), 69–92.

Raaflaub, K. A. (ed.) (2007) *War and Peace in the Ancient World*. Oxford: Blackwell.

Raaflaub, K. and Rosenwein, N. (eds.) (1999) *War and Society in the Ancient and Medieval Worlds: Asia, the Mediterranean, Europe, and Mesoamerica*. Cambridge, MA: Harvard University Press.

Rabinow, P. (1991) *The Foucault Reader: An Introduction to Foucault's Thought*. London: Penguin.

Raccagni, G. (2010) *The Lombard League, 1167–1225*. Oxford: Oxford University Press.

Rae, H. (2002) *State Identities and the Homogenisation of Peoples*. Cambridge: Cambridge University Press.

Rahe, P. A. (2002) 'Justice and Necessity: The Conduct of the Spartans and the Athenians in the Peloponnesian War'. In Grimsley and Rogers (2002).

Ralston, D. B. (1990) *Importing the European Army: The Introduction of European Military Techniques and Institutions into the Extra-European Army, 1600–1914*. Chicago: Chicago University Press.

Ramage, E. S. (1960) 'Early Roman Urbanity', *The American Journal of Philology*, 81 (1), 65–72.

Ramage, E. S. (1961) 'Cicero on Extra-Roman Speech', *Transactions and Proceedings of the American Philological Association*, 92: 481–94.

Ramage, E. S. (1963) '*Urbanitas*: Cicero and Quintilian, A Contrast in Attitudes', *The American Journal of Philology*, 84 (4), 390–414.

Rankov, B. (2007) 'Military Forces'. In Sabin, van Wees and Sabin (2007a).

Ranum, O. (1980) 'Courtesy, Absolutism and the Rise of the French State, 1630–60', *Journal of Modern History*, 52 (3), 426–51.

Rawcliffe, C. (1999) 'Medicine for the Soul: The Medieval English Hospital and the Quest for Spiritual Health'. In Hinnells and Porter (1989).

Ray, J. L. (1989) 'The Abolition of Slavery and the End of International War', *International Organization*, 43 (3), 405–39.

Raymond D'Aguiliers, *Historia Francorum qui ceperunt Jerusalem*. Available at www.fordham.edu/halsall/source/raymond-cde.html.

Reeser, T. W. (2006) *Moderating Masculinity in Early Modern Culture*. Chapel Hill, NC: Studies in the Romance Languages and Literatures.

Reibman, J. E. (1987) 'Kames's Historical Law Tracts and the Historiography of the Scottish Enlightenment'. In Carter and Pittock (1987).

Reinhard, W. (ed.) (1996) *Power Elites and State-Building*. Oxford: Clarendon Press.

Reinold, T. (2013) *Sovereignty and the Responsibility to Protect: The Power of Norms and the Norms of the Powerful*. Abingdon: Routledge.

Reiss, H. (ed.) (1991) *Kant: Political Writings*. Cambridge: Cambridge University Press.

Rengger, N. (2013) *Just War and International Order: The Uncivil Condition in World Politics*. Cambridge: Cambridge University Press.

Reus-Smit, C. (1999) *The Moral Purpose of the State: Culture, Social Identity, and Institutional Rationality in International Relations*. Princeton: Princeton University Press.

Reus-Smit, C. (2011) 'Struggles for Individual Rights and the Expansion of the International System', *International Organization*, 65(2), 207–42.

Reus-Smit, C. (2013) *Individual Rights and the Making of the International System*. Cambridge: Cambridge University Press.

Revel, P. (1989) 'The Uses of Civility'. In Chartier (1989).

Reynolds, H. (1987) *Frontier: Aborigines, Settlement and Land*. Sydney: Allen and Unwin.

Reynolds, S. (1984) *Kingdoms and Communities in Western Europe, 900–1300*. Oxford: Clarendon Press.

Reynolds, S. (1997) 'The Historiography of the Medieval State'. In Bentley (1997).

Reynolds, S. (2003) 'There Were States in Medieval Europe: A Response to Rees Davies', *Journal of Historical Sociology*, 14 (6), 550–5.

Rice, C. D. (1975) *The Rise and Fall of Black Slavery*. London: MacMillan.

Rich J. (1995) 'Fear, Greed and Glory: The Causes of Roman War-Making in the Middle Republic'. In Rich and Shipley (1995).

Rich, J. (2001) 'Warfare and External Relations in the Middle Roman Republic'. In Hartmann and Heuser (2001).

Rich, J. and Shipley, G. (eds.) (1993) *War and Society in the Greek World*. London: Routledge.

Rich, J. and Shipley, G. (eds.) (1995) *War and Society in the Roman World*. London: Routledge.

Richardson, J. (2001) *Contending Liberalisms in World Politics: Ideology and Power*. Boulder, CO: Lynne Rienner.

Rihll, T. (1993) 'War, Slavery, and Settlement in Early Greece'. In Rich and Shipley (1993).

Riley-Smith, J. (1986) *The First Crusade and the Idea of Crusading*. London: Continuum.

Riley-Smith, J. (1992) *What Were the Crusades?* Basingstoke: Macmillan.

Riley-Smith, J. (ed.) (1995) *The Oxford Illustrated History of the Crusades, 1098–1291*. Oxford: Oxford University Press.

Riley-Smith, J. (1997) *The First Crusaders: 1095–1131*. Cambridge: Cambridge University Press.

Riley-Smith, J. (2002) 'Early Crusaders to the East and the Costs of Crusading, 1095–1130'. In Madden (2002a).

Riley-Smith, J. (2002a) 'Crusading as an Act of Love'. In Madden (2002a).

Roberts, A. and Guelff, R. (eds.) (2001) *Documents on the Laws of War*. Oxford: Oxford University Press.

Robertson, J. (2005) *The Case for the Enlightenment: Scotland and Naples 1680–1760*. Cambridge: Cambridge University Press.

Robertson, L. R. (2003) *The Dream of Civilized Warfare: World War I Flying Aces and the American Imagination*. Minnesota: Minnesota University Press.

Robinson, P. (2006) *Military Honour and the Conduct of War: From Ancient Greece to Iraq*. Abingdon: Routledge.

Robinson, W. I., and Harris, J. (2000) 'Towards a Global Ruling Class? Globalization and the Transnational Capitalist Class', *Science and Society*, 64 (1), 11–54.

Rogers, C. J. (1993) 'Military Revolutions of the Hundred Years' War', *Journal of Military History*, 57 (2), 241–78.

Rogers, C. J. (2002) 'By Fire and Sword: Bellum Hostile and "Civilians" in the Hundred Years' War'. In Grimsley and Rogers (2002).

Roodenburg, H. (1991) 'The "Hand of Friendship": Shaking Hands and other Gestures in the Dutch Republic'. In Bremmer and Roodenburg (1991).

Roosen, W. (1973) 'The True Ambassador: Occupational and Personal Characteristics of French Ambassadors under Louis XIV', *European Studies Review*, 3 (2), 121–39.

Roosen, W. J. (1976) *The Age of Louis XIV: The Rise of Modern Diplomacy*. Cambridge, MA: Schenkman.

Roosen, W. (1980) 'Early Modern Diplomatic Ceremonial: A Systems Approach', *Journal of Modern History*, 52 (3), 452–76.

Roper, M. (2004) 'Maternal Relations: Moral Manliness and Emotional Survival in Letters Home During the First World War'. In Dudink, Hagemann and Tosh (2004).

Rorty, R. (1989) *Contingency, Irony, and Solidarity*. Cambridge: Cambridge University Press.

Rosecrance, R. (1986) *The Rise of the Trading State: Commerce and Conquest in the Modern World*. New York: Basic Books.

Roseman, M. (2002) *The Wannsee Conference and the Final Solution: A Reconsideration*. New York: Metropolitan Books.

Roseman, M. (2007) 'Beyond Conviction? Perpetrators, Ideas and Action in the Holocaust in Historiographical Perspective'. In Beiss, Roseman and Schissler (2007).

Rosenbaum, A. S. (ed.) (1998) *Is the Holocaust Unique? Perspectives on Comparative Genocide*. Boulder, CO: Westview Press.

Rosenstein, N. (2007) 'War and Peace, Fear and Reconciliation at Rome'. In Raaflaub (2007).

Rosenstein, N. (2007a) 'Military Command, Political Power, and the Republican Elite'. In Erdkamp (2007).

Rosenstein, N. and Morstein-Marx, R. (eds.) (2006) *A Companion to the Roman Republic*. Oxford: Blackwell.

Rosenwein, B. H. (ed.) (1998) *Anger's Past: The Social Uses of an Emotion in the Middle Ages*. Ithaca: Cornell University Press.

Rosenwein, B. H. (2006) *Emotional Communities in the Early Middle Ages*. Ithaca: Cornell University Press.

Rossi, P. (1984) *The Dark Abyss of Time: The History of the Earth and the History of Nations from Vico to Hooke*. Chicago: The University of Chicago Press.

Rossiaud, J. (1990) 'The City-Dweller and Life in Cities and Towns'. In Le Goff (1990).

Roth, J. P. (2007) 'War'. In Sabin, van Wees, and Whitby (2007).

Rothenberg, G. E. (1977) *The Art of Warfare in the Age of Napoleon*. London: B. T. Batsford.

Rothenberg, G. E. (1994) 'The Age of Napoleon'. In Howard, Andreopoulos and Shulman (1994).

Rouche, M. (1987) 'The Early Middle Ages in the West'. In Veyne (1987).

Rousseau, J. J. (1968) [1754] *A Discourse on the Origin of Inequality*. London: J. M. Dent.

Rowe, C. and Schofield, M. (eds.) (2000) *The Cambridge History of Greek and Roman Political Thought*. Cambridge: Cambridge University Press.

Ruff, J. R. (2001) *Violence in Early Modern Europe, 1500–1800*. Cambridge: Cambridge University Press.

Ruggie, J. (1983) 'Continuity and Transformation in the World Polity: Toward a Neorealist Synthesis', *World Politics*, 35 (2), 261–85.

Ruggie J. (1993) 'Territoriality and Beyond: Problematizing Modernity in International Relations', *International Organization*, 47 (1), 139–74.

Ruggiero, G. (1980) *Violence in Early Renaissance Venice*. New Brunswick, NJ: Rutgers University Press.

Ruggiero, G. (ed.) (2002) *A Companion to the Worlds of the Renaissance*. Oxford: Blackwell.

Runciman, W. (1990) 'Doomed to Extinction: The Polis as an Evolutionary Dead End'. In Murray and Price (1990).

Russell, F. H. (1975) *The Just War in the Middle Ages*. Cambridge: Cambridge University Press.

Ryder, T. T. B. (1965) *Koine Eirene: General Peace and Local Independence in Ancient Greece*. London: Oxford University Press.

Sabin, P. (2007) 'Battle'. In Sabin, van Wees, and Whitby (2007).

Sabin, P., van Wees, W. and Whitby, M. (eds.) (2007) *The Cambridge History of Greek and Roman Warfare, volume one, Greece, the Hellenistic World and the Rise of Rome*. Cambridge: Cambridge University Press.

Sabin, P., van Wees, W. and Whitby, M. (eds.) (2007a) *The Cambridge History of Greek and Roman Warfare, volume two, Rome from the Late Republic to the Late Empire*. Cambridge: Cambridge University Press.

Sadowski, Y. (1996) *The Myth of Global Chaos*. Washington: Brookings Institution Press.

Sage, M. M. (ed.) (1996) *Warfare in Ancient Greece: A Sourcebook*. London: Routledge.

Salter, M. (2000) 'The Visibility of the Holocaust: Franz Neumann and the Nuremberg Trials'. In Fine and Turner (2000).

Sandholtz, W. (2008) 'Dynamics of International Norm Change: Rules against Wartime Plunder', *European Journal of International Relations*, 14 (1), 101–31.

Scaglione, A. (1991) *Knights at Court: Courtliness, Chivalry, and Courtesy from Ottonian Germany to the Italian Renaissance*. Berkeley: University of California Press.

Scales, L. (2010) 'Central and Late Medieval Europe'. In Bloxham and Moses (2010).

Schaps, D. (1982) 'The Women of Greece in Wartime'. *Classical Philology*, 77 (3), 193–213.

Scheidel, W., Morris, I. and Saller, R. (eds.) (2007) *The Cambridge Economic History of the Greco-Roman World*. Cambridge: Cambridge University Press.

Schlereth, T. J. (1977) *The Cosmopolitan Idea in Enlightenment Thought: Its Form and Function in the Ideas of Franklin, Hume and Voltaire, 1694–1790*. Notre Dame: The University of Notre Dame Press.

Schmidt, J. (ed.) (1996) *What Is Enlightenment? Eighteenth-Century Questions and Twentieth-Century Answers*. Berkeley: University of California Press.

Schmidt, J. (2000) 'What Enlightenment Project?', *Political Theory*, 28 (6), 734–57.

Schmidt, U. (2006) *Justice at Nuremberg: Leo Alexander and the Doctors' Trial*. Basingstoke: Palgrave Macmillan.

Schmidt, U. (2007) *Karl Brandt, The Nazi Doctor: Medicine and Power in the Third Reich*. London: Hambledon Continuum.

Schmitt C. (1985) [1934] *Political Theology: Four Chapters on the Concept of Sovereignty*. Chicago: University of Chicago Press.

Schmitt, C. B. and Skinner, Q. (eds.) (1988) *The Cambridge History of Renaissance Philosophy*. Cambridge: Cambridge University Press.

Schofield, M. (2000) 'Epicurean and Stoic Political Thought'. In Rowe and Schofield (2000).

Schroeder, P. W. (1994) *The Transformation of European Politics, 1763–1848*. Oxford: Clarendon Press.

Schwartz, S. B. (ed.) (1994) *Implicit Understandings: Observing, Reporting and Reflecting on the Encounters between Europeans and other Peoples in the Early Modern Era*. Cambridge: Cambridge University Press.

Scott, H. M. (ed.) (1990) *Enlightened Absolutism: Reform and Reformers in Later Eighteenth-Century Europe*. Basingstoke: MacMillan.

Scott, H. (ed.) (1995) *The European Nobilities in the Seventeenth and Eighteenth Centuries, volume one, Western Europe*. London: Longman.

Scott, H. (2007) 'Diplomatic Culture in Old Regime Europe'. In Scott and Sims (2007).

Scott, H. and Sims, B. (eds.) (2007) *Cultures of Power in Europe During the Long Eighteenth Century*. Cambridge: Cambridge University Press.

Scott, H. and Storrs, C. (1995) 'Introduction: The Consolidation of Noble Power in Europe, c.1600–1800'. In Scott (1995).

Seed, P. (1993) '"Are These Not Also Men"? The Indians' Humanity and the Capacity for Spanish Civilization', *Journal of Latin American Studies*, 25 (3), 629–52.

Segal, C. (1981) *Tragedy and Civilization: An Interpretation of Sophocles*. Cambridge, MA: Harvard University Press.

Sekunda, N. (2007) 'Land Forces'. In Sabin, van Wees, and Whitby (2007).

Seneca, 'On Favours'. In Seneca (1995).

Seneca, 'On Anger'. In Seneca (1995).

Seneca, 'On Mercy'. In Seneca (1995).

Seneca, 'On the Private Life'. In Seneca (1995).

Seneca, *Moral and Political Essays* (1995 edition translated by J. M. Cooper and J. F. Procope). Cambridge: Cambridge University Press.

Seneca, *Letters from a Stoic* (2004 edition translated by Robin Campbell). London: Penguin.

Sennett, R. (2002) *Flesh and Stone: The Body and the City in Western Civilization*. London: Penguin.

Sereny, G. (1995) *Albert Speer: His Battle with Truth*. New York: Vintage.

Serrati, J. (2007) 'Warfare and the State'. In Sabin, van Wees, and Whitby (2007).

Setton, K. M. (ed.) (1969) *A History of the Crusades, volume 1: The First Hundred Years*. London: University of Wisconsin Press.

Setton, K. M. (ed.) (1975) *A History of the Crusades, volume 3: The Fourteenth and Fifteenth Centuries*. London: University of Wisconsin Press.

Setton, K. M. (ed.) (1985) *A History of the Crusades, volume 5: The Impact of the Crusades on the Near East*. London: University of Wisconsin Press.

Shaftesbury, Earl of (1978) [1711] 'An Essay on the Freedom of Wit and Humour'. In Earl of Shaftesbury, *Characteristics of Men, Manners, Opinion, Times*. New York: Georg Olms Verlag.

Shani, G. (2014) *Religion, Identity and Human Security*. Abingdon: Routledge.

Shapcott, R. (2001) *Justice, Community and Dialogue in International Politics*. Cambridge: Cambridge University Press.

Shaw, M. (1991) *Post-Military Society: Militarism, Demilitarization and War at the End of the Twentieth Century*. Cambridge: Polity Press.

Shaw, M. (2005) *The New Western Way of War: Risk-Transfer War and Its Crisis in Iraq*. Cambridge: Polity Press.

Shepherd, V. and Beckles, H. McD. (eds.) (2000) *Caribbean Slavery in the Atlantic World: A Student Reader*. Oxford: James Currey.

Sherrard, O. A. (1959) *Freedom from Fear: The Slave and his Emancipation*. London: Bodley Head.

Shik, N. (2008) 'Sexual Abuse of Jewish Women in Auschwitz-Birkenau'. In Herzog (2008).

Shipley, G. (1993) 'The Limits of War'. In Rich and Shipley (1993).

Sidebottom, H. (2007) 'International Relations'. In Sabin, van Wees and Whitby (2007a).

Simpson, G. (2004) *Great Powers and Outlaw States: Unequal Sovereigns in the International Legal Order*. Cambridge: Cambridge University Press.

Simpson, L. B. (1950) *The Encomienda in New Spain: The Beginning of Spanish Mexico*. Berkeley: University of California Press.

Skinner, A. S. (2003) 'Economic Theory'. In Broadie (2003).

Skinner, Q. (1978) *The Foundation of Modern Political Thought, volume one: The Renaissance*. Cambridge: Cambridge University Press.

Skinner, Q. (1981) *Machiavelli*. Oxford: Oxford University Press.

Skinner, Q. (1988) 'Political Philosophy'. In Schmitt and Skinner (1988).

Skocpol, T. (1979) *States and Social Revolutions: A Comparative Analysis of France, Russia, and China*. Cambridge: Cambridge University Press.

Slim, H. (2008) *Killing Civilians: Method, Madness, and Morality in War*. New York: Columbia University Press.

Smith, A. (1910) [1776] *An Inquiry into the Nature and Causes of the Wealth of Nations*. London: J. M. Dent.

Smith, A. (1982) [1759] *The Theory of Moral Sentiments*. Indianapolis: Liberty Fund.

Smith, J. M. H. (2005) *Europe after Rome: A New Cultural History, 500–1000*. Oxford: Oxford University Press.

Smith, K. E. (2010) *Genocide and the Europeans*. Cambridge: Cambridge University Press.

Snowden, F. (1983) *Before Color Prejudice: The Ancient View of Blacks*. Cambridge, MA: Harvard University Press.

Solow, B. L. and Engerman, S. L. (eds.) (1987) *British Capitalism and Caribbean Slavery: The Legacy of Eric Williams*. Cambridge: Cambridge University Press.

Sommer, R. (2008) 'Camp Brothels: Forced Sex Labour in Nazi Concentration Camps'. In Herzog (2008).

Sontag, S. (2003) *Regarding the Pain of Others*. London: Hamish Hamilton.

Sorensen, G. (1999) 'Sovereignty: Change and Continuity in a Fundamental Institution'. In Jackson (1999).

Sorensen, G. (2007) 'After the Security Dilemma: The Challenges of Insecurity in Weak States and the Dilemma of Liberal Values', *Security Dialogue*, 38 (3), 357–78.

Southern, R. W. (1970) *Medieval Humanism and Other Studies*. Oxford: Blackwell.

Spawforth, T. (2007) 'The Court of Alexander the Great between Europe and Asia'. In Spawforth (2007a).

Spawforth, A. J. S. (ed.) (2007a) *The Court and Court Society in Ancient Monarchies*. Cambridge: Cambridge University Press.

Spierenburg, P. (1981) *Elites and Etiquette: Mentality and Social Structure in the Early Modern Northern Netherlands*. Rotterdam: Erasmus Universiteit Press.

Spierenburg, P. (1998) 'Masculinity, Violence and Honor: An Introduction'. In Spierenburg (1998a).

Spierenburg, P. (ed.) (1998a) *Men and Violence: Gender, Honor, and Rituals in Modern Europe and America*. Columbus: Ohio State University.

Spivey, N. (2001) *Enduring Creation: Art, Pain, and Fortitude*. Berkeley: University of California Press.

Spivey, N. (2004) *The Ancient Olympics*. Oxford: Oxford University Press.

Spruyt, H. (1994) *The Sovereign State and Its Competitors: An Analysis of Systems Change*. Princeton: Princeton University Press.

Spufford, P. (2003) *Power and Profit: The Merchant in Medieval Europe*. London: Thames and Hudson.

Stacey, P. (2007) *Roman Monarchy and the Renaissance Prince*. Cambridge: Cambridge University Press.

Stacey, R. C. (1994) 'The Age of Chivalry'. In Howard, Andreopoulos and Shulman (1994).

Stanford, W. B. (1983) *Greek Tragedy and the Emotions: An Introductory Study*. London: Routledge and Kegan Paul.

Staub, E. (2003) *The Psychology of Good and Evil: Why Children, Adults and Groups Help and Harm Others*. Cambridge: Cambridge University Press.

Stearns, P. N. (2005) *Global Outrage: The Impact of World Opinion on Contemporary History*. Oxford: OneWorld.

Steiger, H. (2001) 'From the International Law of Christianity to the International Law of the World Citizen – Reflections on the Formation of the Epochs of International Law', *Journal of the History of International Law*, 3 (2), 180–93.

Steigmann-Gall, R. (2003) *The Holy Reich: Nazi Conceptions of Christianity, 1919–1945*. Cambridge: Cambridge University Press.

Stein, P. (1999) *Roman Law in European History*. Cambridge: Cambridge University Press.

Steintrager, J. A. (2004) *Cruel Delight: Enlightenment Culture and the Inhuman*. Bloomington: Indiana University Press.

Stephens, J. (1990) *The Italian Renaissance: The Origins of Intellectual and Artistic Change Before the Reformation*. London: Longman.

Stepper, R. (2001) 'Roman-Carthaginian Relations: From Cooperation to Annihilation'. In Hartmann and Heuser (2001).

Sternberg, R. H. (ed.) (2005) *Pity and Power in Ancient Athens*. Cambridge: Cambridge University Press.

Stevens, C. (1994) *White Man's Dreaming: Killipaninna Mission 1866–1915*. Melbourne: Oxford University Press.

Stevenson, T. R. (1992) 'The Ideal Benefactor and the Father Analogy in Greek and Roman Thought', *Classical Quarterly*, 42 (2), 421–36.

Stewart, J. (1823) *A View of the Past and Present State of the Island of Jamaica*. Edinburgh: Oliver and Boyd.

Stickler, T. (2007) 'The Foederati'. In Erdkamp (2007).

Stinchcombe, A. L. (1975) 'Social Structure and Politics'. In Greenstein and Polsby (1975).

Stone, D. (ed.) (2004) *The Historiography of the Holocaust*. Basingstoke: Palgrave Macmillan.

Stone, D. (ed.) (2008) *The Historiography of Genocide*. Basingstoke: Palgrave Macmillan.

Stone, D. (2010) *Histories of the Holocaust*. Oxford: Oxford University Press.

Stone, R. (2011) 'Masculinity without Conflict: Noblemen in Eighth- and Ninth-Century Francia'. In Arnold and Brady (2011).

Strachan, H. (1983) *European Armies and the Conduct of War*. London: Routledge.

Strange, S. (1986) *Casino Capitalism*. Oxford: Basil Blackwell.

Strickland, M. (1996) *War and Chivalry: The Conduct and Perception of War in England and Normandy, 1066–1217*. Cambridge: Cambridge University Press.

Stroccia, S. T. (1998) 'Gender and the Rites of Honour in Italian Renaissance Cities'. In Brown and Davis (1998).

Stroikos, D. (ed.) (2014) 'Introduction: Rethinking the Standard(s) of Civilisation(s) in International Relations', *Millennium*, 42 (3), 546–556.

Suganami, H. (2007) 'Understanding Sovereignty Through Kelsen/Schmitt', *Review of International Studies*, 33 (3), 511–30.

Suzuki, S. (2009) *Civilization and Empire: China and Japan's Encounter with European International Society*. Abingdon: Routledge.

Suzuki. S. (2012) 'Viewing the Development of Human Society from Asia', *Human Figurations: Long-Term Perspectives on the Human Condition*, 1 (2), available at http://hdl.handle.net/2027/spo/11217607.0001.207.

Swaan, A. de (1995) 'Widening Circles of Identification: Emotional Concerns in Sociogenetic Perspective', *Theory, Culture and Society*, 12 (2), 25–39.

Swaan, A. de (1997) 'Widening Circles of Disidentification: On the Psycho- and Socio-genesis of the Hatred of Distant Strangers – Reflections on Rwanda', *Theory, Culture and Society*, 14 (2), 105–22.

Swaan, A. de (2003) 'Dyscivilization, Mass Extermination and the State'. In Dunning and Mennell (2003), originally published in *Theory, Culture and Society*, 2001 (18), 2–3.

Swaan. A. de (2015) *The Killing Compartments: The Mentality of Mass Murder*. New Haven: Yale University Press.

Swain, S. and Edwards, M. (eds.) (2004) *Approaching Late Antiquity: The Transformation from Early to Late Empire*. Oxford: Oxford University Press.

Swann, J. (1995) 'The French Nobility, 1715–89'. In Scott (1995).

Swift, L. J. (2007) 'Early Christian Views on Violence, War, and Peace'. In Raaflaub (2007).

Sylvest, C. (2009) *British Liberal Internationalism, 1880–1930: Making Progress*. Manchester: Manchester University Press.

Tacitus, *The Agricola and the Germania* (1970 edition translated by H. Mattingly and S. A. Handford). Harmondsworth: Penguin.

Tacitus, *The Histories* (1972 edition translated by K. Wellesley). Harmondsworth: Penguin.

Taithe, B. (1998) 'The Red Cross Flag in the Franco-Prussian War: Civilians, Humanitarians and War in the "Modern Age"'. In Cooter, Harrison and Sturdy (1998).

Tallett, F. (1992) *War and Society in Early-Modern Europe, 1495–1715*. London: Routledge.

Tarn, W. W. (1933) 'Alexander the Great and the Unity of Mankind', *Proceedings of the British Academy*, 19: 123–66.

Tarn, W. W. (1948) *Alexander the Great: volume 2, Sources and Studies*. Cambridge: Cambridge University Press.

Tarn, W. T. and Griffith, G. T. (1952) *Hellenistic Civilization*. London: Methuen.

Taylor, A. (1999) 'Chivalric Conversation and the Denial of Male Fear'. In Murray (1999).

Taylor, C. (1989) *Sources of the Self: The Making of Modern Identity*. Cambridge Massachusetts: Harvard University Press.

Taylor, F. (2004) *Dresden: Tuesday 13 February 1945*. London: Bloomsbury.

Taylor, P. (1999) 'The United Nations in the 1990s: Proactive Cosmopolitanism and the Issue of Sovereignty'. In Jackson (1999).

Taylor, T. (1971) *Nuremberg and Vietnam: An American Tragedy*. New York: Bantam Books.

Teitel, R. G. (2011) *Humanity's Law*. Oxford: Oxford University Press.

Temperley, H. (1972) *British Antislavery, 1833–1870*. London: Longman.

Terjanian, A. F. (2013) *Commerce and Its Discontents in Eighteenth-Century French Political Thought*. Cambridge: Cambridge University Press.

Teschke, B. (1998) 'Geopolitical Relations in the European Middle Ages: History and Theory', *International Organization*, 52 (2), 325–58.

Thomas, K. (2009) *The Ends of Life: Roads to Fulfilment in Early Modern England*. Oxford: Oxford University Press.

Thomas, W. (2001) *The Ethics of Destruction: Norms and Force in International Relations*. Ithaca: Cornell University Press.

Thomson, J. E. (1994) *Mercenaries, Pirates, and Sovereigns: State-Building and Extraterritorial Violence in Early Modern Europe*. Princeton: Princeton University Press.

Thucydides, *History of the Peloponnesian War* (1928 edition translated by C. F. Smith). London: William Heinemann.

Tilly, C. (1992) *Coercion, Capital, and European States: AD 990–1992*. Oxford: Blackwell.

Tirman, J. (2011) *The Deaths of Others: The Fate of Civilians in America's Wars*. Oxford: Oxford University Press.

Tlusty, B. A. (2011) *The Martial Ethic in Early Modern Germany: Civic Duty and the Right of Arms*. Basingstoke: Palgrave Macmillan.

Tocqueville, A. de (1945) [1840] *Democracy in America: volume two*. New York: Alfred A. Knopf.

Todorov, T. (1984) *The Conquest of America: The Question of the Other*. New York: Harper and Row.

Todorov, T. (2000) *Facing the Extreme: Moral Life in the Concentration Camps*. London: Wiedenfeld and Nicolson.

Todorov, T. (2009) *In Defence of the Enlightenment*. London: Atlantic Books.

Tooke, J. D. (1965) *The Just War in Aquinas and Grotius*. London: S.P.C.K.

Towns, A. (2009) 'The Status of Women as a Standard of "Civilization"', *European Journal of International Relations*, 15 (4), 681–706.

Townsend, C. (1997) 'Introduction: The Shape of Modern War'. In Townsend (1997a).

Townsend C. (ed.) (1997a) *The Oxford Illustrated History of Modern War*. Oxford: Oxford University Press.

Trexler, R. C. (1980) *Public Life in Renaissance Florence*. New York: Academic Press.

Trexler, R. C. (ed.) (1994) *Gender Rhetorics: Postures of Dominance and Submission in History*. Binghamton, New York: State University of New York.

Tritle, L. A. (ed.) (1997) *The Greek World in the Fourth Century: From the Fall of the Athenian Empire to the Successors of Alexander*. London: Routledge.

Tritle, L. A. (2000) *From Melos to MyLai: War and Survival*. London: Routledge.

Turner, B. S. (2004) 'Weber and Elias on Religion and Violence: Warrior Charisma and the Civilizing Process'. In Loyal and Quilley (2004).

Tusa, A. and Tusa, J. (1983) *The Nuremberg Trial*. London: Macmillan.

Tyerman, C. (2005) *The Crusades: A Very Short Introduction*. Oxford: Oxford University Press.

Ullmann, W. (1955) *The Growth of Papal Government in the Middle Ages: A Study in the Ideological Relation of Clerical to Lay Power*. London: Methuen and co.

Vale, M. (1981) *War and Chivalry: Warfare and Aristocratic Culture in England, France, and Burgundy at the End of the Middle Ages*. London: Duckworth.

Vale, M. (1988) 'The Civilization of Courts and Cities in the North, 1200–1500'. In Holmes (1988).

Vale, M. (2000) 'Aristocratic Violence: Trial by Battle in the Later Middle Ages'. In Kaeuper (2000a).

Vale, M. (2001) *The Princely Court: Medieval Courts and Culture in North-West Europe, 1270–1380*. Oxford: Oxford University Press.

Vandekerckhove, W. and van Hooft, S. (2010) 'Introduction'. In van Hooft and Vandekerckhove (2010).

Vardi, L. (2012) *The Physiocrats and the World of the Enlightenment*. Cambridge: Cambridge University Press.

Vattel, E. (1863) [1758] *The Law of Nations or the Principles of Natural Law Applied to the Conduct and to the Affairs of Nations and of Sovereigns*. Philadelphia: T. and J. W. Johnson.

Vaughn, P. (1991) 'The Identification and Retrieval of the Hoplite Battle-Dead'. In Hanson (1991).

Vegetius, *Epitome of Military Science* (1993 translation by N. P. Milner). Liverpool: Liverpool University Press.

Veitch, S. (2007) *Law and Irresponsibility: On the Legitimation of Human Suffering*. London: Abingdon.

Verbruggen, J. F. (1977) *The Art of Warfare in Western Europe During the Middle Ages: From the Eighth Century to 1340*. Amsterdam: North Holland Publishing Company.

Verkamp, B. J. (1993) *The Moral Treatment of Returning Warriors in Early Medieval and Modern Times*. Scranton: University of Scranton Press.

Veyne, P. (ed.) (1987) *A History of Private Life: From Pagan Rome to Byzantium*. Cambridge, MA: Harvard University Press.

Veyne, P. (1993) 'Humanitas: Romans and Non-Romans'. In Giardina (1993).

Vigarello, G. (2001) *A History of Rape: Sexual Violence in France from the 16th to the 20th Century*. Cambridge: Polity Press.

Vigneswaran, D. (2007) 'The Territorial Strategy of the Italian City-State', *International Relations*, 21 (4), 427–44.

Viljamaa, T., Timonen, A. and Krotzl, C. (eds.) (1992) *Crudelitas: The Politics of Cruelty in the Ancient and Medieval World*. Krems: Medium Aevum Quotidianum.

Vincent, R. J. (1986) *Human Rights and International Relations*. Cambridge: Cambridge University Press.

Vincent-Buffault, A. (1991) *The History of Tears: Sensibility and Sentimentality in France*. Houndmills: MacMillan.

Viroli, M. (1990) 'Machiavelli and the Republican Idea of Politics'. In Bock, Skinner and Viroli (1990).

Vitoria, F. de (1917) [1565] *De Indis et de Iure Belli Relectiones*. Washington: Carnegie Institute of Washington.

Vogel, D. (2009) 'The Private Regulation of Global Corporate Conduct'. In Mattli and Woods (2009a).

Vogel, R. J. (2011) 'Drone Warfare and the Law of Armed Conflict', *Denver Journal of International Law and Policy*, 39 (1), 101–38.

Vogel, U. (2000) 'The Sceptical Enlightenment: Philosopher Travellers Look Back at Europe'. In Geras and Wokler (2000).

Vogel, U. (2003) 'Cosmopolitan Loyalties and Cosmopolitan Citizenship in the Enlightenment'. In Waller and Linklater (2003).

Vogt, J. (1974) *Ancient Slavery and Ideal of Man*. Oxford: Basil Blackwell.

Voltaire, (1918) [1759] *Candide*. New York: Boni and Liveright.

Vree, W. van (1999) *Meetings, Manners and Civilization: The Development of Modern Meeting Behaviour*. London: University of Leicester Press.

Vyverberg, H. (1958) *Historical Pessimism in the French Enlightenment.* Cambridge, MA: Harvard University Press.

Walbank, F. W. (1975) 'Symploke: Its Role in Polybius' Histories'. In Kagan (1975).

Walbank, F. W. (1981) *The Hellenistic World.* Glasgow: Fontana.

Waley, D. (1969) *The Italian City-Republics.* London: Weidenfeld and Nicholson.

Walker, N. (ed.) (2003) *Sovereignty in Transition.* Oxford: Hart Publishing.

Walker, R. B. J. (1993) *Inside/Outside: International Relations as Political Theory.* Cambridge: Cambridge University Press.

Wallace-Hadrill, A. (1982) '*Civilis Princeps*: Between Citizen and King', *The Journal of Roman Studies*, 72, 32–48.

Waller, J. (2002) *Becoming Evil: How Ordinary People Commit Genocide and Mass Killing.* Oxford: Oxford University Press.

Waller, M. and Linklater, A. (eds.) (2003) *Political Loyalty and the Nation-State.* London: Routledge.

Waltz, K. N. (1959) *Man, the State and War: A Theoretical Analysis.* New York: Columbia University Press.

Waltz, K. N. (1979) *Theory of International Politics.* Reading, Massachusetts: Addison-Wesley.

Waltz, K. N. (1981) *The Spread of Nuclear Weapons: More May Be Better.* Adelphi Paper 171, London: International Institute of Strategic Studies.

Waltz, K. N. (2012) 'Why Iran Should Get the Bomb', *Foreign Affairs*, 91(4), 2–5.

Walvin, J. (1992) *Black Ivory: A History of British Slavery.* Washington: Howard University Press.

Walzer, M. (1978) *Just and Unjust Wars: A Moral Argument with Historical Illustrations.* London: Allen Lane.

Ward-Perkins, B. (2005) *The Fall of Rome and the End of Civilization.* Oxford: Oxford University Press.

Ware, V. (1992) *Beyond the Pale: White Women, Racism and History.* London: Verso.

Wasserman, E. R. (ed.) (1965) *Aspects of the Eighteenth Century.* London: Oxford University Press.

Watson, A. (1987) 'Hedley Bull, States-Systems and International Societies', *Review of International Studies*, 13 (2), 147–53.

Watson, A. (1992) *The Evolution of International Society.* London: Routledge.

Weber, E. (1977) *Peasants into Frenchmen: The Modernization of Rural France, 1870–1914.* London: Chatto and Windus.

Weber, M. (1948) [1919] 'Politics as a Vocation'. In Gerth and Mills (1948).

Webster, L. and Brown, M. (eds.) (1997) *The Transformation of the Roman World, AD 400–900.* London: British Museum Press.

Wees, H. van (1992) *Status Warriors: War, Violence and Society in Homer and History.* Amsterdam: J. C. Gieben.

Wees, H. van (ed.) (2000) *War and Violence in Ancient Greece.* London: Duckworth/Classical Press of Wales.

Wees, H. van (2001) 'War and Peace in Ancient Greece'. In Hartmann and Heuser (2001).

Wees, H. van (2004) *Greek Warfare: Myths and Realities*. London: Duckworth.

Wees, H. van (2010) 'Genocide in the Ancient World'. In Bloxham and Moses (2010).

Weikart, R. (2009) *Hitler's Ethic: The Nazi Pursuit of Evolutionary Progress*. Basingstoke: Palgrave Macmillan.

Weiler, I. (2002) 'Inverted Kalokagathia'. In Wiedemann and Gardner (2002).

Weindling, P. J. (2006) *Nazi Medicine and the Nuremberg Trials: From Medical War Crimes to Informed Consent*. Basingstoke: Palgrave.

Weisbrod, B. (1996) 'The Crisis of Bourgeois Society in Interwar Germany'. In Bessel (1996).

Weitzman, L. J. (2010) 'Women'. In Hayes and Roth (2010).

Welch, K. E. (2006) 'Introduction'. In Dillon and Welch (2006).

Welch, D. and Fox, J. (eds.) (2012) *Justifying War: Propaganda, Politics and the Modern Age*. Basingstoke: Palgrave Macmillan.

Wells, C. M. (1992) *The Roman Empire*. London: Fontana.

Wells, D. A. (1992) *The Laws of Land Warfare: A Guide to the US Army Manuals*. Westport, Connecticut: Greenwood Press.

Wendt, A. (1992) 'Anarchy Is What States Make of It: The Social Construction of Power Politics', *International Organization*, 46 (2), 391–425.

Wendt, A. (2003) 'Why a World State Is Inevitable', *European Journal of International Relations*, 9 (4), 491–542.

Wesley, J. (1958–9) [1872] 'Thoughts upon Slavery'. In Wesley (1958–9a) [1872].

Wesley, J. (1958–9a) [1872] *The Works of John Wesley*, volume 11. Grand Rapids, Michigan: Zondervan Publishing House.

Whaley, J. (ed.) (1981) *Mirrors of Mortality: Studies in the Social History of Death*. London: Europa Publications.

Wheeler, N. J. (2000) *Saving Strangers: Humanitarian Intervention in International Society*. Oxford: Oxford University Press.

Wheeler, N. J. (2002) 'Dying for Enduring Freedom: Accepting Responsibility for Civilian Casualties in the War Against Terrorism', *International Relations*, 16 (2), 205–25.

White, H. (1972) 'The Forms of Wildness: Archaeology of an Idea'. In Dudley and Novak (1972).

White, S. D. (1998) 'The Politics of Anger'. In Rosenwein (1998).

White, S. (1986) 'Feuding and Peacemaking in the Touraine around the Year 1100', *Traditio*, 42: 195–263.

White, I. (2006) *Scotland and the Abolition of Black Slavery, 1568–1838*. Edinburgh: Edinburgh University Press.

Wiedemann, T. (1992) *Emperors and Gladiators*. London: Routledge.

Wiedemann, T. and Gardner, J. (eds.) (2002) *Representing the Body of the Slave*. London: Frank Cass.

Wight, M. (1966) 'Western Values in International Relations'. In Butterfield and Wight (1966).

Wight, M. (1966a) 'Why Is There No International Theory?'. In Butterfield and Wight (1966).

Wight, M. (1977) *Systems of States*. Leicester: Leicester University Press.

Wight, M. (1991) *International Theory: The Three Traditions*. Leicester: Leicester University Press.

William of Tyre, *A History of Deeds Done Beyond the Sea* (1943 edition translated by E. A. Babcock and A. C. Krey). New York: Columbia University Press.

Williams, B. (1993) *Shame and Necessity*. Berkeley: University of California Press.

Williams, E. (1964) *Capitalism and Slavery*. London: Andre Deutsch.

Willis, J. F. (1982) *Prologue to Nuremberg: The Politics and Diplomacy of Punishing War Criminals of the First World War*. Westport Connecticut: Greenwood Press.

Wilson, P. (1999) 'European Warfare, 1450–1815'. In Black (1999).

Winter, J. (1995) *Sites of Memory, Sites of Mourning: The Great War in European Cultural History*. Cambridge: Cambridge University Press.

Winter, J. (2012) 'Commemorating War, 1914–1945'. In Chickering, Showalter and van de Ven (2012).

Witt, R. G. (2000) *'In the Footsteps of the Ancients': The Origins of Humanism from Lovato to Bruni*. Leiden: Brill.

Wolin, S. (1960) *Politics and Vision: Continuity and Innovation in Western Political Thought*. Boston: Little, Brown and Company.

Wood, M. (2000) *Blind Memory: Visual Representation of Slavery in England and America: 1780–1865*. Manchester: Manchester University Press.

Woolf, G. (1995) 'Roman Peace'. In Rich and Shipley (1995).

Woolf, G. (1998) *Becoming Roman: The Origins of Provincial Civilization in Gaul*. Cambridge: Cambridge University Press.

Wouters, C. (1990) 'Social Stratification and Informalisation in Global Perspective', *Theory, Culture and Society*, 7 (4), 69–90.

Wouters, C. (1998) 'How Strange to Ourselves Are Our Feelings of Superiority and Inferiority: Notes on Fremde und Zivilisierung', *Theory, Culture and Society*, 15 (1), 131–50.

Wright, N. A. R. (1976) 'The Tree of Battles of Honore Bouvet and the Laws of War'. In Allmand (1976).

Xenophon, *Memoirs of Socrates* (1970 edition translated by H. Tredennick). Harmondsworth: Penguin.

Xenophon, *Hellenica* (1979 edition translated by R. Warner). Harmondsworth: Penguin.

Yates, F. A. (1975) *Astraea: The Imperial Theme in the Sixteenth Century*. London: Routledge and Kegan Paul.

Zajac, W. G. (1997) 'Captured Property on the First Crusade'. In Phillips (1997).

Zarakol, A. (2011) *After Defeat: How the East Learned to Live with the West.* Cambridge: Cambridge University Press.

Zaum, D. (2007) *The Sovereignty Paradox: The Norms and Politics of International State-Building.* Oxford: Oxford University Press.

Zelizer, B. (ed.) (2001) *Visual Culture and the Holocaust.* London: Athlone Press.

Zimmerman, M. (2000) 'The National Socialist "Solution of the Gypsy Problem"'. In Herbert (2000).

Zimmermann, M. (2006) 'Violence in Late Antiquity Reconsidered'. In Drake (2006).

Ziolkowski, A. (1995) 'Urbs Direpta, or How the Romans Sacked Cities'. In Rich and Shipley (1995).

Zorzi, A. (1994) 'The Judicial System in Florence in the Fourteenth and Fifteenth Centuries'. In Dean and Lowe (1994a).

Zurbuchen, S. (2003) '"Decorum" and "Politesse": Thomasius's Theory of Civilized Society in Comparative Perspective'. In Hochstrasser and Schroder (2003).

INDEX